# BOATS OF THE WORLD

# BOATS OF THE WORLD

## FROM THE STONE AGE TO MEDIEVAL TIMES

Seán McGrail

OXFORD

UNIVERSITY PRESS

# OXFORD
## UNIVERSITY PRESS

Great Clarendon Street, Oxford OX2 6DP

Oxford University Press is a department of the University of Oxford.
It furthers the University's objective of excellence in research, scholarship,
and education by publishing worldwide in

Oxford  New York

Athens  Auckland  Bangkok  Bogotá  Buenos Aires  Cape Town
Chennai  Dar es Salaam  Delhi  Florence  Hong Kong  Istanbul  Karachi
Kolkata  Kuala Lumpur  Madrid  Melbourne  Mexico City  Mumbai  Nairobi
Paris  São Paulo  Shanghai  Singapore  Taipei  Tokyo  Toronto  Warsaw
with associated companies in  Berlin  Ibadan

Oxford is a registered trade mark of Oxford University Press
in the UK and in certain other countries

Published in the United States
by Oxford University Press Inc., New York

British Library Cataloguing in Publication Data

Data available

Library of Congress Cataloging in Publication Data
McGrail, Seán
Boats of the world: from the Stone Age to Medieval times / Seán McGrail
p. cm.
Includes bibliographical references and index.
1. Boats and boating—History.   2. Boats, Ancient.   3. Ships, Medieval.
4. Underwater archaeology.   I. Title
VM16 .M3823 2001     623.8′21—dc21

ISBN 0-19-814468-7

1 3 5 7 9 10 8 6 4 2

Typeset by Newgen Imaging Systems (P) Ltd., Chennai, India
Printed in Great Britain, on acid free paper by
St. Edmundsbury Press, Bury St. Edmunds, Suffolk

# Preface

James Hornell, the great nautical ethnographer of the early twentieth century, wrote in the preface to his *Water Transport* (1946a: p. vii) that his aim was 'to marshal in due order the major part of the knowledge within our ken concerning the origins of the many devices upon which men, living in varying stages of culture, launch themselves afloat upon river, lake and sea'.

This present study is not a search for origins—indeed, such an aim would be unattainable—but its subject matter is similar to that of *Water Transport*: it is an attempt to document 'the many devices' that have been used on the waters of the world from the earliest times for which there is evidence until the period when technical descriptions and measured drawings of contemporary water transport become increasingly available.

Such technical documentation began at different times in the regions of the world. In Europe it happened during the fifteenth and sixteenth centuries. Elsewhere, this recording phase began in the seventeenth to nineteenth centuries, as European seamen and others recorded what they saw on voyages of exploration and colonization which took them into all the oceans of the world. These 'first contact' reports are even now the earliest firm evidence, from a nautical viewpoint, for water transport in many regions—see especially Chapters 6, 9, and 11. Ironically, during those centuries very few descriptions were compiled of European inshore, river and lake rafts and boats, the equivalent of those noted overseas. It was the large, seagoing European ships that were documented. Small craft in all their variety were not, generally speaking, recorded competently until the late nineteenth century.

The time span of this book is thus from the earliest times that water transport can conceivably have been used, to the late medieval period (using European terminology). This study is also intended to have as wide a geographic coverage as possible. Worldwide coverage is clearly not possible: as Paul Johnstone (1988: p. xxi) put it in the introduction to his *Seacraft of Prehistory*, 'Anyone taking the whole world as his setting can justly be excused of rashness, if nothing more.' No one person can be familiar with everything now known about the building and the use of water transport, worldwide, over a 40,000 year period.

This book is based on fieldwork in Europe and South Asia, on visits to China, South-east Asia, and Egypt, and on study of accessible literature: coverage is therefore not comprehensive. There is little here on the boats of the coasts and rivers of the former USSR or the African continent outside Egypt. On the other hand, there is much about Asia from the Red Sea to the China Sea, about the South Pacific, Australia, and the Americas, and about Europe. The aim has been to present as broad and as detailed a study as the present-day documentation of ancient boats allows.

The idea of writing such a book came to mind as I edited Paul Johnstone's *Seacraft of Prehistory*, but was not pursued further until I moved from Greenwich upstream to Oxford in 1986. There, and later at Southampton, the preparation of lectures, and subsequent questioning by students, clarified my aims and focused my research.

Fellowships and travel grants enabled me to widen the range of libraries I used, and to visit overseas colleagues and examine their ships and boats. During the 1990s I held a Leverhulme Research Fellowship and a Leverhulme Emeritus Fellowship, and I received a research grant from the British Academy. The Academy also financed travel and study in China in association with the Chinese Academy of Science. The British Council similarly funded study tours of Egypt and Poland, and the Faculty of Anthropology and Geography gave me several travel grants during my years at Oxford. Fieldwork in India and Bangladesh during the past six years has been funded by the Society for South Asian Studies. To all these institutions I am indebted: they have my grateful thanks.

I also thank colleagues who have readily answered my questions, criticized sections of the book, and made available the results of their own research: Anwar Aleem, Béat Arnold, Lucien Basch, Carlo Beltrame, Peter Bellwood, Lucy Blue, Ronald Bockius, Arne-Emil Christensen, John Coates, Ole Crumlin-Pederson, Barry Cunliffe, Detlev Ellmers, Basil Greenhill, David Hinton, Yak Kahanov, Eric Kentley, Peter Kuniholm, David Lewis, Jerzy Litwin, Brad Loewen, Pierre-Yves Manguin, Peter Marsden, Yvonne Marshall, Colin Palmer, Patrice Pomey, Himanshu Ray, Eric Rieth, Owain Roberts, Margaret Rule, Dick Steffy, André Tchernia, Lotika Varadarajan, David Waters, Maarten de Weerd, and Ted Wright. I am also grateful to those who provided illustrations, especially Mrs Paul Johnstone, and to Alison Wilkins of the Institute of Archaeology, Oxford, who drew most of the maps and many other figures.

S. McG.

*Chilmark*
*Feast of St Nicholas, 1999*

# Contents

# List of Illustrations

In a few instances we may have been unable to trace the copyright holder before publication. If notified, the publishers will be pleased to amend the acknowledgements in any future edition.

# List of Tables

# Abbreviations

| | |
|---|---|
| *AJA* | *American Journal of Archaeology* |
| *Antiq. J* | *Antiquaries Journal* |
| *BAH* | *Berichte über die Ausgrabungen in Haithabu* |
| *BAR* | *British Archaeological Reports* |
| CBA | Council for British Archaeology |
| *IJNA* | *International Journal of Nautical Archaeology* |
| INA | Institute of Nautical Archaeology |
| ISBSA | International Seminars on Boat and Ship Archaeology |
| *Med. Arch.* | *Medieval Archaeology* |
| *MM* | *Mariner's Mirror* |
| *OJA* | *Oxford Journal of Archaeology* |
| *PPS* | *Proceedings of Prehistoric Society* |
| *SAS* | *South Asian Studies* |

# Conventions used in the text

## MEASUREMENTS

- Dimensions of vessels are given in the order L × B × D, where L = length; B = breadth; D = depth of hull.
- Measurements are given in metres except when the original data were in imperial units when they are given with metres in parentheses.
- Spacings of fastening holes, frames etc., are given from centre to centre.

## DISTANCES AND SPEEDS

- Distances at sea are given in nautical miles, and speeds in knots. 1 nautical mile = 1.853 km. 1 knot = 1.15 statute miles/hour = 1 nautical mile/hour.

## ABBREVIATIONS

b: mean breadth of keel below bottom planking
d: depth of keel below bottom planking
m: moulded dimension of a timber
s: sided dimension of a timber

# I

# SOURCES AND THEMES

## I.I

## Maritime Archaeology and Boat Archaeology

The principal subject of this study is water transport, that is, rafts, boats, and ships. Research into water transport, a subject sometimes known as 'boat archaeology', is just one aspect of the maritime subdiscipline of archaeology which may be defined as 'the study of the nature and past behaviour of Man in his use of those special environments associated with lakes, rivers, and seas' (McGrail, 1989a: 10). In addition to water transport, this research area includes the study of landing places and harbours, as well as the study of the building, use, and performance of rafts, boats, and ships (Fig. 1.1). It also includes: anchors and fishing gear; overseas colonizations and trade routes; trade and cargo handling; changes in past climates, sea levels, and coastlines; and early seafaring and navigational techniques (McGrail, 1995c: 329). A study of all aspects of maritime archaeology by a single author would necessarily be uneven in quality with some parts at an elementary level: such a task would better be tackled by a group of specialist authors. The present work leaves to one side much of maritime archaeology (although every aspect is at least touched upon in some part of the text) to focus on rafts, boats, and ships. Moreover, although planked vessels are dealt with in some detail, emphasis is placed on rafts and non-plank boats whenever the evidence allows, since in all regions of the world these are the craft most likely to have been used in earliest times about which we know least. The aim is to present a history of water transport as it has developed over millennia in the regions of the world, in as much as the evidence available at present allows.

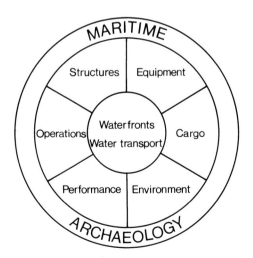

Fig. 1.1. Diagram to illustrate the scope of maritime archaeology (Institute of Archaeology, Oxford).

## I.2

## Sources of Evidence

This study is based whenever possible on archaeological evidence, in particular the excavated remains of water transport. Outside Europe such evidence is rare, and even within Europe there are no excavated remains of logboats before the eighth millennium BC, or of plank boats before the second millennium BC. In later times such finds as there are, are usually isolated in time and space, and it is only from the late-Roman period onwards that sufficient numbers of similar plank boats and ships have been excavated to justify the definition of boatbuilding traditions in certain periods and regions. Remains of other types of water transport are virtually negligible worldwide. Thus other forms of evidence have to be used, often standing alone rather than in conjunction with archaeological remains. The recording, examination, and post-excavation analysis of boat and ship remains is a specialized task, outside the scope of this present work: the reader is referred to publications by Steffy (1994), by Olsen and Crumlin-Pedersen (1967), and by Crumlin-Pedersen (1977).

## 1.2.1 INDIRECT EVIDENCE FOR SEAGOING VESSELS

Evidence for early overseas voyages, and therefore the existence of seagoing vessels, before the time when there is direct evidence from shipwrecks, comes from the distribution patterns of artefacts, and of those ideas which become archaeologically visible as 'monuments', as 'ritual', and as technological innovations. However, not every exotic artefact or structure is a sure sign of seafaring: in continental land masses some goods and ideas may indeed have travelled by sea on coastal routes, but others may have been transported on land routes, albeit including the use of rivers. Only in the case of islands, or between continental land masses, which were demonstrably surrounded by water at the time in question, must people, artefacts, animals, and ideas necessarily have arrived by sea.

Evidence for possible early seafaring must be examined critically and, in the case of non-islands, the balance of probability struck. Even when an overseas voyage seems likely, it does not follow that there was direct contact by sea (Spain to Ireland, for example). Unless there is other evidence, the minimum conjecture must be that a coastal cabotage route was used (Spain, France, Britain, Ireland).

## 1.2.2 ICONOGRAPHIC EVIDENCE

Representations of boats are the only evidence available in earliest times. Furthermore, sails and rigging rarely survive to be excavated, but they are sometimes depicted on stone carvings, engravings on seals, and on pottery decorations. Such representations can therefore be invaluable, but they cannot be accepted without rigorous analysis and interpretation. The bow and stern need first to be identified and the problem of scale tackled. There are several examples in this study of ship and boat depictions which have been the subject of vigorous and lengthy academic debate about how they should be interpreted—for example, the Thera frieze (4.7.2.2). Earlier examples, such as depictions from ancient Egypt (2.4, 2.6.3) and Mesopotamia (3.2), are stylized and even more difficult to interpret.

Without the control imposed by comparisons with contemporary examples of excavated boats, the interpreter of early iconography may allow imagination too much scope. Furthermore, it has to be borne in mind that these depictions are not naval architects' plans: they are (usually) a two-dimensional representation created by someone from a distinct culture, working to specific artistic conventions, who may have only indifferent knowledge of nautical matters. However, systematic analysis of individual elements of a boat depiction, and comparisons between representations from the same artistic environment, may lead to working hypotheses about conventions used: for example, vertical lines across a depicted 'hull' possibly represent the bindings of a bundle raft; vertical lines above a hull may represent the crew; vertical lines extending below a hull may represent paddles or oars; horizontal lines along a hull may represent planking; and short vertical lines or devices, across these horizontal lines, may represent plank fastenings. But these are guidelines rather than rules, and it may be necessary to admit that some representations cannot be interpreted or, at best, it may only be possible to suggest, from the context, that they depict some unspecified type of water transport. On the other hand, a model of a boat can be potentially rewarding since the cross-section, generally unseen in two-dimensional depictions, provides much information about the boat's potential when afloat.

A series of representations from a particular period and place can thus be very useful to the archaeologist in the absence of, but particularly in addition to, excavated evidence, providing the evidence is critically evaluated. It is to be noted, however, that the iconography available probably does not represent the full range of water transport in use: for example, boats, unlike ships, are very seldom found on medieval town seals. Compounding such difficulties is the problem of dating early representations such as the Scandinavian rock carvings: the margin of error in the dating methods used is insufficiently stressed.

## I.2.3 DOCUMENTARY EVIDENCE

Documentary evidence ranges from inscriptions mentioning shipping, and early law codes listing harbour dues, to detailed technical reports written and illustrated by explorers and travellers. The principal aim of most of the authors of the earlier documents was seldom to record the building or the use of water transport; thus the nautical information in them may frequently be inconsequential. To obtain reliable information from such documents even if it is a mere scrap, it is first necessary to determine the standpoint, the reliability and the nautical competence of the observer; and the document must be given a precise provenance in time and space. Translators with an inadequate knowledge of nautical and marine affairs can easily add to inherent difficulties in understanding texts, as may the fact that no twentieth-century English word may now exist to describe a particular feature or operation. As with iconographic evidence, documentary evidence of water transport is unlikely to be comprehensive or unbiased: objects and events that are commonplace to the observer will be noted briefly, if at all, whereas the unusual, which may be in no way representative of its day, will be discussed in some detail.

## I.2.4 ETHNOGRAPHIC EVIDENCE

The documentation of traditional rafts and boats still in use in non-industrial, generally illiterate, small-scale societies can also suggest the sort of water transport those societies may have used in earlier times, providing some form of cultural continuity can be demonstrated. Should there also be excavated remains of early craft, a symbiotic relationship between the two forms of evidence may ensue, as seems to have happened in Norway, leading to a fuller picture of early nautical life than obtainable solely from archaeology.

Such ethnographic evidence may also be useful in a broader sense in the interpretation of excavated remains. A knowlege of a wide range of solutions to specific boatbuilding and boat-use problems (for example, how to close the ends of a boat; how to get the desired shape of hull; and how to steer) enable the archaeologist to escape the constraints of his own culture, and perhaps come closer to understanding the early technology he is investigating. There are undoubtedly problems in using analogies cross-culturally, but the more alike in environmental, technological and economic terms two cultures (one ancient, one recent) can be shown to be, the greater the likelihood that ethnographic studies will be of relevance to the investigation of early nautical technologies and boat use.

Ethnographic studies can thus be of great value in the interpretation of early boats, their structure and their use. There is not, however, necessarily a one-to-one relationship between ethnographic documentation and the incomplete, fragmented, and distorted remains of an ancient boat. Ethnographic evidence can suggest the sort of questions to be asked of the ancient boat and may prompt a range of answers, but, as Grahame Clark (1953: 357) said nearly fifty years ago, '. . . only archaeology, in conjunction with the various natural sciences, can give the right answers'—with the rider that, in the present state of knowledge, no answer may be possible, and any answer will be probabilistic rather than definitive.

The fact that ethnographers have documented the recent use in the west of Ireland of simple forms of water transport such as the hide boat (Hornell, 1937–8) and the bundle raft (Delaney, 1976) does not validate a claim that they must have been used there millennia ago. The possibility is certainly brought to our attention, but, since there is no direct evidence for such early use, it will be necessary to trace evidence back to the protohistoric period. If this can be done, and it can be further shown that appropriate raw materials and analogous tools and techniques were available and used in prehistoric times, then a hypothesis may be formulated that such craft may have been built and used in the Bronze Age or even earlier. Evidence may subsequently be sought to support, or refute, such a hypothesis.

The 'first contact' reports by fifteenth to eighteenth-century European seamen concerning the water transport they encountered in the 'new found lands' of the

Americas, Australia, and the South Pacific are especially valuable in that many of these craft were documented (though not always in the detail one would wish) before European technologies had influenced them.

## 1.2.5 DATING EVIDENCE

Until relatively recently, remains of water transport were generally dated by reference to the archaeological context in which they were found, or from the cargo or other finds associated with them. Such methods are not always satisfactory and, in any case, the margin of error is often unacceptably great since such methods depend ultimately on the most recent stylistic dating of artefacts such as pottery. In recent years, however, direct dating of boats has been undertaken by radiocarbon assay and, latterly, by dendrochronology with its much greater precision. Those boats excavated before the advent of scientific dating must be considered only provisionally dated until definitive dendrochronological dates are published.

## 1.2.6 ENVIRONMENTAL EVIDENCE

In order to understand how and where water transport was used in earlier times, and to appreciate fully the problems faced by early seafarers, and suggest how these might have been solved, it is first necessary to build up a picture of the environment at a particular time and place. Things have not always been as they are today: there have been short-term and long-term climatic changes, and mean sea level has generally risen, at variable rates, during the past 18,000 years. Former weather patterns are of particular interest to our understanding of seafaring and overseas trading routes: especially important are the direction and strength of the predominant winds, and the frequency of winds from other sectors.

Of even more interest, and of fundamental importance to seafaring, is the position of mean sea level at a given time and place, since, in conjunction with other factors, this determines:

- the general form of the coastline;
- river gradients, and hence rates of erosion and deposition;

- the presence or absence of archipelagos, shoals, sands, reefs, skerries, tidal races, spits, and bars.

Mean sea level also indirectly influences local tidal regimes which are, to a degree, determined by the configuration of the coast. Before we can suggest how both Greater Australia and the Americas could have been first settled, mean sea level has to be determined for the period when these migrations are thought to have taken place—see Chapters 7 and 11.

Changes in sea level and in weather patterns are discussed in some detail in the chapters on the Mediterranean (see Ch. 4) and on Atlantic Europe (see Ch. 5), regions for which environmental data is readily available. The reconstruction of earlier coastlines, coastal waters, river channels, and earlier weather experienced at a particular time and place, is a complex matter since the effects of a number of interacting variables have to be estimated. Maps have been published for certain parts of the world showing sea levels and coastlines at intervals of time during past millennia; in the present state of research these must be considered as general guidance for the maritime archaeologist, rather than definitive, and the conclusions drawn by archaeologists about ancient seafaring and navigation from such data are, at best, probabilistic.

When the evidence for the direction, strength, and frequency of a predominant wind in former times in a particular region is well established, it is possible to estimate, in a relative way, whether passages between selected harbours were feasible by using a theoretical 'standard ship' which could be sailed with the true wind one point forward of the beam (leeway being discounted). In monsoon-type climates, where the wind remained in a fixed quarter for much of the sailing season, as in the eastern Mediterranean and in the Indian Ocean, such estimates are probably realistic. In temperate regions, as in Atlantic Europe, winds were probably much more variable and estimates will therefore be less reliable. In several regions of the world, however, there are periods at the beginning and the end of the main sailing season when winds can be fair for passages which cannot be made at other times.

Weather data for earlier times is either derived from dendrology and similar palaeo-research and is therefore generalized, or it is based on averages and extrapolations of observations made in past centuries. The actual weather experienced, in earlier times, over a particular period of, say, three or four days (sufficient for many passages in the Mediterranean and coastal Atlantic waters) could well have been different from these averages. Thus, once again, it is necessary to talk in terms of probability and likelihood of what could be achieved in prehistoric times.

## 1.3

## The Reconstruction and Interpretation of Excavated Vessels

The reconstruction and interpretation of the remains of an ancient vessel is the key phase in a research pro-

ject (Figs. 1.2, 1.3). The record made during excavation, the post-excavation research documentation, environmental data, and the results of sample analyses are brought together and evaluated in the light of known facts about ancient water transport and other comparative data from iconographic, documentary and ethnographic sources. Hypothetical reconstructions of the original full form and structure of the vessel are built up, either as measured drawings or as small-scale models—see Steffy (1994: 189–298) and McGrail (1981a: 9). Two or more reconstructions may be compatible with the evidence. From these reconstructions, predictions of performance can be made (McGrail, 1998: 192–202): stability in various conditions (a sine qua non); payloads at certain drafts; the likely range of speeds; and achievements when tacking if it has proved possible to reconstruct the sailing rig. Only if the reconstruction is authentic, the data accurate, and the arguments rigorous will the predicted perfor-

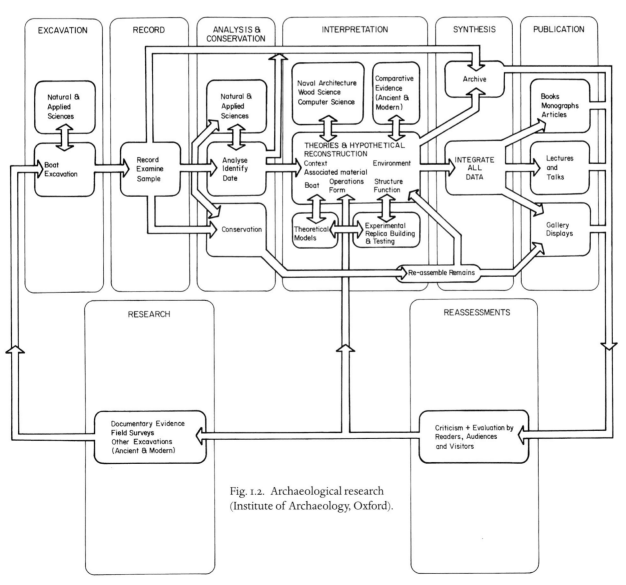

Fig. 1.2. Archaeological research (Institute of Archaeology, Oxford).

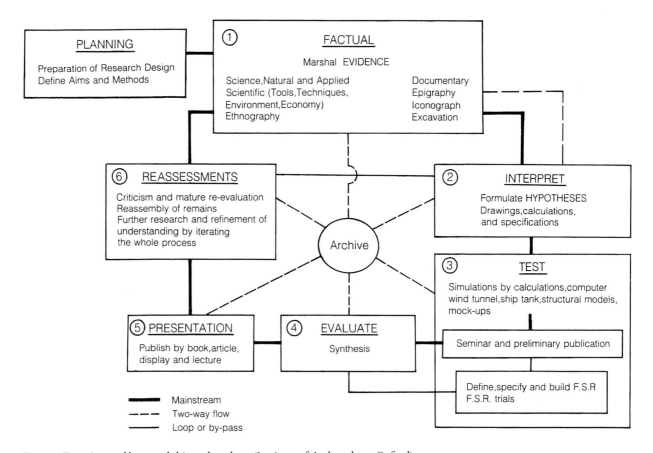

Fig. 1.3. Experimental boat and ship archaeology (Institute of Archaeology, Oxford).

mance be credible. Cargo-carrying abilities may be presented either in the form 'at a draft of *n* metres *x* tonnes of amphorae filled with wine may be carried' or in the form 'if *n* tonnes of wine-filled amphorae were carried the draft would be *x* metres'.

In such estimations of performance it has to be ensured that the vessel would have adequate freeboard (however that is defined), and that she would be stable when carrying the designated loads, using cargo storage factors in the calculations when necessary (McGrail, 1989*b*). For international comparisons it is customary to assess the tonnage that vessels could carry at drafts equivalent to 60 per cent (cargo vessels) and 50 per cent (warships) height of sides amidships, such drafts being considered (on the evidence of medieval Icelandic laws see McGrail, 1998: 199) to give safe freeboard for the two classes of vessel.

Ways of distinguishing cargo vessels from fighting vessels are discussed in 5.8.1.3.5. Another important assessment of a vessel is to determine whether or not she would have been seagoing. By 'seagoing raft or boat' is meant the sort of craft which, without special preparations or additional fittings, could be relied upon to carry a reasonable load on a sea passage of some duration in the weather and sea conditions generally experienced at that time and place, not just on one or two occasions of perfect weather. Evaluating whether an ancient vessel would have been seagoing is an art as well as a science since a number of interacting factors have to be considered (McGrail, 1993*a*: 202–4). The strength, durability, and integrity of the hull have to be taken into account, as do freeboard at operational drafts, stability, and reserves of buoyancy. An open boat below a certain size is unlikely to have been seagoing but a decked vessel, *ceteris paribus*, could have been. Shape is also of importance: a 'boat-shaped' underwater hull, and a sheerline rising towards the ends suggest a seagoing vessel. Manœuvrability, controllability, sea-kindliness, and dryness have also to be considered.

Many of these characteristics contribute towards the safety of vessel and crew, and it is impossible to know now what was the approach to risk assessment in earlier times: in this event it seems best to assume that the ancient mariner was also a 'prudent mariner'. Nowadays the Atlantic Ocean is crossed by adventurers in the most unlikely vessels, and it may be that mavericks similarly put to sea in the past. Nevertheless, as in other aspects of the past, we should deal with the general picture, in averages and in probabilities, when evaluating whether a vessel would have been seaworthy or not. Some boats assessed as 'non- seagoing' may nevertheless have been operable within estuaries in testing conditions—this is because, in the event of trouble, the crew would have the possibility of returning to their base or of running ashore on a nearby beach before some catastrophic failure.

After excavated boat timbers have been conserved it is essential that they are re-examined to confirm any doubtful measurements and assessments, and to seek answers to questions not formulated until conservation had begun. Much may also be learned during the reassembly of the timbers for display. As a result of these two phases of research, the hypothetical reconstruction may need to be amended and performance re-estimated (Fig. 1.2).

After hypothetical reconstructions of an ancient boat have been investigated, it may prove possible to build a full-size reconstruction and undertake sea trials (Coates *et al.*, 1995). Whether such a project should in fact be undertaken depends on the extent it is expected that such an experiment would expand understanding of the building and the use of the original vessel: it is very rare, however, for this to be the only consideration.

An authentic reconstruction can be based on excavated remains of a specific boat and other appropriate evidence; or one can be based mainly on documentary and iconographic sources concerned with a general class of vessel (McGrail, 1997c: 313–15). Both methods are valid ways of finding out more about the past: individual projects should be judged on their merits. What can be learned from full-scale reconstruction depends upon: the quality of the evidence; the rigour used in interpreting that evidence, in building the reconstruction, and in the trials; and the clarity of the subsequent publication (Coates *et al.*, 1995: 295). In other words, what can be learned about the original vessel from such an archaeological experiment depends upon authenticity, rigour, and the use of the scientific method. There have been a handful of experiments which have matched these standards and significantly increased knowledge of the nautical past: these are discussed in the appropriate chapters.

It may prove possible to suggest that a particular wreck was a member of a tradition of building already recognized (for example, a Nordic ship); in this event, data from other similar wrecks may be used in the reconstruction process. At the same time, data from the new wreck will probably be added to the features characteristic of the tradition, possibly causing that tradition to be redefined. Occasionally it is possible to equate a named type of medieval ship with a documented type name (for example, 'cog') and sometimes with illustrations of a distinctive type. In these cases, the conflation of the several types of evidence significantly adds to knowledge of the past. Only very exceptionally can a wreck be identified with a specific known ship, and these are invariably of a late date (for example, *Mary Rose* and *Wasa*).

## 1.4

# Concepts behind Some of the Arguments in this Study

### 1.4.1 TYPES OF WATER TRANSPORT

As James Hornell observed (1946a), a seemingly boundless variety of 'devices' have been, and are being, used by Man in his encounter with the waters of the world. Since no early forms of water transport were mass-produced, in the ultimate analysis, each individual raft or boat is different from all others. Some sort of classification scheme is therefore needed to bring order into what at first sight may seem to be near-chaos. By such means scholars around the world can be sure that they are discussing similar forms of water transport. Furthermore, patterns may be recognized, and fundamental differences and shifts in technology may be identified. Any classification scheme is, however, a construct, an approximation or best-fit to reality: if they were other than this, they would be unwieldy. Moreover, such schemes cannot remain static: as fresh

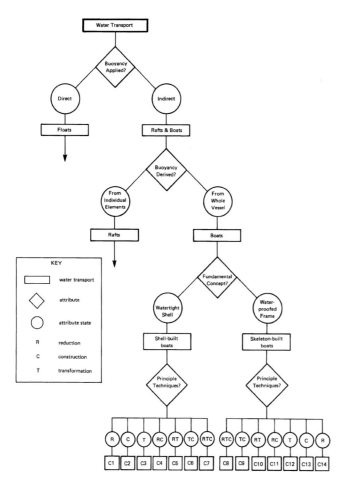

Fig. 1.4. Structural classification scheme for water transport—mainly boats (Institute of Archaeology, Oxford).

bundle rafts, log rafts, and buoyed rafts; and log boats, hide boats, bark boats, plank boats, and (the rare) pot boats, basket boats, and bundle boats (McGrail 1985*b*: 289–90). Little analytical work has been done on raft structure, but boats can be further classified by reference to the sequence in which the boat is built, and, secondly, the principal techniques the builder uses when converting his raw materials into a boat (Fig. 1.4).

### 1.4.1.1 BUILDING SEQUENCES

A fundamental distinction has long been recognized in the way plank boats are built (Hasslöf, 1963; 1972; Greenhill, 1976: 60–88). In one case the planking is fashioned and fastened together to form the hull, then the framing is fastened to the planking; in the alternative method the framing is first fashioned to the hull shape required, then the planking is fastened to the framework. Behind these two sequences lies a more fundamental difference: the builder's concept of his boat. On the one hand, the builder visualizes the form of his boat as a watertight shell of planking which is subsequently reinforced by framing; on the other hand, as a framework or skeleton which is subsequently 'waterproofed' by planking (Fig. 1.4). This fundamental distinction between 'shell-built' and 'skeleton-built' boats can be recognized not only in plank boats but also in boats built of hides and of bark (McGrail, 1985*b*). Whichever sequence of building is recognized in examples of these three types of boat, it also reveals how the builder visualized his boat, how he obtained the hull shape he wanted, and where the structural strength mainly lay.

When dealing solely with plank craft it is now customary to use the more explicit terms 'plank-first' and 'frame-first' to describe these different styles of building. In recent centuries European frame-first ships were not planked-up until virtually the whole of the framework or skeleton had been built and faired (Greenhill, 1995*a*: 266–9), whereas with early frame-first boats, only *part* of the framework was erected before the hull was planked; or alternatively, the lower framework was erected and planked, then the upper framework was erected and planked (4.15; 5.6). To distinguish between the early and later forms of frame-first building, the term 'frame-based' has been coined

evidence emerges and new ways of analysis and synthesis are devised, the classification must be re-examined and revised where necessary.

The scheme used in this study is illustrated in Figure. 1.4. Answers to two questions separate units of water transport into three main groups (McGrail, 1985*b*; 1993*b*: 4–11). How buoyancy is applied segregates 'floats' (in which buoyancy is directly applied) from 'rafts and boats' (in which buoyancy is indirect). How buoyancy is derived divides 'rafts' (from individual elements) from 'boats' (from the whole vessel). Ships are, in general terms, merely large boats—for a more detailed discussion of the differences, see McGrail (1993*b*: 19–21).

Floats are not considered in detail in this study. Rafts and boats may each be further divided into sub-groups based on their principal raw material: thus there are to describe the alternating forms of building, and 'frame-orientated' to describe that builder's approach (McGrail, 1995b, 1997a). The term 'plank-based' may correspondingly be used to describe boats which are built plank-first but in an alternating fashion.

### 1.4.1.2 PRINCIPAL TECHNIQUES

The two groups of boats—those shell-built and those skeleton-built (to use the general terms)—may each be divided according to the techniques the builder uses when converting his materials into a boat. Three main techniques may be identified (McGrail, 1998: 6–7):

(a) *reduction*: the raw material is reduced in volume as in hollowing a log;
(b) *construction*: several elements are joined together as in binding reeds into bundles, or when making a framework by weaving, plaiting, or similar processes, or fastening planks together by lashings;
(c) *transformation*: altering the shape of the material without subtraction or addition, as in the expansion of a logboat, or the bending of a plank.

One or more of these techniques may be used to make the form-determining, watertight envelope of shell-built boats, and the waterproofing outer element of skeleton-built boats. As a result of this second division of boats, fourteen theoretical classes of boat structure are identified—C.1 to C.14 in Fig. 1.4. A survey of a large number of excavated and ethnographic boats (by no means comprehensive) shows that five of the seven shell-built classes have members, and a sixth may have members. Two of the seven skeleton-built classes are known to have members and two others may have members (McGrail, 1998: table 2.1). Table 1.1 lists those classes (C.1 to C.14) in which the seven basic types of boat have members. From this table we see that all logboats are shell-built, and they are represented in classes C.1, 4, 5, and 7; that is, some are built solely by reduction, some by reduction and construction, some by reduction and transformation, and some by all three techniques. Basket boats, on the other hand, are all evidently skeleton-built, and their outer waterproofing element is produced by transforming a solid mass of bitumen or tar into a skin.

### 1.4.2 BOATBUILDING TRADITIONS

The scheme for dividing water transport outlined in Fig. 1.4 deals only with the early stages of classification, merely identifying the major groups of floats, rafts, and boats with some subdivision of the boats. Further work needs to be done to take classification beyond the lowest levels shown in Fig. 1.4. To do this a wide range of characteristics would have to be analysed, mostly structural attributes such as fastening methods, but also the means of propulsion and steering as well as aspects of form. As a result of this, natural groupings should be identified at a deeper level of classification. In this way sewn-plank boats which at present are virtually an undifferentiated group might be divided into meaningful sub-groups. Furthermore, traditions such as the Nordic (5.8.1.3.4) or Romano-Celtic (5.6) which have already been identified by intuitive, ad hoc

**Table 1.1** Classification of boat types

| Boat type | Attributes | | Class |
|---|---|---|---|
| | Concept | Techniques | |
| Logboats | Shell | R | C1 |
| | Shell | RC | C4 |
| | Shell | RT | C5 |
| | Shell | RTC | C7 |
| Plank boats | Shell | RC | C4 |
| | Shell | RTC | C7 |
| | Skeleton | RTC | C8 |
| | Skeleton | (RC) | (C11) |
| Bark boats | Shell | RT | C5 |
| | Shell | RTC | C7 |
| | Skeleton | RTC | C8 |
| | Skeleton | (RT) | (C10) |
| Hide boats | Shell | RT | C5 |
| | Shell | RTC | C7 |
| | Skeleton | RTC | C8 |
| | Skeleton | (RT) | (C10) |
| Bundle boats | Skeleton | T | C12 |
| Pottery boats | Shell | T | C3 |
| | Shell | (TC) | (C6) |
| Basket boats | Skeleton | T | C12 |

R = reduction

C = construction

T = transformation

C1 to C11 = classification—see Figure 1.4.

*Note*: Items in parentheses are doubtful.

methods may be confirmed as valid by this logical approach, or it may be found that their present definition has to be altered to become consistent with the general scheme.

A boatbuilding tradition may be formally defined as: the perceived style of building generally used in a certain region during a given time range. As with any classification it has its drawbacks. For example, it is a theoretical construct which may or may not be similar to the concepts of the people who actually built and sailed such boats. Furthermore, for our purposes, traditions must be given arbitrary start and stop dates, although it may well seem that their earliest and latest phases merge into other traditions. Similarly, spatial boundaries have to be given to such traditions, but these must necessarily be fuzzy, and in some cases it may not be clear whether the boats of a particular area (say, the southern Baltic) should be included within a regional tradition (i.e. the Nordic). There are also problems in giving names to traditions: the solution here is to consider such names as codewords without cultural or ethnic implications. Notwithstanding these and other drawbacks (McGrail, 1995b: 139–40), the concept of a tradition has proved useful in maritime studies both archaeological and ethnographical: it can continue to be so providing that definitions of individual traditions are modified when acquisition of new data demands it.

Within a particular tradition it is not necessary that all boats have all characteristics in common. Each boat has to share with every other boat in the tradition a large number of characteristics, but no one characteristic *has* to be possessed by all boats. Such groups are known as *polythetic* (Doran and Hodson, 1975: 160) and, in not requiring 100 per cent conformity, they reflect an intuitive understanding of the real world.

### I.4.2.I THE ORIGINS OF A WRECK

A ship may be wrecked, abandoned, or dismantled outside those waters where vessels of her tradition predominate, and within waters usually sailed by ships of another tradition. Even when wrecked within 'traditional' waters, a ship may be far from where she was built. As the definition of shipbuilding traditions in terms of structural characteristics is refined, including the recognition of temporal and regional variants, the

identification of a wreck's region of origin should become increasingly practicable. In the long run, it may prove possible to narrow origins down to a particular 'shipyard' where some master builder had given a recognizable personal touch to his ship's structure or her decorative features.

The 'nationality' of the crew (as deduced from their personal possessions), and the nature of the cargo carried, have both been used in the search for a wreck's origins. The crew's likely origins may be one of several clues to be considered in such research, but the sources of the cargo may be misleading: the latter can, however, be of use in tackling a related problem—the route of the ship on her final voyage.

Cargo ships generally need ballast, often of stone, which can be: permanent, embarked when fitting out; temporary, loaded or unloaded many times at different harbours during a ship's life to match the cargo density of the goods embarked; or saleable, embarked on a particular voyage to serve two purposes (McGrail, 1989b). If permanent ballast can be recognized and its source identified, this may be another clue to the regional identity of the ship. The identification of the timber species used in a hull may also help, as can the dendrological examination of hull timbers which may not only date the ship's construction, but may also link the timber to a specific region.

These clues to origins need to be evaluated and integrated with any other pertinent information, so that a likely 'home port' for the wreck may be identified.

### I.4.3 EARLIEST WATER TRANSPORT

There is no direct evidence for water transport until the Mesolithic period even in the most favoured regions, and it is not until the Bronze Age that vessels other than logboats are known. Nevertheless there is sound evidence for the use of lakes and rivers and for overseas voyages from earlier times: for example, the settlement of Greater Australia from 40,000 BC or even earlier (7.2). To investigate which form of water transport was used on these and other early voyages, we can, at present, only have recourse to informed speculation. Table 1.2 is based on theoretical assessments of the types of water transport that could have been used in different technological stages from the European

Upper Palaeolithic to the Bronze Age (*c.*40,000 to *c.*2000 BC) and the equivalent stages elsewhere. Each type of basic float, raft, and boat has been analysed to determine the minimum tools and techniques needed to construct them. This information was then correlated with data concerning the earliest use of these tools and techniques in the manufacture of other artefacts, and deductions made as to which period specific types of float, raft, or boat might reasonably be thought to have been first made. Whether this was so at a particular time and place would depend not only on the availability of the appropriate raw materials, but also on whether the idea of using such tools and techniques in the manufacture of water transport had arisen.

The seagoing abilities of rafts and boats in Table 1.2 are based on theoretical assessments of the structures' ability to withstand the stresses imposed in a seaway. Boats, by their nature, afford some protection to the crew against the elements and therefore those with a suitable structure for seagoing may generally be used in all latitudes (subject to other constraints). Rafts, on the other hand, being flow-through structures, do not protect the crew in conditions of low air and sea temperatures which, combined with exposure to wind and wetness, can soon induce hypothermia and tax the crew beyond endurance. Rafts are thus not used at sea today beyond latitudes *c.*40°S and 40°N; in former times there would have been corresponding limitations. Table 1.2 therefore differentiates between higher

**Table 1.2** A theoretical assessment of early water transport

| Technological stage | Water transport | Use in Mediterranean types of maritime environment | Use in NW European types of maritime environment |
| --- | --- | --- | --- |
| Palaeolithic | Log float | S? | IW |
| | Bundle float | S? | IW |
| | Hide float | S? | IW |
| | Simple log raft | S | IW |
| | Simple hide-float raft | S | NT/IW |
| | Simple bark boat | NT/IW | NT/IW |
| | Simple hide boat | IW | IW |
| Mesolithic | Complex log raft | S | IW |
| | Multiple hide-float raft | S | NT/IW |
| | Bundle raft | S | IW |
| | Simple logboat | IW | IW |
| | Multiple hide boat | S | S |
| | Basket boat | S | NT/S |
| Neolithic | Pot float | S? | NT/IW |
| | Pot-float raft | S | NT/IW |
| | Pot boat | S? | NT/IW |
| | Stabilized logboats | S | S |
| | Paired logboats | S | S |
| | Extended logboats | S | S |
| | Simple plank boats | IW | IW |
| Bronze Age | Expanded logboats | S | S |
| | Bundle boats | S | NT/S |
| | Complex bark boats | NT/S | NT/S |
| | Complex plank boats | S | S |

S=seagoing (includes possibility of inland use)    IW=inland waters only    NT=no known tradition

*Sources:* For definition of types see McGrail (1985*b*; 1998: 4–11.) See also Johnstone (1988: pp. xiii–xiv). For technological evidence see McGrail (1981*b*: 12; 1998: 53–4, 85–7, 96–7, 171–2, 185–7, 191).

and lower latitudes, taking Atlantic Europe and the Mediterranean as being representative of those two regions. The table also takes into account whether there is any known tradition of the use of each type of raft or boat in those regions.

# I.5

# Presentation of the Evidence

The aim of this study is to use all forms of evidence, especially archaeological, to present an account of how rafts, boats, and ships were built, propelled, steered and generally used, from earliest times to somewhere in the period AD 1400–1800. When in that period the study ends depends upon circumstances in a particular region, but generally speaking, it coincides with the introduction of frame-first building and the formal design of ocean-going ships. Where the evidence justifies, methods of navigation, means of exploration, and principal overseas trading routes are also discussed.

For the purposes of exposition, the seafaring world has been divided into ten regions (Chs 2–11). The reasons for defining some of these regions are clear: for example, the early Americas had negligible overseas contact with the rest of the world, apart from the circumpolar zone, from first settlement until the late fifteenth century AD. Australia was similarly virtually isolated until post-medieval times; pre-Hellenic Egypt and early Mesopotamia can also be reasonably dealt with as individual maritime zones, although in both cases documented overseas voyages were undertaken at an early date. The Mediterranean forms a convenient maritime unit up to Classical times when maritime interaction with both Atlantic Europe and the Indian Ocean became increasingly common.

Atlantic Europe, on the other hand, cannot be recognized as an entity in maritime terms until the medieval period although there clearly were maritime contacts within, and sometimes between, each of its subregions (Baltic, North Sea, British and Irish archipelago and the Channel, Biscay and Iberia). The form of the evidence is such, however, that it is convenient to discuss this environmentally disparate region in one chapter.

The Indian Ocean, extending east and west rather than north and south and united in some sense by monsoonal winds, has, on the other hand, been a link between Arabia, east Africa, south Asia, and south-east Asia for millennia. Nevertheless the pattern of evidence dictates that these regions be dealt with separately, but with detailed cross-references where themes overlap. China has extended its cultural/technological boundaries greatly over the millennia, yet it has had periods of enforced isolation from overseas influences. Furthermore, as an entity, it has a relatively well-documented protohistory, unlike surrounding regions. China is thus sufficiently different in culture and in general technology to have its own chapter. Nevertheless, it is clear that there were maritime links between China and south-east Asian countries throughout documented times, and, indeed, the late medieval wrecks recently excavated from Chinese and south-east Asian waters have proved to have similar hull structures. Oceania also has a chapter to itself. There seems to have been much maritime interaction from early times between south-east Asia and Near Oceania. Remote Oceania (east of the Solomon islands), on the other hand, appears to have had a degree of cultural/technological homogeneity since the second/first millennium BC, and its prehistory did not end until the post-medieval European oceanic voyages.

In what sequence to place the chapters has proved difficult to decide. Boatbuilding and seafaring did not originate in one region and spread neatly around the world: all chapters thus greatly overlap chronologically. The solution has been to deal first with Egypt and Arabia, where much early evidence for water transport has survived; then to describe the European evidence in two chapters; followed by south Asia and a generally eastwards progression from south-east Asia to the Americas, via Greater Australia, the South Pacific, and China.

Individual chapters differ in their layout and in the general approach adopted, depending on the strengths of the various types of evidence available within a region. Generally, the environmental setting is described first and then a range of evidence is discussed chronologically by centuries, or by archaeological/historical periods. However, certain themes, such as 'rafts and non-plank boats', and 'navigational techniques', are usually considered for the whole time range within one section.

Underlying all chapters in this study is the theme that rivers and seas connect continents and cultures: it is possible to travel by water from the Swiss Alps to the heart of Ethiopia, or from the Himalayas to the Indonesian archipelago or even the West Indies. Individual people or boats may not have undertaken such voyages until recent times, but ideas can travel great distances in a series of discrete passages. For example, the use of the mariner's compass is thought to have spread from the China Sea to the North Sea within the short space of 100 years (3.8.2.2.1, 5.10, 10.11). Other aids to navigation, hull forms, shipbuilding techniques, and sailing rigs, may have been similarly transmitted about the world, but remain undocumented. The spatial bounds of each chapter are purely for convenience of exposition: it is necessary to bear in mind the interaction (often unknown to history) between different cultures that water transport, especially the sailing boat, facilitates and indeed, encourages.

# 2
# EGYPT

There is no single agreed chronology for Ancient Egypt. Three authors who have recently written about the nautical aspects of Egypt each use a different chronology: Vinson (1994: 5) bases his account on one published by Murnane in 1983; D. Jones (1995: 7) uses dates published by Baines and Malik in 1980; whilst Wachsmann (1998: 345) uses a chronology published by Kitchen in 1987. I have chosen to use the chronology published by James (1983) in a widely available text. For the non-specialist there are only minor differences between these four chronologies.

Herodotus (2. 5) called Egypt the 'gift of the River Nile', and it is undoubtedly true that, without the fertility brought northwards by this great river, Egyptian civilization would not have existed. From headwaters in the vicinity of Lake Tana, and in the Ugandan/Kenyan highlands around Lake Victoria, the Nile brought not only water which annually in late summer (Strabo, 17. 1. 4) flooded the Nile valley north of the First Cataract (*c.*24°N), but also a silt deposited as a rich alluvium which regularly, and almost without fail, renewed the valley's fertility (James, 1983: 21–4).

In ancient times and to a great extent today, the effective land of Egypt was a narrow strip of cultivated land (Herodotus, 2. 8; Strabo, 17. 1. 4) stretching *c.*750 m. from Aswan to the sea (Fig. 2.1). This extended either side of the Nile as far as the rising ground of the desert, from the natural barrier found to the south by the first cataract—just south of Aswan where the river flow is broken by the granite nature of the river bed— through sandstone and then limestone, north to Cairo, where the vast delta lands begin, and on into the Mediterranean.

## 2.1

## The Delta

This delta area formed the principal part of what was known in antiquity as Lower Egypt: the precise position of the ancient boundary between this and Upper Egypt is not known.

Today there are two main channels of the Nile in the Delta, an eastern arm which reaches the sea at Damietta and a western arm which debouches at Rosetta. In Pharaonic times there were three principal channels: *Amun* to the west (known in Classical times as the Canopic); *Ptah* flowing more or less due north (Sebennytic); and the *Pre* (Pelusiac) to the east (James, 1983: 20; Herodotus (2. 15, 154, 179); Strabo, 17. 1. 4., 17. 1. 18). There were other minor channels (Saitic/Tanitic; Mendesian) and canals (Balbitine and Bucolic) in Classical times (Herodotus, 2. 17; Strabo, 17. 1. 4., 17. 1. 18) and probably in earlier times also. In the late summer an immense amount of water had to be dispersed through this delta region to the sea. Although much of the silt the Nile carried was deposited on land, it still contained an appreciable amount when it entered the Mediterranean, and this discharge, as Herodotus (2. 5) tells us, could be recognized out to a distance of a day's sail (say, 70 nautical miles) from the coast, where a sounding lead could pick up samples of the Nile silts.

The regularity of the Nile's 'gift' and the genius of the Neolithic peoples living there, resulted in the evolution of a Bronze Age civilization towards the close of the fourth millennium BC. At about this time the two loose confederacies of Upper and Lower Egypt each became more closely defined and subject to 'kings' with centres at Naqada (Nubt—north of Karna), then Hierakonpolis (north of Edfu) in the south, and Behdet, then Buto (in the Delta) in the north. Subsequently, the north was conquered by the south and emerged from prehistory to form, under a king known as Menes or Narmer (James, 1983: 41; Mark, 1997: 88–121), a unified state rivalling, and in many respects surpassing, the roughly contemporary Mesopotamian civilization. It has sometimes been suggested that this rapid evolution of civilization in the Nile valley was due to direct influences from Mesopotamia, either across the Red Sea to Naqada in Upper Egypt or via the Levant to Buto in Lower Egypt (Hourani, 1963: 6–7; Mark, 1997: 69–87, 129–30). Although there was undoubtedly Mesopotamian influence, it seems unnecessary to postulate large-scale intrusions (O'Connor, 1980a: 129–30; Mark, 1997). The technological achievements of the indigenous peoples within the context of an exceptionally fertile river valley allowed

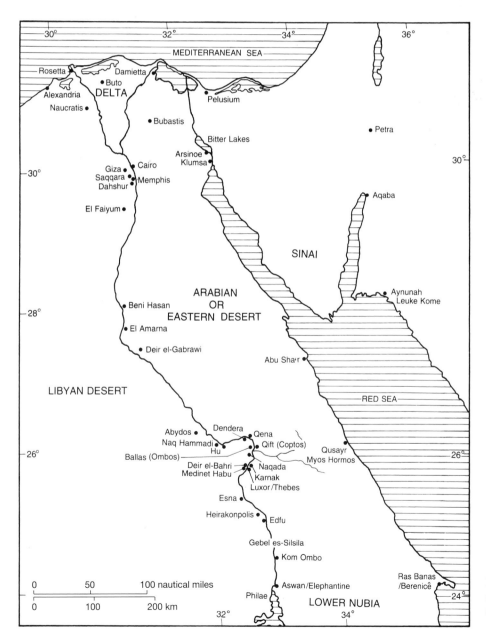

Fig. 2.1. Map of Egypt (Institute of Archaeology, Oxford).

them to evolve economically and politically. This led rapidly to a Bronze Age civilization which was not elsewhere achieved in Africa until very much later. Such Mesopotamian influence as there was probably came indirectly, overland through the Levant, or through Syria and across the Mediterranean to the Nile (Mark, 1997: 122–31).

The Nile, with its special characteristics, was not only a sine qua non for life in Egypt, but also a vital artery, the principal 'highway' of the land with no part of the valley more than about 16 km from the river. In this respect Egypt was similar to Mesopotamia, but it had an added advantage that the Nile flowed northwards against the generally predominant northerly wind. Thus sail could (in time) be used, rather than towing (as in Mesopotamia) to travel upstream. That the river was used whenever possible, in preference to travel by foot or by ass, is suggested by the early use of hieroglyphics showing a boat with sail to mean to go 'south' or upstream, and a boat without sail to mean to go 'north' or downstream (James, 1983: 21–2).

To the west of the Nile valley is the Libyan desert which in Pharaonic times, as now, was a desolate area of sand, dunes, and rocky wasteland and thus was little used by the ancient Egyptians. The Arabic desert plateau to the east, on the other hand, is a mountainous region with peaks up to 2,000 m or more, and with minerals and hard stone much needed in ancient Egypt. Access from the Nile to quarry sites in this eastern desert, and ultimately to the Red Sea, was by *wadi* (rocky watercourses, generally dry) and by mountain pass, the principal route being the Wadi Hammamat (Fig. 2.1). Egypt thus had direct access down the Nile by water transport to Mediterranean lands, especially to the Levant; and indirect access, up the Nile and across the eastern desert, to the Red Sea, thence to Arabia and eastern Africa.

## 2.2

# Egypt's Natural Resources

In addition to the resources of the Nile, ancient Egypt had three main raw materials, stone (sandstone, lime-

stone, and granite), papyrus reed, and river mud, all of which were used for building (James, 1983: 31–2). Papyrus was also used to make ropes, cord, mats, durable writing material, and bundle rafts. Flint, found as nodules within the limestone, was used to make tools. Copper was obtained from the eastern desert but this supply had to be supplemented by imports from Cyprus. Arsenic and tin (needed to make bronze tools) had to be imported from Asia. This deficiency resulted in the late development of bronze tools and weapons compared with elsewhere in the Near East. Furthermore, although iron was used from the twenty-sixth dynasty (seventh century BC) onwards, it was not until the third century BC that iron tools became usual (James, 1983: 34, 218).

Another significant deficiency in natural resources, especially in the context of water transport, was timber. Trees such as the acacia (*Acacia nilotica*), sycamorefig (*Ficus sycomorus*), date-palm (*Phoenix dactylifera*), dom-palm (*Hyphaena thebaica*), persea (*Mimusops schimperi*), and tamarisk (*Tamarix* sp.) did indeed grow within the bounds of Egypt, but these did not produce planking longer than *c*.6 m, and acacia was a hard timber to work: this led to the import of other timber species, especially cedar (*Pinus cedrus*) from Lebanon, which were easier to fashion and gave lengths of 20 m and more (Landström, 1970: 19; Meiggs, 1982; Wachsmann, 1998: 254, 310).

## 2.3

# Seafaring

It has sometimes been said that the ancient Egyptians were not seafarers and that the vessels they built were only suitable for the Nile (e.g. Barnett, 1958: 223). This was not so: their need for copper early led them to trade with Cyprus, and with Asia Minor for tin (James, 1983: 34); their need for long planks from the earliest dynastic period (early third millennium BC) stimulated overseas voyages to the Levant coast for *meru*—probably cedar wood (*Pinus cedrus*)—from the Lebanon highlands. The import of this timber by Sneferu in the fourth dynasty (*c*.2600 BC) is recorded on the Palermo stone, and inscriptions at Byblos in the Lebanon suggest that this trade may have begun in the second dynasty (*c.*2700 BC). By *c.*2400 BC, Byblos was virtually an Egyptian port for the embarkation of timber (Wachsmann, 1998: 9–10).

Furthermore, the Egyptians sent military expeditions into the eastern Mediterranean. For example, Uni led an amphibious assault on the Levant coast (possibly in the region of Mount Carmel) during the sixth dynasty (*c.*2250 BC). In the twelfth dynasty, probably *c.*1800 BC, an Egyptian army was brought back to Egypt from Lebanon in ten ships; and in the eighteenth dynasty, around 1450 BC, Thutmose III led another expedition to the Levant coast (Wachsmann, 1998: 10).

Herodotus (2. 43) who believed that the Egyptians had been a seafaring nation before the Greeks, recounts several seafaring incidents: Haibre Wahibre (Apries) of the twenty-sixth dynasty fought a naval battle against Tyre in the early sixth century BC (2. 161); his successor, Khnemibre Amosis II (Amasis) invaded and took Cyprus (2. 153); and Egyptian ships and crews played a prominent part on the Persian side in the battle of Salamis (8. 17).

On the base of a statue in Amenhatep III's mortuary temple (*c.*1800 BC) at Kom el Hetan there is a list of Aegean place names which appears to be a record of an Egyptian voyage during which Crete was circumnavigated, and the Peloponnese, Kythera, and Ilium (Troy) visited (Wachsmann, 1998: 297).

The Egyptians also sailed in the Red Sea. From the mid-third millennium BC (fifth dynasty) onwards there was trade with the east African coast for exotic goods such as incense, sandalwood, and ebony. Herodotus (2. 102) tells us that Sesostris (probably Sesostris III of *c.*1850 BC) explored the coastal lands of the Red Sea with a fleet of ships.

Pilot was one of the seven Egyptian occupational classes (Herodotus, 2. 164) and their familiarity with piloting vessels along the Nile and in the Delta would have fitted them admirably for similarly guiding seagoing craft along the coasts of the eastern Mediterranean and in the Red Sea. As in Mesopotamia the necessity to forecast river floods led the Egyptians to the early study of astronomy (Herodotus, 2. 4). Merchants travelling through the desert at night were able to navigate by the stars (Strabo, 17. 1. 45). Such knowledge and expertise could also have been used at sea to navigate out of sight of land.

# 2.4

# The Pre-Pharaonic Period
## (*c.*13,000–3100 BC)

Mesolithic hunter-gatherers lived in the Nile valley from *c.*13,000 BC (O'Connor, 1980*a*: 128): what form of water transport they used is not known, but theoretical studies suggest that they were technologically capable of building a range of floats as well as bundle rafts (McGrail, 1988*a*: table 1). Farming and other aspects of the Neolithic way of life began *c.*5000 BC, and this predynastic phase lasted until the late fourth millennium BC when a short proto-dynastic period led to the unification of Upper and Lower Egypt under Narmer (Menes), the first king of the first dynasty (*c.*3100 BC).

There are several finds from the late part of this period—mostly iconographic, from Upper Egypt and the eastern desert—which portray the forms of water transport used by the late Neolithic / Early Bronze Age peoples. The earliest finds are from Naqada 1 period (Amratian) of *c.*3500 BC. A shallow oval dish appears to have a plan-view of a double-ended raft or boat painted on it (Arkell, 1959: fig. 1; Landström, 1970: fig. 4; Casson, 1971: fig. 3); two other dishes have a chequered framework which Landström (1970: 12, figs. 3 and 5) thinks may represent a boat's framework, but his argument is not convincing. A shallowly curved craft with paddles depicted on an Amratian bowl (Fig. 2.2) possibly represents a raft of some sort, probably bundles rather than logs, if we take into account subsequent Egyptian practice. Casson (1971: 12) considers the vessel on the oval dish is propelled by oars, but paddles seem more likely on both depictions, especially when compared with the vessel painted on linen from a grave at Gebelein which depicts helmsmen and crew facing for-

Fig. 2.2. Craft depicted on an Amratian bowl from the fourth-millennium BC (after Bass, 1972: fig. 2).

Fig. 2.3. Boats painted on a fourth-millennium BC linen fragment from El-Gebelein in Upper Egypt (Soprintendenza per leantichita Egizie, Turin).

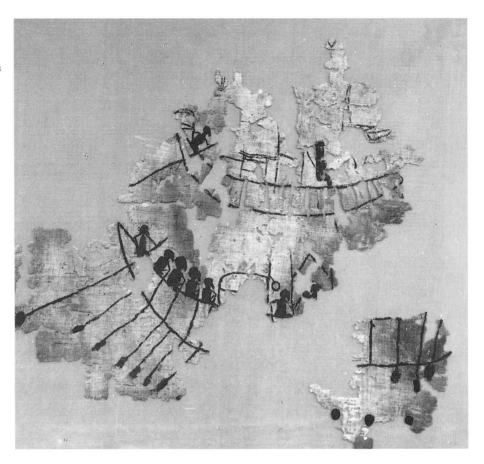

ward (Fig. 2.3). Although oars can be used to propel a vessel by men facing forward (McGrail and Farrell, 1979) it seems more likely in this case that paddlers are depicted. The other features on these vessels—rectangular 'boxes' with a chequerboard pattern—are generally interpreted as cabins or shelters for important passengers, or as shrines (Arkell, 1959).

From the next phase Naqada 2 (Gerzean) of *c.*3200 BC come innumerable stylized drawings on pottery of what are generally thought to represent rafts or boats, although some authors have suggested stockades (Barnett, 1958: 222; Arkell, 1959: 52; Landström, 1970: 13). The parallel curved lines on these drawings (Fig. 2.4) probably represent the hull, most likely that of a boat-shaped bundle raft (to judge by subsequent developments). The numerous lines drawn downwards from the hull may represent paddles or possibly oars. The chequerboard structures may be cabins or shrines; poles next to these cabins/shrines appear to carry the emblem of various *nomes* (political divisions) of Upper Egypt (Bass, 1972: 13). The palm branch at one end (the bow?) may be there to provide shade for the lookout as

Bass has suggested, or it may be to use a following wind to propel the vessel, as known from recent times (Folkard, 1870: 247; Waugh, 1919: 30). Some of these vessels—see, for example, the one published by Landström (1970: fig. 14) and by Johnstone (1988: fig. 7.11)—additionally have a banner-like device set up on a pole towards one end, which may be decorative or may signify allegiance to a particular grouping or, like the

Fig. 2.4. Craft with banners and shrines depicted on a vase of *c.*3200 BC (after Landström, 1970: fig. 14).

palm branch, may be a simple means of using a following wind (R. Bowen, 1960). At least one vessel (Landström, 1970: fig. 10) shows three distinctive steering paddles or oars.

Other pottery paintings of this period show craft with inward turning ends and lines across the hull which suggest that these are representations of reed bundle rafts (Landström, 1970: figs. 11, 12, 13).

From c.3100 BC in the proto-dynastic period (Naqada 3=Samaiden), which appears to merge into Dynasty 1 of the historic period (O'Connor, 1980a: 129), comes the earliest depiction of a true sail (Fig. 2.5). The boat on this pot (BM 36326) has a square sail on a pole mast stepped near one end. The boat has a distinctive shape with high, near-vertical, ends. Such a hull form is also seen (along with curved hull vessels) on the ivory handle of a knife (Fig. 2.6) said to be from Gebel-el-Arak, and in a painting formerly on the brick walls of Late

Fig. 2.6. Two types of craft carved on an ivory knife-handle from Gebel-el-Arak (Louvre, Paris).

Fig. 2.5. Vase from Nagada of about 3100 BC showing a craft with a single square sail (British Museum).

Gerzean tomb 100 in Hieraconpolis, again with curved hull vessels in the vicinity (Bass, 1972: fig. 6; Landström, 1970: figs. 16,17)—both representations are dated to c.3200 BC.

There are two small models from this period which have vertical stripes across their hulls which may well represent the bindings of reed rafts (Landström, 1970: figs. 24, 25). Other models published by Landström (1970: figs. 26, 28, and 29) are difficult to interpret.

Depictions of vessels with high vertical ends and others with low-curved hulls have also been noted amongst petroglyphs in the Egyptian eastern desert (Winkler, 1939) on the Wadi Hammamat route between the River Nile at Coptus (Quft) and the coast of the Red Sea at Qusayr (Hornell, 1941a: 234). Examples of these are given by Bass (1972: figs. 3 and 4) Johnstone (1988: fig. 13.7) Hornell (1946a: fig. 6),

Landström (1970: figs. 30 and 45) and by Mark (1997: figs. 44–8). The high vertically ended vessels have some similarities with the shape of boats depicted on Mesopotamian cylinder seals of the Jamdat Nasr or Uruk periods (Bass, 1972: plate 8; Barnett, 1958: plate 21a; Arkell, 1959: fig. 3; Mark, 1997: fig. 35), contemporary with the Egyptian Naqada 2 and 3 phases. This has led some authors to suggest that the representations found in Egypt depict a Mesopotamian type of vessel, and that, taken together with other evidence of Mesopotamian/Egyptian contact—certain pottery types, a few cylinder seals, some artistic motifs, to quote O'Connor (1980a: 129)—this may indicate that the origin of the Egyptian state was due to intrusions by Mesopotamians. (Hourani, 1963: 6–7; Hornell, 1941a: 235). An alternative, less contentious hypothesis, and with more support from the evidence, is that knowledge of Mesopotamian boat types (among other influences) came to Egypt via trade with the Levant (Hourani, 1963: 7; Mark, 1997: 87, 104). The Egyptian state probably evolved rapidly from internal influences; the similarities between aspects of Mesopotamian and Egyptian cultures were due to imports and influences from the Levant trade and were of minimal significance politically (O'Connor, 1980b: 129–30: Mark, 1997).

If we take the Egyptian evidence (especially the Wadi Hammamat petroglyphs) at face value and evaluate it for the light it throws on early water transport rather than the origins of political power, it seems possible to suggest that travellers on the route between the Red Sea and the Nile in the late fourth millennium BC were familiar with oared or paddled vessels of two types: a low-curved form of hull; and a hull with high vertical ends. The low hull form reappears later in depictions of reed-bundle rafts both in Mesopotamia and in Egypt where it was developed most. Some of the petroglyphs in the eastern Desert have a line from the 'stem' to the bottom of the vessel which may well represent the stay sometimes used to support the ends of a reed-bundle raft (Landström, 1970: figs. 30 and 32). Three other desert petroglyphs (figs. 32, 37, 38) have bundle 'binding lines'. Representations of the hull with high vertical ends are also found in Mesopotamia at about the same time (3.2). Subsequently Egyptian craftsmen of the protohistoric/first Dynasty period reproduced both hull forms on the Gebel-el-Arak knife handle (Fig. 2.6) and on the Naqada 3 pot (Fig. 2.5).

Indigenous evidence for sail in Mesopotamia is from a very much later date and thus it is unlikely that this feature has been copied by Egyptians from Mesopotamian prototypes. The low-curved form of hull seems most appropriate to the reed-bundle raft which may have had independent origins in Mesopotamia and Egypt, and indeed in many other parts of the world. If, as suggested above, the high-ended hull represented a bundle *boat*, this could explain why it does not appear subsequently in Egypt which, unlike Mesopotamia, had no readily available supply of the tar needed to waterproof the reed bundles (3.4.4).

# 2.5

# Non-Plank Craft Throughout Pharaonic Times

From c.3100 BC onwards there is an increasing amount of iconographic and documentary evidence for the building and the use of water transport, and the illustrative material, whilst still not absolutely clear, is more readily interpreted than the prehistoric petroglyphs and pottery paintings. Although planked vessels (which will be discussed later) predominate in this evidence, there are other types of raft and boat, especially reed-bundle rafts. It is convenient to discuss here these non-plank craft over the whole time range of this chapter, rather than dealing with the evidence in chronological periods.

## 2.5.1 POT BOATS AND BUNDLE RAFTS

Strabo (17. 1. 4) mentions two types of non-plank boat which he saw in use on the River Nile: pottery boats used as ferries in the Delta; and a *pacton*. Pots, linked together by a light timber framework to form a raft, have been used in the Mediterranean and in China, Korea, India, and Egypt in recent times (Hornell, 1946a: 34–7; McGrail, 1998: 188), and large pots were also used individually as boats in Bengal in the present century (Hornell, 1946a: fig. 9).

Strabo (17. 1. 50) crossed to the island of Philae, in

the Nile above Aswan, on a *pacton* 'constructed of withes, so that it resembles woven work'. Casson (1971: 342) considers that this was a round bundle *boat* similar to the *quffa* of Mesopotamia (3.4.4.1), whilst Hornell (1946a: 51) thought it was a bundle *raft*. The fact that the passengers were 'standing in water or seated on small boards' suggests that the *pacton* was a raft, through which water flows. Furthermore, Egypt unlike Mesopotamia has no readily available supply of tar which would be needed to make a bundle *boat* water-tight. In the second and third centuries AD, *pactons* were wooden craft capable of carrying up to 14 tonnes of cargo (Casson, 1971: 342) and were propelled by two oars. Of all the forms of water transport, the boat-shaped raft made of bundles of light poles, linked by the coiled basketry techniques seems best to fit Strabo's description. Such rafts were used in the early twentieth century in India (Hornell, 1946a: 68) and in Africa on the upper reaches of the Nile, and in Uganda (Hornell, 1946a: 52, plates 7A, and 7AA) where poles of *ambatch* (*Herminiera elaphroxylon*) were used.

Rafts of reed bundles are also widely used in Africa today: in Morocco, the Lake Tana region of Ethiopia, the Lake Chad area, in and around the Okavango Swamp, and in Lake Ngami (Hornell, 1946a: 51–5), and in many other parts of the world wherever there is a good supply of reeds (McGrail, 1998: 168). They were also extensively used in ancient Egypt and are often depicted in hunting, fishing, and fowling scenes within the marshlands in the Delta, around the lake in the Faiyum, and wherever flood water was trapped after the annual inundation (James, 1983: 31). In the eighth century BC, Isaiah (18: 1, 2) mentions that Egyptian envoys were brought to the Levant in papyrus-bundle rafts.

There are many scenes with reed-bundle rafts on tomb paintings from early dynastic times, and their use continued for millennia, one of the latest representations being on a relief at Kom-Ombo dated to the second century BC showing Ptolemy VIII (Euergetes II) (Hornell, 1946a: 50)—see also the first-century BC boat-shaped bundle raft published by Casson (1971: fig. 116). Pliny (*NH* 13. 22. 71–3) noted that in his time they were used on the River Nile. Strabo (17. 1. 49) described how boatmen tackled the First Cataract passage both upstream and downstream. Although Strabo did not say what sort of vessels were used, it may be that they were reed-bundle rafts as these were used in the eighteenth century AD to shoot these rapids (Hornell, 1946a: 51).

The reed used in ancient Egypt was papyrus (*Cyperus papyrus*) which grew in abundance in the marshes and pools (James, 1983: 92) as it did in Mesopotamia. The only tool necessary to build a bundle raft was a simple blade to cut through the reed; the only techniques needed were rope-making and the ability to

Fig. 2.7. Scene in Ptahhotep's fifth-dynasty tomb at Saqqara showing reed bundle rafts under construction (after Hornell,1946a: plate 6B).

bind bundles of reeds tightly in themselves and to other bundles, using coiled basketry (McGrail, 1998: 165–9). The tighter the bundles, the more rigid the resultant raft, and the longer it will stay afloat without waterlogging.

The sequence of building a reed raft can be seen in several tomb paintings, for example, in the fifth-dynasty tomb of Ptahhotep in Saqqara (Fig. 2.7); in the fifth-dynasty illustration in the Mastaba of Achethetep (Wachsmann, 1998: fig. 10.10); and in a twelfth-dynasty illustration of *c*.2000 BC, published by Bass (1972: plate 23). In these we can see the cordage being made, the bundles being bound together, the builder using his extended foot as a lever to ensure tightness (Fig. 2.8),

Fig. 2.8. Tightening the lashings of a bundle raft (after Bass, 1972: fig. 23).

and the bundles being bent against wooden stocks to give upturned ends. In an unusual scene published by Landström (1970: fig. 307) the bundles are being bound and shaped at the end against a man's humped back. As Hornell (1946a: 47) pointed out, the tightening of the lashings at the ends by pulling towards amidships naturally causes the projecting reed ends to splay out fanwise; later this was a distinctive feature on some planked boats.

These bundle rafts are distinguished in the paintings and models by vertical lines representing the bundle bindings (e.g. Landström, 1970: fig. 295). The ends of some reed rafts are blunt and bent upwards just sufficiently to keep them clear of the water—see, for example, the Theban tomb painting in James (1983: plate 4), and in Johnstone (1988: fig. 7.3) and also some of the

models from Tutankhamun's tomb. Other representations show rising ornate ends with the after end recurved and ending in a lotus or papyrus terminal, or it has a long high curve; the forward end is nearly always lower (Hornell, 1946a: 47; Landström, 1970: figs. 300–2; Casson, 1971: 12–13, figs. 7, 89). Bundle rafts can readily be given a hollowed boatlike form by positioning the smaller side bundles higher than the large bottom bundle—see, for example, the twentieth-century rafts of Lake Titicaca, Peru (Hornell, 1946a: plate 5). Although flat-top bundle rafts predominate in the Egyptian material, there are examples of hollow forms (Casson, 1971: fig. 7). In some of the scenes showing distinguished men hunting or fowling (Landström, 1970: figs. 294, 295, 299, 302; Casson, 1971: fig. 9; James, 1983: plate 4) the hunter is shown standing on what appears to be a decking or a wooden platform laid on top of the bundles. In pre-dynastic times stays at the ends held the upturned end and the bottom of the bundle raft in the correct relationship (Landström, 1970: 16, figs. 32–4, 43; Heyerdahl, 1978: figs. 4 and 5). In later times these relative positions seem to have been maintained by a taut rope lashed to the entire upper rim of the raft (Landström, 1970: figs. 294, 297, 304, 309): an alternative method is seen on the two 'trawling' models from the eleventh-dynasty tomb of Meket-re (Casson, 1971: fig. 8; Hornell, 1946a: plate 6A; Bass, 1972: plate 17; Landström, 1970: fig. 305; D. Jones, 1995: fig. 26) where small reed bundles are lashed to the rim.

These bundle rafts were depicted propelled by pole, sometimes by paddle. Some of the poles have a forked terminal, useful where there is a muddy bottom but also usable in a fight as seen in another painting in Ptahotep's tomb (Hornell, 1946a: 48). Sail is rarely seen on any vessel which is unambiguously a bundle raft—the only example that comes to mind is that noted by Hornell (1946a: 49): a model of a reed raft of the sixth dynasty from Gebrâwi, No. 65 in Petries series, which has a bipod mast made of two sheers stepped on the side bundles and meeting at an apex.

As well as being used for hunting buffalo and fowling, bundle rafts were used for fishing: the pair of models from the Theban tomb of Meket-re are towing a simple trawl net between them. Doubtless simple rafts were also used everywhere as ferries for people and goods: Hornell (1946a: 51) recorded similar twentieth-century uses on the Upper Nile south of Egypt, and on Lake Tana and Lake Chad.

## 2.5.2 LOGBOATS

Hornell (1946*a*: 48, plate 27b) considered that the boat-building scene on the walls of the fifth-dynasty tomb of Ti (Bass, 1972: plate 21; Landström, 1970: fig. 102; D. Jones, 1995: fig. 64) showed planking being added to a logboat base, mainly because some of the builders were adzing the ends and the upper and lower surfaces. However, it seems more likely that a planked boat is represented. Although planks are not depicted on the lower part of the hull, the boat's shape matches other representations of known planked vessels, and the builders are probably using their adzes (in the manner of a plane) to give a final shaping to the vessel. Logboats are, in fact, scarcely known from Egypt, presumably because the indigenous trees did not yield suitable timber, both in size and in woodworking qualities. Casson (1971: 8) gives only one example, a reference to a logboat in the Delta by classical author Heliodorus (I. 31. 2). Models of logboats said to be from a tomb near Giza and from Lake Bardawil, east of Port Said, are held in the National Maritime Museum, Haifa in Israel (Basch, 1976*a*; 1987*a*: 55–6).

# 2.6

## Planked Craft of the Early Dynastic Period

### (*c*.3100–2866 BC)

The oldest excavated planked vessel in the world is the ship from an underground chamber or pit near the pyramid of Cheops/Khufu of the fourth dynasty (Fig. 2.9). This date of *c*.2600 BC receives support from a radiocarbon date, from a fragment of rope, of 3990 + 105 BP (BM-332) which indicates a calibrated date towards the middle of the third millennium BC.

The size and complexity of this ship suggests that the Egyptians must have been able to build planked boats for some considerable time before 2600 BC. From a study of wooden objects from the pre-dynastic period, James (1983: 228) has deduced that fine woodworking—as needed for boatbuilding—was not possible in

Egypt until the Early Dynastic period when copper tools became available: this reflects the worldwide picture. From *c*.3000 BC a range of tools was available in Egypt: axes, adzes, chisels, pulling saws, mallets, wedges, bradawls, bowdrills, and sandstone rubbers; furthermore, examples are known of honing stones with oil flasks, squares, levels, and plumb-rules (James, 1983: 228–30; Landström, 1970: 23; Jones, 1995: 72–3). From these early dynastic times timbers could be joined by lashing with leather thongs, dovetailed cramps, mortise and tenon joints, and wooden dowels (James, 1983: 230; Johnstone, 1988: 74; Hornell, 1946*a*: 220).

The Cheops ship's planks were positioned in relation to one another by joggles, tenons, and 'coaks' (2. 7. 1), and then fastened together by lashings running transversely across the planking. The frames were then lashed to the planking. It seems likely, therefore, that the planks of Early Dynastic-period vessels (first and second dynasties) were also lashed together using flax or grass ropes.

## 2.6.1 BURIED BOATS AND SHIPS

Although the Cheops ship is, to date, the earliest surviving planked vessel, it is not the earliest Egyptian boat or ship known to have been buried. This ritual practice seems to have begun during the first dynasty: nineteen boat chambers or pits thought to be dated to this period were excavated at Helwan beginning in 1947, and six at Saqqara from 1954. When opened, most of these pits no longer contained recognizable boat remains and the publications of those boats that did survive tell us almost nothing about the vessel's structure (D. Jones, 1995: 33–5; Wachsmann, 1998: 219). For example, the reconstruction drawing of the vessel inside a brick-lined pit published in D. Jones (1995: fig. 30) reveals merely that this vessel (assumed to be that of Aha, second Pharaoh of the first dynasty) measured *c*.15 × 1.5 × 1 m, that one end was higher than the other, and that there was some superstructure towards that higher end.

In 1991 further planked boats were discovered near the north corner of Khasekhemmy's first-dynasty funerary enclosure at Abydos (Wachsmann, 1998: 218; Jones, 1995: 35). These twelve boats, 15–18 m in length, had been buried within brick 'coffins'. They are of

Fig. 2.9. The Cheops ship of
*c*.2600 BC on display in Giza
(photo: Paul Johnstone).

enormous potential, but excavation has been post-poned until appropriate resources are available for research and conservation.

Other boat burial chambers dated to later dynasties have also been recognized; with two exceptions, all are at Giza (James, 1983: 23, 27; Jones, 1995: 33–5; Wachs-mann, 1998: 219–23), see list on p. 25.

Senusret III, of the twelfth dynasty (*c*.1850 BC) also had six boat pits within his funerary enclosure at Dahshur (2.8.3.2). Apart from this, the practice of burying boats and ships with important people seems to have lasted for *c*.700 years from *c*.3050 to *c*.2345 BC; this ritual appears to have been replaced by the deposition of model vessels within tombs.

| 4th dynasty | Cheops/Khufu | 5 (possibly 6) pits |
|---|---|---|
| | Meryetes (wife of Khufu) | 1 pit |
| | Redjedef | 1 pit (at Abu Roash, north of Giza) |
| | Chephren/Khafre | 5 (possibly 6) pits |
| | Mycerinus/Menkaure | probably at least 1 pit |
| 5th dynasty | Khentkawes (wife of Userkef) | 1 pit |
| | Unas | possibly 1 (at Saqqara) |

That actual boats and ships were entombed with important people (most frequently a Pharaoh) may mean that they had a symbolic function in addition to any use they may have had during that Pharaoh's lifetime. There are three main theories about this. Such a vessel may have been:

(a) *Funerary barge*. The purely functional use of transporting the Pharaoh's embalmed body to the tomb.
(b) *Pilgrimage boat*. The part symbolic/part practical use by the Pharaoh to visit holy places during his lifetime and in the Other World.
(c) *Stellar/solar boat*. A symbolic use, reflecting an early belief that the dead but resurrected Pharaoh journeyed to the stars; and a later belief that he journeyed daily with the sun.

Of the sixty or so boat pits known, only thirteen remain to be excavated. The twelve boats thought to be interred at Abydos and the second Cheops ship should in time reveal more about the structure of Early Dynastic vessels. For the present, we can only turn to some other early wooden remains and to a limited range of representational evidence.

## 2.6.2 OTHER WOODEN REMAINS

Planks used to line or roof a first-dynasty grave were excavated by Petrie at Tarkhan, south of Cairo in the early years of this century (Vinson, 1994: 18–19; Wachsmann, 1998: 218). Some of these planks have V-and L-shaped holes and some have mortises along their edges. These two features are characteristic of the Cheops ship which suggests that these planks may have been the remains of a first dynasty vessel.

Johnstone (1980: 74) has drawn attention to a rectangular block of wood excavated by Emory from the tomb of Uadji/Djet, third Pharaoh of the first dynasty. This fragment has tenons at both ends pierced with holes for treenails or dowels. Although this timber had no nautical connections, it does show that, as early as c.3000 BC, Egyptian woodworkers used the *locked* mortise and tenon joint which was to become a prime characteristic of Mediterranean ships from the mid-second millennium BC to the mid-first millennium AD.

## 2.6.3 REPRESENTATIONAL EVIDENCE

The earliest suggestion of a plank boat is seen on one of the so-called 'foreign' vessels carved on the ivory handle of a slate knife from Gebel-el-Arak (Fig. 2.6) which is dated to the end of the fourth millennium BC. The horizontal line just below the upper edge of the hull has been taken to depict planking. However, a more dominant feature of this representation is the stay running from the high upturned end to the bottom of the hull which is more characteristic of a bundle boat. Landström (1970: 19–21, figs. 23–4, 64–72) considered that several other proto-dynastic representations, including some ivory models of the Early Dynastic period, may be of planked boats, but his argument is not convincing. It seems more likely that the lines incised along the top edge of the hull and around the chine are decorative features, or possibly a representation of a rim-strengthening rope on a bundle raft, since the model in Landström's fig. 72 has indisputable vertical lines across the hull which almost certainly denote bundle binding lines.

In fact, there is at present no evidence dated before 2600 BC which unambiguously represents a planked boat, with lines showing the run of the planking. Sewn-plank fastenings need not be depicted since they can be invisible from outboard—as in the Cheops ship. Hidden stitching on the underwater hull is used worldwide to ensure that fastenings cannot be damaged when a sewn boat takes the ground or touches a river bank or other hazard (McGrail and Kentley, 1985).

## 2.7

# Planked Boats and Ships of the Old Kingdom

## (*c*.2686–2160 BC)

The Cheops ship of *c*.2600 BC is the main source of evidence for the structure of vessels from this 500-year period. It has to be remembered, however, that even though she may be a representative riverine vessel from her own times—and this is by no means certain—it is unlikely that the technological practices seen in her remained the same for the next 400 years. Furthermore, she furnishes no evidence for mast, rigging, or sail, at a time when the Egyptians were undoubtedly using sail.

### 2.7.1 THE CHEOPS SHIP (Fig. 2.9)

The dismantled timbers from this ship were recovered from an underground chamber in 1954, and between 1957 and 1971, the 1,224 components were reassembled to form the ship now on display in a museum built directly over the pit where she had been for *c*.4,500 years. As reconstructed, she measures *c*.43.4 × 5.9 × 1.8 m—the ends rise to 6–7.5 m. This is a large vessel by any standards. The description that follows relies very much on Lipke's pioneering work (1984), and on commentaries by Steffy (1994) and Haldane (1997*b*).

The hull is cedar, probably from Lebanon, the wooden plank fastenings are sidder ('crown of thorns' tree), other pegs are sycamore, whilst some of the internal framing is of acacia. The lashings by which the planks were fastened together were of Halfa grass (*Desmustachya bipannata*).

This vessel was built in the plank-first sequence: in general terms, the flat bottom of three adjacent strakes (only two towards the bow) and the cluster of timbers which closed the watertight ends of the vessel, were first assembled, then the side planking, and finally the framing.

Planks (120–50 mm thick) within strakes were fastened together in long S-shaped scarfs. Strakes were positioned relative to each other in three ways (Fig. 2.10):

(a) plank edges had projections and notches which fitted into similar joggles on adjacent planks;
(b) unlocked mortise and tenon joints (*c*.40 mm deep) regularly spaced at about 1 m intervals;
(c) dowels or 'coaks' at irregular intervals of *c*.2 m (Haldane, 1997*b*).

These three devices additionally acted to prevent adjacent strakes from sliding relative to one another due to sheering forces experienced when afloat.

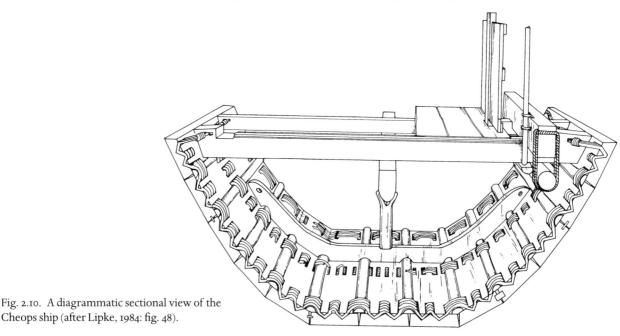

Fig. 2.10. A diagrammatic sectional view of the Cheops ship (after Lipke, 1984: fig. 48).

Fig. 2.11. The interior of the Cheops ship with temporary fastenings in place (photo: Paul Johnstone).

The planking was fastened together by two types of lashings:

(a) lashings between adjacent strakes—called 'strategic' fastenings by the reconstructor Hag Ahmed Youssef (Lipke, 1984: 79, 117). There were 277 sets of these holes.
(b) transverse lashings from sheer to sheer through V-shaped holes in every strake. There were over 4,000 such fastening holes.

It is noticeable that, although there are locked mortise and tenon joints within the vessel's superstructure, the hull mortise and tenons are not locked. Moreover, the holes for the hull lashings are worked within the thickness of the planking and cannot be seen from outbound. The Egyptian shipwrights, as in many other sewn-plank boat technologies (McGrail and Kentley,

1985), avoided making holes through planking below the waterline.

The framing consisted of: sixteen floor timbers notched over the seam battens and lashed to the planking: a central wooden carling/girder/spine notched to receive crossbeams and supported by stanchions; crossbeams notched over the planking at sheer level; and stringers at sheer level along each side (Figs. 2.10, 2.11).

The original hull building sequence is difficult to ascertain, since only Hag Ahmed has been able to study the structure in any detail (Lipke, 1984: 117–20). An informed guess would be:

(1) align and assemble the bottom strakes and the end closure timbers, and fasten them together with the 'strategic' lashings;

(2) align and assemble the side strakes and fasten with 'strategic' lashings;

(3) stabilize the set-up with widely spaced cross-beams let into the sheer strake;

(4) fashion and fit the seam battens. Although no caulking was found with this vessel, it has been (and is) found in all other sewn-plank traditions;

(5) fasten the hull planking with the 'permanent' lashings from sheer to sheer (Lipke, 1984: 79, 119);

(6) fashion, fit, and fasten the floor timbers;

(7) fit the central carling and lash to stanchions and crossbeams;

(8) Remaining crossbeams fashioned, fitted, and lashed;

(9) fashion, fit, and fasten stringers;

(10) add decking, superstructure, and terminals at the ends.

This vessel was evidently propelled by five oars (6.5–8.5 m in length) each side. It seems likely that the oarsmen stood to use them, probably facing forward. She was steered by a rudder (6.5 m in length) on each quarter. The stock of each rudder was bound to a transverse timber so that it could only be turned about its own axis.

## 2.7.2 REPRESENTATIONAL EVIDENCE FOR HULL STRUCTURE

There seem to be three main types of riverborne craft represented in the Old Kingdom (the specialized obelisk transporter is discussed in 2.9.3): the passenger-carrying vessel ('travelling boat'); the cargo-carrying vessel; and the vessels used for religious purposes ('funerary' and 'solar'). All seem to have had essentially the same form and probably the same structure. They were round-hulled, spoon-shaped, relatively broad, double-ended vessels, which from the evidence of the Cheops ship, were built in the plank-first sequence. The planking appears to have been joined together by unlocked wooden tenons in mortises, as seen in the boatbuilding scenes (Fig. 2.12) in the fifth-dynasty Mastaba of Ti at Saqqara (Wachsmann, 1998: 229–30, figs. 10.13–10.21). Since strakes are depicted being pounded down on to tenons to fit closely against

Fig. 2.12. Boat-building scene from the fifth-dynasty tomb of Ti at Saqqara (after Hornell, 1946a: plate 27B).

Fig. 2.13. A vessel being fitted with a hogging hawser depicted in the fifth-dynasty rock tomb of Nefer at Saqqara (photo: Paul Johnstone).

the strake below, it might be that unlocked tenons were sufficient fastenings in themselves. From our present-day viewpoint, however, this seems questionable, and it is likely that the planks were also fastened together by 'hidden' lashings like the Cheops ship and as probably depicted in the fourth-dynasty chamber of Rahotep at Medum, and in the fifth-dynasty tomb of Nefer at Saqqara (Wachsmann, 1998: figs. 10.9, 10.11; D. Jones, 1995: fig. 63).

Other techniques shown in these fourth- and fifth-dynasty scenes include:

- fitting and aligning a strake;
- forming mortises with chisel and hammer;
- tightening lashings using a man's foot (as also used when binding together bundle rafts—see, for example, Fig. 2.8 and Wachsmann, 1998: fig. 10.32);
- sawing logs into planks;
- trimming planks with axes and finishing them with adzes.

In one scene the master boatwright appears to be about to check alignments with a ruler and a plumb bob. On a painting in the sixth-dynasty tomb of Mereraka a line is set from end to end of the boat to help the boatwrights achieve symmetry (D. Jones, 1995: 74).

The Nefer depiction also shows the use of a hogging hawser to prestress the planking against the forces experienced afloat (Fig. 2.13). The stick used to tighten the hawser can be seen inserted between strands. These longitudinal ropes ran from near-end to near-end of the vessel, led over vertical crutches along the centreline. Hogging hawsers are also depicted in a painting from Zawyet el-Molin (Johnstone, 1980: fig. 7.6), on ship reliefs in the Abusir fifth-dynasty pyramid of Sahure of c.2450 BC (Casson, 1971: fig. 17), and on paintings of cargo vessels of the Old Kingdom (e.g. Landström, 1970: fig. 180).

Sahure's seagoing ships also have a distinctive criss-cross feature along the length of the hull (Fig. 2.14), which Hornell (1946: 220) and Wachsmann (1998: 14) believe represent sewn planking. Landström (1970: 64), however, has interpreted them as a horizontal rope girdle attached to vertical rope girdles around the ends and this seems a more plausible hypothesis. Similar girdles may be depicted on Old Kingdom cargo ships (Landström, 1970: figs. 175, 179) to strengthen the hull against cargo-induced stresses.

Fig. 2.14. One of the ships depicted on a relief in Sahure's fifth-dynasty burial temple at Abusir (after Wachsmann, 1998: fig. 2.3).

Superstructure was added to these hulls to suit their role: deckhouses and lookout shelters for working boats; cabins for important passengers; shrines/kiosks and funeral biers for 'religious boats'. As though to emphasize their function, the latter vessels had special ends, similar in shape to the terminals of papyrus bundle rafts: sometimes both were vertical, sometimes the stern terminal was higher and the bow more drooping—Landström calls this the 'papyriform' shape of boat, but it is evidently an ordinary Nile planked craft with special 'figureheads' at the ends. The Cheops ship, having a religious function, is of this form with a near-vertical bow and a forward-curving stern—without these added ends she would be very similar in form (and probably in aspects of her structure) to the near-contemporary seagoing vessels depicted in Sahure's pyramid. These Sahure ships are shown bringing back to Egypt prisoners of war from the Levant and thus must have been, in some sense, 'warships'. However, at this period, warships were relatively unspecialized, seagoing craft, probably galleys, that is, propelled by sail and oar, and capable of carrying armed men or passengers: perhaps they are better called military transport ships.

From a relatively early date sailing vessels were given a specialized deck aft for the helmsman—see, for example, the ship depicted on a relief in the tomb of Kaem'onkh at Giza of *c*.2400–2300 BC (Fig. 2.15): see

also Landström, 1970: figs. 126 and 153. Helmsmen of cargo vessels especially needed a raised deck so that they could see over the cargo piled amidships (Landström, 1970: figs. 175, 180): in some cases they appear to have steered from the roof of an after deckhouse, a usage known from recent times in, for example, Bangladesh (Greenhill, 1995a: fig. 19).

### 2.7.2.1 SHIPBUILDING SITES

The earliest reference to a site which was probably where vessels were built is on a second-dynasty seal of Nimaathap (*c*.2700 BC). There is a reference to such a site in the fourth-dynasty tomb of Rahotep at Meidum, and in the sixth-dynasty mastaba of Kaem'onkh at Giza. Several people buried at Giza and Saqqara had the title 'Captain of the Shipyard' and there are references to shipyards or dockyards, in this region and south of Memphis, from the fifth through to the twentieth dynasty (D. Jones, 1995: 80–1).

### 2.7.3 PROPULSION BY PADDLE AND OAR

It is sometimes difficult to determine whether it is paddling or rowing that is depicted in the Old Kingdom material. Blades of oars and paddles can be very similar

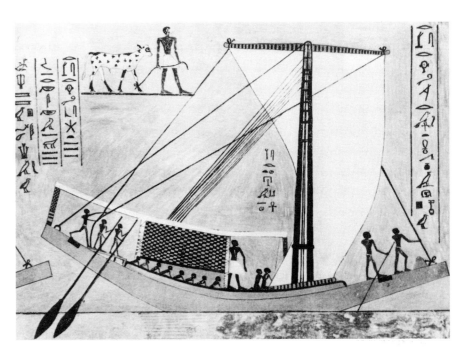

Fig. 2.15. Sailing ship on a relief in the tomb of Kaem'onkh at Giza, of *c*.2400–2300 BC (after Casson, 1971: fig. 19).

in shape and, although paddling is invariably undertaken by a man facing forward, he can be standing, kneeling, or sitting; rowing can be, and often is, done with the man facing aft but it can also be undertaken when facing forward and by men who either sit or stand (McGrail, 1998: 208–11). The best evidence for oars would be the use of pivots, but these are not always depicted even when other features suggest the action is rowing.

Paddling in a relatively conventional way is shown on several paintings from the Old Kingdom, for example, Landström (1970: fig. 96)—probably sitting (figs. 155, 158) or kneeling. A more elaborate paddling style is shown on a relief in the funerary temple of Userkaf at Saqqara in which the crew appear to apply their paddles sequentially, each man reaching high in the air before plunging his paddle into the water (Fig. 2.16). This exaggerated action seems more likely to represent a particular incident (a ceremonial race?) than standard procedure.

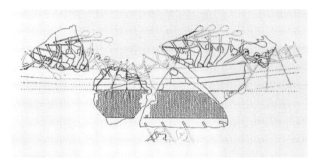

Fig. 2.16. Paddling action depicted in the mid-third millennium BC funerary temple of Userkaf at Saqqara (after Casson, 1971: fig. 15).

There are many illustrations of conventional rowing in the mode sit-pull (McGrail and Farrell, 1979), for example, in Landström (1970: figs. 111, 113) and in Sahure's seagoing ships of the fifth dynasty (Wachsmann, 1998: figs. 2.2, 2.3). In some of these the oars can be seen to be pivoted against the ship's side in grommets: the oar angle seems relatively steep, but this may be due to the perspective. In one illustration published by Landström (1970: fig. 157) there are two scenes which, if taken sequentially, show an oar-pulling stroke which begins with the oarsmen standing and ends with them sitting on a bench. This style is known in other times and places, for example, in twentieth-century Pakistan (Greenhill, 1966: 30).

A mid-third millennium BC galley in a tomb painting (Casson, 1971: fig. 63) is typical of many illustrations where it is difficult to decide whether the vessel is paddled or under oars. No pivots are shown, the blades could be from paddles or oars, and the crew are shown standing up, facing outboard but looking aft, with both arms outstretched and with oar or paddle in the right hand. A possible interpretation is that this is a paddled open boat and the men are spacing themselves to the optimum distance for a particular style of paddling.

### 2.7.4 PROPULSION BY SAIL

Sail was known in proto-dynastic Egypt and is seen to be well developed by Old Kingdom times. The bipod mast is most frequently depicted (Fig. 2.15), and this has led Hornell (1946a: 225–8) and others to deduce that this is a feature taken over from bundle, boat-shaped rafts, the outer bundles of which more readily provided a seating for a mast than the bottom. However, depiction of bundle rafts with a bipod mast are rare and methods are known of stepping pole masts on the centreline of bundle rafts, as for example, in those of Lake Titicaca in South America (McGrail, 1998: fig. 9.4). Furthermore, the earliest known representations of masts in Egypt are undoubtedly pole masts (Fig. 2.5). There is at least one example of a pole mast in the fifth dynasty on a small planked boat (Fig. 2.17), and others are seen in depictions from the sixth dynasty (Landström, 1970: fig. 133).

Fig. 2.17. A fifth-dynasty boat with a pole mast (after Landström, 1970: fig. 98).

The two elements of the bipod mast were joined near the apex by several cross timbers (Landström, 1970: fig. 118), but it is not clear how the two spars were stepped. At deck level they seem to have been held in position by rope cables (Landström, 1970: figs. 116, 192; see also Unas' representations of the fifth dynasty where tripod masts are similarly supported (Wachsmann, 1998: fig. 2.5)). In the sixth dynasty they were lashed to wooden knees (Landström, 1970: figs. 125–6). Masts, whether tripod, bipod, or pole, are invariably shown stepped well forward of amidships, about one-third the waterline length from the bow which, in this context, must mean that with a square sail set so far forward these vessels were probably constrained to sailing with the wind in the stern sector, say, four points ($c$.45°) either side of dead astern, otherwise there could have been steering problems due to the couple generated by the horizontal separation of the centre of effort of the sail and the centre of lateral resistance of the hull. Sailing with a fair, stern wind would, in fact, have generally suited vessels on the Nile where there is a predominantly northern wind. However, such a limitation could have been restrictive for seagoing craft.

The standing rigging primarily consists of a backstay (known from the fourth dynasty) and a forestay (known from the fifth). The backstay may also have acted as a halyard where one was not fitted. No shrouds are shown but a number of auxiliary backstays are frequently there, running from the mast below the main backstay to the deck forward of the helmsmen, as on a relief from the tomb of the fourth- or fifth-dynasty Kaemankh at Giza (Fig. 2.15); from a sixth-dynasty tomb at Kom el Ahmar (Hornell, 1946a: fig. 41). It is conceivable that some of these could have been moved to the windward side to act as shrouds if and when the wind was forward of the quarter, although this use does not seem to have been depicted.

The sail, which in later times was of linen (Wachsmann, 1998: 253), was bent to a yard at the head, and also to a boom at the foot: there is no evidence for a parrel to hold the yard to the mast. The boom appears to rest on the sides of the vessel, abaft the mast and sometimes the crew are depicted sitting on it: see, for example, Landström (1970: fig. 109). With a boom constrained by the mast in this manner, it would be difficult but perhaps not impossible to rotate the sail away from its thwartship position. Sheets appear not to have been always necessary and appear only infrequently

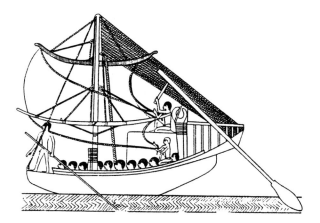

Fig. 2.18. A relief in the mid-third millennium BC tomb of Ipi at Saqqara (after Bass, 1972: fig. 10). The helmsman appears to be holding the braces; the lower man aft, the sheets.

(Fig. 2.18). Without sheets, such a rotation might have been achieved by forcing the boom round and by using the braces which are depicted running from the yardarms to the helmsman (Casson, 1971: fig. 19; Landström, 1970: figs. 95, 97, 104; Bass, 1972: fig. 10; D. Jones, 1995: fig. 33) or to a man stationed on the roof of a deckhouse (Hornell, 1946a: fig. 41). From the relative size of the man with the braces there is an impression that he was in a position of responsibility.

Braces are usually a sign that the sail could be trimmed to get optimum performance when the wind was not in the stern sector. As also is the fitting of a bowline running from the bows to the leading edge (weather leach) of the sail (Fig. 2.19). Landström (1970: fig. 116) also depicts the use of a pole with a forked ter-

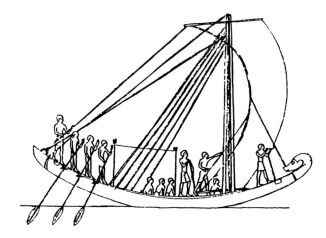

Fig. 2.19. Ship with a bowline rigged, from the fifth-dynasty tomb of Seshemnefer at Giza (after D. Jones, 1995: fig. 34).

minal as a tacking spar to hold the sail leading edge taut to the wind (D. Jones, 1995: 42).

Despite the forward position of the mast and the difficulty in rotating the boom, the use of braces, bowlines, and leading-edge spars suggests that these ships could be sailed with the wind forward of the stern sector, perhaps even on the beam, as would seem to have been necessary on the east–west section of the Nile north of Luxor, between Nag Hammadi and Qena (Fig. 2.1). With this arrangement, special attention to the steering would have been necessary, which may have been one of the reasons why numerous helmsmen are often depicted (Fig. 2.19).

The sail in the fourth- and fifth-dynasties period is generally of high-aspect ratio, i.e. taller than broad—see, for example, Landström (1970: figs. 98, 99, 104) and D. Jones (1995: fig. 31)—and made up of horizontal sail cloths (Landström, 1970: fig. 109; Hornell, 1946a: fig. 41). Landström (1970: 42, 43, 46) considers that these sails are trapezoidal with the head broader than the foot. However, this apparent shape seems more likely to be due to some perspective in the drawings.

Halyards when depicted are single in the fourth dynasty and either double or triple from the fifth (Landström, 1970: figs. 104, 110, 117; D. Jones, 1995: 36). There is no sign of block and tackle, so that the halyards (and all other running rigging) must have been directly hauled, probably through a greased hole in the mast. The mast was lowered aft using the backstays, with the forestay as a preventer (Bass, 1972: fig. 9; Landström, 1970: fig. 122) and stowed in gallows or crutches aft which sometimes were on top of the deckhouse (Figs. 2.18, 2.19). During the sixth dynasty (c.2345–2181 BC) changes to the rig began to appear. On vessels depicted in the mastaba of Mereruka (Landström, 1970: figs. 125, 126; D. Jones, 1995: fig. 33) masts are lashed to knees rather than secured by trusses; the yard is suspended by lifts from a position on the mast just below the backstays; and the sails are now broader than they are tall. The boom has lifts and is well clear of the deck when in use. Yard and boom are shown upcurving at the ends: whether this is due to artistic licence or in order to prevent the yard entering the water as the ship rolled, is uncertain. Such a sail may have been difficult to handle if, as seems likely, the boom was much longer than the beam of the ship; furthermore, a sail of low-aspect ratio is not so weatherly as a comparable one of high-aspect ratio.

A relief from the tomb of Ipi at Saqqara (Bass, 1972: fig. 10; Landström, 1970: fig. 143) also shows a ship with curved boom longer than curved yard, lifts for both boom and yard, and sheets to the ends of the boom which now seems to be forward of the mast. Bass dates this relief to c.2500 BC (i.e. fourth/fifth dynasty), but the rigging depicted seems to lie more happily with the sixth dynasty (c.2345–2181 BC) attribution of Landström.

Tomb paintings from Thebes and Deir el Gebrawi and paintings from the tomb of Mereruka in Saqqara (Landström, 1970: figs. 126, 133, 137, 138) show vessels with pole masts, suggesting that this type may well have persisted from the late fourth millennium BC (Fig. 2.5) through the centuries with little documentation. One ship pictured in Deir el Gebrawi and those in Unas' temple have a tripod mast (Landström, 1970: figs. 152, 192). Another of the Deir el Gebrawi vessels has its mast stepped nearer amidships than previously, suggesting a search for more weatherly performance.

The sum of this evidence from the sixth dynasty, that is towards the end of the third millennium BC, suggests that it was a phase of experimentation, including a search for better windward performance. If we allow for lags in artistic knowledge of the latest trends in ship design, and also possibly for difficulties in giving precise dates to some of this material, this search would seem to coincide with the documented evidence for increasing Egyptian overseas expeditions and trade.

## 2.7.5 STEERING

Vessels may be steered by paddle, by steering oar, or by rudder (for other methods see McGrail, 1998: 239, 241). Paddle steering is usually done from the quarter, using an oversize paddle; a steering oar may be pivoted on the quarter or on the stern; and a rudder, supported so that it can be turned about its own long axis, may be fitted on the quarter or the stern. As with paddling/rowing, there are sometimes difficulties in establishing which form of steering is depicted in the Egyptian material. Nevertheless there seem to be examples of all these different uses in Old Kingdom paintings, reliefs, and models.

The fourth-dynasty steersmen in Landström (1970: figs. 95, 96, 97) all appear to be steering with freely held paddles; those of the fifth dynasty (Landström, 1970:

figs. 98, 99, 104; Casson, 1971: figs. 19) appear to be using a steering oar with one pivot (a grommet?) on the quarter—the angle is relatively steep by today's standards and it may be that in addition to steering by varying the angle of the oar to the fore and aft line, they may be using a push stroke to manœuvre the vessels. Landström (1970: figs. 111, 176, 178) shows helmsmen using tillers through the shafts of what must be quarter or side rudders (turned around their own axes), and his fig. 152 shows a vessel with two quarter rudders each pivoted on the quarter and also against a vertical stanchion. The median rudder with tiller, pivoted on the stern and against a vertical stanchion (Fig. 2.18), becomes increasingly common towards the end of the Old Kingdom (Casson, 1971: 18).

## 2.7.6   OTHER EQUIPMENT

A man standing in the bows, as lookout, is frequently depicted in Old Kingdom illustrations (Fig. 2.15). He invariably holds a pole which is generally thought to be a sounding pole. In some cases, for example, Landström (1970: figs. 95 and 96), the pole can be seen to have a forked terminal and thus could be used to push the boat clear of hazards in the river bed and as a sail tacking spar, as well as to check the depth of water.

A pyramid-shaped stone anchor is shown on the foredeck of one of the seagoing ships pictured in Unas' temple of c.2345 BC, and possibly on others (Landström, 1970: figs. 104, 154, 192).

## 2.7.7   SEAFARING IN THE OLD KINGDOM

On the Palermo Stele there are references to the building of ships of *meru* wood and of cedar; and there are references to the import of cedar—'they came with ships loaded with cedar wood'—during the reign of Sneferu (fourth dynasty, c.2600 BC) (Landström, 1970: 35; Wachsmann, 1998: 9–10).

From the fifth-dynasty burial temple of Sahura at Abusir comes a relief (Fig. 2.14) showing a fleet of ships, first leaving Egypt, then returning with Asian prisoners—this suggests an overseas expedition to the Levant.

### 2.7.7.1   THE LAND OF *PUNT* (Fig. 2.20)

The first reference to *Punt* or 'God's land' comes from a text which states that, in Sahura's reign (i.e. c.2400 BC) Egyptian ships returned from *Punt* with myrrh, electrum, and (ebony?) logs (Landström, 1970: 63; Wachsmann, 1998: 19). There was also an expedition to *Punt* in the reign of Djedkara Isesi, eighth king of the fifth dynasty (James, 1983: 46). There has been much discussion on the location of *Punt*: it is generally agreed that it was on the east coast of Africa not further south than c.10°N, but some authorities believe it was within the Red Sea, north of Bab el Mandeb, in what is now Ethiopia (O'Connor, 1980a: 132; Landström, 1970: 63; Sleeswyk, 1983; Sølver, 1936) whilst others prefer the Gulf of Aden on the north-facing coast of what is now Somaliland (Hourani, 1963: 7; Casson, 1989: 11; James, 1983: 36; Hornell, 1941a: 240; Hornell, 1946a: 48; Ballard, 1920a), whilst Budge (1907: 147) suggested nearly a century ago that it was on the west side of the Red Sea *and* also on the Somali coast west of Cape Guardafui.

It seems likely that certain parts of the *Punt* region, the mines, could be reached overland from the upper reaches of the Nile (Sleeswyk, 1983: 289), but that traded goods were more accessible from the coast. The fishes depicted at the foot of the Deir-el-Bahari relief (2.9.1) are typical of the southern Red Sea and the Gulf of Aden (Ballard, 1920a). The landscape and the animals and the trees which at a later date were said to come from *Punt* suggest that *Punt* is more likely to have been on the southern and western coasts of the Gulf of Aden than on the Red Sea coast. The principal objections to this location are based on assessments of the seaworthiness of Egyptian ships, especially their performance to windward (Ballard, 1920a; Sølver, 1922). Some support for a southern Red Sea location comes from James's remark (1983: 33) that obsidian, which was used occasionally in Egypt from predynastic times onwards, probably came from the coast of Ethiopia and may have formed part of the trade with *Punt*. In the *Periplus of the Erythraean Sea* of the first century AD (Casson, 1989) we read in ch. 5 that in a very deep bay south of *Adulis* (probably Massawa, the only good natural harbour on the west coast of the Red Sea) there is the only source of obsidian in that region (Fig. 2.20). Casson (1989: 109) identifies this site as in Hauochil Bay (Baia di Ouachil) c.50 nautical miles south-east of

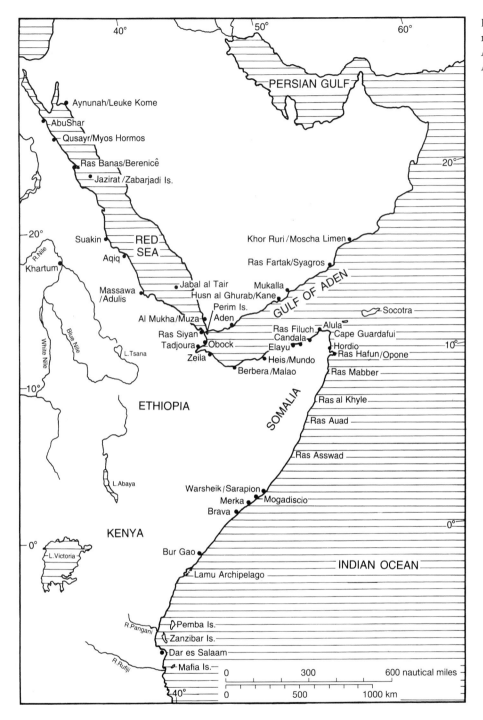

Fig. 2.20. Map of the Red Sea region and the coast of east Africa (Institute of Archaeology, Oxford).

Massawa on the Red Sea coast, where obsidian was found in the early nineteenth century. Clearly, the debate is unfinished, although Horton (1997: 747–9) states that the consensus opinion of today's Indian Ocean scholars is that *Punt* was within the Red Sea, i.e. north of the strait Bab el Mandeb.

In the sixth dynasty both Meryre (Pepi 1) and

Neferkare (Pepi 2) sent naval expeditions to *Punt* (James, 1983: 48; Landström, 1970: 63; Hourani, 1963: 7; Hornell, 1941a). Furthermore, in the tomb of Khui at Aswan there is a reference to a visit there (Wachsmann, 1998: 19): Enenkhet, an official of Pepi 1, was sent to the 'land of the Asians' to build a *kbn* ship for a voyage to *Punt*. This building site was probably at the head of the

Gulf of Aqaba (2.11.4), east of the Sinai peninsula and the nearest part of the Red Sea to Lebanon and its cedars (Hornell, 1941a: 241; Landström, 1970: 63; Wachsmann, 1998: 19). Hourani (1963: 7) translates the term *kbn* as *Gebal*, a Levant coastal city, whilst Sleeswyk (1983: 288) wishes to translate it as *Kubbani*, a site on the west coast of the Red Sea with which he identifies *Punt*. Apart from these authors, it is generally agreed that Egyptian overseas ships, whichever route they were on, came to be known as 'Byblos' ships, after the major harbour on the Levant coast from which Egyptian ships collected timber (James, 1983: 35).

It has been suggested that on their return, Sahure's ships sailed from *Punt* up the Red Sea and via a canal to the Nile. However, it is unlikely that there was a canal there in those times. A more likely route was from *Punt* to a harbour at or near Quseir on Egypt's Red Sea coast (2.11.4). The goods would then have been carried overland through the Eastern Desert along the Wadi Hammamat (Fig. 2.1) to reach the Nile at Coptos (James, 1983: 36).

# 2.8
# Planked Vessels of the Middle Kingdom (*c*.2133–1786 BC)

Political anarchy followed the collapse of central authority at the end of the sixth dynasty, with internal dissension in Upper and Lower Egypt. Little is known about Egypt during this period, which lasted for about 130 years, but it seems clear that there was little, if any, contact with the Levant, Sinai, Nubia, or *Punt* (James, 1983: 48–50; O'Connor, 1980a: 132). Upper and Lower Egypt were reunited again after this First Intermediate Period under Tepya/Nebhepetre Mentuhotpe I in *c*.2133 BC, and remained so under Pharaohs of the eleventh and twelfth dynasties for *c*.350 years.

## 2.8.1 OVERSEAS CONTACTS

During the early years of this Middle Kingdom period Sinai was again re-exploited and close contacts were re-

established with the Levant. Occasional artefacts suggest that Egypt was also involved in a wider trading network which included the Minoan world (O'Connor, 1980a: 132–3). It may be significant, in this context, that around this time of 2000 BC there is the first evidence for the use of sail in the Mediterranean on Minoan seals (4.7.2.1). Trading expeditions were also sent to *Punt*. In *c*.2000 BC, Hunu recorded on a stele in the Wadi Hammamat how he had fulfilled the orders of Sankhker Mentuhotep III of the eleventh dynasty to reopen stone quarries in the Wadi Hammamat and to fit out a seagoing ship on the Red Sea coast for a voyage to *Punt* to bring back myrrh (Sleeswyk, 1983: 288–9; Hornell, 1941a: 241; James, 1983: 52). Wachsmann (1998: 238) considers that, by implication, this vessel was built at Coptos on the Nile, dismantled and transported overland to the Red Sea: this hypothesis requires further consideration.

The quarries and mines in this eastern desert, in Lower Nubia and in Sinai continued to be exploited in the twelfth dynasty, and overseas expeditions were sent to *Punt* as recorded, for example, at Wadi Gasûs, north of Quseir on the Red Sea coast, by two men sent to *Punt* by Ammenemes II (1929–1895 BC) (Hornell, 1941a: 241; Wachsmann, 1998: 238). These voyages to *Punt* are reflected in a Middle Kingdom narrative, *Story of the Shipwrecked Sailor* (possibly one of the sources for *Sindbad the Sailor*). The sole survivor from a wreck in the Red Sea landed on an island where he was befriended by a serpent of fabulous appearance who claimed to be the Prince of *Punt* (James, 1983: 110; Hourani, 1963: 7). This story also describes how Egyptian sailors 'looked to the sky, looked to the land and their heart was braver than the lion's. They foresaw a storm before it had come, and a tempest before it had struck' (quoted by Landström, 1970: 89)—one of the earliest examples of weather forecasting at sea.

## 2.8.2 A NILE–RED SEA CANAL

Strabo (17. 1. 25) tells us that a canal connecting the Pelusiac (eastern) arm of the Nile to the Red Sea was first cut by Khakaure Sesostris 'before the Trojan War', a claim which seems to be supported by Aristotle and Pliny (Huntingford, 1980: 77). Sesostris III of the twelfth dynasty (*c*.1850 BC) was probably the Pharaoh concerned. Herodotus says that this Sesostris *did* cut canals but the implication is that they were within the delta, or were irrigation canals. Herodotus (2. 138, 158) attributes the beginning of the first canal between the Nile and the Red Sea to Wehemibre Necho II (610 to 595 BC) of the twenty-sixth dynasty.

It is not impossible that Sesostris III contemplated the possibility of a canal between the Nile and the Red Sea. The fact that boats were buried around his pyramid clearly shows the importance he placed on water transport: moreover, Herodotus (2. 102) noted that Sesostris was the first Egyptian to take a fleet of warships from the Red Sea along the coast of the Indian Ocean (Arabian peninsula?) 'subduing the coastal tribes as he went, until he found that shoal water made further progress impossible'. He would thus be well aware of the advantages of such an artificial waterway to Egypt's overseas conquests, exploitation, and trade in the Sinai to *Punt* region. The balance of evidence, however, seems to suggest that a navigable canal between the Nile and the Red Sea was cut in the sixth century and not in the nineteenth century BC.

### 2.8.3  BOAT AND SHIP REMAINS

#### 2.8.3.1  TIMBERS FROM EL LISHT

Timbers (of acacia or tamarisk) excavated between 1908 and 1934 and 1984 to 1986 in the vicinity of the pyramid of Senwosrel / Sesostris I (*c*.1900 BC) at El Lisht, south of Dahshur have recently been examined by

Haldane (1988; 1996). The planks and timbers appear to come from one or more vessels and they have joggled edges and two types of fastenings:

(a) unlocked mortise and tenons (105–15 mm deep) at regular intervals;
(b) lashings of halfa grass through L-shaped holes at greater intervals.

The mortises are similar in size to those in the Dahshur boats (2.8.3.2). Many of the surviving tenons are a firm fit within their mortises; others have been wedged in position by pegs and an adhesive inserted on either side. Like Dahshur, but unlike Cheops, the El Lisht vessel relied more on mortise and tenon joints than on lashings. One tenon found to be locked within its mortise by a trans-piercing peg driven at right angles has been interpreted as a repair (Haldane, 1988; Haldane and Shelmerdine, 1990; Wachsmann, 1998: 220–1). A frame from the same site consisted of a 2.4 m curved floor and two futtocks *c*.1 m in length, fastened together in a similar manner to the planking.

#### 2.8.3.2  THE DAHSHUR BOATS

Excavations by de Morgan (1894; 1903) in 1893–5 around the pyramid of Sesostris / Senusret III (*c*.1878–1843 BC) at Dahshur, revealed six boat pits: two of these boats are now in the Egyptian Museum, Cairo, one each in the Field Museum, Chicago (Fig. 2.21) and in the Carnegie Museum, Pittsburgh, whilst the other two cannot now

Fig. 2.21. One of the Dahshur boats of the early second millennium BC (courtesy of The Field Museum of Natural History, Chicago).

Fig. 2.22. Plan and elevation of
a Dahshur boat in the Egyptian
Museum, Cairo (after
Landström,1970: fig. 275).

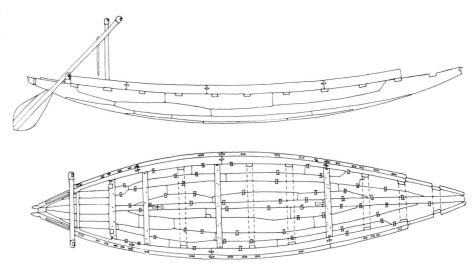

be traced. The boats are similar in size (9.25/9.92 ×
2.15/2.43 × 0.72/0.79 m) and all have a slightly protruding plank-keel and a rounded transverse section (Fig.
2.22). They are relatively broad in the beam, having
L/B=3.8–4.6 and are slightly fuller aft than forward.
They have a gently curving sheerline, the stern being
higher than the bows (Haldane, 1996, 1997a; Steffy,
1994). The planking is cedar, and the tenons are
tamarisk; the planking is hewn to shape and not bent.
The following description relies much on Haldane's
recent examination of these boats.

There are no posts and the plank-keel curves up at
the ends, above which there may formerly have been
ceremonial finial posts. The three planks of the plank-
keel are butted end-to-end and joined by flat wooden
dovetail cramps set into the inboard faces (but see
below) and not locked in position. The three strakes
each side are each made of 2, 3, and 4 planks (from the
bottom upwards): plank lengths range from 1–4.5 m in
length and are thus relatively short. Butts in the lower
planking are joined by unlocked mortise and tenon
joints; in the third strake by dovetail cramps. The hull
planking is fastened together edge-to-edge by
unlocked mortise and tenons (which, at 120–30 mm,
are deeper than those in Cheops), and by more widely
spaced dovetail cramps. Above the three side strakes
are fourth strakes which do not run the full length of
the hull: the two butts in each of these strakes are fastened by lashings. These top strakes are generally fastened to the third strakes by mortise and tenons and by
dovetails, but at their ends they are lashed in position.

There is no framing, but the planked hull is rein-

forced by thirteen non-protruding crossbeams supported on stanchions and let into the third and fourth
strakes: they were lashed in position and then treenailed to the third strake. Deck planks were fitted into
rabbets cut into the upper faces of these beams.

These boats were steered by two quarter rudders
fastened to the hull and to stanchions. There is no evidence for propulsion by sail or oar, and thus poles and
paddles were probably used.

As Steffy (1994: 33–6) has pointed out, with unlocked
mortise and tenons, unlocked and shallow dovetails,
and no frames, there is nothing to prevent the plank
seams opening, should any fastenings be dislodged.
However, the mortise and tenons are arranged in lines
across the hull and the tenons are relatively large. If
these tenons fitted closely into their mortises (possibly
they were dried before fitting, and then swelled on
immersion in water), the lines of fastenings across the
hull, though unlocked, could have ensured hull structural integrity, which the dovetails would have reinforced. It is relevant here to note that in some of the
representations of boatbuilding from the Old
Kingdom, 'pounders' are being used to force down
each strake onto tenons protruding from the strake
below (Fig. 2.12).

Haldane (1993: 220–4, 1996, 1997a; Haldane and
Shelmerdine, 1990: 537–8) has recently examined these
boats in detail and has noted that all four boats show
evidence for post-excavational repair and reconstruction. She considers that the dovetail cramps are modern, and that their mortises were formerly L- or
V-shaped holes within the thickness of the planks,

through which strakes were lashed together. Together with the mortise and tenon fastenings, these lashings would ensure a tight hull. Haldane's conjecture (1996: 240) is supported by de Morgan's record of the hull fastenings, and by Reisner's statement that the hulls had mortise and tenon planking and that most, if not all, the dovetails were modern.

The boatwrights who built these boats were evidently familiar with *locked* mortise and tenon joints as these were used in sarcophagi, furniture, and a sled found with the boats (Haldane, 1988: 146). Locked mortise and tenons were also used in the superstructure of the Cheops ship. Nevertheless, they were not used in the hulls of any of these vessels.

Whatever the fastenings, these boats were unquestionably well built. The cedar for their planking had to be imported, and originally they were all much decorated with red, black, and blue lines over a white or green background. The rudder stanchions had representations of hawks' heads (a symbol of royalty) on their upper ends, and the rudders themselves were painted with flowers and eyes. All these features lead Haldane (1997a) to believe that these were royal funerary boats. Senusret III, a powerful Pharaoh, evidently decided to emulate the boat burial ritual last used by the renowned kings of the Old Kingdom some 500 years earlier.

### 2.8.3.3 THE USE OF SHORT PLANKS

Short lengths of planking, comparable with those used on the Dahshur boats, are depicted on the twelfth-dynasty tomb of Khnemhotep at Beni Hasan (Fig. 2.23). Details of the hull structure are not clear, but one man appears to be using a chisel and wooden beetle to cut mortises in the planking. Landström (1970: 91) deduced that another boatwright (third from the left) was lashing the planking, but, as Wachsmann has pointed out, it is more likely that he is taking the weight of the plank in a rope loop whilst it is being manœuvred into position—an action more clearly depicted in the fifth-dynasty tomb of Ti (Wachsmann, 1998: fig. 10.17).

Short planks are also depicted in later centuries: on a fishing boat painted in the late thirteenth-century BC tomb chapel of Ipy (Bass, 1972: plate 20) and on a boat-building scene in the nineteenth-dynasty (late thirteenth-century BC) tomb of Qaha at Deir el Medinah (Wachsmann, 1998: fig. 10.25).

In the fifth century BC, Herodotus (2. 96) described Nile cargo boats built from acacia timber with thick planks only two cubits (c.0.90 m) in length. A boat of about this date, and with short planks, was excavated in 1987 from a site near Matariya in the vicinity of Heliopolis but has not yet been published in detail (Vinson, 1994: 47–8; Wachsmann, 1998: 222–3). Hornell (1946a: 215–17, plate 35B) has described twentieth-century Sudanese boats on the upper Nile, also built from short planks, 1.2–1.8 m in length, of *sunt* timber (*Acacia nilotica*).

We may conclude from this summary that working boats of the Nile have probably been built of local timber such as acacia and sycamore for 4,000 years or more, even though only relatively short planks could be obtained and the timber was troublesome to work.

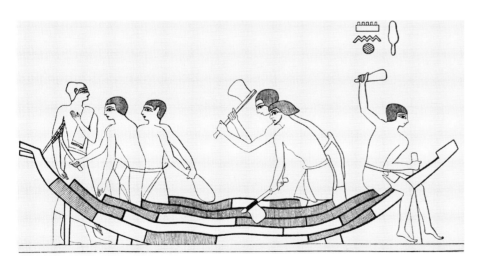

Fig. 2.23. Building a boat with short planks, from the tomb of Khnemhotep at Beni Hasan of c.2000 BC (after Casson, 1971: fig. 11).

Imported timber such as cedar was probably restricted to royal vessels (such as the Cheops ship and the Dahshur boats), to vessels of a religious nature, and possibly to vessels of the king's officials.

### 2.8.3.4 PLANK FASTENINGS

The Nile vessels described by Herodotus and by Hornell were also frameless but had crossbeams like the Dahshur boats—another characteristic that may have persisted for 4,000 years. The only significant change that seems to have taken place is that the planking of the Sudanese boats is fastened by obliquely driven spikes (Hornell, 1946a: fig. 29B) whereas the Dahshur and Herodotus boats had mortise and tenon fastenings. Herodotus' description has recently been reinterpreted by Haldane and Shelmerdine (1990): instead of 'caulking the seams with papyrus' they read: 'bind in the seams from within with papyrus'—that is, they suggest that, in addition to the mortise and tenon fastenings, the planks of Herodotus' boat were lashed together with papyrus ropes within the thickness of the planking.

There is thus a body of evidence recently reinterpreted by Haldane (Dahshur, El Lisht, and Herodotus) which suggests that the Cheop's ship's plank fastenings (unlocked mortise and tenon, and lashings—neither of which penetrate the hull) were generally used in Egyptian-built vessels for millennia, with mortise and tenon joints becoming relatively more important from the second millennium BC onwards. During the late second millennium BC, when the influence of Phoenician shipbuilding techniques began to be felt, locked tenons were probably introduced. The Matariya boat of the mid-first millennium appears to have had not only frames but also locked mortise and tenon plank fastenings (Wachsmann, 1998: 222).

### 2.8.4 REPRESENTATIONAL EVIDENCE

In addition to the excavated and documentary evidence there are numerous models and some representational evidence for riverine planked boats and ships. The general shape and structure of vessels seems to change little from those seen in the Old Kingdom: see, for example, the models from the eleventh-dynasty tomb of Meketre at Deir-el-Bahari and dated c.2050 BC (Bass, 1972: 19; Vinson, 1994: fig. 18; D. Jones, 1995: figs. 22–5). No girdling or hogging hawsers are shown, which might imply more confidence in the integrity of the hull, but is more probably due to the fact that no *seagoing* models or representations are known from this period. Details of the rigging are sometimes difficult to appreciate as some of the models have undoubtedly been restored incorrectly. Nevertheless, it appears that the pole mast, supported by knees at deck level, was now almost exclusively used, and that it was stepped nearer amidships which suggests an attempt to sail closer to the wind. The boom is now consistently forward of the mast and invariably has sheets—thus the sail could more readily be set for optimum performance. The sail now seems generally to have an aspect ratio less than 1, i.e. it is broader than it is tall, as it seems to have been in the sixth dynasty.

There are some other specific improvements to the rigging. Lifts running through a special copper fitting at the masthead are fitted to the yard to supplement the halyards: the sail could now be reduced in area and even furled by lowering the yard to the boom (Wachsmann, 1998: 248). The standing backstay and the backstay/shrouds are fastened to the rudder stanchion; and cleats for shrouds are fitted at the deck edge on both sides of the vessel—another sign of an attempt to improve weatherliness (Landström, 1970: 78–80).

There are changes in rowing fittings also: curved outriggers were fitted to ships' sides to give a better oar angle for standing oarsmen (Landström, 1970: figs. 236, 249, 250, 257). Steering oars no longer feature, and, as in the later years of the Old Kingdom, models show all three ways of using a rudder: on the quarter (Bass, 1972: plate 19); on both quarters (Casson, 1971: fig. 10): and on the centreline (Bass, 1972: plate 18). Vessels with funerary and other papyriform ends were unable to ship a median rudder because of the high rising finial aft, and therefore continued to use quarter rudders (D. Jones, 1995: fig. 22).

Sounding poles continue to be used (Landström, 1970: fig. 236) but the sounding lead now appears (Landström, 1970: fig. 238). A spar is sometimes fitted to the foredeck with a groove in the section projecting beyond the bow: this has been called a 'bowsprit' but more likely uses, as Landström (1970: 75, 76, fig. 226) suggests, are as a fairlead for the anchor cable, or as a pivot for a bow steering oar.

## 2.9

# Planked Vessels of the New Kingdom (*c.*1567–1085 BC)

A second hiatus occurred in Egyptian history for about 200 years from *c.*1786–1567 BC. During this Second Intermediate Period, Egypt was invaded by Asiatics from Palestine, the national government disintegrated, and foreigners (*Hyksos*) became rulers from *c.*1670 BC. Recent excavations have also shown that Aegeans settled in Lower Egypt during this period (Vinson, 1994: 33). Furthermore, the Egyptian parts of Lower Nubia were taken over by people from Upper Nubia (Kingdom of Kush). Only around Thebes were the Middle Kingdom traditions maintained, and from there, under the later kings of the seventeenth dynasty, Lower Nubia was reconquered, the Hyksos expelled (O'Connor, 1980*a*: 133) and the New Kingdom established.

During the second half of the second millennium BC, under the eighteenth dynasty, Egypt developed a strong centralized government and expanded into neighbouring lands: within a short time, Egyptian control extended from Upper Nubia at the Fourth Cataract to the Levant coastal states (Palestine and Lebanon) and into parts of Syria. Trading contacts were re-established with the Levant and *Punt*, and extended to the Mitanni, the Hittites, Babylonia, Assyria, and the Minoan and Mycenaean world (O'Connor, 1980*a*: 133–4).

### 2.9.1 THE *PUNT* SHIPS

Although well documented from the fifth dynasty (2.7.7.1), voyages to *Punt* are best known from the times of Makare Hatshepsut (*c.*1503–1482 BC), Menkhoperre Tuthmosis III (*c.*1504–1450 BC), and Akheprure Amenophis II (*c.*1450–1425 BC), the fifth, sixth, and seventh rulers of the eighteenth dynasty.

The expedition sent by Hatshepsut to *Punt* is shown on a relief in her temple at Deir-el-Bahari (Wachsmann, 1998: figs. 2.11, 2.15–2.18, 2.24–2.26, 2.28–2.34). Five galleys are seen, under sail and oars, approaching the land of *Punt* and preceded by a small Egyptian-style boat with goods on deck. In another scene three of the galleys are seen leaving under oars and loaded with goods, whilst two others are still being loaded by men walking up gangplanks (Fig. 2.24). Among the items to be seen or listed in the text are: gold, electrum, ivory, ebony, sandalwood, leopard and panther skins, fragrant gums and incense, myrrh and myrrh trees, apes, monkeys, dogs, and small cattle, and also some people from *Punt* (Landström, 1970: 123; Hornell, 1941*a*: 242). What the Egyptians gave in exchange is unclear.

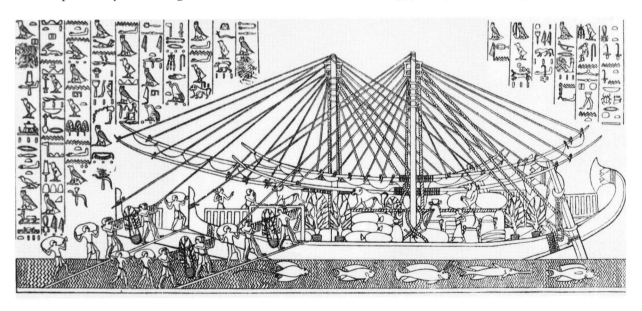

Fig. 2.24. Two of Hatshepsut's ships in *Punt*, from sculptures in her temple at Deir el-Bahri, Thebes (after Hornell, 1946*a*: fig. 43).

The ships depicted on this relief clearly show continuity with those of earlier periods: the longitudinal profile is similar, except that the bow and stern seem to be more prolonged. As with Sahura's seagoing ships (and indeed the Cheops and Dahshur vessels), it is doubtful whether these ships have structural posts at bow and stern. Apart from protruding crossbeams in one ship, other structural details are unclear. However, a hogging hawser (known in the Old Kingdom) can be seen passing over three vertical crutches and fastened to vertical girdles around the ends. There is no horizontal girdle as there seems to have been in, for example, Sahura's seagoing ships of the Old Kingdom.

The oarsmen pull their oars against a pivot (possibly a grommet) at sheer level and are seated at a somewhat higher level than the protruding crossbeams. Jarret-Bell's interpretation of the rowing stroke—quoted by Wachsmann (1998: 247, fig. 1.1)—is physically impossible. It is much more likely to be that proposed by D. Jones (1995: 69) in which the oarsmen begin standing and end sitting. These rowers probably wore a network garment reinforced by a leather patch on the seat as seen on an eighteenth dynasty painting in the tomb of Huy (Landström, 1970: 135, fig. 391).

Hatshepsut's ships are steered by two side rudders pivoted through a grommet on the ship's side and in the crutch of a vertical stanchion: control is by a vertical tiller. The small tender is steered by a median rudder: both systems are known from the Old Kingdom.

The low-aspect ratio, rectangular sail has a boom as well as a yard and is set on a pole mast slightly aft of amidships on the waterline length. The rigging is similar to that in earlier centuries: two forestays and one backstay for standing rigging; two halyards, and lifts for both yard and boom.

Braces and sheets are shown on only one ship (Wachsmann, 1998: figs. 2.15, 2.34). The braces are fastened halfway along the yard and the sheets on the boom are even closer to the mast—possibly these are incorrect interpretations by the artist. The boom, but not the yard, appears to be lashed to the mast. The yard and the boom both curve up at the ends in the ships not underway. When sail is set, the yard becomes horizontal due to the weight of sail, whereas the boom ends remain up-turned (Wachsmann, 1998: fig. 2.18). Some authors have argued that this curvature is to prevent immersion of the long booms (about as long as the ship) when the ship rolls. Another possible reason is

that such a curved boom would give the best bunt (sail curvature) for sailing in the winds generally expected in the Red Sea. That yards and booms are each made from two spars (known from earlier times) may also be so that they can flex and adapt the necessary curvature, rather than due to any inability to obtain the required lengths of timber.

If the distance between the oarsmen depicted in these scenes is taken to be in the range 0.90–1.00 m then these 'Byblos' ships on the *Punt* run were 14–16 m at the waterline when loaded, 20–3 m overall. Their freeboard must have been such that they could still be propelled by seated oarsmen with their oars pivoted at sheer level. The beam measurements of these vessels must have been sufficiently great for a considerable amount of cargo to be carried on deck, along the centreline and between the two files of oarsmen. One loaded ship is portrayed with the same freeboard as the ships before loading, but another one, correctly, has less freeboard. These parameters suggest a broad, spoon-shaped hull of moderate length, similar to that known earlier in Egypt's history.

The only feature that appears to be significantly different in the Hatshepsut's seagoing ships from those of the riverine craft of the Middle Kingdom is that at both ends there is a raised deck surrounded by 'guard rails'—possibly for the ship's master and his assistants aft, and for the lookouts forward. It must be emphasized, however, that we have, as yet, no evidence for the hull structure of New Kingdom ships, comparable with that known from the Cheops ship of the Old Kingdom and the Dahshur boats of the Middle Kingdom: there may have been significant changes in building techniques that are not depicted on New Kingdom reliefs.

## 2.9.2 DEPICTIONS OF OTHER SHIPS

A wall painting in the tomb of Huy at Qurnet Murai, Thebes dated to *c.*1360 BC shows a sailing ship with features essentially the same as those on the Hatshepsut relief (Fig. 2.25). An exception is that the Huy vessel has what appear to be cabins and shelters on the deck. Huy's tomb also contains depictions of cargo ships (Landström, 1970: figs. 390–2). From these and from other eighteenth-dynasty depictions (Landström, 1970: figs. 389, 393, 395, 399, 404) we can see that the tradition-

Fig. 2.25. A cargo ship underway, from the tomb of Huy at Qurnet Murai of c.1360 BC (after Wilkinson, 1983: fig. 51).

al Egyptian shape of hull continued to be used for cargo vessels also. These are generally galleys, sailing ships which can also be propelled by oars at bow and stern when necessary. The cargo is carried on a deck amidships usually in a fenced-off space, as are cattle. Several of the vessels have a hogging hawser, some of them are built from short lengths of planking, and some have protruding crossbeams, all features known in earlier times. On two of the reliefs, ships are shown with a large block at the end of the rudder stock which may well be to counterbalance the weight of the blade when the rudder was rotated upwards in shallow water so that it did not protrude below the ship's bottom.

Two-way trade between New Kingdom Egypt and Syria is shown on a painting in the eighteenth-dynasty tomb of Kenamun (Fig. 4.28) and on the tomb of Nebamun (Johnstone, 1980: 78; Casson, 1971: 35–6, fig. 58) where Syrian vessels are depicted bringing wine or oil, vases and bowls, and cattle. In return, the Egyptians export food, textiles, and sandals. On other tomb paintings, for example, in the tomb of Rekhmire, we see copper ingots, of a distinctively 'ox-hide' shape, being brought to Egypt in Syrian ships (Bass, 1972: 34, plate 28).

The tomb of Nebkheprure Tutankhamun (1361–1352

BC) held thirty-five models of ships and these have recently been published by D. Jones (1990). They are of the same general shape and have essentially the same rigging as known from earlier representations and models. As they are block models they tell us little about the internal structure of the vessels they represent.

### 2.9.3 HEAVY-LIFT VESSELS AND TOWING

From the beginning of the first dynasty, the Egyptians used monumental stone architecture for their tombs and temples (James, 1983: 190) and thus had to evolve a system for transporting stone by water along the Nile, their national 'highway', from quarry to building site. This may be compared with the situation in Mesopotamia where monumental buildings were also erected. Good quality limestone, available south-east of Cairo in the region of Tura and Masara, was widely used into the mid-second millennium BC. From the eighteenth dynasty, sandstone from the region of Gebel es Silsila (between Aswan and Edfu) was used, particularly at Thebes. More highly prized than these two types of stone was granite which came from the region of the First Cataract by Aswan (James, 1983: 192). Other stone was obtained from the Wadi Hammamat region.

After extraction, blocks of stone were lashed to sledges and dragged to the nearest point of the river where they were loaded into vessels and transported to the building site, often late in the Nile inundation period so that the vessels could be positioned close to where the stone would be used.

One of the earliest, if not *the* earliest, depictions of a stone-carrying vessel is on the causeway of Unas, last king of the fifth dynasty *c.*2345 BC (Landström, 1970, fig. 185; D. Jones, 1995: fig. 59. One of the three vessels shown there is carrying two large stone columns set end-to-end on sledges, which the accompanying text states were of granite from the Elephantine region, i.e. Aswan. The structure of these heavy-lift vessels is difficult to deduce from these depictions, but it seems likely that they were specially built for this type of work. Some idea of the size of such vessels may be gained from a sixth-dynasty inscription in the tomb of Weni in Abydos which states that he built a vessel of acacia wood, which was 60 × 30 cubits (*c.*31.5 × 15.75 m) to carry downstream a large stone altar (Landström, 1970: 62; D. Jones, 1995: 65).

In the eighteenth dynasty, Ineni, an official in the reign of Akheperenre Tuthmosis I (*c.*1500 BC), recorded that he had supervised the building of a large vessel some 120 × 40 cubits (*c.*63 × 21 m) to transport two obelisks: these can be seen today and are each estimated to weigh 186 tonnes (D. Jones, 1995: 65).

In the mortuary temple of Makare Hatshepsut (1503–1482 BC), there is a bas-relief (D. Jones, 1995: fig. 60) depicting a large vessel loaded with two obelisks, end-to-end, on sledges (Fig. 2.26), and towed by thirty oared-boats each with about thirty oarsmen. The accompanying text states that this very great vessel was built of sycamore (Landström, 1970: 128). Only certain aspects of the structure of this Hatshepsut stone 'barge' can be discerned: it has three tiers of protruding crossbeams (which stiffened the hull and prevented the strakes sliding relative to one another) and a further structure higher up at sheer level on which the sledges and obelisks are carried. To counteract the tendency of the hull to cave in on itself, it has five, possibly more, hogging hawsers fastened to vertical girdles near the ends and passing over seven pairs of crutches. The vessel is steered by two side rudders on each side (Landström, 1970: fig. 383). Bass (1972: 20) states that one of these granite obelisks survives at Karnak: it is nearly 100 ft (*c.*30 m) in length and is estimated to weigh 350 tonnes.

Several estimates of the size of this barge have been made, most based on the L / B proportions of 1 : 3 given by Ineni; some based on carrying only one obelisk at a time, others based on carrying two obelisks side-by-side. Koster (Landström, 1970: 128–9) estimated the barge to be 84 × 28 m. Ballard (1920b) estimated 207 ft (*c.*63 m) overall and 115 ft (*c.*35 m) on the waterline, with a waterline beam of 69 ft (*c.*21 m). Sølver (1936) deduced waterline length 63 m, beam 25 m. Casson (1971: 17) gives 200 × 70 ft (*c.*61 × 21 m).

If it is accepted that the obelisks were carried end-to-end as depicted, and that the artist represented ship, boat, and obelisks at approximately the same scale, then the room space unit (longitudinal distance between two adjacent oarsmen) may be used to estimate the size of barge and obelisks. Measurements of several groups of room spaces in the oared tugs suggest that the scale of the relief is *c.*1 : 225. This ratio makes the obelisks *c.*10 m and *c.*6.75 m in length, and the length of the barge between the vertical girdles

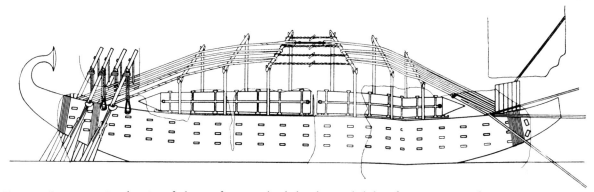

Fig. 2.26. Reconstruction drawing of a barge of *c.*1500 BC loaded with two obelisks (after Casson, 1971: fig. 14).

near the ends as *c*.26 m, i.e. a length overall of *c*.34 m. However, obelisks of *c*.10 m length are small when compared with the one of 30 m mentioned by Bass (1972: 20) and the 57 m obelisk postulated by Landström (1970: 129), and it therefore seems that, as might be expected, the Hatshepsut relief is not to scale and cannot be used as a basis for calculations. Furthermore, it is not certain that the obelisk at Karnak is one of those shipped by Hatshepsut (D. Jones, 1995: 65), thus it is unwise to use the height of 30 m as a basis for estimates of barge size.

There is no doubt that the Egyptians had a good practical grasp of buoyancy, stability, and stresses on a body afloat, as Admiral Ballard (1920*b*) pointed out, even though they may not have recognized such theoretical concepts: large stone objects were indeed moved by water from the early third millennium BC onwards.

There has been speculation as to how obelisks were loaded and unloaded. Pliny of the first century AD described how Ptolemy Philadelphus had a canal dug under a horizontal obelisk, then positioned a ballasted barge in the canal and this took the weight of the obelisk as its ballast was offloaded. Ballard (1920*b*: 271) does not believe this method would work and considers that the barge was positioned alongside the horizontal obelisk in its cradle which was then moved across greased skid beams and planks by driving shores and wedges, the barges' ballast being adjusted as she took the weight. Herodotus (2. 151) was told in Egypt that Cheops used sheerlegs to position large blocks in his pyramid; whilst James (1983: 193) has described how these blocks were manhandled into position by means of baulks of timber, rockers, and ramps of earth and brick—it is possible that some of these devices were used by Hatshepsut's engineers.

The precise method of towing the Hatshepsut barge is unclear from the relief. Ballard (1920*b*) argued that the tugs were each attached to one of three main towing hawsers by a line to their masthead: towing from a mast stepped near amidships ensures that the pull is from the point about which the tug turns hence it ensures the tug's manoeuvrability; the actual point of tow has to be positioned at a height on the towing mast which ensures that the cable is clear of hazards (such as other tugs). Sølver (1936) has argued that the tugs in three lines were each connected by cables from the masthead to the stem of the next astern. As Landström

(1970: 131) has pointed out, on downstream passages (as these were) tugs are needed primarily to give the barge steerage way relative to the river current so that the barges' own rudders would be effective. A further point made by Landström is that it may have been necessary to rig lines from the stern of the barge to the river bank so that it could be more readily controlled. Calculations by Wehausen, Mansour, and Ximenes (1988) show that, on certain assumptions, a Hapshepsut style of barge with obelisks could be safely towed by thirty boats each with thirty oarsmen. They have also demonstrated the theoretical practicability of *c*.50 men towing from the bank a similar barge loaded with one of the quartzite *colossi* of Memnon, weight *c*.720 tonnes, to Thebes from a quarry near Aswan, or one near Cairo.

Herodotus (2. 29) tells us that on the Nile above Aswan boats had to be towed from the bank, as did cargo boats going south on other parts of the river when there was not a fair, northerly wind (2. 96). Herodotus (2. 96) describes another method of obtaining steerage way when such a boat is using the Nile current to proceed northwards against the predominant wind: a stone weighing about 250 kg was towed astern of the barge and this, as it dragged along the river bed, slowed down the barge and gave it motion relative to the current which ensured that the rudder would be effective (albeit in the opposite sense from usual). A wooden raft with a rush mat on top of it was also allowed to drift on a line ahead of the barge thereby reducing yaw and adding to the barge's directional stability as it tended to keep the barge aligned with the main river current.

### 2.9.4 TWENTIETH-DYNASTY INNOVATIONS

Usermore-Meryamon Ramesses III (1198–1166 BC) was the last great king of the New Kingdom: three campaigns were mounted by him to repulse attacks on the Delta by invaders who were collectively known as the 'Peoples of the Sea' (4.9.1): their origin is much debated (Wachsmann, 1998: 178, 360). After Ramesses had repulsed these invasions, there was a general revival of Egypt's prosperity (James, 1983: 67) and Ramesses despatched a fleet to *Punt*, and overseas expeditions to Sinai (Hourani, 1963: 7–8; Hornell, 1941*a*: 243).

On the outer walls of Ramesses' mortuary temple

Fig. 2.27. Battle between ships of Ramesses 3 and those of the Sea People, depicted in his mortuary temple at Medinet Habu, Thebes (after Bass, 1972: fig. 18).

in Medinet Habu is portrayed his third and most decisive battle against the Sea People (Fig. 2.27). This first recorded 'sea battle' took place either in the Nile delta (Wachsmann, 1981; 1998: 166–75) or in a river on the Levant coast (Raban, 1989). Egyptian galleys carrying armed men seem to have made a surprise attack, possibly in conjunction with a land force, on a fleet of sea raiders / mercenaries / immigrants within a harbour.

In Ramesses' texts there are references to three types of vessel in the Egyptian fleet but only one type is depicted. One major change from earlier times is that hogging hawsers and vertical girdles are not shown. This suggests that, since the time of the last known depiction of seagoing ships, in the eighteenth dynasty, some 250 years earlier, confidence in the structural integrity of the hull had markedly increased, possibly due to a significant change in the plank fastening arrangements which may have been the introduction of Phoenician *locked* mortises and tenons (4.9.3.2.3). With the exception of the bow which, in relation to the stern, is lower than in earlier depictions and fitted with a lion figurehead (not a ram as has sometimes been suggested), the shape of the Egyptian vessels shows little change from earlier times. Whether or not these ships had structural stem and stern posts is unclear. It is

clear, however, that these ships, like those of Hatshepsut, had through crossbeams which may also have been used as thwarts by the oarsmen. It also seems likely that there was a deck along the middle line on which marines could stand between the two files of oarsmen. A washstrake has evidently been added to the main hull so that the oarsmen are depicted, for the first time, plying their oars through oarports in the sides rather than through pivots fastened to the top of the sides: the oarsmen thus have some protection both from a rough sea and from the enemy.

Another innovation is that there is a fighting top ('crow's nest') at the masthead from which one man wields a weapon which has been interpreted as a grapnel, but which may be a sling. When on passage, this top was probably used by a lookout. The pole mast is stepped near amidships, as earlier, but there are significant changes to the rigging: there is no longer a boom and thus for the first time the Egyptian sail is depicted as loose-footed. Brails to shorten or shape the sail are also evident: both Vinson (1994: 41, fig. 29) and D. Jones (1995: 60) quote evidence for the use of brails before the time of Ramesses III, possibly as early as the eighteenth dynasty (c.1350 BC). The yard appears to be curved downwards, possibly because sails are furled. A much simpler standing rigging is depicted than in earlier times, but this may be an artistic device to avoid further visual confusion in an already crowded and jumbled scene. The relative lengths of mast and yard depicted suggest that the sails were of low-aspect ratio, as in earlier centuries.

The raised decks at the ends, seen on Egyptian ships in earlier dynasties, here seem more pronounced, especially the one near the stern. When on passage these decks doubtless continued to be used by the lookouts, forward, and by the helmsmen, aft, but, here in battle, archers and other fighting men man them, the after deck being shared with the helmsmen.

Working oars through the sides, the use of fighting tops, and a middle-line decking all have advantages in warfare at sea. The first two features also have peaceful uses: tops for lookouts; higher sides, with oarsmen relatively lower in the hull, increase the capacity for cargo. Compared with a boomed rig, a loose-footed sail can more readily be handled and shifted from tack to tack, and it can be given a more efficient shape relative to the wind. This change suggests that the innovators were seeking to get closer to the wind, although a sail of low-aspect ratio is not as efficient to windward as one with a high-aspect ratio.

In the Middle Kingdom the area of sail was adjusted to match the strength of the wind by lowering the yard or possibly by use of a smaller sail. Brails, as seen in the New Kingdom, allow the useful area of sail to be reduced by bringing the foot of the sail towards the yard. Differential brailing is also a possibility: by such means the shape of the sail can be changed to improve windward performance (Casson, 1971: fig. 188).

In the fifth century BC Herodotus (2. 36) noted that the Egyptians differed from the Greeks in an aspect of their running rigging. The Greek text is usually translated as referring to 'sheets' and to 'ringbolts' fitted inboard or outboard. However, Landström (1970: 111), and others after him, interpret this as a reference to brails rather than sheets: Greek brails were rigged against the leeward (forward) face of the sail, whereas Egyptian brails were to windward (aft): a disparity which may have originated 600 years earlier. On the other hand, this passage also makes sense if the reference is to sheets and ringbolts. Any fitting outboard of a ship's hull is liable to be damaged when the vessel lies alongside a waterfront, and the Egyptians, who probably used such formal harbours more frequently than the Greeks, may have preferred to fasten their rigging to inboard fittings.

Representations of non-fighting ships and boats from the nineteenth and twentieth dynasties show little sign of the innovations incorporated in Ramesses' warships. A sketch in a Theban tomb, paintings in the tomb of Ipuy and a relief in the tomb of Iniwia (Landström, 1970: figs. 356, 396, 403, 405; Bass, 1972: plate 20) depict fishing boats and cargo vessels, some built of short planking and some with protruding crossbeams. The cargo vessels have vertical ends, similar to those depicted earlier in Hatshepsut's and in Sahure's reliefs. The small fishing boats are steered with a median rudder, as appears to have been standard in Egypt by this time. An unstepped mast depicted in the Ipuy painting has a projecting tenon at the foot to fit into a mast step; at deck level the mast was lashed to a knee. The cargo vessels have up-curving yards and booms, rather than the loose-footed sail on the down-curving yards of Ramesses' warships; one of them (Landström, 1970: fig. 403) appears to have a top for a lookout.

## 2.10

# The Late Dynastic Period
### (1085–332 BC)

After the death of Ramesses III in c.1166 BC a period of political instability and decreasing prosperity ensued during which Egypt finally lost control of her Asiatic lands (James, 1983: 69). During the last years of the twentieth dynasty (1114–1085 BC) power in Egypt was effectively divided between the High Priest of Amun at Thebes in Upper Egypt and the governor of Lower Egypt, the King, Menmare Ramesses XI, having withdrawn to his lands in the Delta.

During these disturbed times Herihar, High Priest at Thebes, sent Wenamun by sea to the Levant to buy cedar so that a new state barge could be built for Amun's procession on the Nile from Karnak to Luxor. The hardships, misfortunes, and indignities he experienced in the harbours of Palestine and Syria reflect

Egypt's diminished political and military importance (James, 1983: 116–17; Wachsmann, 1998: 11–12).

The 400 years of the twenty-first to twenty-fifth dynasties (1085–656 BC) are sometimes known as the Third Intermediate Period as these were also unsettled times with competing dynasties and subversive groups setting up their own provinces. This chaotic situation was resolved by conquerors from the south of Egypt, Piankhi (Piye), and then his brother Neferkure Shabaka, who reunited Egypt under the twenty-fifth dynasty (747–656 BC).

There was a cultural revival under Nubian or Kushite kings which continued into the twenty-sixth dynasty (James, 1983: 69–75; O'Connor, 1980b: 193–4). The illustrations noted to date of ships from this period are few in number and Landström (1970: 140–1) has described them as 'generally uninteresting'.

The years 664–332 BC (twenty-sixth to thirty-first dynasties) are usually known as the Late Period. This 300-year period began with a certain stability under the Saite Kings (664–525 BC), but the Assyrians under Ashurbanipal occupied Lower Egypt from c.667–c.656 BC; and Persian kings ruled Egypt from c.525–404 (twenty-seventh dynasty) and again from c.343–332 BC (thirty-first dynasty). Furthermore, although Egypt expelled the Persians in c.404 BC, with help from Carian and Ionian mercenaries, most of the twenty-eighth to thirtieth dynasties Pharaohs (404–343 BC) had a struggle to maintain this independence, having to rely on Greek mercenaries.

The 130 years of relative stability which transpired after Egypt had been reunited by Wahibre Psammetichus I (664–610 BC) and the Assyrian overlordship repudiated in c.656 BC, proved to be years of opportunity for colonists and traders: Greeks in particular were encouraged to settle there: for example, Psammetichus I granted land near the Pelusian (eastern) mouth of the Nile to the Greeks who had helped him (O'Connor, 1980b: 193–4; James, 1983: 75). Herodotus (2. 164) tells us that the remains of the harbour they used on the Nile and their houses could still be seen in his day, 200 years later. During this period Greek influence on Egyptian shipbuilding may well have been great, reinforcing the technological input of the Phoenicians in earlier centuries.

Herodotus (2. 158) and Strabo (17. 1. 25) tell us that the canal through the Bitter Lake region (2. 8. 2) which connected the Nile to the Red Sea was begun by Wehemibre Necho II (610–595 BC). This Pharaoh had triremes built, some on the Mediterranean coast and some in the Red Sea, and used them 'as occasion arose' (Herodotus 2.159). The necessity to have fleets on both Egyptian coasts must have been one of his main reasons for attempting to cut a canal; another was probably an awareness of Egypt's central position on the trade route from the Mediterranean to the east African coast and to India. Necho II further demonstrated his interest in commerce and trade by sending a ship manned by Phoenicians (4.9.3.2.1) to circumnavigate Africa (Herodotus 4. 42; Strabo 2. 3. 4).

### 2.10.1 NAUCRATIS

The greatest of the sixth-century BC Greek colonies in Egypt was *Naucratis* on the Canopic (western) branch of the Nile. Herodotus (2. 178–9) tells us that it was given to the Greeks by Khnemibre Amosis II (Amasis) (c.570–526 BC), whereas Strabo (17.1. 18) believed it was founded earlier, in the reign of Neferibre Psamtek I (664–610 BC). It subsequently became the only legal point of entry to the Nile delta: if vessels were forced to enter any other Nile mouth, and winds subsequently kept them there, their cargo had to be transported by river and canal to *Naucratis* before it could be dispersed.

The fact that Necho II built triremes suggests that, by the early sixth century BC at the latest, there was little if anything distinctive about Egyptian ships and their methods of building them. The *boats* of the Nile doubtless continued to be built in the traditional way—indeed aspects of this tradition continued in use on the upper Nile into the twentieth century AD (Hornell, 1946a: 215–18, plate 35B) but *ships* by now were in all probability part of the general Mediterranean tradition which itself owed much to early Egyptian boat-building techniques (4.8.3.4).

# 2.11

# Graeco-Roman Times

The Persian rule of Egypt was finally ended by Alexander the Great in 332 BC. Three Macedonian kings were followed by the Ptolemies who ruled Egypt from 305 to 30 BC. They organized Egypt on Greek lines, and paid especial attention to the development of commerce: new harbours were built and contacts with both Asian and Classical lands were increased. By the early first century BC, however, the Ptolemies' control of Egypt began to loosen, and dynastic squabbles affected the stability of the regime. From about this time the Romans took an increasing interest in Egyptian affairs, especially in its supply of corn, and in 30 BC, after the Battle of Actium, when Anthony and Cleopatra VII Philopator were defeated by Octavian, Egypt formally became a Roman province ( James, 1983: 78–80).

## 2.11.1 ALEXANDRIA AND THE PHAROS

Alexander the Great ordered a new capital of Egypt to be built on the Mediterranean coast, just to the west of the Canopic branch of the Nile, clear of the Delta with its shifting channels, on a site which was protected from seaward by the island of Pharos. A causeway seven stades (*c.*1.3 km) in length was built linking the island to the mainland, thus forming two harbours, one open to the west and one to the east. A third waterfront to the south of the city bordered the edge of Lake Mareotis, a freshwater lake which gave access to the Nile and thence the whole of Egypt.

The Egyptian Mediterranean coast is, and was, low-lying and Herodotus (2. 5), in the fifth century BC, described how silt was deposited by the Nile well out to sea. It was thus a difficult task to identify a boat's position when approaching the coast and to take her through the ever-changing channels into one of the primary branches of the Nile. In *c.*60 BC Diodorus referred to these difficulties and described how many vessels unexpectedly ran aground and were wrecked. Ptolemy I Soter I (305–282 BC) sought to rectify this situation by building a lighthouse at the entrance to Alexandria harbour on Pharos Island, which could not only be seen by night when the beacon was lit, but also was so tall and distinctive that it could be used as a landmark by day. Homer mentions the building of tumuli in prominent positions near coasts where they could be seen by mariners from afar; he also mentions the use of special beacon fires (McGrail, 1992): but as far as is known the lighthouse on Pharos,

completed during the reign of Ptolemy II Philadelphus (284–246 BC), was the earliest permanent, specialist lighthouse. It has been estimated that it was 455 ft (138.6 m) tall, only 30 ft (9.1 m) less than the Great Pyramid at Giza. The white marble building could thus be seen on a clear day out to more than 20 nautical miles; at night its beacon is said to have been visible out to 35 nautical miles and Pliny tells us (*NH* 36. 83) that it could be mistaken for a low star. The source of the light is not known, but, as wood for burning would have been scarce in Egypt, it has been suggested that animal dung or even petroleum was used; another possibility is reed roots which Pliny (*NH* 13. 22) states were used as firewood by the Egyptians of his day.

Pharos' light was still in working order when the Arabs conquered Egypt in AD 642, but in *c.* AD 700 the lantern was destroyed, probably by an earthquake. This lighthouse had proved so successful that by the end of the Roman Empire in the west there were thirty lighthouses in use in the Mediterranean and the Black Sea, and at Corunna in north-west Spain, Dover in south-east England, and Boulogne in north-west France.

## 2.11.2 ALEXANDRIA AND THE DELTA

Strabo and Pliny are both valuable sources for details of commercial and maritime life in and around Alexandria and the Nile delta in the first century AD. Strabo (17. 1. 9, 16, 18) describes the Grand Harbour with its Pharos lighthouse, moles, warehouses, and ship-sheds, and the canal along which people and goods could be taken to Lake Mareotis and thence to the Canopic branch of the Nile. Another canal led to the town of Schedia where cabin boats were based, for officials to sail to Upper Egypt. There was a raft or pontoon bridge in the canal at Schedia where taxes on imports and exports had to be paid. However, Strabo notes that, at the time of his visit to Egypt, Alexandria was temporarily closed to imports and these had to be brought into Egypt by the Canopic branch, at or near the mouth of which there was a watchtower (Strabo, 17. 1. 6, 17. 1. 18) which had been there in Herodotus' time. Pliny (*NH* 7. 56, 13. 21) notes that rafts of papyrus, rushes, and reeds were still being made in the Delta region and that the inner bark of the papyrus stems was woven into sailcloth and turned up into ropes. He also describes

(*NH* 6. 26) the first stages of the trade route from the Mediterranean to east Africa, Arabia, and India: from Alexandria up the Nile to Keft (*Coptus*) and then by camel across the eastern desert to Egyptian harbours on the Red Sea coast.

## 2.11.3 THE MEDITERRANEAN–RED SEA CANAL

The canal begun by Necho II (2.8.2; 2.10) was probably extended by Darius the Persian (*c*.522–486 BC). Herodotus (2. 158) states that in his day, this canal was of a length equivalent to four days' journey by boat, and that its breadth was sufficient for two triremes to be rowed abreast. It left the Pelusias (eastern) branch of the Nile slightly upstream of Bubastis, and passed through the Bitter Lakes. Strabo (17. 1. 25–6) tells us that it began near the villages of *Phacussa* and *Philo*, and entered the Red Sea near Arsinoe/*Cleopatris*; its breadth was 100 cubits (*c*.50 m.)) and its depth was sufficient for 'very large merchant vessels'. In about 274 BC, Ptolemy II Philadelphus (284–246 BC) appears to have completed Necho's and Darius' work by taking the canal through to Arsinoe/*Cleopatris* (Strabo: 17. 1. 25–6). Ptolemy II incorporated into the canal some sort of removable barrier (a floating boom?) by means of which he could control its use.

In *c.* AD 106 Trajan cut another canal starting from the Nile near Babylon (near where Cairo now stands) running more or less parallel to the Pelusiac branch to join the Necho canal near Thon; he then extended Ptolemy's canal beyond Arsinoe to Klusma (near Suez). This canal was still working 700 years later (Huntingford, 1980: 77–9). Although the final form of the canal does not seem to have been achieved until the early second century AD, it is not impossible that Herodotus and Strabo are correct in stating that it was possible to travel from the Nile to the Red Sea at a much earlier date. Necho in the early sixth century BC, Darius in the sixth/fifth century BC, and Ptolemy II in the mid-third century BC all probably ended their respective canals at a point where it was, at that time, possible to continue to the Red Sea by rivers and lakes: siltation and other natural processes subsequently meant that each canal had to be extended further to ensure a through passage.

## 2.11.4 EARLY OVERSEAS TRADE ROUTES (Fig. 2.21)

There is evidence from early dynastic times (early third millennium BC) of the Egyptian exploitation of Sinai, and of overseas trade with the Levant and with *Punt* (2.7.7). There may have been overland expeditions to *Punt* in the earliest phases, but subsequently, whenever Egypt was politically stable and economically prosperous, ships were used: there is evidence for this from the Old Kingdom, the Middle Kingdom, and the New Kingdom. Some scholars have suggested that these ships sailed down the Nile and then via a canal to the Red Sea, or that ships on the Nile were dismantled and transported overland to the Red Sea. There is some evidence to support these theories but there is stronger evidence that Egyptian ships were built in the Red Sea region, probably at the head of the Gulf of Aqaba, near the source of Lebanon cedars (2.7.7.1; Herodotus 2. 159; Bible: 1 Kings 9: 26–8; 2 Chronicles 8: 17).

Early rock carvings of boats in the Wadi Hammamat show that this was a well-used route across the eastern desert between the Nile and the Red Sea coast, to a port in the vicinity of Wadi Gasûs, north of *Kosseir* (Qusayr or al Qusayr). Stone was quarried in the Wadi Hammamat region and in the eleventh dynasty (if not before) wells were dug so that both quarrymen and merchants could get fresh water. Qusayr or nearby Quseir al-Qadim is probably the *Myos Hormos* (Mussel Harbour) referred to many years later by the geographer Ptolemy (4. 5. 8) (Peacock, 1999: 5).

During the Ptolemaic period, especially in the reign of Ptolemy II Philadelphus (284–286 BC), Greek seamen took merchants and others down the Red Sea as far as the 'cinnamon-bearing country' and to hunt elephants (Strabo, 17. 1. 5)—this may well have been north of the strait at Bab el Mandeb. However, by *c*.200 BC Greek merchants had sailed beyond these straits: to Aden (*Arabia Felix*) for Indian merchandise; and to the south shore of the Gulf of Aden (Casson, 1989: 12) as far west as the promontory *Notuceras*, probably Cape Guardafui (Strabo, 16. 4. 14). By this time the main Egyptian Red Sea port seems to have been changed from Qusayr to *Berenicê* which Philadelphus had founded (Pliny, 6. 168) south of Ras Banas in Foul Bay, on approximately the same latitude as Aswan. Philadelphus also cut a road (more probably resurfaced an old established track) from the Nile to *Berenicê* and built watering stations along it (Strabo, 17. 1. 45). *Berenicê* is over 150 nautical miles south of Qusayr so that, from that time, ships returning from India (6.3), Arabia and east Africa to Egypt had less distance to sail in the Red Sea against the wind which, north of c.20°N, is predominantly northerly. This change may have been precipitated when galleys were replaced by larger ships which it was no longer possible to propel by oar. Previously, galleys had been rowed northwards in foul winds or in no winds; now sailing ships had to wait for a fair wind, delays which were costly.

This Greek/Egyptian seaborne trade from a port in the Red Sea to land further south on the west side of that sea and on to the Somali coast of the Gulf of Aden was extending, if not repeating, the much earlier Egyptian voyages to the land of *Punt*. Descriptions in Strabo (17. 1. 45) and Pliny (*NH* 6. 26. 103) confirm that the Greek merchants' overland route from the Nile to the Red Sea was also similar to that of their Egyptian predecessors. Merchants of Alexandria sailed up the Nile to *Coptus* (Quft) which was connected to the river by a canal. Strabo describes *Coptus* as 'a city common to Egyptians and Arabians' and an emporium where Indian, Arabian, and Ethiopian merchandise came. From at least the early second century AD an association of Palmyrene Red Sea shipowners was based there (Casson, 1989: 20).

There seems little doubt that the position of *Berenicê* is securely located in Foul Bay for it matches the descriptions by Strabo (17. 1. 45) of a natural harbour protected by an isthmus, just north of an island noted for its topaz (or peridots). Pliny (6. 26. 101–4) tells us that it was 257 miles from *Coptus* (Keft or Quft) to *Berenicê*. Merchants on camels took twelve days, travelling by night because of the heat, and staying by day at one of seven or eight named watering places.

Strabo (17. 1. 45) states that watering places had recently been constructed on the route between *Coptus* and *Myos Hormos* and that the journey took six or seven days. Huntingford (1980: 86) located it at or near Qusayr and this has been confirmed by recent fieldwork (Peacock, 1999). *Myos Hormos* therefore had the disadvantage that vessels returning there had further to go against northerly winds. However, as it was primarily a naval base (Strabo, 17. 1. 45), galleys would be the principal ships operated and they would be able to use oars in foul winds: the shorter overland journey from the Red Sea to the River Nile (seven days from *Myos Hormos* compared with twelve from *Berenicê*) would be seen as an advantage by political and naval authorities. That some merchants did use *Myos Hormos* in Roman times is clear from the *Periplus of the Erythraean Sea*—possibly they were able to take advantage of an extension northwards of the region of southerly winds to c.25°N which can occur in April.

## 2.11.5 *PERIPLUS OF THE ERYTHRAEAN SEA*
(Fig. 2.21)

The *Periplus Maris Erythraei* was written by an Egyptian Greek in the middle of the first century AD: the most recent translation and commentary is by Casson (1989). The author evidently had personal experience of trading between Roman Egypt and east Africa, southern Arabia, and the west coast of India, and the first century AD was a period of relatively intensive trade with those regions (Strabo, 2. 5. 12; Pliny, 6. 26. 101). The *Periplus* is a handbook primarily for Greek merchants involved in this booming Indian Ocean trade, with some guidance on pilotage for the seaman. The sections of the *Periplus* dealing with Arabia (chs. 19–37) and India and beyond (38–66) are discussed in 3.7 and 6.3; the Egyptian/African sections (chs. 1–18) are discussed below. Unless otherwise stated, Casson's (1989) identification of the sites is followed.

### 2.11.5.1 EGYPT–AFRICA TRADE ROUTES

The author of the *Periplus* recommends leaving Egypt for *Adulis* and another harbour c.80 nautical miles further on, about the month of September (chs. 5 and 6). *Adulis* is generally identified with Massawa harbour on the west coast of the Red Sea, and the next harbour is thought to be Hanachil Bay (Bia di Ouachil) (Casson, 1989: 102–6, 109). The island of *Dahlach Chebin* (Dahlak Kabir), the largest island in the Dahlak archipelago is midway between these two sites, and Sleeswyk has argued that this island and the mainland opposite may have been the *Punt* of Dynastic Egypt.

The only other part of Africa for which the *Periplus* (ch. 14) gives a recommended departure date (around the month of July) from Egypt is the 'far-side ports', i.e. the southern side of the Gulf of Aden, the northern coast of Somali. These ports were *Malaô* (Berbera), *Mundu* (Heis Island), *Mosyllon* (in the vicinity of Candala), *Neiloptolemaiu* (situation not known), the Spice Port (now Cape Guardafui or Ras Asir—the tip of the Horn of Africa), and *Opônê* (possibly Ras Hafun south of Cape Guardafui).

Two other African ports in the Red Sea region are mentioned. First, *Ptolemais Thêrôn* (ch. 3) which is thought to be in the vicinity of Sualcin and Aqiq, some 200 nautical miles north of Massawa. This had been founded by Ptolemy II Philadelphus (282–246 BC) as a base for elephant hunting (Strabo, 16. 4. 7) and, in the first century AD, was only used by small craft trading in tortoiseshell and some ivory. Second, *Avalitês* (ch. 7) which is thought to be Assab just north of the strait Bab el Mandeb—this was almost 'exclusively' involved in trade with Arabia.

In chapters 15 and 16, twelve other African ports are mentioned beyond *Opônê* (Ras Hafun): *Sarapiôn* thought to be Warsherk; *Nikôn*—in the region of Mogadiscio—*Merka*; seven unnamed harbours—probably between Brava and Bur Gao; *Pyralaoi*—probably the Lamu archipelago; *Menuthias* island—this may be Pemba or Zanzibar or even Mafia island; and the last port used on this coast, *Rhapta*—this is probably either Dar es Salaam or a harbour near the River Rufiji.

There thus seem to have been three main trade routes from *Berenicê* (ch. 18): (a) to the *Adulis* and *Avalitês* region of the Red Sea coast (chs. 6 and 7); (b) to the Somali coast of the Gulf of Aden (chs. 8 to 13); and (c) to ports on the east African coast between *c.*5°N and 7°S (chs. 15 to 17). As no recommended departure date is given in the *Periplus* for this third group of ports, it must be assumed that those vessels that passed through the strait Ras el Mandeb either undertook a tramp-style voyage along the Somali coast and then returned to Egypt, or they rounded Cape Guardafui for the east African ports. It may be that ships trading with these latter ports had first to call at *Muza* (Mocha or Al Mukha on the Arabian coast of the Red Sea just north of the strait Bab el Mandeb), for the *Rhapta* region was under the rule of Mapharifi (Yemen) and the merchants of *Muza* had the grant of it (ch. 16).

### 2.11.5.2 TRADED GOODS AND BALLAST

Goods carried from Egypt and the Mediterranean to the southern Red Sea region, the Somali coast and east Africa are named in chapters 6, 13, and 17 in the *Periplus*; goods to be imported are named in chapters 3–13, and 17. Some of the goods traded have high stowage factors, that is, they occupy a large volume in relation to their weight. For example: olive oil in casks has a stowage factor of 1.67–1.73 m³/tonne; wine in casks, 1.62–1.78; ivory in cases, 1.53–1.67; barley in bags, 1.45–1.67; wheat in bags, 1.34–1.50 (McGrail, 1989b: table 1). Clothing, tortoiseshell, and spices and aromatics also have a high stowage factor, no matter how they are packaged. Only the metals (brass, iron, and tin), the possible obsidian, and slaves have stowage factors near or less than 1. It is not possible to load a vessel with large quantities of high stowage factor goods without compensating quantities of low stowage factor materials otherwise stability can be reduced below safe levels. It may well have been, therefore, that ballast had to be carried on many of these voyages unless the quantities of metals carried were large. As cargo was discharged and embarked, at intermediate ports or at the final destination, the quantity of ballast would probably have had to be varied. Thus ballast of Egyptian stone may have been discharged in Indian ports, and Somali stone in Egyptian ports.

### 2.11.5.3 EAST AFRICAN BOATS AND RAFTS

The *Periplus* briefly mentions some of the water transport used on the eastern coast of Africa. Rafts (whether bundle rafts, log rafts, or buoyed rafts is not stated) were used by the local seamen out of *Avalitês*, and to transport goods across the strait of Bab el Mandeb to Arabia (ch. 7). Sewn-plank boats (chs. 15 and 16) were used from the island of *Menonthias* (Pemba or Zanzibar) and in *Rhapta* harbour (Dar es Salaam).

Sewn-plank boats have been noted on this coast in more recent times: Vasco da Gama saw them in Mozambique in 1498, and they were reported at Zanzibar in the late-sixteenth century (Hornell, 1946a: 235). Hornell (1941b), Prins (1965) and others (e.g. Chittick, 1980b; Gilbert, 1998) have described recent east African boats with sewn planking, including the almost legendary *mtepe* of the Lamu archipelago. This tradition in coastal east Africa must be considered in conjunction with similar traditions in Arabia (3.6) and in India (6.7.3): an Indian Ocean phenomenon for at least 2,000 years.

## 2.11.5.4 SEASONAL SAILING

### 2.11.5.4.1 *To the southern Red Sea*

Ships left *Berenicê* for *Adulis* in September or earlier (ch. 6). They would thus have a fair north-east, north, or north-west wind down the Red Sea. From October to February they would have a fair south or south-east wind for the return voyage as far as 20° or 21°N; if return could be delayed to March/April, however, they would have a fair southerly wind as far north as 25°N and even as far as Suez (*Red Sea Pilot*, vol. 1). Thus in spring, at the change of the monsoon, ships would be able to reach *Berenicê*, and occasionally *Myos Hormos*, under sail. Between October and February, however, they would generally have a foul wind from *c*.20°N (17°N in January) which would mean a broken passage with long delays waiting for the occasional day when progress northwards was possible. If these ships were, as is probable at that time, too large to be propelled by oar, then the only alternative would be towing by oared-boats—an arduous task. The Egyptian coast of the Red Sea is strewn with coral reefs and therefore it is unlikely that coastal passages at night were undertaken except at times of full moon. The *Periplus* (ch. 20) clearly states that a coastal passage along the Arabian coast is 'too risky' as it is 'foul with rocky stretches' and is 'fearsome in every respect'. Day passages in sight of the Egyptian coast, perhaps using an inner lead inside the reefs, would seem to be the best plan, but an alternative mentioned in the *Periplus* was to sail down the middle of the Red Sea as far as *Katakekanmene* (the island Jabal at Ta'ir which is only *c*.200 nautical miles north of the strait Bab el Mandeb): beyond this island a coastal passage was possible (ch. 20).

### 2.11.5.4.2 *To the Somali coast*

Ships left *Berenicê* for the Somali coast in July (ch. 14) and had fair north and north-west winds down the Red Sea. In the Gulf of Aden they encountered the south-west monsoon with winds from the south, south-west, and west—thus a passage along the Somali coast would be possible, although there might be difficult winds on certain days. At their final port of call they awaited the change of monsoon which established a fair east/east-north-east wind in the Gulf of Aden from November to the spring. The return up the Red Sea followed the same pattern described above (2.11.5.4.1): December to February would have fair

winds, but only as far as *c*.20°N; if they could wait to enter the Red Sea until March they could well have fair winds the whole way to *Berenicê*, or even to *Myos Hormos*.

### 2.11.5.4.3 *To the east African coast*

It seems likely that ships would aim to arrive in the vicinity of the Spice Port (near Cape Guardafui) when the autumn change of monsoon was imminent, that is in September/November. Thus they would leave *Berenicê* in the period July to September. They would then be able to choose the best time to round the Cape and have a fair north or north-east wind, and sail with the monsoon and the current along the coast of east Africa. These ships would have until March to get to the vicinity of Dar es Salaam. They could leave there in May or June once the first boisterousness of the south-west monsoon had passed, but would not be able to round Cape Guardafui until the autumnal change of monsoons—thus it could be preferable to delay at Dar es Salaam until, say, September, round Cape Guardafui in October, and have fair east and east-north-east monsoon winds in the Gulf of Aden, and south and south-east winds in the Red Sea. These ships would thus arrive at 17° to 20°N in November/December, with the prospect of a lengthy, broken voyage against the prevailing wind before reaching *Berenicê*: there seems to be no way they could plan their return to catch the March/April favourable period in the Red Sea.

### 2.11.5.4.4 *Length of voyage*

Voyages from *Berenicê* to the southern region of the Red Sea around *Adulis*, and return, took about seven months and there was a reasonable chance that the final 500 nautical miles would be with a fair wind. Voyages to the Somali coast and back, took up to nine months, again with a good chance of a fair wind all the way. On the other hand, as Casson has pointed out (1989: 283–8) the voyage to the east African coast was much longer, taking up to twenty-one months; the stay in *Rhapta* could be for just the month of April during the change of monsoons, or it might be as long as nine months from December to September. Furthermore, on the return route there would appear to have been no way that they could avoid a lengthy, broken passage for the final 500 nautical miles.

### 2.11.5.5 EARLY VOYAGES TO *PUNT*

With this wind pattern in the Red Sea and Gulf of Aden it would have been possible for ships of fifth-dynasty Egypt and later (2.7.7.1, 2.9.1) to voyage to, and return from, *Punt* in one season. This would be so whether *Punt* was near the southern end of the Red Sea or on the Somali coast of the Gulf of Aden or indeed, if *Punt* was both places. Even with their restrictive sailing rig fifth-dynasty ships would have been capable of sailing with a fair wind. If they chose the appropriate time to leave Egypt (July–September) and delayed their return up the Red Sea until March/April, they would have had a fair wind for all but the last 500 nautical miles of the voyage. These early voyages could, in fact, have been made in less time than later ones: since galleys were being used, the last 500 nautical miles in, say, December, could have been under oars. The Egyptian port which they used at or near Khoseir or Qusayr (later known as *Myos Hormos*) had the advantage of being the closest point to the Nile; it also was not so far north of the zone of autumn to spring southerly winds as to make an oared northbound passage intolerably long.

# 3
# ARABIA

This chapter deals with that part of Asia which lies east of the Red Sea, west of the Indian subcontinent and south of the Caspian Sea. It does not include the Black Sea region, Anatolia, or the Levant (except indirectly) which, for historical rather than geographic reasons, are dealt with in Chapter 4 on the Mediterranean. Nor does it include Egypt and the western shores of the Red Sea or the southern shores of the Gulf of Aden which are considered in Chapter 2. The core of this region, in the earliest phases of this chapter, is Mesopotamia (modern Iraq)—the land of the two rivers, Tigris and Euphrates (Fig. 3.1). These rivers, flowing south from Assyria and from the Anatolian highlands into the Persian Gulf, were not only the source of the fertility (water and alluvium) on which one of the world's first urban civilizations was based, but also led to the western Indian Ocean (Arabian Sea) with access by sea to the coasts of the Arabian peninsula, north-eastern Africa, India, south-east Asia and beyond.

The fertile region of southern Mesopotamia (Sumer) was farmed from the seventh millennium BC: crops were grown intensively and animals herded (Oates, 1980: 113); in the delta regions, further south, fish and fowl were hunted. During the sixth and fifth millennia BC permanent settlements were established with an economy dependent on the successful irrigation of the land, and by the late fourth millennium BC substantial settlements recognizable as city states, such as Eridu, Uruk, Nippur, Kish, Ur, and Lagash, had emerged, each one either on a major river or joined to it by a canal. Dykes and channels were built to regulate the irregular flow of the two rivers which not only reduced the risk of settlement sites being flooded, but also maintained and enhanced the fertility of the land

on which this civilization was based—comparable regulatory means were used in the Nile Valley (*c*.3400 BC), the River Indus (*c*.2500 BC), and the Huang ho in northern China (*c*.1800 BC). These channels also formed a network of communications by boat and raft.

The cooperative work needed during the annual cleaning of the irrigation channels and the communication canals of Sumer led, on the one hand, to a centralized administration and, on the other, to the measurement of time and the creation of a calendar, to land measurement and mathematics, and to the invention of writing (in the late-Uruk phase, soon after 3400 BC).

## 3.1
## Overseas Trade

Southern Mesopotamia lacked basic resources such as timber, stone, and metal ores (copper and tin) needed by the city states of the early third millennium BC for their monumental buildings and for their craftsmen; and this need led to external trade both with the high lands of Anatolia and the Iranian Plateau around the headwaters of the two rivers, and also with overseas lands accessible through the Persian Gulf. Furthermore, the hierarchical nature of Sumerian society stimulated the demand for non-utilitarian exotic products which led to the import of luxury goods by an overland route from China and by overseas routes from such places as the Persian Gulf, the Horn of

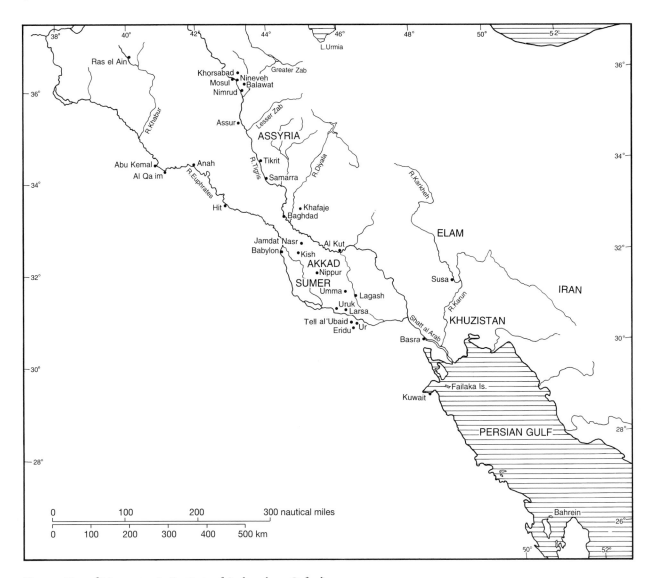

Fig. 3.1. Map of Mesopotamia (Institute of Archaeology, Oxford).

Africa, and the Red Sea coasts, and possibly India. In exchange, the Sumerian city states exported their agricultural surplus of wheat, barley, and wool (Ratnagar, 1981: 3; Potts, 1994). These widespread contacts (direct or indirect) are demonstrated by the maritime distribution of Ubaid pottery of the fifth/fourth millennia BC (Bourriau and Oates, 1997: 720—but see also Roaf and Galbraith (1994) for statistical reservations). Water transport was needed for this trade: river craft to the north for some of the inland routes; seagoing craft to the south for overseas routes. Well-sited landing places such as *Ur* on the Euphrates and *Lagash* on the Tigris became international with bazaars or markets adjacent to beaches and anchorages.

## 3.2

# Water Transport before the Third Millennium BC

During this long period, from the beginning of farming in the mid-seventh millennium BC, there is little evidence for the water transport used, either inland or seagoing. Clay models of the Ubaid period, dated to the early fifth millennium BC, from a grave at Eridu in southern Mesopotamia (Fig. 3.2) are almost elliptical in plan and have a vertical socket in the base and three

Fig. 3.2. Clay model from a grave at Eridu of the early fifth millennium BC (after Casson, 1971: fig. 20).

holes through the top of the sides. Bass (1972: 12) following Barnett (1958: 221) has suggested that these may represent hide boats with fittings for a mast. Strasser (1996) has argued that they are spinning bowls, a hypothesis which is strongly opposed by Bourriau and Oates (1997). It is possible that these models may represent some form of water transport, possibly hide or reed-bundle boats. However, the fittings seem more readily explained as a socket for a ceremonial staff and as fastening points for suspension cords, as proposed by Casson (1971: 22). An alternative hypothesis is that, if the models are of boats, the socket is for a towing mast, for which it is in an ideal position about one-third of the waterline length from the bow. The earliest evidence for sail in Mesopotamia, in fact, is not until some 2,000 years later (3.5.5). This apparent late development, when compared for example with Egypt, may be due to the fact that the generally northerly wind in the region could not be used to sail upstream (as it could on the River Nile), and towing had to be used. During recent excavations at Tell Mashnaqa, in Syria, other Ubaid boat models have been found which appear to resemble reed-bundle rafts (or possibly boats), but which have no fittings which might be interpreted as for sail (Strasser, 1996: 922).

A pictogram in the early form of writing used in Sumeria and the surrounding lands (Walker, 1990: 17–21) and used on clay tablets from Uruk of the later fourth millennium BC shows a double-ended vessel with high curving ends and with vertical lines across the hull which probably depict the bindings around individual bundles of reeds and the coiled bindings which bind bundles together (Bass, 1972: 12–13, 27; Bar-

nett, 1958: 221). Engravings on cylinder seals of the Jamdat Nasr (Uruk III) period dated to c.3200 BC (Fig. 3.3) and from Tell Billa near Nineveh (Oates, 1980: fig. 16.6), show craft with a similar outline shape to that of the pictogram, with their rising ends bent over and tied in position, again suggesting a raft of reed bundles, although Hornell (1946a: 49–50) has argued for wood. At the stern a seated or kneeling man paddles and steers; another man, standing in the bows, has a pole with a forked terminal for propulsion, or possibly to take soundings.

In sum, this representational evidence suggests the use of reed-bundle rafts of elongated boat-shaped form, and of an elliptically shaped boat made (if we may make deductions from a later period) either of hide on a basket framework, or of reed bundles assembled as coiled basketry and waterproofed with tar (3.3.2).

The elliptically shaped boats of hide or of reed bundles were probably river craft. The boat-shaped reed-bundle rafts, on the other hand, may have been used on coastal voyages, as for example, along the coast of eastern Arabia where Ubaid pottery of the mid-fourth millennium BC from Sumer has been found at sites with freshwater springs such as Kuwait, Failaka Island, Tarot Island, Qatif, Bahrain, Oman, and many other coastal sites (Oates et al., 1977; Oates, 1980: 114; Ratnagar, 1981: 10–13; Biagi et al., 1984).

Contact with Egypt in this period is also known from the archaeological record (Bass, 1972: 13; Mark, 1997), including the depiction of similarly shaped vessels in rock carvings in the Wadi Hammamat (2.4) and elsewhere in Egypt, which implies contact by sea, probably via Buto in the Nile delta.

Fig. 3.3. Engraving on a cylinder seal from Tell Billa near Nineveh of c.3200 BC (Staatliche Museen zu Berlin).

# 3.3
# The Third Millennium BC

The evidence for maritime activity increases from the mid-third millennium BC. In c.2350 BC Akkadian-speaking Semites from the lands north of Sumer, and led by Sargon, rose to power at Kish and subsequently overthrew the Sumerian rulers. A capital was established at *Akkad* which was probably where Babylon was subsequently founded, on or near the River Euphrates. The Akkadians were subsequently overwhelmed by the Sumerians and places such as Uruk and Lagash re-emerged as 'city-states' in the period now known as the third dynasty of Ur. Nevertheless overland trade to the Anatolian and Iranian highlands and seaborne trade southwards through the Persian Gulf seems to have continued with little interruption throughout the later third millennium BC (Moorey, 1980). Mesopotamian wheat and barley were exchanged for limestone, basalt, timber, gold and silver, and semi-precious stones from Iran (Doe, 1980; Moorey, 1980: 123). This was almost entirely overland trade as the northern coast of the Persian Gulf has few natural harbours, and south of Bushik there are few, if any, freshwater springs (Ratnagar, 1981: 11). The western and southern shores of the Persian Gulf, on the other hand, do have natural harbours with fresh water, and there was trade between this east coast of the Arabian peninsula and Mesopotamia by sea during the late third millennium BC.

## 3.3.1 MELUHHA, MAKKAN, AND DILMUN

*Dilmun/Telmun* is first mentioned in the late fourth millennium BC, in a Late Uruk recension of the Archaic list from Uruk (Mark, 1997: 10), in the context of tax collection. There are an increasing number of references to *Dilmun* during the Jamdat Nasr period c.3100 to 2900 BC. Some 500 years later in c.2450 BC, Ur-Nanshe of Lagash recorded on a stone stele and tablet that the ships of *Telmun/Dilmun* brought him timber from foreign lands (Kramer, 1963: 112). And, after the conquest of Sumer by the Akkadians, Sargon proclaimed on steles and statues erected at Nippur that 'ships from or

destined for *Meluhha, Makkan/Magan,* and *Telmun/Dilmun* were moored in the harbour which was situated outside his capital' (Oppenheim, 1954: 15). Other inscriptions dated to the late third millennium BC/early second millennium BC mention these places (Kramer, 1963: 112), and they record that grain, dates, dried fish, hides, and some manufactured goods such as garments were exported from Mesopotamia to these place by sea in return for wood, stone, metal ingots; exotic foods, plants and animals; and 'luxury goods' such as ivory and precious stones (Moorey, 1980; Oppenheim, 1954: 7–14).

*Meluhha* is said to be the source of raw materials such as timber, copper, and stone, some plants, and some breeds of animals, monkeys, and dogs; semi-precious stones such as lapis lazuli and etched cornelian beads (Potts, 1994; Ratnagar, 1981: 68–70; Oppenheim, 1954: 6–17). Unlike the other two places, no details are given of *Meluhha* and therefore it is assumed to be furthest away and it is generally identified with the Harappan lands of the Indus valley and the Gujarat coast (6.1). Distinctive square steatite seals and etched cornelian beads of this Indus culture have indeed been excavated from Mesopotamian sites of the later third millennium BC (Chakrabarti, 1980: 165; Moorey, 1980: 121; Doe, 1980: 213; Ratnagar, 1981: 68–71). Furthermore, ivory excavated from such sites may also have come from India (Oppenheim, 1954: 12) and a seal found at Lothal in India is thought to be similar to seals of the third millennium BC from Failaka and Bahrain (Rao, 1963).

*Makkam* or *Magan,* the source of copper, diorite stone and wood, especially boatbuilding timber, is thought to be at the mouth of the Persian Gulf, on both sides of the Gulf of Oman: to the north and east in the present-day Makran on the Iran/Pakistan border; to the south and west in the present-day Oman (Doe, 1980: 212; Ratnagar, 1981: 42). The strait of Hormuz, curving through 180°, forms a natural restriction to movement by sea, and thus a site in that vicinity would make a suitable entrepôt. Copper-mining and smelting sites dated to the end of the third millennium BC have been excavated in this region at Wadi Samad and in Iranian Baluchistan (Doe, 1980: 213). As with other places mentioned in these texts, *Makkam* need not be the *original* source of some of the materials mentioned—they may have been trans-shipped.

In the Flood myth *Telmun/Dilmun* is said to be 'the

place where the sun rises': this need not imply that it was in Persia or even in India as Kramer (1963: 113) argued. In south Sumeria the main rivers flow generally east-south-east, towards the rising sun and this is the direction from which overseas goods would indeed come to Sumeria. At one time it was thought that *Telmun/Dilmun* was solely the island of Bahrain (Oppenheim, 1954) but it now seems more likely that the term referred to a greater area, a cultural, and possibly political and federal, union in the north-west of the Persian Gulf, including the islands of Bahrain, Failaka, and Tarut, and a coastal strip on the mainland (Doe, 1980: 212; Ratnagar, 1981: 25; Crawford, 1997). Islands, especially if they have fresh water, make good entrepôt as they are attractive to seamen as well as to merchants and to the political authority (McGrail, 1983: 310–13). In addition to trading in its own products, it is likely that *Telmun/Dilmun* was a trans-shipment site for goods going to, and coming from, *Makkam/Magan* and *Meluhha*.

*Meluhha*, that is north-west India, is not mentioned in the clay tablets of the early second millennium BC (Oppenheim, 1954: 15), and subsequently only *Telmun/Dilmun* is mentioned. From this evidence it would appear that the Indian trade ended *c.*2000 BC, a date which is close to that usually given for the end of the Harappan civilization (Ratnagar, 1981: 207); and trade with *Makkam/Magan* (Oman-Makran) ceased soon afterwards. Artefacts from India have been found in Mesopotamian contexts of the Larsa period (2000–1760 BC) (Ratnagar, 1981: 207) and it may be that goods continued to flow from India and the Gulf of Oman hinterland to and from Mesopotamia, but that first *Makkam* and then *Telmun* took a grip on the trade, and forced seagoing traders to exchange their goods first at an entrepôt in the Gulf of Oman region, and then on Bahrain island. If this hypothesis is correct, by this later stage *Telmun/Dilmun* had become *the* market place for Mesopotamia's overseas trade.

## 3.3.2  WATER TRANSPORT IN THE THIRD MILLENNIUM BC

For their discussion of third millennium BC boats, Casson (1971: 22–9) and Bass (1972: 12–14) have both drawn on research published by Salonen (1939) who extracted information about boats from Sumerian and Akkadian sources, most of it dealing with river, rather than seagoing, craft. By the later third millennium BC wooden boats were in use on the rivers and canals of Mesopotamia. These craft were generally paddled, poled, or towed, but some had a sail which Casson (1971: 23) believes may have been of wool or of reed matting. Some of the craft were for passengers, others for cargo. The cargo capacity is given in *gur* or *kur* which Casson (1971: 26) quoting Salonen, states was a volume measure equivalent to *c.*121 litres, i.e. 0.121 m³. Oppenheim (1954: 8) notes craft of up to 300 *gur* but the more usual craft appear to have been 60 to 120 *gur* in capacity (Casson, 1971: 26; Bass, 1972: 18). Some of these craft were used for fishing (Oppenheim, 1954: 8), but we may get some idea of the capacity tonnage that could be carried by the cargo carriers if we assume that their cargo was entirely of barley (wheat would be 10 to 13 per cent heavier). Barley in bulk has a stowage factor of 1.36 to 1.50 m³/tonne; if in containers, this factor is 1.45 to 1.67 m³/tonne (McGrail, 1989*b*: 356). Assuming Salonen's conversion factor is correct, the 'standard' size of vessel of sixty *gur* would carry between 4.3 and 5.3 tonnes of barley grain, whilst the exceptional craft of 300 *gur* could carry 21.7–26.7 tonnes. These tonnages would have been subject to the vessels having a safe freeboard when loaded, but as it seems likely that these were river craft, freeboard is unlikely to have been a major constraint.

The largest oared boat mentioned had a crew of eleven (Casson, 1971: 23). Towing crews varied from two to eighteen men. Towed speeds varied depending on the size of the team, 10–20 km (6–12 miles) each day upstream, and 30 to 35 km (18–22 miles) downstream (Bass, 1972: 17). Bass (1972: 14) has stressed the importance of boatmen to the temple economy, for example, at the Lagash temple one-tenth of the temple population were boatmen, and in addition there were cargo handlers.

Clay tablets of *c.*2000 BC list some of the materials used to build water transport, including hide, pitch, and caulking (Bass, 1972: 14). The hide was presumably used to build hide boats, and the caulking was possibly for planked boats, but there may be a translation problem here. The pitch could also have been a plank caulking, but is more likely to have been used to make reed-bundle boats watertight. Reed-bundle *boats* of two distinct shapes are known in this region today: the boat-shaped *zaima* (Fig. 3.4) and *jillabie* and the round-

Fig. 3.4. A twentieth-century *zaima* reed bundle boat of the southern Iraq marshes (W. Thesiger, 1978: plate 45).

Fig. 3.5. Model of a recent *quffa* from the River Tigris (Hornell, 1946a: plate 17B).

shaped *guffa* (Fig. 3.5) (McGrail, 1998: 163–4). They are built of reed bundles linked by coiled basketry with an inserted stiffening of light willows; the linked bundles are then coated externally with bitumen. Bitumen is a mineral tar available in the Iraq / Iran region either as a liquid seepage (*naptha*) from an underground source, at the junction between plain and mountain folds, or as *asphalt*, limestone impregnated with bitumen (Hodges, 1964: 165; Forbes, 1964; Ratnagar, 1981: 3; Strabo, 16. 1. 15). Bitumen is known to have been used to waterproof reeds for housebuilding by 4000 BC (G. Clark and Piggott, 1976: 180). The earliest reference to its use in boats is an inscription dated to *c*.2300 BC in which Sargon of Akkad claims to have been placed in a river as a baby in a basket of rushes (reed bundles

linked by coiled basketry) sealed with bitumen (B. Anderson, 1978: 49): a comparable story is told about Moses (Exodus 2: 3). Bitumen was used on working boats in the time of Hammurabi (1792–1750 BC) and subsequently (Herodotus, 1. 179, 6. 119; Strabo, 16. 1. 15; Pliny *NH* 16. 56, 16. 158; Forbes, 1964: 91–2; Hornell, 1946a: 57–8).

In the absence of excavated remains, the nearest we can get to an understanding of what some of these vessels of the late third millennium BC looked like is from an examination of models and of representations on seals. The models are of clay, bitumen, and silver, some from graves and some as temple offerings (Bass, 1972: 14, 26, 28; Oppenheim, 1954: 8; Barnett, 1958: 221). All of them are similar in shape to the fourth-millennium BC depictions of boat-shaped reed rafts described above: that is, with a flattish bottom and high rising ends (Fig. 3.2): none has any 'conventional' sign of bindings seen on depictions of bundle rafts, and therefore they may represent boats. Some of the clay models from Ur tombs dated to *c*.2250 BC appear to have a framework of withies, paddles and poles for propulsion, and a cargo of pots (Barnett, 1958: 221). These may represent reed-bundle boats waterproofed with bitumen. The silver model from Ur (Fig. 3.6), of about the same date, has twelve paddles and a pole for propulsion (Barnett, 1958: 221; Bass, 1972: 28): there appears to be no internal

Fig. 3.6.  Silver model of a boat from Ur of *c*.2250 BC (British Museum).

framework other than seven transverse members at sheer level, presumably benches for paddlers. There is some possibility that this model represents a planked boat (although as with the clay models, no planks are delineated) but it seems more likely to be a model of a bundle boat, somewhat similar to the twentieth-century *zaima* (Fig. 3.4) but bigger and with rising ends, and with thwarts rather than transverse sticks.

The rather fanciful boat on an Akkadian seal (2350–2000 BC) published by Bass (1972: 28, fig. 9) has the flat bottom and rising (here, vertical) ends generally associated with early Mesopotamia. There is no sign of planking or bundle bindings and so this may be a representation of a bundle *boat*. On the other hand, the craft seen on a seal of *c*.2300 BC (Casson, 1971: fig. 21) although of a similar shape does have the vertical lines across the hull generally understood as reed-bundle bindings and therefore probably represents a bundle *raft*.

Three circular steatite stamp seals, dated to the end of the third millennium BC (*c*.2000 BC—de Graeve, 1981: 29), from Danish excavations on the upper Persian Gulf islands of Bahrain and Failaka, have representations of vessels on them (Figs. 3.7, 8, 9). All three have near ver-

tical ends which seems to be a characteristic of Mesopotamian and Persian Gulf craft of this era, possibly arising from the necessity to take vessels through the reed beds of the delta region. One (Fig. 3.7) has vertical lines across the hull, which suggest this may be a bundle raft or a log raft lashed together, with an animal figurehead, possibly a gazelle or goat, at one end. Johnstone (1988: 174–5, fig. 13.6) has drawn comparisons with the *huwayriyah* (Fig. 3.10) (also *warjiwa*—de Graeve, 1981: 159) used today by Kuwait fishermen: the *sha-shah* used on the Batinah coast of Oman is similar (R. Bowen, 1952: 193–5). In constructional terms, these two twentieth-century craft are boat-shaped, log rafts, rather than bundle rafts, although the 'logs' which are lashed together are date palm boughs. Johnstone's suggestion that the vessel depicted on this first seal is a boat-shaped log raft, may be correct.

The vessel on the second seal (Fig. 3.8) also has a gazelle-like figurehead at one end and its outline is similar to that on the first seal except that its bottom is flat rather than slightly rounded in profile. There is a mast stepped amidships with what may be a furled sail. As Johnstone (1980: 176) suggests, this is probably a representation of a planked boat. The third seal (Fig. 3.9)

Fig. 3.7, 8, 9.  Seals excavated from Bahrain and dated to *c*. 2000 BC (photos: Paul Johnstone).

Fig. 3.10. A twentieth-century boat-shaped lograft made of date-palm boughs in Bahrain (photo: Paul Johnstone).

also appears to show a planked boat, of similar form and with a midships mast. There are birds depicted on each end rather than a gazelle-like figurehead. At the stern sits a man, the steersman(?), holding lines from the masthead as well as a 'baton of authority'. There may be rigging lines at the foot of the mast and possibly a yard with furled sail, at the head.

It seems reasonable to suggest then that, on this evidence, three types of vessels were involved in the late third-millennium BC Persian Gulf trade: boat-shaped log rafts, and bundle boats, for coastal and inshore work, possibly propelled by pole and paddle; and double-ended, planked craft with a single square sail on a midships mast, for overseas voyages.

# 3.4

# Water Transport in the Second and First Millennia BC

Marie-Christine de Graeve (1981) has published many illustrations of Mesopotamian water transport dated between c.2000 BC, the Old Babylonian period, and the sixth century BC, the Neo-Babylonian period. This de Graeve catalogue provides a sound basis for a discussion of the types of water craft in use, their functions, and their methods of propulsion and steering. Unless otherwise stated, examples given in the following discussion refer to the numbered illustrations in de Graeve (1981).

## 3.4.1 FLOATS

Floats may be used to float downstream or as a source of additional buoyancy for a swimmer. Swimmers without floats are shown on two mid-ninth-century BC reliefs: (35) a fugitive fleeing from the Assyrians; and (37) Assyrian soldiers crossing a river. Elsewhere, swimmers use either hide floats or pot floats (40) (Fig. 3.11). In the ninth-century illustrations (35, 36, 37) relatively small hide floats are used to support the upper part of the swimmer; in the seventh century, larger ones are in use with the man either sitting astride them (53, 55) or lying prone (53, 54). Some of the swimmers (35) are shown with one leg of the float in their mouths which may be a method of combating slight air leakage (de Graeve, 1981: 81).

The larger hide floats are used by men fishing (55); towing a bundle raft (51) and guiding a float raft from astern (54) (Fig. 3.12). Men wearing helmets and carrying shields and other weapons can be supported by such floats (59).

The procedures used today in China and India

(McGrail, 1998: 189) to make a hide float are very similar to the techniques illustrated in some of the ninth- to seventh-century BC Mesopotamian reliefs (37, 59): after the skin—goat, sheep, or bullock in Mesopotamia—had been separated from the body, the hair or wool was scraped off, the hide dressed and then all openings except one tied. For the smaller hide floats of ninth-century BC Mesopotamia, inflation was through one of the forelegs (37); in the seventh-century BC, inflation of the larger floats was through the neck (59). In these two illustrations men can be seen directly inflating the floats; however, Worcester (1966: 121) has noted that recently in China larger floats were inflated from smaller ones, and it seems possible that this less-exhausting method may well have been used in earlier times.

On one of the bronze bands from the Balawat gates of Shalmoneser II (858–824 BC), now in the Louvre, Chaldeans are depicted fleeing from the city of Baqanu (40). Two of these are naked swimmers supported by floats (Fig. 3.11) which de Graeve (1981: 43) considers to be hide, but which, from their distinctive shape, may well be large pots. Pot floats are known in recent times from India where the mouths of unglazed pots are closed with a leaf or are stopped with clay (6.6.2).

## 3.4.2 BUOYED RAFTS AND LOG RAFTS

Hide floats linked together by a framework of light poles to form a raft have been used widely from China

Fig. 3.11. A possible bundle boat on the left, and swimmers using pot floats as an aid to flotation. On the mid-ninth century BC Balawat gates (Louvre, Paris).

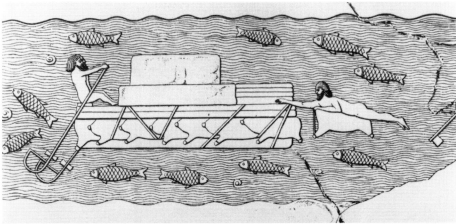

Fig. 3.12. A float raft under oars being guided by a man using a hide float. From the palace of Sennacherib c. 700 BC (after Casson, 1971: fig. 1).

westwards to the Levant, and in Abyssinia, Morocco, Albania, and South America (McGrail, 1998: 187–8). They were also known in Mesopotamia in the early twentieth century (Hornell, 1946a: 106) on the Tigris bringing goods downstream from the Kurdistan mountains to Mosul and Baghdad (Fig. 3.13), and they were used by Layard to transport monolithic statues of a bull and of a lion from Nineveh downstream to Baghdad (Hornell, 1946a: 78): they are known as *kelek* (Akkadian: *kalakku*; Sumerian: *ka-lá*–Barnett, 1958: 220; de Graeve, 1981: 82).

Float rafts are depicted on two reliefs (49 and 54) from the reign of Sennacherib (705–681 BC), and may be on a third one (50). In one scene (49) the float raft is carrying passengers and a fisherman, whereas in a second one (Fig. 3.12) the raft carries two large stone blocks (54). In both cases the raft is propelled by oarsmen pulling an oar from a sitting position at the forward end of the raft. In (54) the raft is evidently being guided from the stern by a swimmer on a hide float. The raft depicted in (50) is seen in plan view and consists of four logs bound together. A large inflated hide float is carried on board which may indicate that under the raft there are also hide floats—on the other hand this hide may hold fresh water and the raft may be a simple log raft. The use of log rafts is not otherwise documented until travellers' reports of the mid-nineteenth century

(R. Bowen, 1952: 192–3). These are usually simple ones of two or three logs lashed together, although Paris (1843: 8) saw a more complex one under sail.

In the fourth century BC Xenophon (*Anab.*, 1. 5. 10; 2. 4. 28; 3. 5. 9–11) saw local people crossing the Tigris on 'leather rafts' and he himself used one to cross the Euphrates near the town of Chaarmande. Julian linked float rafts together to form a pontoon bridge (Casson, 1971: 5). Further afield, but still in south-west Asia, in the first century AD, Pliny (*NH* 6. 35) described their use in the Gulf of Aden, and by pirates off the Hadramaut coast (Pliny, 6. 176), and in the *Periplus of the Erythraean Sea*, ch. 27, we read that frankincense was brought to *Kanê* (probably near the cape of Husn at Ghurab near Bir Ali some 240 nautical miles east of Aden) by rafts made of 'leathern bags' (Casson, 1989: 67, 161). Whether the rafts which Strabo (16. 3. 3) reported were used by Gerrhaeuns from the west coast of the Persian Gulf to cross to the River Euphrates, were float rafts or log rafts is unclear.

### 3.4.3 BUNDLE RAFTS

There are several representations of boat-shaped bundle rafts (probably of reed bundles) in the de Graeve corpus in which the binding lines across the hull are

Fig. 3.13. A large twentieth-century float raft (*kelek*) and two round bundle boats (*quffa*) at Baghdad (Hornell, 1946a: plate 4B).

Fig. 3.14. Bundle rafts being used by armed men on an Assyrian relief of the early seventh century BC (Louvre, Paris).

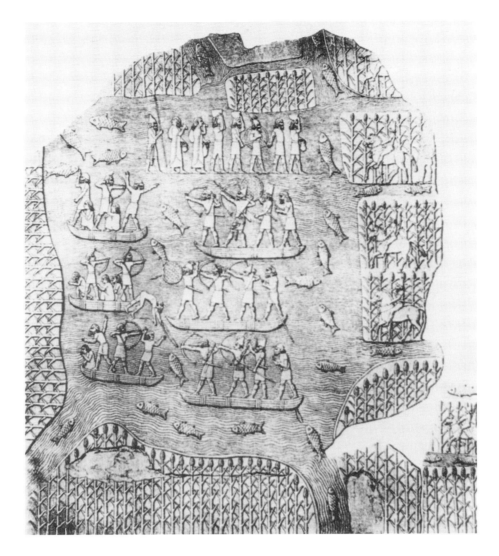

particularly clear: on a Middle Assyrian seal (32); and on depictions (Fig. 3.14) of early seventh-century Assyrian attacks on the marsh dwellers of southern Meso-potamia (51, 52, 60, 62, 63, 64, and 66). The seal depic-tion has high upturned ends surmounted by horned animals. In the marsh battle and deportation scenes the Assyrian and the marsh dwellers' rafts are differentiat-ed, the marsh dwellers' rafts being smaller and with ends not so strongly upturned, and in one scene (60) some of their rafts are either simple flat ones or with only one upturned end. The method of propulsion is not always shown, especially on the marsh dwellers' rafts, but others are poled from near the stern (52) or from amidships (62) or from near the bow (63); propelled by oar pulled from a sitting position near the bow (60 and 66); or towed from the land (62).

### 3.4.4 BUNDLE BOATS

Nowadays two forms of bundle boats are used in the Mesopotamian region: round ones (Figs. 3.5, 3.13) known as *quffa* (Akkadian *quppu* = basket); and boat-shaped ones known variously as *zaima* (Fig. 3.4) or *jilla-bie* (McGrail, 1998: 163–4). Both forms are built of bundles of reeds lashed into the required shape using the coiled basketry technique. The hollowed form, round or elongated, is then strengthened with a light wooden framework, and the hull is waterproofed with bitumen. Outwardly, therefore, the reed bindings are not visible, and the hull externally has a smooth finish, unlike a bundle raft. In the mid-nineteenth century, Layard (1853: 551–2) described the 'black boats' of southern Mesopotamia: although the larger ones (*tara-da*) were of teak, the smaller ones were made of bundles of rushes and bitumen, and were poled from the stern using long bamboos—these may have been bundle boats.

Round bundle boats may be differentiated from round hide boats (3.4.5) in the de Graeve corpus as the former do not have the patchwork appearance of the several joined hides which form the outer skin of the latter. It is more difficult to differentiate the elongated form from any planked-boat depictions as there seems to be no tradition of representing the run of planking even in those vessels which are, from other features, clearly planked boats and indeed ships. Nevertheless an attempt will be made.

### 3.4.4.1 ROUND BUNDLE BOATS (QUFFA)

Hornell (1946a: 101–8) and, following him, Casson (1971: 6) and other authors such as de Graeve (1981) did not distinguish between the two types of round boats depicted in the Mesopotamian illustrations of the first millennium BC: the bundle boat with a tarred outer skin (depicted in outline only); and the hide boat with an outer skin of sewn hides (depicted with a patchwork of lines). The name *quffa*, which these authors apply to both types, is more appropriately applied to the one built with a coiled basketry technique—the tarred bundle boat, as that is the craft to which the name *quffa* is applied in Iraq today (Hornell, 1938). These have been recognized since the mid-eighteenth century as 'baskets made of reeds, perfectly round . . . daubed on the outside and the bottom with bitumen' (Hamilton, 1727: 88). Herodotus may have nodded (3.4.5), like Homer, in confusing the *quffa* (a bundle boat) with the *kelek* (a buoyed raft) (Hornell, 1946a: 106), but Hornell himself nodded by applying the name *quffa* to early Mesopotamian hide boats.

Round bundle boats (*quffa*) are depicted on sculptures from the reign of Ashurnasirpal II (883–859 BC)—figure 36 in the de Graeve corpus. Assyrian soldiers are seen crossing a river, some swimming, some in bundle boats one of which has a chariot on board, the axle resting on the rim of the boat with the wheels outboard; the other boat carries a water jar or a pot float, and some other objects. These boats are propelled by a seated oarsman at each end, one pushing, the other pulling an oar pivoted through a grommet attached to the boat's rim. Two men in a *quffa* depicted on the Bal-

awat gates of Shalmaneser III (858–824 BC) are standing at each end and paddling (or possibly poling). This bundle boat (60) is shown with a curved line parallel to the outer edge of the hull—see also the boat (40) in Fig. 3.11.

*Quffa* are also shown as an element of pontoon bridges depicted on these Balawat gates (43 to 46), although de Graeve (1981: 145) thinks they may be 'barges'. These bridges are sufficiently substantial to take not only marching men but also chariots drawn by paired horses. It seems most unlikely that these were float rafts linked together, as the hulls are of round bundle boat form rather than of hide float shape.

The modern *quffa* (Fig. 3.5) was first noted on the River Euphrates in the late seventeenth century (Hornell, 1946a: 104). In the early twentieth century *quffa* of some considerable size were built, up to 16 ft (4.9 m) in diameter, although the average was *c*.13 ft (4 m) with a depth of *c*.7 ft (2.1 m). The largest size could carry up to 5 tonnes of grain; the smaller, 2 tonnes or about thirty sheep (Hornell, 1946a: 103). De Graeve (1981: 85) quotes *quffa* of up to 5.5 m in diameter which can carry sixteen tonnes.

### 3.4.4.2 ELONGATED BUNDLE BOATS

These are built by the same techniques as the *quffa* but are boat-shaped in form (McGrail, 1998: 163–4). As described above, it is difficult to distinguish them in the de Graeve corpus from planked boats or even logboats. Thus any of the boat-shaped vessels depicted without binding lines may be bundle boats, e.g. (1) to (5) which are on terracotta plaques of the period 2000 to 1600 BC. These craft are generally shown in hunting scenes: they are propelled either by paddle wielded by a man squatting in the stern, or by pole, one with a forked terminal (5). Two fragmentary clay boat models (18, 19) from the same period have representations of framing inside and thus may be bundle boats which are nowadays reinforced by a light framework (Fig. 3.4).

Large double-ended boats depicted on river-crossing scenes at Nimrod in the reign of Ashurnasirpal II (883–859 BC) may also be bundle boats (37, 38). In one of these boats (37) there are two chariots, one evidently on some decking at about sheer level, the other in the process of being loaded. This boat is propelled by a man standing near the bows with an oar; another man in the stern appears to have a steering oar. The other boat carries Ashurnasirpal and his chariot which is amidships, balanced across the sheer with its wheels outboard. Here a man at the stern on a deck is clearly using a steering-oar; two men standing in the bows use paddles or poles whilst a man near the stern is pulling an oar, also from a standing position. Furthermore, the boat is being towed by two men using a rope from the bow. Near the stern a fourth man holds the reins of four horses swimming astern. Other elongated bundle boats are seen on (41) and (42) from the bronze bands on the Balawat wooden gates of Shalmaneser III (858–824 BC). The boats on (41) have a cargo of bales and are poled from forward. The boat on (42) seems to be a ferry propelled by large oars pivoted against large upstanding crutches near each end.

Strabo (16. 1. 15) refers to boats woven with reeds and plastered with bitumen in the first century AD: it seems likely that these were elongated bundle boats rather than *quffa*. In the early nineteenth century, Layard (1853: 552) and Chesney (1868: 78) noted in the marshes of southern Iraq and on the Euphrates at Hir boat-shaped craft which had a hull of rushes or reeds and straw consolidated by an internal wooden framework and waterproofed with hot bitumen producing a smooth external surface which was 'hard, impervious to water and well-suited for river navigation' (Hornell, 1946a: 57–8). If these 'black boats' were made of coiled basketry and not woven basketry then structurally they were bundle boats rather than basket boats (8.3.3).

Today, elongated bundle boats waterproofed with bitumen are small in size and only found in the southern part of Iraq. They have been described by Thesiger, the *zaima* (Fig. 3.4) and by Heyerdahl, the *jillabie* (1978: 35). See also Layard (1853: 551–2).

### 3.4.5 HIDE BOATS

Hide boats have been used in many parts of the world (McGrail, 1998: 173) and are still used in Arabia. Apart from some simple boats which are essentially a 'leather bag', they are skeleton built with a waterproofing envelope of hides moulded around a pre-erected framework: they can have a rounded form or be boat-shaped.

Clay models from Eridu (Fig. 3.2) dated to the early

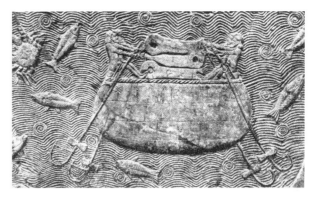

Fig. 3.15. A possible hide boat depicted in Sennacherib's palace of *c.*700 BC (British Museum).

fifth millennium BC may represent hide boats. Subsequent evidence comes from inscriptions from Ur of *c.*2000 BC which include hide and split willow in the boatbuilding materials they list (Bass, 1972: 14; Casson, 1971: 6). The illustrations in the de Graeve corpus that can be identified as hide boats (Fig. 3.15) are those of rounded form and with 'patchwork' marks on their hulls (50, 55, 110)—see also Casson (1971: fig. 4).

Two bas reliefs of Sennacherib (705–681 BC) show hide boats made of several hides and with a reinforced rim (Hornell, 1946a: plate 17A), as is common worldwide (McGrail, 1998: 179). One boat is smaller and more rounded in profile than the others, having a diameter/depth ratio of 1.64 compared with a range of 2.10 to 2.33 for the other four. This smaller boat (the one on the left of 50) is propelled by only two oarsmen who are sitting near one end pulling one oar each. The other boats are propelled by two men sitting at each end, each with an oar pivoted against a thole(?) on the rim. As on the *quffa* depicted in (36) the two groups of oarsmen are shown as though they are pulling against one another (Fig. 3.15), but this, as Hornell (1946a: 105) suggested, must be due to an artistic desire for symmetry rather than an accurate rendering: the more practicable arrangement is that those at the forward end would have pulled and those astern pushed. Although sit/pushing an oar is not as efficient as sit/pulling or stand/pushing, it seems more likely that the two at the after end would be facing forward rather than all four would face astern. An alternative suggested by Hornell (1946a: 105) is that all four should have been shown facing forward but, as it seems incontrovertible that the oarsmen were indeed sitting, this would be a most inefficient arrangement.

The larger hide boats are shown carrying stone blocks or large items of an unusual shape—elongated with a round perforation through one end; de Graeve (1981: 50) has suggested that these may have been 'door panels'.

Herodotus (1. 194) who visited Babylon in the fifth century BC described rounded boats of hides stretched over a framework of withies: these boats surprised Herodotus more than any other sight in that country, apart from Babylon itself. He states that they were built in Armenia to the north of Assyria whence they travelled down the Euphrates with cargoes of wine in casks on a dunnage of straw. The propulsion method described by Herodotus seems to be that the crew *stand*, one at each end, the man at the forward end pulling, and presumably facing astern, the other man pushing his oar, and presumably facing forward. This gives support to the interpretation, advanced above, of the propulsion of the hide boats depicted on the seventh-century reliefs, although there the oarsmen are sitting.

Herodotus goes on to state that, as it is impossible to return upstream because of the current (a statement which is true also today), these boats are dismantled in Babylon, the framework and dunnage disposed of, and the hides returned overland to Armenia on the backs of donkeys which have been brought downstream on board the boat. Several scholars consider that Herodotus confused the hide boat with the float raft (Hornell, 1946a: 106; Casson, 1971: 6; de Graeve, 1981: 87) since float rafts were dismantled in this manner in early twentieth-century Baghdad (Hornell, 1946a: 28): the practice is also known in China (10.2.4). However, there is no reason to think that hide boats could not be similarly used, indeed, they were so used on the River Kaveri in southern India in 1825 (Deloche, 1994: 139). Hornell's other argument (1946a: 29, 107) that float rafts are more likely to be used than hide boats in the upper reaches of the Euphrates has more in its favour. A hide holed below the waterline in a hide boat is a serious matter whereas one burst hide float in a float raft with several floats is of minor concern. Furthermore, the average float raft can carry much more than the average hide boat, possibly even as much as the 5,000 talents (*c*.125 tonnes) mentioned by Herodotus (1. 194). However, hide boats *are* used on the headwaters of great rivers as, for example, in Tibet on the upper Mekong, Indus, and Huang Ho (Hornell, 1946a: 25, 97, 99), and in India on the Kaveri and Krishna (6.6.4).

Away from Mesopotamia, hide boats were used by Arabians to cross the Red Sea in the vicinity of the strait at Bab el Mandeb in the first century BC (Strabo, 16. 4. 19). There is, however, no mention in the *Periplus* of their use in south-west Asian coastal waters. Julian used 500 hide boats to ferry his army across the Euphrates in AD 363 (Casson, 1971: 6). They were still in use in Mesopotamia in the early nineteenth century (Hornell, 1946a: 104). By the mid-nineteenth century they were said to be rare (Chesney, 1850: 640). In their descriptions of the recent history of the hide boat, both Hornell (1946a: 104) and de Graeve (1981: 86–7) confuse the two types of basketry, woven and coiled, and thus confuse two types of boat, the hide boat with a framework and the bundle boat made of waterproofed coiled basketry. A similar confusion may be found in the terminology used by some of the nineteenth-century travellers. However, there is an observation by Layard which has suggested to some that there may be a boat type intermediate between hide boats and bundle boats: '*quffa* are sometimes covered with skins over which bitumen is smeared' (1849: 380–1). In this case Layard was either conflating separate accounts of the building of two distinct boat types or he was describing a temporary repair to a hide boat by sealing the hides with bitumen: whichever it was, there was probably no intermediate boat type.

### 3.4.6 LOGBOATS

A shortage of suitable trees and an abundant supply of reeds may mean that the logboat—widespread elsewhere—did not become prominent in this region (Johnstone, 1980: 182). Evidence for their early use is sparse. De Graeve (1981: 221) thinks that a fragment of a clay model (15) may be part of a logboat with a bulkhead, but this is far from certain: however, Amorianus (24. 4. 8) did note that *monoxylon* were used on the Euphrates in the fourth century AD: and R. Bowen (1952: 198–201) has described how, in the recent past, teak logboats were exported from the Malabar coast of India to Arabia where they were known as *huri*. They were used as ships' boats and, in an expanded and side-extended form, by coastal fishermen.

## 3.4.7 PLANKED VESSELS

As there appears to be no tradition in early Mesopotamian art of depicting the planking of planked boats and ships, it is possible that some of the boats identified above as elongated bundle boats may in fact be planked boats. Strabo (16. 1. 11) and Arrian (*Anabasis* 7. 19. 4) both stressed that, in their time, Mesopotamia had little timber suitable for boat- and shipbuilding. However, there was some timber in the region: the mulberry tree in northern Mesopotamia and the palm tree elsewhere, and Alexander built boats from cypress trees when in Babylonia (Strabo, 16. 1. 11). Furthermore, as Hourani (1963: 91) has noted, a boat can be built from the palm tree alone, including plank fastenings, sail and rigging. Moreover, texts of *c.*2370 BC from the temple at Ban record that ten different kinds of tree were available locally, two of which were specifically recommended for boatbuilding (de Graeve, 1981: 94). On the other hand, it is quite clear that timber was imported to Mesopotamia from western India from early times: Ur-Nanshe, founder of the Lagash dynasty in *c.*2450 BC, recorded that ships of *Dilmun/Telmun* brought wood as tribute; statute B of Gudea mentions wood imports from *Dilmun*, *Magan*, and *Meluhha* (de Graeve, 1981: 94); and the Ur tablets record the import of two different types of wood from *Meluhha*, i.e. western India (Kramer, 1963: 112). Theophrastus, in *c.*300 BC, noted that the wood used to build ships in Bahrain lasted for more than 200 years if kept under water—so this was almost certainly teak (Johnstone, 1980: 182; Hourani, 1963: 90). In the first century AD teak logs and baulks, and logs of sissoo and ebony were imported from the west coast of India to the Persian Gulf (*Periplus*, ch. 36). In the tenth century AD, al Masudi noted that Indian Ocean ships were built of teak.

Thus Mesopotamia made up for natural deficiencies in timber by importing it, not only by sea from northwest India but also overland from Lebanon, especially in the time of Sennacherib (705–681 BC) when cedar was the prime timber (Meiggs, 1982: 53–63; de Graeve, 1981: 94–5); and some of this timber was for shipbuilding.

The fact that this teak and cedar was imported must, however, have made vessels built from it relatively expensive and it thus seems probable that only the most important craft (or most imposing parts of vessels) were built of planks, perhaps only royal boats and ships, and possibly the barges which were specially built to transport monolithic statues. Thus, although the boats identified above as elongated bundle boats cannot be recognized with certainty, it seems likely that most of them were so built rather than of planking. This proposition receives further support from references to the use of bitumen in boatbuilding in, for example, the law Code of Hammurabi (de Graeve, 1981: 105–6). It is clear from these and other texts that the heated bitumen was applied in layers by roller, a technique which may be used to pay a planked boat (Thesiger, 1978: 125–6) but is especially appropriate to the waterproofing of a bundle boat.

Other, mostly larger, vessels depicted in the de Graeve corpus are undoubtedly planked craft, because they have rams or other projections, or because they are multi-level vessels, i.e. *biremes*, or because they have large figureheads at one or both ends. Most of these vessels are Phoenician: the accompanying text says so, or they have characteristic features such as *hippos* figureheads or a particular shape of rowing sweep (Fig. 3.16; 4.9.3.2.2.1). Two notable exceptions are the royal river boats of Sargon (48) and of Ashurbanipal (67): these appear to be Mesopotamian craft with specific

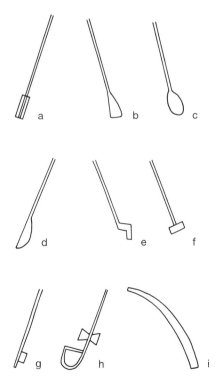

Fig. 3.16. Nine types of early Mesopotamian oar (after de Graeve, 1981).

Phoenician features such as horse figureheads or two levels of oarsmen. They are not considered further here.

### 3.4.8 HEAVY-LIFT BARGES

There are five representations of heavy-lift barges from the time of Sennacherib (54–58). They appear to have been a special design for the transport of huge monolithic statues, capable of being towed on land and by river. As an engineering construction for a specific purpose they were, no doubt, remarkable and comparable with those built by the Egyptians (2.9.3).

# 3.5
# Propulsion and Steering in Early Mesopotamia

### 3.5.1 TOWING

With the predominant, northerly wind blowing downstream, rather than upstream as on the River Nile, sailing up the Tigris and Euphrates was generally not practicable: thus towing was used, as in earlier times (3.3.2), when oar, paddle, or pole were insufficient. A clay model from Tell ed-Der (17) and one from Uruk of the sixth century BC (104) have a step for a towing mast towards one end; and in a scene from a late eighth-century BC sculpture from Sargon II's palace at Khorsabad, four men are shown towing a boat from a short mast close to the bow (47): other towing scenes are less specific about the point of attachment of the tow. De Graeve (1981: 152) quotes Salonen (1939: 118) for the information that towing ropes were made of reed bast and bulrush and were sometimes coated with bitumen. Towing upstream is frequently mentioned in first-millennium BC inscriptions and from these we learn that (as late as Roman times) there was a special force of men who were towers; sometimes cattle were used (de Graeve, 1981: 154). Other sculptures depicting men hauling lines attached to boats (41, 61, 64) seem to show boats being hauled ashore, rather than towed. In

an early seventh-century BC sculpture from Kuyunjik (51), on the other hand, there is clear illustration of a swimmer with a hide float towing a bundle raft loaded with prisoners and guards.

### 3.5.2 POLING

Propulsion by pole, generally from the stern, is shown on many scenes of the marshes of southern Mesopotamia (e.g. 62, 64, 65), but also from near amidships (62) and from nearer the bow (41, 63). The silver boat model from Ur (3.3.2) of the mid-third millennium BC, has a punting pole with a forked end; such a terminal can also be seen with the boat shown on a fragment of terracotta from Nippur (5).

### 3.5.3 PADDLING

On terracotta fragments (12, 34) men can be seen squatting in the stern to use a paddle—the shape of blade cannot be seen. Two Chaldeans stand to paddle (or possibly pole?) a hide boat (Fig. 3.11) in one of the reliefs from the Balawat Gates (40), whilst on the sculpture showing Ashurnasirpal II crossing a river in a large bundle boat (38) two men in the bows appear to be temporarily using their short oars as paddles.

### 3.5.4 OARED PROPULSION

The two principal modes of oared propulsion are well depicted in the de Graeve corpus: sit/pull from near the stern (38), but mostly from the bow (36, 49, 50 (Fig. 3.15), 54, 55/110, and 60); stand/push from the stern (49 and 53). The craft depicted in (42) was probably propelled by stand/push at the stern and at the bow. The action stand/pull is also shown using oars which another oarsman is simultaneously using in the stand/push mode (53). The mode sit/push may also be illustrated (36, 50 (Fig. 3.15), and 55/110).

The detail of oar pivots is seldom clear, but in one case (36) there appears to be a rope grommet fastened to the rim of a rounded bundle boat. A similar grommet is shown in Fig. 3.15 and on the right-hand boat in (55/110). The oars on the latter seem to be constrained in their movement by, if not actually pivoted against, pairs of wooden(?) projections from the rim of this hide boat.

Nine or more different types of oar blade are illustrated (Fig. 3.16). A sweep-type blade (b), i.e. a gradual swelling of the loom, is found on (49) and (60); an elliptical blade (c) on (42) and (49); a broad blade lashed to the loom (f ) and (g) on (36), (38), and (54); whilst the unusual type (h), found only on scenes of the upper Tigris around Nineveh, is on (50), (54) and (55). The double wedge-shaped board on type (h) is probably the main blade; the device at the extreme end is more difficult to explain: de Graeve (1981, 160) considers that a piece of transparent animal skin was fastened to it and thus it could also be used for propulsion, but her explanation is unconvincing: Hornell (1946a: 106) believes that the device must have had 'some quality fitting it to local conditions'. A more probable solution is that this is a combined oar and boat hook or, with less likelihood, a combined oar and pole: comparable, multipurpose artefacts are known in north-west Europe (McGrail, 1998: 204–5).

## 3.5.5 SAIL

Models (17), (103), and (104) have sockets for mast steps near one end, but these are almost certainly for towing masts, and the crutches seen on (42) seem more likely to be where oars were pivoted than for the stowage of masts and spars.

The principal evidence for sail in the de Graeve corpus is on Phoenician vessels, but two of the c.2000 BC seals (Figs. 3.8, 3.9) from Falaika (20) and (21) depict ships with masts. This suggests that, although seagoing vessels in the Persian Gulf had sails, they were only infrequently used by river and canal boats. On the other hand, as has been pointed out by de Graeve (1981: 177), the Sumerians had a word for 'sailing boat' and the Akkadian phrase for going downstream also means sailing boat, so there must have been some sailing on inland waters.

Casson (1971: 23) states that sail was used in this region from the second half of the third millennium BC on vessels which were of no great size. The evidence for this statement is not presented, but Casson appears to be quoting Salonen (1939). In the first century AD Strabo (16. 1. 9) refers to sails made from the reeds of southern Mesopotamia. On the other hand, the Sumerian word for 'sail' is related to the word for 'linen' (de Graeve, 1981: 178).

## 3.5.6 STEERING

Steering is frequently undertaken at the same time as propulsion as, for example, on (49) where a man on a raised deck at the stern of an elongated bundle boat propels the boat in a stand/push mode but also can steer by varying his blade angle and stroke. Paddlers facing forward also can steer. There are, however, five depictions of what may be steering oars (32) (34) (37) (38), and (53) pivoted on or near the stern. In Fig. 3.12, a swimmer with a hide float appears to be guiding a float raft from astern, alternatively he is allowing himself to be towed.

# 3.6

# Sewn-Plank Boats of the First and Second Millennia AD

There is no evidence of how the planking was fastened in the ships depicted on the Falaika seals (Figs. 3.8, 3.9) or on other planked vessels in the de Graeve corpus; nor do early authors who dealt with this region (Herodotus, Strabo, and Pliny) mention fastenings. The earliest evidence, to date, for a specific type of plank boat comes from the *Periplus of the Erythraean Sea*. In ch. 36 we learn that sewn-plank boats were built in the vicinity of *Omana* (in *Persis*, on the Makran coast to the east of the Persian Gulf ) and exported to Arabia (west of the Persian Gulf ). As Omana imported teak, sissoo, and ebony wood from *Barygaza* in north-west India it is possible that the planking of these sewn boats was fashioned from one of these timbers. These boats are said to be of the kind called *madarate*: this word has frequently been translated as 'fastened with palm fibre' (e.g. Hornell, 1946a: 234; Huntingford, 1980: 162) but Casson (1989: 181) has recently suggested that it cannot have such a meaning but may mean that these sewn boats were 'armoured' in some way. The only explanation of this term that comes to mind is that the plank seams were protected by thick pads or pads of coir fibre and palm leaf-stalk strips bound over the seam caulking inboard, as in the *mtepe* of east Africa (Hornell, 1946*a*: 235), the *madel paruwa* sewn boats of Sri Lanka (Wright, 1990: fig. 9.9), and the Arab *sambuq* of Dhofar (Facey and Martin, 1979: 154–5). In other regions of the world, e.g. north-west Europe (5.4) and Egypt (2.7.1) sewn-plank fastenings preceded fastenings of wood and of metal. By analogy, therefore, we might expect sewn fastenings to have been used in Arabia much earlier than the first century AD.

In the sixth century AD Procopius (*Bell. Pers.* 1. 19. 23) mentions sewn boats in the Persian Gulf, which were not covered in tar, i.e. were not bundle boats. The next evidence does not appear until the tenth century when Abu Zayd mentioned sewn boats built at Siraf on the River Tigris, the bottoms of which were payed with oil mixed with other materials (possibly dammar resin and lime which are used today) so that the fastening holes would be filled—this mixture also protects a vessel's bottom from the teredo shipworm (Hornell, 1946*a*: 234). Al Idrisi of the twelfth century noted how oil was produced from whales caught in the Indian Ocean and used to fill the sewing holes along the planking seams of Arab boats (Hourani, 1963: 97): this was a paying of the seams, not a caulking within the seams. A contemporary of Idrisi, Ibn-Jubayr, stated that the bottom of these ships was payed with fish oil, shark oil being the best (Hourani, 1963: 98). This paying was also noted by Marco Polo in the late thirteenth century, at Ormuz on ships that were sewn with coir cord (Hornell, 1946*a*: 234).

Ibn-Jubayr also described something of the sewing techniques: bundles of rushes and grass bound by threads of palm fibre were evidently placed along the seams and the planking fastened together by coir cord made from the coconut husk (Hourani, 1963: 92). Ibn-Jubayr further mentioned the use of *dusur* ('wood of the date palm'). Hourani (1963: 97–8) suggests that this was used as caulking, but the term is elsewhere (e.g. *Koran* 54. 13) used to refer to 'wooden pegs'. Treenails or wooden pegs seem much more likely, as no early author mentions caulking, and the fourteenth-century John of Montecorvino specifically says there was no caulking in the Arabian Sea ships he saw. Furthermore, Marco Polo says that treenails (*artenons*) were used (Moreland, 1939: 68); and treenails within the thickness of the planking were used in recent Arab sewn boats

(R. Bowen, 1956*a*: 284–5, fig. 3D; Facey and Martin, 1979: 154–5).

Friar Odoric of the fourteenth century suggested that the sewing material was hemp, whilst John of Montecorvino of the same century noted that the sewing was renewed annually (Hornell, 1946*a*: 235; Hourani, 1963: 94). In recent times Arab seamen have renewed the sewing during the summer months, between the two monsoon seasons (Tibbetts, 1971: 50). Hornell (1946*a*: 235) has traced other records of sewn boats in the Indian Ocean from the fifteenth century right up to recent times—see also R. Bowen (1952).

### 3.6.1 TIMBERS USED

Descriptions by Theophrastus (5.4) writing in *c*.300 BC, and the author of the *Periplus* (ch. 36) of the first century AD, suggest that Indian teak (*tectona grandis*) was used to build boats in the Persian Gulf region. Al-Masudi of the tenth century says plainly that teak was used; whilst Ibn-Jubayr of the twelfth century states that boatbuilding timber was imported from India (Hourani, 1963: 90). By the fifteenth century Arab merchants had their ships built on the Malabar coast near the source of their timber (Moreland, 1939: 70).

Other timber species could be used. In the tenth century Abu Zaid Hasan of Siraf noted that boatbuilders from Oman went to the Maldives and Laccadives islands and there built vessels entirely from the coconut tree: hull, fastenings, mast, rigging, and sail (Hourani, 1963: 91; Facey and Martin, 1979: 107–8).

### 3.6.2 HULL STRUCTURE

Jordanus of the thirteenth century noted that Indian Ocean seagoing sewn ships were not decked over, and, in one version of his book, Marco Polo agreed that this was so, but in another, longer, version he noted that they did have a deck (Johnstone and Muir, 1962: 59). Polo also noted that the cargo was covered with hides (Hourani, 1963: 98; Johnstone and Muir, 1962: 59). Earlier, in the mid-tenth century, Buzurg had mentioned cabins onboard ships. Ibn Mājid, who was Vasco da Gama's navigator from Malindi in East Africa to Calicut on the west coast of India in 1498 (Hourani, 1963: 83) states in his book, *Instructions and Principles of the*

*Science of the Sea*, that cargo must be protected from rain by a cover, implying that at least the main hold was open (Tibbetts, 1971: 51). That these fifteenth-century vessels had some weather decks is clear from Ibn Mājid's remark that he could stand on the *dabūsa* to observe the sea. Today the *dabūsa* is a cabin aft of the mizzen in Arab *daos* (Tibbetts, 1971: 51) which suggests that in the fifteenth-century vessel there was a weather deck aft, under which was a cabin; there may have been a similar deck forward.

From Tibbetts's (1971: 51) translation of Ibn Mājid's navigational poems other details of ship construction emerge. There was a beam (*kalb*) across the bows which projected to form catheads; the *dastur* was a spar fastened to the main mast which projected beyond the stem post like a bowsprit—this would be where a line from the sail was made fast when sailing close-handed.

Hornell (1942*a*: 13) thought that, in his day, Arab vessels were built frame-first, but there is much evidence (for example in Johnstone and Muir, 1962: 60; Facey and Martin, 1979: 154–5) to show that early twentieth-century sewn Arab boats were built plank-first. The likelihood then is that, in common with the rest of the world, early vessels of Arabia were built plank-first and that, like the rest of the world except for Europe and possibly south-east Asia and China, even their largest seagoing vessels continued to be built in this shell sequence until the late fifteenth century, or even later.

Strabo (15. 1. 15) states that vessels sailing between India and Ceylon were without frames and one of the earliest descriptions of the *masula*, the sewn-plank boat of the Coromandel coast of southern India by Bowrey in the seventeenth century (Hill, 1958: 207; Kentley, 1985) states that they had no floor timbers (6. 7. 3). The *beden seyad*, a recent sewn boat of the Muscat and Omani coast also has no floor timbers (R. Bowen, 1952: 202; 1956: 286). These two types were and are surf boats used in testing conditions and so the possibility that at least some of the early Arabian seagoing sewn boats were also without floor timbers (but with cross beams) must be considered.

## 3.6.3 SHAPE AND SIZE

All representations and models of early boats of Arabia show a hull with (near) symmetrical ends, i.e. double-ended, and the seagoing craft of this region seem to

have retained that form until the coming of the Portuguese in the late fifteenth century, when the transom stern was introduced. With no excavated examples to form a basis it is difficult to estimate the size of the early medieval vessels. However, the Portuguese in the early sixteenth century noted Gujarat sewn-plank ships at Melinde, India which were said to be about 100 tonnes (Moreland, 1939: 177) and they estimated the ordinary merchant ships of the Arabian Sea to be up to 250 tonnes—both these figures presumably being 'tons burden', i.e. an estimate of the cargo capacity or deadweight tonnage, as it would be called nowadays. Tibbetts (1971: 49) has noted that the fifteenth-century navigational text *Aja'ib al-Hind* mentions a ship with a 75 ft (23 m) mast, which would not be out of place on a ship of 250 tons burden.

## 3.6.4 THE HARIRI SHIP

In a manuscript of al-Hariri's *Māqāmat* (Bib. Nat. MS arabe 5847, vol. 119v) dated *c*. AD 1237, by a scribe from Wasit in Mesopotamia, is an illustration of an Arab ship (Fig. 3.17). This is a double-ended vessel, as far as one can judge from the profile, with high ends, a near-vertical stern post, and a slightly raked stem post. The planking is fastened by sewing with intermittent paired stitches and appears, as would be expected, to be flush-laid (i.e. not overlapping). Projecting forward of the bow is what appears to be a *dastur* (Tibbetts, 1971: 51) or bowsprit, and what may be a *kalb* on which a grapnel anchor is catted (again as described by Tibbetts (1971: 51). There are *oculi* (eyes) at both ends.

Two internal decks and a weather deck appear to be depicted: at the lowest level two of the crew are bailing out water; at a higher level there are merchants(?) possibly in cabins; whilst on the weather deck—i.e. on top of the cabins, as deduced from Ibn Mājid's navigational poems by Tibbetts (1971: 51)—there are six further crew. The crew's activities, and the propulsion and steering features of this illustration are discussed further below.

## 3.6.5 PROPULSION BY SAIL

In several accounts by thirteenth- and fourteenth-century European travellers it is noted that Arab vessels

Fig. 3.17. Illustration from a
thirteenth-century manu-
script, al-Hariri's *Māqāmat*
(Bibliothèque nationale de
France, MS.Arabe 5487 fo.
119v.).

had one mast and one sail (Moreland, 1939: 67, 68–70; Johnstone and Muir, 1962: 59). However, Tibbetts (1971: 52) notes that the author of the fifteenth-century *Aja'ib al-Hind* was familiar with two-masted ships, and Ibn Mâjid mentions a ship with two sails. The Hariri ship has two masts—a mainmast just aft of amidships and a foremast close to the bow. In that illustration there is no standing rigging, and only the foremast appears to have sails and running rigging: these lines are held by the master(?) who is seated at the stern in an attitude which reminded Johnstone (1980: 176–7) of the 'master' of the ship depicted on one of the Failaka seals of *c.*2000 BC (Fig. 3.9), even to the detail that both hold a

'baton of authority' in their other hand. The lines on the Hariri vessel appear to be attached to one edge and to the upper corner of a sail of indeterminate shape—in fact there may be two sails on very short yards; such features are difficult to explain.

Strabo (16. 1. 9) noted that, in Mesopotamia, reed sails were similar to rush mats or wickerwork: an echo of this is heard thirteen centuries later when John of Montecorvino notes that in the Arabian Sea the sails are either of matting or 'some miserable cloth' (Moreland, 1939: 67).

In the past few centuries Arab craft have been notable for their use of the lateen sail (Hornell, 1942*a*), and Hourani (1963: 103–5) has attempted to demonstrate that the lateen came from the Indian Ocean to the Mediterranean around the time of the Arab expansion, say, ninth century AD. Casson (1971: 244) has shown, on the other hand, that the so-called 'Arab' lateen (*settee*: a quadrilateral sail with a short luff ) was in use in the eastern Mediterranean from the second century AD, and the triangular form from the fourth century (4.14.1). No representational or other evidence for a lateen from the Indian Ocean region is as early as that. In fact what early evidence there is for sail in this region—the two stamp seals of *c.*2000 BC from Failaka (Figs. 3.8, 3.9)—suggests that the square sail on a mast stepped near amidships was the norm. If we include the early evidence from Egypt (2.7.4) and from Indian waters (6.7.5) the case for the early and widespread dominance of the square sail is reinforced.

It is difficult to suggest what sort of a rig the Hariri ship may have had: this representation is not incompatible with lateen sails or square sails. However, there are some indications that the twelfth- to fifteenth-century Arab vessels did have lateen sails. First, Ibn Mājid in his navigational poems describes sails which have either length of luff and leach, or the length of foot and head, in the proportions 3 : 4 or 10 : 13.5 (Tibbetts, 1971: 52, 116): whichever sides of the sail these ratios refer to, this is clearly not a rectangular sail; it is therefore unlikely to be a square sail, rather a four-sided fore-and-aft sail and of these, the *settee*-lateen is most likely. Second, Ibn Mājid's descriptions of the procedure for going about, the difficulties he describes, and the verb he uses (Tibbetts, 1971: 57) seem more appropriate to wearing than tacking, and wearing, where the stern of the vessel is passed through the wind, is more appropriate to, and almost invariably used with, a lateen rig where sail and the very long yard have to be swung around the mast. John of Montecorvino, when describing how Arab ships change tack, states that, 'it is done with a vast deal of trouble; and if it is blowing in any way hard, they cannot tack at all' (Moreland, 1939: 67): this could well apply to wearing a lateen-rigged vessel. Third, Ibn Mājid's claim that, in certain conditions, Arab ships could sail within four points of the relative wind (Tibbetts, 1971: 57) may be an exaggeration, nevertheless performance to windward, even if it were only within six points, would suggest a fore and aft sail rather than a square sail.

The fifteenth-century Arab vessels described by Ibn

Mājid had adjustable stays rather than shrouds—twentieth-century practice is similar; the yard and sail were raised by a halyard (Tibbetts, 1971: 53). Sulaiman al Mahri tells us that the yard was held to the mast by a *shart*—a combined parrel and truss (Tibbetts, 1971: 54) as is the case today.

Sail area was reduced by lowering the yard and sail somewhat or by substituting a smaller sail, as the lateen could not be reefed (Tibbetts, 1971: 57–8). There is a possibility that a makeshift topsail (an 'Indian' sail) was used (Tibbetts, 1971: 53)—this would be another way of varying sail area.

### 3.6.6 STEERING

The Hariri illustration shows that by the early thirteenth century, Arab ships had a median rudder fastened to the stern post by three or more pintles within gudgeons. John of Montecorvino confirms this: 'they have a frail and flimsy rudder, like the top of a table, of a cubit (*c.*0.45 m) in width in the middle of the stern' (Hourani, 1963: 98–9). Whether side rudders were used in the Arabian Sea earlier in the medieval period is uncertain, but the Graeco-Roman vessels used in the Indian trade may well have introduced them.

Tibbetts (1971: 54–5) considers that the Hariri rudder was controlled by the seated helmsman using lines passing over 'outrigger sticks' to the rudder, as seen, for example, in Hornell's drawing (1942*a*: fig. 4) of a twentieth-century Red Sea vessel, but the Hariri evidence (Fig. 3.17) does not seem to support this interpretation. On the other hand, in the mid-sixteenth century, admittedly some time after the Portuguese arrival, Correa noted that the rudders of the Indian Ocean ships were controlled by ropes on either side (Johnstone and Muir, 1962: 62), so perhaps this *was* the thirteenth-century method.

Muir (1965) has pointed out that a fourteenth-century version of the Hariri ship illustration, now in the National Library of Austria, is steered by a steering-oar pivoted near the stern post. Ibn Mājid used different words for 'steering-oar' and 'rudder' (Tibbetts, 1971: 55), and so perhaps we may conclude that in the thirteenth–fifteenth century period some of the smaller vessels were steered by steering-oar, and the larger ones by median rudder. It is conceivable that the side rudder may also have been in use during these centuries of change.

## 3.6.7 SHIP'S EQUIPMENT

A grapnel, a four-hooked anchor, is seen suspended from a spar projecting forward of the bow of the Hariri ship—this was the form of iron anchor used in the Indian Ocean until the coming of the Portuguese (Tibbetts, 1971: 55). Anchor stones were also widely used, as is known worldwide; Ibn Mājid knew these as 'Chinese anchors' (Tibbetts, 1971: 55).

Fresh water was stored on board in a vessel called a *fantash*. Other equipment noted by Tibbetts (1971) included: the sounding lead and line; the compass box, the binnacle, and a 'latitude-measuring instrument' (3.8.2.2.3).

Ships may also have carried boats or towed them. *Sambuk* was the term used for a ship's boat; *qarib* were longboats capable of carrying fifteen men normally, but up to thirty-three in an emergency—they were sometimes used under oars to tow becalmed or dismasted ships; *dunij* were smaller boats able to hold four men (Tibbetts, 1971: 56; Hourani, 1963: 99). Several boat types are mentioned in Ibn Mājid's poems but the basis for their classification is not always clear: *jilah* appear to be Red Sea craft; *khashab* specific to the Gulf of Aden and the Red Sea; *tararid* to the Orissa coast of eastern India (Tibbetts, 1971: 47).

## 3.6.8 THE SHIP'S CREW

The *Mu'allim* was the ship's master responsible for pilotage and navigation. Under him was the *sarhang*, or mate, who sometimes deputized for the master and appears to have been responsible for berthing and unberthing the ship. The *tandil* was in charge of the *khallasi* (seamen)—possibly the equivalent in our terms was the chief boatswain's mate. Some of these seamen were *sukkangir* or *sahib al-Sukkan* (helmsmen); others were employed as *punjari* (or *al-Fanjari*) or lookouts—one can be seen at the top of the Hariri ship's mainmast and another in the bows; or as a *gunmati*, bailing out the bilges, as again seen on the Hariri ship. Others were *topandaz*, gunners; and some were employed as divers to repair the hull underwater or to

free an anchor (Tibbetts, 1971: 58–9). Ibn Mājid's term for the crew generally was *al-'Askar*, from which the term *laskar* for Indian Ocean seamen evidently derives. On board the Hariri ship two of the *al-'Askar* are lookouts and two are bailing out; two others are handling the lines controlling the sail in some way, whilst the fifth seaman appears to be concerned with one of the sails.

The *nakhoda-khashab* was in charge of the cargo; the *bhandari* in charge of the stores; the *karani* the man who kept the accounts (the clerk).

The day at sea was divided into *zam* or watches of three hours, for example, during a tropical night of twelve hours the watches were changed at about 2100, 2359, and 0300 (Tibbetts, 1971: 63). The *zam* was also a unit of distance, that distance travelled by the average sailing ship in three hours (3.8.2.2.2).

## 3.6.9 AN APPRECIATION OF SEWN BOATS

Several medieval European travellers to Indian Ocean countries adversely criticized the Arab sewn-plank boats they encountered. John of Montecorvino thought that they were 'frail and uncouth'; Jordanus noted that the sewn planking leaked very badly, and that the crew were almost always bailing; and Marco Polo reported that these Arab vessels were very bad, many were wrecked because of their sewn construction, and that it was, 'no little peril to sail in these ships' (Moreland, 1939: 67–8; Hourani, 1963: 94). Needless to say, observers on Vasco da Gama's expedition echoed these earlier opinions: Arab sewn vessels were 'badly built and frail' ( Johnstone and Muir, 1962: 59).

Marco Polo attempted to explain why the Arabs persisted in using this sewing technique instead of using iron nails as in Europe: he advanced two theories, firstly that the wood they used was so hard and brittle that iron nails split and shattered it; and secondly, that the Arabs had no iron (Moreland, 1939: 69; Hourani, 1963: 95). The Arabs, who were aware that Chinese ships, and indeed Arab ships in the Mediterranean, had iron nails in their construction, also sought for explanations: some held the view that magnetic rocks (lodestones) in the Indian Ocean would attract a nail-fastened vessel to its destruction; whilst others, e.g. al-Mas'udi, theorized that the sea water of the Indian Ocean corroded iron (Hourani, 1963: 96).

All these criticisms, at best exaggerations, are generally ill-founded. Teak and other Indian woods can be successfully nailed; iron was available in Indian Ocean countries; there is no significant difference between the chemical composition of the water of the Mediterranean and the Indian Ocean; no iron-fitted vessel has ever been magnetically attracted to destruction—indeed, Procopius (*Bell. Pers.* I. 19) refuted this theory in the sixth century AD (Moreland, 1939: 186–7; Hourani, 1963: 95–6).

There is worldwide evidence for the early use of sewn fastenings in plank boats (McGrail, 1996c). In Europe this technique was used in the pre-Classical Mediterranean (4.9.4), and in pre-Roman Scandinavia and Britain (5.4), indeed it was in use in certain parts of the Mediterranean into the eleventh century AD (4.9.4.7), and in Finland, Estonia and northern Russia into the twentieth century. Sewn-plank boats are also known in Africa, India, south-east Asia, Oceania, North and South America, and China (McGrail, 1996c): of the major land masses, only in Australia is there so far no evidence for this technique. It is thus a long used and proven method of fastening the planking of seagoing vessels. Sewn boats are found to perform better on an open coast than any nailed boat—this is mainly due to the resilient nature of the fastenings. Ibn Battutah and other early Arab travellers noted how well sewn boats rode through heavy surf and withstood the shock of beaching (Hourani, 1963: 96), and twentieth-century owners of sewn boats have emphasized their great strength and flexibility in surf (R. Bowen, 1952: 201). The criticism of Arab sewn boats by medieval European travellers was thus not warranted: as sewn-plank vessels the Arab craft were very good indeed, being demonstrably capable of ocean voyages and usable in difficult inshore waters where European boats would not venture.

## 3.6.10 THE CHANGE FROM SEWN FASTENINGS

Medieval Arab boatbuilders were aware of iron-fastening traditions both to the west and to the east, and iron was available in India, Iran, and inland Sudan, but it was probably relatively expensive (Moreland, 1939: 186–8; Hourani, 1963: 96). There would therefore have had to be a demonstrable major gain in performance

for Arab builders and seamen to be convinced that the change from sewing to iron fastening was worthwhile. The advantages of European practices may not have been sufficient until the coming of the Portuguese in the late fifteenth century in the three-masted, non-edge-joined, frame-first built ships which became the means by which Europeans 'discovered' all the seas of the world (Greenhill, 1976: 289).

As these late fifteenth-century European ships were frame-first and did not use nails to fasten the planking together, there can have been no direct transfer of technology which resulted in Arab sewn planks being replaced by nailed planks, as has been suggested by several commentators (e.g. Johnstone and Muir, 1962: 59–61). However, it may have been that the boats carried by the European ships were still built in the shell tradition and were edge fastened by nails. Whatever the stimulus, it does seem that iron nails began to be used in Arab vessels during the period *c.*1507 to 1512 (Moreland, 1939: 179–80; Johnstone and Muir, 1962: 60–2; Prados, 1997: 190). That this change was selective is evidenced by the survival of Omani and Yemen sewn-plank building into the late twentieth century (Vosmer, 1997; Prados, 1997: 196). Other changes to traditional Arab boatbuilding which probably were stimulated by the arrival of the Portuguese include the introduction of a transom stern and the use of a head sail.

## 3.7

# Harbours and Trade Routes in the First Century AD (Fig. 3.18)

### 3.7.1 HARBOURS

The *Periplus of the Erythraean Sea* (Casson, 1989) mentions several coastal sites in Arabia known to the author as suitable places for Graeco-Roman merchants from Egypt to undertake trade, or as havens which may be used en route to and from India. From details given in the *Periplus*, these places may be grouped into three types: simple landing places with fresh water, regional trading places, and entrepôts for international

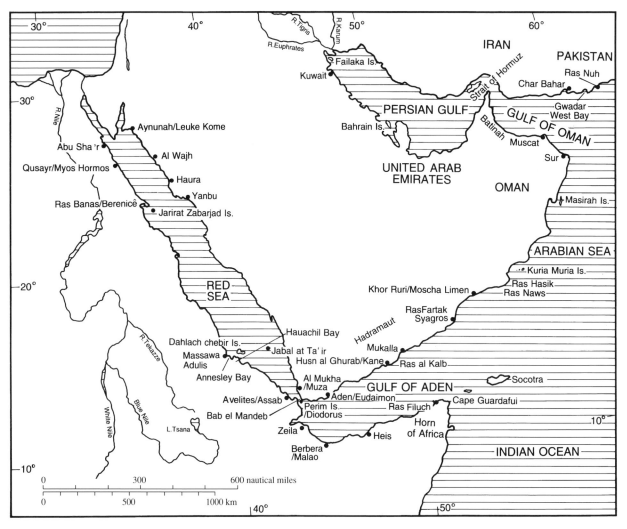

Fig. 3.18. Map of the Red Sea and Persian Gulf region (Institute of Archaeology, Oxford).

trade. Examples are given below: in the identification of place names, Casson (1989) is followed unless stated otherwise.

### 3.7.1.1 LOCAL LANDING PLACES

*Okêlis* (*Periplus*, chs. 7 and 25) on the east side of the strait Bab el Mandeb was a coastal village where there was fresh water. When the *Periplus* was compiled it was involved in some minor trade across the strait with *Avalites* (Assab). *Okêlis* is generally thought to have been on the lagoon Shaykh Sa'id. It was called *Akila* by Strabo (16. 769) and *Cella* by Pliny (*NH* 6. 26. 104) who thought it was comparable with *Kanê* in importance.

By the time of Ptolemy (6. 7. 7) it had achieved the status of an emporion.

### 3.7.1.2 REGIONAL TRADING PLACES

*Leukê Kômê* (*Periplus*, ch. 19) on the Arabian side of the Red Sea near the northern border of Arabia, was a Nabataean trading place with a land route to the regional capital Petra. Small craft brought freight from Arabia, and there was a customs officer and a detachment of soldiers there. It is identified as Khuraybah near Aynunah, where buildings of the early centuries AD have been excavated (Casson, 1989: 144).

There were also regional trading places at: *Sachalitês*

(*Periplus*, chs. 29 and 30) on the Hadramaut coast in a deep bay protected by a fortress on the headland *Syagros* (probably Ras Fartak); and *Moscha Limên* (*Periplus*, ch. 32), over 100 nautical miles to the east of *Syagros* (Ras Fartak), which was a designated harbour with a mole. It is identified as Khor Ruri, an inlet west of Ras Naws.

### 3.7.1.3 ENTREPÔT

*Eudaimôn Arabia*—'prosperous Arabia' (*Periplus*, ch. 26) was an entrepôt *c.*120 nautical miles to the east of Bab el Mandeb. This was a harbour with a good water supply. It had recently been sacked by the Romans, but before that it had been a prosperous entrepôt where cargoes from India destined for Egypt were transshipped and exchanged for Mediterranean merchandise destined for India. *Eudaimôn Arabia* is identified as Aden. From at least the thirteenth century, when Ibn Battutah was there, Aden has had to use reservoirs for storing rainwater and this may have been the case in the first century AD (Casson, 1989: 159). The temporary decline of Aden noted in the *Periplus* may have been due not only to destruction by the Romans but also to the rediscovery (*Periplus*, ch. 57) of the monsoon trade winds across the Indian Ocean—first noted by Eudoxus in the late second century BC (Strabo, 2. 98–9), which enabled open sea rather than coastal voyages to be made (6.3). Thus if a vessel had sufficient fresh water and other supplies, Aden could be bypassed.

Aden, however, is a good landmark. It is situated where westward-bound vessels might have to wait for a shift of wind to take them northwards up the Red Sea, and is, and was, a well-protected natural harbour. Thus its period of disuse was evidently not long. In the second century AD Ptolemy (6. 7. 9) describes the place as *Arabia emporion*, and in the mid-fourth century AD Roman ships regularly stopped there. In the mid-twelfth century it was used by vessels en route to India and China, and in the late thirteenth century Marco Polo noted that much Indian merchandise went through the port (Casson, 1989: 159).

There were also entrepôt at:

(a) *Muza* (*Periplus*, chs. 7, 16, 17, 21, 24, 25, 31) which is thought to be Mocha (al Mukha) *c.*35 nautical miles north of the strait Bab el Mandeb.

(b) *Kanê* (*Periplus*, chs. 27 and 28) which is identified with Quana a site to the east of Cape Hasn al Ghurab, some 200 nautical miles east of *Eudaimôn Arabia*.

(c) *Apologos* (*Periplus*, ch. 35) in the Kingdom of Persis at the head of the Persian Gulf—this was probably near Basra on the Shatt al Arab, the united Euphrates and Tigris.

(d) *Omana* (*Periplus*, ch. 36) another port of Persis, some 300 nautical miles to the east of the entrance to the Persian Gulf. Sewn boats were built there and exported to Arabia. *Omana* may be Chāh Bā har or Tiz on the Makran coast of Iran, or possibly further east at Gwadar West Bay or Pasni in western Pakistan.

### 3.7.2 TRADE ROUTES

Throughout the *Periplus of the Erythraean Sea*, interspersed with commercial information, there is advice for the mariner on the hazards to be faced, on recommended seasons for departure from Egypt for foreign lands, and on the aids to pilotage that can be used. For example, the *Periplus* gives the best months to leave Egypt for *Muza* in ch. 24, and for *Kanê* in ch. 28. In ch. 20, the author advises against a passage close inshore on the central section of the Arabian coast of the Red Sea, as this would be 'altogether risky, since the region with its lack of harbours offers poor anchorage, is foul with rocky stretches, cannot be approached because of cliffs and is fearsome in every respect' (Casson, 1989: 63). The *Periplus* advises that a course down the middle of the Red Sea should be taken until a region with a more hospitable coast is reached. There were other hazards to be faced in the northern parts of the Red Sea, for Strabo (16. 777) mentions that Nabataeans, who lived on the coast and on islands, used rafts to plunder ships from Egypt.

The *Periplus* (ch. 25) also describes the hazards to be faced on a passage through the strait Bab el Mandeb at the southern end of the Red Sea. The narrowing of the channel between Arabia and Africa, and the presence of the island of Diodôros in mid-channel causes a strong north-flowing current. Nowadays during northerly tidal streams, the combined flow can be 3 or even 4 knots. which would almost always mean that a southbound ship had to wait for a more favourable wind or tide. Furthermore, the *Periplus* tells us, there could be a strong cross wind in the strait due to the neighbouring mountains.

There are also descriptions in the *Periplus* to assist the identification of landmarks:

Ch. 20: In the Red Sea an island is called *Katakekau-menê*, i.e. 'burnt': this is probably Jabal at Ta'ir which has an active volcano today and in the early nineteenth century was still used as a landmark (Casson, 1989: 147).

Ch. 27: An island near *Kanê* is called *Orneôn*, i.e. 'of the birds': this is probably Sikha, the peak of which is now white with guano (Casson, 1989: 161).

Ch. 30: A mighty headland facing east called *Syagros* is given as the landfall for the approach to the regional trading place of *Sachalitês*: it is also mentioned by Ptolemy (1. 17. 2–3) and by Pliny (*NH* 6. 100). This must be Ras Fartak, the highest and most prominent headland on the Hadhramaut coast (Casson, 1989: 166).

Ch. 35: The mouth of the Persian Gulf may be recognized by the mountain range of *Asabô* to the west and the distinctive round and high mountain *Semiramis* to the east.

There is also at least one example in the *Periplus* of how to forecast the weather: when off the Horn of Africa if the sea becomes turbid and changes colour, there will be a storm (ch. 12). In western Arabian waters today, fishermen know that changes in water temperature and in currents, and the presence of weed and phosphorescence foretell the change from the south-west monsoon to a north-east wind (*Naval Intelligence, Western Arabia*, 1946: 608).

### 3.7.2.1 COASTAL ROUTES

There was a coastal route from *Barygaza* (Broach) in western India to *Omana* on the Meggan coast, and beyond Hormuz to *Apologos* at the head of the Persian Gulf (chs. 35 and 36). From *Apologos* there was a coastal route to eastern Arabia (ch. 36); and second-century AD dedicatory inscriptions in Palmyra, Syria refer to the sea route from the Shatt al Arab region (known to the Greeks and Romans as *Mesene*) to northern India (Mathews, 1984). From *Moscha Limên* (Khor Rûri) and possibly from *Sachalitês* there was coastal traffic to

*Kanê* (Husn al Gharab) (chs. 29, 30 and 32); and from *Kanê* (chs. 27 and 28) and formerly Aden (ch. 26), there were coastal passages to Egypt. The earlier passage from Aden to India (ch. 26) also appears to have been a coastal one, and a section of this route would have coincided with the *Kanê* to *Persis* and *Omana* route across the mouth of the Persian Gulf (chs. 27 and 28). From western Arabia there was a coastal route up the Red Sea to *Leukê Kômê* of the Nabataeans (ch. 19). From *Muza* there was a coastal route along the east African coast to *Malaô* (Berbara) and *Rhapta* (Dar es Salaam)

### 3.7.2.2 ACROSS THE RED SEA

There were routes from *Myos Hormos* and possibly from *Berenicê* across the northern parts of the Red Sea to *Leukê Kômê* (ch. 19). Further south, in or near the strait Bab el Mandeb, there were crossings between *Okêlis* and *Avalites* (Assab) and between *Mouza* and *Adulis* and *Avalites* (chs. 7 and 24).

### 3.7.2.3 OPEN-SEA VOYAGES

Although the *Periplus* advises keeping clear of the Arabian coast on voyages southwards in the Red Sea from the Egyptian ports (chs. 20 and 21), it seems likely that such passages were generally within sight of the Arabian coast. The voyage between *Mouza* and *Dioscuridês* (Socotra island) across the Gulf of Aden could have been coastal or may have included some time out of sight of land.

From the first century BC/AD when the direct route began to be used by Egyptian-based shipping, there would have been open-sea voyages to India from *Mouza* (ch. 21) and *Kanê* (chs. 27 and 28): the prominent headland of Ras Fartak may well have been the point from which ships took departure. Indian-bound vessels which could not make *Kanê* because they were late in the monsoon season (ch. 32), wintered at *Moscha Limên* (Khor Rûri). This direct route was probably known to Indian and Arab seamen well before the late-second century BC when Eudoxus learned how to use the monsoon winds from a shipwrecked Indian pilot (6.3).

# 3.8

# Seafaring

## 3.8.1 EXPLORATION BY SEA

The necessity to forecast the seasonal flood of the Euphrates and Tigris led, as in Egypt, to the study of astronomy and mathematics as an aid to the compilation of a calendar. This, in turn, appears to have led to the use of stars for navigation on land and sea. The pre-Islamic Persians were early leaders in the fields of overseas seafaring and navigation (Hornell, 1946a: 231–3). They were aware of the fixed direction of the pole and how the rising and setting of certain stars or constellations could form the basis of a direction system, and compiled a treatise of sailing directions which were subsequently used by the Arabs (Hornell, 1946a: 233; Hourani, 1963: 106–7).

By the ninth century, as Islam expanded, a requirement arose to be able to describe land and sea routes and the position of new lands (Aleem, 1980: 583), and in the ninth and tenth centuries we find an explosive burst of activity in the field of navigation, partly based on the translation of Persian, Indian, and Greek works into Arabic (Hourani, 1963: 106). Observatories were established at Junde-Shapur, Baghdad, Damascus, Cairo, Samarkand, Toledo, and Cordova (Hourani, 1963: 105; Aleem, 1980: 584).

By the tenth century Arab seamen were regularly sailing to all parts of the Indian Ocean, in the Red Sea as far north as Jidda (Ras al-Quhhaz) and the east African coast as far as 20°S at Sofola (Tibbetts, 1971: 398; Aleem, 1980: 587). Arab merchants were established in Ceylon as early as AD 414 (Aleem, 1980: 582). A Chinese account

Fig. 3.19. Severin's reconstruction sewn-plank boat *Sohar* off Malaca (Richard Greenhill/Severin Archive).

of *c.* AD 727 speaks of Persian ships sailing to Canton for silk goods; and in *c.* AD 748 along with Indians and Malays, they are noted again on the river at Canton (Hourani, 1963: 62; Aleem, 1967: 459). Later Arab writings describe a mid-eighth century AD voyage by an Omani merchant, Abu-'Ubaydah, to China where he bought aloes and wood (Hourani, 1963: 63). By this time there were regular sailings from the Gulf to China, to exchange cloth, rugs, metalwork, iron ore, and bullion for silk, camphor, spices, and ceramics (Hourani, 1963: 66–7) and the route was described by Ibn Khurdadhbih in *c.* AD 850 and by Ibn Wahab in the *Voyage of Sulayman the Merchant* of about the same date (Hourani, 1963: 66–7; Aleem, 1980: 586–7). This latter contained, in the midst of its epic tales, much useful information about sites of fresh water, tides, typhoons, and landmarks such as volcanoes. Severin's (1982) voyage from Oman to Canton in a sewn-plank boat (Fig. 3.19) during 1980–1, was in part inspired by Ibn Wahab's account. The *Wonders of the Sea of India* compiled by a Persian, Ibn Buzruk, in AD 953 (Aleem, 1989: 61) continued in the same vein, with geographical descriptions and maritime lore embedded in wondrous tales.

Arab seamen also sailed the Mediterranean, and are thought to have ventured into the Atlantic as early as the tenth century AD, thereby repeating some of the pioneering voyages of the Phoenicians some 1,500 years earlier (4.9.3.2.1). In the mid-thirteenth century, Ibn Fatima is reputed to have sailed south along the west African coast and then to have appeared in Madagascar off the east coast (Aleem, 1980: 588), the implication being that he had part-circumnavigated Africa anti-clockwise: the evidence is insufficient to endorse this claim.

Tides and tidal regions were discussed by Arab authors as early as the mid-ninth century. In *c.* AD 907, Ibn al Fakih (Al Hamadani) mentioned not only these sources but also quoted from *Sulayman the Merchant* (Aleem, 1967: 460) in his description of the maritime route to China. He referred specifically to the semi-diurnal tides in the South China Sea. Towards the end of the tenth century Al Mokaddasi was able to relate the tidal flows at Basra at the head of the Persian Gulf to the lunar cycle, and in the thirteenth century, Al Dimiski published detailed descriptions of the semi-diurnal tides at Shatt el Arab. Furthermore, he recognized that the ebb was longer than the period of flow, and that the time of high water each day lagged behind

that of the previous day by one hour 'or rather slightly less'.

### 3.8.2 NAVIGATIONAL TECHNIQUES

The renowned fifteenth-century Arab navigator, Ibn Mājid al-Najdi, recognized that there were three types of voyage on which different aspects of navigation were required (Tibbetts, 1971: 165–70, 273–5):

(1) *Dirat-al-Mul*: The coastal route: on which pilotage techniques were used.
(2) *Dirat al-Mutlaq*: A direct route across the sea between two points. On this route the altitude of the Pole Star (in our terms, the observer's latitude) was taken on departure from the near side and also on making a landfall on the far side. During the passage dead reckoning methods were used: a given course in rhumbs (points of the compass) was steered, and the distance run (in *isba*) was estimated.
(3) *Dirat al-Iqtida*: A route involving a change of course when out of sight of land. A given course (generally near N/S) was steered until the 'latitude' of the destination (by observation of star altitudes) was reached, when course was altered for the destination.

The techniques Arab seamen used between the early ninth and the late fifteenth centuries when undertaking these types of voyages may be considered under two main headings: pilotage; and navigation.

### 3.8.2.1 PILOTAGE IN COASTAL WATERS

A pilot's duties in coastal waters are described in some pre-Islamic literature dated by Tibbetts (1971: 1) to the first century AD: this is similar to (and may be the ultimate origin of) a Sanskrit text *Jatakamata* by Aryasura which Needham (1971: 555) states was translated into Chinese before AD 434. From this we learn that the pilot must know the signs of approaching good and bad weather and be able to recognize different regions by the fish and the birds, by mountains and other landmarks, and by the colour of the water and the nature of the bottom. Depths of water were noted from at least AD 1000, the term for a lead line being *bild* (Tibbetts,

1971: 2, 56) and by the twelfth century (but probably much earlier) the *gama* (fathom, from fingertip to fingertip of outstretched arms) was used to measure this (Aleem, 1980: 586).

In his late fifteenth-century navigational works, much of it in poetic form so that it could more readily be memorized, Ibn Mājid recorded soundings and the nature of the bottom in coastal waters and in harbour approaches over much of the world known to Arabs. He noted the existence of reefs and shoals, especially in the Red Sea, and off the east African coast. He also drew attention to atolls in the Indian Ocean and to other landmarks, including mountain peaks on the west coast of India, southern Arabia, the Red Sea, and the African coast (Aleem, 1968b: 575–6). Ibn Mājid also identified the principal problems a pilot could experience in inshore waters as: inaccurate allowance for tidal drift and leeway; a compass defect or a dozing helmsman; and the ignorance of the pilot when taking star altitude measurements.

### 3.8.2.2 NAVIGATION OUT OF SIGHT OF LAND

#### 3.8.2.2.1 *Directions and courses*

In the simplest form of navigation—that without instruments—a form of dead reckoning can be used, i.e. the navigator steers a course specified at some angle to some (relatively) fixed datum for a given time (measured in units of a 'day's sail'); as the voyage progresses he adjusts the course and his estimate of the time of sighting the next landfall, to compensate for the effects of currents, tidal flows, leeway, and changes in wind velocity, and to allow for any speed differences from the norm which his boat may achieve on a particular voyage (McGrail, 1998: 280–2).

As in all known maritime cultures, the early Arabs based relative directions on the boat's heading, thus there was 'ahead', 'astern', 'windward bow', etc. (Tibbetts, 1971: 40). For absolute directions they are known to have used a system based on the celestial pole (i.e. the null point about which the heavens appear to rotate) from at least the tenth century AD (Aleem, 1968b: 574). It is not clear what datum was used in daytime, or at night when the sky was obscured by cloud. By analogy with the practices of other seafaring cultures, such 'fixed points' could have been: the wind, especially trade winds from a relatively steady direc-

tion such as the Indian Ocean monsoons; the swell, a wind-induced, surface motion of the sea which persists long after the wind velocity has changed; and the sun (at sunrise, noon, and sunset). In the relatively low latitudes in which medieval Arab seamen generally sailed on open-sea voyages (c.25° to 10°S) the heavens appear to rotate at a less oblique angle than, say, in north-west Europe, and thus the sun is seen to rise due east or nearby, and to set on or near due west.

From one of these fixed points, say the celestial North Pole, a system of directions can be derived or, in seamen's language, the horizon can be divided into 'points' (Arabic: *rhumb*). Thus when facing north, the celestial South Pole is at your back, west on your left hand, and east on your right. Points midway between these four cardinal points (N. S. E. W.) can then be recognized: for example, *Sulayman the Merchant* in c. AD 851 described the wind in the Sea of Harkland (Bay of Bengal) as blowing from between west and north, a direction we call north-west or NW. This subdivision can continue until one arrives at the 32-point system of recent times, each point covering an arc of 11¼°. These 'points of the compass' were further identified by medieval Arab seamen with the rising and setting of certain stars or constellations: thus ENE (east-north-east) was recognized as the direction in which Arcturus rose and WNW (west-north-west) as the direction in which it set (Dimmock, 1944; Aleem, 1968b: 570–1, 574; Tibbetts, 1971: 121–56). Ibn Mājid further subdivided his star rose system into 224 *isbâ* (fingers): thus 1 isbâ = 1°37′ in azimuth. This *isbâ* was also used when measuring star altitudes (vertical angle)—see below.

Predominant winds were also associated with particular points on this 'star compass' system and this may have been done by Persians in pre-Islamic times (Aleem, 1967: 461). Ibn Mājid describes the north-east monsoon wind (*saba*) as coming 'from the East, but a little towards North', and the south-west wind (*Dabour*) as coming from 'between the rhumb of Canopus setting (SSW) and West' (Tibbetts, 1971: 142–3; Aleem, 1967: 461). Similarly, the southerly wind (*Janūb*) was from Canopus' rising (SSE); and the northerly wind (*Shamāl*) was from slightly to the west of the Pole. Similar linkages between a system orientated on celestial bodies ('star compass') and a system based on the direction of recognizable winds ('wind compass') are also known from the pre-Classical Mediterranean (4.4.6) and Viking Age north-west

Europe (5.7.3), and were probably widely used elsewhere (Taylor, 1971: 7–8). Ibn Mājid also described how winds could be recognized, and gave an explanation for land and sea breezes (Tibbetts, 1971: 143–4).

Ibn Mājid, and probably others before him, recognized that there was then no star at the celestial North Pole and that Polaris was a rough substitute (Tibbetts, 1971: 123)—in fact, in the fifteenth century, Polaris was *c*.3½° away from the null point. A more precise method of identifying the celestial north Pole was evolved by medieval Arabs using the guards β (*beta*) and γ (*gamma*) of the constellation Ursa Minor, and six phases were tabulated (Aleem, 1980: 590). Ibn Mājid further advised that the Pole could be found by astrolabe, by lodestone, or from the direction of the highest point of the sun (south). It could also be found halfway (i.e. the zenith) between the rising bearing and the setting bearing of any star—thus if the night sky was partly overcast the Pole could still be identified (Tibbetts, 1971: 123–4).

The Chinese evidently knew of the directional properties of the lodestone in the first century AD, but the first documented use of a magnetized needle at sea seems to be towards the end of the eleventh century when it is said to be used by Arab and Persian ships on passage between Canton, Sumatra, and India (Aleem, 1968b: 574): earliest Chinese use seems to have been at about the same time (10.11). As the first known mention in Europe is *c*.1190, by an Abbot of Cirencester, Alexander Neckham (Waters, 1978: 22) and by a French poet, Guyot de Provins (Hourani, 1963: 109), this aid to navigation may have been transmitted from East to West.

In the mid-thirteenth century, Al-Kobgaki saw Syrian pilots on a voyage to Alexandria using a magnetized needle floating on water in a ring of *acacia* wood. Subsequently the magnetized needle was pivoted over a diagram of directional points and enclosed in a box (*huqqa*) to become a compass (*boussole*) which was then mounted on a binnacle (*nasbal huqqa*): it is thought that Ibn Mājid may have been the first Arab to do this (Aleem, 1968b: 574). From Majid's descriptions (Tibbetts, 1971) it seems that the magnetic compass—was generally more of an auxiliary aid at sea rather than a primary method of navigation: in this, they were similar to north European seamen in their attitude to the compass — except in foul overcast weather the compass was used to check the direction of the wind, thereby improving the accuracy of course estimates, but the

mariner continued to conn his ship by reference to the natural elements e.g. the wind (Waters, 1978: 22).

### 3.8.2.2.2 *Distance measurement*

As well as being a unit of angular measure the *isbâ* (finger) was a linear measure, and was used to derive a measure of distance in the north–south direction, i.e. change of latitude. Thus, if the altitude (angular elevation) of the Pole changed by one *isbâ* between two readings, the change in latitude was one *tirfa*: since by definition one *isbâ* = 360°/224 = 1°37′, 1 *tirfa* was equivalent to 97 nautical miles (Tibbetts, 1971: 146–7; Aleem, 1968b: 573). The *zam* was a measure of distance unrelated to latitude: it was an Indian unit adopted by Arabs and defined as the distance sailed in one watch, i.e. three hours, and was generally taken to be 12 nautical miles (Tibbetts, 1971: 62; Aleem, 1980: 586). However, Tibbetts (1971: 48) has noted several examples in Ibn Mājid's text of *zam* being qualified by the type of ship. In fact the theoretical *zam* was 1/8 *isbâ* = *c*.12 nautical miles: in practice, as Ibn Mājid explains (Tibbetts, 1971: 152), the pilot had to estimate what his particular ship did on a specific voyage. The *zam* as a measure of distance may be compared to the European 'day's sail'—that distance usually sailed by a standard ship in fair weather (McGrail, 1998: 282). In these terms, a *zam* is a 'watch sail' and eight *zam* would be equivalent to one (24 hours) 'day's sail'. In other words, one day's sail (8 × 12 nautical miles) due north would increase the altitude of Polaris by one *isbâ*. Aleem (1980: 586) has noted that another unit of linear measure was the *farsakh* which he equates with 6,305 yards (*c*.5,765 m), but how this unit was derived and how it was used at sea is not stated—possibly it was some near equivalent of the European 'league' ('the usual distance sailed in one hour') which was *c*.3 nautical miles, i.e. 6,000 yards (Waters, 1978: 37). On a smaller scale, the *zira* (arm, cubit, ell) was also used to measure by eye the apparent distance between two stars (Tibbetts, 1971: 113; Aleem, 1980: 586).

### 3.8.2.2.3 *Measurement of latitude*

Ibn Mājid (Tibbetts, 1971) gives the latitude in terms of star altitude (angular elevation) for many places within the seas usually sailed by Arabs (Tibbetts, 1971: 398; Aleem, 1968b: 565), and the routes he describes within and across the Indian Ocean, the Red Sea, the Persian Gulf, and the Malayan Archipelago include star altitudes. Such observations of 'latitude' were taken by late medieval Arabs on leaving and on sighting land on a direct voyage between two places (type 2). They were also taken on indirect voyages (type 3) when latitude sailing techniques were used, i.e. the ship was steered (near) north or south until the 'latitude' of the destination was reached, and then that parallel was maintained (by star observation) until a landfall was made. Ibn Mājid had been using this technique for forty years when he wrote, and so latitude sailing was known to the Arabs at the latest by AD 1450 (Aleem, 1980: 591).

The altitude (vertical angle) of Polaris and other stars was at first measured in hand breadths (*dhubban* = four *isbâ*), presumably being held at a standard distance from the eye, e.g. at arm's length (Aleem, 1968*b*: 573; Tibbetts, 1971: 137). In the ninth century, Al Khwarizmi designed a staff for measuring star altitudes (Aleem, 1980: 588). Fatimi (1996) has traced the earliest known reference to the use of wooden tablets (*khashabat*) for star measurement at sea to the second half of the ninth century. These were evidently forerunners of the more widely-known *kamāl* (Aleem, 1968*b*: 573; Tibbetts, 1971: 56; Fatimi, 1996). These tablets were of several sizes, to cater for a range of angles, and were fastened in the centre to a string which had knots tied in it at graduated intervals. The tablet was held at eye level and moved towards the star to be measured until the gap between horizon and star was apparently filled (Fig. 3.20): the length of string, i.e. the number of knots was a measure of the vertical angle in *isbâ*—the fewer knots, the greater the angle (Aleem, 1980: 590–1; Fatimi, 1996: figs. 1 and 2). This was a simple yet very practical aid to navigation, readily usable in the dark when the knots could be counted by touch. The observations were made from a sitting-down position (Tibbetts, 1971: 189) presumably to minimize the effects of ship motion. Ibn Mājid also gives practical advice on the problems associated with sighting the horizon in a heat haze and in conditions of bioluminescence (Aleem, 1968*b*: 575–6; 1968*a*: 361; Tibbetts, 1971: 190).

From the instructions given by Ibn Mājid it seems clear that a high standard of accuracy in reading these star altitudes could be expected. In the case of Polaris the reading was further refined using the guards of Ursa Minor to give the correct latitude, i.e. the vertical angle of the celestial North Pole.

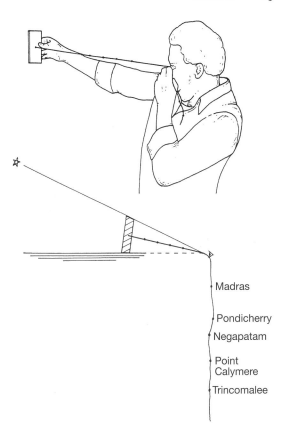

Fig. 3.20 Method of using a *kamāl* calibrated for Sri Lanka and the east coast of India (Institute of Archaeology, Oxford).

Quadrants and astrolabes were also known to the medieval Arab navigator. The first Arabic astrolabe (possibly based on a Greek model) was made in *c*.771 and some of the best astrolabes were made by Arabs as early as the ninth and tenth centuries (Hourani, 1963: 106; Aleem, 1980: 588; Fatimi, 1996) and the quadrant was perfected in the tenth century (Fatimi, 1996). Astrolabes were little used at sea, however, because of inaccuracy resulting from ship motion, and tablets were preferred (Aleem, 1968*b*: 573; Fatimi, 1996).

### 3.8.2.2.4 *Landfall*

Ibn Mājid describes some of the signs which indicate approaching land and, in some cases, may give guidance on position. Thus seaweed and floating grass may be encountered on the north coast of Socotra and sea snakes off Somalia (Tibbetts, 1971: 196). Sea snakes may also be found off the coast of western India between certain latitudes—similar advice was given in the first-century AD *Periplus of the Erythraean Sea* (6.3.3.1). Schools of migratory fish and whales may also be a sign of approaching land (Aleem, 1968a: 364; 1968b: 576). In addition, Ibn Mājid describes the coastal topography and oceanography of many places especially the west coast of India so that the mariner may identify his landfall by the shape or number of mountain peaks, by the depths of water and by other environmental clues (Tibbetts, 1971: 197–203).

### 3.8.2.2.5 *Aids to navigation*

Arab charts were first mentioned by Al Mokaddas, writing in about AD 985. He stated that he had seen charts (*suwar*) of the Indian Ocean, from China to Africa, in the library of the Prince of Khurasan: whether these were practical charts for use at sea or merely decorative is not clear. By the end of the fifteenth century there were certainly seagoing charts in Arab ships, as reported by Vasco da Gama ( Johnstone and Muir, 1962: 59), which the Portuguese were ready to use (Aleem, 1968b: 576).

The earliest treatise on astronomy seems to have been written by Ali-ibn-Isa before AD 830 (Hourani, 1963: 106). Some astronomical tables were published by Al Batlani in the early tenth century (Aleem, 1980: 590). In the mid-eleventh century Al Zarkali published tables giving star altitudes and solar declinations from the observatory at Toledo. Other tables were published by observatories in Baghdad and Samarkand (Aleem, 1980: 588). Much of the instruction on astronavigation given in Ibn Mājid's books and poems was based on similar data for the Indian Ocean and elsewhere.

The first mention of *rahmani*—which is probably best translated as 'rutter' or 'pilot's handbook'—is in the late tenth century: Al Mokaddas states that he had sailed in the Indian Ocean for 2,000 *Farsakh* (c.6,000 nautical miles) and voyaged around the Arabian coast from Suez to Abadan. He talked to ships' masters and pilots and noted that they had books describing the seas, the ports, the winds, and the islands (Aleem, 1967: 462; 1968b: 577; Hourani, 1963: 107). Ibn Mājid mentions some of his predecessors, compilers of early *rahmani*, who lived around the late ninth/early tenth centuries (Hourani, 1963: 107–8).

These marked advances in aids to navigation—Khwarizimi's stick, the *kamāl*, astronomical treatises and *rahmani* (pilot's handbooks) from the ninth century, and charts and the quadrant from the tenth century—seem to be a consequence of the period of spectacular economic growth which followed the foundation of Islamic Baghdad in AD 762. By c. AD 800 the Persian Gulf had become the main route for the transport of raw materials and goods from China, India, and east Africa through Siraf to the markets of western Asia, as can be paralleled by the eighth to tenth century growth in the size of the port of Siraf within the Gulf, and Suhar in the Sea of Oman (Whitehouse, 1983). The prospect of increasing overseas trade seems to have stimulated pilots to search for improved navigational techniques, and the contemporary growth in astronomical knowledge was able to provide them with much of the tabulated data they needed to build upon their own practical e xperience.

### 3.8.3 MASTERS AND PILOTS

Ibn Mājid's own works on navigational techniques and related matters are masterly, and he is not slow to praise his own knowledge and skill on several occasions, but with due acknowledgement to God. He had over fifty years' experience at sea from Africa to China and was a legend in his own lifetime and long afterwards—Richard Burton, the English explorer, stated in 1856 that, before they went to sea, the sailors of Aden said a prayer for Majid as the 'discoverer of the compass' (Aleem, 1968b: 569–70). It seems likely that he was the Arab pilot who guided Vasco da Gama from Africa to India in 1488, although Aleem (1980: 593) has sought to disprove this.

Ibn Mājid's work may be summarized under four headings (Aleem, 1968b: 565):

(a) The training and duties of a master. This became a 'code of practice' for Indian Ocean pilots.
(b) Detailed descriptions of passages in the Red Sea, the Persian Gulf, the Indian Ocean, and the Malay Archipelago. Astronomical observations were an important part of these.
(c) Information of use in coastal waters, including descriptions of coastal profiles, currents, winds, and tides to be expected, and depths of water, the position of shoals and reefs, and descriptions of major landmarks.
(d) Latitudes of places, times and distances between places, and the correct methods of dividing the horizon.

Ibn Mājid covered every conceivable aspect of a master's duties from taking over a new vessel, when the master should assess the ship's facilities, crew, and passengers carefully, and set up a stick with a piece of rag on it to see which way the wind is blowing (Tibbetts, 1971: 192), to navigation on the high seas and pilotage in coastal waters, including knowing such things as the signs which foretell a typhoon (Tibbetts, 1971: 196). Ibn Mājid identified the master's greatest problem as 'the negligence of the helmsman' when he 'dozes off or leans too much on the rudder' (Tibbetts, 1971: 165, 170). Although he tells us that in fifty years at sea he 'never left the helmsman alone without standing over him or my deputy in my place' (Tibbetts, 1971:

170), he mentions the unreliable helmsman so often in his work, as to suggest he may have had a chastening experience with a dozy helmsman in his early days as a navigator: Columbus was equally concerned (McGrail, 1992).

Ibn Mājid's ideal master knew the courses of the stars and could always orientate himself; on the high seas and in coastal waters he was zealous in his observation of winds, storms, currents, rotations of the year and seasons, bays and coastal shallows, capes, islands, coral shelves, entrances of straits, and coasts without fresh water (Needham, 1971: 555; Tibbetts, 1971: 62). There is no doubt that this description matched his own achievements.

# 4
# THE MEDITERRANEAN

This chapter, which deals with the water transport of the Mediterranean apart from Egypt, impinges not only on Chapter 2 (Egypt), but also on the Mesopotamian/Arab world of the western Indian Ocean (Chapter 3) and on the Atlantic region (Chapter 5). The Mediterranean is an extensive, semi-enclosed sea, almost an inland sea, some 2,000 nautical miles in length, east to west, with a greatest breadth of *c.*700 nautical miles (Fig. 4.1). It extends from *c.*6°W at the Strait of Gibraltar to *c.*36°E on the Levant coast; and from 31°–37°N on the coast of northern Africa to *c.*46°N at the head of the Adriatic. It is divided into western and eastern basins by a seabed ridge which runs from Cape Bon, Tunisia, to Sicily. The continental shelf is generally narrow, out to 40 nautical miles in some places, but less than 5 in others. The seabed then drops more or less steeply to depths of over 500 fathoms (*c.*900 m).

The Mediterranean probably has a wider range of evidence for early vessels than any other region. It may not have the volume of representational evidence known from Egypt; nor the number of medieval wrecks documented in Atlantic Europe: but it does have extensive documentary and iconographic evidence, which both precedes and is contemporary with an impressive array of excavated material. On the other hand, with some outstanding exceptions, Mediterranean underwater wreck sites (of which there are, at present, nearly 1,200 dating from before AD 1500—Parker, 1992) have, until recently, been primarily investigated for information about the cargo rather than ship's structure: in this field the full archaeological potential of these sites is not yet being realized.

## 4.1
## Reconstructing Past Sea Levels and Climates

In order to appreciate how water transport was used in the ancient Mediterranean—and indeed, in every region dealt with in this book—it is necessary to reconstruct in as much detail as possible, the environmental context within which these vessels were operated: that is, the sea levels and coastlines, the weather, the currents, and the tides. As systematic observation of these phenomena has only been undertaken in the recent past, it is necessary to ask whether modern meteorological, physiographic, and oceanographic data are also relevant to earlier times (van Andel, 1989; McGrail, 1998: 258–60; W. Murray, 1987; Pryor, 1995).

Changes in sea levels within the Mediterranean region have recently been described by van Andel (1989); and changes in climate have been discussed by Mantzourani and Theodorou (1989), and by Pryor (1995). Their combined views may be summarized:

- *Fifteenth–eleventh millennium BC*
  A time of lowest sea levels within the last glaciation. Levels were some 65–70 fathoms (120–130 m) below today's.
- *Twelfth–eighth millennium BC*
  Rapid rise in sea level causing the flooding of coastal plains, and the isolation of islands. By the eighth millennium BC, the Mediterranean coastline had just about assumed its present configuration.

- *Seventh and sixth millennium BC*
  Increasing temperatures and precipitation. The rate of sea level rise markedly decreased, with the sea level within 3 fathoms (5.5 m) of today's sea level.
- *Fifth and fourth millennium BC* (5000–3000 BC)
  Temperatures a little higher than today; precipitation greater. Sea level still rising slowly.
- *Third and second millennium BC* (3000–1000 BC)
  At first drier and hotter summers, and wetter winters. Later a fall in temperature to around today's values. Oscillations around a very slowly rising sea level led to a level close to today's.
- *First millennium BC and first millennium AD*
  At first cooler, then warmer from 300 BC–AD 400. Warmer again in the tenth to thirteenth centuries. A 'mini-ice age' in the fourteenth and fifteenth centuries, followed by slight oscillations to the present (Pryor, 1995: 206–7).

In general terms, before the fifth millennium BC, mariners would have known a significantly different coastline and a somewhat different climate from today. From late Neolithic times onward, however, the islands and coastlines of the Mediterranean would have increasingly resembled today's, apart from recent changes due to natural erosion and silting, and to man-induced factors.

During the past 7,000 years, from the late Neolithic period onwards, changes in the main climatic parameters have, in general, been insufficient to significantly alter seafaring conditions. Rates of sea level change during these millennia have varied, not only regionally but also locally, so that data from one site cannot necessarily be applied to another nearby. Nevertheless, past sea levels and former coastlines can be deduced with reasonable accuracy from global sea level data, providing tectonic and glacial effects are taken into account (van Andel, 1989). During the past 3,000 years (from the Iron Age) sea level changes have been of limited significance from the seafaring viewpoint, for example, it has been estimated that since the Roman period mean sea level has risen by less than 0.5 m. Of more consequence in that period have been the changes caused by coastal erosion, silting and other forms of deposition, including soil erosion due to changes in vegetational cover.

From at least 1000 BC, the general meteorological situation appears to have been such that the direction of the predominant wind was only slightly different from that of today, when it is generally north-west. Furthermore, the physical principles which determine current flows in the sea (mainly evaporation, precipitation, and differences in water densities) are timeless. Thus, with generally similar coastlines, rainfall, and winds, from the Neolithic onwards, ancient tidal effects and currents would have been similar to today's.

In the absence of more detailed knowledge of earlier Mediterranean environments, it thus seems valid to use modern data on winds, currents, tides, and coastlines to deduce the context within which Mediterranean mariners voyaged from, say, 5000 BC onwards. Observations (usually in literary rather than quantitative terms), made by authors from Classical times onwards, appear to be very similar to today's records of wind directions, current flows, unusual conditions in the Strait of Messina and the Bosporus, and so on (Pryor, 1992: pp. xvii–xix; Murray, 1987); this reinforces the argument for drawing on present data to deduce earlier seafaring conditions—at least until more detailed palaeo-data become generally available. However, for pre-Neolithic and Early Neolithic voyages, account must be taken of the significantly different sea levels and coastlines then prevailing.

# 4.2
# Environmental Conditions

The sea and the rivers have been the main links between the lands of the Mediterranean basin ever since Man took to the water. Environmental features—meteorological conditions, winds, currents and tides, coastal configurations and depths of water—have had a lasting influence on the sea routes used, and on the development of hull forms and sailing rigs.

## 4.2.1 CURRENTS

The almost-closed nature of the Mediterranean, its cloud-free skies, and high temperatures result in the

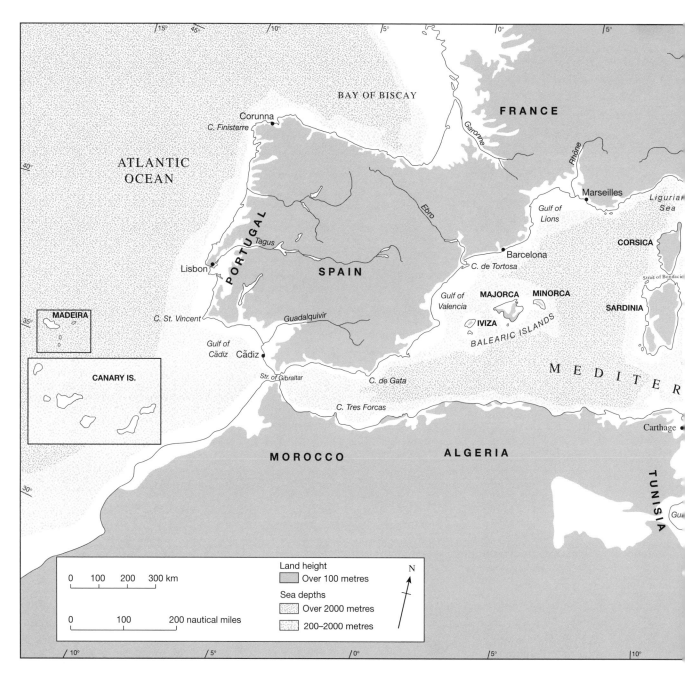

rapid evaporation of surface water. The rivers that flow into the Mediterranean, principally the Nile, Po, Rhône, and the Ebro, replace only about a third of this water loss—this deficit is especially marked in summer when there is generally insignificant rainfall. Dynamic equilibrium is attained and the deficit generally made good by a strong surface inflow from the Atlantic through the Strait of Gibraltar, whilst highly saline and dense water, a product of the rapid evaporation, flows out through this strait at subsurface depths (*Medi-*

*terranean Pilot*, 5, 1988: 15–16). There are comparable, but less pronounced, effects between the Black Sea and the Mediterranean: inflows from the Danube, Don, Dneiper, and Dneister more than compensate for evaporation in the Black Sea and, surface water flows out via the Bosporus and Dardanelles straits into the Aegean (Deacon, 1968). In the narrowest parts of these two straits, south-setting currents flow at up to 4 knots (Neumann, 1991; Labaree, 1957).

Superimposed on the corresponding inflow

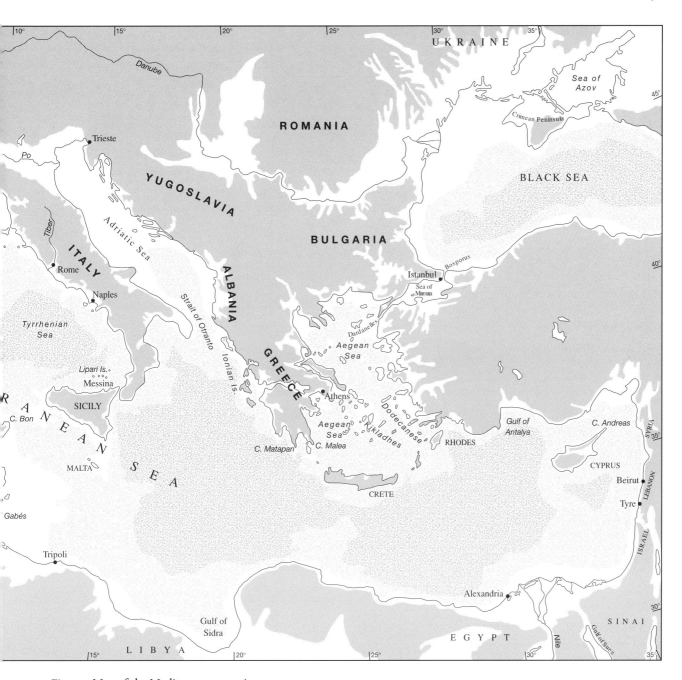

Fig. 4.1. Map of the Mediterranean region.

through the Gibraltar strait (which is probably of the order of 3.5 knots) are tidal flows which alternately oppose and reinforce it (*Admiralty Pilot, West Coasts of Spain and Portugal*, 1921: 10–11). The resultant flow in mid-stream is always easterly, and can be up to 4 to 6 knots during an east-flowing tidal stream, but only 1 to 2.5 knots during westward flows. These flows are less strong inshore, and there are places on the European

coast where they nearly cease. On parts of the African coast, near the shore, the combined stream continually sets westward.

Physically, the Mediterranean consists of two basins connected by the Sicilian channel (Strait of Carthage) and the Strait of Messina, and the general flow of the surface currents is determined by flows into these basins from the Atlantic and, to a much less extent, from the Black Sea. The main current flows eastwards from the Gibraltar strait along the Algerian coast; part of it then flows in a generally counter-clockwise circulation around the western basin, with local circulations around the islands. The remainder of the mainstream continues eastwards through the Sicilian channel to the east basin. From here a current flows generally east-south-east to the Nile delta, with some diversion into the Gulf of Sirte where there is a clockwise circulation. From the Nile delta a weak coastal current continues generally counter-clockwise, passing north of Cyprus and along the south coast of Turkey to the Rhodes channel. Within the Aegean there can be a northerly flow from Rhodes along the Turkish west coast, but generally there is a southerly flow due to the inflow from the Black Sea. The Black Sea itself has counter-clockwise flows on either side of the Crimean peninsula. Within the Adriatic there is a generally counter-clockwise circulation (*Mediterranean Pilot*, 5, 1988: map 1.132). In the summer sailing season these currents average 1 knot or less, except where they are channelled or otherwise constrained, and therefore accelerated, by the configuration of the coast or the seabed: for example, the Strait of Messina, the Sicilian channel, and the Strait of Bonifacio between Corsica and Sardinia.

## 4.2.2  TIDAL FLOWS AND TIDES

In general terms, the Mediterranean is a near-tideless sea. However, in addition to Gibraltar, there are three regions where restrictive channels cause appreciable tidal effects. The Strait of Messina, between the Italian mainland and Sicily, connects the Ionian and Tyrrhenian Seas and tidal effects are mainly experienced within a 3 nautical mile length of channel. Tides ebb and flow at up to 4.5 knots and there are tide rips and races; the seas are further disturbed by winds funnelled by the mountains. At certain times there can be a tidal bore (*taglio*) reaching 1.5 m in height. These phenomena—which were more pronounced before natural changes in the seabed in the nineteenth century—may well have led to the legend of Scylla and Charybdis. In the Strait of Evripou, between the island of *Evvoia* (Euboea) and the Greek mainland, tidal streams at springs can reach 8 knots (*Mediterranean Pilot*, 4, 1987:

355). Diodorus Siculus (book 13: ch. 47) noted that, in 410 BC, tidal flows became very strong when a causeway was built which seriously restricted the channel.

There are also significant tides (range greater than 1 m) at the head of the Adriatic, and in the Gulf of Gabes (Lesser Sirtes). Elsewhere in the Mediterranean, tidal streams are insignificant. Moreover, the tidal range is very small, generally in the region of 0.3 m (1 ft) or less, although in the Aegean, for example, the maximum range is 0.8 m (2.5 ft). Meteorological conditions, especially the wind, often have a greater effect on sea levels, especially on lee shores.

## 4.2.3  WEATHER

The climate of this region is so distinctive that the term 'Mediterranean' is applied to similar areas in other parts of the world. This is one of the most favoured climates: summers are long, hot, and fine, with little rain; winters are usually short and mild. From the seaman's viewpoint the summer, with its long daylight hours, also has welcome characteristics, the main problem being the relatively high number (up to 20 per cent) of days with little or no wind. The winter, however, can be a dangerous time for, in addition to offshore local gale-force winds such as the Bora (see below), there are many occasions when outbreaks of cold air from between north-west and north-east penetrate the region, resulting in very boisterous conditions and considerable seas, with severe squalls and thunderstorms which may develop rapidly with little warning (*Mediterranean Pilot*, 5, 1988: 17). There are also significant differences in cloud cover between summer and winter, with averages of ⅛–⅜ compared with ⅘–⅝. Thus in winter there is a much greater probability of the night sky being obscured by cloud, making navigation by the stars impossible (4.4.6). Furthermore, greater precipitation—most of the rain falls in the winter—and more frequent storms, with their reduced visibility, and changing wind directions, make it more difficult to use the other environmental aids to navigation. Reduced visibility also increases the problems of pilotage in coastal waters, making shipwreck more likely. Vegetius (*Res Mil.* 4. 39) described the winters of his day (fourth century AD) as having dense cloud cover, poor visibility, and violent winds.

There was some winter sailing in the Classical world, mainly in connection with wars or when shortages forced the unseasonal import of grain, but it did not become a regular feature of the Mediterranean until the sixteenth century AD: in earlier times summer was *the* sailing season. The Greek poet, Hesiod, of *c*.700 BC, admittedly a landlubber, advised restricting seagoing to fifty days in July and August (*Works and Days*, 663–5). Vegetius (*Res Mil.* 4. 39) gave what is probably a more realistic picture: June to mid-September was considered safe; mid-March to the end of May, and mid-September to mid-November were risky periods; and from mid-November to mid-March was the period known as *mare clausum*, 'the seas are closed'. Thus, although the end of May to mid-September was considered to be the most suitable season, the conditions prevailing from mid-April to mid-October were those regularly faced by early Mediterranean seamen. In general this period of about six months, 'an extended summer', had clear skies, moderate winds, and slight seas, but in late spring and early autumn storms were much more likely, and even in high summer, occasional strong winds could raise a short, choppy sea.

## 4.2.3.1 SUMMER WINDS

During the main summer months, June to August, the winds in the Mediterranean east of 20°E are almost entirely in the quadrant between west and north, with the predominant wind being from the north-west (60 per cent). In the Aegean, the winds are mostly from the sector north-west to north-east with north predominating (35 per cent). In the Gulf of Sirte (30–35 per cent) and in the vicinity of Sicily (25 per cent), winds from the north and north-west are of equal frequency. The Adriatic has a predominant north-west wind, but also a significant proportion from the south-east. The north-west wind also predominates in the Tyrrhenian Sea (30 per cent), as it does in the Sicilian Channel (30 per cent), but with a 15 per cent chance of a west wind. Along the north coast of Africa, west of Cape Bon, west or east winds blow with about the same frequency (15–25 per cent), with a 20 per cent chance of a north-east wind. Around Corsica, west winds predominate at 25 per cent, with north-west at 20 per cent. Whilst in the Gulf of Lyon, winds are more evenly distributed with 60 per cent being in the sector south-east through south to

north-west (Hodge, 1983). West of the Strait of Gibraltar the predominant wind is north (30 per cent), with north-west at 25 per cent (*Mediterranean Pilot*, 5, 1988: fig. 1.151.3).

From these figures it can be seen that, in the east basin and much of the west, the winds are predominantly in the sector between north and west; this predominance decreases, more or less steadily, from a high of 90 per cent in the eastern Mediterranean to *c*.45 per cent in the western basin and *c*.25 per cent near Gibraltar. Summer winds are, and were, highly predictable in the eastern Mediterranean and Aegean—hence the name *Etesian* wind, the 'annual' wind. In this respect it may be thought of as a 'monsoon' wind, from between north-west and north-east in the Aegean, and between west and north in the eastern Mediterranean. The situation is more variable in the western basin: for example, west of Cape Bon, the chances of there being a wind from the sector east-north-east (34 per cent) are very similar to the chances of a wind from west–north-west (33 per cent). This means that, in an *average* summer week, for a ship which could make good a track at right angles to the wind, the wind in these western coastal waters would be fair for a westbound voyage for three days, and fair for an eastbound voyage also for three days, with one day of light, variable winds or calms. A similar ship, bound for Gibraltar from a position east of Sicily, would have a 42–63 per cent chance of fair wind if the Master chose a passage through the Sicilian channel and along the North African coast, but only a 30–44 per cent chance on the route through the Strait of Messina and via Sardinia and the Balearics. The wind is, how-ever, only one of several variables that have to be evaluated when choosing a route—currents, possibility of storms, visibility, sources of fresh water, ports of trade, the Master's knowledge of alternative routes, and so on, have all to be taken into account. In summer, the adverse effects of some of these factors are minimal; nevertheless, they need to be assessed.

## 4.2.3.2 WINDS IN LATE SPRING AND EARLY AUTUMN

In late April and May, and in September and early October, in the pre-summer and post-summer parts of the sailing season, the winds are somewhat different from those in high summer. In late Spring there is more risk of gale-force winds and there is more variability in wind direction. In particular, the north-west wind is not so prominent in the eastern basin and there can be, for example, calms in Turkish waters in these transitional seasons. In the Aegean there is a 55 per cent (spring), as against an 85 per cent (summer), probability of a wind between north and west, and the probability of a wind from south-east/south-west is 20 per cent (spring) rather than 2 per cent (summer). Thus there were more opportunities for sailing northwards in the Aegean in this early part of the sailing season. There are comparable changes east of 20°E. In late spring the probability of a wind from between northeast and south-east is 30–5 per cent, compared with c.6 per cent in high summer. There was thus a greater probability of a fair wind for a westerly voyage from the Levant in late spring than in summer.

In early autumn, towards the end of the sailing season, there is also more variability, again with the northwest wind not so prominent. This is especially so in the northern parts of the western basin where winds from any quarter may be expected; whilst, further south, along the African coast, east and west winds are equally likely. In the Adriatic, the chances of a wind in the sector between north and west in October are 35 per cent compared with 53 per cent in summer. In the eastern seas, east of 20°E, a north or north-east wind is more likely than one from the north-west. Whilst in the Aegean, there is an increase in the frequency of north-east winds at the expense of north and, particularly, north-west winds. Throughout the Mediterranean in this September–October period there is a greater risk of gales than in summer.

### 4.2.3.3 THE INFLUENCE OF PREDOMINANT WINDS ON THE CHOICE OF ROUTE

There are two main conclusions about open-sea ship operations which emerge from this summary of the distribution of wind directions in the twentieth-century Mediterranean, which, for reasons given above, seem likely to be similar to those of the ancient world. These conclusions are most readily formulated in relation to sailing ships which could make good a track at right angles to the wind.

- In the Aegean and the eastern Mediterranean in the summer months, the Etesian/Meltemi wind is, and was, so overwhelmingly predominant that there was little point in waiting for a fair wind for voyages on headings from west through north to east in the Aegean, and for headings from south-west through north to north-east in the eastern Mediterranean. Alternative routes had to be found; land and sea breezes (4.2.3.4) or other local meteorological phenomena could be used when and where they overwhelmed the Etesian wind; or voyages could be attempted earlier or later in the year.

- Outside this region, and in the pre- and post-summer months in the eastern Mediterranean, there was generally sufficient variability in the wind direction over a period of two or three weeks for voyages in many, but not all, directions to be attempted, providing that the Master was prepared to heave-to, or remain in harbour, during periods of foul winds. Generally speaking, the delays encountered in late spring and early autumn were significantly shorter than in summer.

### 4.2.3.4 COASTAL WINDS

In coastal waters the winds over the open sea, discussed above, are modified by the local topography and by thermal effects due to differential heating of the land and sea. In the Aegean, for example, the mountainous character of the land, the many islands, and the complex coastal configuration deflect, funnel, and change the speed of the wind; there are comparable effects in such channels as the Straits of Messina and of Gibraltar. Local knowledge is required in these waters.

In addition to these local winds there are regional winds which occur in particular meteorological conditions in coastal waters where the hinterland has certain topographical characteristics. The *mistral* of the Gulf of Lyon, the *bora* of the northern Adriatic, and the *vardarac* of the north-west Aegean are north-west to north-east winds which flow from cold mountainous regions down to the coast, due to the pressure gradient and to the katabatic (downsinking) tendency of cold, relatively heavy, air. Funnelling effects in the valleys further accelerate these winds towards coastal waters. Such winds can set in suddenly and may reach gale force; they mainly occur in the winter, but can also appear in the late spring and in the autumn.

In North African coastal waters, the *scirocco* in the west, the *ghibli* in the central section, and the *khamsin* in the east are warm, south, and south-east winds from the North African Desert. Such winds may reach force 6–8 on the Beaufort scale, and they raise quantities of sand and dust which seriously effect visibility in coastal waters: they also have a depressing effect on human beings. As these very dry winds pass over the sea they absorb moisture, bringing fog to northern coastal waters, from Gibraltar to the Adriatic and Aegean. A similar wind can blow from the Arabian Desert north-west across the coastal waters of the Levant. The most severe of these winds seldom, if ever, occur in the summer, but they are encountered in the autumn and in late spring (*Mediterranean Pilot*, 5, 1988: 18, fig. 1.151.5).

Land and sea breezes are a marked feature of Mediterranean coastal waters, particularly in the summer, although they can occur in quiet periods in other seasons. As the land quickly warms up in the morning, air begins to flow from the sea towards the land. This sea breeze generally lasts from the late forenoon to shortly before sunset and can reach force 5 or 6 in favourable situations. The effects can be felt out to 20 nautical miles and more from the land. Conversely, as the land cools relatively quickly after sunset, a lighter breeze blows from the land to the sea. This land breeze is usable from the early hours of the morning until mid-forenoon, out to *c.*5 nautical miles. When there is little or no regional wind blowing, land and sea breezes predominate; otherwise, these breezes modify coastal winds.

Local topographical effects can influence wind velocities at all times of the year. In general they make coastal passages and approaches to, and departures from, harbours more difficult, and local knowledge is required. Regional winds, such as the *mistral* and the *scirocco*, bring gales and poor visibility to coastal waters: they seldom occur in high summer, however, but can be troublesome in the late spring and early autumnal periods of the sailing season. Unlike other winds in coastal waters, land and sea breezes are generally beneficial. They can modify or, indeed, overwhelm regional winds, enabling vessels to leave and enter harbour under sail, and to steer courses in coastal waters which otherwise could not be attempted.

# 4.3
# Overseas Passages

## 4.3.1 ALONG THE LENGTH OF THE MEDITERRANEAN

### 4.3.1.1 NORTHERN ROUTES

The northern shores of the Mediterranean generally have a high coastal profile with mountain ranges or distinctive peaks not far inland; this means that land can be sighted from well out to sea—a distinct aid to navigation. The indented coastline, with relatively deep water close inshore, includes many natural havens with sheltered landing places, and in the sailing season, when the predominant wind is in the northern sector, this is generally a windward shore, although the northern coasts of islands such as Crete and Sicily are lee shores. Furthermore, there are several large islands off this coast which are visible from a boat before sight is lost of the mainland: Cyprus, Rhodes, the Aegean islands, Crete, Sicily, Sardinia, Corsica, and the Balearics. These can be a valuable aid to position fixing (4.4.6), as well as providing shelter when needed, and a supply of fresh water.

The southern shores do not have these advantages (see below). The northern shores were thus more friendly to seafarers; this great advantage, and the fact that the European hinterland had greater economic potential, meant that, where there was a choice, northern, rather than southern, routes were preferred for east–west voyages. On this northern route eastward voyages, generally speaking, had a fair wind in the open sea, but an adverse current, albeit slight. Voyages to the west had a favourable current, but generally foul winds, especially in the eastern basin; a fair wind was more likely early and late in the season. Summer voyages to the west would have been lengthy: using land and sea breezes in coastal waters when they were favourable, remaining hove-to or in harbour when not. Should a fair wind arise offshore—there was more chance of this in the western basin—vessels could use any land breeze to open out from the coast into the region of fair winds. Although this coast was generally not a lee shore, its convoluted configuration meant that there were other hazards to be overcome, especially near headlands. For example, at Cape Malea, the southernmost point of Greece, the westward flowing current could be reinforced by a north-east wind making eastward passages impossible at times—the Corcyrans (Corfu) claimed that conditions such as these prevented their fleet joining the Greeks before the battle of Salamis (Herodotus, 7. 168). Furthermore, the high ground in the hinterland to the north could deflect and intensify the wind, creating a disturbed sea, making even westward passages difficult. Jason is said to have encountered strong northerly winds off Cape Malea, when attempting to sail round the Peloponnese, and was blown to Libya (Herodotus, 4. 179); Aeneas was similarly driven from Cape Malea to the North African shores during a storm (Aeneid, 1. 150). An alternative to sailing around the Peloponnese was a portage across the 6 km isthmus of Corinth. This route was used not only for pack-animal transports between the Aegean and Ionian Seas, but also, from at least the fifth century BC, for the transport of vessels along a stone causeway known as the *dialkos*, across this isthmus (Werner, 1997).

There are also several straits in northern coastal waters: the Dardanelles/Hellespont and the Bosporus between the Aegean and the Black Sea; the Rhodes channel; the channel between *Evvoia* (Euboia) and the Greek mainland; straits east and west of Crete; the Otranto channel between Greece and Italy; the Strait of Messina; and the Bonifacio strait between Sardinia and Corsica. Passage through these depended on the relative velocities of wind and current, on the state of the sea and, in some cases (notably *Evvoia* and Messina—see Strabo, 1. 3. 11) on tidal flows. In foul winds, ships waited in a nearby haven: such delays were especially long at the entrance to the Dardanelles where the predominant wind, from the north-east, reinforced the constantly flowing south-west current from the Black Sea (Neumann, 1991). These problems are not so great in the wider straits (e.g. Otranto), as the funnelling effect is less, and there can also be sufficient searoom to tack. Moreover, even in narrow straits, such as the Dardanelles and the Bosporus, these are usually favourable, though weaker, counter-currents away from the main stream.

### 4.3.1.2 SOUTHERN ROUTES

The southern coast of the Mediterranean was not only a lee shore, often with a heavy swell induced by the pre-

dominant wind, but it was also generally low-lying, especially in the eastern basin, and, in many places, there were reefs and shoals offshore. Havens were few and far between on the African mainland, and islands were rare: only Pharos, west of the Nile; Kerkennah and Djerba in the Gulf of Sirte; and Malta, Gozo, Pantelleria, and Lampedusa in the Sicilian channel.

Open-sea voyages in the summer, eastwards along the southern routes, had a favourable current from Gibraltar to the Nile and a generally fair wind, though with an onshore component which was particularly significant around Tunisia, the Gulf of Sirte and further east. The passage through the Sicilian strait was difficult: a lee shore to the south, the wind funnelled by mountains, and shoals and reefs in the offing. The *Mediterranean Pilot*, 1: 27 (1873) advises staying 'a good distance from shore'. South and south-east of this strait lies the Gulf of Sirte with its low-lying coast, shoal water, and drying sandbanks: vessels can easily be driven towards these hazards. Further east, the Nile delta was difficult to identify from seaward, except by its distinctive outflow and possibly in relation to the island of Pharos (2.11.1). A passage westwards had the added disadvantages that it was against the current, and also generally against the wind: only west of Cape Bon was there a reasonable chance of easterlies. The passage northwestwards through the Sicilian strait was especially difficult, often impossible, as it was against the predominant wind, and the foul current could at times reach 2–4 knots.

### 4.3.2 ACROSS THE MEDITERRANEAN

In addition to coastal routes at the eastern and western ends, the Mediterranean could be crossed from Sicily via islands to Tunis: in good weather, high ground, ahead or astern, is in sight the whole time. Cape Bon (ancient Cape Hermes) was a particularly notable landmark. Summer crossings of the Sicilian channel, on a generally south-west or north-east heading, could be either from and to south-west Sicily at the shortest crossing, or further east. Such crossings could only be attempted, generally speaking, in ships capable of making good a track at right angles to the wind. In late spring and in early autumn there was a better chance, though not a great one, of having a wind from the stern sector. This 70 nautical miles of open sea would have taken a minimum of a long-day's sail, but, in poor visibility, such a voyage would have been lengthened from the afternoon of one day to around noon on the next, so that landfall would be in daylight. Crossings may have been broken by calls at the Maltese islands, at Lampedusa, or Kerkennah, all of which are to leeward, or possibly at Pantelleria which is close to the shortest crossing. The four leeward islands may well have been regarded as a safety net, needed when winds, currents, or leeway proved greater than anticipated.

From Crete it is some 150–180 nautical miles, on a south–south-east heading, to the African coast—say, two days' sail with the wind on the starboard beam or quarter. Such a voyage is feasible. A direct return voyage was probably impossible if the departure point were east of Bay Al Bumbah, since the 'standard' ship used to evaluate these routes could not maintain a track closer to north than north-east: thus the eastern point of Crete would be left to port.

A voyage from Crete to Libya could have been one leg of a counter-clockwise route around the eastern Mediterranean: eastwards along, but well clear of, the African coast to the Nile, with the current and with a fair wind on the port quarter; then northwards along the Levant coast, again with the current (averaging ¼–½ knot), and using land and sea breezes on the beam to track northwards, more or less parallel to the coast. Extensive narrow ledges of rock lie offshore, roughly parallel to its general direction; these would have been more visible in earlier times. To make one of the Levantine landing places for trade or merely for fresh water, it would have been necessary to pass through gaps in these ledges, using a sea breeze. The morning land breeze could have been used to leave harbour. Land and sea breezes would have again been used along the south coast of Turkey—a slow and difficult voyage—followed by a faster reach across the wind from Rhodes to Crete.

From the south coast of Turkey or the northern Levant it was possible to sail direct to the Libyan coast, with the predominant wind on the starboard beam: this would have been the most southerly open-sea route. An alternative route was described by Odysseus who told Eumaeus how he had sailed from the Levant in a Phoenician ship bound for Libya (*Odyssey*, 14: 300–5). In a northerly wind they 'took the central route and ran down the lee-side [i.e. the southern side] of Crete'. The implied northerly route would have been

along the south coast of Asia Minor to Rhodes, then Crete.

Odysseus (Rieu, 1946: 228) also noted that the voyage from Crete to Egypt took four days and nights (though some say three—Strabo, 10. 4. 5). This would have probably been with the north-west wind fine on the starboard quarter. A return direct to Crete was impossible in summer unless the vessel could tack— even then it would have been a lengthy affair—as the track was almost directly into the predominant wind. In late spring, however, there was a 30 per cent chance of a fair wind for the direct voyage. The alternative in summer, and probably also in late spring if the vessel could not tack, was the counter-clockwise coastal route.

## 4.4
## Exploration and Navigation

### 4.4.1 AN EARLY CROSSING OF THE STRAIT OF GIBRALTAR?

Bones and what are thought to be stone tools excavated near Orce in Andalusia raise the possibility that humans were in southern Spain in the Early Pleistocene *c*.1,500,000 years ago (Roe, 1995). Since it is generally agreed that humans (and their hominid predecessors) originated in sub-Saharan Africa, there are two possible routes they may have taken to southern Europe: a long route, by the ridge between Cape Bon in Tunisia and Sicily which may have been above sea level in those days (or even further east via the Levant); or a short crossing via what is now the Strait of Gibraltar (ancient *Fretum Herculeum*) where, even at lowest sea levels it is thought that there would have been a channel 4–6 nautical miles (7–11 km) wide (Clark and Piggott, 1976: 41; van Andel, 1989: 737). Technological affinities between Lower Palaeolithic stone tools in Spain and southern France, and those in northwest Africa, and the presence of African elements in the Early Pleistocene fauna of southern Spain (Roe, 1980: 77; Roe, 1995: 11), suggest that the Strait of Gibraltar was probably the point of entry into Europe.

Crossing the Strait over one million years ago, or indeed any time before the Late Palaeolithic, raises a number of questions. At such an early date, theory suggests that log floats were the only form of water transport technologically possible (Table 1.2). With much lower sea levels in those times, it is not possible to speculate whether currents could have been relied upon to transport groups of humans across the Strait. Swimming (possibly float-assisted) remains an alternative, but whether Man could swim at this time is unknown (Johnstone, 1988: 3–4).

### 4.4.2 EARLY KNOWLEDGE OF OFFSHORE ISLANDS

The Rock of Gibraltar (ancient *Calpe*) with a present-day height above sea level of *c*.425 m can readily be seen from Almina Point near Ceuta in Morocco. It is not possible to see across the full breadth of the Mediterranean elsewhere. However, high ground in the coastal regions on the northern shores, and the many off-shore islands, from the Balearics in the west to Cyprus in the east, mean that land is in sight from sea level in much of the Mediterranean (Fig. 4.2). On days with good visibility a boat on the northern route

could sail the length of the Mediterranean without losing sight of land. Furthermore, the Mediterranean could be crossed by a boat which remained in sight of land, not only at the Strait, but also from the 'toe' of Italy via Sicily to the Cape Bon peninsula. This means that much of the Mediterranean coastal lands and islands were accessible by boat using pilotage methods rather than the more complex techniques needed when out of sight of land (4.4.6).

Rafts and boats were no doubt used on lakes and rivers from early times but there is no direct evidence for this. The earliest coastal voyages may also be archaeologically invisible since, although excavated evidence may suggest overseas 'trade', the use of land routes cannot be ruled out. On the other hand, islands which were surrounded by water even at times of lower sea level must have been explored and colonized by sea.

Table 4.1 gives the theoretical distances at which high ground can be seen from sea level, data which is the basis for the visibility map in Fig. 4.2. Similar methods can be used to estimate whether islands can be seen from the mainland or from another island (see e.g. 9.1). From such calculations it seems likely that, during the early days of seafaring, most if not all, Mediterranean islands would have been visible from the mainland,

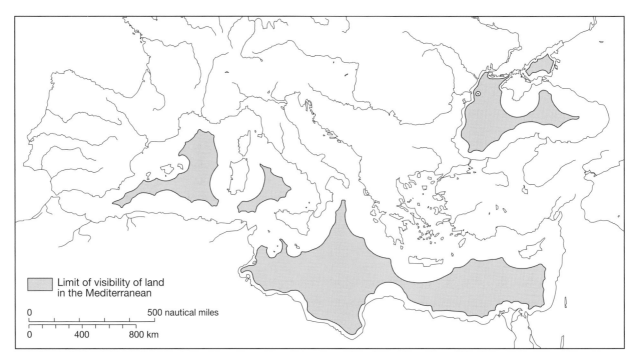

Fig. 4.2. Visibility from sea level in the Mediterranean (after Henkel, 1900: fig. 1).

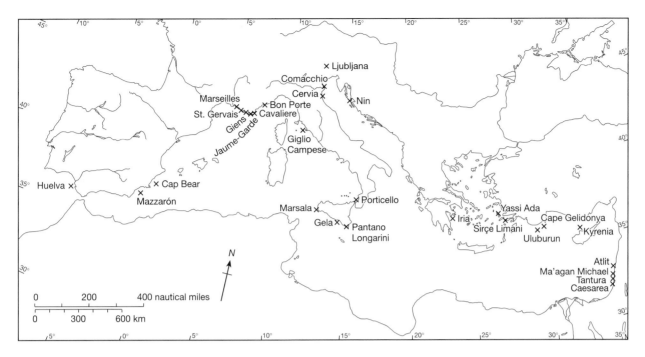

Fig. 4.3. Map of the Mediterranean showing sites.

from another island nearer the mainland, or from a boat which had not yet lost visual contact with already known land. Thus there would have been no necessity to rely on the flight path of migrating land birds, unplanned drift voyages, or other means that had to be used over greater distances in Oceania, for indications of land beyond the horizon: all islands in the Mediterranean were within the ideal horizon when viewed from some part of the European, Asian, or African mainland, or from a boat still within visual range of the mainland.

**Table 4.1** Visibility distances from sea level

| Height of land | Distance (nautical miles) |
| --- | --- |
| 100 ft/30 m | 11.5 |
| 200 ft/61 m | 16.2 |
| 500 ft/152 m | 25.7 |
| 1000 ft/305 m | 36.3 |

*Notes*: In meteorological conditions of refraction, high ground may be seen at more than the theoretical distance. In poor visibility the distance is much less. An approximation is given by: D. (nautical miles) $\simeq$ 1.1 $\sqrt{}$Ht. (ft); D. (km.) $\simeq$3.8 $\sqrt{}$Ht. (m).

*Source: Inman's Nautical Tables, 1920: 12.*

### 4.4.3 MESOLITHIC OVERSEAS EXPLORATION

The earliest evidence for overseas voyages in the Mediterranean comes from the Peloponnes/Melos region in the western Aegean: Melos was undoubtedly an island even at times of lower sea levels (van Andel, 1989). Tools of the volcanic glass obsidian, quarried in Melos, have been excavated from the Franchthi cave in southern Greece, in contexts dated to the tenth millennium BC (Perlès, 1979; Bass, 1980: 137; Renfrew, 1998: 255). This shipment of obsidian would have involved a sea crossing of some 50 nautical miles (93 km) if the direct route were taken, but an indirect route through the western Cycladic islands seems more likely. Such a voyage would have been undertaken over a period of days, with distances between islands being 15 nautical miles (28 km) or less (van Andel, 1989)—see the route taken by Tzalas (1995*b*) on his experimental voyage (4.5.3). Cyprus may also have been explored, or even settled, during the ninth millennium BC (Bass, 1997: 269; Broodbank and Strasser, 1991: 238). Similar early prospecting/exploratory voyages may have been undertaken elsewhere in the Mediterranean leaving little evidence for short stays on islands visited: for example, Crete (Renfrew, 1998: 255).

### 4.4.4   NEOLITHIC SETTLEMENT OF ISLANDS

Many Mediterranean islands were first colonized during Neolithic times, from *c.*7000 BC onwards. Such voyages, or subsequent ones, must have included the carriage of domestic animals and seed corn, as well as sufficient people to form a viable founder population, and water for crew and animals. The earliest settlements seem to have been in the eastern Mediterranean: Cyprus in the ninth millennium BC (Cherry, 1990) with an open-sea crossing at that time of *c.*40 nautical miles (74 km) (van Andel, 1989); Crete, in the seventh millennium BC (Cherry, 1990) with a longest passage of *c.*25 nautical miles (46 km) if from Anatolia via Rhodes, Karpathos, and Kasos (the most likely route—Renfrew, 1998: 255), or *c.*15 nautical miles (28 km) if from the Peloponnese via Kythera and Antikythera. In the central Mediterranean, Sardinia and Corsica (a longest passage of *c.*15 nautical miles: 28 km) were colonized, probably via the Tuscan archipelago in the seventh millennium BC, as was Malta (*c.*35 nautical miles: 65 km) (Perlès, 1979; Calcagno, 1997). The distribution in the central Mediterranean of obsidian from Pantelleria, and Lipari, testifies to voyages to these islands and to Malta and Lampedusa in the early Neolithic (Cherry, 1990; Calcagno, 1997: 48, 64, maps iv.1 and iv.2). In the western Mediterranean the Balearics were first settled in the sixth millennium BC (Martinez *et al.*, 1997: 57–8): a maximum passage of *c.*45 nautical miles (83 km).

### 4.4.5   EARLY VOYAGES

The islands which were the destinations of these early voyages could all be seen, in conditions of good visibility, from a high point on the European continent, or from another island en route: their existence and their relative position would thus be known before an exploratory voyage. These voyages were across sea from which, on a good day, land could be seen, either astern or ahead, throughout the passage: pilotage methods, generally speaking, could therefore be used.

At the time of these voyages—to Melos, and possibly Cyprus, and the Ionian island of Kefallinia, in the Mesolithic, the majority during the Neolithic—sail is most unlikely to have been used, even in the eastern Mediterranean (4.7.2.1). Thus these early craft must have been propelled by paddles, or possibly by oars. Over a long day, in a fair wind and disregarding currents, paddled vessels might be expected to average 1–2 knots (Tzalas, 1995*a*). In a planked boat, under oars, 3–4 knots with the wind (Duff, 1998) or 1–1.5 knots against a moderate wind (Englert *et al.*, 1998: 20) might be expected (less in other craft), provided that the crew could be rotated at intervals so that some could rest.

The longest open-sea legs on these early voyages at times of somewhat lower sea levels (van Andel, 1989: fig. 3B) ranged from 15 (Melos, Sardinia, and Corsica) to 45 nautical miles (Balearics). In Mediterranean latitudes at midsummer there are around 14½ hours of daylight, and 15½ hours between morning and evening twilight. Thus, in optimum conditions, all the voyages described above could have been undertaken by oared craft within daylight hours. Using paddles, however, only voyages to Melos, Crete, Sardinia, and Corsica could have been achieved in daylight, although Malta may have been possible using both periods of twilight.

In other conditions, however (with an adverse wind or current, crew, or boat underperforming; at seasons other than midsummer; or when poor visibility made direction-holding difficult), one day's daylight hours would have been insufficient for the longer voyages—Malta, Cyprus, and the Balearics. Days when the moon could be expected to shine during the evening hours might have been chosen. However, the risk of failure due to poor day visibility, adverse environmental conditions, underperformance, or to cloud obscuring the moon, or a requirement to make such journeys outside the midsummer period, may well have led to the use of elementary navigational techniques, even in this early period. At the very least, these Neolithic seamen would probably have been able to get their directions from the pole star or with less accuracy, from the wind or the swell. As in the settlement of Greater Australia (7.2), this early navigation was more than pilotage.

### 4.4.6   EARLY NAVIGATIONAL TECHNIQUES

Throughout the world, as demonstrated in other chapters of this book, from the earliest times that there is evidence until well into the medieval period, seamen used non-instrumental navigational techniques, based on inherited traditions, personal experience, and detailed observation of natural phenomena (McGrail, 1998: 275–6). Many of these practices are still used today, in the Indian Ocean for example. The only seagoing navigational aid known anywhere in the world before the ninth century AD is the sounding lead and its near relative, the sounding pole (2.1, 2.3, 2.7.6). The lead not only recorded the depth of water but also gave an indication of position from the nature of the sample of seabed recovered. Many leads have been found in inshore waters in the Mediterranean (Kapitän, 1969–71; Oleson, 1988; Grossmann, 1994), the oldest being that excavated from the Gela wreck of the late sixth / early fifth centuries BC (Oleson, 1994; Parker, 1992: 188–9).

Homer's *Odyssey* contains a number of direct references, and many allusions to the navigational practices of his day (McGrail, 1996a). Although Herodotus (2. 53) believed that Homer lived 'not more than 400 years ago', i.e. the late ninth century BC, the version of the Homeric epics that has come down to us was probably written in the early seventh century (Osborne, 1996: 156–60). This saga is, however, the product of a long tradition and it is conceivable that the seafaring elements in the *Odyssey* reflect centuries-old practices. It is clear from many sections of the narrative that, although Odysseus had no sea chart as map, he had a 'mental chart' in his head, giving him the spatial relationships of the coastal lands and the islands of the eastern Mediterranean from the Ionian Sea to the shores of the Levant, Egypt, and Libya. From other passages in the *Odyssey*, a picture can be built up of the non-instrumental methods used at that time.

### 4.4.6.1 DIRECTIONS

When sailing away from Calypso's island, Odysseus kept the Great Bear (Ursa Major) on his port side (*Odyssey*, 5. 270–5). This constellation appears to rotate about the celestial North Pole (the heavenly null point) in a relatively tight circle so it is one of the few star groups which, in Mediterranean latitudes, does not sink below the horizon. The pointers of the Great Bear indicated the position of the Pole, providing Odysseus with a fixed direction from which other bearings could be gauged. Thus if Odysseus kept the Pole on his port

beam he would, in our terms, be steering due east; if just forward of the port beam, north–north-east; if on the port bow, north-east; and so on, around the horizon.

Odysseus also monitored the rising and setting of constellations such as Orion and the Pleiades, and prominent stars such as Arcturus (*Odyssey*, 5.270–5). This suggests that he had a detailed knowledge of the movements of the heavenly bodies, and could use this information to assist his direction keeping.

In addition to this star 'compass', Odysseus also used a wind 'compass'. He knew that winds from different quarters could be recognized by their physical characteristics: a wet wind was from the west; a cold wind from the north; and a hot dry wind from the south (*Odyssey*, 12. 285–90; 14. 455–60, 476–80). Once such a wind had been identified, Odysseus had another fixed direction, at least for as long as that wind continued to

Fig. 4.4. An eighteenth-century engraving of the first century BC Tower of the Winds, Athens (Aegean Maritime Museum).

blow, and he could visualize other bearings in relation to it. Eight elements of such a wind compass could be seen on the first century BC Tower of the Winds in Athens (Fig. 4.4).

### 4.4.6.2 DISTANCES

As in many other maritime cultures Greek seamen in Odysseus' time measured distances at sea in units of a 'day's sail'. For example, Menelaus tells Telemachus that it is a day's sail from the Nile to Pharos island 'for a well-found vessel in a fair wind' (*Odyssey*, 4. 355–60). We can deduce from this, and other examples, that the unit, one day's sail, was the average distance traversed by the usual sort of ship in fair wind and sea conditions, in a twenty-four hour period in the summer sailing season. Equivalent to this standard distance must have been a standard speed. On a particular voyage, any deviations from the standard conditions—adverse winds, a faster than average ship, and so on—would have been reflected in the speed actually achieved: thus distances actually traversed in any one day could have been estimated by Odysseus as greater or less than the standard distance. The passage of time during the night was marked by certain stars reaching their zenith (Taylor, 1971: 48).

### 4.4.6.3 NAVIGATION ON EXPLORATORY AND SETTLEMENT VOYAGES

When in the open sea, Odysseus would have used all the environmentally based methods outlined above to determine the direction he had sailed since last leaving land. When this was combined with his estimates of speeds achieved, and thus distance sailed, he would have been able to 'plot' his position on his 'mental chart'. We may conjecture that earlier seamen had comparable abilities.

On exploration and settlement voyages in the tenth to seventh millennia BC, pilotage methods would have been used for as long as land was in sight. In fair weather, with good visibility, at around midsummer, on these particular routes, land would have been in sight, astern or ahead, throughout the voyage. As experience was built up so voyages could be undertaken in worse conditions when land was not always in sight, provid-

ing that environmental clues had been noted, as seems likely, during the earlier voyages, so that the techniques of 'plotting' directions and distances on a mental chart could be used. Once such non-standard voyages could be undertaken with confidence it is conceivable that night-time voyages with clear skies might be preferred, since keeping directions by the star nearest the celestial Pole (in Odysseus' time this was Kochab and not Polaris—Taylor, 1971: 9–12, 43) would generally have been more accurate and less demanding than using the wind compass, or even a swell or a sun compass (McGrail, 1983b). Such nocturnal voyages would have had to be timed so that dawn broke before the hour that a landfall was expected to be made.

Signs of land over the horizon include: orographic cloud rising over distant land; colour changes in the water; land birds flying out to sea or back to the land. Once in sight of land, Odysseus identified natural landmarks such as Pharos island west of the River Nile or Psyria island when crossing the Aegean. We also learn from Homer that artificial landmarks were sometimes built. For example, the bones of Achilles, Menoetius, and Antilochus were buried under a mound on a foreland where 'it might be seen far out to sea by the sailors of today and future ages'.

## 4.5
# Water Transport before the Bronze Age (before *c.*3800 BC)

Theoretical studies suggest that by Mesolithic times in the Mediterranean, the following craft could have been built and used at sea (Table 1.2): complex log rafts; buoyed rafts; bundle rafts; complex hide boats; and basket boats. Although basket boats were used in Mesopotamia, there is no early evidence or surviving tradition of their use in the Mediterranean, despite bitumen being accessible in Greece. There is evidence for the other four types of craft, but there are no excavated examples: the evidence is literary or iconographic, and none is early.

### 4.5.1 LOG RAFTS

The earliest reference to seagoing log rafts is in the late sixth century BC when Hiram of Tyre sent cedar and juniper logs towed by sea to Solomon (1 Kings 5: 23). In 316 BC, log rafts were used to transport elephants across the Saronic Gulf from Megara to Epidaurus (Diodorus, 19. 54. 3). The sea-goddess, Isis Pelagia, is portrayed on board what seems to be a log raft on a fourth-century AD coin (Fig. 4.5).

Fig. 4.5. A fourth-century AD engraving of a Contorniate coin with a sea-goddess on what may be a log raft (after Evans, 1935: fig. 148).

### 4.5.2 BUOYED RAFTS

Elephants were also transported on buoyed rafts, made buoyant by sealed pots, in 252 BC from Calabria to Sicily (Pliny, *NH* 8. 16). The earliest depictions of these pot-float rafts are on a series of Etruscan gems dated to the sixth century BC (Fig. 4.6).

### 4.5.3 BUNDLE RAFTS

Bundle rafts were used from very early times in Egypt (3.4.3). In the Mediterranean region as defined here, there is both representational and ethnographic evidence. Incised on two stones in the megalithic temple at Hal Tarxien in Malta, are a number of figures which have been interpreted as forms of water transport (Woolmer, 1957). It is impossible to identify these depictions precisely, but some of them may depict bundle rafts: for example, Nos. 5 and 10 on Stone A (Woolmer, 1957: fig. 1). Basch (1987a: 395) dates these figures to c.2000 BC. The craft on a Minoan gold ring from Mochlos, Crete, and on a ring of similar date from Tiryns, Argolid, may also represent bundle rafts (Fig. 4.7). A graffito of Roman date excavated at Bet She'arim, Israel (Johnstone, 1988: fig. 6.4) has, like the Tiryns craft, vertical lines across the hull which are generally thought to represent bundle bindings. Johnstone (1988: 59, fig. 6.11) also considers that an engraving in the 'maison aux stucs' on Delos depicts a bundle raft because at one end there is 'a lashing around the end of the reed bundles': on the other hand, Basch (1987a: fig. 151) believes that it 'vraisemblablement une pirogue monoxyle'.

Fig. 4.7. A possible bundle raft depicted on a gold ring from Mochlos, Crete (after Evans, 1935: fig. 919).

During the twentieth century reed-bundle rafts were built and used in Corfu (Johnstone, 1988: 60), Sardinia (Brindley, 1931: 12–15), and in Morocco (Hornell, 1946a: 55). The Corfu rafts, which had a wooden framework, were used at sea to tend lobster pots, and in 1988, a reconstruction raft (Fig. 4.8) was paddled from Lavrion, south-east of Athens, to Melos via the western Cyclades, in an attempt to simulate a tenth-millennium voyage for obsidian (Tzalas, 1995b).

Fig. 4.6. Sixth-century BC Etruscan gems with Hercules on a raft buoyed by pots (after Casson, 1971: fig. 2).

Fig. 4.8. An experimental bundle raft under way in the Aegean (photo: Harry Tzalas).

### 4.5.4 HIDE BOATS

Lucan (*Pharsalia*, 4. 131–2) refers to the use of hide boats in the Po Valley, Italy, during Classical times. This seems to be the only evidence for their use in Mediterranean countries, although they are known to have been used in Arabia (3.4.5) and on the Iberian Atlantic coast (Strabo 3. 3. 7).

### 4.5.5 MESOLITHIC SEAGOING CRAFT

There is little evidence for the use of hide boats in the Mediterranean in ancient times or today. The evidence for the log raft and the float raft is more substantial and extends back to the third and fourth centuries BC: it is likely that they were used at sea for some considerable time before that.

The evidence for the bundle raft, although possibly extending back to *c*.2000 BC, is more tenuous since it depends on the interpretation of scribings and engravings, a notoriously imprecise task. Nevertheless there are several other considerations which point towards the bundle raft as the seagoing craft of the early Mediterranean. Both Egypt and Mesopotamia used them at an early date, although as far as is known, not on lengthy voyages. Before the days of sail, bundle rafts could have been much more handy, when paddled, than log or float rafts, since they could be fashioned more readily into a directionally stable and hydrodynamic shape. Some species of reed-like materials are better than others for seagoing voyages (McGrail, 1998: table 9.1, 169); nevertheless most types have been used in some part of the world, and these reeds/rushes/sedges/papyrus/palm grow wherever there are lakes or swampy valley floors, especially near river mouths or confluences. Suitable papyrus grows today in, for example, Sardinia, Corfu, and Morocco; and it is known to have been present at Delos in early times (Tzalas, 1995*b*: 443). The fact that bundle rafts are used today in marginal regions of the Mediterranean tends to support the view that there has been a long-standing indigenous tradition. With all these points in mind, it seems that, of the four possible types, the bundle raft is the most likely to have been the seafaring craft of the Mediterranean Mesolithic. The successful experimental voyage (Tzalas, 1995*b*) undertaken in 1988 in a bundle raft, similar to those used off Corfu earlier this century, does not by any means prove this hypothesis, but it does provide substantial support.

Although large bundle rafts have been built in recent times (see e.g. Heyerdahl, 1972) one similar in size to Tzalas's double-ended reconstruction (5.48 × 1.50 × 0.50 m) would seem more appropriate for the Mesolithic. This raft had a crew of four paddlers and one steersman. A major problem with bundle rafts (not discussed by Tzalas) is their susceptibility to waterlogging. Decay and waterlogging are delayed by draining and drying the craft after each use; in the longer term, useful life is prolonged by ensuring that the inner core of each bundle is highly compressed during manufacture (McGrail, 1998: 169).

### 4.5.6 NEOLITHIC SEAGOING CRAFT

The Neolithic colonization of islands such as Crete (Broodbank and Strasser, 1991) had to be undertaken by a small flotilla of seaworthy craft capable of transporting, possibly in more than one wave, a nucleus of people (the minimum is thought to be 40), and of breeding animals, corn for one year and the next year's seed, and water for the voyage.

Theoretical considerations (Table 1.2) suggest that by Neolithic times, in addition to rafts of logs, floats or bundles, and hideboats, seagoing logboats (stabilized, paired, or extended) could have been built. Simple plank boats were also technologically possible, but it may be that these would have been for inland waters rather than seagoing. The earliest known Mediterranean planked vessel, in fact, is dated to the mid-second millennium BC (4.8.3.1).

Logboats have been excavated from Italian inland sites (Calcagno, 1997: 33–5; Castiglione, 1967; Simone, 1990) dating from the third millennium BC and later:

one from Lake Bracciano may be from the sixth millennium BC. With this logboat were found four models which probably represent logboats, the earliest known boat models in the Mediterranean (Calcagno, 1997: 48, fig. 1). Elsewhere in the Mediterranean, logboat studies are in their infancy. Some of the Italian logboats have features which suggest that they may have been one of a pair (Medas, 1993), whilst one may formerly have been extended by the addition of strakes (Delpino, 1991). These excavated boats are generally too recent to throw direct light on the Neolithic, but they do suggest that, in the central Mediterranean Bronze Age, techniques were known which could have been used to build paired and/or extended logboats with sufficient transverse stability to be used at sea: the use of stabilizing timbers at the waterline is also a possibility. Whether such techniques were used during the Neolithic is debatable.

# 4.6

# The Early Bronze Age

## (*c*.3800–2000 BC)

The direct evidence for seagoing planked vessels and for advanced forms of logboat with seagoing potential is thus much later than the Neolithic. There is, however, evidence for seagoing voyages during the Early Bronze Age: the Egyptians raided the Levant coast by sea, and imported cedar logs from Lebanon (2.3, 2.7.7); in the Aegean there was inter-island trade and travel, and a search for metals; objects from the Cycladic islands have been excavated from as far away as Sicily and Dalmatia, whilst there is evidence for contacts between the island of Lemnos and the Anatolian site of Troy (Bass, 1997: 269).

Underwater excavations off Cape Myti Komeni, on the Aegean island of Dokos, have revealed EH2 pottery dated to *c*.2200 BC (Vichos and Papathanassopoulos, 1996: 527). No ship remains have so far been encountered and, for the present, this is a doubtful shipwreck site (Wachsmann, 1998: 205; Parker, 1992: no. 362). Other than this, all evidence for vessels of the third millennium BC is iconographic.

Apart from a curious and incomplete graffito on a vase excavated on the Dalmatian island of Hvar (Lesina), and dated to c.3500 BC (Calcagno, 1997: 49; Bonino, 1990), no Mediterranean representations of boats are earlier than the third millennium BC: most are thought to be from the Keros-Syros culture which is generally dated from c.2800–2200 BC. They may suggest the sort of boats that were being used as ferries and to transport animals, and for warfare and piracy, and possibly cargo in the Early Bronze Age Aegean and Ionian Seas (Vigie, 1980). Before 2000 BC there is no evidence for sail in this region: boats must have been poled, paddled, or rowed.

### 4.6.1 MODELS

Representations readily fall into two groups: models; and engravings/drawings. Models supply the vital third dimension, with plan views and sections, usually missing from other representations: they will therefore be considered first and then used in the interpretation of the two-dimensional figures.

#### 4.6.1.1 LEAD MODELS FROM NAXOS (Fig. 4.9)

Three of these models are held in the Ashmolean Museum, Oxford (Broodbank, 1989: fig. 4; Basch, 1987a: 78–9, figs. 154, 155), whilst a fourth is in the Merseyside Museum, Liverpool (Basch, 1987a: fig. 153). One Ashmolean model appears to be complete, although distorted by hogging of the bottom (Renfrew, 1967: plate 1), but the other three are broken and

incomplete at one end. The remains suggest, however, that in their complete state, these three probably had ends similar to those of the fourth model. If the hogged bottom of this model (as evident from the long section) were to be corrected (as suggested by Roberts, 1987), both ends would probably rise slightly, and their tips would move inwards. However, the central cross-section in Renfrew's drawing (1967: plate 1) shows a deeper hull with no sign of hogging, rather a full section with rounded bilges.

The first question to be asked is, as with all representational evidence, which end is the bow? The plan and sections (Renfrew, 1967: plate 1) show that this model has a tapering end (the bow) rising at c.30° to horizontal and a transom end (the stern) rising at about 20°. A boat built on the lines of this model would float with the stern slightly deeper than the bow: this would accentuate the relative height of the bow. This disparity in height is not significant, however, being only 6–7 per cent.

This complex shape could not represent a logboat, but the relatively high L/B ratio of c.12 : 1 suggests that the vessel was logboat-based, with added ends, and the sides extended by planking. The hull is flared in section showing that the waterline breadth (hence stability) was greater than it would have been if a log alone had been used.

The second point to establish, if at all possible, is the scale of the model. Empirical data, established in relation to paddled logboats (McGrail, 1978: 132), shows that kneeling, double-banked paddlers (two side-by-side) need a minimum internal breadth of boat of 0.85 m. There has to be c.1 m longitudinal separation

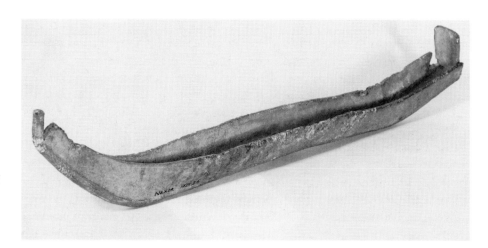

Fig. 4.9. A lead model boat of third millennium BC from Naxos, Greece (Ashmolean Museum, Oxford).

between two such pairs; however, where the breadth of bottom allows only one paddler at a station, three paddlers require only 2 m length of boat if they are alternately port and starboard. If we assume that the ancient boatbuilders would have chosen a shape which would allow maximum use of double-banked paddlers, and subjectively assess this as a region equally disposed about the station of maximum breadth as far as the station where the bow begins to narrow perceptibly, the internal breadth of the model at the foremost and aftermost points of this region is 0.028 m. If this represents 0.85 m (the minimum breadth for two paddlers) then the scale of the model is $c.1 : 30$. From this it follows that the boat represented by this model was $c.12.45 \times 1.06 \times 0.63$ m, a reasonable size for a logboat extended in length and in height of sides from a parent log $c.7.2$ m in length, with a maximum diameter of $c.0.9$ m, the butt of this log being positioned towards the stern of the boat.

With paddlers double-banked in the central region, and alternating port and starboard where there is room forward and aft of this, there would have been space for thirteen to fifteen kneeling paddlers. Additionally there would have been two standing steersmen with longer paddles.

A lookout/steersman at the bow is also known today: there may have been one in this case. Thus the crew of this hypothetical third-millennium BC, paddled Naxos boat, in a maximum propulsion role would have been between fourteen (1 + 13) and eighteen (3 + 15). Unless used in a war/piracy role, the full complement of paddlers and steersmen need not be carried: cargo, animals, and passengers could be placed in the midships region, with paddlers towards the ends. Passengers would have to squat, and animals would be hobbled and thrown, to ensure adequate stability in such a boat. High density/low stowage factor cargo, such as metals, stone, weapons or tools would be preferable to low density/high stowage factor items such as wool and hides: filled ceramic containers would be preferred to empty pots (McGrail, 1989b: table 1). With a half crew complement of eight, and animals, children, and cargo stowed amidships, such a vessel could have been one of a flotilla on an Early Bronze Age summer colonization voyage. On present evidence it is not possible to say whether a similar boat could have been used in the Neolithic Aegean.

## 4.6.1.2 TERRACOTTA MODEL FROM PALAIKASTRO, CRETE (Fig. 4.10)

This model boat (Basch, 1987a: 83, figs. 170, 175; Wachsmann, 1998: 71–3; fig. 5.9) is now in the Heraclion Museum, Crete. No measured drawing can be located and there is only one orthogonal photograph (Basch, 1987a: fig. 171); however, something can be learned from the published photographs and sketches. In plan and in cross-section one end of this model is evidently rounded whilst the other end tapers: Wachsmann (1998: fig. 5.10) has published a drawing of a model from Christos, dated $c.2000$ BC, with a similar shape. This taper converges on a high rising end, some 70°

Fig. 4.10.  A terracotta boat model of third millennium BC from Palaikastro, Greece (Ashmolean Museum, Oxford).

from the horizontal when seen in longitudinal profile. The more bulbous end terminates in a short, horizontal projection low down on the hull. In this case, for reasons of directional stability propounded by Roberts (1987: fig. 1) the probability is that this low, rounded end is the bow, with a projecting forefoot. What seem to be crossbeams are positioned at about one-third and two-thirds the waterline length from the bow (excluding the forefoot).

The boat represented by this model was evidently 'bluff-bowed' with a waterline plan which was 'cod head and mackerel tail', a shape which, in late sixteenth-century Europe, was thought, on the analogy of a fish, to be the best (McGowan, 1981: 26)—see also a cutter of 1768 (Landström, 1961: 174, fig. 401).

The reasons for incorporating a high stern are unclear. If the boat were to float significantly trimmed by the stern (i.e. with the forefoot clear of the water), the high stern would tend to counterbalance the effect of the wind on this, now raised, bow. This seems an unlikely trim, however, since the hull is markedly more capacious towards the bow. The projecting forefoot may have been to ease the bows onto the strand when beaching, although an increase in potential speed (from the increased waterline length) may also have been an aim: this forefoot may also have been used as a means of re-embarking after pushing the boat off the beach. The practicability of some of these uses depends on the scale of the model which, in the absence of measured drawings, is indeterminant. As an approximation one can guesstimate that the maximum beam is about one-third the waterline length (without forefoot). This suggests that with a beam of $c.1$ m, the main hull of the original boat may have been $c.3$ m in length, and the overall length some 4 m. This could have been a planked boat. Alternately, the main hull may have been formed from a log with its butt end towards the bow—however, the stern and the forefoot, at least, must have been added; it is also possible that planks were added to the sides. It is conceivable that a boat of these proportions could have been propelled by oar: a measured drawing of the model would be required before this possibility could be investigated.

This hull is relatively deep, $L/D = c.6$, whereas the corresponding ratio for the Naxos lead models is $c.20$. This feature not only makes it more likely that washstrakes were added to a Palaikastro logboat base, but also reinforces the suggestion that this was a relatively small boat, since in a boat longer than, say, 8 m the sides would be inconveniently high for paddlers, unless they stood, thereby reducing the boat's stability.

The two beams may have been inserted across the top of the hollowed log to hold the sides together during building, and to reinforce the strength of the hull during use. It is possible that they could also be used as thwarts; alternatively or additionally, they may define functional spaces—propulsion by paddlers in the bow, stowage of cargo and/or passengers amidships, steering by long paddle in the stern.

The Palaikastro model seems to represent a small boat suitable for local uses by a ferryman, a fisherman, or a farmer. The reason for incorporating a sharply raised stern is unclear. Its seaworthiness would have been limited by its lack of sheer forward.

### 4.6.1.3 TERRACOTTA MODEL FROM MOCHLOS (Fig. 4.11)

This 0.20 m long, double-ended model is now in the Heraclion Museum, Crete (Wachsmann, 1998: 76–7, fig. 5.16; Basch, 1987: 132, fig. 276). No measured draw-

ing can be traced, only photographs and sketches. The model has high-rising ends ($c.70°$) and a protruding forefoot at bow and stern. Such a form could have been built in planks, alternatively the vessel may have been a logboat extended both in length and in height of sides.

At the forward and after extremities of the main hull representations of frames extend transversely around the hull and project above the sheerline on both sides. These projections may well represent oar pivots: if this is so they could be used by one man at both ends each pulling/pushing two oars, or two men at both ends each operating one oar. For two men to work effectively at each station the beam at that station would have to be greater than 1.5 m; for one man to man two oars the

Fig. 4.11. A terracotta boat model of third millennium BC from Machlos, Crete (after Wachsmann, 1998: fig. 5.16).

beam would have to be of the order of 1 m (McGrail, 1998: fig. 12.9). Both these assessments depend upon the rowing geometry (oar length, oar angle, oar gearing) which can only be investigated in detail using a measured drawing. Having oarsmen towards the ends leaves a relatively capacious hull for the carriage of cargo, animals, and people. An advantage of double-endedness is that either end can be the bow, making beach operations simpler. Furthermore, with such a disposition of oars it seems likely that there was no steersman, rather the steering would be done by the oarsmen at whichever end was the stern, who would have faced forward and pushed their oars. This reasoning suggests this was not a large vessel, perhaps less than 8 m in length—possibly 7.5 × 1.9 × 1.2 m. Like the Palaikastro boat, the Mochlos boat would have been used by ferryman, fisherman, or farmer, but it would have had relatively greater cargo capacity and possibly better stability, and it could have been used in worse sea conditions. If it was propelled by oars, voyages would have been undertaken more effectively than if paddlers had to be used.

## 4.6.2 ENGRAVINGS AND PAINTINGS

There are three groups of two-dimensional representations of boats, dated to the third millennium BC:
engravings on terracotta dishes; carvings on stone
slabs; and figurings on pottery shards.

### 4.6.2.1 TERRACOTTAS FROM SYROS (Fig. 4.12)

About 200 objects, circular in plan, with surrounding
lip and projecting handle, and dated to the third millennium BC, have been excavated from Euboea, the
Cycladic islands, the southern Greek mainland and,
unusually, central Anatolia (Coleman, 1985; Broodbank, 1989). These are mostly of terracotta, but a few
are of stone and two are of bronze. Many of these 'frying pans' have an elaborate incised decoration, including some which are thought to represent boats: these
latter are all on terracottas from the Cycladic islands
(Broodbank, 1989: fig. 3). Although nicknamed 'frying

Fig. 4.12. Incised decorations on Cycladic terracottas—'frying
pans' (after Broodbank, 1989: fig. 3).

pans', these objects have clearly never been used as
such, nor are they thought to be mirrors: other interpretations range from decorated plates to religious/
cultic objects.

The thirteen incised boat figures have a portion
which is near-horizontal (main hull?). Extending to the
right (except for one representation which is to the left)
of this there is a relatively high end rising at an angle of
$67.5° \pm 4.3°$ to the horizontal. Mounted above the top
of this end is what appears to be a fish evidently with its
head pointing away from the vessel, and with a tassel or
pendant hanging down from it. On two representations the other end is incomplete; on two others there
is a break of slope but the angle is imperceptible; on all
the others there is a short rising end at an angle of $22°$
$\pm 8.5°$ to the horizontal. Beyond this low end there is a
further, but slimmer, projection. Short angular lines
are incised above and below the horizontal element
and the low rising end, in all but three cases: one of
these exceptions has single lines across the hull, whilst
the other two have broader zig-zag lines which may
represent sewn planking.

It is generally agreed that these figures represent
boats, although, because of their diagrammatic nature,
this view is not unchallengeable. Much scholarly effort
has been given to the question of what type of boat is
represented and which end is the bow (Johnstone, 1973;
1988: 61–6; Roberts, 1987; Basch, 1987a: 79–89; Wachsmann, 1998: 70–1). Of the three contemporary groups
of model boats described above, these Syros figures
most closely resemble the profile view of the Palaikastro model (Fig. 4.10), with its single high end and its
protruding forefoot, rather than the double-ended
Mochlos model (Fig. 4.11), or the Naxos models (Fig.
4.9) with their two almost equally high ends. It follows
from this that the lower end of the Syros 'frying pan'
boats is the bow. If the analogy with the Palaikastro
model is pursued we may also deduce that the Syros
craft were either planked boats or extended logboats
with crossbeams/thwarts; they were propelled by paddles or possibly oars, and had a relatively capacious
hull.

A significant difference between the Syros boats in
outline and the profile of the Palaikastro model is that
the bow (lower end) of the former, on many, but not
all, representations, rises at an angle of $c.22°$ to the
main hull, whereas the model ends in a horizontally
projecting forefoot. Basch (1987a: figs. 181, 182) prefers

to see the Syros boats trimmed in such a way that their projections lie at the waterline, comparable with the model in this respect. However, the majority of the Syros figures seem to suggest that these vessels floated so that there was a short bow rising at $c.22°$ to the horizontal, quite different from the much longer and much steeper (70°), rising bow of the Naxos models. If this hypothesis is correct then the Syros boats, having more sheer forward, would be more seaworthy than the Palaikastro boat with its near-level sheer.

The short angular lines above and below the hull have been interpreted as representing paddles, oars, or crew. They range in number from twelve to fifty, but there is no set pattern to them—there are not equal numbers above and below (starboard and port?) the hull, and they are not all angled in the same direction; furthermore some of the lines appear against the rising bow where it would not be possible to paddle owing to the high freeboard. These lines cannot be taken to represent a crew one to one, and thus cannot be used to estimate the size of these boats. Broodbank (1989, 1993) argues strongly that the Syros boats represented by these images were lengthy ones ('longboats') with a large crew: so many people would have been required in the crew that one boat would have stretched the manpower resources of an entire island. From this reasoning, he deduces that they were not used for trade but were symbols of prestige and power. There is no reason to think that the Syros engravings represent 'longboats', if by 'longboats' is meant a L/B ratio greater than, say, 6 : 1. The 'frying pan' depictions being two-dimensional cannot themselves give any guidance on this ratio. By analogy, however, we can deduce that the Syros boats L/B were probably nearer the 4 : 1 of the Palaikastro models, rather than the 12 : 1 of the Naxos lead models.

In an archipelago such as the Cyclades there would probably have been several sizes of boat ranging from small ones with little sheer forward used for local work (represented by the Palaikastro model), to larger, seagoing ones with a raised bow of which some of the Syros figures may be representations. These would have been able to carry passengers, animals, and cargo; in war, piracy, or raiding roles, the 'passengers' would have been armed men.

The undoubted symbolic nature of the depictions on the Syros 'frying pans' probably means that some of these vessels, perhaps only one or two, were of extra importance, either because they were the basis for economic prosperity (by overseas trade?) or because they were a symbol of some authority.

### 4.6.2.2 ENGRAVINGS ON STONES FROM NAXOS (Fig. 4.13)

Two rock carvings from Korphi t'Aroniou, Naxos (Johnstone, 1988: fig. 6.7; Basch, 1987a: fig. 152, 169; Broodbank, 1989: fig. 5; Wachsmann, 1998: fig. 5.8) are generally assumed to be from the third millennium BC. Both may depict boats similar in profile to the Syros engravings and the Palaikastro model. On one stone a

Fig. 4.13. Engraving on a stone from Naxos, Greece (Paul Johnstone, 1988: fig. 6.7).

man appears to be driving a quadruped (goat?) on board the boat: if this is so, it suggests, once again, that the lower end is the bow. Tholes are thought by some to be depicted on this boat.

### 4.6.2.3 DECORATIONS ON CERAMICS

An incised decoration on a shard from an Early Helladic vase handle from Orchomenos (Fig. 4.14) may

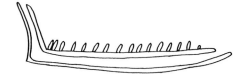

Fig. 4.14. Incised decorations on an early Helladic vase from Orchomenos (after Wachsmann, 1998: fig. 5.11).

represent a similar type of boat. The rising end of another boat may be depicted on a shard from Phylakopi, Melos which is thought to be third millennium BC (Casson, 1971: fig. 46). Wachsmann (1998: 73, fig. 5.12) considers that a 'steering oar' with a short tiller is also depicted: it is more likely to be a steering paddle.

### 4.6.3 EARLY BRONZE AGE BOATS

The iconographic evidence reviewed above suggests that there were three types of boat in the Aegean Early Bronze Age. It should be remembered, however, that there are no excavated boats against which these hypotheses can be evaluated:

1. A logboat extended in height and length, with a rising (30°), tapering bow and a rising (20°), but broader, transom stern, and with a rounded transverse section and flared sides. Dimensions may have been of the order of 12.45 × 1.06 × 0.63 m, the crew, fourteen to eighteen paddlers and steersmen: with a smaller crew, cargo, passengers, and possibly animals could have been carried. A seagoing vessel of adequate stability, more suitable as a passenger ferry/fighting craft than as a low-density cargo carrier. *Basis*: Naxos lead models.

2. Planked boats of good cargo capacity, and with a tapering and high stern rising at *c.*70° to the horizontal. There were two versions:

(a) A small boat, say, 7 × 1.75 × 1.15 m, with bluff bows and a projecting forefoot, but no sheer. Crossbeams may have been used as thwarts and it is possible that oars were used, although there may have been paddle steering. A local fishing boat, ferry, or farm boat with good transverse stability.

(b) A larger vessel, with a short bow rising at *c.*22° to the horizontal. Its stability was probably as good as that of the smaller boat, and the sheer at the bow would have made it more seaworthy. Some of these boats may have been built for prestige reasons as a display of power. *Basis*: Palaikastro model; engravings on the Syros 'frying pans' and the Naxos stones; and decorations on the Orchomenos and Phylakopi ceramics.

3. Double-ended planked boats with high ends rising at *c.*70°, and a protruding forefoot at bow and stern. These were relatively small, general purpose boats of adequate stability and cargo capacity, probably propelled by oars and with a helmsman. Dimensions

may have been of the order of 7.5 × 1.9 × 1.2 m. *Basis*: Mochlos model.

# 4.7
# The Middle Bronze Age
## (*c.*2000–1500 BC)

The eastern Mediterranean Middle Bronze Age opened in *c.*2000 BC with an evident marked increase in seafaring associated with the Levant coast and with Crete. The end of this period is usually taken to be the collapse of the Minoan 'thalassocracy' based on Crete. Conventionally, this event is dated by cross links with the Egyptian chronology to 1450–1500 BC; however, the end of Minoan civilization on the island of Thera / Santorini has been linked to a catastrophic volcanic explosion which has recently been dated to *c.*1628 BC on the assumption that perturbations in dendrochronological data were also due to this explosion (Kuniholm, 1990; Wachsmann, 1998: 83–4, 351–2). The validity of this argument is still under evaluation.

In *c.*2000 BC maritime city-states appear to have been established on the southern coast of the Levant, and there are other indications of the emergence of a Syro-Canaanite culture throughout the Levant coast. Egyptian sources (2.3, 2.7.7) describe trading voyages between Egypt and the Levant, and seaborne invasions of the Levant.

At about the same time, there is textual and iconographic evidence for Cretan contacts with Cyprus, the Levant coast, and Egypt (Wachsmann, 1998: 83–6). Articles manufactured in Crete have been excavated widely from Sicily to the Levant, including the southern Aegean, the west coast of Anatolia and Rhodes. It is possible that only Egyptian or Syro-Canaanite ships were involved in this overseas trade. However, Middle Bronze Age Crete and its legendary ruler, Minos, earned a reputation for seafaring, according to Herodotus (1. 171, 3. 122), Thucydides (Warner, 1954: 15) and Strabo (10. 4. 8), and it seems not unreasonable to assume that at least some of this trade was undertaken by Cretan ships.

## 4.7.1 TRADE ROUTES

Predominant winds, local winds, and currents suggest that ships trading between Egypt, the Levant, and Crete would have adopted an anti-clockwise circulation since this would be the best for vessels with limited, or no, tacking ability (McGrail, 1991b: 89). A similar (but smaller) triangular pattern is suggested for direct trading between Crete and Cyprus (Mantzourani and Theodorou, 1991). Although such long-distance routes may have been used in the Middle Bronze Age it is probable that much trading was undertaken on voyages which consisted of several short-distance legs—cabotage or tramping.

The difficulties and the distances involved, even on cabotage routes, make it very likely that sail was used, except for short passages between places less than, say, 20 nautical miles apart when a small oared boat may have sufficed.

## 4.7.2 SHIPS AND BOATS

During 1973–5 excavations off Sheyton Deresi, east of Bodrum, Turkey, Bass recovered Aegean and Anatolian pottery, thought to be dated c.1600 BC, but no ship remains (Wachsmann, 1998: 205–6; Parker, 1992: no. 1079). Other than this the evidence for Middle Bronze Age boats and ships is entirely iconographic.

Although sail was known in Egyptian waters from the late fourth millennium BC (2.4) it does not appear to have been used in the Mediterranean until c.2000 BC. It is possible that sail was used on the Levant coast at an earlier date, but the earliest depiction of what is probably a Levant vessel is dated to the eighteenth century BC (Fig. 4.15): an engraving on a locally made copy of a Syrian seal excavated within a Syro-Canaanite context

Fig. 4.15. Ship depicted on an eighteenth-century BC Syrian cylinder seal from Tel el Daba (after Wachsmann, 1998: fig. 3.1).

at Tel el Daba in the Nile delta (4.9.3.2.2.1). This is a sailing ship with a mast stepped near amidships, supported by forestay and backstay. In profile the hull is flat-bottomed with rising ends, one (the stern?) being nearer the vertical than the other.

## 4.7.2.1 MINOAN SEALS (Fig. 4.16)

Ships engraved on small stone seals from c.2000 BC are the earliest depictions of mast and rigging in the Mediterranean (Casson, 1971: figs. 34–6; Wachsmann, 1998: figs. 6.29). The mast is stepped near amidships but the sail is not shown. On one (Wachsmann, 1998: fig.

Fig. 4.16. Sailing ship on a Minoan seal of c.2000 BC (Ashmolean Museum, Oxford).

6.29A), a lowered yard is depicted supported by two pairs of halyards: this suggests that, on several of the other seals where no yard is visible, halyards rather than multiple stays may be represented. It is not impossible to sail a vessel without stays (McGrail, 1998: 218, 224), but there would be restrictions imposed by wind strength and angle to the wind. Both ends of the engraved hull curve upwards and so these vessels may be considered seaworthy. On most, one end is significantly higher than the other: the general impression is that the higher end is the stern (as might be expected in a vessel with limited tacking ability) but this is difficult to justify objectively.

Later seals (Casson, 1971: figs. 37–40; Wachsmann, 1998: fig. 6.21) show vessels with a low aspect ratio sail.

Patterns of lines on these sails suggest that they may have been made of several small pieces sewn together (Wachsmann, 1998: 102). The rigging is stylized but multiple sheets as well as multiple halyards may be depicted. These hulls have ends of almost equal height. Angular lines from the lower part of the hull have been taken to represent oars (Casson, 1971: 31), but this is by no means certain.

### 4.7.2.2 FRESCOS FROM THERA

During excavations by Spyridon Marinatos in 1972 at Akrotiri on the Cycladic island of Thera, frescos with a maritime theme were revealed on the inside walls of a structure that came to be called the West House (Marinatos, 1974; P. Johnston, 1997; Wachsmann, 1998: 83–122). Ships and boats are depicted on the north and south walls of Room 5 in friezes which are c.0.40 m high. In Room 4 there are eight larger paintings of what are interpreted as *ikria*, decorated cabins, which are also featured in the stern of some of the ships in Room 5.

The frescos are not continuous: windows, doors and niches in the walls limit the area available for painting. Furthermore, none of the scenes was complete when excavated, and much is missing (Fig. 4.17). The parts that had survived were fragmented and have had to be

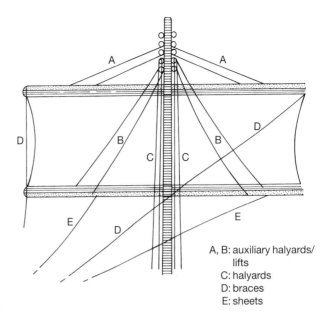

A, B: auxiliary halyards/
         lifts
C: halyards
D: braces
E: sheets

Fig. 4.18 Thera sailing ship's rigging reconstructed (after Wachsmann, 1998: fig 6.20).

restored and missing sections reconstructed (Fig 4.18). This has its critics—see, for example, Giesecke (1983).

#### 4.7.2.2.1 *Date*

The excavator deduced that the Bronze Age town of Akrotiri had been devastated by earthquakes, and then covered by deposits of pumice and ash from a major volcanic eruption. This eruption has been dated indirectly, through frost damage recorded in an American dendrochronological sequence, to 1628–1626 BC (Warren, 1984). Dating, again indirectly, by a peak of acidity in ice-core records suggests c.1645 BC (Tzalas, 1995a). The latest pottery excavated at Akrotiri was Late Cycladic IA which is dated archaeologically, via Egyptian chronologies, to 1550–1500 BC. The date of the frescos is thus unclear: they may have been painted in the mid-sixteenth century BC, when the ships and boats depicted could be Mycenean, or in the mid-seventeenth century BC when they would be Minoan. Some authors have seen parallels between decorations on the Thera ships' hulls and known Mycenean motifs, whilst others have noted that the ships themselves are similar to those depicted in Minoan art (Wachsmann, 1998: 95). The matter is not yet resolved, but the balance of archaeological opinion now seems to be in favour of a seventeenth-century BC date and a Minoan attribution.

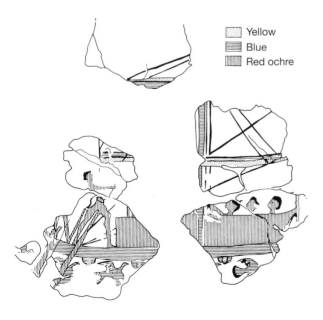

Yellow
Blue
Red ochre

Fig. 4.17. Remains of the Thera sailing ship depiction as excavated (after Wachsmann, 1998: fig. 6.19).

### 4.7.2.2.2 *Interpretation*

These fragmentary remains have generated numerous publications, including two books (Marinatos, 1984; Morgan, 1988), chapters in several books (e.g. Wachsmann, 1998) and at least twenty-five specialist papers in the English language. The conflicting views expressed in these accounts well illustrate how subjective can be the interpretation of ancient iconography. Not only are there differences about the date of the paintings, but also about such fundamental matters as whether the several scenes are related sequentially to one another (Basch, 1985; Giesecke, 1983); whether they are unconnected, merely a series of sailor's yarns (Giesecke, 1983; P. Johnston, 1997); or whether they are a geographical or a temporal sequence (Morgan, 1988).

The excavator, Spyridon Marinatos (1974), suggested that some of the scenes were set in Libya; Basch (1987a) prefers the Nile delta; whilst Morgan (1988) and Wachsmann (1998) argue for the Cyclades. One particular scene in the south frieze has been interpreted as a procession of ships in connection with religious ceremony or cultic pageant (Morgan, 1988; Wachsmann, 1998: 105); a celebration of good relations between Cretans and Acheans (Giesecke, 1983); Minoan ships returning to harbour after a naval triumph (Tilley and Johnstone, 1976; Wachsmann, 1980); and the return of a fleet after a peaceful mission (Marinatos, 1974). A fragmentary scene on the north wall, in which there are apparently contorted bodies in the vicinity of ships, has been interpreted as depicting ships attacking a coastal town through waters in which there are drowning men (Casson, 1975); a sea battle (Wachsmann, 1980); and as Cretan ships, on a festive visit to the Aegean, with sponge divers nearby (Giesecke, 1983).

Since this book is focused on ships and boats it might be thought that such controversies could be set aside and the Thera vessels interpreted in isolation. Enigmatic features of the ships prevent this: the question must be asked whether the vessels are depicted in their usual role (as warships or cargo ships) and are representative of their times; or whether they are unusual and perhaps incorporate features which by then were archaic. A ship capable of being sailed is depicted being paddled (Fig. 4.19): was this the usual way of propelling a ship on windless days and/or in confined or shoal waters? Or was there some symbolism in the depicted action and thus the usual practice would be that oars were used whenever it was impractical to sail? War helmets and possibly long spears are depicted on some of the ships yet, apart from the seaman steering and propelling the ships, most of the occupants are shown sitting at their ease within some structure near amidships. Are these warships or passenger-carrying ships? Furthermore, interpretation is not a sequential action—first identify the context, then analyse the technical features of the vessels: rather it is an iterative process, since the identification of nautical fittings can influence the general interpretation of the entire scene, reinforcing or challenging.

Fig. 4.19. The Thera 'flagship' restored (S3 in Fig. 4.20) (after Johnstone, 1980: fig. 7.2).

Interpretation of these friezes is made difficult because of their incomplete, fragmentary nature, but more importantly, because (due to the exigencies of excavation), they appear to have not been fully record- ed until after conservation, and this conservation included restoration work. The great majority, if not all, published photographs and drawings were pro- duced after this restoration: this is not a sound basis for the interpretation of what was excavated, nor for the reconstruction of missing parts. Nautical scholars who published papers on these remains in the early days of research and presumably examined the remains (Basch, 1983b; Casson, 1975; Giesecke, 1983; Gillmer, 1975; Prytulak, 1982; Tilley and Johnstone, 1976; Wachs- mann, 1980) have felt able to evaluate the ships and boats. Gillmer, who seems to have worked with the excavator in the early days of post-excavation research (1978, 1985a, 1989, 1995) and Giesecke (1983) have felt justified in publishing full reconstruction drawings and evaluation of performance. Reconstructions were also produced by Toby (1986) and by Gifford (1997).

Before representation of vessels can be described it is necessary to identify the bow or stern, and to esti- mate the waterline. With the Thera friezes, the stern is readily identified by the proximity of the steering device. These vessels clearly have a finer bow than stern, and this feature can therefore be used to identify the bow and stern of incomplete remains. In all vessels, the bow is to the right.

The waterline is more difficult to assess. In general terms early depictions of vessels seem to be either a floating view (the lowest line is the waterline) or a 'high and dry' view (the lowest line is the keel or the founda- tion plank). Most commentators have not made clear which type they consider the Thera depictions to be. Gillmer, however, believes that the depictions are 'high and dry' and has located the waterline 'where the pad- dlers' blades seemed to be properly immersed' (1985a: 409). Basch (1983b, 1985) has criticized this view, draw- ing attention to anomalies in the depictions and to other aspects not considered by Gillmer. Basch (1985: 414) concludes that there may not be 'sufficient evi- dence . . . to become sufficiently certain' of the posi- tion of the waterline. As we shall see, this justifiable doubt influences a general appreciation of the artist's accuracy, and raises questions about some of the inter- pretations of the near-horizontal projection from the sterns of some of these ships.

A further difficulty impeding informed discussion of these friezes is that there is not an agreed system of ref- erence to individual vessels depicted. Marinatos (1974) did assign letters to certain vessels but his scheme did not include all depictions, and it did not proceed in a systematic order. Giesecke (1983: 130) attempted to rec- tify this but his numbering system also does not run systematically. Another identification system has been published by Doumas (1978)—see Ernston, 1985: fig. 1 —but in this, boats are numbered separately from ships; furthermore one boat is unnumbered and the scheme covers only the southern frieze. Basch's scheme (1987a: fig. 232) also covers only that frieze, and boats are allotted letters whereas ships have numbers. A further scheme has therefore been devised (Figs. 4.20 and 4.21) based on Doumas' layout for the southern frieze, and Televantous' layout for the northern frieze, as set out by Wachsmann (1998: figs. 6.8–6.11). The ships are numbered in sequence from the left using the stern of each one as a datum: S1–S11 on the south frieze; N1–N9 on the north.

### 4.7.2.2.3 *The friezes*

The main features of the southern frieze (Fig. 4.21) are town (A) to the left and town (B) to the right, with a flotilla of nine vessels (seen in profile) evidently pro- ceeding in company from (A) to (B), in line ahead with- in two columns. There are three ships in the port column, the middle one (S5), being more ornate and distinctive than all the others, is probably the flagship; and four ships in the starboard column, with smaller vessels (boats) ahead (S9) and astern (S1). In the small bay to the left of town (B) two boats (S10 and S11) appear to be berthed. If the, evidently temporary, bow adornment or spar is removed from the seven ships, the profiles of their hulls are alike and very similar to that of the two boats: flat bottomed longitudinally, with a rising bow, and a more sharply rising, and slightly high- er, stern (Fig. 4.20).

All the ships have a structure on deck near the stern within which a man is evidently seated. This structure is probably an *ikria*, a small cabin for important people (M. Shaw, 1982), in this case probably the captain or master. Each ship (except possibly S6) has, further for- ward, a structure extending almost half the overall length of the ship, within which ten to fifteen formally

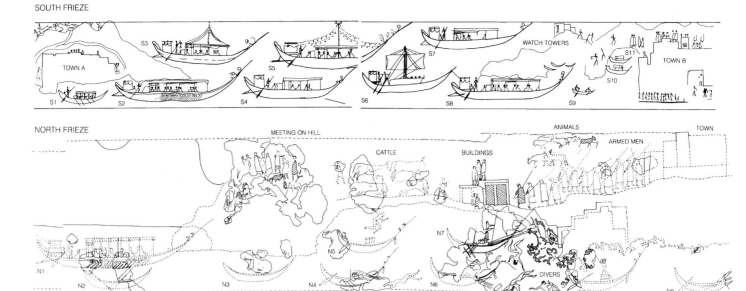

Figs. 4.20, 4.21.  Diagrammatic representations of the Thera south and north friezes as restored (Institute of Archaeology, Oxford).

robed people sit. There is a steersman in each ship (two in S6), and one or two other members of the crew squat in his vicinity. All ships except S6 have an animal figurehead at the stern, and all ships' hulls are decorated in colours: this is especially so in S5 which has lines rigged fore-and-aft and is 'dressed overall'. All ships, except for S6, have a triangular-shaped object projecting horizontally from the stern. Ship S6 is under sail whilst the other ships are probably paddled.

Three of the boats (S1, S10, and S11) have the long structure seen in the ships, but without occupants, and an *ikria* with someone sitting inside. Boat S1 is steered in a similar manner to the ships, but is propelled by oars. Boat S9 has a crew of two, but neither has a steersman's stance: it seems most likely that they are using either paddles or oars both to propel and to steer. Boats S10 and S11 are not underway.

### 4.7.2.2.3.1  *The stern projection*
This enigmatic device has been interpreted in several ways:

- an underwater skeg to increase directional stability (Casson, 1975);
- an underwater stabilizer to dampen down 'porpoising' (Kennedy, 1978; Basch, 1983*b*, 1985);
- a landing ramp or gangway (Marinatos, 1974: 50; Gillmer, 1975: 323; Reynolds, 1978);

- a means of pushing the ship into the water (Tilley and Johnstone, 1976);
- a means of securing the ship to shore by a hawser (Rubin de Cervin, 1977).

Several authors (for example, Wachsmann, 1980, and Casson, 1975) believe that projections on models and engravings from the Bronze Age Aegean (4.6.1) must all have the same function, and thus they seek for an explanation which will satisfy *all* depictions. Their premise is very doubtful.

Projections are not fitted on all vessels on the southern frieze: they are *not* fitted on boats, nor on the one ship under sail. There is thus an apparent correlation of projections with propulsion by paddling, and also with an animal figurehead at the stern of these ships. No logical argument can be envisaged to support this conjectural relationship and therefore it is considered a mere coincidence. There may, however, be a negative relationship with the use of sail, and a positive correlation with the embarkation of passengers: in these two relationships may lie the key to interpretation. It is generally agreed that this device is probably a temporary fitting which can be removed, stored, and replaced. It appears to consist of a bifurcated timber which takes against the trailing edge of the stern and extends some distance forward, on both sides of the ship (Casson, 1975: fig. 6). It is reinforced and held to the stern by a wooden knee; there were probably other fastenings which are not depicted. Gillmer has shown that such a fitting could be used as a gangplank to embark and disembark dry-shod from a beach or jetty off which a ship was anchored 'in a Mediterranean moor' with her stern overhanging but not touching the embarkation place (Gillmer, 1985a: fig. 5; 1989: fig. 9). Notwithstanding the one main drawback to this hypothesis (for such use a hanging, rather than a standing, knee would give more support to the structure) and the problem of establishing the waterline, this function for the projection seems more likely than any other suggested. The ship under sail, S6, did not need such a landing ramp since she had no passengers and presumably her crew were sufficiently agile to shin up ropes, climb on board from the water, and the like. The *boats* could readily be manned. On the other hand, the dignatories embarked in certain ships needed to embark and disembark in a dignified manner—hence the gang plank.

#### 4.7.2.2.3.2 *Ikria*
By comparison with other depictions of these, often ornate, cabins, Shaw (1982) has deduced that they consist of oxhide covers on the sides of a wooden framework, probably mounted on a wooden base. They are evidently open forward, although it is possible for people to sit forward of them and lean on the framing. The captain or master is seated in this position of authority on the deck right aft, and is able to see over the top of the hide 'walls': his helmet is hung on the *ikria* framing. Extending astern from the *ikria* is a long pole: the details are indistinct but it is thought to have a crossbar near the tip. This may be a spear (Prytulak, 1982) or perhaps a pole for use in shoal water (Giesecke, 1983): alternatively it may be a symbol of the office held by the captain.

#### 4.7.2.2.3.3 *The structure amidships*
There are two main schools of thought concerning the principal function of this framework:

- To support the mast, yard and sail when sent down, and other spars where necessary;
- To act as a framework for a decorated awning over the area in which people were seated; weapons (Prytulak, 1982; Basch, 1986: 425) or oars (Gifford, 1997) may also be stowed there.

The structure is seen, in conjunction with an *ikria*,

on boat S1, S10, and S11, and on ships S2, 3, 4, 5, 7, and 8. Boat S9 has neither features, whilst ship S6, under sail, has an *ikria* but, instead of a framework structure, has a sub-rectangular shaped object which Gillmer (1985a, 1989) has interpreted as a weather screen of hide or possibly canvas. The vertical elements in the structure appear to be stanchions which divide the midships section of the boat into open compartments in which robed figures sit facing one another. The after stanchions are generally shown in pairs; the forward ones end in a crutch, and the foremost ones in S8 are possibly supported by a diagonal strut (Toby, 1986). On the two non-sailed ships which have their mast stepped, S3 and S5, the mast also acts as a divider between compartments. The horizontal lines across the heads of these stanchions have been variously interpreted as spars and poles (Casson, 1975), weapons (Prytulak, 1982; Basch, 1986: 425), oars (Gifford, 1997), as roller blinds (Giesecke, 1983), or as yard, boom, and sail.

Examination of available illustrations and a review of the many scholarly opinions expressed leads to the conclusion that the original functions of this structure were:

- as a stowage for yard, sail and boom when sent down;
- as a gallows on which the mast could be pivoted during stepping and unstepping
- as a stowage for extra spars and possibly oars

This structure was of such a height that the steersman standing on the after half-deck could see over it. From the stability viewpoint, this would have been too high a stowage position for yard, sail, and boom at sea, but not in harbour or in other calm waters. The mast would normally remain stepped in harbour; if it had to be unstepped whilst at sea, it would have been positioned with one end on the after deck and the other in the crutch forward (see below).

Leaving to one side S6, there seems to be a distinction drawn between S3 and S5, on the one hand, and S2, 4, 7, and 8 on the other. The stanchions in the former group appear to be supporting some combination of yard, boom, sail, and spars, whilst those on board S2 and S4, and possibly S7 and S8, appear to have a striped awning. The details in boats S1, 10, and 11 are unclear.

The most likely explanation here seems to be that, for the particular special occasion featured, the flagship (S5) and another important ship (S3) had their yard, boom, and sail sent down and stowed on this structure, some of the rigging in S5 being extended to form (or being replaced by) dressing lines; the mast remained stepped. Seats or benches for 'passengers' were installed within this open structure. The remaining ships had their mast, yard, sail, and boom stowed ashore. An awning was then rigged on these ships, over the structure, and seats/benches installed. Whether spars, oars, or weapons were stowed under these awnings is not clear: the hanging of helmets on the stanchions, on the other hand, is clearly depicted. The ship depicted under sail, S6, had a weather screen installed rather than gallows and crutches. In this case, when required, yard, sail, and boom could have been sent down to the deck.

### 4.7.2.2.3.4 *Steering*

Steering may be undertaken by the same means as propulsion when a vessel is paddled or under oars that are pushed on the power stroke (McGrail and Farrell, 1979): the boat S9 is being steered in this manner. All other vessels depicted, except S10 and S11, which are evidently not underway, are steered by a helmsman (two in S6—both on the weather side) from the starboard quarter. As only the profile of vessels is shown, it may be that there was a second helmsman to port. In all cases the steering device projects only slightly below the hull as depicted. There appears to be no tiller, but it is not clear whether a steering oar or a steering paddle is being used. A steering oar needs to be pivoted on the hull, and there is no sign of a fulcrum: this absence may, however, not be significant. Steering sizeable vessels by large paddles appears to be depicted on Egyptian vessels of the Old Kingdom (fourth dynasty = *c.*2500 BC)—see Landström (1970: figs. 95–7). By the fifth dynasty (*c.*2400 BC), steering oars, pivoted on the starboard quarter, were used (2.7.5). Whereas the helmsmen in the ship under sail (S6), are clearly involved in some steering action, other steersmen seem merely to be holding their paddle or oar and not actually using it: it could be that steering was actually being undertaken by the paddlers (or someone in charge of them) and that the steersmen were poised ready to take over if necessary. However, the steersman in S1, a boat under oars, must be steering, and he holds his paddle or oar in a similarly languid manner. This relaxed posture suggests that a steering-oar, rather than a paddle, was being used.

### 4.7.2.2.3.5 *Propulsion*

Ship S6 is clearly under sail; boat S1 is clearly under oars in the mode sit-and-pull; boat S9 may be under oars (stand-and-push) but is more likely to be paddled. The other ships are thought to be propelled by paddlers (see, for example, Gillmer, 1978; Casson, 1975; Tilley and Johnstone, 1976). However, Giesecke (1983) considers that the angled lines interpreted as paddles actually represent oars on lanyards; that the paddlers' 'backs' are the curved tops of shields; and that the paddlers' 'heads' are blemishes on the frieze. It may not now be possible to resolve this matter, since the frieze has evidently been restored in a manner which emphasizes the paddlers interpretation. Since Marinatos (1974) saw the frieze before conservation, perhaps his opinion that paddlers *are* represented may be given the greater weight.

### 4.7.2.2.3.5.1 *Paddling*

Paddles may be plied from a sitting, standing (as in S9) or kneeling position (McGrail, 1998: 205–7). The paddlers depicted in S2–5, 7, 8, and N1 are probably kneeling. They appear to be very close together, and are evidently leaning over the side, in an uncharacteristic manner, so that they can reach the water with their paddles. Lambrou-Phillipson (1996) has convincingly argued that the artist has not depicted the correct use of a paddle and that these representations are not true to life. Nevertheless it does appear that ships which could be sailed are actually being paddled, and paddlers having to lean outboard and stretch down would be consistent with the ships having too great a freeboard for the standard paddle action. Gillmer has argued that the paddles are plied in sequence from the bow, and he compares their action with that depicted in the Egyptian funerary temple of Userkaf at Saqqara (2.7.3 and Fig. 2.16). But such an exaggerated style is not practical, and can only have been used in some ceremonial display. Furthermore, Lambrou-Phillipson (1996) has pointed out that, although the first seven paddles in S3 appear to be deeper than the remainder, this is in relation to the keel and not to the waterline: all other paddles end at the keel. It thus seems unlikely that paddling was the usual method of propulsion on the Thera ships when sail could not be used (Gillmer, 1978). The depicted scene was probably a re-enactment of some significant voyage in the past when, with smaller boats, paddles could be used in a practical fashion. This explanation would be consistent with the main scene on the south wall being interpreted as a symbolic enactment of an ancient ritual involving archaic practices but in current vessels, perhaps at the beginning of the sailing season (Casson, 1975; Morgan, 1988; Wachsmann, 1998: 105–13). During this unusual evolution, it is highly likely that there was a 'paddle-master' in each vessel to give the time, since paddlers on one side could not see paddlers on the other.

4.7.2.2.3.5.2 *Under oars*    Since oarsmen are depicted in boat S1 yet there is no sign of oar pivots, it seems probable that the omission of pivots from the ships is not significant, and that the secondary method of propulsion for the Thera sailing ships was usually by oar. The freeboard suggested by the depicted paddlers could suit oared propulsion. These ships may have been galleys, with a full complement of oars for use over a lengthy period when sailing was impossible. Alternatively, but possibly less likely at this date, oars may have only been relied on as a last resort, to enter or leave harbour, to round a headland, or avoid a lee shore: in which case there would probably have been a few oars towards each end of the ship, leaving the area in the vicinity of the mast for cargo and passengers. Galley oarsmen were probably double-banked, i.e. two to each bench, and may well have occupied almost the entire breadth of the ship. Paddlers take up signficantly less space transversely than oarsmen, thus allowing the passengers on this important occasion to sit inside the midships structure. Giesecke's controversial idea that oars rather than paddles are depicted means that oarsmen would have to be stationed below decks, underneath the prestigious passengers, resulting in an unconvincingly deep hull in his reconstruction drawing (1983: fig. 4).

4.7.2.2.3.5.3 *Under sail*    There is a mast stepped on S5, and a mast and yard on S3, but the best evidence for sail comes from S6 which Casson (1975) notes has been much restored (Fig. 4.17). Gillmer (1983) assures us it has survived sufficiently for us to recognize the sail and the rigging. Morgan (1988: fig. 171) has published the generally accepted interpretation of the running rigging (Fig. 4.19): two halyards to the yard; two auxiliary halyards (sometimes called 'running lifts' or 'topping lifts') (Emanuele, 1977) to each side of yard and boom; a brace to each yardarm; and a sheet to each end

of the boom. The halyards and auxiliaries are not taken aft or to one side to act as back stay or shrouds, and there appears to be no depiction of any standing rigging. The halyard and auxiliaries pass through 'loops' near the mast head: these were probably rope grommets or wooden deadeyes, rather than the blocks or sheaves proposed by some authors. It is assumed that the mast was stepped in the bottom of the ship. The mast, which is approximately three times taller than the sail is deep, can be unstepped, and when not sent ashore can be stowed in the crutch seen forward on S3. The mast is about half the overall length of the ship, whilst the yard and boom are *c*.80 per cent of the length of the mast.

The sail shown on S6 has an aspect ratio (AR) (Height/Breadth) of *c*.1:3. This is low by twentieth-century standards and thought to be not so efficient as a sail of higher AR (say, 1:0.67 for good windward performance) since there is greater leakage of air over the yard, and the sail cannot so readily be shaped to the aerodynamic optimum. However, Kay (1971: 99) found experimentally that a sail of 1:3 AR gave good results on a broad reach, and that point of sail is probably what Aegean Bronze Age sailors aimed to achieve. When underway, sail area could have been decreased by using the auxiliary halyards to raise the boom towards the yard, and then possibly lowering yard and boom if stability were adversely affected. The sail shape could have been varied by differential use of the auxiliary halyards, thus matching shape and area to changing wind velocities. The sail could be furled by sending down the yard to the boom, and then lowering yard, sail, and boom to the centreline stanchions.

4.7.2.2.3.6 *Station-keeping*
With vessels of different sizes being propelled by three, if not four, different means (one or two ways of paddling, oars, and sail), keeping station within the flotilla would have posed a problem. In post-medieval terms, S5 (the 'flagship') would have been the datum, giving S3 the relatively easy task of following in her wake. Ships forward of S5 (S6, 7, and 8) would have had more difficulty. The oared boat (S1) and the oared or paddled boat (S9), being astern and ahead of a mainly paddled column of ships would doubtless have maintained somewhat fluid relative positions. The ship under sail (S6) would have had the most difficult task, not only being on the starboard bow of the flagship, but perhaps

more importantly, not easily being able to maintain the same track as the rest of the flotilla or to hold a matching speed. Ship S6 appears to be out of line with S1, 2, 4, and 8, and it might be thought that she was sailing between the two columns at her own speed, thereby giving her captain and helmsmen an easier time. This deduction may be more than the evidence can bear: as, indeed, may the idea that Bronze Age ships kept station as known in recent times.

### 4.7.2.2.4 *Reconstructions of a Thera ship*

At least four attempts have been made to produce a hypothetical reconstruction in the form of a scale drawing and/or lines plan (Gillmer, 1975, 1978, 1985a, 1989, 1995, Giesecke, 1983; Toby, 1986; Gifford, 1997). Gillmer also had a scale model built. The four reconstructions differ in several ways, not least in their overall dimensions (Table 4.2).

**Table 4.2**  Reconstructions of a Thera ship

| L | B | D | Author | B/D ratio | L/B ratio |
|---|---|---|--------|-----------|-----------|
| 24.0 | × 3.7 | × 1.9 m | Gillmer | 1.95 | 6.49 |
| 35.0 | × 4.0 | × 2.3 m | Giesecke | 1.74 | 8.75 |
| 34.0 | × 2.2 | × 0.8 m | Toby | 2.75 | 15.45 |
| 17.6 | × 2.6 | × 1.4 m | Gifford | 1.86 | 6.77 |

In theory, these four authors (at least two of whom, Gillmer and Gifford, are naval architects) have based their reconstructions on the same evidence, the Thera friezes, and should therefore have evolved very similar reconstructions. However, some looked further afield than others for parallels, and each individual made different assumptions. Gillmer and Toby took some account of all reconstructions published before their own paper, whereas Giesecke and Gifford did not. All approached the subject in a quantitative, rather than qualitative, manner, but Gillmer's ideas are the most closely argued, although even he does not explicitly state all his assumptions, nor does he state, for example, precisely how he estimated the dimensions of the reconstruction. Nevertheless, Gillmer's reconstruction may have the edge on the others in that he was first in the field, and, over a period of fifteen years, has steadily refined his assessment. Furthermore, he seems to have worked with the excavator, S. Marinatos.

However, there is a major inconsistency in his calculations (see below), and there are a number of reasons why his general approach, and that of the others, cannot be supported.

#### 4.7.2.2.4.1 *Reconstruction techniques*
These reconstruction techniques may be compared with the general method of hypothetically reconstructing a vessel from two-dimensional evidence discussed in 1.3. Gillmer, for example, first estimated the scale of S3 and S5 by measuring the proportion of the overall length of the depictions occupied by the paddlers. The spacing of the paddlers was then assumed to be a length which Gillmer estimated from past experience, and from this the scale was determined, and the overall length and the depth of hull amidships calculated. This scaling was not always used rigorously: for example, depth of hull was chosen by Gifford to suit twentieth-century paddling geometry.

Gillmer estimated the general hull shape by considering the apparent distribution of body volume along the profile of the representation, and the difference in longitudinal curvature at bow and stern. Gillmer then 'borrowed' the sections of the Dahshur boats (2.8.3.2) of *c*.1800 BC. Others used different methods: for example, Toby was convinced that the vessel was designed for speed, and therefore chose a high L/B ratio which resulted in a beam of only 2.2 m, almost half of that estimated by Gillmer.

Gillmer based his reconstruction of the mast, sail, and rigging on the evidence from ship S6, whilst various methods were used by the others. One result of these differing approaches is that the sail areas postulated vary: 45 m² (Gifford); 61.5 or 58.8 m² (Gillmer); and 183.9 m², or even 204.3 m² (Toby).

As a result of devising these greatly differing reconstructions, the performance assessments varied from author to author.

#### 4.7.2.2.4.2 *The problem of scale*
Assessing the scale is the first step in the reconstruction: if this is wrong, any reconstruction is flawed. Gillmer's method of estimating the scale has been criticized by Lambrou-Phillipson (1996: 359–60). She has demonstrated that, in order to deduce an overall length of 24 m for ship S3, Gillmer must have allotted each paddler only *c*.0.5 m. In fact, although paddlers occupy much less space athwartships than oarsmen,

they need only slightly less length longitudinally if they are to paddle efficiently (McGrail, 1978: 131–2). If this spacing is taken as *c*.0.9 m, the overall length of S3 should be over 40 m instead of Gillmer's 24 m. Gifford has chosen an even closer spacing of 0.35 m which results in an overall length of only 17.6 m. A tightly packed but realistic spacing of 0.7 m would result in an overall length of *c*.34 m (the figure proposed by Giesecke and by Toby).

### 4.7.2.2.5 *The Thera ships*

Before the performance of an ancient vessel, be it excavated or some form of representation, can be estimated, a hypothetical reconstruction of the original form, propulsion, and steering has to be undertaken (Coates *et al.*, 1995: 296). The methods used by the four reconstructors may be faulted on two main counts: inappropriate means were used (a) to deduce the scale of the representations; and (b) to reconstruct the transverse section from what is essentially two-dimensional evidence. As Lambrou-Phillipson (1996: 360) pointed out, the Bronze Age artist probably did not aspire to the reliability and accuracy attributed to them by twentieth-century naval architects: the ships and boats and the spacing of the men on board are not necessarily depicted at a standard scale; and there is insufficient consistency in the depictions to enable an operational waterline to be chosen. It seems clear that the Thera depictions, even if the effects of inappropriate restoration are allowed for, cannot bear the weight of some of the conclusions drawn by the four reconstructors.

Nevertheless, something *can* be deduced about Aegean boats and ships, even if the surviving evidence to date is insufficient to support a reconstruction from which detailed performance could be estimated. A Thera ship in its every day role may be described in the following way.

#### 4.7.2.2.5.1 *Form*
Longitudinally the flat bottom curves upwards to join the bow and the stern. The stern is fuller, and rises more sharply, and to a slightly greater height than the bow. It is not possible to estimate the length of such a ship; the beam over the central part of the ship was probably greater than the minimum needed for two oarsmen on a bench; the depth of hull was probably not more than that needed to use oars at sheer level.

#### 4.7.2.2.5.2 *Structure*
These ships were probably planked vessels, most likely built plank-first, but it is not possible to describe the fastenings. They may or may not have had a keel, since masts may be stepped on a plank-keel, or even on the foundation plank of a vessel without any sort of keel (McGrail, 1998: 218–29). Moreover, if there were a mast beam, to which the mast could be secured, a mast step would not be essential (Blue *et al.*, 1997: 202–3). There was probably a deck aft for the captain and helmsman, and a deck forward for a lookout or an armed man, otherwise these were probably 'open boats'. It seems likely that oarsmen sat on the crossbeams with their oars pivoted on or near the sheer.

#### 4.7.2.2.5.3 *Propulsion and steering*
These ships could be propelled by sail or by oar. It seems likely they could be used in one of two roles:

- under sail, with a few auxiliary oars: there would be no need to unstep the mast;
- under sail, but able to man a full set of oars: the yard, sail, and boom could be sent down to a spar stowage on the centreline above the oarsmen; if needs be, the mast could be unstepped and stored in a crutch at deck level.

The main rigging consisted of halyards and auxiliary halyards, braces, and sheets. Although not depicted, it is likely that some of this rigging doubled-up as stays and/or shrouds when sailing conditions required it. It is not possible to specify the number of oarsmen, but the likelihood is that they pulled one oar each.

The helmsman (or men) was stationed on the quarter and probably used a steering oar.

#### 4.7.2.2.5.4 *Crew*
There was a captain/master stationed aft, one or two helmsmen and a few (four?) seamen. In those ships in which a full set of oars could be manned there would also have been a number of oarsmen (who may have doubled as armed men when needed).

#### 4.7.2.2.5.5 *Function*
It seems likely that the same hull could be fitted out in one of two roles defined by their means of propulsion. It is likely that this hull was a general-purpose shape rather than being an optimum design (as known today) for one or other of these roles:

- A cargo or ferry role. Ships were under sail, with a few auxiliary oars available.
- A fighting or piracy role. Ships were under sail or under oars, as conditions dictated.

### 4.7.2.2.6 *Thera Boats*

Boats were similar in form, and probably structure, to the ships, even having a deck aft. They could be propelled by sail, oar or paddle, and were steered, when necessary, by a steering oar. They had a helmsman when needed, and a master/captain. They were probably used for fishing, and as ferries and tenders.

### 4.7.2.2.7 *Reinterpretation?*

These deductions, and those of most (all?) other commentators, have been made from photographs, drawings, and descriptions of the vessels as restored. The only way to improve on such observations would seem to be for a small group of specialists to hold a seminar on site with the conservators and curators of the National Museum in Athens.

# 4.8

# The Late Bronze Age (*c*.1550–1100 BC)

Overseas trade, as evidenced by the excavation of imported goods from the Levant in the east and as far west as Sardinia (and possibly Spain) markedly increased during the Late Bronze Age (Bass, 1991; 1997; A. Knapp, 1993). Whether there was a single thalassocratic power dominating this trade and, if so, whether this was Minoan/Mycenaean, Cypriot, Levantine/Syrio-Canaanite, or even Egyptian, has been argued at length. It is increasingly possible to identify the source of raw materials and traded goods, and even ballast, by scientific means, but this information does not lead directly to the identification of the origins of the shipbuilder, the shipowner, or the merchant. The excavation of a number of eastern Mediterranean wreck sites dated to this period (see e.g. that at Ulu Burun (4. 8. 3. 1) has intensified, rather than simplified, this problem.

Such matters, and the related one of determining the countries visited by a ship before she was wrecked, have been discussed in more detail in 1.4.2.1.

On some aspects of overseas trade there is more of a consensus. It is generally agreed that trading voyages resembled those of the later 'tramp' ships—cabotage, as it is sometimes known. Ships went from port to port, often on coastal routes, loading and unloading a variety of merchandise and raw materials, as the occasion arose. It appears that, from the evidence principally of the wreck sites excavated off Cape Gelidonya and Ulu Burun, off the south-west coast of Turkey, there were three main types of cargo:

- prestige items such as personal decorations, beads, pins, pendants, jewellery, scarabs, special drinking cups, and ivory carvings;
- relatively low cargo-density goods such as textiles, pottery, and glass; medium cargo-density liquid and solid contents of large pottery containers, and raw materials such as logs of wood.
- high density raw materials such as copper and tin in ingot form.

Such a range of commodities has led some authors to believe that, whilst the trade in ingots may have been between regional authorities, much of the trade could be described as commercial. The range in cargo density of the items in such cargoes, suggests also that Bronze Age seafarers were aware of the necessity to ensure a ship was loaded to a stable condition (McGrail, 1989*b*).

## 4.8.1 DOCUMENTARY EVIDENCE

By this date there are a number of texts which refer, directly and indirectly, to seafaring and overseas trade. Texts, dated from the early fourteenth century to the late twelfth century BC, excavated from Ugarit, a city state and entrepôt north of Latakia on the northern stretch of the Levant coast (Wachsmann, 1998: 333–44), indicate that trading voyages were relatively commonplace within an arc which extended from Egypt in the south, along the Levant coast to Cyprus, the Anatolian coast in the north, and the Aegean in the west. There are no descriptions of ships in these accounts, but we learn, for example, that one ship had a crew of nineteen; and that another had nine oars, a hatch and a mast with rigging. Ports named include Acco, Byblos, Sidon, and Tyre. Cargo included barley grain, copper, stone, and jars of oil (see also Linder, 1972).

Other documents, written in Akkadian, originating in the Levant and excavated from El Amarna in Egypt, confirm the existence of trading by sea between the Levant and Egypt.

Clay tablets, dated towards the end of the Late Bronze Age, excavated from Knossos, Pylos, Mycenae, and Thebes have accounts and decrees written on them in archaic Greek (Linear B). Some tablets contain lists of oarsmen, whilst others have an outline or an ideogram of a ship on the reverse. It also seems possible that some of the names given are ships' names (Wachsmann, 1998: 123–8). Many tablets remain to be transcribed and translated, thus there is a possibility that more may be learned about the Aegean aspects of the overseas trading network.

## 4.8.2 ICONOGRAPHIC EVIDENCE

Wachsmann (1998: 130–58) has described numerous Mycenaean representations of vessels dated to the Late Bronze Age. These ships and boats are generally depicted upwards from the 'keel', rather than from the waterline. Their orientation can generally be deduced from the steering equipment near the stern. From this corpus a general description of a Mycenaean vessel may be compiled: this cannot be detailed since all depictions that can be interpreted give a broadside-on view only. These vessels are generally long in relation to their depth of hull. They have a flat bottom longitudinally with the ends curving up at bow and stern. Occasional vessels have a bow set at an angle to the bottom, and a few have a projecting forefoot. They appear to have a deck raised up above the hull on stanchions, evidently for use by armed men. At the stern there is a smaller deck for the helmsman, and another at the bow for the lookout. The fighting ship depicted on shards from Livanates (on the Greek mainland west of the island of Euboea and thought to be the site of ancient Kynos) is a near-typical example of such vessels (Dakoronia, 1990; Wachsmann, 1998: fig. 7.8).

These vessels are generally galleys: the oarsmen ply their oars below (and possibly outboard of) the raised deck; and a single mast is stepped near amidships, supported by stays and with a rigging block near the mast-head. The helmsman appears to have only one steering device (probably a side rudder rather than a steering oar) which he uses on the starboard quarter.

There are also several models from this period, many of them fragmentary: they add only a little to our knowledge (Wachsmann, 1998: 148–53).

The terracotta model from Phylakopi (Wachsmann, 1998: 149, fig. 7.42) has oculi near the bow which ends in an unusual protrusion. Painted bands across the inside of the hull appear to represent frames.

There are two models from Tanagra (Wachsmann, 1998: 148–9, figs. 7.39, 7.41). Both have lines painted inside which may represent a keel or keelson and some of the framing.

Both ends of a model from Argos (Palaiologou, 1989; Wachsmann, 1998: 152–3, figs. 7.53, 7.54) are broken but one end is more pointed than the other which is probably the stern. In section, the hull is flat-bottomed with rounded sides. There is a mast step near amidships and two painted strips from sheer to sheer probably represent frames. The feature in the stern is probably a raised deck for the steersman. This model is not unlike the general run of the two-dimensional depictions.

## 4.8.3 WRECKS (Fig. 4.3)

There are three underwater sites of this period that have been excavated in the eastern Mediterranean: one dated c.1200 BC in the Gulf of Argolid, off the eastern coast of the Peloponnes; and two off the south-west coast of Turkey, one of c.1200 and one of c.1300 BC.

### 4.8.3.1 ULUBURUN (Parker, 1992: no. 1193)

This wreck site off the south-west of Turkey was excavated between 1984 and 1994. The ship had been carrying a wide range of raw materials and goods from nine or ten different cultures, including c.10 tonnes of copper and c.1 tonne of tin (Bass, 1987, 1991; Bass et al., 1989; Pulak, 1998). The distribution and weight of the cargo and the size of her twenty-four anchor stones suggest that this was a relatively large ship, and it has been estimated that her overall length was 15–16 m (Steffy, 1994: 36–7).

Only about 2 m length of the hull has been exposed (Fig. 4.22): a plank-keel, sided 275 mm, and several

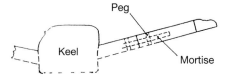

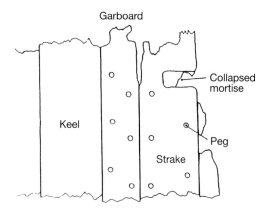

Fig. 4.22. Uluburun wreck remains (after Wachsmann, 1998: fig. 10.2).

planks of cedar were recorded. The planking, which is *c*.60 mm thick and 170–260 mm broad, is fastened together by oak mortise and tenon joints, spaced at 240–60 mm intervals within the thickness of each plank. These joints are larger and more widely spaced than those noted in first millennium BC hulls of similar size and structure. The Uluburun mortises are unusually deep, sometimes extending to within a centimetre or so of the opposite plank edge; occasionally they intersect joints from the far edge (Pulak, 1998: 211). Unlike Egyptian vessels with this form of joint, the 20

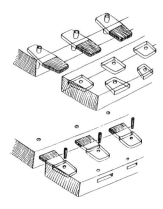

Fig. 4.23. Locked mortise and tenon fastenings (after Pomey, 1997: 94).

mm thick tenons were locked in position within their mortises by transpiercing pegs *c*.22 mm in diameter (Fig. 4.23).

No framing timbers were revealed and there were no signs of frame fastenings in the lengths of planking investigated.

Fragments of oar blades have been excavated, and five round and pointed stakes with associated withies are thought to be part of a wicker fencing/bulwark as seen, for example, on the Levantine ship depicted in the fourteenth-century tomb of Kenamun at Thebes in Egypt (Fig. 4.27). The Uluburun cargo may be compared with that depicted being unloaded from these Kenamun ships, and with reference to traded goods in the near-contemporary Amarna letters. Pulak (1998: 215) interprets the variety and richness of the Uluburun cargo as evidence for an official gift exchange between two specific states, one in the Levant or Cyprus and one in the Aegean. The anchor stones appear to be typical of the Levant coast, and the wooden writing boards, cymbals, trumpet cups, a bronze statuette, and some of the personal possessions and tools seem to be Near Eastern in style. All this leads Pulak to suggest a Levantine origin for the ship which has been dated by dendrochronology to 'a few years after 1305 BC' (Pulak, 1998: 214).

### 4.8.3.2 CAPE GELIDONYA (Parker,1992: no. 208)

This wreck site was excavated during 1960 and again in 1987–9 (Bass, 1967, 1991; Lambrou-Phillipson, 1995). The cargo included copper, bronze, and tin ingots on a matting and brushwood dunnage: there were also ballast stones. It has been estimated that the ship was 9–11 m overall in length. Only a few fragments of hull were investigated but these showed that the planking had been fastened together with locked mortise and tenon joints which were somewhat smaller than those on the Uluburun wreck (Pulak, 1998: 210). The wreck is dated by radiocarbon to *c*.1200 BC, and the excavator considers it to be that of a Canaanite/Syrian ship.

### 4.8.3.3 POINT IRIA

This wreck site in the Gulf of Argolid on the east coast of the Peloponnese, was excavated from 1990 to 1994 by the Hellenic Institute of Marine Archaeology (Delgado, 1997: 190). Pottery on board, from Crete, Cyprus and Greece, has been dated to *c.*1200 BC: there are no reports of hull remains.

#### 4.8.3.4 TRANSFER OF TECHNOLOGY

The hull remains of the Gelidonya and Uluburun wrecks raise the problem of the relationship of their plank fastenings to those used in Egypt in the third and early second millennium BC (2.7.1 and 2.8.3.4). The Egyptian mortise and tenon joints were not locked, and they were used in conjunction with other forms of fastening. The eastern Mediterranean joints of the mid-to late second millennium BC, on the other hand, were locked; whether there was also a second type of fastening (e.g. sewing) is uncertain due to the limited extent of planking so far investigated. It seems likely that there was some transfer of technology between Eygpt and the eastern Mediterranean, perhaps via the Levant: this must remain a hypothesis, however, for lack of direct evidence.

# 4.9
# The Early Iron Age (*c.*1100–550 BC)

The Late Bronze Age civilizations of the eastern Mediterranean appears to have ended during the early twelfth century BC, possibly as a result of intrusion into the region by marauders known to the Egyptians as the 'Sea People' who had been raiding the Levant coast from the fourteenth century BC (2.9.4). Mycenaean sites in Greece were destroyed and depopulated; the Hittite culture of Anatolia collapsed; cities in Cyprus and the Levant were violently destroyed; and displaced people tried to settle elsewhere, adding to the confusion and disruption.

### 4.9.1 SHIPS OF THE 'SEA PEOPLE'

A fleet of Ramses III attacked a group of Sea People's ships in harbour in *c.*1176 BC, and scenes from this battle appear in relief on that Pharaoh's mortuary temple at Medinet Habu (Fig. 2.28). Four Egyptian and five Sea People's ships are depicted (Wachsmann, 1998: 166–75;

figs. 8.1–8.15), their nationality being indicated by the different headdress worn by each crew. The two types of ship differ in their longitudinal profile: the Egyptian hulls have a smooth curve between bottom and rising ends; whereas, the Sea People's ships have near-vertical ends capped by a bird figurehead (Wachsmann, 1998: fig. 8.2). Otherwise Egyptian and Sea People's ships are similar, being galleys propelled by a single square sail on a mast stepped near amidships, and by oarsmen along each side. They both have a raised deck/fighting platform at each end, probably connected by a raised gangway/deck along the centreline between the two lines of oarsmen. Both have loose-footed sails with brails, and there is a fighting top/lookout at the masthead. Two Sea People's ships (N1 and N5 in Wachsmann, 1998: fig. 8.2, 8.10, 8.12) appear to have two quarter rudders: the Egyptian ships depicted appear to have only one, but two are known from ships, models, and depictions from earlier times (2.7.5). Sea People's ships N4 and N5 (Wachsmann, 1998: figs. 8.11, 8.12) have a short pointed projection at the junction of stern post with 'keel' which may indicate a special method of joining the two timbers.

Assuming that these depictions of Sea People's ships are generally typical of the Levant, ships from these two regions appear to have much in common, apart from the form of their ends which seems to perpetuate the much earlier distinction between Egyptian and Mesopotamian vessels (2.4). This superficially suggests that the Egyptian hull form may have been introduced to the Aegean (as, for example, depicted on the Thera reliefs (Figs. 4.21 and 4.22); whereas the Mesopotamian hull may have been introduced to the Levant, to be subsequently used by the Sea People. Such differences in form are merely suggestive, however, and depictions such as those of Medinet Habu do not preclude significant structural differences between the two types. It may be, for example, that Egyptian hulls were still partly fastened by sewing whilst the 'Levant' hulls were fastened by the locked mortice and tenon joints found on the second millennium BC Cape Gelidonya and Uluburun wrecks. This again is speculation: detailed investigations of the structure of further wrecks from this period are needed to turn this into a hypothesis.

The Medinet Habu relief also shows that an improved sailing rig was used in the eastern Mediterranean: it may be that this change originated in the Levant.

## 4.9.2 THE POST-MYCENAEAN EASTERN MEDITERRANEAN

Homer's *Iliad* and *Odyssey*, epic poems first written down during 750–700 BC, but probably based on much earlier oral traditions (4.4.6) contain references to ships and to seafaring. The Greek historians Herodotus (*c*.480–420 BC) and Thucydides (*c*.460–400 BC) discuss similar matters, from the eighth century BC onwards.

Depictions of ships also appear on Greek pottery of the Geometric (ninth and eighth century) and Archaic (seventh and sixth centuries) periods. From the same centuries there are depictions of Phoenician ships and boats on Assyrian reliefs.

### 4.9.2.1 HOMER'S SHIPS

The ships described in the *Iliad* and the *Odyssey* are black, and sometimes have blue bows (Rieu, 1946: 48, 124, 204). There appear to be two sizes of what might be called 'general purpose ships': smaller ones of twenty oars and larger ones of fifty-two (Rieu, 1946: 29, 124). Fifty-oared ships are mentioned in the *Iliad* (Seymour, 1907: 308; Rieu, 1950: 58). Cargo ships could be propelled by twenty oars; their distinguishing feature was their broad beam (Rieu, 1946: 150, 199).

How such ships were built is described in a passage (*Odyssey*, 5: 234–57) which has been understood in several ways. Casson (1964) has interpreted the passage in the light of information from the Cape Gelidonya and Uluburun wrecks: the planking of Odysseus' ship was fastened together with mortise and tenon joints locked by pegs. Subsequently the framing was fastened to the planking by treenails to reinforce the planking shell. This method of building is generally agreed by Morrison (1995: 142–3). On the other hand, Mark (1991) considers that the passage describes the building of a sewn-plank boat as evidenced by the sixth-century BC boats of the eastern and central Mediterranean (4.9.4). Casson (1992) argued strongly against this hypothesis and stimulated a rejoinder from Mark (1996).

Homer's description is enigmatic and incomplete: it would be impossible to reconstruct a practical method of building a boat from that text alone. A knowledge of sewn-plank or mortise and tenon techniques is needed to fill the gaps in Homer's description and produce a coherent sequence. Homer could have been describing either a sewn-plank boat or one fastened with mortise and tenon joints: in both cases, however, there are anomalies. A third possibility is that both sewn and wooden fastenings were used in Homer's boat. In the Egyptian vessels of the third and second millennium BC known to date, *both* techniques are used (2.7.1 and 2.8.3.4). Furthermore, as Morrison (1995: 143) and others have pointed out, the Greek ships at Troy may well have had sewn planking since Homer (*Iliad*, 2: 135) states that their planking had rotted and the cords had worked loose (Rieu, 1950: 43 prefers 'rigging' to 'cords'). The fact that the Cape Gelidonya and Uluburun wrecks had locked mortise and tenon planking need not undermine the suggestion that Homer's ships were sewn (at least in part): only minor samples of the Cape Gelidonya planking have been recovered and only *c*.1.8 m of the Uluburun hull has been examined: in both cases, the use of sewing as well as mortise and tenon fastenings remains a possibility.

What is probably beyond argument is that Homer describes a plank-first sequence of boatbuilding. Alder, poplar, and fir timber was used; some superstructure, perhaps an *ikria*, was added to the vessel at the stern. A washstrake of wattle-fencing was fastened to the sides to keep spray from blowing inboard.

In other sections of the *Odyssey* and the *Iliad* (Rieu, 1946: 46, 47, 124, 163, 198/9, 205, 206, 245, 336; Rieu, 1950: 34, 35; Seymour, 1907: 312–13), we learn that masts of fir were set in a mast step and supported by two forestays and a backstay; the mast rested in a notch in the mast beam, and could be lowered into a crutch at the stern. Sails were of white linen and, when not needed, they were stowed under the thwarts in the bottom of the boat. These sails were controlled by braces, brails/halyards, and sheets, and these and other ropes could be made from oxhide/plaited leather, wood, or papyrus. Oars were of pine and were worked against a thole through a leather grommet.

#### 4.9.2.1.1 *Ship operations*

Victuals embarked for a voyage of several days included: wine in jars or in skins, water in skins, and barley meal or corn in sewn skin bags (Rieu, 1946: 42, 94).

Ships could be anchored offshore in a sheltered cove using an anchor stone. After anchoring, the stern was brought to the beach in 'Mediterranean moor' fashion (Seymour, 1907: 314). For an overnight stay mast and sail were sometimes put ashore. At times boats were dragged up the beach and held upright with props. On occasions, a vessel could be propelled up the beach so that half the keel's length was ashore. When a storm was expected anchored ships would be beached stern first, and dragged inland for shelter. Boats that had been beached were 'run down' into the sea; beached ships could be launched by the use of levers (Rieu, 1946: 26, 78, 94, 202–3, 210–11; Rieu, 1950: 36). Navigation at the time of Odysseus has been considered in 4.4.6.

### 4.9.2.2 HERODOTUS

Herodotus (1. 163, 165–6) identified the Phocaeans, from the Aegean coast of Anatolia, as the foremost and earliest of Greek overseas explorers: in the Adriatic, to Italy and Corsica in the Tyrrhenian Sea, and as far west as Tartessus on the Atlantic coast of Iberia. He also mentioned, almost in passing, how the Greeks had traded and settled overseas; at *Bubastis* and *Naucratis* on the River Nile; on the coasts and rivers of the Black Sea region; and on the Libyan coast in Cyrenaica (2. 154, 2. 178, 4. 24, 4. 51, 4. 151–8).

Three types of early seagoing sailing ships are mentioned by Herodotus (1. 163, 1. 152, 1. 166, 3. 136, 4. 148, 4. 153, 4. 156, 6. 26, 6. 95, 6. 101, 7. 25, 7. 97, 7. 147):

(a)  Ships used for settlement voyages: these were either thirty-oared or fifty-oared, and could also be sailed.

(b)  Merchant ships: these were distinguished from other types by being 'broad-beamed'. In early times, the Phocaeans used fifty-oared ships for trading voyages; it may be that, in contrast, the later broad-beamed merchant ship had no oars, or possibly just a few for manœuvring.

(c)  Fighting ships: these always appear to be galleys, i.e. capable of being propelled both by sail and by a full complement of oarsmen. Spartan ships were fifty-oared, whilst those of the Phocaeans had rams. Sea battles are described in the Sardinian Sea, off Artemisium (Rieu, 1946: 501) and off Salamis (Herodotus, 8.84–92).

Pentaconters (fifty-oared ships) were evidently the mainstay of Greek shipping, being used for exploration, settlement, trading and fighting. It could be that the phrase 'fifty-oared' was a measure of size of vessel, regardless of how many, or how few, oars were embarked. On the other hand, a pentaconter may have actually been propelled by fifty oarsmen as well as by

sail, a general purpose ship used in many roles. Such a ship, with twenty-five oarsmen each side would have been *c.*30 m in length overall, and at least 2 m broad at the waterline for much of this length.

There is little on the operation or the performance of ships in Herodotus. He does, however, note that fighting ships were hauled ashore to dry out (7. 59); that Cape Malea was difficult to make eastbound in the *Etesian* wind; and he seems to imply that Greek ships could tack on a fine reach, i.e. making good a track some seven points off the wind (6. 139–40).

### 4.9.2.3 THUCYDIDES

Thucydides, writing in *c.*411 BC, mentions three groups of Greeks as being active in the maritime field in earlier times: the Athenians who colonized Ionia (Aegean coast of Asia Minor) and the offshore islands, and who, in later years, took part in several battles at sea, and sailed from Cyprus up the River Nile as far as Memphis; the Phocaeans who defeated the Carthaginians in a sea battle and founded a settlement at Massalia/ Marseilles; and the Corinthians of the Peloponnesian isthmus, who not only are thought to have built the first triremes in Greece in *c.*700 BC, but also to have taken part in the first recorded sea battle, against the Corcyraeans in the mid-seventh century BC, and attained eminence in overseas trade (Warner, 1954: 20, 21, 70; Loseby, 1992).

Most of these voyages and battles were undertaken in 'longboats' and fifty-oared vessels without decks, i.e. they were 'open boats' (Warner, 1954: 18, 21). In the mid-sixth century BC, however, Polycrates, ruler of Samos, added forty triremes to his fleet (Warner, 1954: 21; Papalas, 1999: 12), and by the early fifth century, triremes were being used in great numbers (Warner, 1954: 21).

## 4.9.3  SHIPS IN THE EASTERN MEDITERRANEAN

### 4.9.3.1 AEGEAN

Ships which appear to be 'longships', some of them possibly pentaconters, are depicted on Greek Geometric pottery from the ninth and eighth centuries BC (Casson, 1971: figs. 62–8, 70–2, 74, 77; Wachsmann, 1998: figs. 7.11–7.14). Most of these depictions seem to represent

Fig. 4.24. Ship depicted on a Late Geometric vase from Dipylon (Louvre, Paris).

warships. Herodotus' penteconter merchant ships and those used on settlement voyages were probably broader in the beam than the warships, and had greater height of sides and therefore more freeboard, although, as Coates (1990a) has pointed out, a monoreme penteconter has inherently more space for cargo and people than a bireme or trireme.

These ships are all depicted in profile, and most have a high curving stern and a ram (4.12.3). Some of these vessels (Fig. 4.24) have one tier of oarsmen, but others (Fig. 4.25) appear to have two tiers. It has been argued that the apparent bireme in Fig. 4.25 is actually a distorted perspective plan view of a monoreme, and this may be so, since only the oars of the lower/nearer oarsmen appear to enter the water to starboard. However, other fragments of pottery dated 760–735 BC (Morrison, 1995a: fig. 175; Morrison, 1995b: 55; Casson, 1971: 70–2; Wachsmann, 1998: figs. 7.12–14) do appear to show biremes, which, if they still carried fifty oarsmen,

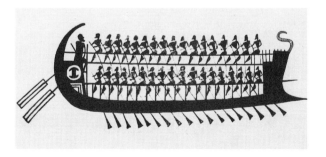

Fig. 4.25. Ship depicted on an eighth-century bowl from Thebes (after Casson, 1971: fig 7.4).

would have been much shorter and therefore more manoeuvrable than the monoreme.

Both types have raised decks at bow and stern and some of the monoremes appear to have a deck for armed men above, and probably inboard of, the single tier of oarsmen. Most of these depictions appear to be propelled by oars alone, however, there is a mast on a shard from the Acropolis, Athens, dated late eighth century (Casson, 1971: fig. 70; Morrison, 1995b: fig. 175A; Wachsmann, 1998: fig. 7.14), and this suggests that these warships/pirate ships were galleys which used a sail in fair winds, but oars in action and in foul winds.

Ships depicted on Archaic pottery of the seventh and sixth centuries BC (Morrison, 1995b: figs. 177–9; Casson, 1971: figs. 81–5, 88–91) are generally similar (both monoremes and biremes) but almost always have a mast stepped, sometimes with a sail set. In a number of these depictions, the ram is clearly being used offensively—see, for example, the Aristonothos vase of the mid-seventh century BC (Basch, 1987a: fig. 482).

### 4.9.3.2 LEVANT COAST

Around 2000 BC, a number of city-states emerged on the Levant coast. The inhabitants became active in maritime trade from the early second millennium BC, and there was a continuity in their nautical terminology from the Late Bronze Age to the sixth century BC (Stieglitz, 1999: 415). These seafaring people subsequently came to be called 'Phoenicians' by the Greeks, although they were known to themselves from at least 1450 BC as 'Canaanites' (Aubet, 1993: 8–9). In the *Iliad* (23. 743–4) these people are referred to as 'Sidonians' after one of their principal cities (Herodotus, 1. 2; 2. 116). These were the seafarers and overseas traders in fast, black ships that the early Greeks met in the Aegean (*Odyssey*, 13. 272–86). Herodotus (7. 89, 1. 1) believed that they originally came from the Persian Gulf region to settle in the part of Syria known as Palestine. He knew them as experienced seafarers who made long trading voyages from their ports of Tyre and Sidon, with Egyptian and Assyrian goods (1. 1, 1. 2, 2. 116). Although literate (they taught the Greeks to write—Herodotus, 5. 58), they left almost no descriptions of their ships or their seafaring activities, and we have to rely on accounts by Egyptians, Greeks, and Hebrews, and on representations of their ships mainly from Assyria and Egypt.

### 4.9.3.2.1 *Phoenician seafaring*

From the mid-second millennium BC onwards, the Canaanite/Phoenicians made exploratory trading voyages eventually encompassing the length and breadth of the Mediterranean. They principally sought out raw materials, mainly metals—gold, silver, copper, tin—which were needed in the Levant and neighbouring countries: in return they supplied timber to the Israelites (1 Kings 5: 8–9; 10: 11); timber, slaves, and wine to the Egyptians (2.9.2); and resins and spices to the Greeks (Herodotus, 3. 107, 111). They also traded with Cyprus, Sicily, Sardinia, Malta, southern Spain, and places along the north African coast. By the mid-first millennium BC they were trading with Atlantic harbours beyond the Pillars of Hercules (Herodotus, 4. 196).

In the eighth century BC a Phoenician colony was established at Carthage and in the mid-first millennium BC, Himilco and Hanno were sent out from there to explore the Atlantic coasts. Himilco sailed along the European coast, possibly only as far as Cape St Vincent (the Sacred Cape) but maybe as far north as Coruña and beyond (Avienus: 116–29); whilst Hanno sailed along the African coast possibly as far as Senegal, Cameroon, or even Gabon (Ramin, 1976; E. Taylor, 1971: 46; Oikonomides and Miller, 1995). Other Carthaginians probably visited the Canary Islands since Punic coins have been excavated there.

In addition to Carthage, Phoenicians settled in Malta in the eighth century BC, Sardinia, and the region around Gadir (Cadiz) in southern Spain, by the ninth century (Aubet, 1993: 222). The Phoenicians appear to have had an eye for natural harbours (Aubet, 1993: 140): many of these, like Tyre and Sidon, were on islands or peninsulas: Gadir in Atlantic Spain; Motya in western Sicily dominating the Carthage strait; Mogador and Lixus in Atlantic Morocco; and notably Carthage. They built artificial basins (*cothon*) at some of these sites to increase harbour capacity and to improve loading facilities.

The seafaring abilities of the Phoenicians were clearly recognized by the Egyptians, the Persians, and the Israelites, and, grudgingly, by the Greeks. Pharaoh Necho II (twenty-sixth dynasty, *c*.600 BC) chose a Phoenician ship to investigate the possibility of circumnavigating Africa clockwise, i.e. south down the Red Sea and back into the Mediterranean through the Strait of Gibraltar (2.10). Herodotus (4. 42) says that they took about two-and-a-half years and when they returned to Eygpt, they reported that, as they sailed south and west around southern Africa, the noon sun was to the north. Although they were not believed by their contemporaries, or by Herodotus, their statement is clear proof that they had been in the southern hemisphere and probably had circumnavigated the continent. For a recent critical appraisal of the evidence, see Kahanov (1999).

The Persians also much valued the Phoenicians' experience and included them in their war fleets; indeed, Herodotus (3. 19) states that the whole naval power of Cambyses (*c*.530–522 BC), son of Cyrus, depended on the Phoenicians, and they were very prominent in Xerxes' fleet at the Battle of Salamis (480 BC).

To the rulers and scribes of Israel, the Phoenicians were men 'who knew the sea' (1 Kings 9: 26–8) and 'rulers of the sea' (Ezekiel 26: 16), who did 'business with the nations in innumerable islands' (Ezekiel 27: 1–3). The Phoenicians 'whose traders were princes, whose merchants, the great ones of the world', 'whose goods travelled over the sea, over wide oceans' (Isaiah 23: 1–8).

The Greeks, who rivalled the Phoenicians in exploration and trading from the eighth century onwards, did not eulogize so. Nevertheless, from Homer to Strabo, they testify to the Phoenician abilities at sea. Strabo (1. 1. 6) gives precedence to the Phoenicians in matters of navigation, a view which was subsequently endorsed by the Roman Pliny (*NH* 7. 57) who understood that the Phoenicians were the first in the Mediterranean to apply a knowledge of astronomy (learnt from the Chaldeans) to the problem of navigation in the open sea. For example, the Phoenicians identified the constellation Ursa Minor and realized that, since it orbited the celestial North Pole in a tighter circle than did Ursa Major, it gave them a more accurate direction of North (Fig. 4.26). It is significant that the Classical world called this most useful, but not easily recognized, constellation, 'Phoinike' (Aubet, 1993: 142).

### 4.9.3.2.2 *Canaanite/Phoenician ships*

Cargo ships from the Levant coast are mentioned by Egyptian pharaohs in the mid-second millennium BC

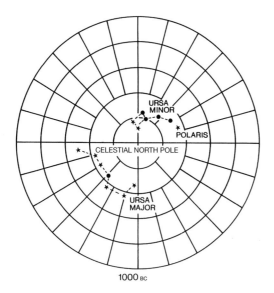

Fig. 4.26. Night sky in c.1000 BC (after Taylor, 1956: fig. 5A).

and there are references to overseas traders in ports along this coast in the Armana texts and in Ugarit documents (Wachsmann, 1998: 39–41). Although much is said about the cargo these ships carried, and these merchants dealt in, the only fact about the ships is that they had cedar planking.

### 4.9.3.2.2.1 *Iconographic evidence*
A cylinder seal (Fig. 4.15) found at Tel el Daba in the Nile delta, and dated to the eighteenth century BC, is thought to be Syrian in origin (Wachsmann, 1998: 42).

The ship on the seal is schematic rather than realistic, but it appears to be near-double-ended, with a mast amidships supported by forestay and backstay. More can be learnt from ships depicted in the early fourteenth century BC tombs of Nebamun and Kenamun at Thebes, Egypt (Fig. 4.27). These ships, which are identified as Syrian by the dress of crew and merchants, are bringing wine or oil, pottery, and cattle to Egypt in return for food, textiles, and sandals (2.9.2) (Wachsmann, 1998: figs. 3.2–3.9, 14.6). One feature which differentiates them from contemporary Egyptian vessels is the vertical post at the stern, rather than the curvacious finial at the stern of Hatshepsut's ships of c.1500 BC (Fig. 2.25). However, vertical stern posts are depicted on seagoing vessels of the Egyptian Old Kingdom (those of Unas and Sahure—Fig. 2.14) and it may be that, in this respect, Hapshetsut's ships are unrepresentative of Egyptian merchant ships of the mid-second millennium BC. No hogging stay is depicted on the Syrian ships. This absence of evidence may not be significant: on the other hand, the Levantine ships appear to be relatively much shorter than Egyptian vessels and would therefore be less likely to need a hogging stay. It may be that, by the mid-second millennium BC, the Syro-Canaanites had developed a 'round' ship with a keel, and a stronger hull (4.9.3.2.3) which was not so susceptible to hogging, and more suitable for a seagoing cargo vessel.

As in the rest of the eastern Mediterranean, there is a dearth of information about Levantine ships until the

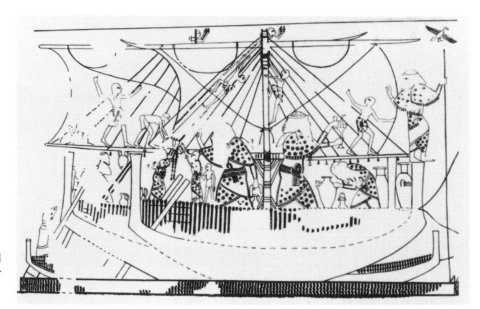

Fig. 4.27. Syrian ships depicted in the tomb of Kenamun (after Casson, 1971: fig. 57).

Fig. 4.28. Phoenician vessels depicted on the Tell Balawat gates (British Museum).

Fig. 4.29 (*below*). Phoenician vessels towing timbers, depicted in the palace of Sargon II at Khorsabad (Louvre, Paris).

ninth century, by which time the Assyrians had the Levant coastal city-states under their control. Bronze reliefs on the Tell Balawat gates of Shalmaneser III of *c*.850 BC, depict Phoenician vessels bringing tribute from their island kingdoms to their Assyrian overlord (Fig. 4.28). These coastal craft have near-vertical ends with horsehead figureheads (*hippoi*) at both ends. They appear to be steered by a steering oar to starboard, and propelled by oars in the stand/pull mode. A Judaean seal of *c*.725 BC (Stieglitz, 1999: fig. 3) has a ship with a square sail and a *hippos* at the bow.

A wall relief from the palace of Sargon II (722–705 BC) at Khorsabad has similar craft, but with a *hippos* at the bows only, towing two, three, or four baulks of timber astern (Fig. 4.29). Tribute rather than trade is probably depicted, since such reliefs appear to have been designed to commemorate some Assyrian triumph. The craft appear to be propelled by oars in the mode stand/push: the oar blades are similar in shape to those on other Assyrian reliefs (3.5.4 and Fig. 3.16). One craft that is not towing timber (Fig. 4.29, left of second register) has a mast stepped near amidships with stays fore

Fig. 4.30. Phoenician warships and cargo ships on a relief in the palace of Sennacherib at Khorsabad (British Museum).

and aft; there is a structure at the masthead, possibly a top or lookout platform.

In 1848, Layard excavated several depictions of Phoenician seagoing ships which had been carved (705–681 BC) in low-relief on limestone in Sennacherib's palace at Khorsabad. Only fragments of these now remain, but Layard had drawn some of them soon after exposure, and photographs were taken of some of the reliefs in 1903–4, although by this time, they had deteriorated significantly. Basch (1987a: 303–18) has pointed out that some of the detail in Layard's drawings are 'improvements' on the original. However, he has concluded that, in general, Layard's drawings are a reasonable record of the reliefs as found.

The scene depicted (Fig. 4.30) is the evacuation of the population of Sidon and Tyre by sea to Cyprus in advance of the invading Assyrians in c.701 BC (Basch, 1969: 144; Morrison, 1995b: 145). Warships and cargo

ships are depicted: both types have two levels of oars manned, the upper tier pivoted at sheer level, the lower through oarports. At a third, higher, level, there are passengers and/or armed men behind a bulwark on which there are shields: these people are probably sitting on benches (cargo ships), or standing (warships), on a deck which appears to run from bow to stern and which may extend the breadth of the vessel (and thus be over the upper oarsmen's heads) or merely be a catwalk along the middle line. Both cargo and warships have steering devices on each quarter: these seem to be steering oars rather than rudders.

Neither type has a figurehead: nevertheless, in later centuries, Phoenician and Carthaginian ships could be identified by a characteristic *hippos* at the bows (3.4.7; Pliny, *NH* 7. 57; Aubet, 1993: 147). Strabo (2. 3. 4), quoting Poseidonius, noted that Eudoxus had found a horse-headed figurehead (*hippos*) when he was shipwrecked in Somalia on his return from his second voyage to India in the late second century BC (6.3). Eudoxus was told, on his return to Egypt, that such a figurehead could only have come from a Phoenician ship based at *Gades*/Cadiz (Johnstone, 1988: 93; Dilke, 1985: 61).

The Khorsabad cargo ships have a 'rounded' hull in longitudinal profile, and are double-ended with near-vertical posts. In contrast, the warships have a less curvaceous hull with a metal-sheathed pointed ram at the bow (Morrison, 1995a: frontispiece) and a stern which, at the tip, curves back on itself. Unlike the cargo ships, the warships have a mast stepped near amidships with stays fore and aft and braces from yardarm to deck: the sail appears to be furled to the yard.

These warships appear to have a series of plain and cross-hatched panels between the upper oarsmen and the upper bulwarks. An incomplete relief from Kuyundjik (Nineveh), also dated to the reign of Sennacherib, depicts a similar warship on which the stanchions that support the deck above the upper level of oarsmen can clearly be seen (Fig. 4.31). Basch (1969: 147) has interpreted the panels as protective screens for the upper oarsmen which he suggests the craftsman has misplaced. Morrison (1995b: 146), on the other hand, considers that the panels represent an unmanned third level of oars: that is, he believes these warships were triremes rather than biremes. A third possibility has been put forward by Sleeswyk (1999) who presents cross-sectional scale drawings of oarage systems in support of his thesis. Sleeswyk suggests that two types

of warship are depicted: those with tumblehome (sides curving inwards); and those with outriggers. These theories depend upon the detailed interpretation of certain features (e.g. the precise position of the foremost upper oar in one of the warships) which may not have been the intention of the craftsman. Furthermore, Sleeswyk does not explain the series of plain and cross-hatched panels except to conclude that they could not be protection for the upper oarsmen in the way Basch visualized.

It must be accepted that these depictions are diagrams rather than draughtsman's scale drawings. The minimilist interpretation is that these Phoenician ships are biremes (two tiers of oars) and not triremes. The cargo ships have, at a third level, a deck with a bulwark behind which passengers (and others) can sit. The warships also have a deck at a third level, with a higher bulwark behind which armed men stand.

#### 4.9.3.2.2.2 *Description*

Ezekiel (27: 3–10), writing in the early sixth century BC, mentioned a warship of Tyre. Parts of his description are difficult to translate, however, it is generally agreed that the mast was of cedar and the oars of oak, the sails were of linen, and she had a purple and scarlet awning (Jerusalem Bible, 1974: 1202–3; Wachsmann, 1998: 227; MacLaurin, 1978). The hull planking was fir or juniper; the deck planking was cedar or cypress. MacLaurin, however, translates the latter phrase as 'lattice bulwarks of tamarisk'. Another phrase in this passage is

usually thought to refer to caulking seams: Wachsmann has pointed out, however, that an equally valid translation would refer to fastening planking together.

### 4.9.3.2.3 *Early mortise and tenon joints*

Locked mortise and tenon joints were used in the superstructure of the mid-third millennium BC Egyptian Cheops ship, although the comparable joints used in the hull were unlocked (2.7.1). The Dahshur boats of *c.*1850 BC also had unlocked mortise and tenon joints in the hull, and locked ones in wooden artefacts found with the boats (2.8.3.2). By the mid-first millennium BC, on the other hand, the hull of the Egyptian Matariya boat (2.8.3.4) appears to have been fastened with locked mortise and tenon joints.

The earliest recorded use of locked mortise and tenon fastenings in the Levant region is on a wooden table from a tomb in Jericho dated to the mid-second millennium BC (Wachsmann, 1998: 241, figs. 10.28 and 10.29): this is roughly contemporary with the Uluburun ship. Sleeswyk (1980) has shown from documentary evidence that the Romans knew this type of joint as *coagmenta punicana*—'Phoenician joints'.

Bass (1991; 1997: 269), and Wachsmann (1998: 206–8) following him, believe that the mid-second-millennium BC wrecks off Cape Gelidonya and off Uluburun were Levantine (i.e. Phoenician) in origin. Others have argued for Cyprus or the Aegean: whilst Cyprus is almost indistinguishable from the Levant, in terms of archaeological evidence from this period, an origin in Greece would have very different implications for the history of shipbuilding. Identifying the 'nationality' of a shipwreck is a difficult task and a definitive answer cannot be expected (1.4.2.1), but the evidence at present available seems to suggest Levantine / Cyprus rather than the Aegean. The Uluburun wreck (4.8.3.1) of *c.*1305 BC, provides the earliest evidence for the use of locked mortise and tenon joints to fasten together hull planking, a technique which, by the mid-first millennium BC, seems to have become widespread in the Mediterranean.

It is therefore conceivable that, in the mid-second millennium BC, the Phoenicians may have pioneered the use of locked mortise and tenon joints to fasten the underwater planking of seagoing ships, thus giving the hull more structural integrity. Improved woodworking techniques could have enabled them to do this without an increase in water seepage into the hull. The frames may have continued to be lashed in position by methods that did not involve boring holes through the planking (2.7.1). Such an innovation could well have led to the Phoenician reputation for seafaring excellence (4.9.3.2.1).

## 4.9.4 EARLY SEWN-PLANK VESSELS (Fig. 4.3)

Sewing was the principal means by which the Cheops ship's planking was fastened together: this may also have been the case for the Dahshur boats. References in Homer (4.9.2.1) suggest that Greek ships of the eighth century had sewn planking. Statements by Virgil (*Aeneid* 6. 413–14) and by Pliny (*NH* 24–65) support this interpretation. The next evidence for sewing comes from the sixth century BC and later, when there are several excavated ships which are either fully or partly sewn.

### 4.9.4.1 GIGLIO (Parker, 1992: no. 451)

This wreck, in Campese Bay, Giglio, off the west coast of Italy, carried ingots of copper and lead, and a cargo of Etruscan, Samian, Punic, and Ionian origin which has been dated to 600–590 BC. Part of an oak keel, the two garboards and three other strakes from one side were exposed and recorded (Bound, 1985). The pine planks were positioned by treenails within the plank-

ing thickness and then sewn together through diagonally disposed holes which had a trapezoidal notch inboard: the stitches were then wedged within their holes. In a preliminary report, the excavator considers that the ship was Etruscan.

### 4.9.4.2 BON PORTÉ; (Parker, 1992: no. 106)

Keel fragments, some frames and a few strakes were excavated in 1973–4 from this wreck off the south coast of France, near St-Tropez (Jestin and Carrazé, 1980). The cargo, which was mostly Etruscan, Ionian, and Massilian pottery containers, has been dated to 530–525 BC. Initially this ship was thought to have had wooden plank fastenings, but re-evaluation by Basch (1976*b*) and Pomey (1981, 1997*a*) has demonstrated that this was a sewn-plank vessel, although no sewing survived. The 20 mm thick planks were first positioned by 9 mm diameter treenails across the seams and within the planking thickness, at 160–140 mm spacing. The planks were sewn together (probably over caulking) by diagonal continuous stitches which were wedged within paired holes. The seams were then treated with pitch internally. The relatively heavy frames (m. 140, s. 120 mm) were spaced at *c.*1 m, and appeared not to be fastened to the planking recorded. A large mast step was fastened to the framing by mortise and tenon joints (Pomey, 1981: fig. 5). Pomey (1981) believes this was an Etruscan vessel not more than 10–12 m in length, with a round hull, but a flattish bottom.

### 4.9.4.3 VENICE LAGOON

Fragments of planking excavated in 1968 from Venice, and dated to *c.*530 BC, are thought to be the remains of a sewn boat (Beltrame, forthcoming).

### 4.9.4.4 PLACE JULES-VERNE, MARSEILLES

Two of the boats excavated during 1992–3 from the Place Jules-Verne in Marseilles have sewn planking (Pomey, 1995, 1996, 1999): Wreck 9, a fishing boat some 5 × 1.5 m; and Wreck 7, a cargo ship *c.*14 × 4 m. Both vessels are dated to the end of the sixth century BC. Wreck 9 had locating treenails within the seams, and appeared to have been sewn throughout with the stitches countersunk outboard (Fig. 4.32). She had a rectangular keel with rabbets, and a gently curving

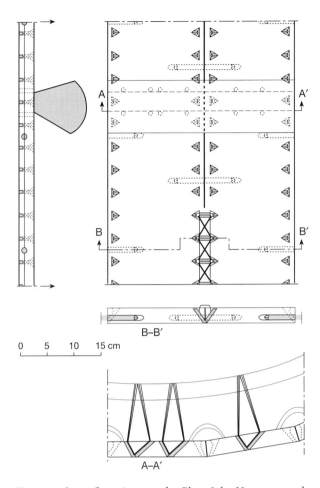

Fig. 4.32. Sewn fastenings on the Place Jules-Verne 9 wreck (after Pomey, 1997c: 92).

transverse section (Pomey, 1996: fig. 5). The frames were notched to fit over the caulking running along the seams, and were lashed to the planking.

The planking of Wreck 7 is mainly fastened by locked mortise and tenon joints, but sewn fastenings were used at the ends of the hull, and for a number of plank repairs. The tenons measure 140–50 × 30–5 × 5 mm, and are spaced at 190–120 mm apart. The framing is nailed to the planking by iron nails, the earliest known use in the Mediterranean. Pomey (1995) believes both vessels are of Greek origin, and come from a period when mortise and tenon fastenings were replacing sewn fastenings. Research is still in progress.

### 4.9.4.5 GELA (Parker, 1992: no. 441)

This relatively well-preserved wreck from off southern Sicily has been dated to the late sixth/early fifth cen-

turies BC by reference to the cargo of Greek, Ionian, and Phoenician pottery (Freschi, 1991): 6–7 tonnes of ballast was also carried, laid on matting in sand. The plank fastenings in the lower hull are similar to the earlier examples described above, with a layer of 'fabric' as a caulking along the inner seams before the planks were sewn together. The inner hull was then payed with pitch (see also Pliny, *NH* 16. 21, 23). In the upper hull mortise and tenon joints were used to fasten the planking together (Kahanov, forthcoming). The framing was fastened to the planking with copper and iron nails—second only to the Marseilles wrecks. A keelson was notched to fit over the frames, and a mast step was associated with it (Freschi, 1991: fig. 202). Research is still in progress.

### 4.9.4.6 MA'AGAN-MICHAEL (Parker, 1992: no. 612)

This wreck of *c*.400 BC was excavated from close inshore, some twenty nautical miles south of Haifa (Kahanov, 1999). Research is still in progress. The ship had been carrying *c*.13 tonnes of stone which mainly had its origins in Corsica and Calabria in the Tyrrhenian Sea, but some also came from Cyprus: this ballast was on grass matting laid in a dunnage of pine and oak. There was also Cypriot and Ionian pottery, cordage, shipwright's tools, and a one-arm wooden anchor (Rosloff, 1991).

The 40 mm thick pine (*Pinus halepensis*) planking was fastened together generally by mortise and tenon joints spaced at *c*. 87 mm, locked by tapered oak treenails. However, the ends of the first three strakes were sewn to the posts and to both post-knees ('dead wood'), and the garboard strake was sewn in places to the keel, the details being similar to sewn fastenings of the earlier ships (Fig. 4.33). The tenth strake was a wale, being thicker than the others. Fourteen pine frames, spaced at *c*.0.75 m, were similar to those in the Bon Porté and Gela ships, each consisting of a floor and two futtocks joined by treenail-fastened hooked scarfs. These frames were probably assembled before installation and were fastened to the planking (but not to the keel or the post-knees) by copper nails clenched inboard by turning the tip through 180° (hooked) (Kohanov *et al*., 1999).

The pine keel was joined to the posts in short scarfs which were fastened by locked mortise and tenon

The Ma'agan
Michael Ship c.400BC

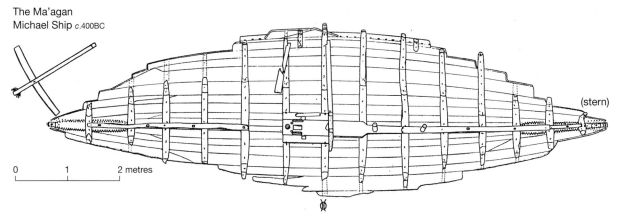

0    1    2 metres

(stern)

Fig. 4.33. Plan of the Ma'agan-Michael wreck (Yak Kahanov).

joints. The keel had no rabbets and the deadrise of the garboards was determined by a bevel worked along their inner edges. A false keel was fastened below the keel, whilst above it, on the centreline and over the floors, were timbers forming a discontinuous keelson. One element of these timbers was a pine mast step which was notched to fit the framing near amidships, and had partners on both sides.

The ship was originally *c.*13.5 m in length and had a wine-glass shaped transverse section, rather than the full-form of earlier sewn plank ships: such a reverse-curve hull maximizes both strength and resistance to leeway. Kahanov's hydrostatic calculations (forthcoming) indicate that, in addition to the 13 tonnes of stone, she could have carried *c.*3 tonnes of cargo. She appeared to be relatively new when excavated: there were no shipworm holes or barnacles in the planking, freshly worked chips of wood were found in the bilges, and there was no observable wear on the keel, false-keel, wale, bow, or stern, or on the anchor. Kahanov (1996) has summarized the evidence for her origins and for her final voyage:

| | |
|---|---|
| *stone* | Aegean or Cyprus |
| *food* | South-west Anatolia or the Aegean |
| *ceramics* | Cyprus and Greece |
| *wood species* | Levant coast, Turkey, Cyprus, and Greece |
| *copper for nails* | probably north-west Cyprus (Kahanov *et al.*, 1999: 284) |
| *hull structure* | the nearest parallels come from the central Mediterranean |

The stone may well have been recycled ballast from another ship. The wood species used in the hull, and for tools and dunnage—Allepo pine (*pinus halepensis*), eastern plane (*Platanus orientalis*), olive (*Olea* sp.), Pistacia pine (*Pistacia Palaestina*), and oak (*Quercus* sp.)—could all have been found on the Levant coast in the fourth century BC, and the ship may have been built in that region. She may have been wrecked on return from a voyage to Cyprus and western Anatolia.

### 4.9.4.7 ROMAN AND MEDIEVAL SEWN-PLANK BOATS

The Cavaliere wreck of *c.*100 BC (Parker, 1992: no. 282) has sewn planking as part of the superstructure and as a repair in the stern. The second-century BC wreck, La Jeanne-Garde B, has two reinforcing framing timbers sewn to the planking (Carrazé, 1977: fig. 7); whilst in the late first-century BC wreck Cap Bear C (Parker, 1992: no. 171) lashings and treenails were used alternately to fasten framing to planking. The seventh-century BC wreck from Playa de la Isla, south-eastern Spain (Negueruela *et al.*, 1995) appears to have mortise and tenon-fastened planking, whereas the framing is lashed to the planking. On the evidence of the cargo, the excavators believe this to have been a Phoenician ship. Work continues on this site so that these early observations may not be conclusive.

A number of sewn-plank boats dated from the late centuries BC to the eleventh century AD have been excavated from coastal sites in the Adriatic, in Croatia, and in the delta of the River Po. This seems to be a relict population which survived for over 1,000 years despite fundamental technological change in adjacent regions, because they fitted well into a particular environment: lakes, lagoons, and deltas (Beltrame, forthcoming; Pomey, 1981, 1985; Brusić and Domjan, 1985).

The two Nin/Zaton boats (Parker, 1992: no. 1248–9) of the early centuries AD, and the Ljubljana/Laibach boat of the late centuries BC were all from Croatia. The latter had a flat bottom connected to flared sides by a hollowed transition strake (Fig. 4.34). The planking was caulked with limebast, and fastened together with limebast rope by continuous stitching through holes 80–100 mm apart. Numerous floors were notched to fit over the seams and treenailed to the bottom planking, whilst knees were similarly fastened to the sides and bottom. Four longitudinal stringers were treenailed and iron nailed to the bottom through the floors. The iron nails were clenched by turning their tip along the outer face of the bottom planking (McGrail, 1981: fig. 4.1.17).

The Nin boats (McGrail, 1981b: fig. 4.1.16) were round-hulled and had a keel to which the planking was fastened by continuous sewing over a longitudinal lath, which presumably trapped caulking (Fig. 4.35). The stitches were wedged within the sewing holes, the holes blocked with resin and the outboard part of the stitch cut away—a technique also used recently in boats of the Lamu archipelago, east Africa (Prins, 1986), so that the stitching cannot be damaged when the boat takes the ground or is dragged across the foreshore.

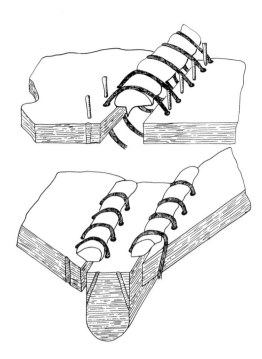

Fig. 4.35. Plank fastening details of the Nin boats (after Brusić, 1968: fig. 8).

Six other boats came from the River Po region: Comacchio/Valle Parti (Parker, 1992: no. 1206) of the first century BC; Venice Lido and Corte Cavanella 1 and 2 (ibid. 339; Beltrame (forthcoming) of the first or second centuries AD; Cervia (ibid. 293) of the second to fourth centuries AD; and Pomposa (ibid. 862) and Borgo Caprile (ibid. 109) with early medieval dates. Generally these six boats were fastened with continuous sewing, but nails were also used in the Comacchio wreck to fasten scarfs and to fasten plank-ends to the posts. Nails were also used in the Cervia boat. The frames of Comacchio were lashed to the planking, whereas those of Corte Cavanella (and possibly others) were treenailed.

None of these boats was recorded in detail, nevertheless, it is clear that on eastern and western coasts of the Adriatic, boats with their planking mainly sewn together continued to be built and used in lakes, rivers, and deltas from Roman times (and probably much earlier) into the medieval period.

### 4.9.4.8 SEWN-PLANK BOAT CHARACTERISTICS

Boats with sewn planking are known worldwide: from mid-third-millennium BC Egypt to twentieth-century AD India (McGrail, 1996c). The sewn-plank boats so far

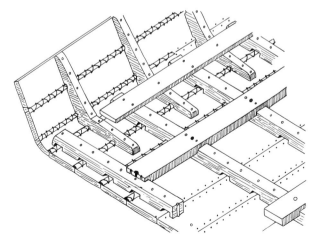

Fig. 4.34. Constructional details of the Ljubljana boat (after Müllner, 1892).

excavated in the Mediterranean appear to have some characteristics which are universal and some which are regional:

(a) They are built plank-first: as is the case worldwide (Prins, 1986; McGrail, 1996c).

(b) There are no examples of Mediterranean (or Egyptian) vessels which rely solely on sewing to position and fasten the planking together. They have either treenails or mortise and tenon fastenings within the seams, as well as sewn fastenings across the seams. The majority of sewn boats in use today also do not rely solely on the stitching (Prins, 1986). Exceptions have been noted on the east coast of India and in Sri Lanka (Kentley, 1985). The known ancient sewn-plank boats from north-west Europe (5.4) do not have any fastenings other than their sewing, but they do have framing/transverse timber, wedged or lashed to the planking which enable the planks to be aligned and also reduce shearing stress on the plank fastenings.

(c) There are no Mediterranean examples of planking being fastened by individual stitches/lashings, as found, for example, on the Bronze Age Ferriby boats of the Humber estuary (5.4.2.1) and on the fourth-century AD Pontian boat of Malaysia (8.3.5.1.1). The Mediterranean (and Egyptian) vessels all have continuous sewing.

Within the Mediterranean, the technique of sewing planking together has been found on vessels wrecked off the Levant coast in the east, the south coast of France and Spain in the west, and the estuary of the River Po in the north. The vessels range in date from c.600 BC to medieval times. The technique is mentioned by Homer (*Iliad*, 2. 135; *Odyssey*, 5. 244–57) in the eighth century BC, and by a range of others, from fifth-century BC Aesychlus (*Suppliantes*, 134–5) to fifth-century AD St Jerome (*Epistolae*, 128. 3). Generally speaking, these references are within a Greek context. The ships and boats described and excavated are used in a range of environments from lake, river, and estuary to fully seagoing.

The early vessels had their planking positioned by treenails within the seams and then fastened together by continuous sewing, with each stitch wedged within its hole. From the late sixth century BC, possibly as an outcome of the early sixth-century orientalization of Greece by Phoenicians (O. Murray, 1993: 81; Osborne,

1996: 167–8), mortise and tenon joints began to be used over much of the hull, sewing being restricted to the regions where leaks were most likely: either the underwater hull (Gela), or the ends and repairs (Jules-Verne 7 and Ma'agan-Michael). Caulking, which is found worldwide in sewn-plank boats, has only been reported on the Gela and Jules-Verne 9 wrecks: it seems likely that it was used (but not recognized) in the other vessels, possibly in the form of resin or tar/pitch.

How the frames of the early sewn vessels were fastened to the planking is unclear from excavation reports, but by 500 BC they were fastened with copper or iron nails (Jules-Verne 7 and Gela). Precisely how these nails were used is not clear, but by 400 BC (Ma'agan-Michael) they were clenched by turning the tip through 180° back into the frame. By comparison with early Egyptian vessels, with the seventh-century BC Playa de la Isla wreck off south-east Spain (4.9.4.7), and with late prehistoric/early medieval boats of north-west Europe (5.4.6–7, 5.7.1. 2, 5.7.1.4.1), it may be that frames of the early Mediterranean sewn-plank boats (Giglio, Bon Porté, and Jules-Verne 9) were lashed to the planking, though not necessarily to every strake. Should the framing of these early vessels prove to have partly rounded cross-sections, this lashing hypothesis would be supported.

## 4.9.5 SHIPS AND BOATS OF THE CENTRAL MEDITERRANEAN

The Etruscan city-states appear to have grown out of the Early Iron Age Villanovan culture which flourished in central Italy between the Rivers Arno and Tiber up to c.800 BC. By the seventh and sixth centuries BC, almost the entire Italian peninsula was under Etruscan dominance. In the late third century BC they were conquered by the Romans, and by the first century, Graeco-Roman culture was all-pervasive.

As with the Phoenicians, more is known about Etruscan seafaring from Greek than from Etruscan sources. During the first millennium BC, probably stimulated by Phoenician and Greek seafarers and traders, Etruscans became active in both the Tyrrhenian and Adriatic Seas (Hagy, 1986). In c.535 BC, allied with Carthaginians, they fought a Phocaean Greek fleet armed with rams off Alalia in Corsica (Herodotus, I.

166–7). Pliny (*NH* 8. 209) attributed the invention of the ram to the Etruscans, but this seems unlikely: it is possible, however, that Phoenicians / Carthaginians introduced the ram to the Etruscans at an early date.

There were trading connections between Sardinia and Italy from early times, and it is convenient to discuss evidence for boats and ships from both places in this section.

### 4.9.5.1 SARDINIAN MODELS

More than one hundred (eighth to fifth centuries BC) bronze boat models of the Sardinian Nuragic culture are known today, mostly from that island but some from Italy and one from Corinth, Greece (Calcagno, 1997: 51; Basch, 1987a: 404–6). All models are hollow and most of them have a large ring amidships by which they were presumably hung and possibly used as lamps or incense burners: thus it seems likely that a flat bottom on a model is authentic and not a craftsman's device to stabilize a standing model. On this assumption, there are two distinct groups: those with rounded hulls (Fig. 4.36); and those with flat bottoms (Fig. 4.37). In general, the models show very little sheer, which brings into question whether they can depict seagoing craft. Protruding from one end (the bow?) of every model is a representation of a horned deer or a bull's head. On many models a variety of animals stand on the top of the sides (Fig. 4.37).

Although these models strongly suggest that boats had a key role in Sardinian life, they tell us little about structure or propulsion. Johnstone (1988: 142) considers that they represent logboats rather than hide or bark boats, whilst Bonino (1995) believes that zig-zag features along the sheerline, and circular features at one end, identify them as sewn-plank boats. Casson (1971: 68) believes that some of them represent seagoing craft. All these hypotheses are very speculative: more might be learnt about structure and function if detailed, measured drawings could be compiled.

Fig 4.36. A Bronze Age round-hulled boat model from Sardinia (British Museum).

Fig. 4.37. A Bronze Age flat-bottomed boat model from Vetulonia, Sardinia (Sopritendenza alle Antichita, Firenze).

## 4.9.5.2 VILLANOVAN AND ETRUSCAN REPRESENTATIONS

The Villanovans placed model boats in their graves, and this tradition was continued by the Etruscans from the eighth century BC. The Villanova models, mostly of clay and dated from *c.*1000 BC onwards, are generally flat-bottomed and with little sheer. They have a figure-head at one end which appears to be that of a bird: one model (Basch, 1987*a*: fig. 842) has these at both ends. Another model (Basch, 1987*a*: fig. 843) has seven holes through each side, just below the sheerline: these may represent oar ports; on the other hand, they could be points from which the model was suspended.

In addition to the burial of boat models, some of which are similar in form to Sardinian models but with a bird rather than an animal figurehead, the Etruscans depicted boats and ships on pottery (Basch, 1987*a*: figs. 865–77). The earliest depiction is that incised on a vase from the early seventh century BC (Basch, 1987*a*: fig. 865): this appears to represent a galley curved longitudinally at both ends where the bottom meets the rising posts. A mast is stepped amidships and four oars are depicted. The vessel is steered by a steering oar, or possibly a rudder, on each quarter, and has a raised deck at bow and stern. Towards the stern there are lines to a fish which suggest that a fishing boat is depicted, however, there is an underwater projection from the bow which has the appearance of a ram, an interpretation which has been much debated. Similar forward projections appear on other depictions of Etruscan vessels, most of them being above the deduced waterline with a tendency to point downwards (Basch, 1987*a*: figs. 482, 868–71). It may be that this enigmatic feature represents a bow which has been shaped for directional stability or for potential speed, rather than a ram.

Sail is frequently depicted on these Etruscan ships and some have a feature at the masthead which is probably for a lookout. A ship depicted in the early fifth-century BC Tomba della nave at Cerveteri (Basch, 1987*a*: fig. 880) has two masts, one amidships, one forward. This is one of the earliest depictions of a two-masted vessel, close in date (late sixth century) to the two-masted vessel on the rim of a Corinthian krater published by Casson (1980)—see also Basch (1987*a*: figs. 499–500). The Tomba della nave ship is probably typical of the Etruscan cargo ships which traded in the Tyrrhenian Sea during the mid-first millennium BC.

This, and the other evidence, indicates that the Etruscans played their part in overseas trade in the first millennium BC central Mediterranean.

## 4.9.6 NAUTICAL DEVELOPMENTS THROUGH THE EARLY IRON AGE

There are no significant wrecks dated to this period except those of sewn-plank boats of the sixth century BC (4.9.4). The mortise and tenon-fastened wreck off Playa Isla in Spanish waters has been provisionally dated to the seventh century BC (4.9.4.7). Thus reliance has to be placed entirely on representational evidence, and information from the few documentary sources.

### 4.9.6.1 CENTRAL MEDITERRANEAN

The evidence here is much less substantial than in the eastern Mediterranean, but it is possible to conclude that indigenous vessels in the Tyrrhenean Sea used sail from at least the early seventh century BC. Rams were in use on warships by the sixth century, and by the fifth century, a distinctive cargo sailing ship with two masts was in use.

### 4.9.6.2 THE EASTERN MEDITERRANEAN

By the eighth century BC in the eastern Mediterranean a distinction was being made in written sources between warships and cargo ships. The earliest depictions of undoubted cargo ships are from *c.*700 BC in the Levant (Fig. 4.30), and from the late sixth century BC in the Aegean (Casson, 1996: fig. 1; 1971: figs. 81, 82, 97). Warships with thirty and with fifty oars (i.e. fifteen or twenty-five each side) are mentioned by Homer, and there are depictions from the ninth century BC onwards with approximately these numbers of oars. The earliest are monoremes, but biremes are depicted in the Aegean from the mid-eighth century BC (Fig. 4.26) and a little later in the Levant (Fig. 4.31)—these Phoenician biremes have a third level deck on which soldiers and/or passengers can be carried. The change from one level (monoreme) to two levels (bireme) of oarsmen resulted in a shorter vessel (*ceteris paribus*). As Coates (1990*a*) has pointed out, this has several advantages: agility is improved all round with increased rate of turn, acceleration, and speed. Furthermore, a bireme penteconter probably cost less than one that was a monoreme, and, since its longitudinal bending problems were reduced, the bireme was much less likely to suffer major damage in a seaway, and with less leakage, would have had a longer, useful life. These qualities would have been of most use to warships, but they would also be useful in a cargo ship seeking to evade pirates—probably the reason why the merchant galleys of *c.*700 BC were biremes.

The ram is first depicted in the late ninth/early eighth-century BC Aegean (Fig. 4.24), and in the early seventh century in the Levant (Fig. 4.31). The earliest rams are pointed (4.12.3), but during the sixth century BC, blunt-ended ones appear (Casson and Linder, 1991: fig. 5.4). The bireme warship galley, armed with a ram, was widely used in the eastern Mediterranean in the sixth and fifth centuries BC: it led to the trireme.

# 4.10
# The Trireme of the Seventh–Fourth Centuries BC

Some ten years after the Persian, Darius, was defeated by the Greeks at Marathon, his son, Xerxes, led another invasion by land and by sea. In Xerxes' fleet there were said to be 1,207 triremes drawn from Egypt, the Levant, Cyprus, Asia Minor, and some of the Aegean islands (Herodotus, 7. 89–95). In 480 BC, at Salamis, this fleet was defeated by a Greek fleet in which there were 380 triremes (Herodotus, 8. 82). Herodotus (3. 44; 2. 159) also refers to the use of triremes in the sixth century BC: Polycrates, ruler of Samos, had 40 triremes in *c.*540 BC; and Nechos II of Egypt (*c.*600 BC) had triremes built, some on the Mediterranean coast, others on the Arabian Gulf, though Wallinga (1993: 45–6) has questioned this. In the sixth and fifth centuries the trireme evidently was the main warship in the eastern Mediterranean, but its origins must lie in the seventh century BC or earlier.

The earliest known reference to a trireme is by Hipponax in the mid-sixth century BC (Papalas, 1997: 25). However, Herodotus (1. 166) described a battle in *c.*600 BC (Morrison, 1995*c*: 152) in the Tyrrhenian Sea

between Phocaean Greeks and a Tyrrhenian and Carthaginian fleet in which Thucydides (Warner, 1954: 21) believed there were triremes. Thucydides (1. 13) also noted the belief that the first Greek triremes were built in Corinth and that a Corinthian shipwright, Ameinocles, built four ships (presumably triremes, but Meijer (1986: 35) doubts this) for Samos, around 700 BC. Basch (1969: 139) has argued that the trireme was evolved in Sidon *c.*700 BC, and Morrison (1995*d*: 54–7) generally supports this view. Wallinga (1993: 1–32), on the other hand, has argued that the trireme did not emerge until the late sixth century BC. Papalas (1997) recently evaluated these views, and others, and concluded that the trireme appeared in *c.*700 BC, but was not used offensively until *c.*525–500 BC when the Greeks evolved the *diekplous* and other ramming tactics.

These opinions on the origins of the trireme are based on the interpretation of documentary sources: no wreck resembling a trireme (or even a bireme) has so far been excavated. It has been argued that, since triremes were so lightly built and needed no ballast, they did not sink when damaged in battle but remained crippled on the surface until they could be towed away (Morrison and Coates, 1986: 128; Casson, 1991: 82); thus it is suggested that remains are unlikely to be excavated. However, triremes wrecked in a storm or by other marine hazards may well have become waterlogged and eventually sank to the sea bed where, in some circumstances, they may remain to be excavated. Moreover, triremes were sometimes run ashore and abandoned (Herodotus; 6. 16); and after the battle of Salamis, captured Phoenician triremes were dedicated and displayed at the Isthmus, at Sunium, and at Salamis itself (Herodotus, 8. 12). Fragments of triremes may yet remain buried on land.

## 4.10.1 EVIDENCE FOR THE TRIREME

Since there is as yet no direct evidence for the trireme, documentary, iconographic, and some indirect archaeological evidence has to be used to establish its characteristic features, a task that has intrigued scholars since the Renaissance (J. Shaw, 1993*b*). From *c.*1975 there has been a relatively concerted attack on the matter, resulting in the building of the full-size reconstruction *Olympias* in 1985–7 by Dimitrios Tzakakos at Piraeus, under an Hellenic Navy contract and to a design (Fig.

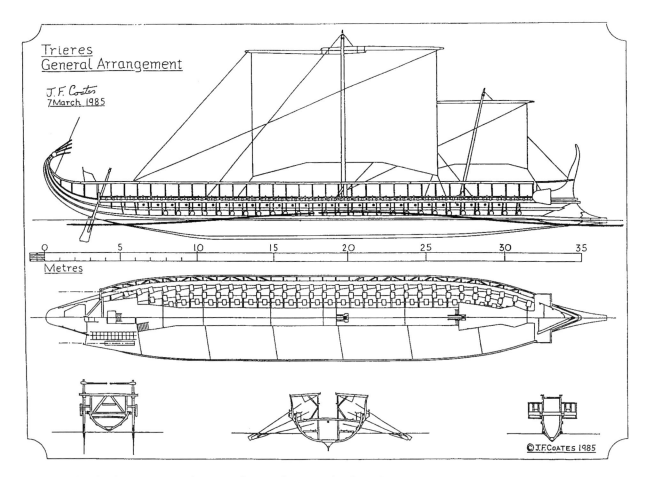

Fig. 4.38. Plans for the reconstructed trireme *Olympias* (drawing: John Coates).

4.38) and specification by the British Trireme Trust (Coates and McGrail, 1984; Morrison and Coates, 1986, 1989; Coates, Platis and Shaw, 1990; Shaw, 1993a; Morrison, Coates, and Rankov, 2000).

A fundamental point in the interpretation of the documentary evidence has been the meaning behind the Greek term *trieres* (trireme): the Trust has translated this as 'three-fitted' or 'three-rowing' (Morrison, 1995d: 63) and has taken this to mean that there were three files of oarsmen on each side of the ship. A remark by Vitruvius (1. 2. 4) that a warship's *interscalium* (distance between oarsmen) was two cubits suggests that this was the standard spacing in a trireme in his day. Other sources show that there was one man to each oar; that some oars were slightly longer than others; that outriggers were used; that a hogging stay or hawser was needed; and that ships had large and small masts, yards, and sails. Representations of vessels thought to be triremes suggest how oarsmen may have

been arranged within their groups of three (Morrison and Coates, 1986: figs. 36, 41). Fifth-century ship sheds thought to have been used by triremes at Zea, Piraeus, suggest maximum lengths and breadths for triremes of that era.

Evidence for the sailing rig has also had to be drawn from literary and iconographic evidence (Roberts, 1990; 1993). Triremes are seldom, if ever, shown under sail since their intrinsic characteristic was their ability to use the ram under oars, therefore depictions of other ships' rig have been used. Roberts has incorporated brails, halyards, parrels, braces, tacks and sheets, and stays, but no shrouds, in his rig design: the area of the low-aspect ratio main sail (95 m²) was calculated so that, in a steady Force 4 (a moderate breeze), the hull would not heel more than 9° so that the lower lee oarports would remain above water. The evidence considered by O. Roberts (1990: 288; 1993: 34–5) suggests that, generally, when under sail, the mainmast and sail were used alone; the smaller mast was embarked instead of the mainmast before a battle and used, presumably in the main mast step near amidships, for a speedy retreat downwind if necessary. Nevertheless, both masts were included in the reconstruction as 'a reasonable archaeological experiment' and to ensure the directional stability of *Olympias* when running before the wind.

Since no trireme has been excavated it was necessary to draw upon structural evidence from later wrecks such as the Kyrenia ship of the fourth century BC (4.12.1) and the Marsala ship of the third BC (4.12.2). The main features here were that eastern and central Mediterranean hulls of this era were built planking-first; their planking was fastened by locked mortise and tenon joints; and framing was fastened to planking by iron nails through treenails. The 'wine-glass' midships section of these ships, the framing pattern of the Masala wreck, and the remains of hull structure inside the third-century BC Athlit ram (4.12.3) were used when designing the reconstruction (Fig. 4.38) (Coates, 1984, 1989a, 1989b, 1990b, 1993, 1995b).

## 4.10.2 AN ASSESSMENT OF THE TRIREME RECONSTRUCTION, *OLYMPIAS*

There are a number of theoretical and practical difficulties in undertaking any reconstruction project (Coates *et al.*, 1995) but the Trireme project had difficulties specific to it. Most projects of this nature are concerned with establishing a rigorous method of transforming the recorded, but incomplete, remains of an ancient vessel into a hypothetical reconstruction drawing or model, from which a full-size version is built. Since there are no excavated triremes the problem for the Trireme project has been to design a hypothetical reconstruction which would match documented aspects of performance whilst meeting constraints imposed by iconographic, historical, and archaeological evidence. With hindsight it is possible to criticize aspects of the Trust's research and trials—as indeed, the Trust has itself done (Shaw, 1993a). The Trireme Trust's general approach has also been criticized, not least by Westerdahl (1992). However, *pace* Westerdahl, there is no intrinsic reason why a scientifically based reconstruction should not be made of a ship type for which there are no physical remains, so the Trust's reconstruction cannot be dismissed for rea-

sons of principle alone. The Trust's interpretation of some of the evidence has also been criticized, notably by Tilley (1976, 1992, 1995) and by Basch (1987b, but see Coates (1995a)). Nevertheless, a balanced assessment must be that both theoretical and practical aspects of the Trireme project have greatly increased understanding of early shipbuilding and seafaring in the eastern Mediterranean. *Olympias* is a 'floating hypothesis' (McGrail, 1992b) which is probably as near as anyone could get, at the first attempt, to the Athenian trireme of the fifth century BC, with the evidence at present available.

### 4.10.2.1 SPEEDS ACHIEVED

Much emphasis during the sea trials of *Olympias* was laid on achieving a sprint speed of 9.5–10 knots since it was considered that this was the equivalent of a cruising speed of 7.5–8 knots which is the average speed needed to undertake the passage from *Byzantium* (Constantinople) to *Heraclea* (on the Black Sea coast of Asia Minor) in 'a long day under oars' (Xenophon, *Anabasis*, 6. 4. 2)—a 'long day' in summer in these latitudes being taken as sixteen to seventeen hours (twilight to twilight). The Trust's position seemed to be that achieving this sprint speed was a necessary, but not a sufficient, condition for validating the claim that *Olympias* was an authentic reconstruction of a fifth-century BC trireme. Xenophon's knowledge of nautical matters has been questioned by some scholars (notably Wallinga, 1993) but even if we allow that Xenophon was familiar with seafaring, his statement is hardly precise. For example, a case can be argued that the phrase 'from *Byzantium* to *Heraclea*' meant 'from the position when departure is taken from (lose sight of) *Byzantium*, to the position when a landfall is made at first sight of *Heraclea*'. In this way the 'distance' would be of the order of 110–100 nautical miles, giving the average speed required as 6.5–6 knots.

Over five seasons of trials *Olympias* achieved:

- a sprint speed of over 8.4 knots for a minute or so, with 8.9 knots momentarily.
- with a flying start, *c*.7 knots has been held for a nautical mile or so.
- over a period of one hour, 5.8 knots has been averaged.

It is therefore not unreasonable to say that *Olympias*

has probably been close to achieving the sort of speeds under oars that would be required to make the passage in a trireme from *Byzantium* to *Heraclea* in a long day.

### 4.10.2.2 OTHER ACHIEVEMENTS

The trials have certainly demonstrated that a three-level oar system is practicable, and that, with training, an inexperienced crew can achieve a relatively high standard. Although there are dissenters, it is also generally agreed that this oar system is compatible with the literary and representational evidence; as is the overall shape and layout of *Olympias*. The reconstruction also conforms to the excavated evidence for hull shape and structure, albeit from a period two centuries later, and from cargo ships rather than warships. Furthermore, the steering arrangements and the sail propulsion outfit generally are not incompatible with the, admittedly inadequate, evidence.

It had been thought by the Trust that, since the trireme was at the extreme of performance, the interacting constraints imposed by the ancient evidence and by naval architectural requirements were so tight that her hull form and structure, her displacement, and her oar system were defined closely with little, if any, scope for variations. It is now clear, however, that some parameters were not as fixed as was once thought: the *interscalium*, a fundamental unit in *Olympias* design, is now thought to have been 0.98 m rather than 0.88 m, and the overall length, rather than 36.8 m, may well have been 40 m, which is also compatible with the evidence from the Zea ship sheds (Shaw, 1993a: 108–11). This change in the perception of what was a fundamental unit does not mean that the original trireme experiment was flawed. *Olympias* had to be designed, built, and tested so that there was a focus for discussions: the hard reality of building a ship rather than flights of fancy on paper. Questions of how the ancient evidence should be interpreted have had to be tackled in the light of physics and engineering. Everyone involved, including the strongest critic, has benefited.

Much has also been learnt, from theoretical and practical studies in connection with *Olympias*, that otherwise could not have been. Coates (1990a) has shown, for example, that the change during the seventh–sixth centuries BC from bireme penteconter to trireme as the main warship had both advantages and disadvantages. There would have been a substantial gain in speed: for example, when cruising under oars, from *c*.5.5 to 7.5 knots. Against this gain had to be balanced a reduction in acceleration, and building costs increased threefold. Furthermore, the trireme hull was still of a length which induced increased longitudinal bending problems and leakage, and reduced length of life. This bending problem meant that a hogging hawser had to be fitted, and that it had to be arched if it was to relieve hogging stresses in the upper hull by raising the ends and imposing sagging forces (Coates, 1990a: 113–15).

Calculations and trials showed that ballast was not needed in a fully loaded trireme. *Olympias*'s quarter rudders proved to have such a high resistance that it seems likely that, in ancient times, whenever possible, one was triced up clear of the water. Against a head wind gusting to 25 knots, *Olympias* under oars averaged 3 knots for over an hour: the crew were then exhausted. Under sail in light winds, *Olympias* evidently made *c*.1¼ knots headway when six or seven points off the wind (leeway discounted); on a broad reach she could make over 2½ knots (Fig. 4.39): Roberts (1993) believes that stays (which were fitted to the mast by *Olympias*'s builder) could be dispensed with providing the mast tabernacle was firmly fastened to beams and floors.

The fact that *Olympias*'s hull became hogged after three season of trials (Shaw, 1993a: fig. 12.1) focused attention on the important role that tenons play in the

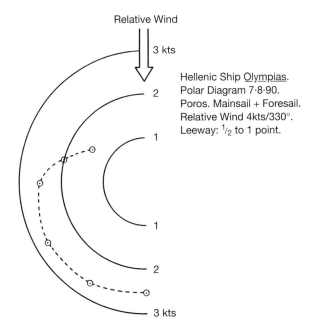

Relative Wind

3 kts

Hellenic Ship *Olympias*.
Polar Diagram 7·8·90.
Poros. Mainsail + Foresail.
Relative Wind 4kts/330°.
Leeway: ½ to 1 point.

Fig. 4.39. *Olympias*'s performance under sail.

structural strength of an ancient Mediterranean hull (Coates, forthcoming). The hogging occurred just above the waterline where shear stress, and the tendency for planks to slide upon each other, are greatest. Analysis has shown that, to minimize hogging, tenons must make an interference fit with their mortises in the longitudinal (fore-and-aft) direction; furthermore the tenons must be aligned so that their growth rings run across the breadth of the mortise, i.e. the tenons' radial dimension (along which shrinkage is least) must lie in the fore-and-aft direction. This alignment is similar to that found in treenails used to plug thickness gauge holes bored through the bottom of large logboats in north-west Europe and elsewhere (5.3.1).

### 4.10.2.3 FURTHER TRIALS

It seems clear that there are still useful trials to be done with *Olympias*. The oar system can be refined, and the methods used to measure speeds, to estimate closeness to the wind, and to plot the ship's track over the seabed need to be optimized. Once these are done, further trials, including lengthy passages, can be carried out under oars and especially under sail. The optimum design and use of the rudders needs to be investigated further, as do manœuvring and simulated ramming runs. A satisfactory means of exercising command and control without electronic assistance must be devised. Further theoretical studies are needed on the hogging hawser, and also on ramming tactics, before practical trials. Having proved herself, *Olympias* can now become a test bed for a wide range of activities which should significantly increase understanding of seafaring and warfare in the early Mediterranean.

# 4.11

# Shipbuilding before the Third Century BC

Parker (1992: 10–11) lists 117 wreck sites dated to *c.*300 BC or earlier: of these, only eleven have any hull structural details noted. This proportion of *c.*10 per cent may reflect the apparently poor survival rate of hulls in the Mediterranean, but probably is more indicative of inadequate excavation, recording, or publication. Furthermore, the fact that hull structure is mentioned in an excavation report is no guarantee that even a partial structural analysis can be made, since descriptions, measurements, and drawings are seldom of the standard required—see also Steffy (1995a: 423–4). Three other early wreck sites with structural remains have been reported since Parker's work went to press: Place Jules-Verne, Marseilles sixth-century Wrecks 7 and 9; and the seventh-century wreck from Playa de la Isla in south-east Spain.

### 4.11.1 PLANK FASTENINGS AND FRAME FASTENINGS

These fourteen wrecks may be divided into three groups (Table 4.3) according to the nature of their primary plank fastenings.

Although certainty is impossible, since no complete hull has been excavated, it seems likely that the later hulls in Group 1, from the fifth century BC onwards, were entirely fastened by locked mortise and tenon joints. On the other hand, so little of the remains of the earlier wrecks has been investigated or reported, that it is possible that their planking was also sewn together.

Of the three wrecks in Group 2, Giglio and Bon Porté may have had some mortise and tenon fastenings in addition to their sewing, but sufficient of the hull of Place Jules-Verne 9 seems to have been recorded to make it highly probable that this was entirely sewn.

Group 3 wrecks have both types of fastenings: in Place Jules-Verne 7 and Ma'agan-Michael, the sewing is at bow and stern; in Gella the lower hull is sewn.

For the earlier wrecks and some of the later ones, the method of fastening framing to planking is inadequately documented. However, in the seventh–fifth centuries BC western Mediterranean, there are two examples of frames being lashed. From *c.*500 BC frames in eastern and central Mediterranean wrecks were fastened by copper or iron nails. In the Porticello, Place Jules-Verne 7, and Ma'agan Michael wrecks these nails were clenched by hooking the point back into the frame. In the Kyrenia wreck the nails were driven through treenails, and then hook- clenched.

**Table 4.3** Plank and frame fastenings in vessels of the fourth century BC and earlier

| Date (BC) | Vessel (Parker nos.) | Frame-to-plank fastening |
|---|---|---|
| *1. Planking fastened by locked mortise and tenon joints* | | |
| c.1305 | Uluburun (1193) | Unknown |
| c.1200 | Cape Gelidonya (208) | Unknown |
| Seventh century | Playa de la Isla | Lashed |
| 440–420 | Porticello (879) | Hooked copper nails |
| c.400 | Plane B (820) | Unknown |
| c.350 | El Sec (1058) | Unknown |
| c.300 | Halkoz Adasi (496) | Unknown |
| c.300 | Kyrenia (563) | Hooked copper nails through treenails |
| *2. Planking fastened by wedged sewing* | | |
| 580 | Giglio (451) | Unknown |
| 530–525 | Bon Porté (106) | Unknown |
| c.500 | PJ-V9 | Lashed |
| *3. Planking fastened mainly by locked mortise and tenon joints but with some wedged sewing* | | |
| c.500 | PJ-V7 | Hooked iron nails |
| c.500 | Gella (441) | Hooked copper nails and iron nails |
| c.400 | Ma'agan-Michael (612) | Hooked copper nails |

*Notes*: Only minor elements of the Uluburun and Cape Gelidonya hull structures have been investigated. Gella and PJ-V9 had dowels across the seams within the plank edges; Ma'agan-Michael had none.

*Source*: Parker (1992), and in the present volume. *Sites*: see Fig 4.3.

## 4.11.2 DEVELOPMENTS FROM *C.*1300 TO *C.*300 BC

The fourteen wrecks in Table 4.3 were excavated from the eastern, central, and western Mediterranean: they range in time (irregularly) from the fourteenth to the fourth centuries BC. Clearly there are too few of them and they are too widespread in time and space to allow firm conclusions to be drawn about hull structural changes. Furthermore, several of these wrecks, excavated decades ago, were not documented to the standards now used. Moreover, identifying any regional patterning in this data is difficult since a ship is not necessarily wrecked in home waters, and the origin, 'culture', or 'nationality' of a wreck is not easy to determine (1.4.2.1; 4.8; 4.9.3.2.3). Nevertheless the Uluburun and Cape Gelidonya (Group 1 in Table 4.3) wrecks have been identified as 'Canaanite' or 'Cypriot' by Bass (1991), and the early sewn-plank boats of the central Mediterranean (Groups 2 and 3) as 'Greek' or 'Etruscan' (4.9.4). Whilst the arguments advanced in both cases are not conclusive, the available evidence sug-

gests that there could well be two traditions of shipbuilding: a 'Levant' tradition with its characteristic locked mortise and tenon plank fastenings (4.8.3.1–2; 4.9.3.2.3); and a 'Greek?' tradition of wedged sewn planking (4.9.4.8).

In the light of this discussion, and of matters considered in 4.8.3.4, 4.9.2.1 and 4.9.4.8, a hypothesis concerning the sequence of developments in Mediterranean shipbuilding between the third millennium BC and 300 BC may be outlined for evaluation by others. A primary assumption is that the Group 3 ships in Table 4.3 were following in the tradition of Uluburun and Cape Gelidonya (4.8.3.1, 4.8.3.2).

1. *In the third millennium* BC and earlier, Mediterranean hulls had sewn planking (without or with interplank dowels) and frames were lashed to that planking. This technological phase would be comparable with what appears to have happened (not necessarily contemporaneously) in other regions, for example, southeast Asia (8.3.5.1 : 8.3.7), north-west Europe (5.4), and in Egypt (2.6 and 2.7).

2. *Second millennium* BC. In the Levant, the locked mortise and tenon joint (known earlier in Egypt—but not in underwater hulls) began to be used as the main plank fastening. Sewing was retained in difficult/vulnerable parts of the hull. This implies that, in addition to having locked mortise and tenon fastenings, the Uluburun and Cape Gelidonya ships had sewn-plank fastenings, perhaps towards bow and stern and in other key areas. Frames continued to be lashed.

3. *In the first millennium* BC. The locked mortise and tenon joint was adopted widely, but not universally, in the eastern and central Mediterranean, but sewing continued to be used in those parts of a hull considered to be 'a problem'—for example, in the bottom strakes (Gela), or at the ends (PJ-V7, Ma'agan-Michael). At about the same time, frames began to be fastened by metal nails clenched by turning the point through 180° (PJ-V7; Gella, Ma'agan-Michael). In the far west similar mixed fastenings may have been used, but with lashed frames retained (Playa de la Isla). In the western (PJ-V9) and central Mediterranean, some fully sewn boats continued to be built, culminating in the Adriatic sewn-plank boat tradition of Roman and early medieval times (4.9.4).

4. *In the late first millennium* BC to c.300 BC Widely in the Mediterranean, hulls were built with locked mortise and tenon plank fastenings, and with metal-fastened framing (Porticello, Plane B, El Sec, Kyrenia, and Halkoz Adasi).

## 4.11.3 THE CHANGE FROM SEWN TO MORTISE AND TENON FASTENINGS

### 4.11.3.1 THE ADVANTAGES OF SEWN PLANKING

The advantages and disadvantages of using sewn-plank fastenings and lashed frames have never been investigated systematically, although Coates (1985; forthcoming) has shown how this might be tackled, both theoretically and experimentally. Unlike prehistoric north-west Europe and twentieth-century India (McGrail and Kentley, 1985), there are no known examples of pure sewn planks from ancient Egypt and the early Mediterranean. Egyptian and Mediterranean planking was positioned and fastened together by additional wooden fastenings—mortise and tenon

(unlocked or locked), dowels/treenails/'coaks', or possibly double-dovetail cramps (2.7.1; 2.8.3; 4.9.4). Apart from locked mortise and tenon joints, these wooden fastenings and the sewn fastenings did not involve boring holes right through the planking, thereby minimizing leakage.

Most of the sewn-plank vessels so far known from the Mediterranean had dowels across the seams—from plank edge to plank edge—as well as stitches. Three of these vessels, PJ-V7, Gela, and Ma'agan-Michael, had mortise and tenon joints in addition to dowels and sewing (Table 4.3). Mortise and tenon joints were not found in the excavated parts of three other sewn-plank (with dowels) ships—Giglio, Bon Porté, and PJ-V9: it is possible that they were used in the first two, but unlikely in the third.

The use of dowels with sewn fastenings has two main advantages over sewing alone:

- adjacent planks can be positioned more easily relative to one another, not only before initial sewing, but also when re-sewing after periodic renewal of stitching.
- the dowels, *ceteris paribus*, have a greater resistance to shear forces in the planking than stitching, especially if the rays of the dowels are aligned with the plank seams (Coates, forthcoming). In the case of the Bon Porté wreck, Coates has calculated that the shear carrying capacity of her dowels would have been almost twice that of her sewing.

Shearing forces, which cause the side planks in a hull to slide longitudinally in relation to each other, lead to stressed plank fastenings and loss of hull integrity. These longitudinal forces are caused by the vertical hogging of the hull: that is, the ends of the boat are pulled down. Hogging occurs whenever a vessel is afloat due to the imbalance of weight and buoyancy along the length of a hull (other than a rectangular box shape): weight is greater than buoyancy towards the ends, and less than buoyancy amidships. These sustained hogging (hence shear) forces are supplemented by further shear forces, varying in magnitude and direction, which are generated as the immersed volume of the hull (hence buoyancy) constantly changes when the vessel is at sea in waves.

On certain assumptions, Coates (forthcoming) has calculated that, since shear forces are directly proportional to displacement, a warship (a long, narrow, and low vessel), held together by stitches alone could not have a displacement greater than 10 tonnes: thus a triaconter (thirty-oared warship) as reconstructed by Coates (1990b) would not have needed dowels. On the other hand, cargo ships, generally with shorter, broader, and deeper hulls, are less severely stressed than warships, and therefore the displacement limit for sewn fastenings alone, would have been greater.

The advantages of using dowels across the seams of sewn-plank seagoing vessels are therefore clear. However, unless they are locked (as in south-east Asia— 8.3.5.2.3) dowels cannot be used alone as plank fastenings: another type of fastening such as sewing has to be used to bind the hull planking together.

### 4.11.3.2   THE ADVANTAGES OF LOCKED MORTISE AND TENON FASTENINGS

There are also clear advantages in the change from sewing with dowels to locked mortise and tenon fastenings. Like seam dowels, unlocked mortise and tenon fastenings need a second form of fastening (double-dovetail tenons, lashings, or sewing) to bind the hull planks. Locked mortise and tenon joints, on the other hand, like clenched nails (5.7.1, 5.8.2), are positive fastenings on both sides of a seam, and can be used as the sole plank fastening in a hull. Furthermore, when fitted tightly in the longitudinal direction within mortises, they have significantly more resistance to shear forces, which occur during launching and during beach landings, and, more importantly, when afloat due to the stress reversals imposed on the planking as the hull alternately hogs and sags in response to the motion of the sea (Coates, 1996). Moreover, the tenons act as discontinuous internal frames, reinforcing the hull transversely.

The change to locked mortise and tenon fastenings would have necessitated improved woodworking skills so that joints and seams without caulking leaked minimally. The change to metal-fastened framing would also have needed increased woodworking abilities. The two innovations taken together would have increased the cohesiveness of the planking shell, both in strength and in watertightness.

It seems likely that these changes would have been stimulated by warship requirements, particularly on the introduction of the ram in the ninth/eighth centuries BC (4.12.3). Locked mortise and tenon plank fas-

tenings and nailed frames would result in a better fighting machine than one with sewn planking and lashed framing.

Mark (1991) has suggested that fewer tools, and less knowledge and skill are needed to build a sewn-plank boat than one with mortise and tenon fastenings. Sewn-boat builders certainly need special skills to ensure that stitches are not exposed outboard in the underwater planking otherwise they would be broken during launching, landing, or unintentional grounding: in Egypt and the Mediterranean, the stitches are retained within the thickness of the planking by boring angled holes from the inner face to the edge (for other techniques see 3.6; 5.4; 6.7.3). These holes have to be precisely aligned with holes in adjacent planks if internal wear is to be minimized. The manufacture and positioning of dowels is equally skilful. On the other hand, sewn boats probably need more maintenance— ethnographic evidence suggests that they were frequently dismantled and re-sewn, sometimes annually— as in Orissa, India.

Evidence discussed above suggests that, at first, locked mortise and tenon joints were used in conjunction with sewn fastenings. Since this sewing was a design feature and not merely a repair, and seems to have been in the underwater hull and/or at the ends, the skill that had to be acquired before sewn fastenings could be entirely dispensed with, was probably the ability to cut mortises at an angle, within the thickness of a bevelled plank: this was especially needed where the hull shape changed rapidly, both longitudinally and transversely. Until this technique was perfected, mortise and tenon joints were used only in the less-curvacious parts of the hull where mortises were more nearly aligned with plank faces.

# 4.12

# The Hellenistic Age (Fourth–First Centuries BC)

The 'Golden Age' of Greece, in which the arts and sciences flourished, as well as shipbuilding and seafaring, was over by c.380 BC. From the middle of the fourth century BC, the peripheral northern Greek state of Macedon, led by Philip II and his son, Alexander the Great, began to dominate, mostly by land battles, first the Aegean states, and then the Persian Empire (Asia Minor, the Levant, Mesopotamia, and Egypt); northeast India was also invaded. After Alexander's death in 323 BC this Macedonian Empire separated into a number of large states each ruled by a Greek.

In the central Mediterranean, Rome had from the early fifth century BC expanded from its Etrurian heartland to dominate most of Italy by the middle of the third century BC. Subsequently Rome came into conflict with the Carthaginians in a series of three Punic Wars. In the first of these (264–241 BC) there were several battles at sea in a dispute over the possession of Sicily. The second war was mainly fought on land (220–200 BC) when Hannibal invaded Italy. In the third war (149–146 BC), Rome invaded and destroyed Carthage. By this time, Roman territory outside Italy included Sardinia, Corsica, Sicily, and parts of North Africa; Greece, western Anatolia, Spain, France, and the Netherlands followed. Julius Caesar invaded Britain twice, in 55 and 54 BC, extending Roman influence to its northern limits. The civil war which followed Caesar's death was resolved in the sea battle at Actium in 31 BC.

Greek culture and technology dominated the eastern Mediterranean during the fourth and third centuries BC, and continued to have a strong influence there. By this time (the Hellenistic Age), the nautical technology of the eastern and the central Mediterranean (apart from the Adriatic) may well have been very similar: ships and boats built plank-first; planking mostly fastened together by locked mortise and tenon fastenings; framing mostly fastened to the planking by metal nails. Archaeological evidence, scarce though it is, generally supports this hypothesis.

### 4.12.1 THE KYRENIA SHIP (Parker, 1992: no. 563)

This wreck site, off the north coast of Cyprus, was excavated in 1968–9 (Fig. 4.40). The remains were lifted and conserved, and are now on display in the medieval castle in Kyrenia. The hull, which is dated *c.*300 BC by associated coins, has a 'wine glass' transverse section (Fig. 4.41), and is similar in form to that of the Ma'agan-Michael wreck (4.9.4.6). The locked mortise and tenon

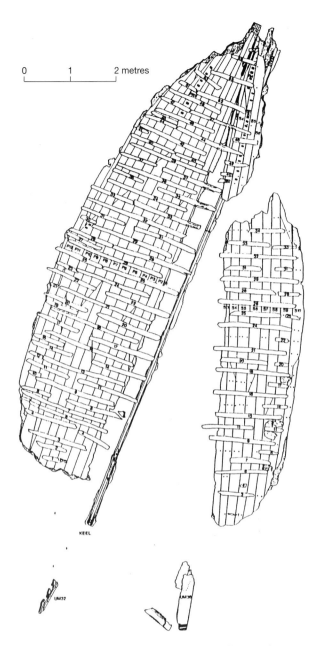

Fig. 4.40. Plan of the Kyrenia wreck (after Steffy, 1994: fig. 3.23).

plank fastenings are also similar and they appear to have been used throughout the ship (unlike Ma'agan-Michael). Hooked copper nails with a round cross-section and driven through treenails were used to fasten the framing to the planking. All these structural features were to persist for 500 years or so.

The ship (Steffy, 1985*a*, 1989, 1994: 42–59, 1995*b*) was mainly built of Aleppo pine (*Pinus halepensis*), whilst Turkey oak (*Quercus cerrus*) was used for the plank

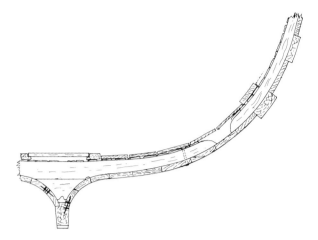

Fig. 4.41. Transverse section of the Kyrenia ship (after Steffy, 1994: fig. 3.31).

fastenings and the false keel. The keel (m/s = 200/120 mm) has a horizontal length near the middle of the ship, otherwise it is rockered. The L-shaped, two-piece stern is fastened to the keel in a horizontal hooked scarf with locked mortise and tenon joints. The curved stern post has a fixed tenon which is set into a mortise in the aft end of the keel and locked by a horizontal peg (Steffy, 1994: fig. 3.24): a large knee is fastened to the inboard faces of the post and keel.

The strakes were made up of two or three 40 mm thick planks fastened together in a horizontal scarf by locked tenons: these joints were mostly aligned with similar joints in the plank seams indicating that each plank had been fitted separately; some strakes were completed before they were fastened to the hull—in these cases the scarf mortises were cut at right angles to the scarf seams. The plank scarfs were shifted throughout the hull so that those in adjacent seams were not close together.

Plank seam mortises were *c*.6 mm thick and thus occupied *c*.12½ per cent of plank thickness: they were angled where necessary to match the changing shape of the hull and they were offset longitudinally from joints in adjacent strakes. Mortises averaged 43 mm broad (siding) and 80 mm deep: the average spacing was 117 mm. The tenons were 150–200 mm in length (i.e. approximately twice the depth of a mortise) and had rounded corners. After each strake had been fashioned and satisfactorily fitted to the tenons protruding from the lower strake, the tenons were locked within their mortises by multi-sided tapered pegs which were

driven generally from inboard into 60 mm holes, above and below the seam, through planking and tenon. Steffy (1994: 48) has estimated that there were more than 4,000 mortise and tenon joints in the original Kyrenia ship.

After at least eight, probably nine, strakes had been fastened together (Steffy, 1995b: 26), the lower framing was added to the hull. Floor timbers spanning six to nine strakes each side alternated with paired half-frames, which did not reach as far as the keel. Side frames were added in line with, and in some cases butted to, the floors and the half-frames, but they were not fastened to them (unlike those in the Ma'agan-Michael ship). There were occasional top timbers (Steffy, 1994: fig. 3.34). None of the floors touched or were fastened to the keel, but they were fastened by unlocked mortise and tenon joints to a chock inserted in the cavity between floor and keel. The majority of framing timbers were compass timbers chosen so that their grain followed the transverse curvature of the hull. Both floors and half-frames were frequently crooked along their length and wandered somewhat across the planking. The forty-one frame stations (floors and half-frames) were about 0.25 m apart. Limber holes were cut over the seam between the second and third strakes, and over the seam between the fifth and sixth strakes, also in each chock.

Frames were generally square in section with 85–90 mm sides. They were fastened to the planking by copper nails driven from outboard through treenails and generally clenched inboard by turning the point

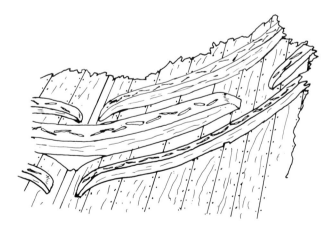

Fig. 4.42. Methods of clenching the nails fastening the framing to the Kyrenia planking (Institute of Archaeology, Oxford).

through 180° back into the frame (Fig. 4.42). Along the garboard and second strakes, where the distance through plank, floor, and chock was 0.30 m or more, copper spikes were used. The treenails were tapered and driven from inboard. The advantages of driving fastening nails through treenails are that leakage through fastenings is reduced, the stresses produced by the nail are distributed around the hole and thus the risk of splitting is reduced, and framing timbers, which are natural crooks and therefore of value, may be re-used more readily, since removing the nails need not damage the actual fastening holes.

The framing in the plank-first Kyrenia ship may be compared with that of the frame-first, Romano-Celtic Barland's Farm boat (5.6.1). Both use a mix of floors and half-frames with associated, but unconnected side timbers and the occasional top timber. The Barland's Farm boat does not have the regularly alternating framing pattern of Kyrenia, however, and her half-frames overlap (but are not fastened together) across the bottom of the boat.

Frame fastenings of these two boats are also similar: they differ in that iron instead of copper nails are used in the Romano-Celtic boat. A more fundamental difference is that in Kyrenia the frames were fastened to the planking, whereas in Barland's Farm, the planking was fastened to the framing.

The tenth strake (the first side strake) was the Kyrenia ship's main wale: that is, a specially chosen plank twice as thick as the ordinary planking. The twelfth strake, probably at the loaded waterline, was also a wale being 60 mm thick, i.e. 1½ times that of the planking. Steffy has estimated that there were two more strakes above this wale. Inboard of the main wale a stringer or beam shelf 50 mm thick was nailed to the inner faces of the framing.

The ship had loose bottom boards for access to the limber holes, and outboard of these was a ceiling of planks nailed to the framing. Kyrenia had no full-length keelson but a mast step timber was notched to fit over frames F33, 35, and 37. The mast step itself was 160 × 90 mm. Alongside the mast step are steps for stanchions which in conjunction with two of the three crossbeams (at beam-shelf level) are deduced to have supported longitudinal mast partners either side of, and c.60 m above, the mast step (Steffy, 1989: fig. 7). Other frames F47 and F44 were also rabbeted and may have been an alternative position for the mast-step tim-

ber; however, these frames are even nearer the bow than F33, 35, and 37.

A timber, heavily eroded by teredo, was found astern of the wreck and is thought to have been part of a rudder or steering-oar blade.

The Kyrenia ship is the earliest known to date to have been fastened solely by mortise and tenon joints. By this date, in the eastern Mediterranean at least, the locked mortise and tenon joint was well understood. This elegant fastening was fashioned to such fine limits that, unlike sewn-plank boats, no caulking was needed; its major disadvantage must have been the time needed to make the joints, and to fit and fasten each plank. Other advances seen in the Kyrenia ship of c.300 BC, when compared with the Ma'agan-Michael ship of c.400 BC are that the Kyrenia keel had rabbets for the garboards to fit into, thus improving the integrity of the lower hull, the framing pattern of alternating floors and half-frames had been evolved (this was to become the standard pattern for the next few centuries), and the keel was rockered. As well as being operationally advantageous in steering and in beach operations, this last feature also increased the hull's resistance to the stress reversals experienced in a seaway and thus minimized the working of plank seams (Coates, forthcoming). Furthermore, the Kyrenia underwater hull had been sheathed with lead during service, mainly as a barrier against teredo crustacea and as anti-fouling; lead sheathing would also have increased watertightness (Kahanov, 1994; Hocker, 1995).

### 4.12.1.1 THE KYRENIA RECONSTRUCTION

As with most ancient wrecks, the bow, stern, and upper sides of the hull were incomplete, when excavated. Using three-dimensional models, Steffy has reconstructed the Kyrenia hull as a lines plan (1985a: fig. 20; Katzev, 1989a: fig. 1). The bow and stern regions are conjectural to varying degrees. In his interim report, Steffy records that the sheer line was based on 'the pattern of isolated nails and scattered remote fragments which were recorded during excavation. But this evidence was slim . . .' (Steffy, 1985a: 99).

From these reconstructed lines (and possibly from the three-dimensional models), construction drawings for a complete ship appear to have been produced and from these drawings a ship known as Kyrenia 2 was built in Greece in 1982–5 (Katzev, 1986, 1987, 1989a and b, 1990).

This vessel measures 14 × 4.2 m and has an estimated cargo capacity of c.25 tonnes. She is double-ended with a sweeping sheer, a stern higher than the bow, and soft bilges. Katzev (1989a: 165) has noted that the bow configuration is conjectural, and the curvature of the stern post somewhat hypothetical. The twin quarter rudders are based on the fragmentary remains of a blade. The sailing rig is more conjectural, presumably being based on representational evidence, as is the case in almost all reconstruction experiments.

The fact that the mast step was found so far forward, with no balancing second step further aft, has been a problem for the reconstructors. In the on-site drawings the mast step appears to be approximately one-third the overall surviving length from the foremost part of the ship to survive: in published photographs of the reconstruction, the mast appears to be in this one-third position relative to the waterline of the ship as built. A square sail on a mast so far forward would not necessarily be in balance with the hull, resulting in steering problems, and it is noteworthy that rudders and tillers were broken during sea trials of Kyrenia 2. Differential brailing could be used, however, to change the effective shape of the sail and thus reduce this tendency. If the bow were to be reconstructed with a protruding forefoot, the mast step would be nearer amidships, possibly sufficiently far forward of amidships to give the lead (of centre of effort of the sail over the centre of lateral resistance of the hull) that a square sail needs to optimize directional stability and minimize steering problems (O. Roberts, 1995).

An alternative approach would be to consider a fore-and-aft sail such as a lateen or a sprit. On a mast stepped well forward, as in Kyrenia 2, such a sail should in theory be more in balance than a square sail. The iconographic evidence for fore-and-aft sails in the Mediterranean does not appear until some 200–50 years after the date of the Kyrenia wreck (4.14.1) but this should not deter experimenters from trials with different forms of sail.

Steffy's publications of the Kyrenia ship's structure, her sequence and method of building and repair, and her significance to archaeological studies is very well argued and presented, and unchallengeable. The design, building and trials of Kyrenia 2 have not yet been comprehensively published: the future publica-

tion of the final report on the Kyrenia project may dispel doubts about the value of Kyrenia 2.

### 4.12.2 THE MARSALA WRECKS (Parker, 1992: nos. 661 and 662)

Marsala wreck 1 ('Punic' wreck) was excavated off Punta Scario, western Sicily during 1971–4 (Frost, 1976). The remains, consisting of the lower parts of one end of the vessel (which the excavator believes is from the stern) with a fragment of the post, and parts of sixteen strakes to port and four strakes to starboard, were lifted, conserved, and displayed in a temporary museum at Marsala where they seem to have deteriorated. The bow of a second wreck was discovered near Marsala 1, after the main excavation had finished: this was photographed underwater, but not recorded in such detail as Marsala 1. These wrecks are dated from pottery types, and by inscriptions on the ship's timbers, to the mid-third century BC. The 200 painted inscriptions, identified as Punic letters or words, suggest that these vessels were built by Carthaginian craftsmen; the timber species and other evidence suggest that Marsala 1 was built in Sicily or Italy.

Marsala 1 is similar in many respects to the Kyrenia ship: the hull transverse sections and the keel cross-section are similar, as is the framing pattern; the frames are not fastened to the keel; the plank fastenings and the frame to plank fastenings are similar in form, size, and spacing; and both hulls were sheathed in lead (Steffy, 1994: 59). A main structural difference is that the after end of Marsala 1 keel turns upwards to form, as it were, the lowest part of the post, to which an outer post is fastened by mortise and tenon joints. A second difference is that in Marsala 1, whereas up to the eleventh strake the planking (30–40 mm thick) is flush-laid, above this level the planks, which seem to have been hewn externally to shape, are thicker at their lower edge than at their upper edge giving a superficial resemblance to clinker planking when seen from outboard (Frost, 1996: fig. 194). This feature is probably best interpreted as a way of planking around the turn of the bilge without having to bevel the plank edges and without leaving the planking over-thin outboard of the tenons. The excavator, on the other hand, has interpreted these 'simulated clinkers' as 'spray deflectors' (which may well be a secondary effect), and sought their origin in some hypothetical influence from northern Europe (Frost, 1996; 1999)—see also Farrar (1987, 1988).

Phoenician letters painted on the port face and the inner face of the keel appear to be at frame stations. Lines were also incised across the planking marking the forward and after faces of each frame (Frost, 1990: 183). Frost (1997: 261) deduces from this that the 'design of the vessel had been preconceived'. The general design of this vessel almost certainly had been conceived in the mind of the shipwright before work began. A more fundamental question is whether this shipwright had a *detailed* design, either in his mind or in some other form. Since this ship, like all others considered so far in this chapter, was built plank first, the hull shape was determined, in conjunction with the posts and keel, by the angle and breadth of each succeeding strake: this shape was achieved before the framing was fashioned, fitted, and fastened. The shipwright would then have marked on the planking the required position of each frame. The incised lines on the planking appear, as Frost suggests, to have been drawn after fitting and before final trimming of each frame. Thus neither symbols nor lines played a part in determining the hull shape.

Circular imprints (interpreted as having been made by the dirty bottom of a paint pot) span the seams of certain pairs of planks in the hull above the turn of the bilge. This has suggested to Frost (1990) and Farrar (1990) that these particular planks were fastened as one unit to the hull, i.e. 'prefabricated'. These pairs of planks (not strakes) must have been close alongside one another (inner face uppermost) when the paint pot (if such it was) was placed on them: this could have happened after the planks had been sawn from the log, but before their final shaping, and well before they were fastened together. By itself, the 'paint pot' evidence does not prove 'prefabrication'.

Frost (1975*a* and *b*) has suggested that a wooden projection from what is thought to be the bow of Marsala 2 was a ram, an opinion generally supported by Sleeswyk (1996*a*). As Basch (1983*a*: 132) has noted, such projections are not necessarily rams: it seems more likely that this Marsala upcurving timber (Frost, 1975*b*: 24) is a protruding forefoot incorporated in the hull to increase the structural integrity of that part of the vessel, to increase speed potential, or to improve directional stability.

Several attempts have been made to formulate a reconstruction of the original shape and structure of Marsala 1, incorporating the bow of Marsala 2 (Adam, 1977; Frost, 1977, 1981; Farrar, 1989, 1990). This project seems overambitious when the extent of the remains is considered (Coates *et al.*, 1995). In line with an overriding idea that Marsala 1 was an oared warship (although no evidence survived for oared propulsion), the reconstructions have been given galley L/B proportions of *c.*1 : 7 by inserting approximately 14 m of parallel body between a Marsala 1 stern and a (more conjectural) Marsala 2 bow. As Owain Roberts has noted (personal communication), if most of this inserted section is removed, the L/B ratio (*c.*4 : 1) becomes more like that of the Kyrenia ship (3 : 1) which was a merchant ship. The large quantity of ballast excavated from Marsala 1, the variety of pottery excavated, the lead sheathing and the several structural similarities with the Kyrenia ship suggest that she was also a cargo ship rather than a warship.

### 4.12.3 RAMS

The earliest representations of rams are dated to the ninth/eighth centuries BC (Fig. 4.24): these are pointed rams, probably at or below the waterline and intended to hole the planking. During the sixth century BC, blunt-ended ones appear: these were intended to spring the planking (Casson and Linder, 1991: fig. 5.4). The first depictions of waterline 'trident' rams are dated *c.*400 BC: these have three broad horizontal fins, disposed vertically and separated by a vertical post at the head (Basch, 1987*a*: figs. 582, 633). This type appears to have continued in use into the first century AD (Casson and Linder, 1991: figs. 5.5 and 5.6).

Only two undoubted rams have been excavated: a small ram of unknown provenance, now in the German Maritime Museum at Bremerhaven (Casson and Linder, 1991: fig. 6.5), and a much longer one found in 1980 on the foreshore at Athlit (between Haifa and Caesarea, Israel), and now in the National Maritime Museum at Haifa (Casson and Steffy, 1991: figs. 2.12 and 4.1). The Athlit bronze ram of the 'trident' type, dated by the style of its decorations to the first half of the second century BC, weighs about 465 kg and measures 2.26 × 0.76 × 0.96 m. It formerly enveloped the foremost 2 m of the bow of a large warship. Steffy (1991) extracted fragments of sixteen bow timbers from inside the ram and reconstructed the forepost of the parent ship from this evidence. These timbers included fragments of the keel, the stem post, the bottom, and some side planking, the waterline wales, a central ramming timber, and a chock, a nosing piece and a false stem. Steffy concluded after detailed examination of these timbers that the hull planking of the parent ship had been assembled and fastened together without the stem post being in place. The post had then been fastened to the ramming timber by a locked mortise and tenon joint, and the two timbers added as one unit to the hull. Subsequently the ram was cast in bronze to match the complex bow structure. How far aft the ramming timber extended is unknown, but Steffy conjectures that it may have led into a keelson, otherwise unknown at this time.

Early rams, which were pointed, would penetrate a hull more readily than blunt or finned rams; consequently their retardation would be less and would make less demands on the strength and hull integrity of the attacking ship. Coates (personal communication) cannot see why a sewn boat should not use such a ram. There are differences of opinion about the strength of the impact and the degree of retardation when a blunt or finned ram is used. Such rams are generally thought to be an advance on pointed rams in that they minimize the problem of withdrawal (probably experienced when using a pointed ram) since they merely thump the planking and start the seams. A preliminary theoretical study by John Haywood (Shaw, 1993a: 99–100) of the use of a three-finned ram suggests that if one fin of the ram were to penetrate the waterline wale of a target ship, there would be no great and sudden impact, rather a relatively slow retardation. Sleeswyk (paper at Henley) and Steffy (1991), on the other hand, consider that the impact would be much greater and thus the ramming ship would need to have the stiffness and strength which could only be given by closely spaced mortise and tenon joints.

Further research in this area, and into ramming tactics (Shaw, 1993a; Casson, 1991), is needed if a better understanding of the building and use of early eastern Mediterranean warships is to be obtained. The use of rams to break the oars of a target ship poses few theoretical problems although it may well have been difficult in practice. The use of rams to cause a hull to leak heavily, in one way or the other, is still controversial.

# 4.13
# The Roman Age (Mid-Second Century BC–Fourth Century AD)

In the early years of this period Rome defeated both Greece and Carthage, and in time absorbed their overseas settlements: from the first century AD Rome was the undisputed seafaring power and overseas trading country in the Mediterranean. More than 60 per cent of the Mediterranean wreck sites documented by Parker (1992: figs. 3 and 4) are from these five and a-half centuries. There is also much literary and iconographic evidence for ships and seafaring (Casson, 1971: 141–7; Basch, 1987a: 418–98; Morrison, 1995a: 78–90; Morrison and Coates, 1996: 112–254). Furthermore several important specialist studies have been focused on this period: for example, that by Dubois (1976) on Roman keels, and that by Rival (1991) on Roman woodworking techniques and their choice of timber for seagoing ships. Here we shall concentrate on the structural evidence from selected excavated hulls. Since there was evidently a general continuity in building techniques from the Hellenistic to the Roman world, we shall focus on variations and changes within a generally homogenous Mediterranean technology.

The technological advance during this period was stimulated, in the main, by the growth of Rome's population and by Rome's increasing domination of the Mediterranean. From the fourth century BC, grain had to be imported to Rome in increasing quantities. Opportunities in overseas trade in other goods increased significantly from the second century BC, both to the west, France and Spain, and to the east, the Levant and Egypt, and via Egypt to India (6.3). The virtual eradication of piracy during the first century BC, and the relative peace that ensued when the Civil War ended in 31 BC set the scene for a marked increase in overseas trading voyages: this appears to be reflected in the increase in the number of known wrecks from the beginning of the second century BC (Parker, 1992: fig. 3).

## 4.13.1 SMALL BOATS

Two open boats, which Steffy (1994: 65–71) was able to document provisionally during excavation and before they were removed from site for conservation, show that the techniques used to build the Kyrenia ship generally continued in use into this period. The boat from the bed of Lake Kinneret (Sea of Galilee) Israel, dated to the period 100 BC–AD 67, is estimated to have been c.9 × 2.5 × 1.2 m (Wachsmann, 1990). The second boat (Parker, 1992: no. 501) was excavated from Herculaneum, near Naples, where she had been overturned and carbonized by outflow from the AD 79 eruption of Mount Vesuvius (Steffy, 1985b). She was similar in size to the Kinneret boat but was lighter, more graceful and generally better built. Both boats were built plank-first with locked mortise and tenon joints spaced at c.120–130 mm. The Kinneret framing, of alternate floors and half-frames spaced at c.0.25 m, was fastened to the planking by spikes and by treenails with occasional nails clenched outboard by hooking (Steffy, 1994: fig. 3.53). The Herculaneum framing was generally similar but with two sets of double frames near amidships, probably in the region of the mast step (Steffy, 1994: fig. 3.56).

## 4.13.2 LARGE MERCHANT SHIPS

The increasing demand for cargo space is reflected in the emergence, from the second century BC onwards, of merchant ships of relatively great tonnage—up to c.600 tonnes cargo capacity, which may be compared with the 25 tonnes of the mid-fourth-century BC Kyrenia ship. It has been estimated that the first-century BC wreck from La Madrague de Giens (Fig. 4.43) (Parker, 1992: no. 616) was 40 × 9 m with a hold some 4.5 m deep which was loaded with nearly 400 tonnes of amphorae, stacked in three tiers, with boxes of ceramics stowed above them (Tchernia, Pomey, and Hesnand, 1978; Pomey, 1982). The first-century BC wreck from Albenga (Parker, 1992: no. 28) in Italy is thought to have been slightly bigger with a capacity of 500–600 tonnes (Delgado, 1997: 24). Other large ships from this century include: Antikythera 1 (Parker, 1992: no. 44), from Greek waters; Mahdia (Parker, 1992: no. 621) off Tunisia; the wreck from Caesarea Maritima, Israel (Oleson, 1994: 163–223) of the first century AD. Second-century BC Italian wrecks from Punta Scaletta (Parker, 1992: no. 960) and Spargi (Parker, 1992: no. 1108) are also estimated to have been over 30 m overall length (Fitz-Gerald, 1994: table 6.3). Some of these wrecks were first excavated thirty (and one even 100) years ago, and we cannot now be certain of details of their hull structure. Nevertheless something can be said in general terms about how these large ships differed from the earlier, smaller ones.

Fig. 4.43. Transverse sections of the Madrague de Giens wreck, amidships (upper) and at the mast step (lower) (after Pomey, 1997c: 99).

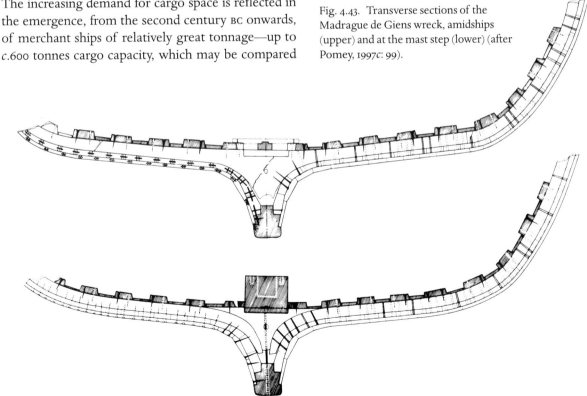

### 4.13.2.1 THE PLANKING

Planking was enhanced by making it thicker, and by increasing the proportion of plank length that was tenoned. The Kyrenia ship of *c*.300 BC and the Ma'agan-Michael ship of 400 BC had 40 mm planking. Two of the large cargo ships had planking *c*.90 mm thick: Caesarea and Antikythera 1 (FitzGerald, 1994: 179, table 6.3), with the mortises staggered (Steffy, 1994: fig. 3.58). Others had inner and outer planking separated by a layer of wool or some other fabric saturated in wax or pitch: Punta Scaletta, possibly 70 and 65 mm thick; Albenga, possibly 40 and 40 mm; Mahdia, possibly 50 and 36 mm; Madrague de Giens, 60 and 40 mm; Dramont 1, *c*.35 and 27 mm thick; and Île du Lévant (*Titan*) a total of 56 mm. In these double-planked vessels the mortises were only slightly staggered, if at all (FitzGerald, 1994: 179–81; Delgado, 1997: 24, 131, 252–5). As FitzGerald (1994: 178) has pointed out, these thick planks, ranging from 56–135 mm are approximately within the range recommended by Juvenal (*Sat.* 12. 58–9) for merchant ship's planking: four to seven finger breadths, i.e. 70–130 mm. Data from some practical, successful wooden fishing boats of the 1950s show that their plank thickness is a linear function of length (Palmer, personal communication). Fishing boats of a similar length to Kyrenia (14 m) had planking *c*.48 mm thick; those similar in length to Madrague de Giens and Caesarea (40 m) had planking *c*.99 mm thick. Thus, by twentieth-century standards, these three ancient ships had near-ideal plank thicknesses (Table 4.4).

Unlike multi-planked medieval Chinese hulls (10.5.1) in which the outer planking was merely fastened to the inner planking, *both* inner and outer planking in the Mediterranean hulls were edge fastened by mortise and tenon joints, with the garboard strake of each layer fitting into its own keel rabbet. As Steffy (1994: 62–5) and FitzGerald (1994: 185) have pointed out, double planking has several theoretical advantages over a single layer of comparable thickness. There would be less wastage when fashioning planks to shape and there would have been less movement and distortion of the tenons when compared with the staggered (near double) row of joints in the single planking. Where the planking had to be bent to achieve the required hull shape, especially at bow and stern, two thin planks would have been easier to fit than one thick plank. Furthermore the lamination effect of two layers would in itself probably result in a stronger hull, and the paying of tarred wool in between inner and outer planking would have added to the hull's watertight integrity. Steffy also considers that the outer planking (often thinner, and frequently of soft wood) would, to a degree, have been sacrificial, protecting the main, inner planking from physical and teredo damage.

Planking strength was further increased by having more fastenings per unit length. The data in Table 4.4 shows that in the main (inner) planking of the double-planked Madrague de Giens, the percentage of strake length occupied by tenons was 49 per cent greater than that of Kyrenia, whilst the outer planking was the same as Kyrenia. The two ships with single planking had percentages some 57 per cent (Antikythera), and 81 per cent (Caesarea) greater than Kyrenia.

### 4.13.2.2 THE FRAMING

The pattern of framing in the large merchant ships was generally the same as that of the smaller vessels, i.e.

**Table 4.4** Mortise breadths per unit length of planking

| 1<br>Vessel | 2<br>Date | 3<br>Average mortise breadth (mm) | 4<br>Average mortise spacing (mm) | 5<br>Breadth/spacing (%) | 6<br>Average plank thickness (mm) |
|---|---|---|---|---|---|
| Kyrenia | 300 BC | 43 | 117 | 37 | 40 |
| Madrague de Giens | 75–60 BC | | | | |
|     Inner | | 80–5 | 150 | 55 | 60 |
|     Outer | | 55–7 | 150 | 37 | 40 |
| Antikythera 1 | 1st century BC | 80 | 138 | 58 | 90 |
| Caesarea | 1st century AD | 90 | 135 | 67 | 90 |

*Sources*: Steffy, 1994: 43–6, 65, 71; FitzGerald, 1994: 178–80.

floors with futtocks alternating with half-frames. One exception to this rule was the Dramont 1 wreck (Parker, 1992: no. 371), of the first century BC, which had eight consecutive floors under her mast-step timber (Delgado, 1997: 131). In the Caesarea and Antikythera and other wrecks of the first century BC, these frames were fastened to the planking by hooked nails through treenails, as in the earlier and smaller ships (FitzGerald, 1994: 192–7, table 6.5). In the ships with double planking frames were similarly fastened to the inner planking but merely nailed to the outer planking. Dramont 1 was again an exception, her frames being fastened by nails through treenails to both planking layers.

The frames of these large merchant ships were clearly of greater dimensions than that of the Kyrenia ship but, in the few examples with reliable quantified evidence (Table 4.5), this increase in frame size was less than commensurate with increase in ship size (measured by length overall). The section modulus (row 8 in Table 4.5) of the frames actually reduces with increased length of vessel (row 2). The main reason for this deficit is that the moulded dimension of the frames was not increased sufficiently to produce the required stiffness. Furthermore, the increased sided dimension of the frames in the larger ships was offset by their increased spacing (especially in the Caesarean ship) so that there was no consistent increase in the percentage of planking in direct contact with a frame (row 9), with increased size of ship.

It has been suggested that these large ships were the first to have composite framing and to have their frames fastened to the keel. In fact, the floors of an earlier and smaller ship, that for Ma'agan-Michael (4.9.4.6)

were each scarfed to two futtocks before her composite frames were fastened to the planking. Similar techniques were used in the gigantic Lake Nemi ships of the early first century AD (Parker, 1992: no. 732–5; Steffy, 1994: 71–2) but they were probably royal barges and not in the mainstream of cargo-ship building. FitzGerald (1994: 189) has noted the two instances where composite frames may have been used in large merchant ships, but these are doubtful evidence. FitzGerald (1994: 198, 222) has also noted evidence for the fastening of frames to the keel. The late second-century BC Spargi wreck, and the first-century BC wrecks from Madrague de Giens and L'isola di Mal di Ventre, all estimated to be over 30 m in length, had at least some frames fastened to the keel. This technique does not appear in small merchant ships until the mid-first century AD (St Gervase 3—Parker, 1992: no. 1002).

### 4.13.2.3 LONGITUDINAL TIMBERS

Longitudinal timbers such as wales, stringers, keelsons, and ceiling planking all strengthen a hull. Earlier, small merchant ships such as Kyrenia had wales and some ceiling planking nailed to the floors but no full-length keelson, only a short mast-step timber; and the only stringer-like timber was a beam shelf spiked to the framing inboard of the main wale (Steffy, 1994: 52).

An innovation in the Madrague de Giens ship was that alternate planks in the ceiling were substantially thicker (60–100 mm compared with 25–40 mm) than the others, and also broader (200–300 mm rather than 150–250 mm). These were effectively stringers. This ship also had a substantial mast-step timber which, if

**Table 4.5** Comparison of the framing in three ships

|  | Kyrenia | Madrague de Giens | Caesarea |
|---|---|---|---|
| Date | 300 BC | 75–60 BC | First cent. AD |
| L × B (m) | 14 × 4.2 | 40 × 9 | 40 × 10 |
| Average frame (m) |  |  |  |
| Moulded | 0.085 | 0.135 | 0.188 |
| Sided | 0.090 | 0.135 | 0.180 |
| Spacing | 0.117 | 0.150 | 0.250 |
| (M.S).$10^{-3}$ | 7.65 | 18.23 | 33.84 |
| $\text{Log}(e)\frac{M^3S}{12}$ = section modulus | 12.29 | 10.49 | 9.20 |
| % of planking in contact with a frame | 77 | 90 | 72 |

*Sources*: FitzGerald, 1994: 187–8; C. Palmer (personal communication).

not a full-length keelson, did nevertheless add to the spinal strength of the hull.

#### 4.13.2.4 STRUCTURAL INNOVATIONS (SECOND CENTURY BC TO SECOND CENTURY AD)

The number of large and small merchant ships used in the foregoing analysis is very small, and the data from them is incomplete and, in some cases, challengeable. Any conclusions drawn must therefore be provisional and need to be tested on future well-documented merchant ships from this period. Two of the features of large merchant ships—increased plank thickness (per se), and stouter frames (per se)—which, it has been suggested, clearly differentiate them from smaller ships, are in fact merely a reflection of the greater hull size, and not a great leap forward in technology.

The innovations incorporated in these large ships (in as much as we have the evidence) are:

(a) the use of double-planking, probably resulting in a disproportionately greater hull strength and integrity;

(b) greater than proportionate increase in breadth of tenons, leading to a greater percentage of the planking having 'internal, discontinuous frames', and thus strengthening the planking shell;

(c) keels of greater dimensions with complex scarfs adding to structural strength;

(d) the fastening of some frames to the keel consolidating the keel/frame assembly—structural strength;

(e) the fitting of prototype stringers and keelsons (elongated mast-steptimbers)—structural strength;

(f) hulls became fuller and flatter in transverse section—greater capacity.

In many ways the structure of these large merchant ships was a natural development from the smaller ones: they continued to be edge-fastened with closely spaced, locked mortise and tenon joints and tight-fitting tenons, and were built plank-first; their framing pattern and the frame to plank fastenings were essentially the same; and the transverse hull shape, as far as can be seen, changed but little. The first two innovations listed above seem to have been discontinued after the second century AD, when huge merchant ships were evidently no longer built. Frame/keel fastenings,

stringers, and keelsons, on the other hand, became part of the standard technology.

#### 4.13.3 TECHNOLOGICAL CHANGE IN THE THIRD AND FOURTH CENTURIES AD

After the second century AD, wrecks of large merchant ships are rare: wrecks are seldom more than 20 m overall length. Importantly, there are signs of a shift in emphasis from the strength of edge-fastened planking towards better framing, keelson, ceiling, and decking. Steffy (1994: 77–8, 83–5), has suggested that these technological changes were the result of social and economic changes. There was a decline in slavery, resulting in labour becoming more expensive; and shipowners had become independent businessmen who preferred smaller, less costly ships. Shipbuilders, in turn, sought to use their resources more efficiently. Since the 'classic' style of building was very labour intensive, especially in the fashioning, fitting, and fastening of the thousands of mortise and tenon joints in even a moderate-sized hull, efficiency meant adopting techniques that significantly decreased the man-hours needed for each ship; it also demanded the economical use of timber resources. Other, more fundamental, reasons have been suggested: changes in types of cargo, improvements in tools and techniques, deforestation, the introduction of fore-and-aft sails (Steffy, 1995b: 27). However, economies gained by reducing manpower, especially of skilled shipwrights, and by more efficient use of available timber seem to have directly affected the shipbuilder's approach to his work (Jezegov, 1985: 142–3).

#### 4.13.3.1 YASSI ADA 2

The fourth-century AD wreck Yassi Ada 2 (Parker, 1992: no. 1240) provides an example of this changing technology. This wreck in Turkish waters was excavated in 1967, 1969, and 1974. The original dimensions of this small cargo ship are estimated to have been 20 × 8 m. Her hull was 'conventional' in many respects: she was built plank-first, her 42 mm thick planking was fastened by mortise and tenon joints, and her frames were alternately floors and half-frames. However, her joints were smaller than in comparable ships from earlier centuries, and were more widely spaced, being 150–200 mm, where the planking was relatively weak because of a concentration of scarfs, but elsewhere up to 320 mm (Steffy, 1994: 79–80). Her tenons were given a double trapezium shape to match the tapering mortises: they did not fit the mortises in breadth or in depth, leaving gaps of 6–7 mm at each end, and 17–18 mm at each side (Steffy, 1994: fig. 4.1). Van Doorninck (1976: 126–7) has suggested that the paired midship half-frames were fastened to the lower hull after five strakes had been erected, and used as a master frame for the upper hull. His argument includes an assumption that 'the ability to assemble hulls with finished planking was a precondition' to the rise of frame-first techniques: this is not so—planks are finally fashioned to shape *after* being fastened to framing in Tamil Nadu frame-first boats and ships (Blue, Kentley, and McGrail, 1998).

Wrecks of the late fourth century / early fifth century AD with similar characteristics to Yassi Ada 2 include: Fiumicino 1 (Parker, 1992: no. 408) from Portus Claudius near Rome (Boetto, forthcoming), where average spacing of joints is 347 mm, and some of these are not locked; and Dramont 5 and 6 (Parker, 1992: nos. 375 and 376).

# 4.14
# Propulsion, Steering, and Seafaring

## 4.14.1 PROPULSION BY SAIL AND STEERING

The single square sail is depicted from 2000 BC until Roman times. From the late sixth century BC onwards, ships are occasionally depicted with a second sail, a square sail on a foremast (Casson, 1971: fig. 97), and descriptions from the mid-third century BC refer to a third sail set on a mizzen (Casson, 1971: 240). In the first century AD, the foremast is depicted with a forward rake, and is sometimes stepped at the bow as an *artemon*. From *c.* AD 200 main topsails are depicted.

Fore-and-aft sails are illustrated during Roman times, invariably on boats rather than ships: the sprit-

sail from the second century BC (Casson, 1971: figs. 175–9); the lateen from the second century AD (Casson, 1971: fig. 181). R. Bowen (1956c), however, disputed the identification of this sail as a lateen, and considered it to be a lugsail. In the Bay of Bengal today lug-shaped sails grade into lateen-shaped sails, and both are taken forward of the mast when changing tack (Blue *et al.*, 1997, 1998): the difference between Bowen's and Casson's interpretation may be of little consequence. Steffy's work on the fourth-century AD Yassi Ada 2 has suggested that she was rigged with a fore-and-aft sail such as a lateen rather than a square sail; his research on seventh-century Yassi Ada 1 indicates that she had two lateens (4.15.2.2). The fact that the single mast step of the Kyrenia ship was set so far forward suggests that a similar fore-and-aft sail may have been in use in 300 BC (4.12.1.1).

Theophrastus of the fourth century BC stated that Egyptian sails were of papyrus; however, Black (1996) has pointed out how very brittle such sails would be. Linen, made from flax, was used to make the sails of Egyptian boat models of the mid-second millennium BC, and this seems a more likely material for actual craft. Ezekiel's statement in the late-sixth century BC that Phoenician sails were linen gives some support to this contention (Black and Samuel, 1991). Part of a second-century BC linen shroud from the temple at Edfu, Egypt has been identified as a fragment of sail cloth with a wooden brail ring attached (Black, 1996: figs. 5 and 6). This is the earliest sail cloth to have survived anywhere; the next earliest appears to be part of a medieval sail from China (10.4.2.3). Casson (1971: 234) has deduced from a study of several representations that the edges of Mediterranean sails were reinforced with bolt rope and the corners with leather patches.

Ships in this period were generally steered by a side rudder on each quarter (Casson, 1971: figs. 108, 109, 119, 128, 147–51). The sea trials of the trireme reconstruction *Olympias* showed that such rudders induced a disproportionate amount of drag, it may be that, whenever possible, only one of the pair was used, especially on warships when under oars.

## 4.14.2 NAVIGATION AND SEAFARING

By the mid-first century AD there is literary evidence that it was customary for seamen to measure the zenith altitude of particular stars by reference to the length of the mast (Lucan, *Bel. Civ.*, 8. 177–81). In this manner they had a measure of 'relative latitude': that is, they knew whether they were north or south of a haven for which they already knew the star zenith altitude (E. Taylor, 1971: 47–8; McGrail, 1983*b*: 308, 318). Apart from this, navigation and pilotage methods appear to have been very similar to those practised in earlier times by the Greeks (4.4.6) and the Phoenicians (4.9.3.2.1).

In the fourth century BC, written sailing directions (*periploi*) for coastal voyages began to be compiled from an accumulation of oral accounts. The earliest of these surviving is now known as 'pseudo-Scylax', written between 361 and 357 BC: this describes passages along the Mediterranean coast (Dilke, 1985). In *c*.320 BC, Pytheas of Massilia/Marseille undertook a voyage of scientific exploration, possibly more than one (Dilke, 1985: 136), along the Atlantic coast of Europe possibly as far north as the Faeroes and the Baltic (Roseman, 1994; Hawkes, 1977, 1984). His account has not survived but parts of it can be reconstructed from later writers.

By the mid-first millennium BC, the Phoenicians had sailed the Atlantic coast of north-west Africa (4.9.3.2.1), and they and the Greeks subsequently traded along the Atlantic coast of south-west Iberia (4.9.2.2). A *periplus* from the sixth century BC seems to have survived, incorporated by Avienus into his fourth-century AD poem, *Ora Maritima* (Hawkes, 1977: 19; Murphy, 1977; McGrail, 1990*b*: 36). This describes what was evidently an established trade route southwards along the Atlantic coast of Europe (Fig. 5.1), then eastwards through the Pillars of Hercules to Massilia/Marseille. The route is described in three stages: Ireland/Britain to western Brittany; from there to *Tartessus* (near modern Cadiz); thence to Massilia, with a subsidiary route to Carthage. The text seems to imply that the northern section of this route was undertaken by the 'hardy and industrious peoples of the islands and coasts around Ushant' (Murphy, 1977: lines 94–116), whilst the southern sections seem to have been used by Mediterranean merchants. The direct crossing from Ireland to Brittany (possibly via Britain) was certainly within the capabilities of Celtic seamen in the first century BC (McGrail, 1983*b*), and there is every reason to think it could have been done much earlier. Whether the voyage from the Ushant region to north-west Iberia was direct across the Bay of Biscay or coastal (very much

longer) is difficult to say. In general terms, the Bay is a lee shore and straying to the east of the direct route across could lead to embayment. However, if a prudent course could be held from Ushant in the direction of Cape Finistere in north-west Iberia, the mountains of northern Iberia should be sighted with ample sea room to adjust course (wind permitting), even though the predominant wind from the south-west may have set the ship into the Bay. An alternative route could have been via a haven in the Gironde estuary (McGrail, 1983*b*: 319–21). The leg along the Atlantic coast of Iberia may have involved keeping well out to sea to avoid the lee shore. The problems of entering the Mediterranean have been considered above (4.2). In general terms, this southbound route would have been more arduous and would have taken longer than when northbound. The fact that a lighthouse was built at Coruña in north-west Iberia during the Roman period (Hague, 1973) must mean that these difficult voyages were relatively frequent by that date. Nevertheless, much traffic between the Mediterranean and north-west Europe seems to have gone via French and German rivers (McGrail, 1983*b*; 5.5.4; 5.6.6). Roman trade routes to India are considered in Section 6.3.

# 4.15

## Early Frame-First Vessels (Fig. 4.3)

### 4.15.1  UP TO THE SIXTH CENTURY AD

All the planked boats and ships described so far in this chapter were built plank-first, i.e. the shape of the hull was determined by the planking, and much of the structural strength of the vessel came from that shell of planking (1.4.1.1). Basch (1972: 47), quoting Herodotus (1. 194), has suggested that the Greeks of the fifth century BC were also 'conversant' with the use of 'active' frames, i.e. frames that determined the hull shape, and thus must have built boats frame-first. This may be true, but only in relation to the building of hide boats, in which the framing does indeed determine the shape. Morrison (1976: 165) has taken Basch's argument a step further by quoting a description by Herodotus (2. 96) of how a Nile plank boat was built. However, Herodotus was clearly describing a boat which had no frames at all: the Dahshur boats of nineteenth-century BC Egypt were similarly frameless (2.8.3.2), as were Sudanese Nile *nuggar* boats of the early twentieth century (Hornell, 1946a: plate 35b).

Basch (1972: 43–5) has also approached the question of early frame-first building from another direction. He points out that in the fifth and fourth centuries BC, large Greek fleets had to be built in a hurry; that, quoting Polybius (I. 20, 13; 38. 5; 59. 8) and Pliny (*NH* 16. 192), the Romans in 260 BC and 242 BC copied Carthaginian hulls and built a fleet of ships; and that in 254 BC they built 220 ships in three months. He then argues that in all these instances moulds must have been used; that is, active frames would have determined the hull shape and therefore this was the frame-first sequence of building. Furthermore, Frost has hinted that formal design methods lay behind the building of the mid-third-century BC Marsala 1 (4.12.2), and Bellabarba (1996: 264, figs. 4.5 and 6) has argued that this ship was built using moulds (equivalent in this sense to active frames) which reproduced the shape of the master frame, the rising and narrowing of the hull being determined by some predetermined procedure.

To twenty-first century people, such arguments have their attractions; however, there are archaeological arguments against them. Mediterranean wrecks dated before c. AD 600 were clearly edge-fastened by sewing or by mortise and tenon joints which were locked by pegs driven from inboard. As far as can be determined, they were all built plank-first: the shape of the hull was determined by the planking; frames were passive rather than active.

There have also been attempts to show that certain early wrecks were built frame-first. The Madrague de Giens of the first century BC was at first thought to have been built partly in this sequence (Tchernia, Pomey, and Hesnard, 1978). Subsequent research showed that the fourth and fifth strakes were replacements: this ship was built plank-first throughout (Pomey, 1988: 406; Parker, 1992: no. 250; Pomey, 1994; Pomey, 1998: 61–2, 66–8).

Gassend (1989) has used the fact that some of the pegs which lock the joints were driven from outboard, and some floors are fastened to the keel, to suggest that the late second-/early third-centuries AD ship Marseille-Bourse (Parker, 1992: no. 668), the second-cen-

tury Laurons 2 (ibid. 578), and the Pont Vendres 2 wreck of c. AD 400 (ibid. 874) were all built frame-first. Pomey (1988: 399, 406–9) has argued strongly against this hypothesis, pointing out that these vessels are all clearly edge-fastened by mortise and tenon joints, that the 'inverted' locking pegs are consistent with a repair, that fastening frames to the keel is not proof of the pre-erection of active framing, and that the evidence from these three ships is entirely consistent with a plank-first sequence of building. Pomey has conceded, however, that some pre-erected framing may have been used to control the shape of the upper hull.

### 4.15.2 SEVENTH CENTURY AD ONWARDS

#### 4.15.2.1 ST GERVAIS 2, TANTURA 1, AND PANTANO LONGARINI

Three seventh-century ships, from France, Israel, and Sicily were all built (at least partly) frame-first. The earliest of these is St Gervais 2 (Parker, 1992: no. 1001) of AD 600–25 (Jezegou, 1985) (Fig. 4.44). Planking at the bow and stern had widely-spaced (usually more than 1 m) mortise and tenon joints which were not locked: these joints were thus used to position the strakes and not to fasten them together. The rest of the 25–30 mm thick planking had no such joints: these strakes were not fastened together (not even the garboards to the keel), but were treenailed and nailed to pre-erected framing, and caulked. All floors, and some of the half-frames, were fastened to the keel with iron bolts: a total of seventeen out of twenty-seven surviving frames (63 per cent). The half-frames were fastened together by hooked nails where they overlapped near the centre-

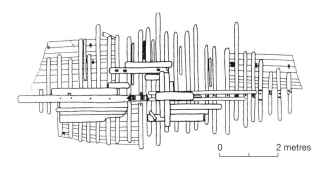

Fig. 4.44. Plan of the St Gervais 2 wreck (after Pomey, 1997c: 100).

line. Two wales each side were fastened by treenails to planking and framing. It is clear that in this ship, some 15–18 m in length, the framing played a more important role than the planking, at least in the underwater part of the hull. Whether plank-first or frame-first methods were used in the upper hull cannot be known since this did not survive.

The early seventh-century vessel recently under excavation in an Israeli coastal lagoon, Tantura 1, appears to have comparable features (Wachsmann, 1994; Kahanov, personal communication). None of the 25 mm thick strakes investigated were edge-fastened; they were nailed to the frames which were spaced c.0.33 m apart. Kahanov has estimated that she was originally 12 × 4 m.

A seventh-century wreck found in a drainage ditch at Pantano Longarini in Sicily (Throckmorton, 1973; Parker, 1992: no. 787) had unlocked mortise and tenon fastenings in her underwater hull widely spaced at c.1 m.

## 4.15.2.2   YASSI ADA I

Yassi Ada wreck 1 (Parker, 1992: no. 123a), dated to c. AD 625 was sparsely preserved but intensive study of the remains by Steffy (1982; 1994: 80–3) has revealed the essential details of her construction. In essence: this ship of c.20 × 5 m and capable of carrying c.60 tonnes of cargo, was built plank-first in the lower hull where there were complex shapes, and frame-first in the upper hull with generally flat sides and a naturally curving sheerline. The garboards were mainly nailed into the keel rabbet (nails often being driven at varying angles), with a few unlocked mortise and tenon fastenings at least 2.25 m apart. The remaining underwater hull had similar mortise and tenon joints (Steffy, 1994: fig. 4.4) spaced 350–500 mm in the stern region, but elsewhere c.900 mm: like those in the garboards, these joints were principally for aligning the strakes until they could be fastened to the framing by iron spikes. After five or six pairs of strakes had been positioned in this manner, the first floors were installed and fastened in the hull. A further six or five strakes were then added out to the turn of the bilge, when the larger floors were added. More strakes were added, still edge-fastened out to the light load waterline, the sixteenth strake. The remaining half-frames and most of the futtocks were then added. The upper hull was then planked up

in the frame-first manner, the planks being nailed, and the wales fastened by forelock bolts, to the framing. The deck, fastened to cross-beams supported by knees, was continuous except for the hatch area and the galley near the stern, thus increasing the structural integrity of the hull.

## 4.15.2.3   SERÇE LIMANI

The movement away from an edge-fastened, plank-first hull towards a frame-first hull evidently culminated, between the seventh and the eleventh centuries, in a frame-first ship with none of the planking fastened together. This innovation did not necessarily take place in the Byzantine Empire, although the best documented example is from those waters. Serçe Limani 1 (Parker, 1992: no. 1070), dated to c. AD 1025, is the earliest known Mediterranean ship of this type. Again, detailed post-excavation work by Steffy (1994: 85–91) has revealed her probable building sequence, and something about the methods of design used (Fig. 4.45). This ship is estimated to have been 15.36 × 5.12 m, not much bigger than Kyrenia (14 × 4.2 m) yet, because she had a hold of box-like proportions (Steffy, 1994: fig. 2.8), she had a much greater cargo capacity—c.35 tonnes compared with c.25.

Steffy's building sequence may be summarized:

1. Posts scarfed to keel.

2. Two composite master frames, some 0.32 m apart, nailed to the keel near the midships station. The heads of these frames would have been at, or near, the intended sheerline.

3. A pair of floors, shaped to give slightly more rising and narrowing of the hull than that of the floors of the master frames, were then nailed to the keel, one c.1.28 m forward of the forward master frame, and one c.1.28 m aft of the after master frame.

4. A second pair of floors was then fastened to the keel, half way between each master frame and the floors placed in 3.

5. Two further pairs of floors were then installed in the interstices between the floors and frames already fastened. At this stage two full frames and eight floors had been fastened to the keel at an average spacing of 0.30 m centre to centre. Each floor was fashioned from a crook, the curve of which matched that required for

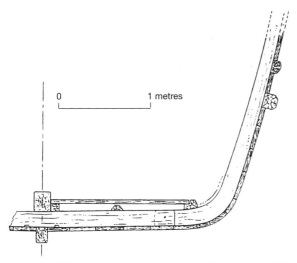

0          1 metres

Fig. 4.45. Midship section of the Serçe Limani ship (after Steffy, 1994: fig. 4.10)

the turn of the bilge: these floors were positioned so that the curve of the crooks were alternately to port and to starboard.

6. Although the evidence is limited, Steffy (possibly drawing on his knowledge of later documented practices in the central Mediterranean (4.16) believes that a further pair of floors or frames was fastened to the keel about half-way between the master frames and each post. These two frames/floors would have been much narrower, and have had more rising than other floors and frames; the after one more than the forward one.

7. The bottom was planked with five strakes each side, the planks being spiked to the floors and subsequently treenailed.

8. The lower sides were planked; and then the turn of the bilge.

9. All remaining frames were installed and the upper planking and wales fastened to them.

10. The keelson was bolted to the keel, between the frames, by forelock bolts (similar to those used in Yassi Ada 1).

11. Stringers and removable transverse ceiling were added to the area of the hold; then a fixed ceiling, clamps and deck beams.

#### 4.15.2.3.1 *Designing the frames*

The shape the builder/owner visualized for the Serçe Limani hull was encapsulated in the framing. A key question is, how were the individual frames designed?

Steffy believes that an elementary form of geometric projection and ratios were used, and he believes he has identified a unit of measurement upon which the design was based: in our terms this *unit* was 0.16 m, which Steffy believes may have been equivalent to a handspan, or perhaps some proportion of a Byzantine foot. It may be that a smaller unit of a 'palm' (i.e. *c*.80 mm) is more appropriate.

The transverse section amidships (the master frame) of this box-shaped hull can be represented by two straight lines: the bottom rising only a few degrees from the horizontal, equivalent to a rise of a quarter of Steffy's *unit* at the ends; the sides rising at *c*.72° to the horizontal—this angle may be constructed by drawing a simple right-angled triangle since the tangent of 72° is 3. These two straight lines were then joined by a curve representing the turn of the bilge (Steffy, 1994: fig. 4.12).

The shapes of the other active or control frames may have been derived from that of the master frame as is done today in Tamil Nadu (6.7.4.3) when building the traditional wooden sailing *thoni* merchant ship and the *vattai* fishing boat (Blue *et al.*, 1998), and as was done in the later Middle Ages in the Mediterranean and in Atlantic Europe (4.16, 5.9.4). The shapes of the frames in the forward and after parts of the ship, where the hull's transverse shape was changing rapidly, may have been derived from temporary ribbands or planking acting as ribbands (5.6.1.3)—a reversion, in a sense, to plank-first methods.

Other Mediterranean ships that appear to have been frame-first include: Plane 6 (Parker, 1992: no. 821) and Agay (ibid. 8) of the tenth century; Pelagos (ibid. 796) of the twelfth century; and Culip 6 (ibid. 349) of the fourteenth (Palou *et al.*, 1998; Rieth, 1999).

### 4.15.3 THE CHANGE FROM PLANK-FIRST TO FRAME-FIRST METHODS

From the first century BC to the sixth century AD, there are suggestions that the earlier, dominant importance of the planking to the structural integrity of Mediterranean ships and boats was being reduced. It is not until the seventh century AD, however, that there is clear evidence that the internal structure of framing and longitudinal timbers was significantly improved. During this transitional phase, planking became less important structurally as the mortise and tenon fastenings became smaller, more widely spaced, and finally not locked: their role now was merely one of aligning strakes (instead of fastening them together in a water-tight seam) until they could be fastened to the framing, and the seams caulked. Ironically, the role of the unlocked mortise and tenon joint when it first appeared on the nautical scene—in Egypt in the third millennium BC—was also that of aligning planking before it could be fastened by other means (2.7.1).

By AD 1025, and probably much earlier, edge-fastened planking began to be abandoned entirely. The framing structure was now clearly the most important feature, not only in the realm of structural integrity, but also in the matter of obtaining the shape of hull the builder had visualized. These frames had to be 'designed': precisely how this was done is not clear but the methods may have been similar to those used from the fifteenth century onwards (4.16).

Possibly induced by social and economic changes, this shift to frame-first construction was to have important technological and, indeed, political, effects in the Mediterranean. Frame-first techniques gave builders the ability to build bigger, but more importantly, more seaworthy hulls suitable for long ocean passages, and to build them more quickly. It also meant that, as the art and science of generating hull shapes developed, significant improvements could be built into a design, and a successful design could be repeated again and again.

# 4.16
# The Design of Medieval Frame-First Ships

It is not until the mid-fifteenth century that the methods of designing the framework of Mediterranean vessels and of building them frame-first appears to have been written down (R. Anderson, 1925; Bellabarba, 1988; 1993; Steffy, 1994: 93–100; Johnston, 1994; Greenhill, 1995b: 256–73; Rieth, 1996). The two documents that have received the most critical attention, the *Timbotta* MS. and the *Fabrica di galere*, originated in Venice,

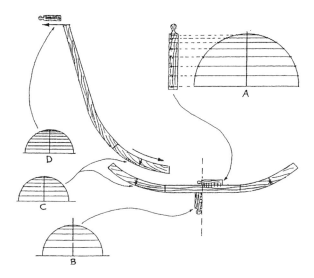

Fig. 4.46. Diagram to illustrate the fifteenth-century Venice method of designing frames A: narrowing the floors; B: rising the floors; C: fairing the junction of futtock and floor; D: widening the futtocks (after Bellabarba, 1993: fig. 4).

and there are indications that design methods similar to those described were used in that region during the thirteenth century, and even earlier (Bellabarba, 1996).

In this Venetian method the main dimensions of the hull were known as proportions of a modular unit, usually the keel length, the length overall (Bellabarba, 1993: 274), or the maximum beam (Steffy, 1994: 93). The dimensions of fittings such as the rudder, the mast, the yards, could also be a proportion of this unit. The shape of the posts was probably obtained by simple geometric construction with measured offsets, or by a batten bent to the required curve through two control points (Steffy, 1994: fig. 4.20A). The shape of the master frame was encapsulated in a 'rule' giving the orthogonal co-ordinates of the required curve at four points (Bellabarba, 1993: fig. 3). A master mould was made from this curve, and a master frame, made from this mould, was set up on the keel near amidships. Geometrically similar frames were set up on either side of this master frame, the number depending upon the length of main hull (of constant transverse section) required. The shapes of the remaining designed frames were obtained from the master mould by simple geometric means—this was the essence of the design system.

A series of horizontal lines was inscribed on a semi-circular wooden tablet known as a *mezza luna* (half moon) using a construction which made the intervals between lines decrease steadily in accordance with a geometric progression (Fig. 4.46). A measuring stick marked with this scale was then used to derive the shapes of pairs of frames (one forward, one aft) from the master mould so that each pair of these frames had the appropriate rising and narrowing to give the shape of the designed part of the hull. These designed frames extended almost to the ends of the keel: beyond this point the hull transverse section changed too rapidly for shapes to be calculated by this Venetian method (Bellabarba, 1993: 282). The bow and stern frames were thus not designed: their shapes were obtained late in the building sequence from ribbands or planking run-ning from post to post—in contrast to the designed frames, these bow and stern frames were passive.

By the sixteenth century similar design methods were used in southern Italy, Spain, Portugal, France, southern Netherlands, England, and possibly else-where (Bellabarba, 1993: 286, 290; Rieth, 1996: 177–99; 1998). The ships of the European explorers of the late fifteenth/early sixteenth centuries were probably designed by these methods (5.9.4) since the earliest known Portuguese text on shipbuilding, *Livro da Fábrica das Naus* by Fernando de Oliveira dated *c.*1570, pre-scribes similar methods to the Venetian (Steffy, 1994: 128–41; Loewen, 1998: 213–14).

# 5
# ATLANTIC EUROPE

This chapter deals with the 'Atlantic arc' of Europe: those seas and coastal lands which lie on a broad sweep from the Strait of Gibraltar through maritime Spain, Portugal and France, the British and Irish archipelago, the Low Countries, coastal Germany, and Scandinavia, including the southern shores of the Baltic (Fig. 5.1). This maritime zone extends in latitude from 36° to c.63°N, in longitude from c.11°W in the Atlantic to c.20°E in the Baltic.

This long coastline, much of it open to the Atlantic Ocean, has a diversity of geology and topography. (Cunliffe, 2001) The Baltic and the North Sea are regions of deposition with relatively shallow seas and low-lying coasts. The Baltic is virtually tideless, but numerous tidal rivers flow into the North Sea: for example, the Elbe, Weser, Ems, Schelde/Meusse/ Rhine, Thames, Humber, and Forth. By and large these rivers flow relatively slowly through low-lying, easily-flooded landscapes, with reeds and marshes at their margins, and widespread sandbanks on their approaches from seaward.

The coasts of Norway, France (from Normandy to the River Loire), Spain, Portugal, and the western and south-western coasts of Ireland and Britain, on the other hand, are formed of more resistant, compact solid rock: the harder rock has weathered to form headlands, promontories, peninsulas, and capes; the softer rock forms bays and inlets. These are generally rugged, rocky coasts with bold cliffs, and deep water relatively close inshore. Along these coasts, from northern Norway as far south as River Minho (at the Spain/Portugal northern border), with the exception of the south-east part of the Bay of Biscay (Golfe de Gascogne) there are numerous off-lying islands. In certain parts of these coastal lands, the coast is broken into a series of deep-water inlets such as fjords and rias, some of which form spacious, natural harbours: Vigo and Corunna in north-west Spain; Morlaix in Brittany; Falmouth and Plymouth in south-west England; Milford Haven in Wales, Killary in western Ireland; Trondheim, Hardangar, and Stavanger in Norway. In other parts there are great tidal rivers such as the Guadalquivir, Tagus, Douro, and Minho in the Iberian peninsula, the Severn and Clyde in Britain, and the Shannon in Ireland.

The Baltic Sea is a tideless, relatively shallow body of brackish water with a mean depth of c.30 fathoms (55 m) The Skagerrak, the channel between Norway and Denmark, and the Kattegatt, between Denmark and Sweden, lead to three entrances to the Baltic: Oresund, in the east between the large Danish island of Sjaelland and south-west Sweden, and the Stora Bält and the Lille Bält which pass through the Danish archipelago. These channels are only c.10 fathoms (c.18 m) deep and form a sill to the Baltic.

The North Sea is also relatively shallow, since it is part of the continental shelf, as is the Baltic. At the seaward limit of this shelf the seabed plunges precipitously thousands of fathoms down to the ocean bed. Since late-medieval times this outer edge has been recognized as approximating to the 100 fathom line (c.180 m). Landward of this line a vessel is said to be 'in soundings' (Waters, 1978: 18). Along the coasts of Norway and of Iberia, and at some points in the west and south-west of Ireland, this 100 fathom line is only 10 to 20 nautical miles from land. Entering soundings when approaching these coasts can thus be a warning of the nearness of land. On the other hand, the 100 fathom line is some hundreds of miles from the coasts of the Irish Sea, the North Sea, the Channel, and the north-

Fig. 5.1. Map of northern Atlantic Europe and the Baltic region.

ern parts of the Bay of Biscay. On a passage from the Mediterranean to the Channel a ship passes out of soundings when only *c*.20 nautical miles off north-west Spain and enters them again when *c*.100 nautical miles south of Ushant. Other methods then have to be used to identify the entrance to the Channel so that the ship would be well clear of both Ushant and Scilly. Similarly, for vessels bound for Ireland or the Irish Sea, the channel between Scilly and Cape Clear, off west Cork, has to be identified.

## 5.1

# The Early Environment

Much work has been done to elucidate past changes in the climate of Atlantic Europe, and changes in sea level (Lamb, 1977; Devoy, 1982; Tooley, 1990; Robinson, 1990; van Andel, 1989, 1990; Flemming, 1996), nevertheless these changes can, even now, only be described in very broad terms. This is especially true of changes in the maritime environment: only in rare places such as the Netherlands are regional palaeo-geographic maps available showing details of former coastlines and rivers at particular periods. Elsewhere, although certain sites have been studied intensively, there are insufficient high resolution temporal and spatial data on which regional maps can be based.

If we are to understand the problems ancient mariners faced, we need to have detailed data on sea levels, coastlines, rivers, estuaries, tides, and weather patterns (especially predominant winds) at the specific time and place being investigated. Of these environmental characteristics, changes in sea level have most importance since mean sea level determines the general form of the coastline and river gradients, and hence rates of erosion and deposition, the presence and extent of shoals, sands, reefs, tidal races, spits and bars, and it indirectly influences local tidal effects. Such precise data is not yet available. Furthermore, changes of sea level have not been uniform throughout Atlantic Europe: during the past 13,000 years there has been a general rise in sea level but at a diminishing rate, with occasional regressions, whereas in Scandinavia, north of an axis running north-east/south-west through Denmark, there has been a significant rise in relative land levels, i.e. an apparent fall in sea level.

Bearing in mind these limitations, the general changes in these environmental data may be summarized:

*Eighteenth–seventeenth millennium* BC (*c.*18,000–16,000 BC). The maximum extent of the last glaciation with ice covering Scandinavia and the Baltic (except for eastern Denmark), the northern North Sea, and much of Britain and Ireland. Sea level was at its lowest, at least 60 fathoms (*c.*110 m) lower than today, with the result that the Atlantic coast of Europe extended from the south-east corner of the Bay of Biscay to western Ireland, thence north of the Shetland Islands to the Norwegian coast at *c.*63°N (Cunliffe, 1994: 43).

*Eleventh–ninth millennium* BC (*c.*11,000–8000 BC). Rapid rise in sea level, and a general increasing air temperature. From *c.*9,000 BC the rate of sea level rise decreased. By this time the Baltic (including Denmark and the extreme south of Sweden and Norway), the North Sea, and Britain and Ireland were clear of ice. The northern North Sea was flooded as was the eastern Baltic, however, Sweden remained connected to Denmark (Cunliffe, 1994: 84).

*Eighth–sixth millennium* BC (*c.*8000–5000 BC). Sea levels continued to rise, albeit more slowly, and islands became isolated. Ireland appears to have become separated from Britain by the North Channel by *c.*8000 BC, and Britain from the Continent by *c.*6000 BC (Cunliffe, 1994: 45). By 8000 BC mean sea level would generally have been *c.*16 fathoms (30 m), and by 5000 BC some 9 fathoms (17 m) below the level of today (McGrail, 1998: 258–9). In 8000 BC oak (*Quercus* sp.) was growing south-west of a line from Brittany to the Bosporus; by 5000 BC it had become established throughout Ireland and Britain and in the Continent as far north as southern Sweden, Denmark, and the western Baltic. Lime (*Tilia* sp.) (which was subsequently used for boatbuilding in parts of northern Europe) was established there from *c.*6000 BC (Cunliffe, 1994: 84–5). From *c.*6000 BC a 'climatic optimum' was established for the next 2,500 years or so, with mild winters, and westerly winds.

*Fifth–second millennium* BC (*c.*5000–1000 BC). The sea level continued to rise slowly and by *c.*3000 BC, relative to the land, the mean sea level, except for Scandinavia, was within today's tidal range; by 1000 BC it was only one fathom or so below today's mean sea level. From *c.*3500 BC there was a generally warm settled climate but with some serious interruptions and fluctuations of temperature and humidity.

*First millennium* BC *and first millennium* AD (*c.*1000 BC–AD 1000). During the first millennium BC there was a decisive shift to a colder, wetter climate so that from the mid-first millennium BC the weather would generally have been comparable with today. The winds were generally north-west/north in summer and west in winter. In the first millennium AD the weather was generally similar with fluctuations: a warmer, drier period in the second–fourth centuries AD; a reversion to colder, wetter weather during the fifth–eighth centuries; from the ninth century the weather generally improved again. By AD 1000 the mean sea level was generally within 0.5 m of today.

From the seaman's viewpoint (and disregarding Scandinavia), this generalized environmental synopsis may be summarized:

Before *c.*10,000 BC, the Atlantic coastline of Europe would have been significantly different from today. It is not possible to speculate about such factors as the tides.

Between c.10,000 and c.3000 BC, the coastline would have been different from today, but increasingly converging towards it in appearance.

From c.3000 BC onwards, mean sea level has been within today's tidal range, i.e. high water mark would have been above today's low water mark, and converging slowly onto today's high water mark. The general features of the coastline would have increasingly resembled those of today and the tidal regime (tidal cycle and tidal streams) would probably have been generally as it is today. However, there would have been significant local differences since there would have been much less accumulation of silt in estuaries and, if spits and bars had been created across estuary mouths by this time, they would not have been so prominent as they are today. On the other hand, coastal erosion would have been less.

The characteristics of past climates is more difficult to assess. In the circumstances it seems best to assume, as in the Mediterranean (4.2.3), that from c.1000 BC the weather, including the predominant wind, has been not unlike today's, with many minor, and some major, fluctuations which at present cannot be quantified. Assessments of weather before 1000 BC must be speculative.

## 5.1.1 THE SEAFARING ENVIRONMENT

In the absence of specific information about earlier times, it seems permissible, therefore, to use twentieth-century data on currents, tides, and winds as a basis for any discussion of the environmental and seafaring problems faced by early seamen.

## 5.1.1.1 CURRENTS

Currents off the Atlantic coast originate in the Gulf Stream which leaves the Gulf of Mexico between Florida and Cuba, and flows strongly northwards along the American coast. South of Nova Scotia it is deflected eastwards by the south-flowing Labrador Current, widens and slows down to become the North Atlantic current flowing in an east to north-east direction towards the Bay of Biscay and the British and Irish archipelago. The southern part of this current is deflected

to form the south-flowing Portugal and Canaries Currents. The northern part of the North Atlantic Current splits into three elements: one into the eastern North Sea through the Channel; and weaker ones flowing northwards to the west and to the east of Ireland, then north of Shetland to the Norwegian coast. In the approaches to the south of Ireland and to the south-west of Britain, these currents average ½ knot and reach a maximum of 1½ knots in strong westerly winds.

The current pattern is thus: south-flowing currents of up to ½ knot in the Bay of Biscay and of up to 1 knot off the Iberian coast; eastward-flowing currents into the Mediterranean; northward-flowing currents on Ireland's west and east coasts; north-east currents along the Norwegian coast; weakish anti-clockwise circulation in the North Sea; and parallel weak flows into the Baltic along the Danish coast, and out of the Baltic along the Swedish and Norwegian coasts. Within the Baltic currents are weak and variable, but can become strong during gales when funnelled—for example, up to 8 knots between Öland island and Sweden.

## 5.1.1.2 TIDES AND TIDAL FLOWS

These surface currents are generally slight—for example, in the Channel the north-east-flowing current averages only 6 nautical miles a day. Superimposed on them and of more importance to the ancient mariner are the regular ebbs and flows of the tidal stream generated by astronomical forces, modified by weather and by local topography. Off the Atlantic coast tides are semi-diurnal: that is, there are two periods of low water and two of high water each day. During each cycle the tidal stream (a horizontal movement of the water) flows with increasing and then diminishing strength in one direction for about six and a-quarter hours, and then similarly in the opposite direction for six and a-quarter hours. The tidal wave runs northwards along the west coast of Iberia and then into the Bay of Biscay, where it traces out an ellipse on a south-east/north-west alignment. From the western approaches to the archipelago this flood stream divides into three: east-north-east into the Channel and around to the Thames; north-east into the Irish Sea towards the Isle of Man; along the west coast of Ireland through the North Channel towards the Isle of Man, and around the north of Scotland across to Norway and southwards into the North Sea towards the Rhine and the Thames. Ancient seamen had to memorize these timings (in terms of the moon's phases) for their own part of the coast and for any other regions they might visit. They also had to learn where contraflows were established inshore.

The northern part of the Bay of Biscay and the Channel are to leeward of the predominant wind, in the path of Atlantic depressions, and downstream of the North Atlantic Current. The Bay and Channel have to absorb much of this energy: in particular, the wedge-shaped Channel restricts, funnels and intensifies these natural elements, and strong tidal streams of complex patterns are generated. Rates of flow vary, not only within each tidal cycle but also according to the phases of the moon 'the chief arbiter of tides'. They also vary inshore and in narrow channels: for example, at spring tides with a general rate in mid-Channel of approximately two and a-half knots, the stream at Dover can be 4 knots, and in the channel between Alderney and France up to 10 knots may be experienced. Strong tidal flows are also found within archipelagos such as Orkney; around promontories and headlands such as Cape Finisterra in Spain, Cape Finistère in France, and Land's End in Britain; and off the estuaries of north-westwards-flowing rivers between the Rhine and Elbe. This variable pattern had also to be memorized by the mariner.

The corresponding vertical movement of the tidal sea is most apparent along the coast, as the level moves from high water to low water about every six and a-quarter hours. As with tidal flows, these heights vary with the lunar cycle and also with the weather, in particular the wind. The times of high and low water are seldom, if ever, the same as those of the associated slack water (the period of about 40 minutes when there are no tidal flows), thus increasing the complexity of the data mariners had to memorize.

Tidal ranges, the vertical height between high and low water, vary with the lunar cycle. They also vary according to local topography, being greatest at the heads of bays, gulfs, and estuaries. Whereas the range of spring tides on an Atlantic coast is generally 1–2 fathoms (2–4 m) the range in the Bristol Channel and in the Baie du Mt. St-Michel, can reach 7–7.5 fathoms (13–14 m).

As in the Mediterranean, in the Baltic there is little, if any, astronomically generated tide and therefore negligible tidal flows, but when winds prevail from one quarter for several days, and where there is a reasonable fetch, sea levels can alter by up to 3 feet (c.1 m).

### 5.1.1.3 WINDS

Today the predominant winds and the resultant swell off Atlantic Europe between Iberia and Denmark are from the sector between south-west and north-west throughout the year, although with travelling depressions moving north-east from the Atlantic, winds from the south through west to north can be experienced. In February to May north-east and east winds are common in the North Sea region, and in the autumn there is a significant proportion of days with easterly winds in the north of the Bay of Biscay. In general, similar conditions were probably experienced back to 1000 BC, and possibly earlier. As in the Mediterranean, local features such as headlands modify the general wind pattern inshore, and in settled summer conditions there can be land and sea breezes although not on the scale of the Mediterranean.

From the north-west corner of Iberia southwards, the predominant winds are from the northerly sector, and there is more settled summer weather than further north. Off the Norwegian coast the winds are generally northerly in summer, backing north-west in the south. In the Skagerrak west and south-west winds predominate in the summer; in the Kattegat and the Danish archipelago there are variable winds with a preponderance of westerlies; within the Baltic, from the sector north-east to south–west.

# 5.2

# Early Seafaring

## 5.2.1 THE SETTLEMENT OF ISLANDS

There is clear archaeological evidence that, as in the Mediterranean (and indeed, around the world), islands off Atlantic Europe were settled at an early date. Ireland was first settled before 7000 BC; Britain was resettled after the Strait of Dover was created by rising sea levels in c.6000 BC. The Hebridean and Danish archipelagos were settled during the Mesolithic period (Cunliffe, 1994; 80); and the Orkney group of islands off the north of Scotland and Öland and Gotland, east of Sweden, in the Neolithic (Dennell, 1983: 125). These islands were all visible from the mainland of Europe or from another island already settled. Moreover, the distances involved were such that even the longest legs could have been accomplished in a paddled craft, in daylight, in settled summer weather. Thus visual pilotage skills rather than navigation out of sight of land would have been needed. Nevertheless, these early explorers may well have had rudimentary navigational skills and been aware of the direction they were heading relative to the celestial North Pole, the wind, or the swell.

### 5.2.2 COASTAL VOYAGES

Voyages along the Continental coast (not necessarily lasting more than daylight hours) would have been in the lee (i.e. to the east) of the chain of islands that lay along the coast of Norway, the west coast of Denmark, Germany, and the Netherlands as far south as the Rhine estuary. There was a similar inshore route in the Bay of Biscay to the leeward of islands on the route between Quimper in Brittany and the Gironde estuary.

The evidence for oar and for sail is late in Atlantic Europe (5.6.5, 5.6.6)—not until the mid-first millennium BC—and these Mesolithic and Neolithic seamen would have used paddles. Their speed and range of action was thus limited and it is unlikely that long voyages were undertaken: raw materials and 'traded' items such as stone axes (Cummins, 1979; 1980; Mandal and Cooney, 1996), and Neolithic pottery (Peacock, 1969; Mercer, 1986) which have been excavated far from their place of origin, probably arrived there at the end of a series of short sea passages. Maximum use would have been made of the tides and tidal flows which are a prominent feature in Atlantic Europe. Coastal voyages along the Channel between France and England, for example, would have been timed to coincide with favourable tidal flows, vessels being anchored or beached during the period of foul tides. Tidal propulsion, unheard of in the Mediterranean, would have also been used in the Atlantic estuaries: a 'free ride' upstream as far as the flood tide extended, and a 'free ride' down on an ebb tide. Timing was all important. Early boatmen must also have had a detailed knowledge of sands and grounds in these estuaries and of the swashways, relatively deep-water channels through otherwise shoal waters.

Late fifteenth-century sailing directions for the 'Circumnavigation of England' and for a voyage to the Strait of Gibraltar' (Gairdner, 1889) contain numerous references to tidal streams and their timing in relation to the moon's phases, the tidal cycle and depths of water to be expected, the sands and other shoal waters to be avoided, prominent headlands and other coastal features to be noted, and the directions that such landmarks lay from one another, in terms of intermediate points—east-north-east, south-south-west, etc. It is likely that Neolithic seafarers had a similar range of knowledge (transmitted orally) for the coast and estuaries they frequented.

### 5.2.3 SEASONAL SEAFARING

It is likely that, as in the Mediterranean, there was a summer seafaring season in early Atlantic Europe. Today gales of force 7 (Beaufort scale) and above are eight times more frequent in winter than in summer; rough seas may be expected every fourth day in winter compared with every twelfth in summer; sea and air temperatures are significantly lower in winter; rain falls more often and lasts longer in winter; and cloud cover is greater in winter and the whole area may be overcast for several successive days. There were thus good reasons why winter coastal voyages would only have been undertaken in exceptional circumstances, and estuary voyages would have been restricted. As in the Mediterranean, late spring and early autumn with their differing weather patterns would have presented new opportunities to early seamen along coasts, across channels, and in estuaries. The resultant season for maximum use of the seas would have been May to September, with some voyaging in April and October (McGrail, 1998: 259–60).

# 5.3

# Water Transport before the Bronze Age

Water transport was probably used on the inland waters of Atlantic Europe during the Palaeolithic period: these could have been various types of float, simple log rafts, and simple hide boats (Table 1.2). From the seventh millennium BC there is evidence for voyages across channels, such as the North Channel between Scotland and Ireland, and to offshore islands and within archipelagos. Theoretical studies suggest that, by this time, multiple hide boats could have been used at sea, with complex log rafts, bundle rafts and simple logboats inland. By 3000 BC the Shetland islands, some 40 nautical miles north-north-east of Orkney, had been settled. By these Neolithic times (from c.4000 BC) complex logboats may also have been used at sea and, possibly, simple plank boats inland. These theoretical conclusions are not yet supported by excavated remains: no prehistoric hide boats, log rafts, or bundle rafts have been excavated; and the earliest known plank boats are Bronze Age. On the other hand, simple logboats have been excavated from the Mesolithic onwards.

It is convenient to deal here with all aspects of these rafts and non-plank boats, rather than restricting discussion to the Neolithic and earlier.

## 5.3.1 LOGBOATS

Logboats have been found and excavated from all the countries in the Atlantic region from Scandinavia to Iberia (McGrail, 1978; Booth, 1984; S. Andersen, 1987, 1994; Hirte, 1987; Switsur, 1989; C. Christensen, 1990; Arnold, 1995–6: 1999c; Lanting and Brindley, 1996; Mowat, 1996; Ossowski, 1999; Fry, 2000) Simple logboats are made by hollowing out a single log, and shaping the ends and the outside. They are thus generally similar in form to coffins, troughs, mill-chutes, slipes, and the like, and, where remains are fragmentary, identification can prove difficult (McGrail, 1978: 2; Mowat, 1996: 137–48). By adding fittings and using more advanced woodworking techniques, complex logboats can be built.

### 5.3.1.1 SEA OR RIVER?

The diameter of the parent log inherently limits a logboat's waterline beam measurement, and its depth of hull: transverse stability and freeboard are therefore also limited. Logboats built from exceptionally large trees on the western coasts of North America (11.4.6.1) had sufficient inherent stability and freeboard to be seagoing: those built from European trees, however, were only suitable for seagoing in unusually calm weather, unless they were modified in some way. Ethnographic examples of such modifications are known from many parts of the world. The effective beam of the boat (and hence stability) can be increased by: expansion, forcing the sides apart after heat treatment; fastening stabilizing timbers each side along the waterline or booming out wooden floats on outriggers on one or both sides; or by pairing two logboats, side by side (McGrail, 1998: 66–73). Furthermore, freeboard can be increased by adding washstrakes to the sides (McGrail, 1978: 41).

Several logboats, from the late-Neolithic onwards, have a series of horizontal holes through their sides near the top edge—the earliest ones are Øgårde 3 of c.3190 BC and Verup 1 (Fig. 5.2), of c.2770 BC, from Amose, Denmark (Troels-Smith, 1946: 17, fig. 2; C. Christensen, 1990: figs. 8, 11 and 12). One interpretation is that the holes are where the sides of the boat were lashed together, during building, until a transom board or beam-tie could be fitted to the stern. An alternative explanation is that they are where washstrakes were once fastened to the sides: if running sewing was used at this early date the strakes could have overlapped the sides; otherwise they would have been flush-laid. It may be then that some logboats had washstrakes fitted from an early date, however, there is no evidence, to date, that any prehistoric logboat was modified to enhance its stability by expansion (McGrail, 1998: 66–70; Arnold, 1996: 157–8), or by fitting stabilizers (McGrail, 1996b: 28–31), and the evidence for pairing logboats is very slim (McGrail, 1978: 48–51).

Logboats were very important economically and socially, and possibly in warfare, on the inland waters and sheltered archipelagos of Atlantic Europe, but it is

Fig. 5.2. Forward part of the Neolithic log boat Verup I, St. Åmose (Danish National Museum).

unlikely that they were used at sea or in the outer reaches of estuaries.

### 5.3.1.2 DATE RANGE

The oldest logboats so far dated are those from Pesse in the Netherlands (Fig. 5.3), of c.7920–6470 BC (Gro-486), and Noyen-sur-Seine, France of c.7190–6540 BC (Gif-6559). Dates earlier than these are hardly to be expected since before this time, neither sizeable trees nor the appropriate tools were available. Generally speaking, the early logboats seem to be within an arc from Denmark, through north-west Germany and the Low Countries to north-west France (Arnold, 1995: 16–19; Lanting and Brindley, 1996). They feature in Ireland from c.4000 BC (ibid.) and in Britain from the fourth millennium BC (Delgado, 1997: 438). Logboats do not appear to have been used in Sweden until 500 BC, Norway, AD 700, and Finland, AD 1200 (ibid.: fig. 3). They continued to be used into the eighteenth century AD, and beyond, in parts of the Atlantic region.

Fig. 5.3. Mesolithic log boat from Pesse, Netherlands (photo: Paul Johnstone).

## 5.3.1.3 MESOLITHIC AND NEOLITHIC

The two oldest logboats were of pine (*Pinus sylvestris*); later in the Mesolithic, alder (*Alnus* sp.), poplar (*Populus* sp.), and lime (*Tilia* sp.) were used. Oak (*Quercus* sp.) was used sporadically from the middle Neolithic, and by the Bronze Age it was clearly the preferred species. Logboats from the pre-oak period were relatively light-weight, making them readily portable across land. They were probably used in the Mesolithic for fishing, fowling, possiby sealing, and as ferries on lakes and rivers and within sheltered archipelagos. During the Neolithic the transport of agricultural produce and of flint may have been added to their roles.

The two pine logboats have rounded transverse sections, similar to their parent logs. Pesse has thick integral ends and measured *c*.2.98 × 0.44 × 0.31 m. Noyen-sur-Seine probably also had integral ends: this boat measured 4.05 × 0.55 × 0.20 m. The Danish early boats also had rounded sections and were even longer in relation to their breadth, L/B being of the order of 10–15 : 1 (C. Christensen, 1990; S. Andersen, 1994). These boats had thin sides and bottoms: 50–80 mm generally, but some were only 20–30 mm. They were up to 10 m in length, and had a shaped bow and a rectangular stern in plan. Two or three of these boats had integral sterns, but the majority were open: these were made watertight by the insertion of a transom in one of several ways (C. Christensen, 1990: fig. 15): within a groove in a thicker part of the bottom; fastened by tenons protruding from the lower edge of the transom into mortises cut in the boat's bottom and wedged; and by vertical treenails partly driven into the bottom forward and aft of the transom and wedged. In one case there was no transom, merely a mound of clay held in position by a bark sheet caulked with moss.

Towards bow and/or stern of several of these Danish boats there was a 'fireplace' of clay on a bed of fine sand: these are thought to have been associated with the night spearing of eels by the light of a flare (S. Andersen, 1994). Large stones found in some boats have been interpreted as 'ballast'; a more likely use would have been to hold the boats underwater when not in use so that the timber did not dry out and impair the hull's integrity, especially those with inserted transoms. Several of the boats had had splits repaired by sewing. Dovetailed grooves were also found on some of these boats (Arnold, 1996: 158).

## 5.3.1.4 THE BRONZE AGE

During the Bronze Age, large oak logboats were built, over 10 m in length, and of commensurate breadth, depth, and thickness: they were also of some complexity in structure. These boats may have been built in response to an increase in trading activity (Arnold, 1996) since they could carry many times the weight and volume of earlier boats. On the other hand, these large boats were not readily manœuvrable and only with certain types of load could their great capacity be used effectively (McGrail, 1988a). One of the most effective loads in this sense was a full complement of paddlers. It may be, then, that there were at least elements of display and prestige in these large boats, built from specially selected, and probably rare, oaks: that the paddlers may also have been armed leads to the speculation that these were also boats of war.

The Brigg logboat of *c*.1000 BC (Fig. 5.4) may be taken as typical of the Late Bronze Age. This boat was excavated, near-complete, but damaged, in 1886 from a site close to the River Ancholme, a tributary of the River Humber. It was destroyed by fire during an air raid on Hull in 1942 (McGrail, 1978: no. 22). This boat had been hewn from an oak with a bole at least 15 m long and a girth of *c*.6 m (diameter 1.9 m) near its butt end. The upper end of the log became the bow and large knot holes on either side were fitted with 0.30 m diameter protruding wooden plugs as the 'eyes' of the boat.

The lower or butt end of the Brigg parent log had heart rot or was damaged during manufacture. This end, the stern, had to be fitted with a two-piece transom which was caulked with moss and wedged within a groove worked around the inside of the stern. Above and aft of the transom some form of strengthening timber or beam tie (or possibly a lashing) was fastened across this open end of the boat to force the sides tight against the transom.

Transverse ridges were left in the solid wood across the boat's bottom, spaced 1.4 and 1.85 m apart. These may have marked stations for paddlers, two at each ridge port and starboard, with cargo further aft. Such ridges have been found in many logboats (McGrail, 1996b: 27) and there may be more than one explanation for their function: skeuomorphs from plank boats; marking functional divisions of the boat; foothold for paddlers; or supports for bottom boards. Arnold (1996:

Fig. 5.4.  The Brigg log boat after excavation in 1886 (E. V. Wright).

157–8) has suggested that these ridges were *nervures*, left in the solid as 'thickness ridges' by means of which the thickness of the bottom could be gauged. The precise means of such control of thickness is not clear: moreover, the Brigg logboat and several other logboats of the Late Bronze Age and the Iron Age with ridges also had thickness gauges, holes bored before hollowing along the centreline to a depth equivalent to the required bottom thickness: after hollowing the log down to these holes, they were plugged with treenails. Furthermore, ridges were seldom left at regular intervals along the length of the boat which would seem to have been a requirement if the bottom thickness was to be controlled. Ridges were still being used in medieval logboats and in logboat-based boats of recent times (McGrail, 1978: 55–6). Clearly, the last word on these ridges has not been said.

At the stern of the Brigg logboat there was probably a platform or deck for two steersmen. There was a smaller platform at the bow for a lookout or possibly a bow steersman. A 3.66 m split low down on the star-board side had been repaired using several oak patches caulked with moss; some of these were sewn to the logboat with a fine rope of natural fibres. Another patch, over 1.5 m in length, had three integral cleats which projected inboard through the split and were locked on the inside by wedge-shaped keys or cotters through the holes in the cleats (Fig. 5.5): this arrangement is similar to the cleat and transverse timber method of linking together the planking of Bronze Age sewn-plank boats such as those from Ferriby, Brigg, Caldicot, and Dover (5.4), and the lower bow of the Iron Age Hasholme logboat to the main hull—see also the method of fastening washstrakes to the hull of this boat (5.3.1.5). The action of these transverse timbers may also be compared with that of the iron 'fore-lock bolts' used to fasten wales to the hull of Yassi Ada 1 in the seventh century AD Mediterranean (4.15.2.2), and the keelson to the keel of the eleventh-century Serçe Limani wreck (4.15.2.3).

Originally the Brigg logboat measured *c*.14.78 × 1.37 × 1 m, the broadest and deepest dimensions being at

Fig. 5.5. A patch with cleats from the Brigg log boat (photo: E. V. Wright).

the stern: the boat thus retained the tapered shape of her parent tree. It is estimated that this boat had a full complement of two steersmen and twenty-six paddlers at a draft o 0.35 m. Alternatively, with a five-man crew the boat could have carried 5.5 tonnes of cargo at a draft of 0.60 m.

This boat was probably used in the tidal creeks and rivers of the Humber estuary to carry people and goods. She was steered and propelled by paddles or poles. Poles have not been excavated or, if they have, they have not been recognized. Paddle-shaped objects may be used in the dairy, the bakery, and the brewery,

and thus excavated boat paddles may have been misidentified. Such objects have been found in Britain and Germany from c.7500 BC onwards, Denmark from 5500 BC, and Sweden and Finland from 2200 BC (Lanting and Brindley, 1996; Mowat, 1996: 136–7). Paddles associated with some of the early Danish logboats had elliptical or heart-shaped blades some of which were decorated (Fig. 5.6A). Paddles were of ash or hazel and rarely oak, and most were for seated or kneeling paddlers although a few could only have been used when standing (C. Christensen, 1990: 133, figs. 18, 19).

### 5.3.1.5 THE IRON AGE

From the Late Bronze Age, mid-second millennium BC, plank boats became more in evidence, but logboats continued to be used on lakes, rivers, and inner estuaries for fishing, fowling, reed gathering, and ferrying of goods and people. Large logboats became a rarity after the Bronze Age. Whether this significant decrease in the size of the average logboat was due to supply conditions (fewer large oaks available) or to demand (plank boats were considered to be better in these roles) is not clear: probably a combination of the two.

The Hasholme logboat, a c.13 m boat of c.300 BC, demonstrates the range of woodworking and boat-building techniques used in a region which was probably not at the forefront of technological innovation in Iron Age Atlantic Europe (Millett and McGrail, 1987; McGrail, 1988a). This boat was excavated in 1984 from land below sea level where there had formerly been a tidal creek of the Humber estuary (Fig. 5.7). The parent oak was 600–800 years old when felled: the bole was at

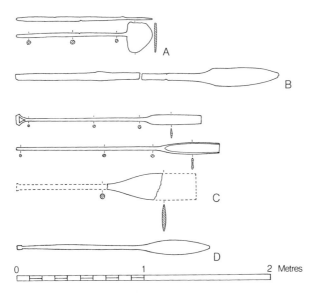

Fig. 5.6. Prehistoric and medieval paddles. A: Tybrind Vig, fourth millennium BC. B: Canewdon, c.1000 BC. C: Hjortspring, fourth century BC. D: Arby, AD 900 (Institute of Archaeology, Oxford).

moss inside a groove near the stern (Fig. 5.8), generally similar to the Brigg logboat (5.3.1.4). Two beam ties held the boat's sides together and also forced the transom further into its groove; a third tie was treenailed to the top edge of the sides *c*.1 m forward of the transom. The forward end of the boat was fitted with two oak 'block-stem' or bow timbers. The after edge of the lower bow sat on rabbets cut along the edges of the foremost part of the main hull, and was locked in position by two large treenails driven horizontally through the boat's sides and through holes in cleats projecting from the lower bow timbers' upper face. The upper bow timber enveloped the leading edge of the lower bow, the forward ends of two washstrakes (fastened to the foremost 4 m of the main hull to give a level sheerline), and the upper forward parts of the main hull. The upper and lower bow were then locked together by three large treenails driven vertically through holes in both timbers.

The washstrakes, also of oak, were fastened into a rabbet worked along the outer upper edge of the main hull (a 'shiplap' joint—see Greenhill, 1995a: fig. 36 (5)) by treenails driven from outboard and locked inboard by wooden keys or cotters—a dovetail-shaped repair block was similarly fastened to the hull at the stern (Fig. 5.9). On the starboard bow of the main hull a semicircular area, some 0.75 m in diameter had been carved *c*.10 mm deep into the timber. This is thought to have been an 'oculus' one of the 'eyes' of the boat. The port bow of the boat was badly damaged before excavation but there was probably an oculus there also. There is much ethnographic evidence for oculi, mainly in the Mediterranean region (Hornell, 1938b; 1946a: 285–9). The *c*.550 BC (OxA-1718) wooden model from Roos Carr (Sheppard, 1901, 1902; B. Coles, 1990: 315–19), which probably represents a logboat with warrior crew, has at the bow a carved animal head which has sockets for quartz eyes. Other logboats which appear to have oculi include those from Brigg and from Loch Arthur in Scotland of 150 BC–AD 200 (McGrail, 1978: figs. 84, 112; Mowat, 1996: 50–2).

A series of large holes through the sides of the Hasholme boat (Fig. 5.10) just below the sheerline are probably where temporary lashings were fastened to hold the sides of the end-less hull together during hollowing. An alternative interpretation that these were fastening points for additional washstrakes is unlikely since calculations show that this boat had ample free-

Fig. 5.7. Hasholme logboat during excavation in 1984—stern nearest camera (photo: Martin Millett).

least 14 m in length with a lower girth of 5.4 m (diameter 1.72 m) and an upper girth of 4.15 m (diameter 1.32 m). Either the log was damaged at both ends during manufacture or, more likely, there was heart rot throughout its length: thus *both* ends of the boat had to be closed to make her watertight.

A transom board was wedged and caulked with

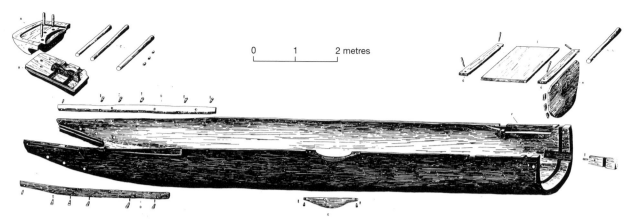

Fig. 5.8. Hasholme logboat reconstructed (Institute of Archaeology, Oxford).

board when fully loaded. A third possibility—that sta-bilizers were once fastened here—can be ruled out as the holes are well above the loaded waterline.

This boat was originally c.12.78 × 1.40 × 1.25 m and retained the tapered shape, in plan and elevation, of her parent oak. She probably had a similar role to that of the Brigg logboat. She could carry a maximum of two steersmen and eighteen paddlers at a draft of 0.46 m. With a five-man crew she could carry 5.5 tonnes of cargo at a draft of 0.75 m.

A boat of this size and shape would not have been the most convenient to use in Humber creeks, and it may be that the choice of such a large oak was not

made solely on economic grounds, but also as a sym-bol of status. The oculi in the bows, and the anthropo-morphic look of the boat when seen from astern (with a superficial resemblance to two eyes and a nose) may be further evidence of the special status of this boat.

### 5.3.1.6 COMPLEX LOGBOATS

With an increasing range of tools and techniques, the addition of fittings to logboats became increasingly more common: for example, thwarts supported by knees. Beam ties were treenailed across the ends of boats to oppose the tendency of oaks to split longitudi-nally. Low ridges were succeeded by dwarf bulkheads dividing the boat into functional compartments. The use of fitted transom sterns decreased, probably because smaller, younger oaks, without heart rot were being selected. Two logboats of the early centuries AD, Zwammerdam 3 and Pommeroeul 2 had their bows replaced by planking, presumably after being damaged (Arnold, 1995: 117–19). These two boats had L-shaped ribs treenailed inside the hull. In Zwammerdam 3 this seems to have been done so that washstrakes could be fastened to them. The reason for fitting ribs to Pom-meroeul 2 is unclear—it may be that this was an unnec-essary copying of plank boat fittings, or possibly to

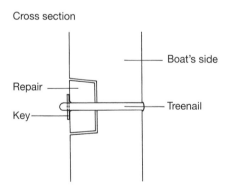

Fig. 5.9. Repair to the Hasholme logboat (Institute of Archae-ology, Oxford).

Fig. 5.10. A 1 : 10 reconstruction model of the Hasholme logboat (Institute of Archaeology, Oxford).

support thwarts. In some of the post-medieval Irish logboats, ribs were fastened in position so that oars could be manned by seated crew, but this use seems unlikely in earlier times.

### 5.3.1.6.1 *Expanded*

Many of the first–third centuries AD boat-grave burials at Slusegard, on the island of Bornholm in the Baltic, were in small oak logboats, and Crumlin-Pedersen (1991*a*) has argued that these boats had been expanded; that is, their sides had been forced apart, and ribs inserted to hold this expanded shape. An increased waterline beam would give them greater stability. Some of the criteria Crumlin-Pedersen used to decide whether or not a logboat had been expanded are qualitative and thus difficult to evaluate objectively. Furthermore it has not yet been demonstrated that oak logboats, unlike those of more malleable species such as aspen (*Populus tremulens*), can be successfully expanded. The research on this matter reported by Gifford (1993) is inconclusive since only short lengths of oak were used, whereas the critical part of logboat expansion is to prevent the ends of a hollowed log from splitting.

Crumlin-Pedersen (1991*a*: 261) has also suggested that medieval logboats from other European countries were expanded. The British logboats he names are so identified because they had fitted ribs. However, none of these three boats (Stanley Ferry, Smallburgh, and Walton) had the thin sides and bottom needed for expansion: they are, in fact, up to 60 mm thick. Furthermore, Stanley Ferry has flared sides which meet the bottom in a hard chine, and such an angular section is probably incompatible with expansion. The support of thwarts or washstrakes, or use as footrests, are more likely reasons for fitting ribs in these boats (McGrail, 1981*c*). Logboats of the right timber species can certainly be expanded after heat treatment (Arnold, 1995: 150–150–5): however, there is no incontrovertible example, to date, of an expanded logboat in Atlantic Europe before the medieval period.

### 5.3.1.6.2 *Washstrakes*

There are a number of early boats with a series of holes through the sides near the top edge which are assumed to have had washstrakes (5.3.1.1). However, no washstrake has (so far) been excavated in association with a prehistoric logboat, apart from the short length at the forward end of the Hasholme boat. From the early centuries AD on, however, there are a number of plank boats built on a logboat base: Zwammerdam 3 of second–third centuries AD (one pair of strakes): Bjorke of *c*.320 AD (one pair); Utrecht 1 of *c*.885 AD (three pairs); and Kentmere 1 (four pairs) of *c*.1315 AD (Arnold, 1995: 118–19, 154, 156, 159). Although having the appearance of planked boats, analytically, they are extended logboats.

### 5.3.1.6.3 *Stabilizing timbers*

The use of stabilizing timbers fastened at the waterline is also difficult to demonstrate on any prehistoric boat. The medieval Kentmere 1 boat has them, however, and they are known from the recent past (Arnold, 1995: 168–9).

### 5.3.1.6.4 *Paired logboats*

Paired logboats are also difficult to identify in prehistoric Europe (McGrail, 1978: 48–51), although Cifton 1 and 2 (*c*.300 BC) from the River Trent near Nottingham, may have been such a pair: they are very similar to one another, and were recovered from the same site. Paired boats were used by the Celtic Helvetii to cross the River Saône in the first century BC (Caesar, *BG* 1. 12), and they are known from recent times (Arnold, 1995: 108; 170–1; McGrail, 1978: 44–51).

### 5.3.1.6.5 *Regional characteristics*

Arnold (1995: 144–5) has drawn attention to the possibility of identifying distinctive styles of logboat building within particular regions during the medieval and later periods. Two groups of British logboats may satisfy such criteria:

- A group of four logboats recovered from the River Lea, a tributary of the River Thames: Walthamstow of *c*. AD 750, Clapton of *c*. AD 950, Sewardstone of *c*. AD 960, and Waltham Cross, probably of a similar date (Arnold, 1995: 124, 125, 137; McGrail, 1989*c*). These are all small oak boats, less than 5 m in length and 0.75 m in breadth, with a rounded transverse section and a central bulkhead in the solid.
- A group of nine twelfth/thirteenth-century boats from the River Mersey: Warrington 1, 2, 3, 4, 5, 7, 11, Barton, and Irlam (Arnold, 1995: 144–5; McGrail and Switsur, 1979). These are all short logboats less than 4.17 m

in length, each made from half an oak log. They had a rounded transverse section, and rounded ends with a beaked protrusion from the bow. Most of them had ridges left proud of the bottom near both ends. Naturally curved timbers were treenailed to the ends to minimize risk of splitting the boat.

Such studies can only be taken further when many more logboats have been scientifically dated, preferably by dendrochronology. In this way not only may other regional groupings emerge, but it should also lead to the investigation of technological changes over time, and possibly establish links with techniques used in contemporary plank boats in Atlantic Europe.

## 5.3.2 RAFTS

There are no excavated examples of log rafts earlier than two of the second century AD recovered from the River Rhine near Strasbourg in 1938 (Ellmers, 1972: 106, figs. 83, 84). An earlier reference to their use comes from the first century BC: Caesar (*BG* I. 12, 6. 5) noted that Celtic people used them to cross rivers in Gaul. From medieval times onwards there are occasional documentary references to log rafts—always on inland waters (McGrail, 1998: 54).

Bundle rafts are even more elusive: none has been excavated, and the earliest reference to them appears to be a late nineteenth-century account of their use on Lough Erne in the north of Ireland (Wakeman, 1872–3). In 1962 a reed bundle raft, with a light wooden superstructure for the oarsman's bench and oar pivots, was built as a copy of an early twentieth-century one, and used on the River Suck, Co. Roscommon, Ireland (Delaney, 1976): this raft is now in the National Museum of Ireland. The raw materials for bundle rafts are, and were, widely available throughout Atlantic Europe and it is likely, but unprovable, that they were used from earliest times.

No matter how structurally sound rafts were, they are unlikely ever to have been used at sea off the Atlantic coast, with the possible exception of the western and southern coasts of Iberia. The relatively low sea and air temperatures generally in coastal Atlantic waters, combined with exposure to wind and wetness from rain or sea, would have soon taxed the endurance of the crew, if this had been attempted (McGrail, 1998:

5). On the other hand, rafts were probably widely used on lakes, rivers, and inner estuaries.

### 5.3.2.1 STONEHENGE BLUESTONES

Some forty years ago, Atkinson (1960: 105–16) suggested that log rafts were used to bring the Stonehenge bluestones by sea from Milford Haven, near their source in the Preseli Hills, Pembrokeshire, along the northern coast of the Bristol Channel into the Severn estuary. From Portishead, he considered that they would have been taken by multiple logboats up the Avon beyond Bath and up the River Frome to Frome; thence overland to the River Wylie at Warminster, down the Wylie to Salisbury, and up the Avon to Amesbury near Stonehenge. It has been argued by Thorpe *et al.* (1991), on the other hand, that the bluestones were glacial erratics deposited on Salisbury Plain by glacial action some 400,000 years ago: this view has recently been supported by Burl (1998: 110–15). The debate continues.

Atkinson undertook 'experiments' on the river and the land sections of his proposed route. On the River Avon near Salisbury, he used simple plank boats, rather than the logboats he had envisaged (1960: 113, pl. 22A), with three boats side by side, and a simulated bluestone (though of insufficient weight) on the central boat: four boys were able to pole this composite vessel along the Avon 'with the greatest ease'.

A coastal voyage from Milford Haven to Portishead would have been much more ambitious, and Burl (1998) has emphasized the natural hazards which would be encountered on such a passage. There is no reason to think, however, that Late Neolithic / Early Bronze Age seamen, whose ancestors had settled the British and Irish archipelago, could not have coped with the races, sands, rocks, and shoals of the Bristol Channel and estuary. They would certainly have used tidal flows to advantage—the tide would, in fact, have been their prime mover, paddles being used mainly to steer and to avoid hazards. A period of fine settled summer weather would have been chosen.

The two questions that remain open, however, are whether they had suitable water transport, and whether they had the means to load and unload the stones.

Of the three types of water transport that Atkinson discusses, plank boat, hide boat, and log raft, there is archaeological evidence only for logboats at the time the bluestones were incorporated into Stonehenge, *c.*2000 BC. Sewn-plank boats are known in Britain from a few hundred years later (5.4); log rafts were likely to have been in use, but, as we saw above, not at sea. Although the evidence for early paired logboats is slim (5.3.1.6.4), from the seaman's viewpoint, multiple logboats would be the preferred craft for the coastal voyage. Three logboats linked side by side, and sized so that the composite vessel was 'boat-shaped in plan', with a bluestone on the central, longer boat and paddlers in the others, would have given the best combination of buoyancy, freeboard, stability, speed, and manœuvrability, together with a robust structure and some protection for the crew. Whether such a craft could also have been used on the rivers of Somerset and Wiltshire is not clear, since the palaeo-environmental data is not available: it is certain, however, that such a craft would be smaller and more manœuvrable than a comparable log raft.

The difficulties of such a voyage should not be underestimated. Nevertheless, with sufficient incentive, the natural hazards could have been overcome. Moreover, the rise and fall of the tide may have been used, in some way, to solve the problem of loading and unloading the bluestones. Should the bluestones prove not to be glacial erratics, transport by sea (possibly by linked logboats) provides an alternative, but hypothetical, explanation.

### 5.3.3 HIDE BOATS

The excavated evidence for early hide boats (sometimes known as skin boats) is insubstantial: an unprovenanced antler fragment from Husum in Schleswig-Holstein (Ellmers, 1984), enigmatic evidence from an Early Bronze Age grave at Barns Farm, Dalgety, Fife (Watkins, 1980) and possible Roman period graves at South Ferriby near the River Ancholme, Lincolnshire (Sheppard, 1926), and at Corbridge near the Roman Wall (Bishop and Dore, 1988: 7); and possibly a small shale bowl from Caergwrle, Wales (Denford and Farrell, 1980). There are also minute boat models of gold from Nors, Denmark which Johnstone (1988: 126) thinks represent Bronze Age hide boats, whilst others, including Crumlin-Pedersen (1990: fig. 14.5), consider them to be sixth century AD representations of

Fig. 5.11. Rock carvings outlined in chalk at Evenhus, Norway (photo: Paul Johnstone).

extended logboats. There are also difficulties in interpreting and dating the many rock carvings of boats in Scandinavia (Marstrander, 1963; Kaul, 1998): however, the boats depicted (especially at Nämforsen and Evenhus) with relatively deep hulls (a low L/D ratio) may represent hide boats (Fig. 5.11)—see, for example, Johnstone (1988: fig. 10.4) and Marstrander (1963, pl. 64, figs. 15–17). The full-scale reconstruction of one of the boats depicted at Kalnes, Norway, built for Marstrander and filmed by P. Johnstone (1972), is unconvincing.

From the mid-first millennium BC to the present day, on the other hand, there is documentary and representational evidence—intermittent yet persistent—for hide boats, seagoing as well as those used on rivers and lakes. The sixth-century BC *periplus* extract incorporated in Avienus' fourth-century AD poem *Ora Maritima* (Hawkes, 1977; Murphy, 1977) notes that 'hardy and industrious peoples' of western Brittany used hide boats (*netisque cumbis*) to obtain tin and lead from Ireland and Britain, whilst Pliny (4. 104) quoting the early third-century BC historian, Timaeus, describes how Britons used seagoing boats of 'osiers covered with stitched hides'. Roman authors from the first century BC to the third century AD also refer to British hide boats, at sea and on inland waters: Caesar (*De Bello Gallico*, 1. 54); Pliny (*NH* 7. 206); Lucan (*Pharsalia*, 4. 130–8) and Salinus (*Polyhistor*, 2. 3). Medieval and later references to British and Irish hide boats have been published by Hornell (1936; 1937; 1946a: 9–13, 297–303). Currachs are still used off the west coast of Ireland as are coracles on the rivers of Wales.

A small gold model of the first century BC from Broighter on the margins of Lough Foyle, Co. Derry, Ireland, probably represents a seagoing hide boat (Fig. 5.12). Farrell and Penney (1975) think it might represent an extended logboat, but its proportions do not support this view. This vessel was propelled by a square sail on a mast stepped near amidships, or by nine oars each side, or by poles in the shallows. She was steered by a steering oar pivoted on the quarter.

Such a long-standing tradition for over 2,000 years, suggests firm roots which could well stretch back to the Bronze Age in Ireland, Britain, and adjacent parts of the Continent. Hide boats were also used in recent centuries in the circumpolar zone, so it would not be surprising if evidence were to be found for their use in early northern Scandinavia and Russia.

Nowadays, *umiaks* (from Greenland) and currachs (from Ireland) do not have keels, and their wooden framework is made of laths fastened together by lashings, treenails, or iron nails. However, a late seven-

teenth-century drawing, now in the Pepys Library at Magdalene College, Cambridge, has a large Irish sailing currach with prominent keel and stem outside the hide (Fig. 5.13). Medieval authors, such as Adamnan in his sixth-/seventh-century *Vita St. Columba* (A. Anderson and M. Anderson, 1961; Marcus, 1953–4: 315), and Classical authors, such as Caesar (*BG* 1. 54), Lucan (*Pharsalia*, 4. 136–8), Pliny (*NH* 7. 205–6) and Dio Cassus (*Epitome*, 48. 18–19), describe British and Irish hide boats built on an osier or woven wicker framework, with prominent keels. With such a keel, ancient hide boats (from at least the mid-first millennium BC) would have been able to sail somewhat closer to the wind than their keel-less twentieth-century equivalents; and the woven framework would have been stronger yet more resilient than its present-day counterpart. It may be that the putative Bronze Age hide boats were structurally similar.

### 5.3.3.1 MESOLITHIC HIDE BOATS?

Seagoing hide boats could theoretically have been built from Mesolithic times (McGrail, 1990b: 34). Hide boats are quickly built, and readily repaired; they fit well into

Fig. 5.12. Gold boat model of first-century BC from Broighter (National Museum of Ireland).

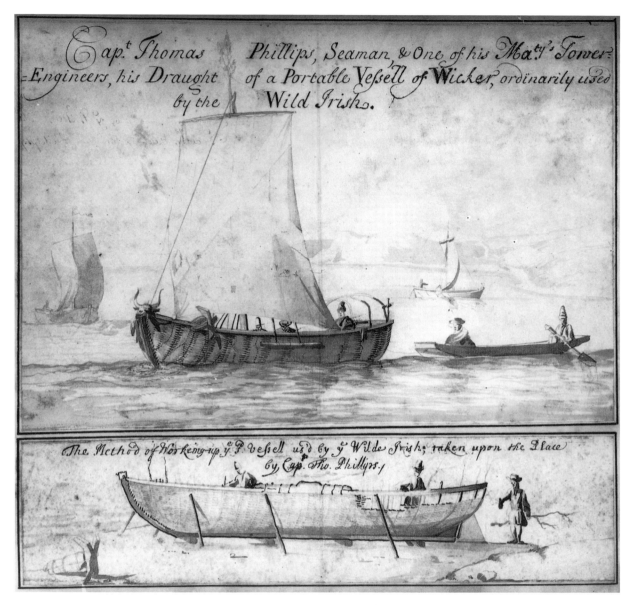

Fig. 5.13. A seventeenth-century drawing of a large Irish sailing currach (Magdalene College, Cambridge).

a crofter economy (i.e. Mesolithic) and can be used from informal landing places, and are excellent boats in a surf. Their lightweight structure, only half the weight of an equivalent planked boat, gives good freeboard when loaded, and they are more seaworthy and sea-kindly than a plank boat. Such boats would have fitted well into the environment, technology, and economy of early Atlantic Europe.

There are no remains of an early hide boat to support the arguments presented above: the case for a Bronze Age (or even Mesolithic) seagoing hide boat can only be taken further if and when a prehistoric example is excavated.

Although the hide on woven framework construction results in a resilient and energy-absorbing hull, the hide contributes little to structural strength: thus hide boats are limited in length (the largest seagoing *umiak* ever recorded was *c*.18 m—Adney and Chapelle, 1964: 175–6) and could never have been developed into ships.

## 5.4
# Bronze and Iron Age Plank Boats

No plank boat has been found in Atlantic Europe dated to the third millennium BC or earlier. However, planks could clearly be fashioned from oak in the Neolithic: for example, see Morgan's (1990) account of a planked mortuary chamber in Cambridgeshire, dated to c.3700–4000 BC. Moreover, Danish logboats of the third and fourth millennium BC, including Øgårde 3 and Verup 1 (5.3.1.1), have a row of holes near the top edge of the sides through which washstrakes may have been sewn or lashed (Westerdahl, 1985a: 138–40; Arnold, 1995: 42–3). It seems possible to suggest, therefore, that Early Bronze Age, and even Neolithic, sewn-plank boats may await excavation.

The remains of ten or so Bronze Age plank boats have been excavated in Atlantic Europe: all are of sewn-plank construction, without 'conventional' stemposts or keel, and most are from southern Britain, the one exception being from Denmark (Wright, 1990; 1994; McGrail, 1981b, 1996b, 1997b; Rosenberg, 1937). There is also some evidence that sewn plank boats were built in prehistoric Switzerland (Arnold, 1985), and since they were used in northern Scandinavia and other Baltic countries (Rank, 1933; Forsell, 1983; Westerdahl, 1985a and b) during the post-Roman period (in some places on into the twentieth century), it seems possible that earlier remains may await excavation in that region.

Tools and weapons of the twelfth century BC have been excavated from two underwater sites: Langdon Bay, Dover; and off Moor Sands near Prawl in Devon. Boat remains were not found, but it seems possible that these bronzes had once been on board one (Muckelroy, 1981).

There are suggestions in Scandinavian rock art and bronze engravings (Hallström, 1960; Marstrander, 1963; Hale, 1980; Malmer, 1981; J. Coles, 1993; A. Christensen, 1996; Kaul, 1998), and in certain British log coffins and logboats (Elgee, 1949; McGrail, 1978) that, in contradistinction to the known sewn-plank boats, there was another Bronze Age tradition of boats with prominent keel and posts. Whether these were hide boats or plank boats is considered further below (5.4.8).

### 5.4.1 DATING

It has proved possible to date dendrochronologically only one of the sewn-plank boats (Goldcliff); the others have been dated by radiocarbon assay which is inherently less precise. Furthermore, the accuracy of both methods ultimately depends on estimates for the number of missing annual growth rings. It should not be assumed, therefore, that the fragment from Caldecot (Severn estuary), for example, is necessarily older than the oldest Ferriby boat (Humber estuary) or the Dover boat, although the summary dates given below appear to suggest that.

### 5.4.2 THE HUMBER BASIN

Parts of four sewn boats have been found on the Humber foreshore at North Ferriby (Wright, 1990, 1994; Wright, Hutchinson, and Gregson, 1989; Switsur and Wright, 1989; Wright and Switsur, 1993): these are known as Ferriby 1, 2, 3, and 5. A fifth fragment comes from Kilnsea on the coast north of the Humber (Van de Noort et al, 1999); and the remains of a sixth boat were excavated at Brigg in a former channel of the River Ancholme, a Humber tributary (McGrail, 1981b, 1985a). The fragment of timber known as Ferriby 4 is dated c.530–375 BC (Wright, Hutchinson, and Gregson, 1989). It has no features suggesting it might be from a sewn-plank boat. Moreover, it is alder (Alnus sp.) which, although used for logboats in Neolithic Denmark (5.3.1.3), has not been noted in any other early boats of Atlantic Europe. This fragment most likely came from a non-nautical structure. The Kilnsea fragment is similar to a Ferriby 1 or 2 cleat; Ferriby 2 and 3 differ in detail from Ferriby 1, but are generally similar: these four finds will therefore be discussed under one heading. Ferriby 5 fragment is similar to a Brigg 'raft' cleat and these will be discussed together.

#### 5.4.2.1 FERRIBY BOATS 1, 2, 3, AND THE KILNSEA FRAGMENT

The remains of the Ferriby boats were discovered on the northern foreshore of the Humber estuary at North Ferriby in 1937, 1946, and 1963 (Fig. 5.14). They have been dated: F1—c.1390–1130 BC; F2—c.1440–1310

BC; F3—*c.*1310–1060 BC. The Kilnsea fragment was discovered in 1996, and is dated *c.*1870–1670 BC. Ferriby 1 has the most remains, the greater part of the bottom and part of one sidestrake, and these are all of oak (Fig. 5.15). The central of three bottom planks was made of two lengths joined in a simple half-lap. This plank was thicker than the other two and protruded below them as a plank-keel, the ends of which had been given an upward curve by external shaping and internal hollowing to form the bow and stern of the boat. The edges of all three bottom planks were cunningly shaped so that they interlocked, and they were fastened together by individual lashings of yew (*Taxus* sp.) at *c.*0.25 m spacing, over a caulking of moss held within and over the seams by longitudinal laths. These lashings, which were wedged within their holes, had been made pliable by twisting single withies to separate the fibres. The greater part of these lashings was within the interlocking seams (Fig. 5.16) so that the plank fastenings would not be damaged when the boat took the ground.

The three bottom planks were further linked by horizontal transverse timbers wedged within holes through cleats which had been left proud of each plank at intervals along its length. This arrangement helped to keep the bottom planking tight transversely, and kept it aligned both longitudinally and vertically; thus reducing the stresses on the plank fastenings (see also 5.3.1.4, 5.3.1.5). The transverse timbers were also probably used to realign the planking before it was fastened

Fig. 5.14. Ferriby 1 on the foreshore of the River Humber in 1946. The ruler is 60 cm long (photo: E. V. Wright).

Fig. 5.15 (*below*). Plans of Ferriby 1 (E. V. Wright).

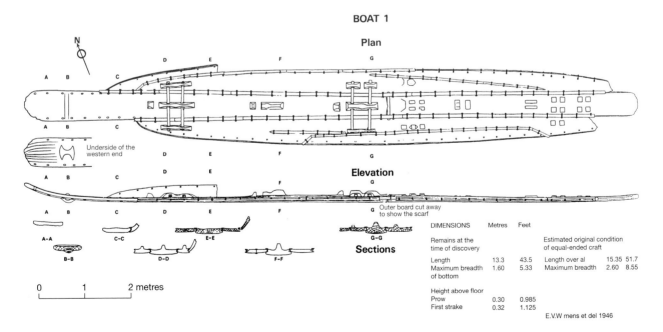

**BOAT 1**

**Plan**

Underside of the western end

**Elevation**

Outer board cut away to show the scarf

**Sections**

| DIMENSIONS | Metres | Feet | | | |
|---|---|---|---|---|---|
| Remains at the time of discovery | | | Estimated original condition of equal-ended craft | | |
| Length | 13.3 | 43.5 | Length over al | 15.35 | 51.7 |
| Maximum breadth of bottom | 1.60 | 5.33 | Maximum breadth | 2.60 | 8.55 |
| Height above floor | | | | | |
| Prow | 0.30 | 0.985 | | | |
| First strake | 0.32 | 1.125 | | | |
| | | | E.V.W mens et del 1946 | | |

0   1   2 metres

together after periodic dismantling for which there is much ethnographic evidence (McGrail, 1981a: 242).

The end of the lowest side strake was curved in two dimensions to form the bilge of the boat and to blend with the uprising curve of the plank keel to form the lower bow. To achieve this, the strake was hollowed internally and shaped externally, and a changing bevel was worked along its lower edge to fit *within* the rabbet in the edge of the outer bottom plank; yet further forward the edge of this lowest side strake enveloped the edge of the plank-keel.

The upper edge of this strake was given a half-lap rabbet, and fastening holes were worked along its length so that a second side strake could be fastened there (Fig. 5.16): the large fragment from Caldicot could have been part of such a second strake (5.4.3.1).

The minimum reconstruction compatible with the excavated remains is shown in Figure 5.17. It is assumed that the boat was double-ended, and that side strakes had cleats on them similar to those on the bottom planks. This second assumption received support from the subsequent find in Dover (5.4.4). Transom boards were inserted towards bow and stern to form the true watertight ends of the boat, and a girth lashing with a tourniquet was passed through the cleat under bow and stern to bind the ends together. Three composite frames wedged within bottom cleats and lashed to side cleats, and conjectural crossbeams/thwarts strengthen this shell of planking.

This reconstruction measures 15.4 × 2.6 × 0.70 m Such a boat could have carried crew and cargo up to a total of *c*.3 tonnes at a draft of 0.30 m; or 5.5 tonnes at

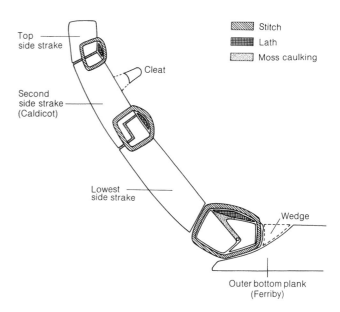

Fig. 5.16. Composite reconstruction drawing: a Ferriby outer bottom plank and lowest side-strake with a Caldicot second side-strake (Institute of Archaeology, Oxford).

0.40 m. She would have been propelled by poles in shoal waters and paddles elsewhere, within the Humber estuary and the many rivers that flow into it, as a ferry of men, animals, and goods. Such a flat-bottomed boat with a plank-keel, working in tidal waters, may be compared with the third-century AD Barland's Farm boat working the Severn estuary (5.6.1).

E. V. Wright (1994), excavator of the Ferriby boats, has proposed a radically different reconstruction, with three side strakes and a rockered bottom. It is not absolutely clear that a rockered keel is compatible with

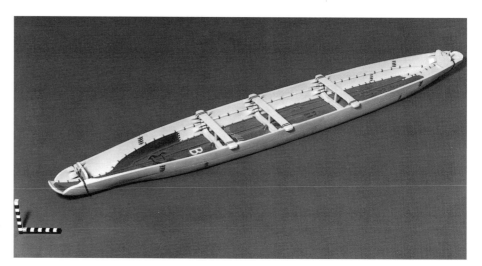

Fig. 5.17. A 1 : 10 reconstruction model of Ferriby 1 (National Maritime Museum, Greenwich).

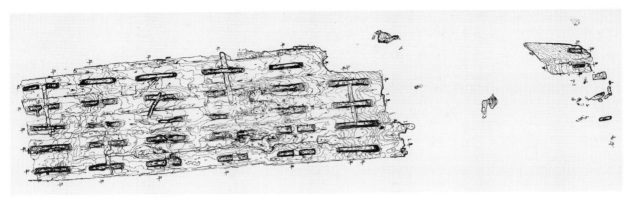

Fig. 5.18. A photogrammatic plot of the Brigg 'raft' during excavation (National Maritime Museum, Greenwich).

the remains as excavated, and it may be an unnecessary embellishment. Some other features of this reconstruction are taken from the Ferriby 4 fragmentary remains which are probably not from a boat, and which are dated 1,000 years or so after Ferriby 1.

### 5.4.2.2 THE BRIGG 'RAFT' AND FERRIBY 5

The oak fragment known as Ferriby 5 was found on the foreshore at North Ferriby in 1989. It is similar to a cleat from the Brigg 'raft' and has been dated to c.410–350 BC. This so-called 'raft', actually a flat-bottomed boat, was excavated from the site of a former tidal creek of the Humber estuary at Brigg in 1886: the remains were re-excavated in 1974 when about three-fifths of the bottom planking and part of a lowest side strake were recovered (Fig. 5.18).

The bottom of this boat (dated c.820–790 BC) consisted of five planks of equal thickness, butted edge to edge and fastened together by a continuous zig-zag stitching of a two-stranded willow (*Salix* sp.) rope, over a moss caulking capped by a longitudinal hazel (*Corylus* sp.) lath. Since the planks were thinner at their edges, the stitching was well above the bottom of the boat (Fig. 5.19). Transverse timbers, as in Ferriby boats 1 and 2, also linked the bottom planking: the Brigg cleats, however, were bigger, and more closely and regularly spaced. The outer edges of the outer bottom planks were left thick and the lowest side strake was fastened there in an overlap by running sewing which emerged through the edge of the bottom plank. Holes along the upper edge of this strake were where a second side strake had been fastened in a bevel lap joint.

Both ends of the remains were incomplete. The minimum reconstruction of the Brigg 'raft' is thus in the form of a lidless box with transom boards in grooves at both ends. The boat would have been some 12.2 m in length, slightly tapering in plan towards both ends from a maximum of c.2.27 m at a position c.8 m from one end (Fig. 5.20). Height of sides would have been 0.34 or 0.55 m, depending on the breadth of the second strake. No sign of framing other than transverse timbers through cleats was found in the boat, but it is possible that there were four crossbeams hooked at their ends over the sides (Greenhill, 1988: 38). These would not only brace the otherwise unsupported side strakes, but could also serve to pen any animals carried. Owain Roberts (1992) has proposed an altogether different reconstruction as a seagoing, round-hulled vessel with a rockered bottom. A round hull is not compatible with the evidence, but the possibility of some rocker requires further consideration.

The Brigg 'raft' was a poled and paddled ferry on the middle reaches of a tidal Humber creek at a point where east–west land routes converged. She could

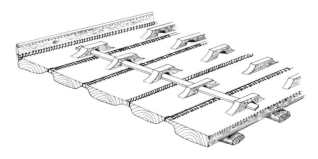

Fig. 5.19. Diagram to show the structure of the Brigg 'raft' (National Maritime Museum, Greenwich).

Fig. 5.20. A 1 : 10 reconstruction model of the Brigg 'raft' (National Maritime Museum, Greenwich).

have carried loads varying from twenty-six sheep with four men (1.54 tonnes at 0.25 m draft) to seventeen cattle with six men (7.16 tonnes at 0.46 m draft).

### 5.4.3 THE SEVERN ESTUARY

Parts of sewn-plank boats were excavated from two sites on the northern shores of the Severn estuary: in 1990, a large fragment of planking (dated c.1880-1690 BC) from the former bed of the River Naddern, a tributary of the River Severn (Nayling and Caseldine, 1997: 210–17); in 1992, two small fragments from the tidal northern foreshore of the Severn at Goldcliff (Bell, Caseldine, and Neumann, 2000: 74–82), east of the River Usk (dated to c.1000 BC by dendrochronology).

### 5.4.3.1 THE CALDICOT FINDS

The substantial oak plank fragment excavated was 3.55 m long, broken in antiquity at one end and having a rounded point at the other: its maximum breadth was 0.66 m and its thickness varied from c.60 to 90 mm (Fig. 5.21). The remains of three cleats protruded from the inboard face of the plank; the outboard face had been fashioned to a curved shape in three dimensions, including chamfering of the edges. The upper edge was worked square; the lower edge had a rabbet which had probably been part of a half-lap joint. Along both edges L-shaped holes had been worked from the

inboard face to emerge within the edge: they could not be seen from outboard. Average spacing of these fastening holes was c.0.35 m, thus these holes were for individual lashings like Ferriby 1 rather than running sewing as in the Brigg 'raft'. The holes were bigger even than the Ferriby holes (c.35 × 25 mm), being c.134 mm × 42 mm: this suggests that this fragment would have been well above the boat's waterline. The most likely position would have been at the end of a second side strake of a boat that was generally but not precisely like Ferriby 1. The rabbet along the lower edge of the Caldicot fragment is the mirror image of the rabbet on the upper edge of Ferriby 1's lowest side strake (Fig. 5.16); and the Caldicot plank's rounded end and expanded rabbet would have blended into a Ferriby bow or stern. A narrow third strake would have been lashed to the upper edge of the Caldicot strake in a butt joint. In this configuration, the cleats on the inboard face would have housed side timbers, elements of the boat's upper framing as in the Dover boat (5.4.4).

Found near this plank and similarly dated were two fragments of yew withy which had each been twisted upon itself to form a rope. These ropes were much less substantial than the Ferriby lashings, being only c.30 mm in girth (10 mm diameter). It is unlikely that these were used as plank fastenings, but they may have been used in other parts of a boat.

From another Caldicot context, dated to c.1100 BC, came a minor fragment of planking 0.33 m in length, worked from a radially split oak board (McGrail, 1997b:

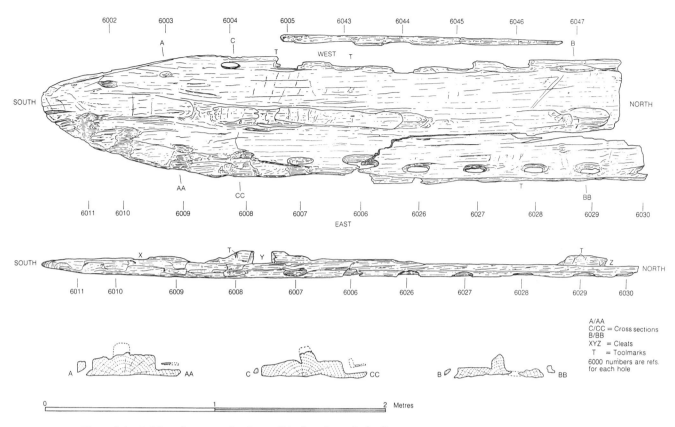

Fig. 5.21. Plans of the Caldicot fragment (Institute of Archaeology, Oxford).

fig. 136). The size of these holes and the character of the fragment suggest that it came from one edge of a plank similar to those of the Brigg 'raft'.

### 5.4.3.2 THE GOLDCLIFF FRAGMENTS

Two fragments of planking, probably from the sides of a boat similar to the Brigg 'raft' were found to have been reused in a small platform on the foreshore. Along the centreline of each fragment were the remains of an integral cleat ridge with holes at c.0.50 m intervals. Holes along one edge were similar in size (8 mm) and spacing (c.40 mm) to fastening holes on the Brigg 'raft'.

### 5.4.4 DOVER

In 1992 a large proportion of an oak sewn-plank boat was excavated from a former channel of the River Stour at Dover: the boat is provisionally dated to the fourteenth century BC (Marsden, personal communication). The bottom of this boat consists of two thick planks, butted together along the centreline, which are not lashed or sewn together but linked by tapered transverse timbers driven through holes in cleat rails which run the length of each plank, beside the seam (Fig. 5.22). The transverse timbers also hold down the moss caulking and lath along the centreline seam. These two bottom planks are further linked by other occasional transverse timbers which run through holes in the cleat rails and through Ferriby-style cleats proud of each plank.

The lowest side strakes have a hollowed cross-section (as in the Ferriby boats) and thus form a transition between bottom and sides around the bilge. They interlock at their lower edges with the outer edges of the bottom planks where there are rope lashings over moss and lath. A half-lap bevel on the upper edges of these side strakes is similar to that on Ferriby 1 and a second side strake (such as the Caldicot large fragment) was formerly lashed on here. Occasional side

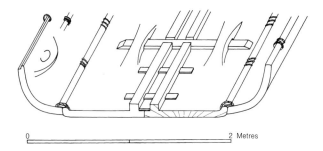

0                                                          2 Metres

Fig. 5.22. Diagram to show the structure of the Dover boat (Institute of Archaeology, Oxford).

cleats appear not to be in line with the bottom cleats: these would have formerly housed side timbers.

At the surviving end of this boat the bottom planks and side strakes were scarfed to a now-missing transom board. This scarf was held together by tapered timbers wedged through a yoke-shaped cleat rail, and made watertight by moss and lath as on the centreline seam.

Although details of the Dover boat have not yet been published, it is clear that it is generally comparable with Ferriby boat 1 in size and timber scantlings, but differs in certain features, such as wedge-fastening rather than lashing together some of the planking. As the Dover boat is keel-less whereas Ferriby 1 has a plank-keel, and the two boats have different shapes in plan and evidently different L/B ratios, different performance may be expected. How and where this boat was used depends not only on its form and structure but also on its contemporary environment, and research on all three aspects is still in progress.

## 5.4.5  CHARACTERISTICS OF BRITISH SEWN-PLANK BOATS

Although the finds discussed above differ in detail, there are several features they have in common. They were built in the plank-first sequence, i.e. their shape and their main strength came from the hull of planking and not from their transverse and side timbers which were secondary. Substantial oak planks were fastened together by individual lashings, by running sewing, or, in the case of the Dover boat, by tapered timbers wedged within holes through integral cleat rails. The plank seams were caulked (before assembling) by moss held in position by longitudinal laths. The bottom planking was linked together by transverse timbers,

and the side planking by side timbers, through integral cleats. Special woodworking techniques were used to ensure that when these boats took the ground (were beached) the plank fastenings were not damaged. The two finds that can be reconstructed, Ferriby 1 and the Brigg 'raft' were narrow, relatively long boats: L/B = c.6 to 8 : 1. The Dover boat, on which research continues, was probably similar.

Some of the differences in detail between these craft were undoubtedly functional: for example, Ferriby 1 had a 'conventional boat shape', suitable for a ferry across the fast-flowing Humber estuary, whereas the Brigg 'raft' was built as a ferry across the relatively quiet, upper reaches of a creek and thus had a more rectangular shape giving maximum capacity. Whether other differences in detail were regional, temporal or indeed, cultural, remains to be investigated.

In the light of present information, these finds may be divided into two groups by reference to their date and their plank fastenings.

*Group A*. Ferriby 1, 2, 3, Dover, and Caldicot 1. The Kilnsea fragment may also belong to this sub-group. These are dated to eighteenth–thirteenth centuries BC, i.e. the Middle Bronze Age. Interlocking, edge-to-edge or half-lap planking is fastened together by individual lashings through large holes. Dover also has wedges through cleat rails as bottom plank fastenings.

*Group B*. Brigg 'raft', Caldicot 2, and Goldcliff. Ferriby 5 may also belong to this sub-group. These are dated to eleventh–ninth centuries BC, i.e. the Late Bronze Age. Edge-to-edge and bevel-lap planking is fastened by continuous stitching through small holes.

### 5.4.5.1  THE IDENTIFICATION OF FRAGMENTARY FINDS

The finds from Ferriby, Brigg, and Dover, although incomplete, survived to be excavated in an articulated state and they had sufficient recognizable features, including caulking associated with sewn planking to make this identification as plank boats almost a certainty. On the other hand, Ferriby 5, Kilnsea, the Caldicot, and Goldcliff finds are minor in extent, as is a fragment from a recent Bronze Age excavation at Testwood Lakes, Southampton, which appears to be part of a cleat (Fitzpatrick *et al.*, 1996) They have been identified as fragments from sewn-plank boats since they have the characteristic features of cleats with holes for transverse timbers, and/or lashing/sewing holes along the plank edges. This identification may be questioned: could there be other Bronze Age artefacts or structures with similar features, say, causeways, rafts, mud sledges, all of which could be deposited in or near sea, river, or lake?. Flat-bottomed boats can be differentiated from rafts since boats are made watertight and rafts are not. The presence of materials, such as moss and laths, which can be used to make seams watertight could also be used to differentiate fragments of sewn-plank boats from other Bronze Age structures, but moss and laths are seldom, if ever, excavated in association with minor fragments of timbers. The possibility must be borne in mind therefore that fragments of timber with only sewing holes or only cleats may not be from sewn-plank boats.

## 5.4.6 THE HJORTSPRING BOAT

This Iron Age boat, dated 350–300 BC, was excavated in 1921–2 from a former lake near the centre of the island of Als off the eastern coast of southern Denmark (Rosenberg, 1937; Jensen, 1989; Rieck, 1994). The shape of this boat in profile (Fig. 5.23) resembles the outlines of a class of boats depicted in some Scandinavian rock carvings (especially the Mikkelsborg group) and on swords generally dated to the Bronze Age, so the boat may be representative of a pre-Iron Age tradition.

Like the British sewn-plank boats, the Hjortspring boat was built plank-first. Furthermore, her planks were sewn together, and her transverse timbers were associated with cleats on the planking. In many other ways, however, the Hjortspring construction is significantly different from that of other Bronze Age plank boats. The hull was built of only seven main parts, all lime (*Tilia* sp.): a slightly hollowed bottom plank; two hollowed block stems; and four side strakes. It is not clear whether the varied cross-sections of the 20 mm thick bottom plank was obtained solely by hewing or by expansion after heating, probably the former. This plank was extended at both ends by an upcurving timber to form a lower projecting 'beak'. The block stems stood on the bottom plank and were sewn to it. They each had an extension which formed an upper 'beak' parallel to the lower 'beak'. The base of this upper 'beak' was fastened to the bottom plank by a vertical

oak timber held within mortises by horizontal treenails, with a paying of an animal fat with traces of linseed oil. A second vertical timber, similarly fastened, joined the upper and lower 'beaks' towards their tips: the function of these 'beaks' is unclear.

The side strakes were sewn to the wings of the block stems in a bevelled lap, with the planking outboard. They were sewn together and to the bottom plank in bevelled laps similar to the joint used to fasten together the first and second side strakes of the Brigg 'raft' (5.4.2.2): such joints have the overlap within the thickness of the planking and thus the sides of the boat appear smooth. The cord used for sewing was probably two-ply roots of birch or fir (Valbjørn *et al.* forthcoming), and the sewing holes were outside the lap—as in the Brigg 'raft' (McGrail, 1981*b*: fig. 4.1.14). These holes were subsequently stopped with a mixture of animal fat and linseed. The planking was generally 20 mm thick, but the upper edge of the upper strake was thickened to strengthen the rim of the shell.

Ten hazel (*Corylus* sp.) ribs were bent to the shape of the hull and lashed to several cleats projecting from each plank: such prestressing of the ribs helped to force the planks together (Fig. 5.24). Upper crossbeams of lime (*Tilia* sp.) were fashioned as thwarts, and these, and the lower crossbeams of ash (*Fraxinus* sp.) were linked to each rib through holes near their ends: this arrangement meant that each set of framing had to be assembled before installation in the boat. Further support was given to each thwart by vertical ash timbers which ran from mortises in the thwart through the lower crossbeams to the lower part of the rib. A pine (*Pinus sylvestris*) plank from Vasternorrland, Sweden, similar to a Hjortspring upper crossbeam, has recently been dated to *c*.220 BC (Jansson, 1994).

Several light and slim propulsion paddles were

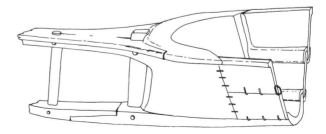

Fig. 5.23. Reconstruction drawing of the bow of the Hjortspring boat (after Greenhill, 1995*a*: fig. 48).

Fig. 5.24. Reassembled framing of the Hjortspring boat (Danish National Museum).

found with the Hjortspring boat, as well as fragments of larger-bladed steering paddles (Fig. 5.6C). Rosenberg, the excavator, deduced that she had been propelled by twenty paddlers, two to a thwart, with a steersman at bow and stern. Rosenberg's reconstruction drawing gives her size (without the projections) as c.13.61 × 2.04 × 0.71 m. At a draft of 0.31 m she could have carried a total of 2.11 tonnes. Having a smooth hull, a waterline L/B ratio of c.10 : 1, and a very low volumetric coefficient, she should have had a good turn of speed when propelled by a full crew in fair conditions.

This relatively lightweight, keel-less, round-hulled, double-ended craft with sewn planking and a refined framing system would have been used (possibly as a war boat) within the Danish archipelago and adjacent coasts and rivers. Similarities with Bronze Age representations and with the Själevad fragment from northern Sweden suggest that this sort of boat may have been widely used in Scandinavia over several centuries.

### 5.4.7 SEWN PLANKS AND LASHED FRAMES

The earliest evidence for lashing as a boatbuilding technique may be from Danish logboats of the fourth and third millennia BC which possibly had washstrakes lashed to the sides to increase freeboard. Repairs in second millennium BC logboats are probably first evidence for the use of running sewing (5.3.1). Plank boats of the earlier second millennium BC have lashed planking; those of a later date have running sewing. Transverse timbers (i.e. elementary framing) were wedged within cleats during the second millennium BC, but they were not lashed to cleats until the fourth century BC Hjortspring boat; as argued above, however, boats of the Hjortspring type may have been used at an earlier date.

The Valderøy boat fragments, from a boat grave on the west Norwegian coast, are dated to AD 245 ± 105 (Westerdahl, 1985a: 132; Brøgger and Shetelig, 1971: 24–5). This boat had fully overlapping pine clinker planking (rather than the Hjortspring bevelled lap) which was fastened by sewing, with a caulking of tar-impregnated wool. The framing was lashed to cleats proud of the planking. The planking and the frames of the boat from Halsnøy in south-west Norway dated to c. AD 335 ± 65, were similarly fastened (Brøgger and Shetelig, 1971: 34–5). Wooden rowlocks were found with both these boats.

In Finland (and elsewhere in northern Scandinavia and Russia) sewn planks and lashed frames seem to have been used from this time on into the twentieth century (Westerdahl, 1985a; Forsell, 1983; 1985; Litwin, 1985; Cederlund, 1985). In Norway, Sweden, and Denmark, on the other hand, iron fastenings began to take over from the fourth century. The Bjorke extended logboat of c. AD 320 has washstrakes fastened by clinker nails, however, its ribs are generally lashed to cleats with a nail at the very top, and there is a sewn repair (Greenhill, 1995a: 67–8; 176–73; Westerdahl, 1985a: 128–9; Myhre, 1980). The frames of the fourth century AD Nydam boat 2 were lashed to cleats (two per plank generally, compared with the four or five on the Hjortspring planks), and there is a sewn or lashed repair on Nydam 1 (5.7.1.2). The Barset boat of the eighth century AD is generally built in the clinker tradition but the top strake is fastened with sewing and intermittent treenails (Westerdahl, 1985a: 130).

### 5.4.8 OTHER TRADITIONS OF PLANK BOATS?

None of the boats dated before the fourth century AD described so far had a conventional stem or a prominent keel, although Ferriby 1 and 2 had a plank-keel. However, there are suggestions, mere hints, in the archaeological record that there may have been Bronze Age plank boats with 'conventional' keel and stems. A boat-shaped log-coffin (Fig. 5.25) excavated in 1937 from an Early Bronze Age round barrow at Loose Howe, north-east England has a prominent keel and stem fashioned in the solid oak (Elgee, 1949: fig. 4). A recent examination of the remains in the British Museum confirmed that these features were not natural but had undoubtedly been worked. Rather than a boat reused as a coffin, this is more likely to be a coffin with the shape of a boat. Since keel and stem are unnecessary on a logboat, the features on the Loose Howe coffin are likely to have been copied from a contemporary plank boat (or possibly, but less likely, from a hide boat). Two Iron Age logboats, Poole (400–180 BC) and Holme Pierrepont 3 (probably 400 BC–AD 50) also have stems shaped in the solid, at a time when there is still no evidence in Atlantic Europe for plank boats with stems.

Scandinavian rock art and bronze engravings, often ascribed to the Bronze Age, include representations which some have claimed may be plank boats with keels (Hallström, 1960; Marstrander, 1963; Hale, 1980;

Malmer, 1981; Coles, 1993; Kaul, 1998). Comparable rock engravings have been noted in Spain in the vicinity of Vigo, and on rock paintings near Cadiz (Alonso, 1994). Such 'diagrammatic silhouettes' are difficult to date and to interpret, and little information has so far been obtained from them.

The evidence for an early tradition of boats with keel and stems is thus not substantial. The possibility should be borne in mind, but the discussion can only be taken further if and when a prehistoric boat with such features is excavated.

### 5.4.9 SEAFARING BEFORE THE ROMAN PERIOD

There were undoubtedly coastal and cross-channel voyages in Atlantic Europe in the prehistoric period (McGrail, 1993a: 199–201). Some authors appear to have interpreted this indirect evidence of excavated exotic materials and objects as evidence for long-distance overseas voyages, out of sight of land. For example: R. Bowen (1972) and Chevillot and Coffyn (1991): Britain and Ireland to Spain; Butler (1963) and O'Connor (1980a): across the North Sea. J. Coles (1993: 30) generally supports these suggestions; Muckelroy (1981) is more cautious; whilst Thrane (1995) denies that there were direct crossings between Scotland and Norway or from England to Denmark. Such transfers of artefacts, and of people/ideas (archaeologically visible as 'monuments', as 'ritual', or as technological innovations), can only be evidence for Bronze Age overseas voyages to and from islands; elsewhere such transfers may have taken place over land or by river. For islands, unless there is evidence to the contrary, it must be assumed (if for no other reason that sail and oar were unknown and thus these boats were paddled) that the sea crossings took the shortest route, e.g. the North Channel between Ireland and Scotland; and the Dover Strait between France and England. Short-haul coastal passages, generally in sight of land, could then have been used to transport goods and people as far south as Spain, and as far north as Scandinavia (4.14.2). These early seafarers would have needed pilotage skills and rudimentary navigational techniques (5.2.1—see also 4.4.6 and 4.9.3.2.1).

Evaluation of the Bronze Age plank boats known today strongly suggests that they were lake, river, and

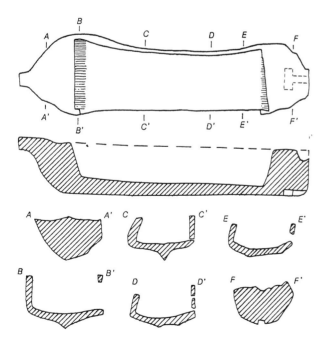

Fig. 5.25. A boat-shaped log coffin from Loose Howe (after Elgee and Elgee, 1949: fig. 4).

estuary boats and would not have been seagoing except on rare occasions of settled fair weather. This is not because they were sewn boats—there are many recent examples of seagoing plank boats (McGrail, 1981*a*: 29–30, 47–8, 51, 54–5, 58, 63–4, 69, 80–1)—but their shape, their lack of sheer, and their structure were such that they would have insufficient stability, freeboard, and sea-kindliness qualities for such a role (McGrail, 1993*a*: 202–4). It has been suggested that the Dover boat was a seagoing vessel, mainly because she was found at Dover. It seems unlikely, however, that the wedged fastenings (Fig. 5.22) along the centreline and around the transom (as they are presently understood) would give the boat the hull integrity needed for even a short sea crossing. A recent assessment of this boat by Owain Roberts (personal communication) suggests that she was probably an estuary boat with restricted abilities in coastal waters. If an authentic full-scale reconstruction of one of these sewn-plank boats could be built, and scientific trials undertaken, these conclusions might be reinforced or challenged. Archaeological experiments which can tell us anything worthwhile about the past are difficult to plan and expensive to undertake (Coates *et al.*, 1995), and, in their absence, the hypothetical Bronze Age hide boat (5.3.3), with a keel, a wicker framework, and of a shape suitable for paddlers, may be considered as a possible seagoing vessel of early Atlantic Europe. Alternatively, the equally hypothetical and elusive Bronze Age plank boat with prominent plank-keel and 'conventional' stems (5.4.8) may be considered.

# 5.5
# Vessels Built Mediterranean Fashion

## 5.5.1 COUNTY HALL SHIP
(Parker, 1992: no. 607)

A large part of the bottom, and one side of a ship were excavated in 1910–11 from the County Hall site near the River Thames in London. This vessel had several of the characteristics of Mediterranean ships of the early cen-

turies AD (Marsden, 1994: 109–29); Riley and Gomme, 1912; Steffy, 1994: 72). Recent dendrochronological work has shown that growth ring thickness patterns from this ship match the master oak chronology for the south-east of England, and thus she was most probably built there; she is dated *c.* AD 290–300 (Marsden, 1994: 124–5).

The planking was fastened by locked mortise and tenon joints with a spacing of *c.*6 inches (0.15 m) at the keel, and somewhat greater elsewhere.

The evidence from the framing pattern is not as clear, especially as Riley noted scarfs in only six of the forty-one frames recorded. Marsden (1994: fig. 111) in a re-evaluation of the evidence, suggests two possibilities: (a) floor timbers alternating with full frames, or (b) half-frames alternating port and starboard. Steffy (1994: 72) prefers the second alternative. Riley (1912: 10) stated that '. . . every alternate rib only being carried up the sides'. The frames he noted with scarfs were probably pairs of Mediterranean-style half-frames, to port and starboard and ending near the centreline with a chock to fill the gap between the two half-frames (Riley and Gomme, 1912: fig. J). The scarfs of these frames (numbered 8, 12, 16, 20, 28, and 36 on Marsden's figure 106) are close to the keel on Riley's plan, and these frames are in such a position that, if we assume that scarfs on frames 10, 14, 18, 22, 24 (incomplete), 26, 30, 32, and 34 were not recorded by Riley, the framing pattern would be 'floors alternating with half-frames' as usually found in contemporary Mediterranean ships (4.13.2.2).

The average spacing between frame stations in County Hall's main hull was *c.*10 inches (0.245 m). The frames were fastened to the planking by oak treenails 1¼ inches (32 mm) in diameter; they were not fastened to the keel. The oak strakes were generally 2 inches (50 mm) thick, but garboards were 3 inches (75 mm). Plank scarfs were horizontal (Riley and Gomme, 1912: figs. B and C) with a nail through the tip, as again commonly found in the Mediterranean.

Features only infrequently noted in Mediterranean wrecks include: stringers nailed to the framing near the bilge—mortises in these stringers appear to have housed stanchions to support decking (ibid., fig. F); wales at eleventh strake level to which deck-supporting crossbeams were nailed outboard (ibid., figs. E and D); and treenails through the keel where a false keel had once been fastened (ibid., fig. A).

## 5.5.2 BOATS FROM THE NETHERLANDS AND FROM THE RIVER DANUBE

The planking of two first–second centuries AD boats, one excavated from Vechten near Utrecht in 1893, and one (boat 2A) from Zwammerdam in 1968–71, were fastened together with locked mortise and tenon joints (de Weerd, 1988: 180–3, 185–94; de Weerd and Haalëbos, 1973: 395–6, figs. 10 and 11); as were the three parts of the blade of a steering-oar also excavated from Zwammerdam (de Weerd, 1988: 162–80). The first side strake of Zwammerdam boat 6 (5.6.2.1.1) was fastened edge-to-edge to the transition strake by mortise and tenon joints, as well as angled nails (de Weerd, 1988: 155–61).

Two river boats from a Danube site at Oberstimm in central Germany were also built in the Classical manner (Hockmann, 1989).

## 5.5.3 A BOAT FROM LOUGH LENE, IRELAND

In 1968 an extended logboat was excavated from Lough Lene, Co. Westmeath near the centre of Ireland. It was thought to be medieval: part was acquired by the National Museum, and part was re-sunk in the lough (O hEailidhe, 1992). The logboat base was retrieved in 1987, and a tenon of yew (*Taxus baccata*) was dated by radiocarbon to the third or fourth centuries AD. The broad oak washstrakes were fastened edge-to-edge to the logboat base by mortise and tenon joints at c.0.35 m intervals. Damage to the base appears to have been repaired by sewing. There is ample evidence that traders, if not Roman military, from Britain were in Ireland from the first century AD (Warner, 1996).

## 5.5.4 ROMAN INFLUENCES DURING THE FIRST TO FOURTH CENTURIES AD

The County Hall ship seems to have been almost entirely Roman in design and techniques, but dendrochronology shows that she was built of oak from the south-east of England and thus was probably built in the Thames region. The Netherlands and Irish craft described above also show that certain Atlantic boatbuilders were familiar with the Mediterranean method of fastening planks together by mortise and tenon joints.

De Weerd (1988, 1990, 1994) considers that he has identified a particular Roman unit of measurement, the *pes monetalis*, in the frame-spacing of several northwest European vessels (5.6) of the early centuries AD. As Arnold (1990) has pointed out, however, precise measurements cannot be derived from small-scale drawings, and the sequence of frame spacing postulated in order to derive this 'standard unit' is hardly practicable. The most that the evidence will support is that the builders of the boats cited by de Weerd used a unit of c.0.30 m or approximately one human foot. Units of c.0.55 and 0.56 m, i.e. two human feet, have been identified in two of the seagoing Romano-Celtic vessels (5.6.1.3): the use of such natural units is not evidence of 'Romanization', however the use of sawn timber (5.6.1) probably is.

During Caesar's campaigns in Gaul (*BG* 3. 9. 1), he had warships (*naves longas*) built on the River Loire which he subsequently used against the Veneti, a maritime people of Brittany (*BG* 3.11. 5). Morrison and Coates (1996: 120–1), writing about this battle, and quoting Dio Cassius, a third-century historian, state that these Roman ships were fast ships from the Mediterranean. Parker (1999) considers that this is a mistranslation, and that Dio was referring to the ships built on the River Loire. It seems likely that these ships were built Mediterranean fashion (though in France by Gallic builders) since later in Caesar's account (*BG* 3.14. 2–8) we are told that they were oared-warships the sides of which were much lower than those of the Veneti sailing vessels.

Whether the Romans ever made passages from the Mediterranean along the Atlantic coast to Gaul and Britain has been considered by several authors. Parker (1999) believes that there is no evidence that Roman warships made such passages; Marsden (1994: 175–6) considers that it was rare for any Mediterranean shipping to use this route. Boon (1977: 21–5) quotes evidence to support his argument that some Mediterranean ships did reach Britain even before Caesar's time—see 4.14.2 and 5.6.6. It is clear that much of the trade between the Mediterranean and Gaul and Britain in the first century BC was up the Rhône and Aude, and down the Garonne, Loire, Seine, and Rhine (Cunliffe, 1982, 1984; McGrail, 1983b) and then, possibly in Celtic vessels, along the Atlantic coast. Nevertheless, as Marsden (1994: 175) has pointed out, Portuguese amphora have been excavated from Vindölanda in northern

Britain, and a Roman lighthouse was built at Corunna in the north-west of Iberia. Furthermore, not only were voyages along the Atlantic coast of Iberia practicable, but also, it is not impossible that direct voyages across the Bay of Biscay from the vicinity of Corunna to the vicinity of Ushant could be undertaken by this date (4.14.2).

# 5.6

## Romano-Celtic Boats and Ships

It is possible to recognize a degree of continuity, in the north-western region of Atlantic Europe, in the methods used to build plank boats and logboats from the early second millennium BC through to the late centuries BC (McGrail, 1990b; 1993a, 1995a, 1996b). There is then an apparent discontinuity. During the Roman period, however, it is possible to recognize at least two main strands of boatbuilding, both of them with features clearly different from those used in the contemporary Mediterranean: the Nordic, which will be considered in Section 5.7.1; and the Romano-Celtic, which is discussed here.

A ship is depicted on two bronze coins of the first century AD issued by the Celt Cunobelin of the Catavellauni of south-east Britain (Muckelroy, Haselgrove, and Nash, 1978). These vessels were propelled by a square sail set on a midships mast, and steered by a side rudder. Braces to the yard suggest a bid for weatherly performance, as do the protruding forefoot

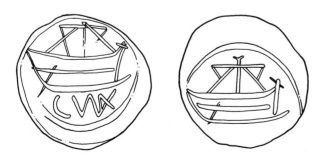

Fig. 5.26. Two bronze coins of first-century BC Cunobelin. (Institute of Archaeology, Oxford).

and the spar at the stemhead which may have taken a bowline (Fig. 5.26).

Caesar (*BG* 3. 13) and Strabo (4. 4. 1), in the first century BC/AD, described the seagoing sailing ships of the Veneti Celts of south-west Brittany, which were more seaworthy and better suited to the difficult seas of the Channel than were Caesar's own ships: they could sail closer inshore and take the ground readily in those tidal waters. The Veneti ships had flush-laid oak planking, caulked with 'seaweed' or possibly moss, and fastened to 1 foot (30 cm.) thick framing timbers by iron nails 1 inch (25 mm) in diameter of shank. They were propelled by leather sails and used for coastal passages and cross-Channel voyages to Britain.

Aspects of Caesar's description may be seen in a group of twenty-five wrecks excavated in the Severn estuary, the Thames at London, Guernsey, the Schelde/Meuse/Rhine delta, the Rhine at Xanten and at Mainz, and Lake Neuchâtel in Switzerland (de Weerd, 1988; Lehmann, 1978; Hockmann, 1982; de Boe and Hubert, 1977; Marsden, 1976; 1994; Arnold, 1992; 1998; 1999; Rule and Monaghan, 1993; McGrail and Roberts, 1999). The description of these vessels as 'Romano-Celtic' has not been unchallenged (e.g. Parker, 1991; Milne, 1996), but it seems more appropriate than other names proposed since it describes the distribution in both time and space: 'Celtic' reflects their spatial dispersion which is, by and large, in regions formerly occupied by Celtic-speaking peoples; 'Romano' reflects the temporal range, first to fourth centuries AD, and acknowledges the possibility of Roman technological influence.

The antecedents of this tradition are unclear, but some scholars have seen parallels with the British prehistoric sewn boats (Basch, 1972: 42; Arnold, 1977, 1999; Wright, 1990). What happened to this style of building after the fourth century AD is also unclear: Ellmers (1996) considers that Germanic peoples used these techniques to build their river and lake boats (see also 5.7.1.4.3.3), whilst others (5.8.2.6) think that aspects of this tradition appeared in the medieval cog (Runyan, 1994: 47). Until further evidence is excavated, these theories must remain speculative.

The distinctive features of this polythetic group of ships and boats are:

• The framing consists of relatively massive and relatively closely spaced groups of timbers, including

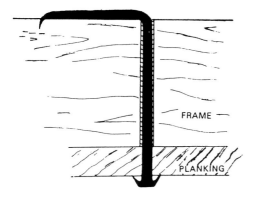

Fig. 5.27. A hooked nail fastening plank to frame in Blackfriars 1 (after Marsden, 1994: fig. 48).

floors spanning bottom and bilges, asymmetric timbers (half-frames) spanning the bottom and one side, and side timbers.

• Relatively large nails (sometimes driven through treenails—reasons for this technique are given in 4.12.1), clenched by turning the emerging point through 180° ('hooked'), or 90° ('turned'), fasten planking and framework together (Fig. 5.27). Caulking of macerated wooden twigs, twisted fibres, or moss, was placed in the seams.

• The sawn planking was generally flush-laid, edge to edge and was generally not fastened together.

This combination of characteristics both defines this tradition, and also differentiates it from the contemporary Nordic and Mediterranean traditions. In the light of present evidence, the twenty-five finds may be divided into two sub-groups: boats for inland waters; and vessels for estuaries and the sea. This division by operating environment coincides with differences in shape, structure, and means of propulsion: it may also coincide with the degree of Roman influence, and with differing ways in which the builders visualized the shape of their vessels.

## 5.6.1 SEAGOING AND ESTUARY VESSELS

The three vessels in this sub-group (code name 'Blackfriars') are: Blackfriars 1 (Fig. 5.28) of the mid- second century AD from the River Thames in London (Marsden, 1994: 33–96)); St. Peter Port 1 from Guernsey of the late-third century (Rule and Monaghan, 1993); and Barland's Farm (Fig. 5.29) of c. AD 300 from the northern shores of the Severn estuary (McGrail and Roberts,

1999). The New Guy's House boat of the late-second century AD and the fragments from Bruges may also belong to this group, but details of their structure are unclear (Marsden, 1976, 1994: 97–104). When reconstructed, Blackfriars 1 measures c.18.5 × 6.12 × 2.86 m, St. Peter Port 1, c.25 × 6 × 3 + m so they may be called ships; the Barland's Farm vessel was c.11.40 × 3.16 × 0.90 m, and so may be considered a boat. These three vessels have L/B ratios of 3–4 : 1; L/D ratios are 6.5–8.3 : 1 (ships), 12.7 : 1 (boat). The two ships have a full-bodied transverse section with a firm bilge (Rule and Monaghan, 1993: figs. 8, 12, 13, 20; Marsden, 1994: figs. 58, 69, 70). The boat is flat in the floors which gives her a flat bottom internally, but she has curved, flaring sides (McGrail and Roberts, 1999: fig. 4). The structure and

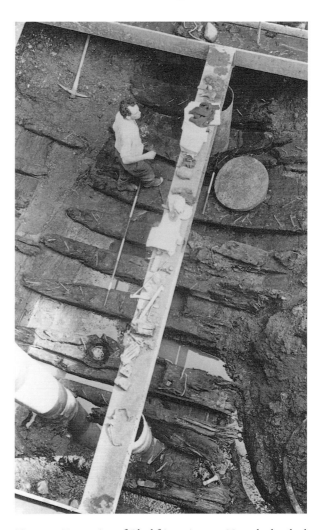

Fig. 5.28. Excavation of Blackfriars 1 in 1962. Note the hooked nails on the upper faces of the floor timbers (photo: Peter Marsden).

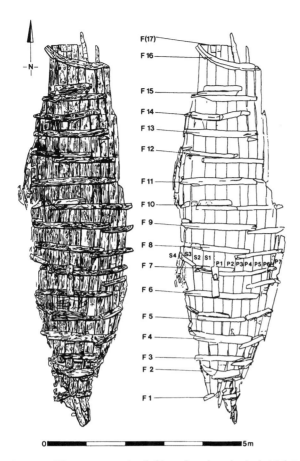

Fig. 5.29. Photogrammatic (left) and archaeological (right) plans of the Barland's Farm boat during excavation (after Nayling, Maynard, and McGrail, 1994).

the lines of the two ships and theoretical analysis of performance confirm that they were seagoing: the Barland's boat was clearly suited for passages in the eastern reaches of the Bristol Channel, in the Severn estuary, and in the numerous rivers of that region (McGrail and Roberts, 1999).

All three vessels have a mast step at approximately one-third the waterline length from the bow: Barland's in a short fore-and-aft timber, the other two in a floor. It is clear that all three were designed as sailing cargo vessels, with the boat additionally capable of being propelled by oars. Theoretical analysis of the Barland's boat's lines by Owain Roberts shows that, for sail balance and for windward performance, a fore and aft sail such as a lug is a better rig than a square sail, although documentary and representational evidence for lug-sails is from a much later date (McGrail and Roberts, 1999: 138, 141–2; Moore, 1970; Sleeswyk, 1986). The evidence considered by Marsden (1994: 67–74) may be

interpreted as suggesting that Blackfriars 1 also had a fore and aft sail, although Marsden seems to favour a square sail.

### 5.6.1.1 STRUCTURE

#### 5.6.1.1.1 *Posts and plank-keel*

These three vessels have posts and a plank-keel. The posts have a long, near-horizontal arm, the inboard end of which is joined to the plank-keel. St. Peter Port has a three-plank plank-keel (thickness *c*.120 mm), whilst the other two have plank-keels of two-planks (thickness *c*.60 mm). These planks are thicker than other bottom planking and protrude below them: like the other planking in these vessels, the planks of the plank-keels are not fastened together.

#### 5.6.1.1.2 *Framing*

All three of these vessels have a stout floor timber positioned immediately above the crucial joints between posts and plank-keel. In the Barland's boat a tongue, protruding from the lower end of the post, forms a half-lap scarf with a recess worked in the upper face of the plank-keel, whilst a notch worked in the outer face of the floor forms a double-notch joint with the post, directly above that scarf. Two large iron nails driven from outboard through these two joints, and hook-clenched by turning through 180° into the inner face of the floor, together with a third nail through post and floor, firmly lock together the plank-keel and the posts to form the backbone of the boat (Fig. 5.30). The two ships have comparable but not exactly similar arrangements.

St. Peter Port and Blackfriars (Fig. 5.31) have sizeable floors generally alternating with side frames. Barland's, on the other hand, has paired half-frames extending from one bilge across the bottom and up the opposite side in a graceful curve to the sheerline; these generally, but not always, alternate with floors which extend to the turn of the bilge. Side timbers partly overlap these floors and extend to the sheerline (Fig. 5.32). Thus in the Barland's boat, there are two or three timbers at each framing station, but adjacent timbers are not fastened together.

#### 5.6.1.1.3 *Planking*

The sawn-oak planking is flush-laid, edge to edge, with butts at frame stations. Average thickness are: Bar-

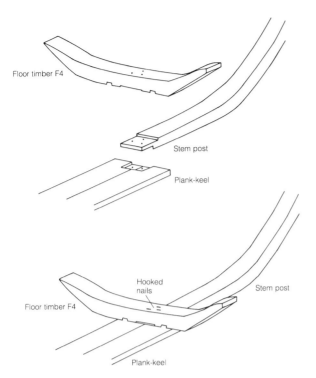

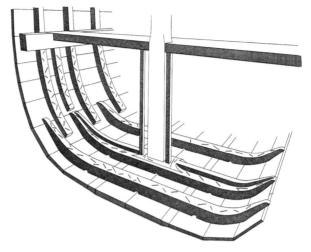

Fig. 5.30. Diagram to show the structure of the Barland's Farm joint between the plank-keel, the stern post, and floor timber F4 (Institute of Archaeology, Oxford).

Fig. 5.31. Reconstructed section of Blackfriars 1, near the mast step (after Marsden, 1994: fig. 58).

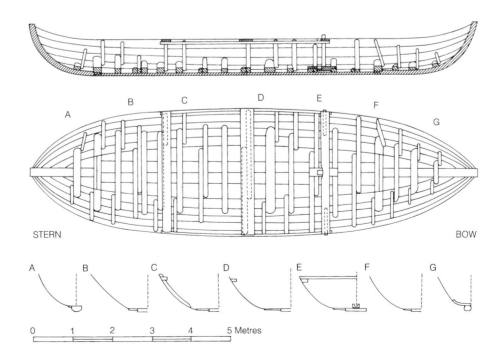

Fig. 5.32. Reconstruction drawings of the Barland's farm boat (Institute of Archaeology, Oxford).

land's Farm 25 mm; St. Peter Port, 50–60 mm; Black-friars, *c*.50 mm. A caulking of macerated wood with tar or resin was nailed by tacks or possibly 'glued' to the plank edges before the planks were fastened to the framing by nails which were hook-clenched inboard. Typical nail lengths are: Barland's Farm, 100–250 mm; St. Peter Port, 320–790 mm; Blackfriars, up to 736 mm.

### 5.6.1.2 DESIGN

The plank-keels of the 'Blackfriars' vessels project below their outer bottom planking, and some framing elements must have been in place *before* this planking was installed. Apart from an unquantified reference by Marsden (1994: 77) to enigmatic, plugged holes in some loose plank fragments saved from the bottom of Black-friars 1, there is no evidence in the three vessels that planking had been temporarily fastened together before it was fastened to the framing. (5.8.2.6), as has been suggested for other vessels in this tradition (5.6.2.1.4).

The hull shape of these three vessels was deter-mined by their framing: they were frame-based vessels and their builders were 'frame-orientated' (McGrail, 1995*b*: 141–2): possibly a better description would be that they were built 'framing-first'. This is not to say that a full framework or skeleton was erected before any planking was installed (as known in nineteenth-century Europe and America—see Greenhill, 1988) rather that, before any element of planking was added to the structure, some framework was there to define hull shape, and to which it could be fastened. In the ter-minology used by Basch (1972) these framing elements were *active*. Since the boat's five pairs of half-frames define hull shape from plank-keel to sheerline, at an early stage in her construction, before any planking had been added to the structure, the full shape of her hull was outlined by posts, plank-keel, and active floors and half-frames. There are no full-height half-frames in the two ships: thus the shape of their upper hulls had to come from active side timbers extending upwards from the planked lower hulls. Most, if not all, side tim-bers in the Barland's boat were passive, as were a few framing timbers at the bow and stern of all three ves-sels: their shape was determined by the plank-keel, a post, and the planking (or possibly ribbands). For an opposing view, however, see Arnold (1999) who con-

siders that these 'Blackfriars' vessels were built plank-first 'within a cradle': this seems an over-elaborate interpretation of the evidence (5.8.1.1).

How individual frames were designed is still a mat-ter of conjecture (Nayling and McGrail, forthcoming). There was probably an element of design 'by eye'; and 'rules of thumb'; simple ratios, and ribbands may also have been used, as they are when building Tamil tradi-tional frame-first vessels in southern India today (6.7.4.3). Units of measurement have been recognized in the frame spacing of the Barland's boat and the St. Peter Port ship. These were respectively, 0.55 m and 0.56 m: probably equivalent to the length of two human feet.

### 5.6.1.3 SEQUENCE OF BUILDING

The general sequence of building these three vessels can be deduced, although details vary and in some cases, are unclear. (McGrail and Roberts, 1999: 141, Marsden, 1994: fig. 70; Rule and Monaghan, 1993: fig. 14; Nayling and McGrail, forthcoming). Marsden's diagra-matic sequence omits some of the distinct steps. Builders' marks and the position of plank butts give some guidance, as do recent frame-first building prac-tices, but the overriding requirement is that some framework has to be in position before planking can be fastened to it.

The preferred sequence and the arguments for it are presented in detail in Nayling and McGrail (forthcom-ing). A summary of that sequence is:

- The elements of the plank-keel are forced together (by levers, ropes, and tourniquets ?), and selected floors are fastened to them.
- The two posts and the floors that lock them in posi-tion are fastened to the plank-keel.
- The remaining floors in the main body of the hull and, in the case of the boat, the half-frames, are fas-tened to the plank-keel. The framework is faired.
- The lower hull is planked, including the outer bot-tom planks and the bow and stern bottom planks.
- With side timbers being fastened to the lower strakes as necessary (to define the hull shape and to receive plank butts), the rest of the hull is planked, not from lowest strake to highest, but in an order which stabilizes the structure.
- The bow and stern frames and remaining side tim-

bers are fashioned by spiling from the planking, and are then fastened to the hull.

#### 5.6.1.4 PERFORMANCE

With a crew of three (Fig. 5.33) and at a draft of 0.34 m the Barland's boat could carry *c*.4.5 tonnes of cargo; at 0.52 m draft (60 per cent draft) she could carry *c*.6.5 tonnes (McGrail and Roberts, 1999). Marsden (1994: table 17) has estimated that, at 60 per cent; draft, Blackfriars 1 could carry 63.7 tonnes.

#### 5.6.2 INLAND WATERS

In this sub-group of first–third centuries AD boats are those from: Abbeville, Bevaix (Fig. 5.34), Druten, Kapel Avezaath, Pommeroeul 4 and 5, Mainz 1–5, Woerden, Yverdon 1 and 2, Zwammerdam 2, 4 and 6 (Fig. 5.35), Xanten 1 and 2, and a fragment from Avenches. They were excavated from the Sheldt/Maas/Rhine delta, from the lower and middle Rhine, and from Lake Neuchâtel in Switzerland. They are not as homogeneous as the 'Blackfriars' vessels, and it is more difficult to identify their common characteristics. Furthermore, some were excavated over one hundred years ago and constructional features were not recorded in detail, and some of the more recent finds have not yet been fully published. Whilst generally of this subgroup, the five Mainz finds have certain distinctive features and these boats are considered separately.

#### 5.6.2.1 NEUCHÂTEL/ZWAMMERDAM

The fifteen boats in this set may be code-named Neuchâtel/Zwammerdam. Most of these boats were originally 20–22 m in length, with two (Zwammerdam 4 and Kapel Avezaath) being *c*.35 m. Their L/B ratios are in the range *c*.6–8 : 1 and their L/D ratios are *c*.22–28 : 1. They are thus much longer in relation to both beam and depth than the three 'Blackfriars' vessels. They have little, if any, sheer; in plan they are generally rectangular, narrowing towards the ends (the Neuchâtel boats—Bevaix and Yverdon 1 and 2—are more curvaceous); and they have a near-rectangular transverse section. They are all thus of barge-like proportions and capacity.

These were flat-bottomed, keel-less boats without

Fig. 5.33. Reconstruction model of the Barland's Farm boat (Newport Museum, Gwent).

posts. Many of them had a mast-step well forward of amidships, some in floor timbers, others in a keelson: these were probably for towing masts, although a sail might be set in fair winds. Fragments of a poling walkway with ridges survived in Pommeroeul 4, and most of these boats were probably poled on occasions. Yverdon 2 had rowlocks and supports for thwarts and therefore could be rowed.

##### 5.6.2.1.1 *Bottom planking and transition strakes*

The bottom planking of these boats is generally aligned fore-and-aft; Bevaix (Fig. 5.34), Yverdon 1, Woerden, and Kapel Avezaath have diagonally laid or 'mosaic' planking, which may be repair work (Arnold, personel communication). As in the 'Blackfriars' vessels, this planking is generally not fastened together. There are, however, angled nails between some of the planks of Yverdon 2; this may also be the case with Pommeroeul 5 which has not yet been fully published. The planking is fastened to the framing by large iron nails (additionally, Zwammerdam 2 has some treenails) which are generally driven from *inboard* and

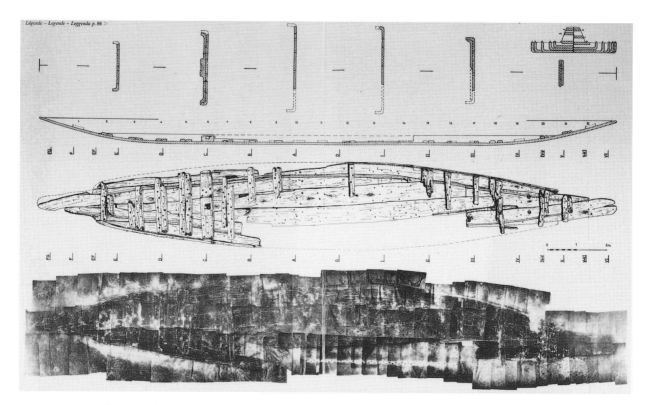

Fig. 5.34. Plans and vertical photograph of Bevaix boat 2 (photo: Béat Arnold).

Fig. 5.35. Vertical photograph of Zwammerdam 6 (photo: Maarten de Weerd).

clenched outboard by turning the tip through 180° although many of the nails in the Neuchâtel boats appear to be turned through only 90°. The bottom planking of the Neuchâtel and Pommeroeul boats has nails driven both ways. Typical nail lengths are 190–200 mm (Abbeville) and 60–80 mm (Druten).

Outboard of these bottom planks are transition strakes (*iles*; chine strakes) hewn internally and shaped externally from a half-log of oak to an L-shaped or rounded cross-section. Some transition strakes are in one piece, others are made in two or three sections scarfed together longitudinally in a horizontal lap. It has been suggested that logboats were hewn out and then split longitudinally to form such transition strakes: this is unlikely if only because of the difficulty of splitting precisely down the middle of the log. These were more likely hewn from half-logs: a tradition which extends back to the Bronze Age Ferriby boats (5.4.2.1).

The caulking differs in composition and possibly in

use from that in the seafaring craft. It consists of either rope or moss and rope and, according to Arnold, it is driven into the seams *after* the planking has been assembled and the plank edges chamfered. It is generally held in place by a longitudinal lath fastened along the seam outboard by many small nails (*c.*25–30 mm length) driven into one or other plank edge (Fig. 5.36).

### 5.6.2.1.2 *Framing*

The frames are generally closely spaced, L-shaped half-frames with the lower arm extending across the bottom of the boat. In many boats these frames are paired, one with its vertical arm to port, one to starboard; Pommeroeul 4 had at least one group of three. Adjacent frames are not fastened together. In Zwam-mer-dam 6 single half-frames alternately rise to port and starboard; Zwammerdam 2 is similar, but also has side timbers set into mortises in the lower end of each half-frame.

### 5.6.2.1.3 *Side strakes*

Pommeroeul 4 had no further side planking beyond the transition strake, but most boats had one or two strakes. Pommeroeul 5 had one overlapping strake, but fastening details are, as yet, unknown. The Neuchâtel boats had one flush-laid strake fastened to the framing

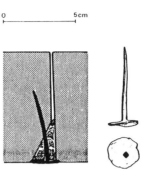

Fig. 5.36. Method of holding the caulking within the seams of Bevaix 1: moss, lath, nail (after Arnold, 1992: 87).

by large iron nails driven from inboard and clenched outboard by turning. Woerdan had two overlapping trakes—fastening method not yet published. Zwammerdam 2 and 4 each had one overlapping strake fastened to the framing by iron nails driven from inboard and possibly turned outboard: they were also fastened to the transition strake by angled nails. Zwammerdam 6 had two side strakes (Fig. 5.37): the lower one was flush laid and was fastened to the frames by turned nails driven from inboard; it was also fastened by angled spikes driven from inboard (and two mortise and tenon joints) to the upper edge of the transition strake. The second was an overlapping strake fastened to the framing by turned nails driven from inboard, and

Fig. 5.37. Interior of Zwammerdam 6 (photo: Maarten de Weerd).

also fastened to the lower side strake by turned nails driven from *out*-board. Inboard of this second strake is an inwale.

### 5.6.2.1.4 *Design*

As Arnold (1991) has pointed out, the initial shape of the Zwammerdam/Neuchâtel hulls is obtained by placing shaped planks of equal thickness alongside one another, and binding them together by some means to form the bottom. The starting line for the shape of the sides is determined by this shape, specifically the outer edge of each outer bottom plank. The initial design of these boats is thus 'bottom-based'. The (varying) angle at which the side planking lies to the bottom may then be determined either by making the cross-sectional shape of the transition strake conform to that of the rising arm of the framing ('framing-first'), or by making that rising arm conform to the shape in section of the transition strake ('plank-first').

In the Neuchâtel boats, transverse lines of holes mark the position of temporary battens or 'external moulds' which Arnold (1999) considers held the bottom planking and transition strakes together until after permanent framing had been inserted. That fastening nails were generally driven from frame to strake lends support to this hypothesis. The Neuchâtel boat-builders were plank-orientated in their approach to the 'design' of the sides of these boats, since the angle at which any further side strake lay would be determined by bevels worked along the upper edge of the transition strake if flush-laid; or by bevels along that strake's outer face, if overlapping.

In the Zwammerdam boats, and others of this type, the sequence of building is more difficult to establish from the information published. It seems, however, that the builder's approach was different from that of the Neuchâtel builder. There were evidently no temporary battens or 'external moulds' holding the bottom planking together, and therefore permanent framing must have been used from the start. Furthermore, the transition strakes were evidently fastened to the framing by spikes driven from outboard (de Weerd, 1988: fig. 54). The building sequence seems to have been : bottom planking; framing; transition strakes; side planking. The shape of the sides was controlled by the framing: the Zwammerdam builders (and probably other builders of this type of boat) were frame-ori-

entated in their approach to the 'design' of the sides.

The 'Neuchâtel/Zwammerdam' group of boats are difficult to analyse structurally; moreover, there is not a uniformly high standard of recording and publication. Some future detailed examination of those boats still surviving might throw light on these matters.

### 5.6.2.2 MAINZ BOATS

In 1981–2 the remains of five late fourth-century AD boats were excavated from a site near the River Rhine at Mainz (Hockman, 1982; 1997). These are light and slender oak river boats with a mast stepped forward of amidships. Four of them (nos. 1, 4, 7, and 9) are generally similar in size and shape: $c.22 \times 2.5 \times 0.94$ m with L/B ratio of $c.8.8$ and L/D ratio of $c.23$—these are similar to the ratios of the 'Neuchâtel/Zwammerdam' boats. Boat 3/5 ($c.14.75 \times 3.07$ m) is relatively broader with an L/B ratio of $c.4.8$.

All five boats differ from the 'Neuchâtel/ Zwammerdam' boats in that they have posts and a plank-keel, and their transverse sections are not box-like, but full near amidships with flared sides, tending towards V-shaped at the ends. In these aspects the Mainz boats have similarities with the 'Blackfriars' vessels. The Mainz craft, lacking any sheer, are clearly river boats, and Hockmann has described them as oared military boats (M1, 4, 7, and 9) and a government inspection sailing boat (M3/5).

The Mainz floors, spaced at $c.0.30$ m, are generally flat with rising ends, comparable with the Barland's Farm floors, and side timbers are butted at their ends. Floor and side timbers are not fastened together except for those in Mainz 3, which are nailed.

As in all other Romano-Celtic craft, the sawn-oak planking of the Mainz boats is not fastened together, but is fastened to the framing by iron nails driven from outboard and clenched inboard by turning: the few nails driven in the reverse direction may be ascribed to repairs. Towards the ends there are passive frames. Again, these features are comparable with 'Blackfriars' vessels.

The Mainz boats differ from the 'Blackfriars' vessels, in that they have transverse lines of plugged holes through their planking, some of which lie under framing timbers. In this they are similar to the Neuchâtel boats.

### 5.6.2.2.1 *Design*

Hockman (1997: 244) has interpreted the transverse lines of holes through the hull as showing that the planking was temporarily fastened to active moulds (rather than passive battens as suggested by Arnold, 1999) which were subsequently replaced by permanent framing. He has claimed that this meant that these boats were 'not built frame-first' but were 'mould first'. Whether 'frame-first' or 'mould first' the Mainz boatbuilders evidently did not use planking to get the hull shape, but were as much frame-orientated as the builders of the Barland's Farm boat. Moulds are not otherwise known at this date, either in north-west Europe or in the Mediterranean (4.15.1). If Hockman's hypothesis were correct the Mainz builders would have been centuries ahead of their time.

## 5.6.3 EARLY FRAME-FIRST BOATBUILDERS

Northern and southern European craftsmen were familiar with the use of a framework to control the shape of a hide boat from the late centuries BC, and probably from much earlier times (4.5.4, 4.15.1, 5.3.3). The earliest evidence for framing-first plank boats in Atlantic Europe, as argued above, is from the second century AD 'Blackfriars' vessels. The earliest Mediterranean evidence is from the seventh century AD (4.15.2). Some Roman tools and techniques were clearly used in the Romano-Celtic frame-first wrecks so far excavated, but the difference in date, as now understood, makes it unlikely that the idea of building planked vessels frame-first could have been transmitted from the Mediterranean to Atlantic Europe. Transfer of technology from Atlantic Europe to the Mediterranean is possible, but remains to be proved.

## 5.6.4 TURNED AND HOOKED NAILS

Hooked bronze nails were used in the Mediterranean to fasten framing to planking from 400 BC (4.9.4.6). Hooked, or sometimes just turned, iron nails were used in Romano-Celtic vessels to fasten planking to framing from the first century AD. Béat Arnold has pointed out that turned and hooked iron nails were used in assembling the beams of the second-century BC *murus gallicus* and, even earlier, during the Halstatt period before 500 BC, in the manufacture of cartwheels (Arnold, 1999*a*: 42, fig. 7; forthcoming; Drack, 1989). The central Mediterranean and north-west Atlantic Europe were connected by two overland routes from at least sixth-century BC Etruscan/Phocaean times (Cunliffe, 1988: 8–9, 19–23): up the Rhône valley to the Seine and Rhine valleys; up the River Po to the Rhine valley. Ideas as well as goods could have been carried along these routes in both directions. However, as with frame-first methods, it is not yet clear whether there was transfer of technology, and, if there was, which way it went.

## 5.6.5 PROPULSION AND STEERING

There is evidence for propulsion by oar on the Mainz boats, by pole on the Pommeroeul boats, and towing on the Zwammerdam boats. Masts steps were excavated on the three 'Blackfriars' vessels: these were well forward of amidships, a position which, for reasons of sail balance and windward performance, favours the use of a fore-and-aft sail such as a lug (McGrail and Roberts, 1999: 138–41). A mast is shown stepped in this position on the first-century AD Celtic monument from Blussus (Fig. 5.38). On the other hand, the first-century BC gold model from Broighter (5.3.3) in the north of Ireland (Fig. 5.12) has its mast stepped amidships, as is the mast of ships depicted on first-century AD coins of Cunobelin from Canterbury and Colchester (McGrail, 1990*b*: figs. 4.11 and 4.12). It may be that mast steps were moved forward and fore-and-aft sails used from the second century AD on seagoing vessels such as Blackfriars 1 (5.6.1.2) as an alternative to the earlier square sail.

The Mainz boats may have been steered by a Mediterranean-style pair of side rudders. Steering oars have been excavated at Zwammerdam, Lake Neuchâtel, and Bruges, associated, directly or indirectly, with Romano-Celtic boats; they are depicted on the Blussus monument and on a first-century AD altar to Nehellannia from Colijnsplaat in the Netherlands; and one was found with the Broighter model, as were model oars and poles (McGrail, 1998: fig. 12.2). The Cunobelin ships may have had a side rudder, but this is

Fig. 5.38. Boat on a first-century BC monument to Blussus (Mittelrheinisches Landesmuseum, Mainz).

far from certain. On balance, it seems that, when necessary, inland boats generally used a steering-oar; seagoing vessels may have used a steering-oar or a side rudder. Metal terminals for poles from the Roman period have been excavated in the Rhine region, and oars were found with the model boat from fifth-century BC Durrnberg (McGrail, 1998: 204–5; fig. 12.10).

### 5.6.6 CELTIC SEAFARING IN THE ROMAN PERIOD

The sixth-century BC *periplus* (sailing directions) incorporated by the fourth-century AD Avienus into his *Ora Maritima* (Hawkes, 1977; Murphy, 1977) tells us that the Celtic peoples of Brittany sailed to Ireland in two days

(5.3.3), and that Britain was sighted on this voyage. Pliny (*NH* 4. 104) writing in the first century AD, and quoting from an early third-century BC history by Timaeus, noted that Britons were involved in similar overseas trade. Caesar (*BG* 3. 13) and Strabo (4. 4. 1) of the first century BC/AD describe the boats of the Veneti people of south-west Brittany, in which they traded with Britain. The fact that Cunobelin of the Catuvellauni, from north of the River Thames, had sailing ships depicted on his first-century AD coinage (5.6.5) probably reflects important overseas trading voyages undertaken by his ships.

The Celts were clearly seafarers of some competence, able to deal with the hazards of the Atlantic coasts, channels, and archipelagos, and also take advantage of tidal flows which extended their voyages well inland. In addition to describing specific instances of Celtic seafaring, Classical authors mention Bay of Biscay, cross-Channel, and southern North Sea trade routes (as far north as the Rhine/Thames crossing) which were also probably undertaken by Celts, although this is not specifically said (Strabo, *Geog.* 4. 1. 14, 4. 2. 1, 4. 3. 3–4, 4. 4. 1, 4. 5. 1–2; Caesar, *BG.* 3. 8, 4. 21–36, 5. 2–23; Diodorus, 5. 21. 3, 5. 22. 22–4, 5. 38. 5; Pliny, *NH* 4. 101–2; McGrail, 1983*b*: fig. 4, table 1). The landing places at the ends of each of these routes may now be difficult to recognize since they could have been informal ones, in natural harbours or within estuaries, where boats took the ground on a falling tide, or were held off the foreshore at anchor, or made fast to a simple mooring post.

During the two-day voyage between Brittany and south-east Ireland, boats would be out of sight of land for a considerable time; as also they would be on the western cross-Channel route from Brittany to Cornwall. On the mid-Channel routes between Brittany/Normandy and Poole/Spithead (McGrail, 1983*b*: table 3) even in good visibility there would be a minimum of 10 nautical miles when land could not have been seen either to north or south; whilst on the Rhine/Thames route this distance would be 30–40 nautical miles, because of the relatively flat terrain on both coasts. The non-instrumental navigation and pilotage techniques that the Celts used on such crossings would have been generally similar to those used in the Mediterranean (4. 4. 6, 4. 9. 2. 1. 1) and, indeed, elsewhere. The Atlantic seamen would, however, have had to place greater emphasis on weather forecasting skills, and although celestial navigation was probably used as much as possible, it would have been limited in comparison with the Mediterranean because of greater and more frequent cloud cover. A further difference would have been that the Atlantic seaman needed a detailed knowledge of tides and tidal flows. The Celtic apprentice navigator/pilot thus had much to learn from his seniors, but stereotyped phrases and rules of thumb would have assisted his memory. Like many illiterate peoples, the Celts paid great attention to memory training for the transmission of learning and culture (McGrail, 1983*b*: 318–19) and Caesar (*BG* 6. 14) noted that the Gauls studied the motion of the stars and related topics, with particular emphasis on the moon. This learning could have been used to maintain reckoning when out of sight of land, and also to predict the tides (McGrail, 1995*a*: 273–6).

## 5.7
# Boats and Ships of the First Millennium AD

In the 1970s Crumlin-Pedersen (1978, 1997*a*: 28) advanced the hypothesis that some of the basic boat types used during the 'Iron Age' (say, fourth century BC–fifth century AD) formed the structural basis for the hulls of the main types of medieval ship: the Nordic ship, the 'cog', and the 'hulc'. This thesis has stood the test of time, although more emphasis than heretofore is now placed on the role of the Romano-Celtic tradition in that transformation. The early evidence for the three types of trading ship will be considered in this section.

In Neolithic times a limited range of tools, but a relatively wide range of woodworking techniques, were used to build rafts and boats (5.3). By Roman times the variety of tools had widened to become the kernel of the medieval shipbuilders' tool kit. Some of these tools, for example, the saw, were not widely used in first-millennium AD north-west Europe but, like some of the Iron Age boatbuilding techniques, they returned to prominence in later times.

A wide range of boatbuilding techniques was used in the Romano-Celtic tradition: some were built framing-first, some evidently plank-first; planking was fastened to the framing, or was edge-fastened together sometimes flush-laid and sometimes in an overlap; fastenings could be clenched iron nails, iron spikes, treenails, or wooden mortise and tenon; caulking was nailed within the seams. With the exception of mortise and tenon fastening, all these techniques were to be used again in medieval Atlantic Europe.

### 5.7.1 THE NORDIC TRADITION

#### 5.7.1.1 OVERLAPPING PLANKS

The overlapping planking of the Romano-Celtic Pommeroel 5, Woerdan, Zwammerdam 2 and 4 (5.6.2.1.3) is not the earliest known, although it is the earliest with a visible, full overlap. Two Danish logboats (Øgarde 3 and Verup 1) of the fourth and third millennium BC may have had washstrakes, possibly overlapping (5.3.1.1). Later examples of overlapping strakes presented a smooth surface, both inboard and outboard, and the fastenings were outside the lap. These include:

- the Dover and Ferriby 1 boats of the mid-second millennium BC—the second side strakes were lashed to the strake below in a half-lap (5.4.2.1, 5.4.4)
- the second side strake of the Brigg 'raft' (early first millennium BC) was sewn to the first strake in a bevelled lap (5.4.2.2);
- the planking of the Hjortspring boat, of 350–300 BC, was sewn together in a bevelled lap (5.4.6);
- the washstrakes of the Hasholme logboat (c.300 BC) were fastened to the foremost part of the hull in a half-lap by treenails locked by wooden cotter pins or keys (5.3.1.5).

During late-Roman times fully overlapping planking appeared in Scandinavia: the west Norwegian Valderøy and Halsnøy boats, probably third–fourth centuries AD, had overlapping planking sewn together outside the lap (5.4.7). The Swedish extended logboat from Bjorke of c.AD 320 is probably the earliest known example of a clinker washstrake; that is, the strake was not only overlapping but it was also fastened through the lap by iron nails which were clenched inboard by deforming the point over a rove (metal washer)–the type of caulking used is not known. In contradistinction to this apparent innovation, the Bjorke ribs, as in earlier boats, were lashed to cleats proud of the logboat base (5.4.7).

### 5.7.1.2 THE NYDAM BOATS

In 1863 three clinker-built boats were excavated from a former freshwater lake at Nydam on the east coast of Jutland, only c.6 miles from Hjortspring (Engelhardt, 1865; Shetelig, 1930; Åkerlund, 1963; Rieck, 1994; forthcoming; Crumlin-Pedersen, 1990). All three had clench-fastened, fully-overlapping planking, comparable with the Bjorke washstrake, and were clearly linked with earlier boats in that their framing was lashed to cleats integral with the planking; furthermore, the top strake of Nydam 3 was sewn or lashed to the one below. All three boats had been deposited, over a period of time, in the lake along with military equipment and

Fig. 5.39. Nydam 2 on display in the Schleswig-Holstein Landesmuseum.

other artefacts, possibly after a battle which the crews of these boats lost, though other explanations are possible. Boat 1 had been broken up so that only fragments of oak planking with cleats were recovered. Boat 3 was mainly of pine with a lime topstrake lashed or sewn on by lime bast rope—little of this boat survived the war between Prussia and Denmark. Although the bottom planking of Nydam 2 had been holed, it survived almost entirely and, after a chequered career, is now on display in the Archaeologisches Landesmuseum, Schleswig (Fig. 5.39). Recent re-examination by the Institute of Maritime Archaeology at Roskilde has shown that, during the past century, new parts were added; for example, none of the rowlocks are original. The surviving original parts consist of: the port side to the sheer; the starboard side to the fourth strake; bow and stern planking only up to the second strake; the whole of the forestem, but only the lowest part of the after stem. Very little of the original framing survives. Examination of the planking during dendrochronological research revealed scarfs in the planking that had previously escaped attention: planks within strakes were 8–12 m in length (Rieck, 1994) rather than the 18–21 m formerly attributed. Dendrochronological research has shown that the oaks used to build this boat were felled AD 310–20, and that she was deposited in Nydam lake in AD 340–50.

The forthcoming publication by the Roskilde Institute of Maritime Archaeology (Rieck, forthcoming) should provide a definitive description of Nydam 2's structure: until that is available, earlier publications must suffice. Nydam 2, a large, double-ended open boat, now measures, c.23.7 × 3.75 × 1.20 m, however, Åkerlund (1963) demonstrated that the planking had probably shrunk in breadth by 13–14 per cent and so the depth of the original hull would have been greater. All timber excavated was oak, the frames and posts being fashioned from naturally curved timbers with the pith present (Shetelig, 1930: figs. 8, 9). She has a plank-keel (m/s ratio of 0.33) of low T-shape form (Fig. 5.40) to which the stems are scarfed in a horizontal lap fastened by two vertical treenails. Her planking of five strakes each side is fastened together by iron nails driven through the lap and clenched inboard by deforming the tip over a rove; the ends of each strake are fastened within stem rabbets by iron nails which can be clenched inboard since the inboard face of each stem has been hollowed. The caulking within the plank laps

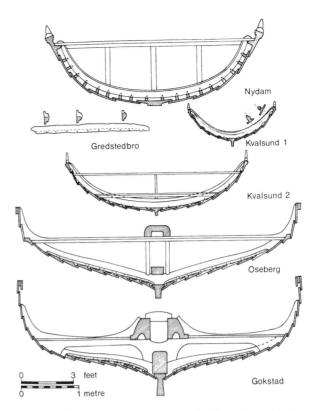

Fig. 5.40. Transverse sections, near amidships, of several Nordic vessels (after Bruce-Mitford, 1975: fig. 291).

has proved to be a 'textile soaked in a sticky fluid', probably tar or resin. The top strake is significantly thicker than the others and contributes towards the boat's longitudinal strength. The frames run from top strake to top strake at c.1 m intervals, and have a rounded inboard face and a narrower, squared face outboard (Fig. 5.40). They lie against small cleats which are proud of the planking (usually two cleats per strake), and are lashed to them through holes in both frame and cleat. Crossbeams, which also act as thwarts, are notched at their ends to take against the frame heads; the fillet on their under surface has mortises into which pillars (usually three) fit, thereby transmitting stress in the beam/thwarts to the frames. This arrangement of frames, pillars, and beams has affinities with the Hjortspring boat (5.4.6). Two oarsmen would have sat on each thwart, each man working a single oar against a curved thole timber lashed to the top strake. A withy grommet through a hole in each thole held oar to thole when trailing or when being used to back-water. There were probably fifteen oarsmen each side.

The present oar/rudder, which is not original, is difficult to match to the hull and the best fit is as a steering-oar yet it seems too short for this role. During fieldwork at Nydam in 1993, a 1.8 m pine side rudder, probably from Nydam 3, was excavated (Rieck, 1995: fig. 3) which suggests that Nydam 2 was also steered by side rudder rather than steering-oar: this rudder has a transverse tiller and a vertical handgrip with grooves for the helmsman's fingers.

These excavations have also shown that the Nydam boats had bottom boards held together by lime bast rope, and pole-shaped wooden mooring bitts with a carved head at the top. Pine timbers of a distinctive waisted shape, 1.04–1.57 m in length, with holes through their enlarged ends (Rieck and Jørgensen, 1997: fig. 3) found in and around boats 2 and 3 had formerly been interpreted as supports for a longitudinal bracing (Åkerlund, 1963: figs. 48,49), or possibly as parts of a fish weir or stake net system (McGrail, 1983a: 45). Similar timbers excavated during 1996 had toggle and rope through the holes, and other poles nearby had the same diameter as these holes: the excavator now suggests that these timbers were tent framing (Rieck and Jørgensen, 1997: 222).

Until the Roskilde reassessment of Nydam 2 is published, (especially the revised lines) it is not possible to be certain of this boat's performance. Basing his judgement on Åkerlund's (1963) reconstruction drawings, Crumlin-Pedersen (1990: 113) believes that she was seagoing, and possibly similar to the boats used by the migrating Jutes and Angles on their short-haul series of coastal voyages under oars in waters sheltered by the line of islands which formerly extended from Esbjerg in Jutland all the way to the entrance to the Channel, east of Calais.

### 5.7.1.3 SIXTH- AND SEVENTH-CENTURY VESSELS

The Nydam 2 boat was bigger and stronger than the Hjortspring boat, and further increases in size seem to have occurred during the seventh century AD. The earliest evidence for structural changes comes from two large frames dated c. AD 600 from Kongsgärde on the east coast of Jutland (Crumlin-Pedersen, 1997a: fig. 9.1.2). The ship from which they came must have been over 4 m broad amidships. These frames had been lashed to planking cleats, as in the Nydam boats, except

at the top strake where they were treenailed. Evidence also comes from Kvalsund in Sunmøre, Norway (Fig. 5.40) where a ship and a boat dated c. AD 690 ± 70 have been excavated (Christensen, 1996; Myhre, 1980); from fragments of a ship of c. AD 700 at Gretstedbro on the west coast of Jutland (Crumlin-Pedersen, 1997a: 289–92); and from three ship burials dated c. AD 630 at Sutton Hoo (Fig. 5.41) and Snape in Suffolk, England (Bruce-Mitford, 1974; 1975; Carver, forthcoming; Evans, 1994). These three East Anglian vessels survived only as a fragile impression of the planking in the sand of the burial trench, crossed by a number of sand casts of frames, and with the highly corroded remains of iron fastenings. The lines of Sutton Hoo 2 (the ship in

Fig. 5.41. Sutton Hoo 2 during excavation (British Museum).

Mound 1) were reconstructed from measurements noted and photographs taken during excavation in 1939 and re-excavation in 1965–7. It is unclear how the reconstructor allowed for the distortion, compression, and damage when these drawings were compiled: the overall shape of the lines may approximate to the hull of the original vessel, but some of the details are not beyond challenge. The reconstruction shows a vessel $c.27 \times 4.5 \times 1.5$ m with high rising ends, nine strakes each side, and twenty-six square-section frames. The number of oarsmen is uncertain, since no tholes were excavated in the midships region where the wooden grave chamber had been erected: if there had been tholes amidships there would have been a total of forty oarsmen, otherwise probably twenty-eight.

When evidence from these seventh-century finds is compared with that from Nydam it can be seen that many features are very similar, whilst others had changed over the centuries. These Nordic vessels of the fourth and seventh centuries AD were all built plank-first and had similar hull forms. They were double-ended with L/B ratios of $c.6:1$, L/D ratios of $c.18–20:1$, and high-rising ends. They had plank-keels (m/s 0.70), with the Kvalsund keels, of $c.$ AD 690, being significantly deeper than that of Sutton Hoo 2 (McGrail, 1998: table 8.1). Plank-keels were joined to rabbeted posts in a horizontal scarf fastened by treenails (Sutton Hoo 2 had been repaired by iron nails; Gretstedbro had iron nails). The deadrise of the garboards was moderate, ranging from 11° Nydam to 24° Gretstedbro. The split oak planking was thin (of the order of 25 mm generally but with thicker top strakes) and was fastened clinker-fashion by iron clench nails. Grown oak crooks were fashioned into frames which were fitted symmetrically about the centreline at $c.1$ m spacing. Bottom boards were probably fitted. These vessels were steered by a side rudder on the starboard quarter, and propelled by oars held to grown crook tholes by grommets: no evidence for sail was excavated. Oared plank vessels pictured on sixth-century Gotland stones (Crumlin-Pedersen, 1990: fig. 14.14) have an additional helmsman at the bow and it may be that the Sutton Hoo and Kvalsund vessels also had them.

The changes over the period of nearly 400 years are fewer but signpost the way ahead. In the seventh century tholes were spiked to the top strake rather than lashed. Planks became narrower and shorter, for exam-

ple, Nydam 2 planks ranged in length from 8–12 m, whereas the largest Sutton Hoo 2 plank was 5.45 m. This could mean that the tall oaks from which the early fourth-century Nydam planks were split were not available in the early seventh century. On the other hand, it could be that the builders of Sutton Hoo chose to use shorter planks so that they could more readily build the hull shape they wanted.

There were also changes in frame fastenings but these were not so uniform. Frames in the Kongsgärde vessel were generally lashed to cleats proud of the planking but treenailed to the top strake. The Sutton Hoo frames, on the other hand, appear to have been only treenailed, whilst the Gretstedbro vessel had treenails but not at every strake and not to the keel, and the top of each frame was fastened with a treenail or an iron nail. The frames of the larger Kvalsund vessel were lashed to the lower planking, and nailed and treenailed to the upper: those of the smaller Kvalsund were solely treenailed, unusually, through integral cleats. By and large, there was a move from lashed to treenailed frames.

### 5.7.1.3.1 *Sail in seventh-century northern Europe?*

Sail was probably used in the British and Irish archipelago from the sixth century BC (5.6.6), if not earlier. From the first century BC sail was certainly used off Brittany, and off Ireland (5.3.3, 5.5.4, 5.6.6), and Blackfriars 1, an indigenous British ship of the second century AD, had sail (5.6.1). In Scandinavia, and the Baltic generally, no direct evidence for sail has been found on any excavated vessel dated before the eighth century AD. However, ships, with an angular junction between bottom and stems, depicted on Gotland stones from the seventh century (Crumlin-Pedersen, 1990: fig. 14.18, 1997: fig. 5) have a square sail on a mast stepped near amidships. It has therefore sometimes been suggested that Sutton Hoo 2 and the larger Kvalsund vessel had a sail. Both Christensen (1996, 79–84) and Crumlin-Pedersen (1990: 111, 1997*b*: 188) have pointed out that the light, flexible early Nordic hulls were not suited to withstand sailing stresses. The rounded, almost semi-circular transverse sections of these vessels, their lack of a prominent keel and sharp ends, and their limited freeboard are better suited to rowing than sailing.

Furthermore, both Crumlin-Pedersen (1997*b*: 188–90) and Westerdahl (1995) have argued that there was little impetus in early Scandinavia (and presumably early Anglo-Saxon England) for change from oar to sail. Society was organized on a ship basis in units of a rowing crew, and all available men were needed both for coastal defence and for overseas raids. Even on peaceful voyages there was prestige for leaders in having many men with them, and there is no doubt that a rowing crew can give a greater impression of power and efficiency than the crew of a ship under sail. Economy of manpower was not needed, oared-ships could admirably fulfill the tasks required of them, and the introduction of sail would have involved significant structural alterations to ships. The Gotland stones depictions suggest that sail was used in the Baltic from the seventh century. However, Crumlin-Pedersen, Christensen, and Westerdahl all agree that on the vessels of this date so far excavated there is no evidence for sail.

Sail only became more attractive when there was royal control of havens and coastal waters, and specialized cargo ships could be used in safety to transport bulky cargoes. Westerdahl (1995) dates this transition to the eighth–tenth centuries. It was during this period, too, that sail had advantages on overseas settlement voyages, such as those to Iceland, and on overseas raiding voyages to Britain, Ireland, and Normandy. Thus was developed the sailing merchant ship which could be used also for settlement voyages, and the sailing warship—in the form of the galley—a sail-assisted, oared-vessel. Gotland stone carvings of the eighth–ninth centuries depict such ships (Crumlin-Pedersen, 1997b: fig. 6; Westerdahl, 1995: fig. 5). The late ninth-century voyages of Ohthere/Otar, along the northern coast of Norway and of Wulfstan in the Baltic, show that there was wide use of sail for overseas trade by this time (Lund, 1984). The ships they used would probably have been similar to the Norwegian Klåstad ship and the Swedish Äskekärr ship of the ninth/tenth century (Westerdahl, 1995).

A half-scale model of the Sutton Hoo 2 ship has been built with mast and sail, and trials undertaken (Gifford, 1995, 1996). The reconstructors argue for sail on three main grounds:

(a) Sutton Hoo 2 has a midship section and waterline shape generally associated with sailing vessels. This view may be contrasted with those of Christensen, Westerdahl, and Crumlin-Pedersen quoted above.

(b) Sutton Hoo 2 is so suited to sailing that it is difficult to believe that she was not intended for that purpose. Such an argument is unsound and does not constitute proof.

(c) Extra framing on the quarter, projection of the posts beyond the planking, and closely spaced (sic) framing are all more appropriate to a sailing than an oared-vessel. The Nydam oared-boats described above provide a counter argument.

The Giffords make the fair point that speeds achieved by a scale model may be converted to speeds achievable by a similar full-size boat. However, scale models can mislead on other aspects of performance. Since the crew remain full-size, rowing, launching, recovering, loading and unloading the boat, and handling the sailing rig can all be affected by such disparities of scale (McGrail, 1997c: 314–15). Furthermore, the structural and sailing properties of a vessel change when it is scaled down as it becomes considerably stiffer (Coates, 1997: 148). Thus this experiment may be criticized on two main grounds: the arguments that Sutton Hoo 2 had sail are inadequate; and the consequences of a reduction in scale need to be considered before conclusions are drawn from such trials.

### 5.7.1.4 THE NINTH AND TENTH CENTURIES AD

#### 5.7.1.4.1 Scandinavia

During this period the main evidence comes from ships in three Norwegian burial mounds, and from two late nineteenth-/early twentieth-century excavations at Äskekärr near Göteborg in Sweden, and from Klåstad in the vicinity of Kaupang, Norway (Table 5.1). The Oseberg ship was built c.815–20 and buried c.834 (Shetelig, 1917; Bonde, 1994; Christensen, 1997); Gokstad was built c.895 and buried c.900–5 (Nicolaysen, 1882), and Tune c.910 and 910–20 (Shetelig, 1917). The Äskekärr ship was built c.955–60 (Humbla, 1934; Westerdahl, 1982; Crumlin-Pedersen, 1985, 1997a: 292–3). Unlike the others, the Klåstad ship has not been dendro-dated, but a radiocarbon date suggests she was built in the ninth or even the tenth century (Christensen, 1974; Christensen and Leiro, 1976; Crumlin-Pedersen, 1985; 1997a: 292–3).

Some authors have suggested that the Oseberg ship

was merely a 'royal yacht' for sailing inshore in fair weather. Christensen (1996; 1997) prefers to see all three burial ships as typical, non-specialized, Early Viking Age ships used for war, trade, or prestige as occasion arose. He sees the structural differences between the Oseberg ship, and the Gokstad and Tune ships as not due to different functions but to improvements incorporated from experience gained on North Sea voyages during the ninth century.

### 5.7.1.4.1.1 *Oseberg*

The Oseberg ship was excavated in 1904 and, since so much of the ship had survived, confidence can be placed in her reconstruction, as now displayed (Fig. 5.42), although some timber and fastenings are twentieth century. She measures 22 × 5.2 × 1.6 m, with L/B ratio of 4.2:1 and L/D of 13.75:1, and was relatively broad in the beam with fine ends (Fig. 5.40). Like the other ships, she was built of oak. Her keel is T-shaped

Fig. 5.42. The stern of the restored Oseberg ship (photo: S. McGrail).

and is joined to the high, curving stems (via a transition timber at the stern) in a vertical scarf.

There are twelve, relatively thin, strakes each side, fastened together in standard clinker style, i.e. as in Nydam 2. Before the planks were brought together a caulking of tarred animal hair was inserted between them. Scarfs within strakes were similarly fastened. The strake ends were fastened into stem rabbets by nails driven alternately from port and starboard and clenched on the opposite side. The tenth strakes, transition strakes between bottom and sides, have an inverted-L cross-section, similar in form to the top strake of Nydam 2: such strakes, near the waterline and of substantial scantlings, were later known as *meginhufr*, the strong strake. The eleventh and twelfth strakes were near vertical, and the twelfth strake, thicker than the others, was pierced by fifteen oar ports.

The naturally grown floor timbers spaced at *c.*1 m and symmetrical about the centreline, are not fastened to the keel but are lashed to cleats on the first eight strakes with baleen strips, and their upper ends are nailed to low cleats on the ninth strake. In the ends there are deeper frames, almost bulkheads. Across the heads of each floor, at tenth strake level, lie crossbeams which are rabbeted to take bottom boards. The eleventh and twelfth strakes are supported by some side timbers and by natural knees fastened by nails and treenails to beam and strake.

Extra strong framing on the starboard quarter supported a side rudder (Fig. 5.42) which was held to this frame by a flexible withy rope and, higher up, by a plaited leather band.

The mast step is in a short keelson which is near amidships and spans two floors; above it is a longer mast partner which spans four beams, with an opening aft through which the mast was stepped. The only other sailing fittings that were excavated were a parrel, and some rigging cleats on the upper strakes. Near-contemporary depictions of ships indicate that Oseberg would have had a square sail and that the minimum rigging would have been a forestay and shrouds to the mast, and possibly a bowline to the luff of the sail. A full-scale reconstruction built in 1987 was fitted with a 100 m2 sail, subsequently reduced to 90 m2: she sailed well but proved unstable at 10 knots with a 10° heel and was swamped by the bow wave (Christensen, 1997).

### 5.7.1.4.1.2 *Changes between the sixth/seventh centuries and the early ninth century AD*

The principal changes arose from the adoption of propulsion by sail as well as by oar (Table 5.1). The midships section became more V-shaped than rounded; the keel protruded more, and was more foil-shaped (d/b = 1.27 as against *c.*0.80); and the garboard strakes had a greater deadrise (31° against *c.*16°). The relative depth of hull also increased from a L/D of 18–20 : 1 to 13.75 : 1; and the relative breadth increased from a L/B of *c.*6 : 1 to 4.2 : 1. These two changes gave the extra stability and freeboard required when under sail rather than oars. Increased freeboard led to a change from

**Table 5.1** Hull data of selected fourth–tenth-century Nordic vessels

| Vessel | Approx. date | Overall, L × B × D (m) | L/B | L/D | B/D | Keel, d/b | Garboard deadrise | Average frame spacing (m) | Oars |
|---|---|---|---|---|---|---|---|---|---|
| Nydam 2 | 310–320 | 23.7 × 3.75 × 1.2 | 6.3 | 19.7 | 3.1 | 0.14 | 11° | 1.00–1.10 | 2 × 15 |
| Sutton Hoo 2 | 630 | 27 × 4.5 × 1.5 | 6.0 | 18.0 | 3.0 | 0.35 | 13° | 0.91 | 2 × 14, or 2 × 20 |
| Kvalsund 1 | 700 | 9.6 × 1.5 × 0.5 | 6.4 | 19.2 | 3.0 | 1.25 | 13° | 1.05 | |
| Kvalsund 2 | 700 | 18 × 3.2 × 0.8 | 5.6 | 22.5 | 4.0 | 1.80 | 20° | 1.30 | |
| Oseberg | 815–820 | 22 × 5.2 × 1.6 | 4.2 | 13.75 | 3.3 | 1.27 | 31° | 1.00–1.10 | 2 × 15 |
| Gokstad 1 | 895 | 24 × 5.2 × 2.2 | 4.6 | 10.9 | 2.6 | 2.40 | 28° | 0.90–1.05 | 2 × 16 |
| Tune | 910 | 20 × 4.5 × 1.3 | 4.4 | 15.4 | 3.5 | 1.80 | 39° | 1.00 | |
| Klåstad | 800–1000 | 21 × 4.8 × 1.7 | 4.4 | 12.4 | 2.8 | 1.33 | 40° | | |
| Äskekärr | 955–960 | 15.8 × 4.5 × 1.9 | 3.5 | 8.3 | 2.4 | 1.10 | 31° | | |

*Note*: Keel (d/b) is derived from the depth and average breadth of the keel protruding below the planking.

*Sources*: Shetelig and Johannessen, 1929; McGrail, 1998: tables 8.1, 11.4, 11.5.

Fig. 5.43. The bows of the restored Gokstad ship (photo: S. McGrail).

rowlocks above the sheerstrake to oar ports through that strake, and the crossbeams were relatively lower at bottom board level, and could not be used as thwarts: it is assumed that seamen's chests were used by the oarsmen and trials have shown that these are at about the right height.

Structural changes include the introduction of a short keelson as a mast step timber, and a mast partner at crossbeam height. The keel/post scarf changed from a horizontal to a vertical one, as the keel changed from a plank-on-face plank-keel to a plank-on-edge keel: the scarf remained short, with a gradient of c.50 per cent. The Oseberg thicker strake near the waterline distributed sailing stresses, transmitted through the mast partner, beams, and knees, around the hull. The unusual cross-section of this strake (McGrail, 1998: fig. 8.9.4) marks an obvious discontinuity in the hull's transverse section at the transition between bottom and sides: possibly, this may have been an attempt to dampen rolling motion in a beam sea.

### 5.7.1.4.1.3 *Changes during the ninth century* AD

The Tune and Gokstad ships were built within fifteen years of one another, about one hundred years after the Oseberg ship. All three vessels were of similar size (for example, Gokstad measured 24 × 5.2 × 2.2 m) and, in general terms, the distinctive hull form (Fig. 5.43) and structure changed little over the century separating Tune and Gokstad from Oseberg. The light flexible hulls were shell built with cleft oak planks fastened in clinker fashion; the elements of the framing were unchanged and the frame spacing remained at *c*.1 m; the lower frames were lashed to cleats, the upper treenailed; the keel/post scarf remained relatively short; chests had to be used by the oarsmen; the elements of the mast support system remained unchanged; and the L/B ratio was virtually the same; thicker planking was used at the waterline and at the sheer in all three vessels. There were, however, significant changes in detail and much of this appears to be aimed at improving performance under sail.

The later ships have a more V-shaped lower hull in transverse section: the keel is more foil-shaped (d/b = 2.4 and 1.8), and the garboards are steeper (28° and 39°). The *meginhufr* are now more wedge-shaped in section (McGrail, 1998: figs. 8.9.5 and 8.9.3), leading to a smoother transition between bottom and sides, and the above-water strakes seem to be part of the hull rather than an after-thought. With sixteen strakes and a L/D ratio of 10.9 : 1, the Gokstad ship had greater freeboard than Oseberg, having two strakes above the oar port strake (Fig. 5.40): the oar ports had lids. Tune survived less well than Gokstad, and it seems likely that, originally, she had more than the ten strakes excavated; her surviving upper strakes flare outwards strongly, increasing her stability when heeled under sail.

The Gokstad mast was stepped nearer amidships than in Oseberg, leading to a better balance between hull and rig. The mast support system was stronger, the keelson (now braced by knees to the floors) spanning four frames in Gokstad and three in Tune, compared with only two in Oseberg; and the Gokstad mast partner, with knees to the beams, spans five frames, one more than that in Oseberg. In longitudinal profile, Gokstad does not have the exaggerated sheer at the

ends of Oseberg, thereby reducing hull windage and leeway.

Other ninth-century changes include:

- ends of planks were fastened into the stem rabbets by spikes rather than by clenched nails, and stealer planks were used to ensure sufficient space on the stems for strake fastenings;
- there were transition timbers at both ends of the keel;
- the floor timbers were not fastened to the first strakes (nor the keel);
- lashings were of birch or spruce roots;
- the upper two strakes were supported by side timbers at alternate stations;
- stations for sixteen oarsmen each side rather than fifteen;
- Gokstad had three pairs of rigging cleats aft, and, just forward of the mast, *beitiass* blocks supported by knees were treenailed to the planking on each side: sockets in the upper face of these blocks were for the heel of the tacking boom which kept the weather edge (luff) of the sail taut.

### 5.7.1.4.1.4 *Early cargo ships?*

The ninth-/tenth-century Klåstad ship is generally similar in shape and structure (Fig. 5.44) to the ships dis-

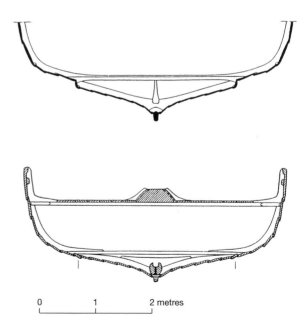

Fig. 5.44. Transverse sections of the Klåstad (*upper*) and Åske-kårr ships (after Crumlin-Pedersen, 1997a: fig. c3.8).

cussed above, but with her S-shaped *meginhufr* has the marked discontinuity in transverse section that is a feature of Oseberg, albeit relatively lower in the hull. Unlike Oseberg, however, her framing is not lashed to planking cleats, but is fastened by treenails, in the underwater hull to alternate strakes, but to each strake above the waterline. Her reconstructed dimensions are 21 × 4.8 × 1.7 m with L/B = 4.4 and L/D = 12.4 : 1. With a protruding keel ratio (d/b) of 1.33 and a garboard angle of 40°, she had a sharp lower hull suitable for sail.

This ship was found to be carrying whetstone blanks on a dunnage of hazel sticks and for this reason, the excavator considers she may have been a specialized merchant ship. Although Klåstad is marginally less broad in relation to length than Oseberg, her hull is deeper in relation to both length and breadth (Table 5.1). Her general proportions are slightly different from those of Oseberg, and approach those of Gokstad. Rather than a specialized cargo carrier, it may be that she was one of the non-specialized ninth century ships visualized by Christensen (1996, 1997) which was being used for trade on her final voyage.

The tenth century Äskekärr ship (Fig. 5.44), on the other hand, with reconstructed dimensions of 15.8 × 4.5 × 1.9, has L/B ratio of 3.5 : 1 and L/D ratio of *c*.8 : 1. Thus she is relatively broader and deeper than the ninth-century ships, and, as she has more of a rectangular transverse section (high block coefficient) and thus a greater volume of hold (Crumlin-Pedersen, 1997a: fig. C3.8.3), she may well have been a specialized cargo ship. This ship has an S-shaped *meginhufr* but it is not as pronounced as that of Klåstad and therefore there is no abrupt change in hull curvature. With a garboard angle of 31° and a projecting keel (d/b) ratio of *c*.1.1, she has a somewhat less pronounced V-shaped lower hull than has the Gokstad ship.

Structurally there is a significant innovation in the Äskekärr ship as reconstructed by both Leiro and by Åkerlund: a second level of crossbeams is positioned at the twelfth (out of thirteen) strake, with standing knees fastened to it and to the top strake: this thwartship strengthening further enhances her potential for cargo carrying. Äskekärr's framing—a lower crossbeam across the ends of a floor timber braced by standing knees to the planking; and a higher crossbeam (at certain stations) also braced by standing knees—seems to have been a step on the way to a pattern of crossbeams at three levels of the later Viking Age (5.8.1.3.2).

### 5.7.1.4.1.5 *Early warships?*

Two burials, one at Hedeby dated late ninth century (Crumlin-Pedersen, 1997a: 252–4) and one at Ladby, Funen in Denmark of mid-tenth century (Thorvildsen, 1957; Sørensen, 1999), may have been specialized warships. Both graves had been heavily disturbed and were excavated at an early date (1908 and 1934), thus there is only limited information on hull structure. The Hedeby ship measured *c*.17–20 × 2.7–3.5 m (L/B 4.8–7.4 : 1) and probably had nine strakes. The keelson spanned four floor timbers and the frame spacing was *c*.0.80 m. The Ladby ship measured 21.5 × 3.2 × 1 m with a L/B of 6.7 : 1 and L/D of 21.5 : 1. She had a mast stepped near amidships with shrouds fastened to four rings in each top strake. There were probably fifteen oars each side. The floor timbers were spaced at *c*.0.91 m and were nailed at their upper ends to the fourth and third strakes, the former appears to have been a *meginhufr*. The frames were lashed to cleats on the lower strakes.

### 5.7.1.4.2 *Southern Baltic*

Boats, and parts of boats, of similar general form and structure to the early-medieval Scandinavian vessels discussed above, have been excavated along the southern coast of the Baltic, from the Jutland peninsula in the west as far east as the lands beyond the River Vistula/Wista (Smolarek, 1994; Litwin, 1997; Crumlin-Pedersen, 1969; 1997a: 20–1, 96–9). Some of these boats (for example those from Mechlinki, Frombork, and Bagert) are fastened with iron nails and a caulking of animal hair—as generally in Scandinavia at this time—but others have small, headed, and wedged treenails and a moss caulking (Fig. 5.45): for example, the boats

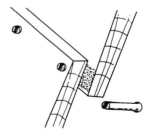

Fig. 5.45. Clinker planking with moss caulking and treenail fastening (after Crumlin-Pederson, 1988: fig. 21).

Gdańsk-Ohra 1, 2, and 3; Charbrow Ralswick 2.4 and Walin; and Fibrødre on the Danish island of Falster (Madsen, 1991). Different views have been put forward about the origins of this latter group of boats but the most reasonable interpretation is that they are an adaptation of an existing Nordic technique (as evidenced primarily in Scandinavia) by a seventh-century people (Western Slavs?) with limited access to iron, and who preferred to use moss rather than animal hair (Crumlin-Pedersen, 1997a: 21). Several of the excavated boats built in this 'Slavic' variant of the Nordic tradition have masts stepped in a floor timber rather than in a keelson, but it is not yet clear whether this is a characteristic of this sub-group or whether it reflects the small size of the vessels excavated to date.

Treenail plank fastenings have also been found in medieval Scandinavian boats where the principal technique was clench nail fastening: these include Skuldelev 1 and 5, Schuby, Kalmar 1, and Sjøvollen (Crumlin-Pedersen, 1981; Christensen, 1968b: 140). The late tenth-century Hedeby 2 also had some treenail plank fastenings (Crumlin-Pedersen, 1997a: 96–8): her lower strakes of oak were fastened with iron nails clenched in the Nordic fashion; whilst the upper strakes of beech and pine were fastened with juniper treenails of c.10 mm diameter, wedged with oak, and spaced 60–70 mm apart. There would thus seem to have been an intermingling of fastening techniques in the western Baltic region during the seventh to eleventh centuries.

### 5.7.1.4.3 Southern North Sea region

#### 5.7.1.4.3.1 Treenail-fastened clinker planking

Treenailed-fastened clinker planking has also been excavated in south-eastern England from sites dating from the eighth to the tenth centuries (Marsden, 1994: 141–54; 170–4; Goodburn, 1987, 1994; Milne and Goodburn, 1990: 635). Reused, moss-caulked, oak planking, dated to 920–55 from New Fresh Wharf was fastened by 15 mm diameter willow/poplar treenails with oak wedges inboard. Fragments of clinker planking from Billingsgate dated to after 970 were also treenail fastened, as were late-Saxon fragments from the Thames Exchange site (which had moss caulking) and fragments from Vintners Place and Bull Wharf. These five sites are in London, and the fact that the New Fresh Wharf and Billingsgate timbers best match the master

oak chronology from south-east England suggests that they were locally built (although Tyers, 1994: 206, states this must be tentative). A small fragment of planking, possibly of c.800, from Medmerry foreshore north-west of Selsey Bill, Sussex, also appear to have been treenail fastened.

The closest parallels in time and space for treenail-fastened, moss-caulked clinker planking are the twelfth-century Utrecht boat 1 (Vlek, 1987), and the possibly eleventh-century Antwerp boat 7 (Ellmers, 1972) both of which are extended logboats (McGrail, 1988a: 137). Crumlin-Pedersen (1997a: 21–2), has raised the possibility that this technique may have been transmitted to southern England during the sixth/seventh centuries by groups migrating from the southern Baltic coast. It should be noted, however, that the Hasholme logboat of c.300 BC (Fig. 5.8) had overlapping washstrakes fastened by treenails locked by wooden cotters or keys. It may be that the early medieval English use of treenail fastenings had its origins in the Iron Age. Another possibility is that Slav ships sailed from the Baltic to the River Thames during the eighth–tenth centuries and the technique was copied locally, although Marsden (1994: 174) has emphasized the lack of evidence for such contacts during the Saxon period.

#### 5.7.1.4.3.2 The Graveney boat

The Graveney boat (originally, c.13.5 × 4 × 1 m) was excavated from a former tidal creek of the River Thames, east of Faversham, Kent, in 1970 (Fenwick, 1978, 1997; McKee, 1978; Fletcher, 1984): about two-thirds of her original length, and about half the planking was recovered (Fig. 5.46). It has been claimed that she is 'recognised as belonging to a distinct non-Scandinavian tradition' (Fenwick, 1997). Goodburn (1986, 1994) has argued further that there was a distinctive tradition in southern England from the ninth to the fourteenth centuries, of which Graveney was an early member, which can be distinguished from the generality of the Nordic tradition. This boat is built plank-first with overlapping planking fastened clinker fashion, and tarred animal hair caulking. Furthermore, she has cleft oak planking and a framing of oak crooks which is fastened to the planking by willow-headed treenails with oak wedges. She was probably double-ended and steered by a side rudder, and there is a possibility that she had a square sail on a mast stepped near amidships. These are some of the primary characteristics of the

Fig. 5.46.  The Graveney boat during excavation (National Maritime Museum, Greenwich).

Nordic tradition, the origin of which seems to lie in late prehistoric and early medieval Scandinavia with a possible input from the Rhine delta region (5.7, 5.7.1.1).

Graveney features which differ from those in near-contemporary vessels, such as Gokstad, in the mainstream Nordic tradition, include:

*Form*. She has a much fuller transverse section which, because her plank-keel protrudes but little, is almost flat-bottomed out to the third strakes rather than a V-shaped lower hull. She has raking, overhanging ends in elevation, with an angular forefoot rather than rising, more nearly-vertical ends blending into the keel-line in a continuous curve. She is relatively broader (L/B 3.4 : 1) and has a less deep hull (L/D 13.5 : 1).

*Structure*. For her size, her floor timbers are relatively massive (m = *c*.200 mm, s = *c*.110 mm), and they are much closer together (*c*.0.52 m) than those of Gokstad (*c*.1.00 m). The floors are not symmetrical about the centreline, but are L-shaped half-frames alternately port and starboard, with a side timber scarfed to one end to make a composite frame from sheer to sheer. There are no knees but there are longitudinal stringers set into the frames towards their upper ends.

Her raking post has a prolonged horizontal part which is joined to a plank-keel in a horizontal, rather than a vertical, scarf. There are clenching grooves worked in the inner face of the post so that nails can be clenched rather than the post being hollowed or stepped; the strake ends are hooked to allow more nails to be used rather than the use of stealers.

The plank-fastening nails are driven through treenails inserted in holes through the laps. Graveney does not have the distinctive *meginhufr* of Gokstad, rather two binding strakes which are somewhat thicker than the rest.

Some of these differences may be considered variants within a polythetic group: clenching grooves; hooked strake ends; possibly the binding strakes. Other differences may be explained by the Graveney boat having a specialized function (transporting heavy loads) in a specialized operating environment (tidal estuary with beach landing places): full form; flattish bottom; broader, shallower hull; plank-keel with horizontal scarf; angular forefoot; heavy, closely spaced frames.

This leaves three features unexplained:

- raking posts with a prolonged horizontal element;
- asymmetric half-frames with side timbers scarfed to make composite frames; stringers; no knees;
- plank-fastening nails driven through treenails

The third characteristic was known in southern England before the ninth century. Articulated oak clinker planking, reused as burial bier or lid in graves at Caistor-on-Sea dated to 720–820, had clenched nails driven through hazel treenails (Rodwell, 1993); and late-Saxon clinker planking reused in a waterfront site at Thames Exchange, London, had similar nails driven through alder treenails (Milne and Goodburn, 1990: 633); planking with clench nails through treenails has also been excavated from Vintner's Place and Bull Wharf in London (Goodburn, 1994). Clinker planking is also known from seventh-century East Anglia, at Sutton Hoo and Snape (5.7.1.3), but as these three vessels survived only as fragile impressions in burial mounds, it cannot be known whether their clench nails were

also driven through treenails. In the Classical Mediterranean (and in the County Hall ship) nails fastening framing to planking were driven through treenails (4.12.1, 5.5.1) as were the nails fastening planking to framing in some vessels of the Romano-Celtic tradition (5.6). In both these cases, however, the nails were clenched by hooking rather than by deformation of the point.

The Barland's Farm Romano-Celtic boat of similar size to the Graveney boat, had asymmetric half-frames from one sheer to the opposite bilge, but in pairs, and not joined to other timbers. And this boat and the two Romano-Celtic ships, St. Peter Port 1 and Blackfriars 1, had raking posts with a prolonged horizontal element (5.6.1).

Future boat finds from the Rhine / Thames and Severn regions of the first millennium AD could well throw considerable light on how the Graveney boat is related to the north-west and northern European traditions of boatbuilding as now understood. She was clearly a boat designed for a specific task in coastal and estuarine waters. Some of her features are similar to corresponding features in the seagoing and estuary craft of the Romano-Celtic tradition, but this is not a direct, one-to-one, relationship, and she certainly does not have the distinctive Romano-Celtic characteristic of being built frame-first. On balance, the Graveney boat appears to be derived from a plank-first iron-fastened, clinker, cleft-oak tradition (i.e. Nordic), but having some affinities with the post-Roman version (if such existed) of the Romano-Celtic tradition.

### 5.7.1.4.3.3 *Romano-Celtic techniques in the Early Middle Ages?*

Twenty-five years ago, McKee (1976: fig. 4) suggested that there were 'heavy' and 'light' traditions of framing in the boats and ships of post-Roman north-west Europe. He was able to quote several examples of his 'light' tradition from Nydam to Kalmar 1, all of them Nordic vessels. There were fewer examples of the 'heavy' tradition: it began with the Graveney boat, and the next example was *Grace Dieu* of *c*.1400. Relatively heavy framing, but in a frame-first orientation, can, in fact, be traced back to Caesar's description of the Veneti seagoing craft in the first century BC, and to the Romano-Celtic tradition of the early centuries AD, as Arnold (1999a: 42) has noted (5.6). It remains to be seen whether the Romano-Celtic style of building, or aspects of it, lived on in north-west Europe through the Migration Age when there were significant changes in dominant culture and technology: the fifth–eighth-centuries wreck Port Berteau 2, from the River Charente near the town of Saintes, may be such an example (Rieth *et al.*, 1996; Rieth, forthcoming). Some future find of an early frame-first, Romano-Celtic style of boat in Ireland could resolve the enigma posed by McCaughan (1988, 1991) that a seemingly indigenous tradition of frame-first plank boats survived into the mid-nineteenth century on the remote and culturally retentive Irish western seaboard, whilst clinker-built, plank-first boats were built only on the innovative north-east coast (McCaughan, 1988: map 2).

Another characteristic feature of Romano-Celtic vessels, the use of turned or hooked iron nails (Fig. 5.27), appears again in the medieval ship type known as a 'cog' (5.8.2), but here as a clinker plank fastening, rather than a plank to frame fastening. An eleventh-century garboard strake from Fennings Wharf, London (Marsden, 1994: 156–8, 174) was fastened to its keel by turned (possibly hooked) nails—future finds with such fastenings may help to clarify the possible linkage between Romano-Celtic techniques and medieval shipbuilding methods.

## 5.7.2 OTHER TRADITIONS

The author of the Anglo-Saxon Chronicle, known as Parker Ā, recorded for the year 897 that King Alfred ordered warships to be built which were 'neither after the Frisian design, nor after the Danish' (Garmonsway, 1967: 90). The 'Danish' warships may be equated with the Nordic tradition discussed above; the 'Frisian' tradition is more difficult to identify. The Frisians appear in the historical and archaeological record from the sixth century AD, living on the coast between the Elbe and the Rhine delta and on the chain of islands to the west and to the north as far as Syldt (McGrail, 1990*a*: 85–97; Crumlin-Pedersen, 1997*a*: fig. 2.6). They were notable for their seafaring abilities and as international traders, and by the ninth century not only traded between the Rhine and Thames but also played a direct role in Anglo-Saxon maritime affairs (Stenton, 1967: 219; Gordon, 1949: 343; Stevenson, 1959: 60). In this cen-

tury also, and probably from earlier times, the North Sea was known as the 'Frisian' Sea (Lebecq, 1990: 88). Linking together documentary and iconographic sources, and using research by earlier authors (e.g. Crumlin-Pedersen, 1965), Ellmers (1990) has suggested that the Frisians used two different kinds of overseas trading ships: the 'cog' on coastal voyages to the Baltic, and the 'hulc' across the sea to Britain.

### 5.7.2.1 THE 'PROTO-HULC'?

The problem of linking documented names of ship types with depictions of vessels is considered below (5.8.3.1): here it suffices to note that among the early ninth-century representations thought to be hulcs are:

- Quentovic coins issued by Charlemagne (Vlek, 1987: fig. 3.2.1–3.2.2);
- Dorestad coins issued by Louis the Pious (Vlek, 1987: fig. 3.2.3);
- a coin from Norfolk issued by Athelstan I of East Anglia (Fenwick, 1983: fig. 1).

The main features of these double-ended, single-masted ships appears to be that they are curved in longitudinal profile, and their planking ends, not on stems, but on a near-horizontal plane above the presumed waterline.

Goodburn (1994; forthcoming) has suggested that there are parallels between the features of some articulated planking from Bull Wharf, London, dated to 966–90, and two twelfth-century boats excavated from Utrecht in the Netherlands (Vlek, 1987). The London clinker planking is fastened together by headed and wedged treenails, and has a moss caulking, held in position by iron staples (*sintel*) over a lath, within a V-shaped groove worked in the *in*board, upper edge of the lower plank (Goodburn, 1994: fig. 6). Goodburn finds support for his contention that the Bull Wharf timbers came from a Netherlands' vessel, in a dendrochronological analysis which showed that these timbers match both the eastern England and the north German oak chronologies. He extends his hypothesis to conclude that these timbers are the remains of an early 'hulc' (Goodburn, forthcoming). The suggestion that this form of planking is representative of the tenth-century Rhine delta region (not to mention a 'hulc') must await the publication of this find and of the dendro report.

## 5.7.2.2 THE 'PROTO-COG'?

Crumlin-Pedersen (1965) has suggested that ships depicted on ninth-century coins issued at Haithabu/Hedeby in the western Baltic (Lebecq, 1990: fig. 11.3.2) may represent early versions of the medieval cog. Like the contemporary Nordic ship and the 'proto-hulc', these vessels are double-ended and have a single sail: their distinctive feature appears to be the sharp junction between bottom and posts. Remains of medieval ships have been found which have this feature, thus, unlike the 'proto-hulc', the 'proto-cog' evidence may be linked, somewhat tenuously, with the evidence from excavations. Whether there is also a link with earlier vessels excavated from the Rhine region—those of the Romano-Celtic tradition—is discussed below (5.8.2.6).

## 5.7.3 SEAFARING IN THE FIRST MILLENNIUM AD

Celtic seafarers undertook overseas voyages out of sight of land, probably from the sixth century BC, certainly from the first century BC (5.6.6). During the Migration period, say, fourth to seventh centuries AD, trading, raiding, and missionary voyages continued in the Celtic West and across the Irish Sea, and in the early eighth century, Irish monks settled on some of the northern islands including the Faeroes and islands off Iceland (E. Taylor, 1971: 69–70, 76; Graham-Campbell, 1994: 165–6, 170). Although hide boats had been used on earlier overseas voyages (5.3.3) the type of craft used in early medieval times is uncertain. Some idea of the navigational techniques used by Irish seamen in those days may be gained from a ninth-century account of the voyages of the sixth-century St. Brendan (McGrail, 1989d).

The migration voyages undertaken by Continental peoples from north of the Rhine delta were coastal and cross-Channel (5.7.1.2). In subsequent centuries, voyages (evidently made by Frisians) between the Rhine region and the Baltic continued to be coastal. Traded goods not transported overland across the Jutland isthmus via Hollingstedt, and the River Traene to Hedeby, or (in the tenth–twelfth centuries) by boat along the Limfjord route (Crumlin-Pedersen, 1997a: 36–8, 202), may have been taken across the Skagerrak, along the south Norwegian and west Swedish coasts and through the Kattegat, keeping well clear of the Skaw (northern tip of Denmark) which was difficult to round because of dangerous reefs and an indistinct coastline. Early versions of the cog could have been used for these coastal passages, and possibly the 'proto-hulc' undertook similar voyages in the southern North Sea.

From the late eighth century, however, and possibly earlier, Scandinavians (and Frisians?) undertook overseas voyages out of sight of land. These early Vikings raided and subsequently settled major and minor islands of the British and Irish archipelago. From the mid-ninth century, they settled the Faeroe islands, Shetlands, and Iceland, and there were comparable voyages within the Baltic. In the late tenth century, Greenland and then Vinland (probably the west coast of Newfoundland—Clausen, 1993) were discovered and settled (Graham-Campbell, 1994: 174–9). On present evidence, ships similar to those from Klåstad, Gokstad, and Äskekärr would have been used, or possibly an earlier version of the eleventh-century Skuldelev 1 cargo ship (5.8.1.3).

Evidence in the medieval Icelandic sagas (Bill, 1997a: 197–8) has been used to deduce how Scandinavian seamen navigated the North Atlantic in the ninth–fourteenth centuries (Thirslund, 1987). These methods are essentially environmental, similar to those deduced to have been used by the Celts (5.6.6), in the Homeric Mediterranean of the early first millennium BC (4.9.2.1.1), and in late second-millennium BC Oceania (9.5.4).

It has been claimed that the Vikings used a 'sunstone' of felspar which polarized light. The suggestion that, using this mineral, the sun's bearing could be determined when the sky was obscured by cloud seems doubtful (Bill, 1997: 199). Thirslund (1995; Vebaek and Thirslund, 1992) has demonstrated in theory and practice that, if the lines inscribed on an early Icelandic fragmented wooden disc constitute a gnomic curve for latitude 60°, the device can be used at sea as a sun compass whenever the sun cast a shadow. The validity of this hypothesis depends on the identification of the incised lines and this has been questioned (Bill, 1997a: 199). It has also been suggested that the Vikings practised latitude sailing between Bergen in Norway and Greenland, but this technique requires accurate observations of Polaris altitude, the altitude of the noon sun, the amplitude of the sun or the length

**Table 5.2** Hull data of selected eleventh–twelfth-century Nordic vessels

| Vessel | Approx. date | Overall, L × B × D (m) | L/B | L/D | B/D | Keel, d/b (tonnes) | Garboard deadrise | Average frame spacing (m) | Oars | Deadweight at 60 per cent draft |
|---|---|---|---|---|---|---|---|---|---|---|
| Hedeby 3 | 1025 | 22 × 6.3 × 2.5 | 3.5 | 8.8 | 2.5 | 1.0 | 28° | 0.83 | | 60 |
| Skuldelev 1 | 1040 | 16.0 × 4.8 × 2.1 | 3.6 | 7.8 | 2.1 | 0.72 | 13° | 0.92 | 5 | 24 |
| Skuldelev 3 | 1040 | 14 × 3.8 × 1.3 | 3.7 | 10.8 | 2.9 | 0.47 | 35° | 0.93 | 7 | 4.5 |
| Galtabac | 1100 | 14 × 4 × 1.85 | 3.5 | 7.6 | 2.2 | | | | | 13 |
| Lynaes | 1140 | 24 × 6 × 2.5 | 4.2 | 10.0 | 2.4 | | | 0.72 | | 60 |
| Ellingå | 1200 | 14.8 × 4 × 1.8 | 3.7 | 8.2 | 2.2 | | | | | 15 |
| Hedeby 1 | 985 | 30.9 × 2.7 × 1.5 | 11.4 | 2.1 | 1.8 | 0.33 | 38° | 0.84 | 2 × 27–31 | |
| Skuldelev 5 | 1050 | 17.5 × 2.5 × 1.1 | 7.0 | 16 | 2.3 | 0.63 | 20° | 0.91 | 2 × 13 | |
| Skuldelev 2 | 1060 | 29.3 × 3.8 × 1.8 | 7.7 | 16 | 2.1 | 0.46 | 44° | 0.71 | 2 × 28–30 | |
| Fotovik | 1100 | 10.3 × 2.4 × 1.0 | 4.3 | 10.3 | 2.4 | | | 0.83 | 2 × 7 | |

*Note*: Keel (d/b) is derived from the depth and average breadth of the keel protruding below the planking.

*Source*: Crumlin–Pedersen, 1981: 60–1; 1983b: 16; 1991b, figs. 7,10; 1994: fig. 5; 1997a, tables 4.1, 4.2; 2000: table 2.

of daylight hours, and a knowledge of celestial data by which these observations may be turned into latitude. It is doubtful that the necessary instruments and tables were available (McGrail, 1998: 284).

# 5.8

## Medieval Vessels (Eleventh–Fourteenth Centuries)

This period includes the centuries between the end of the Viking Age and the beginning of European oceanic voyages of exploration. Of the three types of north European seagoing vessels identified in the previous section, the Nordic vessel (subsequently known in English manuscripts as the *ceol* or 'keel'), the cog, and the hulc, there are now many excavated wrecks of vessels from the first two traditions. This is especially true of the Nordic type, so much so that Ole Crumlin-Pedersen (1991b: 72) has claimed that such finds 'are now so numerous that it is possible to make statements about basic patterns in shipbuilding with reasonable certainty, as well as discuss some of the variations'. Furthermore, from the late-tenth/early eleventh century onwards, differences in form and structure between warships and cargo ships can be recognized archaeo-

logically. Moreover, by size, cargo capacity and structural features, it is possible to differentiate between coastal and overseas merchantmen (Crumlin-Pedersen, 1991b: fig. 10).

## 5.8.1 THE NORDIC OR 'KEEL' TRADITION

Examples of this tradition include: the eleventh-century Skuldelev (Olsen and Crumlin-Pedersen, 1967) and Hedeby (Crumlin-Pedersen, 1997a) wrecks; the twelfth-century Lynaes (Crumlin-Pedersen, 1981: 52) and Ellingå (Crumlin-Pedersen, 1981: 36–8) wrecks; and the thirteenth-century Gedesby (Bill, 1997b), Magor Pill (Rednap, 1998), and Kyholm (Crumlin-Pedersen, Nymark, and Christiansen, 1980) wrecks (Table 5.2). Timbers and planking from dismantled Nordic ships have been reused in waterfront structures, or as fill when tidal foreshores have been enclosed: examples are in London (Marsden, 1996), Bergen (Christensen, 1985), and Dublin (McGrail, 1993b). Much can be learned, even from individual loose timbers, not only about timber selection and conversion, and woodworking techniques, but also about the size of parent vessels. Ships of this tradition are also depicted on the eleventh-/twelfth-century Bayeux tapestry (Wilson, 1985; Sleeswyk, 1981), and, in later centuries, on town seals (Ewe, 1972). Not all the wreck sites from this period have been fully published, nevertheless there is sufficient reliable information in the public domain for descriptions of individual ships to be collated and generalizations made about their structure. The forthcoming publication of the Skuldelev ships and other vessels of this era may well lead to some revision of the picture presented here.

### 5.8.1.1 HOW WERE VESSELS DESIGNED?

How early plank-first boats were designed has long intrigued scholars (Hornell, 1946a: 189–98; Hasslöf, 1972; Christensen, 1972; McGrail and McKee, 1974: 44–5): in the past twenty-five years there has been some, but not much, progress in tackling this question (Greenhill, 1995a: 47–71; McGrail, 1998: 98–111). As far as is known, scale models were not built, nor were constructional drawings compiled in Europe until a much later date: thus the question is not about 'design' (as known today), rather the question is: how did the builder obtain the shape of planked hull that he wanted; how was the idea of a boat with particular characteristics turned into reality? Were such vessels as Skuldelev 1 (or the Nydam and Gokstad vessels of earlier centuries) built entirely 'by eye' as was evidently done earlier this century in western Norway (Christensen, 1972; Crumlin-Pedersen, 1997a: 14–15) and in other regions of the modern world (McKee, 1983: 114; Greenhill, 1995a: 26–72; Blue et al., 1997)? Or were there rules of thumb; simple geometric constructions; or such building aids as boat ells or boat levels with key measurements marked on them; or were temporary moulds used? (McGrail, 1981a: 32)

Arnold (1999a) has suggested that some Romano-Celtic boats were built on a 'cradle': by 'cradle' Arnold appears to mean stocks which were shaped and arranged so that they were effectively a large, external mould giving the required shape of the bottom and lower sides of the boat (1999b: 108–15). If such an unlikely method had been used, we would still be left with the problem of how such a 'cradle' was itself designed.

Partly worked stemposts in the Nordic tradition have been recovered from bogs (formerly ponds) in Scandinavia (Brøgger and Shetelig, 1971: 41) and in Britain (McPherson, 1877–8), where they had probably been stored to stabilize the timber and keep it moist (McGrail and McKee, 1974: 39–40). Landings for the ends of six pairs of strakes, and scribed lines represent-

ing the run of each strake, had been worked on one of the unused stems from Eigg. It is clear from this that, before fashioning this stem, the builder must have had a very good idea in his head of the shape of the boat as defined by the planking runs. How then did he fashion such stems? Crumlin-Pedersen (1986b: 220–2) has proposed that the hollow stem of Skuldelev 3 (slightly larger, but similar to the Eigg stem) was 'designed' by a simple geometric procedure involving the use of string and chalk/charcoal. He believes that the outline of the stem was determined by circles of radii which were simple proportions of the keel length. Such information could be 'stored' in the form of rules of thumb defining appropriate ratios for vessels of differing size and function (as are used to store comparable information in Tamil Nadu today—Blue et al., 1997).

Crumlin-Pedersen has not yet gone on to investigate how the shapes and angles of the plank landings, and the curves of the simulated planking, were determined: these are more closely related to hull design than is the outline of the stem. Steffy (1994: 85–91) has used comparable methods when investigating the design of the eleventh-century ship from Serçe Limani (4.15.2.3). Such investigations are promising, not only in relation to the stems of Nordic vessels, but also to find answers to other questions: for example, was the keel length the basic unit of measurement from which other key dimensions were obtained by proportions, as done in later years in frame-first building? (5.9.4)

### 5.8.1.2 SELECTION AND CONVERSION OF TIMBER

Oak (*Quercus* sp.) was used for the main elements of a vessel whenever it was available, otherwise pine (*Pinus* sp.) or ash (*Fraxinus* sp.) (McGrail and McKee, 1974: 39–44; McGrail, 1993: 84, 87–90; 1998: 26–35). The timber was chosen to match the job in hand: long, straight-grained, knot-free boles for planking; natural crooks for framing and tholes (Fig. 5.47). Oak logs were converted into planking by splitting them radially into half, then half again, and so on—experimental work has shown that a maximum of sixteen planks can be obtained from a good oak bole in this way (Crumlin-Pedersen, 1986c). Pine logs were converted by splitting the log into two, each half then being worked down to one plank. Keel, stems, and framing timbers were obtained by reducing a log or half-log to the shape

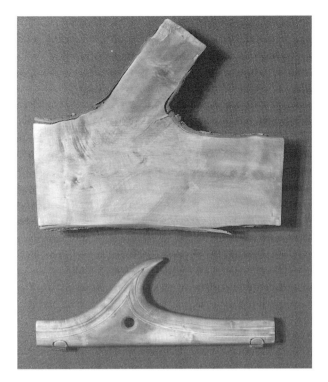

Fig. 5.47. An oar thole fashioned from a crook.

required, following the natural run of the grain whenever possible. It seems highly likely that trees were converted into ship and boat timbers soon after they had been felled (McGrail and McKee, 1974: 39–40). Generally bark and sapwood was removed, but in almost every early ship excavated so far sapwood has been found on a few timbers, especially where a particular breadth was needed, often on a curve.

Crumlin-Pedersen's study of three eleventh-century wrecks from Hedeby (1997b: 184–6) shows that, although oak was the principal timber species, a wide range of other species was used, mainly for treenails, rowlocks, cleats, and other fittings for sailing. He has concluded that species were chosen so that their individual properties matched the requirements of particular fittings. Crumlin-Pedersen has also drawn attention to the disparity in the choice of timber for these three ships: the builder of Hedeby 1 (a 'Royal Danish warship') had access to large, high quality oaks, as had the builder of Hedeby 3 (a 'large Danish cargo ship'); whereas the builder of Hedeby 2 (a hybrid Slav/Nordic ship) had to use beech (*Fagus* sp.) and imported pine (*Pinus* sp.), as well as some (reused) oak.

Nordic shipbuilding practices seem to have presupposed a good supply of quality oak logs to provide the necessary high-grade 'clove boards' and the crooks for framing: Nordic workmanship clearly matched the

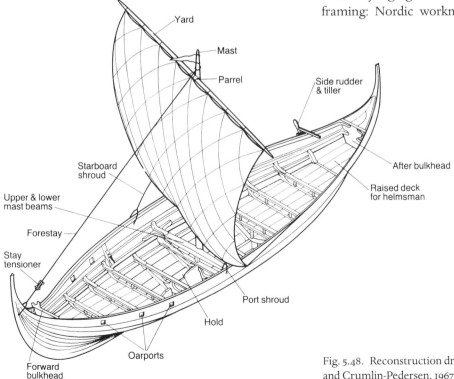

Fig. 5.48. Reconstruction drawing of Skuldelev 3 (after Olsen and Crumlin-Pedersen, 1967: fig. 44).

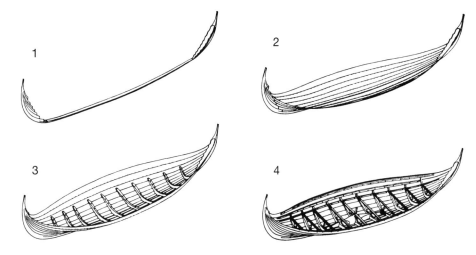

Fig. 5.49. The sequence of building a Skuldelev ship (after Crumlin-Pedersen, 1986a: fig. 3).

quality of this raw material. From the eleventh century, however, there appears to have been a shortage of such quality oak logs leading to the recycling of planks as in Skuldelev 5 and Fotovik 1 (Crumlin-Pedersen, 1994). Oaks that were available were evidently felled at a younger age leading to shorter and narrower planks (Crumlin-Pedersen, 1986c).

A considerable number of tools for wood and iron-working have been found on northern European sites, and many of these could have been used in shipbuilding (Olsen and Crumlin-Pedersen, 1967: 154–62; McGrail and McKee, 1974: 45–7; Christensen, 1985: 209–13; 1986; McGrail, 1998: 149–58). Trees were felled and trimmed with axes, and logs split by hardwood (sometimes hafted metal) wedges driven by mallets: saws were not used in northern shipbuilding until the thirteenth century (Crumlin-Pedersen, 1983b). Planks

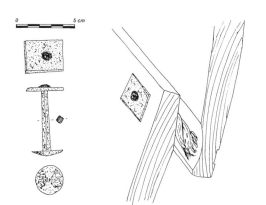

Fig. 5.50. Clinker planking with hair caulking and clenched nail fastening (after Christensen and Leiro, 1976).

were fashioned by axe but planes were sometimes used to work the bevels in the lap. Augers with a spoon-shaped bit were used to bore holes; profile or moulding irons to cut decorative linear patterns; draw-knives and adzes for curved shapes such as found in framing; chisels, shaves, and possibly the Nordic equivalent of a bargebuilder's slice, for fine work (Crumlin-Pedersen, 1986b). Blacksmiths' tools including hammer, metal shears, draw plates, and files would have been used to make the hundreds of nails. Block and tackle, rollers, sheerlegs, Spanish windlasses, cramps, shores, and spalls were also needed on the building site.

### 5.8.1.3 ELEVENTH AND TWELFTH CENTURIES

The typical Nordic vessel of this period may be described under three main headings.

#### 5.8.1.3.1 *Form*

A (near) double-ended vessel with a smooth keel/post transition, a distinctive sheerline leading to high ends, and a generally rounded bottom with flaring sides (Fig. 5.48).

#### 5.8.1.3.2 *Structure*

The hull was built plank-first (Fig. 5.49) from relatively thin split planks. The uppermost and the waterline strakes were generally thicker than the others, and, with the keel, constituted the main longitudinal strength members of the hull. Planks within strakes were joined in a simple overlapping scarf, and strakes were fastened together clinker fashion by nails clenched inboard by distorting the point over a rove

(Fig. 5.50). Planks frequently had a decorative line or pattern (moulding) scribed near their edges.

The keel, of T-shaped cross-section, protruded moderately well below the hull, and was joined to the stems in a vertical scarf fastened by clenched nails. Stems were either rabbeted to receive the ends of the planking, or they were hollowed in section and stepped in profile. Hollowing meant that the planking could be clench-fastened rather than merely spiked, and steps ensured that there was sufficient timber to which each plank end could be fastened.

Evenly spaced, symmetrically placed floor timbers were fastened to the lower planking (but not to the keel or the garboards) by treenails. Above these, at every station, there was a lower crossbeam supported by standing (vertical), and sometimes by lodging (horizontal), knees to the planking. A second level of crossbeams and knees was installed at every station in warships and at selected stations in cargo ships (Fig. 5.51). In cargo ships there could be a third level of beams, for example, above the mast step and at the ends of the hold. Pillars or *snelles* (combining the function of a stanchion and two knees) were fastened between floor and beam, and between lower and higher beams. Side timbers supported the planking between the frame stations in the upper hull. Warships with their high L/B ratios were vulnerable to longitudinal stresses, as were cargo ships with their hold amidships: both were stiffened by one or more sets of stringers treenailed to the planking.

Even the largest vessels in this period had the nature of an 'open boat', although cargo ships appear to have had a short deck at each end. As far as can be ascertained, there was no fixed ceiling planking, although there may have been movable bottom boards.

### 5.8.1.3.3 *Propulsion and steering* (Fig. 5.48)

Large boats and ships were propelled by a square sail on a mast stepped near amidships in a longitudinal keelson. This keelson was joggled to fit over several floors so that it rested on the keel, but it was not fastened to it, merely to the floors. The mast beam further supported the mast, replacing the earlier mast spur projection from the keelson. Standing rigging was probably forestay, shrouds, and a parrel between yard and mast; running rigging: a halyard and sheets. Braces do not appear to have been used, but may have been introduced towards the end of this period, as may reef

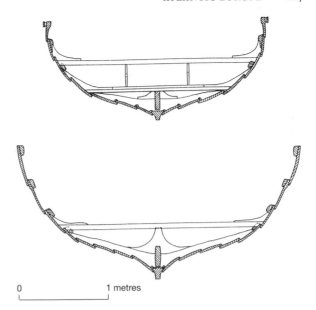

Fig. 5.51. Transverse sections of Skuldelev 5 (*upper*) and 3 (after Crumlin-Pedersen and Vinner, 1993: fig. 14).

points. The tacking spar was used from the eleventh century, and may subsequently have been supplemented by the bowline. Warships could also be propelled by oar with two oarsmen, each with one oar, on each bench. Small cargo vessels could be propelled by two or three oars at bow and stern, but it seems likely that cargo *ships* did not retain that facility.

Steering was by a side rudder held to the hull structure on the starboard quarter at two points on its shaft so that it could be rotated about its long axis by a thwartships tiller. Rudders protruded well below the level of the keel, thereby tending to offset some of the leeway induced when sailing across the wind. Some rudders could still be used when the upper shaft was canted forward to a position where the entire blade was above keel level, as would be desirable in shoal waters. (McGrail, 1998: 244–51; Hutchinson, 1995)

### 5.8.1.3.4 *Characteristics and capabilities of the Nordic ship*

The Nordic method of construction could be adapted to build different sizes of vessel, and vessels with different functions. It was essentially a light buoyant structure with resultant advantages in the cargo ship version, as well as in the warship operating in relatively shallow coastal waters and up rivers. The lines were generally very graceful: the disjointed transverse section of Skuldelev 1 (Fig. 5.52) with its angular junction of bottom and sides (reminiscent of some of the earlier Nordic vessels) does not seem to have been widely used. In the warship version the volumetric coefficients were especially low, and the lines were appropriate to a vessel with the potential for high speed under oars rather than top-rate performance under sail. The cargo ship's lines were a compromise between cargo capacity and performance under sail. Until the twelfth century Nordic merchant ships did not need formal harbours but were loaded and unloaded whilst at anchor or, in tidal waters, whilst beached.

Trials and passages undertaken by *Saga Siglar*, a full-size reconstruction of Skuldelev 1 based on studies by the institutions at Roskilde, have shown that this type

Fig. 5.53. *Roar Ege*, a reconstruction of Skuldelev 3, underway in Danish coastal waters (Danish National Museum).

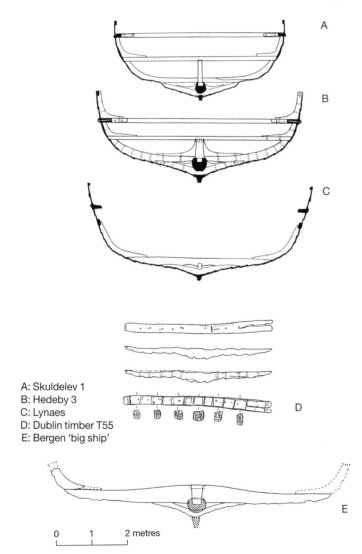

A: Skuldelev 1
B: Hedeby 3
C: Lynaes
D: Dublin timber T55
E: Bergen 'big ship'

0    1    2 metres

Fig. 5.52. Transverse sections of five Nordic ships (Institute of Archaeology, Oxford).

of vessel was capable of ocean voyages under sail in difficult weather (Crumlin-Pedersen, 1986b: 211–13). *Roar Ege*, a reconstruction of Skuldelev 3, was built under the supervision of Crumlin-Pedersen in the boatyard of the Viking Ship Museum and sea trials have been undertaken in Roskilde Fjord and elsewhere over a period of years (Crumlin-Pedersen, 1986a and b: 213–16; Andersen *et al.* 1997). She has proved to be very seaworthy in coastal waters (Fig. 5.53).

In controlled tacking trials during 1983 and 1984 in Roskilde Fjord, these two reconstructions made ground to windward (VMG) at 1.2–1.5 knots (*Saga Siglar*) and 1.3–1.9 knots *Roar Ege* (Bill, 1995: 7). Plotted tracks over the seabed showed that *Roar Ege* could sail up to 64°–72° off the true wind, whilst *Saga Siglar* could hold 65°–68°. In fair winds both vessels reached a maximum speed of *c*.8.5 knots (Fig. 5.54). Full publication of the Skuldelev wrecks, the two full-size reconstructions, and their trials is awaited. Nevertheless it seems clear from several preliminary publications that, given that these reconstructions accurately replicate Skuldelev 1 and 3, and that these two vessels are representative of their type and times, eleventh-century Nordic cargo ships were very capable sailing vessels. By this date Greenland had been settled, and Vinland encountered: Skuldelev 1 may well have been capable of such voyages, but a ship such as the near contemporary Hedeby 3 of *c.*60 tonnes capacity (Crumlin-Pedersen, 1997: 103) may have been preferred.

### 5.8.1.3.5 *Warships and cargo ships*

Excavators of wrecks from this period have identified some as warships and others as cargo ships, but the criteria used to make this distinction are not always clear. On rare occasions, significant cargo remains have clearly identified a cargo ship. Otherwise some of the following features may be used to identify merchantmen:

- A hold located amidships—recognized by the absence of upper crossbeams (except a mast beam), and/or the presence of bulkheads forward and aft.
- Dunnage in the hold.
- Relatively heavy framing for a vessel of her size.
- Rowing stations at the end only: warships have such stations along most of their length.
- L/B ratio < *c.*5 (Table 5.2) } relatively broader and deeper of hull than a warship
- L/D ratio < *c.*10 (Table 5.2) }
- Inter-frame distance generally less than 0.60 m (Table 5.2). There are, however, some anomalies here. McKee (1983: fig. 113) gives 0.91 m as the optimum spacing (centre to centre) between oarsmen sitting/rowing one behind the other, and 0.76 m as the minimum. This suggests that if the frames of a wreck are more closely spaced than *c.*0.75 m, the vessel is likely to be a cargo ship. The frames of Skuldelev 2, however, are spaced at *c.*0.71 m yet, on other grounds, this vessel is recognized as an oared warship. Conversely, the mid-twelfth century wreck from Lynaes (McGrail, 1998: table 11.5), which is thought to be a cargo ship, has a frame spacing of *c.*0.72 m (Crumlin-Pedersen, 1983*a*).

Skuldelev 3 with relatively little depth of hull (*c.*1.3 m) and a cargo capacity of only 4.5 tonnes may be thought of as an inter-island trader. Two other Nordic vessels of the eleventh/twelfth centuries identified as cargo vessels have an overall length of *c.*14 m, and capacities of 13–15 tonnes (Table 5.2): these are examples of medium-sized cargo vessels probably used in the coastal trade. Skuldelev 1 with a load of *c.*24 tonnes is an example of a small overseas merchant ship; Hedeby 3 and Lynaes at 60 tonnes were relatively large cargo ships for their time (Fig. 5.52).

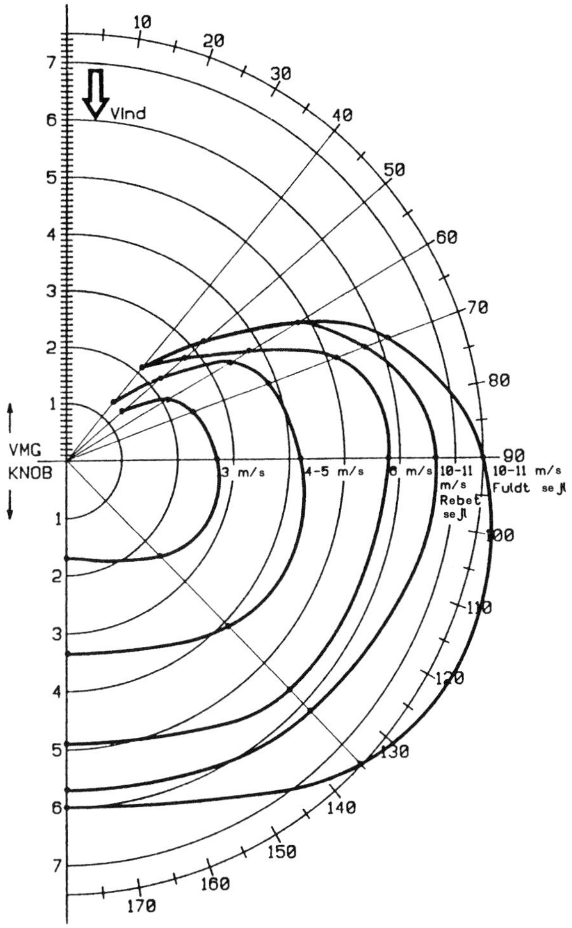


Fig. 5.54. Polar diagram showing *Roar Ege*'s speed and heading relative to the apparent wind during sea trials in 1984 (after Crumlin-Pedersen and Vinner, 1993: fig. 11).

The four vessels of this period identified as warships are long, low, and slender, designed primarily for propulsion by oars, but capable of being sailed in fair winds on long passages. Two of them, Hedeby 1 and Skuldelev 2, are around 30 m in length and had 54–62 oars, and may be considered large warships. The proportions and lines of Skuldelev 2 are such that a long overseas passage would be practicable, as indeed she must have undertaken at least once in her life since she was built of Irish oak, probably in the vicinity of Dublin.

Hedeby 1 as reconstructed, on the other hand, is exceptionally long in relation to both her breadth and her depth of hull (L/B = 11.4; L/D = 21) and cannot have been as seaworthy: possibly more emphasis was put on potential speed and her role as a display of power within the islands and coasts of Greater Denmark, than on seagoing capabilities.

Skuldelev 2 has the relatively short spacing of 0.71 m between oar stations, compared with the 0.83–0.91 m of the others. This unusual spacing raises the question of the style of rowing adopted: in the sit-pull mode a shortish stroke is best at sea, but 0.71 m spacing seems to imply an excessively short stroke, possibly making it difficult to develop the propulsive power that would give the speeds of which her hull appears to be capable. This apparent paradox may be resolved in Crumlin-Pedersen's forthcoming publication of the Skuldelev ships.

Skuldelev 5 (Fig. 5.51) has much the same proportions as Skuldelev 2 but is only 17.5 m long overall, with twenty-six oar stations: she seems to have been built for a coastal defence role (*leding*). Fotovik 1 is more difficult to place: she is only 10.3 m long, with fourteen oar stations. Her L/B of 4.3 : 1 and L/D of 10.3:1 are much less than other warships and are within the range of vessels identified as cargo ships (Table 5.2). However, her maximum beam of 2.4 m is almost as narrow as it can be if she is to be rowed by two men to a bench and still have room along the centreline for the mast and its fittings; and her depth of hull at 1 m can scarcely have been less for a seaboat. Given that her length is only 10.3 m (for timber supply or operational reasons) she could not have had more warship-like proportions.

### 5.8.1.4 THIRTEENTH AND FOURTEENTH CENTURIES

From the thirteenth century onwards wrecks of the Nordic tradition became rarer. There are sufficient, however, to provide an archaeological context within which other evidence, notably iconographic (Ewe, 1972; Crumlin-Pedersen, 1983b) and documentary (Whitwell and Johnson, 1926; Johnson, 1927; R. Anderson, 1928; Tinniswood, 1949; Sandahl, 1951, 1958, 1982) can be discussed. Examples of such wrecks are those from Sjøvoll (Christensen, 1968b); Ellinga, Kyholm, and Kalmar 1 (Crumlin-Pedersen, 1980; 1983a); Bergen

(Fig. 5.52) (Christensen, 1985); Gedesby (Bill, 1997b; Bill and Vinner, 1995); and Magor Pill (Rednap, 1998).

#### 5.8.1.4.1 *Structure and size*

Boats and ships continued to have an open-boat structure into the thirteenth century, sometimes with a deck at each end. The fact that ocean-going voyages were undertaken in such vessels reflects the physique and hardiness of the seamen rather than the suitability of their vessels (O. Roberts, 1994: 12). Entries in late thirteenth-century financial accounts concerning the building of galleys for the English king (Whitwell and Johnson, 1926; Johnson, 1927; R. Anderson, 1928; Tinniswood, 1949) suggest that a canvas awning spread above the deck was all the protection the crew had. However, the position of the beams on the Nordic ships depicted on the thirteenth-century seals of Winchelsea (Fig. 5.55), Sandwich, and Hythe, and the 1300 seal of Yarmouth (Ewe, 1972) suggests that the bigger ships may by then have had a deck under which the crew could have slept and ate. In addition to protecting the crew, such a deck would have significantly strengthened the structure and, if it could be kept mod-

Fig. 5.55. The thirteenth-century town seal of Winchelsea (National Maritime Museum, Greenwich).

**Table 5.3** Hull data for thirteenth–fourteenth-century Nordic cargo ships

| Vessel | Approx. date | Overall, L × B × D (m) | L/B | L/D | B/D | Keel, d/b | Garboard deadrise | Frame spacing (m) | Deadweight tonnage at 60% draft (tonnes) | Hold index |
|---|---|---|---|---|---|---|---|---|---|---|
| Sjøvoll | c.13th C. | 15–18 × 5.0 × 2.5 | 3.6 | 7.2 | 2.0 | | | 0.35–0.60 | | |
| Kyholm | after 1205 | 13 × 3.4 × 1.5 | 3.8 | 8.7 | 2.3 | 0.55 | 55° | 0.69 | | 48 |
| Magor Pill | c.13th C. | 14.3 × 3.7 × 1.2 | 3.9 | 11.6 | 3.0 | 1.35 | 26° | | | |
| Bergen | 1188 | 30 × 9.5 × 3.7 | 3.2 | 8.0 | 2.6 | | | | 120–160(?) | |
| Gedesby | late–13th C. | 12.6 × 5.2 × 1.4 | 2.5 | 9.0 | 3.6 | | | | | |
| Kalmar 1 | c.13th–14th C. | 11.1 × 4.6 × 2 | 2.5 | 5.6 | 2.3 | 1.1 | 4° | 0.48 | | 48 |

*Notes*: Keel (d/b) is derived from the depth and average breadth of the keel protruding below the planking. Hold index = Length of hold / overall 'length' of ship.

*Sources*: A. E. Christensen, 1989; Crumlin-Pedersen, 1991*b*; 2000: table 2; Bonde *et al.*, 1993; M. Rednap, 1998; McGrail, 1998.

erately watertight, increased the vessel's seaworthiness.

As seen in profile on town seals, thirteenth- and fourteenth-century ships were much the same shape as earlier ones. The L/B ratios of the seven excavated cargo boats in Table 5.3 may be compared with those of earlier centuries in Table 5.2: a range of 2.5–3.9 and a mean of 3.3 in the eleventh/twelfth centuries, compared with 3.5–4.2, and 3.7, indicating an increase in relative breadth in the thirteenth/fourteenth centuries. L/D ratios are in the range 5.6–11.6 with a mean of 7.2, compared with 7.6–10.8, and 8.8, suggesting relatively deeper hulls in the later period.

Town seals also suggest that vessels became bigger. For example, the ship on the thirteenth-century Sandwich seal has a boat on board, and the thirteenth-century Winchelsea (Fig. 5.55) and Pevensey seals depict a windlass being used to weigh anchor: a windlass could also be used to work the bilge pumps (O. Roberts, 1994: 20), and to raise and lower the heavier yards. A base for a windlass was found on the Ellingå wreck of the thirteenth century (Crumlin-Pedersen, 1983*a*). The evidence from boat and ship timbers reused in Dublin (Fig. 5.52) suggests that there was a significant increase in the size of vessels using the port in the late twelfth/early thirteenth century (McGrail, 1993*b*: 98). Merchant ships were not only larger but also had relatively bigger holds, the hold index increasing from 0.278–0.338 in the eleventh to c.0.480 in the thirteenth century (McGrail, 1998: table 11.6).

There were also significant structural changes. Superstructures known as 'castles' were built at bow

and stern (Ewe, 1972: seals of Dunwich, 1200; Winchelsea (Fig. 5.55), Dublin, and Hythe of the thirteenth century). A top (for lookout and fighting purposes) was fitted near the masthead (1200 seal of Dunwich, thirteenth-century seal of Sandwich). On the 1200 Dunwich and the 1300 Yarmouth seals, protruding crossbeams are depicted: the beams on the thirteenth-century Sandwich and Hythe seals have fairings over their ends so that they do not snag when alongside other ships or waterfront structures. Protruding beams are a feature of the eleventh-century Hedeby 3 (Fig. 5.52) wreck as reconstructed, and they have been found on thirteenth-century wrecks Kalmar 1 (O. Roberts, 1994: 24) and Gedesby (Bill, 1997*b*).

Decorative mouldings disappeared from near plank edges and shorter lengths of planking were used (Bill, 1998). Ceiling planking of split beech (*Fagus* sp.), nailed to the floors of the mid-thirteenth-century Magor Pill boat (Rednap, 1998), would have increased the hull strength. Plank scarfs became longer—in Dublin, for example, they decreased in gradient to 8–16 per cent from the c.21–33 per cent of earlier centuries; thirteenth-century scarfs were also less carefully shaped and had a protruding lip (McGrail, 1993*b*: 43–4). A more fundamental change is seen in the Gedesby boat: most of her planking was split, as in earlier centuries, but some was sawn. By the late thirteenth/early fourteenth centuries, English galleys were built from sawn planking, generally 12 feet (c.3.6 m) or less in length, but selected planks were up to 28 feet (c.8.5 m) (Tinniswood, 1949).

The late thirteenth-century Gedesby wreck had

other significant features: her planking was prolonged to cover the faces of the stern post; and she had knee-shaped lower posts—both these are characteristic of the cog (5.8.2.2). The Kyholm and Kalmar 1 ships have straight outer edges to their raked posts, another cog characteristic (Crumlin-Pedersen, 1981, 1983a).

### 5.8.1.4.2 *Propulsion and steering*

A single square sail set on a mast near amidships continued to be the norm until the fourteenth century when topsails were introduced (Sandahl, 1958). In the early thirteenth century the yard was held to the mast by a composite parrel with trucks and ribs (balls and laths); the earlier parrel (Fig. 5.48) made from a crook continued in use (McGrail, 1993b: 72). Reef points are depicted on the sail of the 1297 Dublin seal, and bonnets were introduced in the fourteenth century (Sandahl, 1958). Reefs and bonnets enable the area of sail to be varied to match the wind. A bowsprit is featured on thirteenth-century Poole and fourteenth-century Stubbekøbing seals, whilst the ship on the Yarmouth seal of 1300 seems to have a bowline running from the luff of its sail to a bowsprit: the term 'bowline' is attested from the late thirteenth century (Sandahl, 1982). Braces to the yardarms appear for the first time on the thirteenth-century Winchelsea seal (Fig. 5.55). The term 'brace' has not been noted before 1353 although 'yard-rope' is known from 1294–5. Braces (yard-ropes) are used to trim the yard (and sail) to the wind. It is difficult to believe that they were not used before the thirteenth century.

The side rudder on the starboard quarter continued in use into the thirteenth century (seals of Dunwich and Faversham); the thirteenth-century Winchelsea seal (Fig. 5.55) has a side rudder worked on a sponson protruding from the hull planking. Stern or median rudders are depicted on hulcs on the late twelfth-century fonts at Winchester (Fig. 5.61) and Zedelgem (McGrail, 1998: 251), and on cogs on the mid-thirteenth-century seals of Elbing and Wismar: they first appear on Nordic ships on the thirteenth-century seals of Poole and Ipswich. The late thirteenth-century Gedesby boat had two gudgeons for a stern rudder (Bill, 1997b). Late thirteen to early fourteenth-century accounts for the building of English galleys specified timber which was to be fitted as a deadwood to the stern post presumably so that a stern rudder might more readily be hung there (Tinniswood, 1949).

### 5.8.1.4.3 *The Nordic ship and the cog*

During the thirteenth century the Nordic merchant ship began to be challenged by the cog (5.8.2.5). The economics of the market place seem to have forced builders in the Nordic tradition to respond to this challenge and reduce the costs of building and operating cargo ships (Bill, 1997a: 200–1). Less effort was put into embellishments, and planking and framing techniques were simplified. Ships were increased in size and holds were made relatively longer, and techniques were 'borrowed' from the cog—sawn planking, planking overlapping the posts, raked posts, and the like (5.8.1.4.1). Ships became more utilitarian: a tool of trade, perhaps no longer a delight to the eye. By the fifteenth century the Nordic ship and the cog were almost indistinguishable.

The last large ship to be built in the Nordic tradition may have been Henry V's warship *Grace Dieu* of 1418 (5.9.2). Subsequently ships, both merchant and warships, were built frame-first with non-edge- fastened planking (5.9.3–4). Nordic traditional building techniques lived on, however, in the small craft of northern Europe, particularly in northern Norway and in Shetland (McGrail and McKee, 1974: 6–7; Bill, 1997a).

### 5.8.2 THE COG

The type name 'cog' was first noted in ninth-century documents referring to Frisian shipping and trade (Jellema, 1955: 32), and Crumlin-Pedersen (1965) has suggested that the ninth-century Frisian ships referred to by King Alfred (5.7.2) may have been early cogs. References to cogs increase markedly in the thirteenth and fourteenth centuries when this type of cargo vessel seems to have been the 'workhorse' of the Hanseatic League in coastal voyages from the Rhine region in the south, to Scandinavia in the north, and to Rostock and even Gdansk Bay in the east. Cogs also traded between Britain and Ireland and the Continent (Hutchinson, 1994: 15; Ward, 1995). They were also used as troop transports and as warships during these centuries (Brooks, 1929: 29; 1933: 75–7; Crumlin-Pedersen, 1983b; Runyan, 1994). Crusaders and pilgrims from northern Europe were transported to the Mediterranean in cogs (Runyan, 1991) and in 1304 the Florentine chronicler, Villani, noted that, after buccaneers from Bayonne in the Bay of Biscay brought cogs to the Mediterranean,

Genoese, Venetian, and Catalonian shipyards began to build cogs which they found cheaper and more seaworthy (Ellmers, 1994: 39).

### 5.8.2.1 ICONOGRAPHIC EVIDENCE AND WRECKS

Fliedner (1964) established a vital link between documentary and iconographic evidence when he realized that the fifteenth-century citizens of Stralsund had called their fourteenth-century town seal 'the cog'. The ship portrayed in profile on this 1329 seal (Ewe, 1972: no. 194) has some features in common with Nordic ships (single mast and sail set amidships; clinker planking above the waterline) but it also has distinctive features: straight, raked bow and sternposts; moderate sheer towards bow and stern; relatively deep hull; castles at bow and stern; and a centreline rudder (Fig. 5.56).

The large, almost complete, ship excavated from the River Weser downstream from Bremen, in 1962 had many of these features and thus could be identified as a cog (Fig. 5.57). Dendrochronological analysis gave the felling date of the oaks from which she was built as 1378: thus this vessel, which is believed to have been on building stocks when she was swept into the river, is a late example of the cog tradition, since documentary

Fig. 5.57. The Kiel-built reconstruction of the Bremen Cog under sail in the Baltic in 1991 (photo: S. McGrail).

sources suggest that, by the mid-fifteenth century, the Hanseatic towns ceased to build them.

Ships similar to the Bremen cog and to the cog on the Stralsund seal appear on thirteenth–fifteenth-century seals of many ports, from Elbing in the east to Damm, near Bruges, and possibly Ipswich, in the west (Ewe, 1972). Thirteenth–fifteenth-century vessels with some of these characteristics have been excavated from the Ijsselmeer region of the Netherlands, and from Danish, Swedish, German, and, possibly, Polish waters (Crumlin-Pedersen, 1979, 1981, 1983b, 1985, 1989, 1991b; Bonde and Jensen, 1995; Ellmers, 1979, 1994;

Fig. 5.56. The 1329 town seal of Stralsund (photo: S. McGrail).

**Table 5.4** Hull data for twelfth–fifteenth-century cogs

| Vessel | Approx. date | Overall, L | × B | × D (m) | L/B | L/D | B/D | Keel, d/b | Garboard deadrise | Average frame spacing (m) |
|---|---|---|---|---|---|---|---|---|---|---|
| Kollerup (S) | 1150 | 20.1 | × 4.8 | × 2.2 | 4.2 | 9.1 | 2.2 | 0.09 | 0° | 0.63 |
| OZ 43 | 1275–1300 | 43 | × 6–8 | × ? | 5.5/7.2 | | | | | |
| Kolding (S) | 1250 | 18 | × ? | × ? | | | | 0.15 | 0° | |
| NZ 43 | 1300 | 11.8 | × 4.25 | × 1.2 | 2.8 | 9.8 | 3.55 | 0.32 | 8° | 0.36 |
| Q 75 | 1300–1325 | | | | | | | 0.36 | 7° | |
| N 5 | 1325–1350 | 14.5 | × 4.5 | × 1 | 3.2 | 14.5 | 4.5 | 0.24 | 2° | |
| Vejby (S) | 1372 | 16–18 | × 5.6 | × ? | 2.9/3.2 | | | 0.13 | 6° | |
| NZ 42 | 1350–1400 | | | | | | | 0.17 | 2° | |
| M 107 | 1375–1400 | 15.5 | × 4.5 | × 1.4 | 3.4 | 11.1 | 3.2 | 0.18 | 13° | |
| Bremen (S) | 1378–1380 | 22.7 | × 7.6 | × 4.3 | 3 | 5.3 | 1.8 } | 0.19 | 5° | 0.50 |
| | | 23.3 | × 7.0 | × 4.3 | 3.3 | 5.2 | 1.6 } | | | |
| Almere | 1410 | 15.95 | × 4.2 | × 1.93 | 3.8 | 8.3 | 2.2 | 0.07 | 0° | 0.25 |

*Notes*: S=Seagoing. Two sets of dimensions have been published for the Bremen cog and three estimates of deadweight tonnage. Keel (d/b) is derived from the depth and average breadth of the keel protruding below the planking. Hold index=Length of hold/overall length of ship.

*Sources*: Crumlin–Pedersen, 1979, 1981, 1983, 1985, 1991, 1994; 2000: table 1; Ellmers, 1972, 1979, 1994; Reinders, 1979, 1985; McGrail, 1998: tables 8.1, 11.4, 11.5, 11.6, 12.7; Steffy, 1994: 114–124; van Moortell, 1991a, 1991b.

Fliedner and Pohl-Weber, 1972; Hocker, 1991; Hoekstra, forthcoming; Lahn, 1992; Reinders, 1979; 1985; van de Moortel, 1991a and b; Litwin, 1995: 21–2; Adams, 1990; Cederlund, 1995: 14; Hörberg, 1995). Goodburn (forthcoming) has suggested that some thirteenth-century fragments of planking reused in London may have been from cogs. Ellmers conjecture (1979: 3) that hooked nails, excavated from ninth-century Hamburg and tenth-century Birka, came from cogs has been questioned by Reinders (1985: 18), since such nails are known to have also been used in housebuilding.

### 5.8.2.2 COG CHARACTERISTICS

The wide range of evidence for the medieval cog from iconographic and literary sources has been reasonably well dated, and, after critical evaluation can mostly be satisfactorily interpreted (in so far as it is possible) in terms of shipbuilding practices and seagoing abilities. The wreck evidence is not so well placed: very few, if any, of the presumed cogs have been fully published, and only a handful have been dated scientifically. It is therefore difficult to define cog characteristics in, say, the late twelfth century and then detail subsequent changes. Moreover, shipbuilding traditions are, by their nature, polythetic groupings (McGrail, 1995b).

This means that there may be no one diagnostic characteristic of a shipbuilding tradition, rather a group of characteristics many of which are found in most of the vessels of that tradition.

A provisional group of such characteristics may be identified for the cog tradition, using evidence from nine moderately well-documented wrecks (Table 5.4) and from a dozen or so depictions on thirteenth- and fourteenth-century seals (Ewe, 1972).

### 5.8.2.2.1 *Form*

These double-ended vessels, generally with straight, raked posts, have a flat bottom longitudinally with a sharp transition between bottom and posts (Fig. 5.58). Of those reconstructed, only the Almere Wijk 13 wreck and N243 (Steffy, 1994: figs. 4.42, 4.47) have a bottom which rises towards the ends. The thirteenth-century seal of Ipswich depicts a ship with straight stern post but a slightly curved stem. The ship on a series of seals from Lübeck (1224–81) has similarly curved posts at bow and stern. There is no excavated evidence for such curved posts, but a medieval model from Ebersdorf church, clinker-built on a keel but with protruding beams and large standing knees as in the cog, has a curved stem at the bow (A.-E. Christensen, 1987). It is not clear how such curved posts fit into the general

| Deadweight tonnage at 60% draft | Hold index | Mast Position as % of LOA | Keelson length |
|---|---|---|---|
| | | | Plank-keel length |
| 30 | 0.40 | 0.29 | – |
| | | 0.34 | – |
| | | 0.34 | 0.50 |
| 9 | | 0.34 | – |
| | | 0.30 | 0.10 |
| | | 0.24 | – |
| | | 0.42 | 0.80 |
| | | 0.27 | 0.18 |
| | | 0.33 | 0.13 |
| c.80 | 0.42 | 0.43 | 0.72 |
| | 0.49 | | |
| 24.5 | 0.50 | | |

technological picture. It may be that the Lübeck seals are misleading or depict archaic features for these ships not only have curved posts, but also are steered from the quarter rather than the stern, and the 1281 seal appears to depict reverse-clinker planking. Each of these features is unusual in the context of the thirteenth-century Baltic: the combination suggests that the Lübeck depictions may be more artistic than realistic.

The cog sheerline rises gently at the stern, more so at the bow where the stempost extends above the planking. In transverse section one of the cogs thought to be for inland waters (Almere Wijk 13) has a flat bottom, as has the Kollerup cog (Fig. 5.58) from the west coast of Jutland (Crumlin-Pedersen, 1979: fig. 2.12). Other cogs have a full form, with a slight deadrise of the garboards from a plank-keel, and with rounded bilges. The upper sides of seagoing cogs are flared; inland vessels have near vertical sides.

The cog depictions on seals give the impression that they are high-sided in relation to their length (L/D < 3). Of the wrecks, only the Bremen cog bears out this with a L/D of 5.3; other cogs have a mean L/D c.9.4 ± 2.9 which in fact suggests that they were relatively less high-sided than their Nordic contemporaries (c.8.3 ± 1.7), although they no doubt had more freeboard than Nordic *war*ships. Comparison, of L/B ratios (cog c.3.37 ± 0.58; Nordic c.3.30 ± 0.54) suggests little difference in relative breadth. These comparisons are from the few wrecks for which the data is available (seven, thir-

teenth-century Nordic; five, late twelfth- to mid-fifteenth-century cogs). When more wrecks are fully published the position may change; nevertheless, on present evidence, seal-makers in the Nordic north and in the West seem to have been more realistic than those in Hanseatic lands.

### 5.8.2.2.2 *Structure*

The cog had a plank-keel roughly twice the thickness of the garboards. Transition timbers fashioned from a crook to give a skeg and a heel were scarfed to plank-keel and posts, so that the upper arm of this 'hook' or 'stem knee' became the lower post.

The bottom planking over most of its length was laid edge-to-edge and was not fastened together or to the plank-keel. Towards the ends, however, this planking became overlapping as it was turned through 90° by notching, sculpting, bevelling, and probably by charring, so that it could be nailed into rabbets in the 'stem hook' and the lower stems. The side planking was laid overlapping and fastened together by nails which were clenched inboard by hooking. In the later wrecks the side planking overlapped the posts, with a false stem forward. Caulking, using tarred moss and sometimes cattle hair, was done after the planks were fastened: in the bottom planking by forcing the caulking between the outboard seams and holding it in place by butterfly-shaped iron clamps (*sintels*) driven across a lath placed along each seam (Fig. 5.59); the clinker planking was caulked inboard by placing the caulking

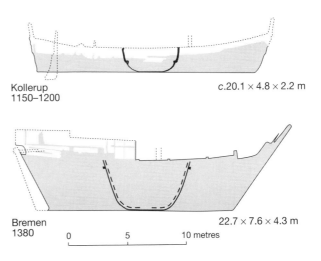

Kollerup
1150–1200                          c.20.1 × 4.8 × 2.2 m

Bremen
1380          0          5          10 metres
22.7 × 7.6 × 4.3 m

Fig. 5.58. Silhouettes of the Kollerup and Bremen cogs (after Crumlin-Pedersen, 1991b: fig. 11).

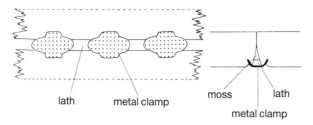

lath    metal clamp

moss    lath
metal clamp

Fig. 5.59. Cog caulking methods (after Reinders, 1979: fig. 3.8).

in a cove cut in the upper outboard edge of each lower strake, and securing it with lath and *sintels*. Occasionally, some side seams were also caulked outboard (N5, NZ43, Almere). Planks within strakes were joined in vertical scarfs, with a moss caulking, fastened by hooked nails; some scarfs were lipped as in the thirteenth-century Nordic ships (5.8.1.4.1). All cogs excavated have relatively thick, sawn planking, except for the Kollerup cog, the oldest known to date, which had planking fashioned from half-logs (Crumlin-Pedersen, 1989: 32).

Floor timbers were generally laid with a longer arm to port and starboard alternately (e.g. Kollerup, NZ43, Almere, Bremen cog) but in the Bremen cog some floors (e.g. nos. 10 and 20) were symmetrical about the plank-keel. In NZ43 and the Almere wrecks, half-frames were fitted over the stem hooks. Floors, which were treenailed to the planking, were substantial ones when compared with those in Nordic ships: the cross-section area (m × s) of Almere floors was 195–273 cm², those of NZ43 were *c*.262 cm² and the largest floor in the Kollerup wreck was 629 cm²: these may be compared with the average for Nordic vessels of 100–50 cm², with a maximum of 240 cm² (Crumlin-Pedersen, 1997*a*: 117). Above the floors were futtocks and top timbers to the sheer strake. In the Kollerup cog there appears to have been no contact between floor and futtock (Crumlin- Pedersen, 1979: 30). Almere futtocks were scarfed to the floors but it is not clear how they were fastened. The floors and futtocks of the Bremen cog, and several others, were treenailed together and to the planking. Stringers were fitted in the Kollerup cog and most later ones, and the top strake was reinforced. Kollerup had loose bottom boards, but later cogs had ceiling planking, sometimes intermittent as in Vejby, which in several cases was treenailed through the floors to the hull planking. The Bremen cog's ceiling planking extended up the sides: in effect these were stringers.

Crossbeams had been fitted above the waterline in all cogs so far known except for three of the Dutch wrecks which were probably inland water craft. These beams were more or less regularly spaced along the hull, generally one as mast beam, and one at each end of the hold. They rested on tenons protruding from the futtocks in the Bremen cog, and were fastened to the planking by hanging and standing knees. In the Kolding cog of *c*.1300 these beams were notched and protruded through the planking, and seals of this date also show this feature: the 1350 seal of Elbing shows the ends of these beams protected by fairings; the Bremen cog projecting beam ends are rounded. In some of the Dutch wrecks (for example, Q75, NZ42, and N5) the beams do not appear to protrude. The Bremen cog has a fifth crossbeam forward at a higher level, to which bitts for the anchor cable were fastened. Large, deep knees stand on the main beams of the Bremen cog and are treenailed to them and to the side planking—these are also found in the Kolding cog of *c*.1300 and some of the later finds. Fore-and-aft beams (carlings) are let into the upper face of the large knees and are themselves supported by small knees: removable deck planking was laid on these beams athwartships.

The ship on the 1299 Gdansk seal has crenellated platforms on stanchions at bow and stern, and possibly a fighting top near the masthead. On the 1329 Stralsund seal the after-castle seems to be more integrated into the hull; the forecastle is reduced in size (Fig. 5.56). There is little, if any, archaeological evidence for forecastles, but the Bremen cog has a well integrated raised superstructure aft from which the ship was conned and sailed. There seems nothing that would prevent such a cog being adapted for warfare by crenellating the after superstructure and fitting a crenellated platform at the bow.

### 5.8.2.2.3 *Propulsion and steering*

Cogs propelled by oars are known to have been used as late as the mid-fourteenth century (Friel, 1995: 38), but these were probably galleys. Some of the smaller Dutch finds may also have had oars, but the other vessels thought to be cogs were probably propelled by sail alone. The Kollerup cog had her mast step in a floor timber, as did the early fourteenth-century Dutch cog N5. The late thirteenth-century Dutch OZ43 had her mast step in a chock on one side, and there may have been a second on the other side. The other known cogs had a mast step in a keelson, a central longitudinal timber which was treenailed to the floors but not to the plank-keel.

When compared with the length of their associated plank-keel, length of keelson ranged from 10 per cent, in the early fourteenth-century Q75, to 72 per cent in the late fourteenth-century Bremen cog, and possibly 80 per cent in the near contemporary cog from Vejby (Table 5.4). This was no simple increase with time, however, since the keelson of the Kolding cog of the thirteenth/fourteenth centuries was 50 per cent of her plank-keel, and that of the Almere cog of c.1433 only 14 per cent. There is probably a correlation with function: seagoing vessels have relatively longer keelsons, 50–80 per cent in Kolding, Vejby, and Bremen cogs; inland cogs from 10–18 per cent. The apparent anomaly here is the Kollerup cog which almost certainly was seagoing yet had no keelson: the two Romano-Celtic seagoing ships of the second and third centuries AD, were similarly without keelsons, and had their mast step in a floor timber (5.6.1, 5.6.5) so the Kollerup cog's seagoing abilities cannot be challenged on these grounds.

The Kollerup mast step is well forward, before the hold (Fig. 5.58), at a point which is c.29 per cent of the overall length of this ship: again, Romano-Celtic ships had their masts in a similar relative postion (5.6.1, 5.6.5). Crumlin-Pedersen (1979: fig. 2.13) illustrated a sequence of the cogs then known showing the mast moving closer, over time, towards the midships station. On present evidence, this does appear to be the case for the four seagoing cogs, with Kolding at 34 per cent, Vejby at c.42 per cent, and Bremen at 43 per cent. This may indicate that there was a change in seagoing rig during the early fourteenth century from a fore-and-aft sail such as a lug or sprit (Kollerup and Kolding) to a square sail. That cog masters used square sails in a way that gained some of the advantages of a fore-and-aft sail seems to be suggested on the 1365 seal of Kiel where the sail is canted.

Dutch vessels used on inland waters continued to have their masts well forward (24–34 per cent: Table 5.4) at the ideal station for being towed on rivers and canals, and where they could also perhaps set a sail in fair winds: there are parallels with Romano-Celtic river and canal boats (5.6.2). Seagoing cogs (like ships of the Romano-Celtic tradition—5.6.1.1) had plank-keels which scarcely protruded below the bottom planking (d/b from 9–19 per cent), and had negligible rise of gar-

boards (0° to 6°). Leeboards are thought to have been first used in north-west Europe in the late sixteenth century Netherlands (Prins, 1970: 349–53; Reinders, 1983: 337): the possibility that they might have been used on the smaller, seagoing Dutch cogs in earlier times should be borne in mind.

No sail or rigging has been excavated with a cog, and so representational evidence has to be used. A bowsprit is depicted in the 1242 Elbing seal, and a possible bowline on the 1263 seal of Hardwijk, otherwise the rigging seems to consist of stays and shrouds, and sails appear to be square sails. The Bremen cog had a windlass aft for hoisting yard and sail, and a capstan at a higher level for working the sheets.

Three seals of Lubeck, dated 1224–81, show the helmsman steering over the port quarter. In the two earlier seals his posture suggests he is using a side rudder, although no pivot is evident. The helmsman in the third seal appears to be using a paddle. Ellmers (1994: 32–3) has suggested that the engraver has depicted the use of a *firrer*, a steering device which depends for its turning effect on changes in the immersed length of blade by moving the device up or down—similar to the action of *guares* on log rafts (6.6.3, 8.3.1, 10.2.5, 11.4.1.2). Such vertical movement is not suggested on these seals: Ellmers's conjecture is unlikely.

Seals, from 1242 onwards, show a median rudder with a fore-and-aft tiller, and this use is confirmed by fittings on the thirteenth- to fourteenth-centuries Kolding and later cogs. This evidence for the earliest use of the median rudder is, like several other cog features, contemporary with that for Nordic ships. It cannot be said that one 'borrowed' from the other: more likely there was a general move in northern Europe towards bigger merchant ships, steered by median rudders, and with castles for command and control and/or for defensive/offensive operations.

### 5.8.2.3 SEQUENCE OF BUILDING

With the bottom planking not fastened together and the sides edge-joined with iron nails, it might be thought that the cog was built partly frame-first (the bottom), then plank-first (the sides). However, in two wrecks (NZ43 and Almere), small square holes plugged with treenails have been found throughout the bottom planking and in some of the clench-fastened side planking, and it is concluded that these holes are where battens were temporarily fastened to hold the bottom planking firmly together before floors were fitted. Thus the hulls of these two vessels were built plank-first and their builders visualized the ship's shape in terms of her planking. However, no evidence for temporary fastenings has been found on the Bremen cog, (Ellmers, personal communication): whether similar evidence has been found on other cogs is not clear. The builders of the Hamburg full-scale reconstruction of the Bremen cog used temporary battens, those building the Kiel reconstruction used temporary lashings, to keep the central parts of the bottom strakes in position until floor timbers could be fastened to them (ibid). Full publication of other cog finds may throw further light on this important matter.

The building sequences proposed for the three best-published cogs, Bremen, Almere, and NZ43, are very similar, and a composite sequence, based mainly on the Bremen cog, may be summarized:

- plank-keel scarfed to the stem hooks, then hooks to the main posts;
- bottom planking fashioned, fitted, and fastened at the ends in an overlap; the central parts of these bottom planks temporarily fastened together with lashings or battens;
- floors fashioned, fitted, and fastened to bottom planking; keelson fastened to floors; temporary battens removed; bottom caulked externally;
- the first five side strakes fashioned, fitted overlapping, fastened together and to hooks and posts, and caulked inboard;
- main crossbeams inserted and supported by knees; possibly some futtocks added;
- after two more strakes, higher crossbeams, and all remaining futtocks inserted;
- two more strakes, and the washstrake added; then the top timbers;
- great knees / half-bulkheads added;
- ceiling planking, longitudinal timbers, and decking added;
- superstructure, etc.

## 5.8.2.4 PERFORMANCE AND CAPABILITIES

Two full-size reconstructions of the Bremen cog have been built (Fig. 5.57) and have undergone preliminary trials (Hoheisel, 1994; Baykowski, 1994; Brandt and Hochkirch, 1995), and theoretical estimates of performance have been made for other cogs. The hold index for three cogs ranges from 0.40–0.50 (Table 5.4), not unlike those for contemporary Nordic cargo ships (Table 5.3). Two cogs from inland waters could carry 24.5 tonnes (Almere) and 9 tonnes (NZ43). It has been estimated that the seagoing Kollerup cog could carry c.30 tonnes. Estimates for the Bremen cog have been in the range 70–130 tonnes (McGrail, 1998: table 11.4; Crumlin-Pedersen, 1991b: fig. 10; Steffy, 1994: 121; Ellmers, 1994: 38; Tipping, 1994). In their comprehensive trials report on the Kiel-built reconstruction of this vessel, Brandt and Hochkirch (1995) estimate her maximum useful cargo capacity to be 87 tonnes at a draft of 2.25 m.

Sailing trials in the Baltic showed that this cog reconstruction could sail up to 67–75° off the true wind, depending on sail area and wind strength. In such conditions the ship could make c.1 knot to windward for a short period of time: generally, however, the best she could achieve was to make good a track 90° off the wind. The ship performed best on a broad reach and when running, when the maximum speed was 8 knots. In any sort of seaway, the ship developed a short cycle, jerky motion 'leading to considerable strain on the crew'. Her operational performance was also limited by her not having a watertight weather deck. The general conclusion was that the Bremen cog, as represented by the Kiel reconstruction, was not a windward vessel and would have had to wait for fair winds. When evaluating this trails report it has to be borne in mind that, although the reconstructed hull is probably authentic (so much of the original having survived), the reconstructed rig has had to be based on seal depictions supplemented by calculations.

## 5.8.2.5 THE COG AND THE NORDIC SHIP

Vessels which appear to have been what we now call cogs came in a variety of sizes, from seagoing ships to boats for inland waters. As well as having similar structural features and similar methods of propulsion and steering, these vessels had in common a shape which maximized, in as much as operational constraints allowed, the volume of cargo that could be carried. In the cogs for which details have been published, a box-like hold is combined with an underwater shape which allows the vessel to take the ground in tidal conditions and sit upright, yet with sufficiently fine ends to give reasonable performance under sail. The stern rudder could more readily be fitted to the cog than the contemporary Nordic ship, even though both were double-ended (5.8.1.4.3).

Cogs probably had a stiffer and stronger hull than Nordic ships and, size for size, they were heavier since the frame scantlings were greater: in this respect the cog may be seen as a continuation of the 'heavy' structural approach to shipbuilding as seen 1,000 years earlier in the Romano-Celtic tradition (5.6, 5.7.1.4.3.3). Since the stress per unit area in such a structure would be less than in a 'light' tradition such as the Nordic, high quality timber was not essential (Crumlin-Pedersen, 1989, 1991b: 77–8). The cog could be built from oaks widely available rather than from limited, and therefore expensive, stocks of high quality trees with knot-free, straight-grained boles, and potential crooks in the crown, as were needed by the Nordic vessel. Furthermore, sawn rather than split timbers could be used in the cog.

### 5.8.2.6 COGS AND THE ROMANO-CELTIC TRADITION

The cog tradition of boat and shipbuilding was not a strictly homogenous group: most of the excavated vessels thought to be cogs have many features in common, but there are regional differences, changes over time, and the function of a particular vessel sometimes determined which characteristic features should be incorporated, or even enhanced, and which should be omitted. Such variability is most readily appreciated in the Dutch finds (Reinders, 1985), most of which were used on inland waters: it is by no means certain, however, that all such vessels were called 'cogs' by their builders and users.

It is generally considered, mainly on documentary grounds, that the cog style of boatbuilding originated in Frisian lands in and near the mouth of the Rhine (5.8.2). Much of the evidence for the inland boats of the first–fourth centuries AD Romano-Celtic tradition (5.6.2) also comes from this region. There is a gap of c.1,000 years between excavated examples of these two traditions, and there are significant structural differences between them; nevertheless, there are certain striking similarities.

Both types were evidently 'designed' to have maxi-mum possible space for cargo and to be used either on rivers and canals or in tidal waters. Thus there were two versions of each type: (a) rounded hulls of full form, with plank-keels protruding only slightly below the bottom planking; and (b) flat-bottomed hulls.

Both types were built in the 'heavy' tradition of framing and were built from sawn planking. The plank-keel, stem hook, raked stempost combination of the cog may be compared with the plank-keel and 'curved L-shaped' stems of the Romano-Celtic vessels. Hooked nails were used in both traditions (albeit in different ways), and the cogs caulking sequence of moss, lath, metal fastening is also found in some of the Romano-Celtic boats. In both traditions the bottom planking was not fastened together or to the plank-keel.

Romano-Celtic vessels had their mast steps well forward and several of these were in a floor timber: early cogs were similar. Furthermore, other characteristic features of the cog were within the Romano-Celtic technological repertoire although maybe not in the mainstream, if the boats and ships so far excavated are representative of the tradition. Overlapping planking fastened by metal nails through the overlap is found in some of the second–third century AD Zwammerdam boats, as are mast-steps within a longitudinal keelson. Both frame-first, and plank-first techniques are found in the Romano-Celtic tradition, albeit not in one particular vessel. Furthermore, the building sequence of some of the inland Romano-Celtic boats involved temporarily fastening together hull planking until floor timbers could be inserted (5.6.2.1.1): this technique is a key aspect of the cog (5.8.2.3), and indeed, reappears again in the Rhine mouth region in large seagoing Dutch ships of the sixteenth–seventeenth centuries (Maarleveld, 1992, 1994; Moortel, 1991), a procedure sometimes called 'Double Dutch' (5.9.3).

The similarities presented here can only be provisional since a high proportion of cog-like wrecks remain to be published and the structure of certain Romano-Celtic boats is not yet fully understood.

### 5.8.3 THE HULC TRADITION

The first documentary reference to the 'hulc', a medieval merchant ship, comes in the laws of Aethelred II of England: in c. AD 1000 tolls of equal value were to be paid by hulcs and by *ceol*/keels discharging cargo at

Billingsgate on the River Thames in London (Robertson, 1925: 71). Regulations of c.1130 concerning ships importing Rhenish wine state that keels were to pay a greater toll than hulcs; whereas by the fourteenth-century hulcs were to pay more than keels (McCusker, 1966: 279–80). These variations in tolls suggest that hulcs continued to carry much the same amount of cargo during the late tenth to the mid-twelfth centuries, but that by the fourteenth century, they had been enlarged and carried a greater load. Waskönig (1969) has suggested that this increased cargo capacity was stimulated by a marked increase in overseas demand for salt, grain, and timber. The cog could not be developed for this role (Waskönig does not give reasons for this statement) and the Hanseatic League turned to the larger version of the hulc currently in use in the Channel region. Thirteenth–fifteenth-century documents show that in c.1400 Hanseatic merchants began to use hulcs in the Baltic, and by the mid-fifteenth century hulcs had entirely replaced cogs as the Hanseatic workhorse (Ellmers, 1994: 44–5).

### 5.8.3.1 ICONOGRAPHIC EVIDENCE

The link between these references to the hulc and representational evidence was made by Heinsius (1956) who pointed out that the Latin inscription on the seal of New Shoreham in Sussex of 1295, referred to this hulc (Fig. 5.60). In translation this text reads, 'By this symbol of a hulc I am called mouth which is a worthy name.' The West Sussex Record Office hold a reference dated 1302 to a ferry 'across the water' of Hulkesmouth with appurtenances in New Shoreham , and a 1457 reference to sixty acres of land 'in the port of Hulkesmouth *alias* Shoreham'. As with other port seals, it may be taken that the citizens of Hulkesmouth/Shoreham had the representation of a ship which traded from their port engraved on their town seal. The features of that ship, insofar as they can now be understood, should thus be characteristic of the hulc type of ship as used in the Channel region in the late thirteenth century.

In profile this Shoreham hulc is double-ended, with castles at bow and stern. There are no visible stems and a keel is not discernible. The planking, which appears to be laid in reverse-clinker, runs in a uniform curve, parallel both to the sheerline and the bottom of the hull, and ends on a horizontal line at the base of each

castle, well above the waterline. A mast is stepped near amidships, and the ship appears to be steered by a rudder on the starboard quarter; an anchor seems to be catted on the starboard bow. This is clearly a different type of vessel from both the cog and the Nordic ship, and its most distinctive feature seems to be its planking which does not end at posts but on the sheerline, high at bow and stern. It might be suggested that the craftsman had been forced to engrave a curved hull with curved planking by the circular shape of the seal. However, similarly curved planking on other ship depictions not so constrained (for example, the ship on the font in Winchester Cathedral (Fig. 5.61) of a hundred years earlier) demonstrate that this was not so.

As with the cog, once the link between the type name 'hulc' and features depicted on the Shoreham ship, had been established, scholars sought out both earlier and later depictions with such features. Numerous 'hulcs' have been identified in twelfth-to fifteenth-centuries illustrated manuscripts and paintings, and as engravings on stone, wood, seals, and coins (Greenhill, 2000; Hutchinson, 1994: figs. 1.4–1.6, 2.1, 3.2, 3.5; Friel, 1995: figs. 1.1, 2.4, 2.5, 5.3).

It has been suggested that hulcs are depicted on ninth-century coins from Quentovic, south of Bologne (Vlek, 1987: figs. 3.2.1 and 3.2.2), Dorestadt (Vlek, 1987:

Fig. 5.60. 1295 town seal of New Shoreham (National Maritime Museum, Greenwich).

Fig. 5.61.  Scene from the life of St. Nicholas on the late twelfth-century font in Winchester Cathedral (National Maritime Museum, Greenwich).

fig. 3.2.3; Lebecq, 1990: fig. 11.3.1), and from West Harling, Norfolk (Fenwick, 1983). A vessel engraved on a seventh-century Merovingian strap-end from the Pas de Calais–Somme region (Joffrey, 1978) is of the same general hull form, though not so highly curved: this ship has a mast with stays, a rudder on the port quarter, and possibly a number of oars (Fig. 5.62): its relationship, if any, to the hulc tradition is unclear.

These seventh- and ninth-centuries ship depictions generally show undifferentiated, though curved, plank runs, but clinker planking with its prominent fastenings is clearly indicated on many of the twelfth- to fifteenth-century representations. In some of these, reverse-clinker planking is depicted: that is, each succeeding strake overlaps inboard the upper edge of the strake below rather than overlaps outboard as in the Nordic tradition. The most convincing representations are: in *John of Worcester's Chronicle* dated before 1140 (Hutchinson, 1994: fig. 1.5); in the 1240 *Life of St Thomas of Canterbury* (Hutchinson, 1994: fig. 3.2); possibly on

Fig. 5.62.  Ship engraving on a seventh-century strap-end from the Pas de Calais-Somme region (after Joffrey, 1978).

the New Shoreham seal (Fig. 5.60); a ship depicted on the Sea of Galilee in an early fourteenth-century manuscript (Friel, 1995: fig. 5.3); and on the *c.*1446 seal of the Admiralty Court of Bristol (Fig. 5.63). It might be thought that such depictions were a mistake by the engraver, since reverse-clinker is otherwise not known in Europe until the late twentieth century (McGrail, *et al.*, 1999: 145–6). However, the technique is a practicable one (reverse-clinker boats are used widely in Bangladesh, West Bengal, and Orissa—Blue *et al.*, 1997; McGrail *et al.*, 1999; Kentley *et al.*, 1999) and the medieval craftsmen should, for the present, be given the benefit of the doubt.

Some medieval seals appear to depict a 'hybrid hulc' with hulc-like planking ending on a horizontal surface at the bow, but ending at a post or an upward-turned, extension of a plank-keel at the stern. Examples range in date from the thirteenth-century seal of Poole (Friel, 1995: fig. 2.6) to the seal of the Admiralty Court of Bristol of 1446 (Fig. 5.63). It has been suggested that this variant arose during the change from side rudder to stern rudder. However, there is no clear correlation between these two features, and in any case, one of the earliest depictions with hulc planking at both ends (on the late twelfth-century font in Zedelgem near Bruges) has a stern rudder (see also Fig. 5.61). There are also a number of representations with hulc planking in the upper hull when the lower planking runs to a hog, post, or transom. Examples are in the 1230–40 *Life of St. Thomas of Canterbury* (Hutchinson, 1994: fig. 3.2),

Fig. 5.63. The fifteenth-century seal of the Admiralty court of Bristol (photo: Basil Greenhill).

the early fourteenth-century illustration of Christ on the Sea of Galilee (Friel, 1995: fig. 5.3), and depictions noted by Greenhill (1995a: fig. 320, 1995b: figs. 9.1 and t32.11).

### 5.8.3.2 EXCAVATED EVIDENCE

It has sometimes been suggested that hulcs or parts of hulcs have been excavated, but such claims have not been generally supported. Finds in the Low Countries, Utrecht boats I and II (Vlek, 1987; Hoekstra, 1975), Velsen (de Weerd, 1987), Zwammerdam 3 (Marsden, 1976: 49), and Antwerp (Ellmers, 1972: fig. 35) are all extended logboats rather than hulcs. Goodburn (1994: 103; forthcoming) has sought to show that some tenth-century timbers reused at Bull Wharf, Queenhithe, London, are from a Netherlands based 'hulc', but his arguments are not convincing.

There are two other finds which may be from reverse-clinker built vessels, not necessarily hulcs. A thirteenth-/fourteenth-centuries floor timber from the sea off Kastrup, Denmark (Crumlin-Pedersen, 1981: 46) appears to have been joggled on its lower face to match reverse-clinker planking. Crumlin-Pedersen, however, prefers to see it coming from a Nordic vessel with an upper strake positioned in an irregular fashion.

A group of incomplete strakes excavated from a late sixteenth-century waterfront site in 1987 (Marsden, 1996: 136–44) have been interpreted as being from the stern of a boat built in reverse-clinker. At present, it seems unlikely that isolated finds such as this can be unambiguously identified as clinker or reverse-clinker. Future finds of overlapping planking, fastened to other timbers which can be orientated with certainty, should help research forward.

### 5.8.3.3 ETHNOGRAPHIC EVIDENCE

Thus there are no unchallengeable excavated remains which have features thought to be diagnostic of a medieval hulc. This means, in turn, that there is no archaeological control on the interpretation of the iconographic evidence. As Greenhill (2000) has pointed out, however, ethnographic evidence from the reverse-clinker boats of south Asia can suggest what the structure of a medieval hulc may have been like.

Following in the footsteps of Greenhill in the 1950s (1971), fieldwork in Bangladesh, West Bengal, and Orissa during 1996–8 confirmed that there were three main types of boat with hulc planking (6.7.4.2).

(a) Round-hulled boats with a plank-keel or a hog which extends upwards at the ends to take the place of posts. These boats have reverse-clinker, hulc-like planking which ends on a diagonal line from a high point on the extended plank-keel; the gap between the two ends is filled with conventional (European-style) clinker planking. Example: the *pattia* of Orissa (Blue *et al.*, 1997; Kentley, McGrail, and Blue, 1999).

(b) Flat-bottomed boats and round-hulled but keel-less boats with block stem (sometimes plank) ends. These boats have reverse-clinker, hulc-like planking which ends on a near horizontal line. Above these strakes are further strakes which run from block stem to block stem—these can be a combination of reverse-clinker strakes, conventional clinker strakes and standing strakes; occasionally there is just one full length reverse clinker strake forming the gunwale. Example: the *Sylheti nauka* from Bangladesh (McGrail, Blue, and Kentley, 1999).

(c) A variety of boats, mostly round-hulled, which have hulc-planking patterns but are not reverse-clinker. Their planking overlaps, but within a half-lap so that, externally and internally, these boats are smooth skinned. The planks are fastened together within this half lap by boatbuilder's staples (Greenhill, 1995a: fig. 36, no. 5). The hulc planking in the lower hull is capped by a number of near-horizontal full-length strakes. Examples are: the *pallar* and the *patam* of Bangladesh; the *salti* and *chhoat* of Orissa and West Bengal (McGrail, Blue, and Kentley, 1999; Greenhill, 1971: figs. 9, 10, 11).

There are also some reverse-clinker boats in Bangladesh which have asymmetric planking patterns with some similarities to the 'hybrid hulcs' depicted on certain medieval seals (5.8.3.1). These boats have hulc planking running to a horizontal line at the bow, but at the stern the strakes run to the turned-upwards garboard strake as though it were a sternpost (Greenhill, 1995a: 254, fig. 327).

There is thus a wealth of information about twentieth-century south Asian boats with hulc planking (with and without reverse-clinker) which have features comparable with those seen on European medieval representations of what are thought to be hulcs (6.7.4). Greenhill's recent work (2000) has already thrown light on a singular advantage of hulc tplanking. A small-scale model of one of the Bangladesh boats has shown that all the strakes are straight or virtually so. The hulc hull could have been built without using the shaped planking of the cog or the Nordic vessel. Straight runs of sawn planking could be used, making the hulc quicker and therefore cheaper to build than the cog. Hulc-planking patterns are clearly very suitable for a beamy, full-ended, and capacious hull. If and when parts of a hulc are excavated, ethnographic evidence from south Asia may prove even more useful in the interpretation of the remains.

# 5.9
# Late Medieval Ships

During the decades around 1300, Genoa and then Venice, both near the height of their overseas commercial activities, established annual convoys sailing to and from the Low Countries and England. The first recorded voyage was in 1277/8 when Genoese merchant galleys traded with Bruges and Southampton (Hutchinson, 1994: 84–7). By this date Mediterranean ships had been built frame-first for some time (4.15). Whether any element of framing-first building, as practised during Romano-Celtic times (5.6.1, 5.7.1.4.3.3) survived in north-west Europe is impossible to say: the fact that the cog, with its apparent origins in the Rhine mouth region and with its bottom planking not edge-fastened, was mainly built plank-first (5.8.2.3) tends to suggest that framing-first was no longer used in the mainstream of late medieval Atlantic European shipbuilding.

Ships similar to Genoese galleys must have been seen by the crews of Crusader ships in earlier centuries, but the late thirteenth century was probably the first time a lateen-rigged, frame-first, flush-laid Mediterranean ship could be studied at length, as Italian ships overwintered in north-west Europe. Equally, this may have been the earliest that Mediterranean seamen could study square-rigged, plank-first, mainly clinker-built ships. Perhaps even more significant is the fact that, from 1293 and throughout the fourteenth century, Genoese shipwrights and others from Marseilles and Narbonne built two-masted galleys in the French 'le clos des galées' dockyard at Rouen on the River Seine (Rieth, 1989, 1996). The idea of building frame-first must, once again, have been abroad in north-west Europe from this time. However, possibly because Italian vessels were galleys and not carriers of bulk cargo, north Europeans evidently saw no advantage in adopting this Mediterranean technology. During the course of the fifteenth century, this attitude was to change (5.9.3).

## 5.9.1 COGS, *COCHA*, AND CARRACKS

The medieval chronicler, Giovanni Villani, noted that in c.1304, Bayonnese cogs undertook buccaneering voyages in the Mediterranean. From this time on Genoese, Venetians, and Catalans began to use cogs because of their greater seaworthiness and lower cost (Greenhill, 1995a: 227). These Mediterranean 'cogs' became known as *cocha* (Ciciliot, 1998). It is most unlikely that they were direct copies of the northern cog, rather, a frame-first version with emphasis on the capacious hull form. The northern median rudder may also have been taken over, as may the square sail on a central mast since it matched the hull. A mizzen lateen was added at about this time or subsequently (van der Merwe, 1983). The first reference to a *cocha* in Venetian literature is from 1312: by 1340 they had replaced galleys on the trading voyages to north-west Europe where they appear to have become known as 'carracks' (Hutchinson, 1994: 42–4). The earliest illustration of a three-masted *cocha*/carrack is in a Catalan manuscript of 1406 (Mott, 1994).

From the middle of the fourteenth century carracks were known and used in northern Europe. For example, from 1371 onwards carracks came into the King of England's possession by default or by capture (Friel, 1995: 172–8). Although these vessels were put into active service, the English had to recruit foreign carpenters and caulkers to repair and refit them (Rose, 1982: 12, 20–55). The situation may have been similar in Flanders and France. Northern shipyards continued to build plank-first in the Nordic, hulc, and cog traditions: the innovative frame-first methods were not immediately taken over. It may be that this was not because northern shipwrights and shipowners did not perceive the virtues of frame-first building, nor an unwillingness to change from traditional methods: rather that they did not have access to the 'mystery' of how to design a ship's framework—not even in the Rouen dockyard where Frenchmen building barges worked in the same yard as Mediterranean shipwrights building galleys (Rieth, 1989). Genoese carpenters and caulkers might readily explain how to shape and fasten planking to the framing and caulk the seams, but only a master builder would know how to design and fashion the framework to give the required hull form.

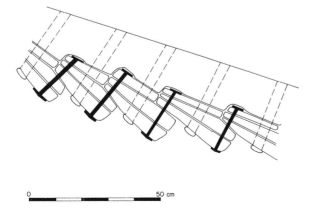

0                    50 cm

Fig. 5.64. *Grace Dieu*'s clinker planking (after Hutchinson, 1994: fig. 2.3D).

## 5.9.2 THE FINAL PHASE OF THE NORDIC TRADITION OF SHIPBUILDING

Henry V's *Grace Dieu*, built in Southampton between 1416 and 1420, was, in essentials, a ship of the Nordic tradition, albeit a late and very large one; her capacity is said to have been c.1,400 tons and she measured c.40 × 15 × 6.5 m (R. Anderson, 1934; Prynne, 1968; Friel, 1993). *Grace Dieu*'s planking was an elaborate form of clinker (Fig. 5.64)—in the overlaps there were five layers of planking, elsewhere three (Clarke *et al.*, 1993; fig. 5). This planking was caulked with moss and tar, and clench-fastened in the overlap by iron nails some of which were 220 mm in length. Her floor timbers, which were evidently added after the planking had been fastened together, averaged 200 × 200 mm, and were spaced at c.0.40 m: they were treenailed to the planking. Futtocks, stringers, and through-beams completed her framing (McGrail, 1993c).

A boat or small ship in the Nordic plank-first tradition can clearly be built 'by eye' using some elementary building aids (McGrail, 1998: 98–103). For a large complex ship such as *Grace Dieu*, building by eye—in effect, 'designing' the hull as the work progressed—would seem to be impracticable: some aids to controlling hull shape were necessary. In the presumed absence of models and drawings there would seem to be two possibilities: the shape was known as a set of plank breadths and bevel angles at selected stations along the length of the ship, possibly recorded in code on a boatbuilder's level, if one existed in those early days; alternatively, moulds might have been used (McGrail, 1993c: 48). Louwen (1997) has shown that there was a third possible method.

Henry V had another ship building at Bayonne in 1419, and details in a letter to Henry from his agent, John Alcetre, have led Louven to suggest that, although this large ship (capacity 1,826 to 1,937 tons—Carr Laughton, 1923), was probably clinker-built, some of her frames were designed, that is, they controlled the hull shape in some way.

The Bayonne ship has not survived, as far as is known, but the bottom of *Grace Dieu*'s hull lies in the River Hamble not far from Southampton (Clarke *et al.*, 1993). Some future excavation of this designated wreck site might establish whether *Grace Dieu* was built in the Bayonne manner: for example, by demonstrating that *some* floors could have been in position before the planking. A near-contemporary wreck off the north Breton coast at Aber Wrac'h (L'Hour et Veyrat, 1994) has some features similar to *Grace Dieu*, with cleft clinker planking, relatively heavy oak frames, and through beams. Although this ship of *c.*1435 is nowhere near the size of *Grace Dieu* or the Bayonne ship, being only *c.*25 × 8 m, it may be that the forthcoming publication will throw some light on the matter. *Grace Dieu*, the Bayonne ship, and the Aber Wrac'h wrecks were in the final phase of Nordic shipbuilding: they (and the hulc and cog) gave way to an entirely different method of shipbuilding, in which the framing became all-important. On the other hand, boats continued to be built in the plank-first Nordic tradition right up to the twentieth century.

### 5.9.3 THE *CARAVELA* AND CARAVEL SHIPBUILDING

By *c.*1430 another southern ship type had appeared in northern Europe: this was the *caravela*, a relatively small Portuguese frame-first ship which appears to have been developed from a fishing boat to become a vessel capable of voyages of exploration and trade along the Atlantic coasts of Africa and Europe. In 1438–40, a caravel is said to have been built in Brussels (Sleeswyk, 1990: 345), and in 1451, a caravel was built in Dieppe for a Breton owner. Others were bought or captured (Friel, 1995: 175–80). The mid-sixteenth-century compiler of the *Chronicles of Zeeland* stated that, in about 1459, instead of hulcs and *craiers*, caravels began to be built in Flanders following the example of a Breton named Julian (Fliedner and Pohl-Weber, 1972: 27). In 1462 a French-owned caravel, *Peter de la Rochelle*, was abandoned in Gdansk and from this the local shipwrights are said to have learned how to build them (van der Merwe, 1983: 121). The first caravel known to have been built in England was a three-master at Dunwich between 1463 and 1466 (Friel, 1995: 164–5). The Tudor royal ship, *Mary Rose*, was built frame-first fashion in 1509–16 (Rule, 1982).

Unlike the thirteenth-century galley and the carrack of the fourteenth century, the fifteenth-century caravel seems to have inspired northern European ship owners and shipbuilders, and frame-first (carvel) ships began to be built in increasing numbers by overseas trading nations. By the end of the sixteenth century the frame-first building of seagoing ships was undertaken almost everywhere in Atlantic Europe, a principal exception being the Netherlands where some large ships were still built plank-first in a cog-like 'Double-Dutch' (5.8.2.6) manner (Maarleveld, 1992; 1994; Moortel, 1991). Although certain aspects of hull, fittings, and rigging are mentioned in contemporary documents and something can be learned from illustrations of ships thought to be caravels (Friel, 1995), it is not possible to describe their significant features in detail since no vessel which might be a fifteenth-century caravel has been excavated.

### 5.9.4 THE DESIGN OF LATE MEDIEVAL FRAME-FIRST SHIPS

The real 'mystery' of the late medieval Mediterranean frame-first shipbuilder lay in the method he used to define a hull's three-dimensional form (Bellabarba, 1993: 278). That caravels were built in northern Europe from the mid-fifteenth century, and that frame-first shipbuilding gradually ousted plank-first over much of Atlantic Europe, must mean that, by then, the technique of designing a ship's framework had been transmitted from the Mediterranean. The earliest references to such design methods come from early fifteenth-century Venice (4.16). It seems likely that these methods or similar ones were used in earlier times to design the galleys, *cocha*/carracks, and caravels of the thirteenth–fifteenth centuries (Rieth, 1989).

By the sixteenth century similar design methods were used in southern Italy, Spain, Portugal, France, southern Netherlands, England, and possibly elsewhere (Bellabarba, 1993: 286, 290; Rieth, 1996: 177–99). The ships of the European explorers of the late fifteenth/early sixteenth century (Dias, Vasco de Gama, Columbus, and Magellan) were probably designed by these methods since the earliest known Portuguese text on shipbuilding, *Livro da Fábrica das Naus* by Fernando de Oliveira dated *c.*1550, prescribes methods similar to those of Venice (Steffy, 1994: 128–41).

Nearest in date to the ships used by the fifteenth-century Iberian oceanic explorers are seven early sixteenth-century wrecks, two in the Mediterranean, three in American waters, and two off the south coast of England. The American (Highborn Cay, Molasses Reef, and Red Bay) and the British (Cattewater and

Studland Bay) wrecks may all have been built in the tIberian peninsula (Rednap 1984; Grenier, 1988; Grenier, Loewen, and Proulx, 1994; Keith, 1988; Oertling, 1989; Hutchinson, 1991; Thomsen, 2000). These five ships have several features in common. The 'backbone' consists of a raked stern post with a transom, a gently curved stem, and a substantial keel. The five ships appear to have a full body with heavy frames closely spaced: where the futtocks overlap the main floors at the turn of the bilge there is little, if any, space between timbers. Except for the Studland Bay wreck, which has 'square lap' joints (Thomsen, 2000), floor and futtock are held together by a dovetail scarf (Fig. 5.65) and fastened by treenails and iron nails driven from opposite faces (Loewen, 1999) (Steffy, 1994: figs. 5.4 and 5.5): these main frames were assembled before they were erected and fastened to the keel. The master frame near amidships, has futtocks fastened to both after and forward faces of the floor: the other designed frames forward of the main frame have futtocks fastened to their forward face; those aft of the main frame have futtocks on their after face. Towards the ends of these ships, beyond the region of standing frames, frame components are not fastened together: these are not designed frames, their shape being derived from the planked hull. It is possible that the upper framing (futtocks) of these ships is similarly passive (Loewen, personal communication). However Thomsen (2000, 72–3) considers that the second futtocks (which were not joined to the first futtocks) were fastened to, and projected above, the lower planking, and thus determined the shape of the lower part of the upper hull; the third futtocks were also active and were used in a similar manner to define the shape of the remainder of the hull. If Thomsen's view is correct, these ships were designed and built framing-first; similar, in this respect to the Romano-Celtic ships from Blackfriars and St. Peter Port (5.6.1.2).

Two Mediterranean wrecks, Villefranche 1 which may have been the Genoese *Lomellina* (Rieth, 1991; Guérout, Reith, and Gassend, 1989) and Yassi Ada 3 (Steffy, 1994: 134) appear to be generally similar to the wrecks described above, but floor and futtock are interlocked rather than held together by a dovetail (Steffy, 1994: figs. 5.10 and 5.11*b*).

The fourteenth–sixteenth-centuries design methods for frame-first ships (4.16), did not necessarily originate in Venice. Frame-first methods (strictly-framing-first methods) were used in Celtic Europe before the second century AD (5.6.1.2, 5.6.3). From the seventh century AD Mediterranean ships were partly built frame-first (4.15.2). The change from plank-first ('free-arm/by eye') hulls to frame-first (designed) hulls in that region appears to have been a progression, over some centuries, from the dominant structural role of planking to the dominance of framing by the eleventh century. The formal design methods described in Venetian and subsequent texts were probably preceded by informal methods using units of measurements and ratios as suggested by Steffy for the Serçe Limani ship (4.15.2.3).

Vestiges of the 15th/16th century Venetian/Iberian design system (sometimes known as 'Mediterranean moulding') have been found in use in twentieth-century Newfoundland, Brazil, and Tamil Nadu (Taylor, 1988; Sarsfield, 1984, 1985, 1988; Carrell and Keith, 1992; Barker, 1993; Blue, Kentley, and McGrail 1998: 66–70; Kentley *et al.*, forthcoming). When the Tamil Nadu and the Mediterranean/Atlantic design methods are compared, it is readily seen that they have much in common (McGrail, forthcoming, *a*). Both are based on parameters such as a basic length module, the shape of a master frame, the number or spacing of frames, and the total narrowing and rising of the designed hull. The shape of hull is obtained by a combination of 'equal' (identical to the master frame) and 'unequal' (allowing for rising and narrowing of the hull) frames; passive (non-designed) frames are subsequently added. The shapes of the 'unequal' frames are derived from that of the master frame using the tablet (Fig. 4.46) (in the Mediterranean/Atlantic) or a scrieve-board system (Fig. 6.31) with rules of thumb (in Tamil Nadu). The passive frame shapes are obtained from ribbands.

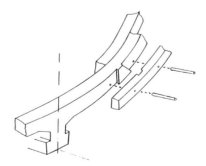

Fig. 5.65 A dovetail mortise on the Cattewater wreck (after Barker, 1991: fig. 4).

Furthermore the position of the foremost and after-most designed frames is emphasized by giving these frames a specific name. There is also the remarkable similarity in the use of dovetail joints to lock together the floors and futtocks in the Tamil Nadu boats and ships. It seems likely therefore that the Tamil design methods were taken there (and to Brazil) by the Portuguese in the sixteenth century. The twentieth-century Tamil design seems to be a simplification of the late medieval Iberian process, more suitable for less complex hull forms (6.7.4.3).

Tamil frame-first vessels are not fully designed: there is still an element of 'building by eye' and the use of personal experience in such matters as fairing the framework before it is planked; when determining the run of the sheerline; in working bevels on the 'unequal' frames; and when spiling the passive frame shapes from planking used as ribbands. A similar blend of techniques, frame-first mainly but with 'by eye/free arm' elements, was probably used in the late medieval shipyards of Atlantic Europe, as they changed to Mediterranean frame-first methods in the fifteenth century. The transition would also have been smoothed if, as seems likely, northern builders of large plank-first ships (cogs, hulcs, and Nordic tradition ships such as *Grace Dieu*) had been using some sort of active framework to get hull shape, which on that scale was probably difficult to conceive tin the mind's eye alone (5.9.2; McGrail, forthcoming, *a*).

The adoption of frame-first techniques in Atlantic Europe meant that stronger, more seaworthy ships could be built, ships capable of coping with long periods at sea on some of the most difficult ocean passages. It also meant that a design which proved itself at sea, whether as a cargo ship or a warship, could be repeated again and again, and, as theory and practice developed together, modifications could be made to optimize aspects of performance.

# 5.10
# Atlantic Seafaring

There is evidence from Neolithic times that boats were used within estuaries and coastal waters and to cross channels such as those between France and Britain and between Britain and Ireland (5.2.2, 5.4.9). The Phoenicians and the Greeks sailed the coasts of southern Spain (4.9.2.2, 4.9.3.2.1), the Phoenicians/Carthaginians may, in fact, have sailed even further north (4.9.3.2.1). Pytheas, the fourth-century BC explorer from Marseilles may well have sailed along this coast from the Pillars of Hercules to the River Rhine and beyond, not in a single voyage but in several short-haul passages between places where he could land to make astronomical observations and enquiries (4.14.2).

Trade between the Mediterranean and north-west Europe in Roman times seems to have been mainly by French and German rivers, but the final leg of these routes was along the Atlantic coast, from the estuaries of the Garonne, Loire, Seine, and Rhine. Some ships at least sailed the Iberian Atlantic coast to and from the Bay of Biscay (4.14.2; 5.5.4). In the ninth century the Vikings sailed the Atlantic coast southwards into the Mediterranean (Graham-Campbell, 1994: 127, 146–7); and in the tenth century Arab seamen ventured from the Mediterranean into Atlantic coastal waters (3.8.1).

Chaucer's fourteenth-century shipman (Coghill, 1951: 35–6) knew the harbours and havens of much of the Atlantic coast from Gotland to Cape Finisterre, and the creeks of Brittany and Spain. He could reckon his tides, tidal streams, phases of the moon, and tracks and distances. Similar expertise had been used by Atlantic seamen in the Neolithic and it continued to be used in parts of north-west Europe into the twentieth century (McGrail, 1998: 282–5). During the medieval period navigational instruments began to be used at sea. By the late twelfth century the mariner's compass was available: its use was at first restricted to periods of foul weather to check the wind direction, since the mariner continued to con his ship by reference to the wind (Waters, 1978: 22). The fifteenth century saw an influx of navigational aids (McGrail, 1998: 285): sand-glass, traverse tables, astrolabes, quadrants, printed sailing directions (rutters), and charts (portolans). Nevertheless, vessels still sailed from the vicinity of one known landmark to the next, and the course was frequently referred to as 'caping the ship' (Waters, 1978: 11; Gairdner, 1889).

In the early fourteenth century, Genoese and Iberian seamen undertook exploratory voyages along the coast of north Africa, rediscovering the Canary Islands (Gaspar and Vallejo, 1992: 120), and discovering the Madeiras and the Azores, the latter some 800 nautical miles out into the Atlantic (Waters, 1988: 286–94). Dias, in 1488, and Vasco da Gama, in 1497–9, pioneered the route to India (6.5), and da Gama met Arab navigators using the *kamāl* to measure star altitudes (3.8.2.2.3). As a result of these voyages enormous improvements were made in the art of navigation.

In 1492, therefore, Columbus was heir to a great wealth of navigational knowledge. In his journal of his first transatlantic voyage (Ife, 1990), Columbus noted that he had both quadrant and astrolabe on board *Santa Maria*, but he did not use them effectively on this voyage (McGrail, 1992a: 85). He used a magnetic compass for courses and bearings; time was measured by sand-glass and by the relative positions of the two 'guard' stars (Kochab and Pherab) in Ursa Minor; speeds and distances were estimated. Columbus' navigation, both westwards and eastwards across the Atlantic, was thus what is now known as 'dead reckoning', the simplest form of navigation when using a chart and compass. It is clear that he preferred tried and tested techniques rather than the newfangled methods of instrumental astronavigation. Without chart, compass, or sand-glass, Viking seamen had used similar non-instrumental/environmental means to cross the northern Atlantic in the tenth century (5.7.3). Indeed, comparable methods had been used in the Mediterranean, the Indian Ocean, and in the South Pacific Ocean (and doubtless other regions of the world) from the earliest days of seafaring.

# 6

# INDIA

The 'India' of this chapter is the Indian subcontinent or 'south Asia', including Pakistan, Bangladesh, and Sri Lanka (Fig. 6.1). In latitude it extends from north of the Tropic of Cancer at *c*.30°N, to near the Equator at *c*.5°N; and in longitude from *c*.65°E to *c*.95°E. The subcontinent is effectively a large peninsula bounded by the Arabian Sea to the west, the Bay of Bengal to the east, and the Indian Ocean to the south, and separated

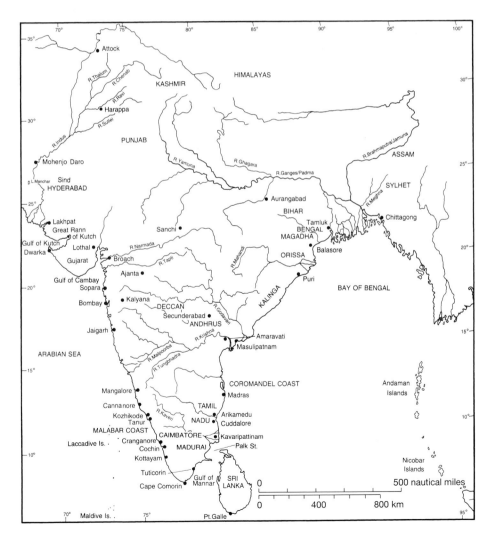

Fig. 6.1. Map of south Asia (Institute of Archaeology, Oxford).

from the rest of Asia by the Hindu Kush, Karakoram, and Himalayan mountain ranges.

Generally the climate is tropical with seasonal monsoon winds having a profound effect on the sailing season (Deloche, 1994: 209–16). On the west coast the stormy wet winds of the south-west monsoon virtually prevent sailing from May to August and later. From the end of this monsoon until November the wind strength abates, and sailing becomes increasingly practicable. The winter months from December to March are the main sailing season using regular land and sea breezes. From March to the onset of the south-west monsoon, as the land and sea breeze effect slackens, it becomes increasingly more difficult to make coastal passages. The south-west monsoon is not felt so keenly on the east coast, and sailing can be undertaken through the late summer months of June to September except at times at the head of the Bay of Bengal. The north-east monsoon, on the other hand, brings sailing to a halt on this coast from October to December and later. From December or January until the onset of the south-west monsoon is usually a good sailing season, with the north-east wind giving way to regular land and sea breezes followed in April and May by south-east and south winds.

The two great river systems of northern India both have very large catchment areas and collect water from a range of different climatic regimes, and have immense flood plains and enormous deltas. They differ in one main respect (Allchin and Allchin, 1997: 22–30): throughout the Ganges-Brahmaputra system there is moderate to high rainfall, whereas the Indus, despite high rainfall in its upland reaches, flows, in its lower reaches, through a desert with virtually no rainfall. In this respect, the Indus is like two other major rivers, the Nile (2.1) and the Tigris-Euphrates (3.1). These three perennial rivers became early natural highways for water transport, and their annual flooding ensured the success of early agriculture which in turn led to early civilizations. Both the Indus and the Ganges-Brahmaputra river systems became the principal means of communications within their vast regions and also a gateway to the sea and overseas trade. They remained so until the coming of the railways.

In the peninsular part of India, there are other rivers of some considerable size which, within their individual regions, are comparable, but on a smaller scale,

with the two northern river systems. This is especially so on the east coast, in the large delta areas of the River Mahanadi in Orissa, Krishna-Godavari in Andhra Pradesh, and Kaveri in Tamil Nadu. Iron Age and later kingdoms were founded on these nuclei.

With an immensely long coastline and innumerable lakes, rivers, and tidal estuaries, water transport was needed from very early times for estuary and coastal fishing, to cross unfordable rivers and to move along them, and also for fowling and the gathering of reeds and similar aquatic activities. There are very few documented finds, however, to help us visualize what early water transport was like, and the two that have been published are very late in date: a logboat from the Kelani Ganga in the Colombo district of Sri Lanka (6.6.6), dated to the sixth/fourth centuries BC (Vitharana, 1992); and the chance find of a sixteenth-century barge-like vessel (probably of European design) on an abandoned tributary of the River Boro Bulong at Olandazsahi near Balasore in Orissa (Behera, 1994: 67). Biswas (1981: 26), writing about Bengal terracottas, has mentioned, but not described, a third find, that of a boat from the River Gumani at Farakka on the west bank of the Ganges, some 250 km north of Calcutta, dated by radiocarbon to AD 80 ± 40. It may be that other early boats are known which have not yet been brought to public attention.

# 6.1

## The Neolithic and Bronze Ages

Agriculture, and other features of Neolithic times, spread into India from the north-west, into the Indus valley from eastern Iran, Baluchistan, and Afghanistan (Chakrabarti, 1980: 162). Along the lower Indus and on the Gujarat coast the Bronze Age Harappan civilization subsequently developed. This culture is first recognizable in the early third millennium BC and it lasted for 1,500 years or so (Thapar, 1990: 24–5), with grid-planned cities, monumental architecture, the art of writing, measurement units (for example a foot of *c.*335 mm and a cubit of *c.*520 mm) and a wide trading network (Chakrabarti, 1980: 163–4). This was a river-based economy, as were its near-contemporary civilizations in Egypt and Mesopotamia, and it early became involved in overseas trade.

In the late third millennium BC Sargon of Agade in Mesopotamia (3.3.1) proclaimed on steles and statues that ships from *Dilmun* (the Bahrain region in the Persian Gulf), *Makkan* (the Makran coastal region of Iran and Pakistan), and *Meluhha* (probably the River Indus region), came to the harbour outside his capital (Oppenheim, 1954: 15). Subsequently, *c.*2000 BC, the Larsa tablets show that at *Dilmun*, merchants from *Makkan* and *Meluhha* traded copper, wood, ivory, beads, and precious stones for goods brought there by the merchants of Ur (Oppenheim, 1954: 6–17). Cornelian beads, a product of India, excavated from royal graves at Ur and dated to the mid-third millennium BC (Chakrabarti, 1980: 165) give some archaeological support to this idea of overseas trade between Mesopotamia and the Indus valley. More convincing is the evidence from recent excavations at several sites in Oman (Reade, 1996: 122–4): at Asimah, for example, 32 per cent of the pottery excavated was from the Indus valley, suggesting to the excavator that this trade was by sea rather than overland. Excavations in India have revealed several sites in the Rann of Kutch region on the coast south of the Indus, which were probably Harrapan harbours (Deloche, 1994: fig. vi).

At Lothal, an Harrapan site near the head of the Gulf of Cambay, an excavated walled structure measuring *c.*214 × 36 m, has been interpreted by Rao (1965) as a dock; there is some questionable support for this view from an analysis of foraminifera in a sample of sediment taken from the site some twenty years after the excavation (Nigam, 1988). The walled structure is, however, at some distance from the deduced position of the Harappan tidal River Sabarmari; and it has been estimated that the sill of the supposed dock was at such a level that vessels could only cross it when the surrounding countryside was flooded (Allchin and Allchin, 1997: 167). Moreover, vessels of that period are unlikely to have needed a dock, but would have been beached or anchored in the river shallows when loading and discharging cargo—this is especially so where there is a good tidal range, as in the Gulf of Cambay. The Lothal 'dock' is more likely to have been a freshwater reservoir or irrigation tank (Deloche, 1994: 45–6).

The undoubted importance of the Gulf of Cambay as a harbour for trade by sea is emphasized by the exca-

vation in that region of five clay models of boats (Rao, 1965: 35–6). The mast, sail, and rigging seen on one of these models (Johnstone, 1988: fig. 13.4) are recent additions. Although it seems reasonably certain that these models do represent boats, precisely what form of boat is uncertain (6.7.1). On the other hand, impressions on a seal (Fig. 6.2) and another on a baked clay amulet (Fig. 6.3) from Mohenjo-Daro, an important Harappan site on the River Indus, do seem to represent river bundle rafts with some superstructure amidships and twin steering oars aft, and propelled by means other than sail.

A graffito on a potsherd from Mohenjo-Daro of *c.*2000 BC (Fig. 6.4) seems more likely to represent a planked boat, possibly with a 'spoon-shaped' hull. There are echoes of this shape in some of the early twentieth-century boats of the Indus (Greenhill, 1971). The vertical and near-horizontal lines above the graffito hull may well be depictions of mast and yard: if so, this is the earliest evidence for the use of sail in India.

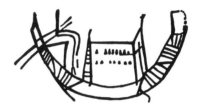

Fig. 6.2. Impression on a seal from Mohenjo-Daro, possibly a bundle raft (after Johnstone, 1980: fig. 13.1).

Fig. 6.3. Vessel on a backed clay amulet from Mohenjo-Daro (University of Pennsylvania Museum, Philadelphia).

Fig. 6.4. Graffito on a potsherd from Mohenjo-Daro (after Johnstone, 1980: fig. 13.3).

# 6.2

# The Iron Age

By the mid-first millennium BC, several hundred years into the Iron Age, the focus of economic activity had shifted from the Indus to the Ganges-Brahmaputra (Thapar, 1980: 257; Ray, 1987). From *c*.600 BC towns appear in northern India, in the middle Ganges valley, and in the east coast deltas of the River Krishna and the River Vaigai-Tambraparni. Written sources from these times stress the high status given to merchants and traders in these urban centres (Thapar, 1980: 258; Ray, 1990: 1–2). A written script and a coinage system were evolved and, together with the development of religions such as Buddhism and Jainism which provided a suitable social environment, these stimulated economic activity and facilitated long-distance trade (Ray, 1985: 15).

## 6.2.1 EARLY EUROPEAN CONTACTS

In *c*.519–512 BC, Darius I, King of the Persians, sent Scylax, a Greek from Caria in Asia Minor to investigate the course of the River Indus (Herodotus (4. 44); Dilke, 1985: 134). Scylax travelled overland, probably via the River Kabul and the Khyber Pass, and reached the River Indus near the modern town of Attock. From there he sailed downstream to the coast and then westwards coastwise into the Red Sea.

After Alexander the Great had subjugated central Asia he planned to do the same to India and crossed the Himalayas in 330 BC, taking a similar route to the River Indus as had Scylax. On the River Jhelum, a tributary of the Indus, he had vessels built (Deloche, 1994: 53, 156) in which his army sailed downstream to the island of Patala near Hyderabad within the Indus delta (Pliny, *NH* 6. 21–3). From there Alexander took an eastern arm of the Indus to Lakhpat, then on a bay open to the sea, now the salt marshes of the Great Rann of Kutch in Gujarat. From Lakhpat, Alexander's admiral, Nearchus, took about one-third of the army through coastal waters to the Persian Gulf using the north-east monsoon. One aim of this passage was to survey the Makran coast seeking out landing places where some future eastbound fleet could find drinking water, but

this second expedition never materialized as Alexander died in 323 BC.

## 6.2.2 THE MAURYAN PERIOD

From the late fourth century to the second century BC the Indian subcontinent (except for parts of Afghanistan, the southern parts of the Deccan, and Sri Lanka) was dominated by the Mauryan emperors such as Chandragupta, Bindusara, and Ashoka. This centralization of authority and the Mauryan expansion into the northern Deccan encouraged the growth of trade between regions (Ray, 1989: 46; 1990).

### 6.2.2.1 THE WEST COAST

Textiles, pottery, precious and semi-precious stones, and metals (and possibly the *malabathron* and *nard* of the first-century AD *Periplus*—see 6.3.1) were transported from the Ganges area southwards to peninsular India. One branch of this east coast route went overland to the westward flowing River Narmada, thence to ports such as *Bhrigu kaccha* (probably the *Periplus'* *Barygaza*, modern Broach in the Gulf of Cambay) and Sopara, north of Bombay. By the late first millennium BC there was an extensive coastal trading network along this west coast (Ray, 1990: 1; 1993). Inscriptions from the time of Ashoka show that gold, diamonds, and other minerals were transported from mines in the Deccan (Andhra Pradesh and Karnataka) to the north, probably by west-coast shipping from Sopara and Broach to Gujarat, Sind, and the lower Indus valley.

### 6.2.2.2 THE EAST COAST

From the state of Magadha in southern Bihar, raw materials such as timber and iron ore were transported down the Ganges to the port of *Tamralipti* (Tamluk) on the west bank of the River Hugli whence they were transported by sea to *Kalinga*, a fertile area around the delta of the River Mahanadi in Orissa. By the second century BC there appears to have been a well-established seaborne trading system along this section of the east coast (Ray, 1989: 43). Landing places (*ghat*) have been identified further south on this coast at Dharanikota opposite Amararati on the River Krishna, at

Arikamedu on the River Ariyankuppam, south of Pondicherry on the Coromandel coast, and at Kaveripattinam on the River Kaveri in Tamil Nadu—all of them were probably involved in coastal trade by the third/second centuries BC (Ray, 1990: 2). Rao (1970; 1981) has suggested that these places and the landing place on the island of Elephanta near Bombay (Ray, 1987: 98; Rao, 1981) had 'wharfs' and 'docks' which, whilst not impossible at this time, does seem to be an over-elaboration of the evidence (Deloche, 1994: 45–6): these remains were probably river-bank reinforcements and causeways (McGrail, 1983a).

## 6.2.3 POST-MAURYAN

In the post-Mauryan period, from the second century BC onwards, smaller kingdoms prevailed, such as that in the Deccan controlled by the Andhra or Satavahana dynasty, and Gujarat under Ksatrapa rule (Thapar, 1980: 260). From the first century BC or earlier there was overseas trade from west coast harbours with the Mediterranean via Egypt. This trade was at its height during the first and second centuries AD (6.3.1), and lasted until the fifth, possibly sixth, century AD (Horton, 1997). Indian goods such as spices, textiles, semi-precious stones, ivory, and peacocks were traded for gold coins, pottery, beads, lamps, intaglios, and glass.

Kaveripattinam and Arikamedu continued to flourish as landing places on the east coast. The earliest phase at Arikamedu, probably the *Poduke* of the *Periplus* (6.3.1), has recently been re-dated by Begley (1996) to the third century BC. Excavations by Wheeler, Ghosh, and Deva (1946) and by Begley (1996) have revealed evidence for trade with other regions in the west and north of the Bay of Bengal from the third century BC, as well as with the Mediterranean from the first century BC: the latter probably indirectly through a west coast port.

Roman coins have been found in many places in peninsular India especially in the Tamil region in the district of Coimbatore (Ray, 1985: 29); coin hoards have also been found in the Laccadive (Lakshadweep) islands (Ray, 1994: 178). Indian coins were also in circulation during this period: a unique series of Mauryan copper punch-marked coins and unbaked terracotta sealings with a ship symbol have been excavated from the earliest levels of Chandraketugarh in the lower

Ganges valley (Ray, 1989: 44; 1990: 8; 1994: 177, plate 17).

There are many references to trade by sea in the *Arthaśāstra* (Sangam literature of the Tamils) which is now thought to be of the second century AD, and in the roughly contemporary *Tandulanāli Jataka* (Ray, 1985: 19–21). Traders had to pay duty in ports, and those merchants who used the king's ships had to pay hire charges for the voyage. Members of the crew mentioned in the *Arthaśāstra* include *sasaka* (captain), *niryamaka* (master), *rasmigrahaka* (sailors), and *utsecaka* (bailers) (Ray, 1990: 14). We learn that merchants travelling overland by caravan were navigated across the desert by pilots (*thalaniyāmaka*) who were well acquainted with the stars: similar techniques would have been useful at sea.

Some merchants were known as *dvināvadhana* (having two boats); others as *pancanavapriya* (sailing with five ships). *Maha-navika* (master mariners) are mentioned in the *Jataku*; and also in an inscription from Ghantasda on the Andhra coast (Ray, 1989: 46; 1990: 13–14); *sagarapaloganas* (maritime traders) in other inscriptions (Ray, 1985: 22, 24, 25). A first-century BC inscription from northern Sri Lanka refers to *duta-navika* (envoy mariner) see Ray (1989: 45). Inscriptions in the early Brahmi script found at Andiyagala in north-west Sri Lanka refer to a mariner of *Bhojakataka* (probably Bhatkuli in Amaravati on the south bank of the River Krishna). This indicates overseas trading between the Coromandel coast and Sri Lanka (Ray, 1985: 22). The Palk strait between India and Sri Lanka has long been famous for pearls and for conch-shells and these have been traded far afield: for example, to Bhattiprolu and Amaravati in the lower Krishna valley, and even to China (Ray, 1989: 45). The *paradvar* communities of the Tamil coast dive for pearls today (Hornell, 1910: 50; Ray, 1994: 14; Blue, Kentley, and McGrail, 1998: 45). Similar diving is referred to in the *Periplus* (ch. 59), and in first century BC Sri Lanka inscriptions (Ray, 1989: 45).

## 6.2.4 EARLY DEPICTIONS OF INDIAN VESSELS

Outlines of vessels with a mast are found on coins dated to the second/first centuries BC, from Chandraketugarh in the Ganges delta. A monument in Duvegala in Sri Lanka, and terracotta seals of the first

Fig. 6.5. Medallion of the second-century BC from Baharhut (after Ray, 1986: fig. 4.1).

Fig. 6.6. Boat depicted on a first-century BC stupa at Sanchi (after Mookerji, 1912: 32).

Fig. 6.8. Vessel depicted in the Buddhist cave at Aurangabad (after Ray, 1990: fig. 4).

Fig. 6.7. Second-century AD coins of the Satavanhanas (after Ray, 1990: fig. 4.2).

century BC show a similar ship but with 'double-rigging' (Ray, 1990: 8). Planked boats are depicted on a second century BC medallion from the monastery at Bharhut (Fig. 6.5) and on the first-century BC southern pillar of the east gate in Stupa 1 at Sanchi (Fig. 6.6) (Mookerji, 1912: 32; Cunningham, 1879: plates 34, 56; Ray, 1986: 117, fig. 4.1; 1994: 176). The plank fastenings depicted on these two boats do not appear to be sewing, as some have thought, but flat wooden clamps of double-dovetail shape (6.7.2).

Two-masted and possibly three-masted ships (Fig. 6.7) are depicted on coins found along the Andhra coast, which were issued by the Satavanhanas in the second century AD (Mookerji, 1912: 51; Ray, 1989: 46; 1990: 8). The masts on these vessels have forestay and backstay but evidently no shrouds. There is a steering oar on each quarter and the ships have a rising sheerline towards the ends. A ship symbol is also found on later coins from the Coromandel coast possibly issued by

the Pallavas in the fourth century AD (Ray, 1989: 46). These finds supplement other evidence which indicates that, by the second century AD, settlements in the lower Krishna and Godavari valleys in the east Deccan reached an economic peak due to overseas trade under Satavanhana rule.

Ships are also depicted in the fourth-to sixth-centuries AD Buddhist centres at Aurangabad and Ajanta. The ship depicted in the Aurangabad cave (Fig. 6.8) appears to have three masts with stays; there is one steering oar (possibly rudder) on the starboard quarter, and the bow has much more sheer than the stern. The wall paintings in the Ajanta caves (near Hyderabad, north-east of Bombay) illustrate a variety of ships (Mookerji, 1912: 40, 42, 44; Ray, 1990: figs. 5, 6, 7). In cave 17, of the fifth century (Fig. 6.9), two large open boats propelled by oars are depicted transporting fighting men with their horses and elephants to Sri Lanka as in the *Divyavadana* (Ray, 1996). Another illustration from the same cave shows a three-masted vessel with the masts all in the fore part (Ray, 1990: 8). A vessel in cave 1 has a curved hull with planking terminating above the waterline on a near-horizontal line at the ends and not at posts (Fig. 6.10). Such a run of planking is similar to that found on the early nineteenth-century reverse clinker-built *pattooa* (Mookerji, 1912: 252–3), the twentieth-century reverse-clinker *patia* (Blue *et al.* 1997), the twentieth-century flush-laid *pallar* of Bangladesh (Greenhill, 1971: 92): this 'hulc planking' is discussed further below (6.7.4.2). The cave 1 vessel may aso be multi-masted but this is uncertain because the centre is obscured by a pavilion-like superstructure. There is a steering-oar over the starboard quarter and what may be a paddle over the starboard bow, and there are *oculi* at both ends. On a fresco in cave 2, another three-masted ship is depicted (Fig. 6.11). The sails on these masts have a high-aspect ratio, recalling the lugsails of the Chinese (10.7.3) and south-east Asian tradition (8.3.6, 8.3.8). This vessel also has a sail on an artemon-type mast projecting forward from the bow, and twin steering-oars on the quarters.

# 6.3
# Graeco-Roman Trade with India

Strabo (2. 3. 4) quoting Poseidonius, tells us that in the reign of Ptolemy II, who ruled Egypt from 146 to 117 BC, the Greek Eudoxus of Cyzicus was sent on a voyage to India guided by an Indian pilot who had been shipwrecked in the Gulf of Aden. This seems to be the first occasion on which a seaman who was neither an Arab nor an Indian used the monsoon winds to cross the Arabian Sea (Fig. 6.12). Eudoxus was subsequently sent on a second voyage by Cleopatra III in *c.*112 BC but was shipwrecked on his return (4.9.3.2.2.1).

After the Romans had conquered Egypt in 30 BC they encouraged Greek merchants to renew their trading voyages to India. This trade did indeed increase, and Strabo (2. 5. 12) wrote that 120 ships left *Myos Hormus* (presumably each year) for India, whereas under the Ptolemies only a few did so. Moreover, Pliny (*NH* 6. 26. 101) states that, in his times, Rome 'invested' not less

Fig. 6.9 (*right*). Wall painting in cave 17 at Ajanta (after Ray, 1990: fig. 5).

Fig. 6.10 (*below*). Wall painting in cave 1 at Ajanta (after Ray, 1990: fig. 6).

Fig. 6.11 (*below right*). Wall painting in cave 2 at Ajanta (after Ray, 1990: fig. 7).

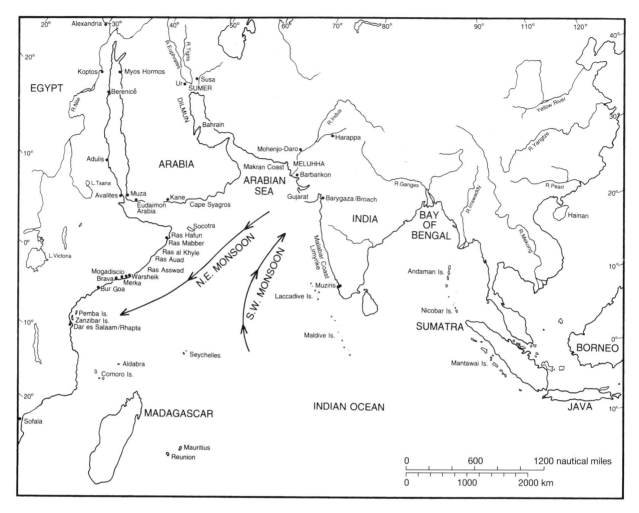

Fig. 6.12. Map of the Indian Ocean (Institute of Archaeology, Oxford).

than fifty million sesterces in Indian products. The merchants of Alexandria sailed up the River Nile as far as Coptos where desert roads led to *Myos Hormos* or *Berenicê* on the Egyptian coast of the Red Sea (Pliny, *NH* 6. 26. 102–4) (2.11.4).

During Tiberius' reign 14–37 AD, Roman ships bound for India were said to leave the Arabian coast with the 'Hippalus' wind (Pliny, *NH* 6. 26. 100; *Periplus*, ch. 57). Pliny believed 'Hippalus' was the Arabic name for the south-west monsoon, whilst the author of the *Periplus* (6.3.1) thought that it was the name of the first Greek seaman to use the open sea route to India. Since Eudoxus had made this voyage in the second century BC, the *Periplus* is wrong on this point. Furthermore, Mazzarino (1987) has shown that 'Hippalus' is a misguided, ancient textual correction to the word

'Hipalum' with the meaning 'wind from (under) the sea' (Tchernia, 1995: 992–4).

This Egypt/India trade continued until the fifth, or even sixth, century AD (Horton, 1997: 747–9), in ships of the Mediterranean tradition, built in the Red Sea region (2.11.4). It is not clear how much Indian ships were involved in this trade: probably they continued their earlier trading voyages to the Persian Gulf (Strabo 2. 3. 4) along with Arab ships (*Periplus*, ch. 21).

### 6.3.1  THE PERIPLUS OF THE ERYTHRAEAN SEA

*Periplus Maris Erythraei* is the Latin title of a work written in Greek, probably *c*.50 AD (Reade, 1996: 312; Casson, 1989). It is an example of a group of early

Mediterranean texts called *periploi* or 'circumnavigations' which gave information about harbours and watering places along a particular coast or regional litoral, about pilotage between such places—directions and distances, landmarks, shoals, rocks, and other hazards—and about the goods that were traded between them. They were, in other words, a combination of what we would today call a 'sailing pilot', a regional handbook, and a trading guide. These *periploi* were probably written versions of pilotage information which had formerly been memorized by rote.

The *Erythraean Sea* was not just the Red Sea, as its name seems to imply: to the unknown author of this *Periplus* it seems to have been the Indian Ocean from Burma to Zanzibar, including the Persian Gulf and the Red Sea (Casson, 1989). From internal evidence it is clear that the author lived in Egypt, and he was most probably a trader who may also have been a ship's master. From the detailed descriptions he gives it seems very likely that he had himself sailed to the west coast of India as far south as the 'pepper coast' of Travancore. His description of the Coromandel coast, the Ganges region, Burma, and other parts of south-east Asia, on the other hand, seem to be based more on informants than on personal experience.

## 6.3.2 ROUTES FROM THE RED SEA TO INDIA

The *Periplus* describes two coastal routes, the first one from the Egyptian port of *Myos Hormos* on the western side of the Red Sea along the coast of Sudan / Eritrea, around the Horn of Africa (Somali), and south to the region of Zanzibar (2.11.5). The second route begins at *Berenicê*, crosses to the western side of the Red Sea, then the southern coast of Arabia, past the entrance to the Persian Gulf, and continues coastwise to India and beyond. As with a present day sailing 'pilot', the author mentions several places on this coastal route whence an open sea passage may be made to the west coast of India using the south-west monsoon.

In ch. 21 we are told that Arab merchants sailed from *Muza* to *Barguza* (probably Broach, on the west coast of India). *Muza* is probably Mocha, some 40 nautical miles north of the strait Bab el Mandeb (Casson, 1989: 147).

*Eudaimon Arabia*, now Aden, also seems to have formerly been a point of departure for Arab ships bound for India but was no longer so used when the *Periplus* was written (ch. 26). *Kanê*, thought to be Hisne Ghurab some 200 nautical miles east-north-east of Aden (Fig. 3.18), was one of the two principal ports of departure for *Barugaza* (Broach) and *Skuthia* (the Indian coast north and west of the River Indus). Ships from *Kanê* (Hisne Ghurab) also traded with Oman and ports along the Persian coast (*Periplus*, ch. 27) (3.7.2.1). The second main point of departure for the direct route to India was *Aromata* or *Aromaton Emporion* (ch. 57)—this was close to Cape Guardafui, the north-west tip of the Horn of Africa (Fig. 3.18).

*Moshka*, probably modern Salalah in Muscat (Fig. 3.18) was a port where ships engaged in the coastal trade with India, sometimes wintered (*Periplus*, ch. 32). The *Erythraean Periplus* shows that in the first century AD, the coastal route to and from India continued to be used by traders discharging and loading goods at ports on the Arabian coast where they knew they would be welcome. Those merchants involved in the direct trade between Egypt (thence the Mediterranean world) and India (thence beyond) after emerging from the Red Sea, either called at the major port of *Kanê* and then stood out to sea, or they crossed the Gulf of Aden, made ground to the south-east towards the Horn of Africa, and took departure from Cape Guardafui and the island of Socotra (Fig. 6.12). Which of these two routes they took probably depended on whether they needed to embark water at *Kanê*, and also on the precise wind conditions within the Gulf of Aden.

Pliny (*NH* 6. 26. 99–105), writing at about the same time as the author of the *Periplus*, gives a slightly different version. At first the direct voyage to India was from *Suagros* (Ras Fartak—a prominent cape on the Hadramaut coast of Arabia) with the south-west wind to *Patale* (near the Indus delta). Later the destination was changed to *Sigerus* (Jaigarh, 120 nautical miles south of Bombay). Subsequently the most advantageous route was found to be from *Ocelis* (Sheikh Sa'id at the mouth of the Red Sea in the Bab el Mandeb) to *Muziris* (Cranganore) on India's west coast, and then to *Becarê* (Pirakad) further south, on the Malabar coast.

## 6.3.3 SEAFARING IN THE ARABIAN SEA

The best time of departure from Egypt for ships going only as far as *Mouza* (Maushij) or *Kanê* (Hisne Ghurab) was September (*Periplus*, ch. 24) although it could be earlier. September, however, was too late for Indian-bound ships to use the south-west monsoon across the Arabian Sea and these, the *Periplus* (chs.39, 49, 56) tells us, had to leave the Egyptian ports of *Myos Hormos* or *Berenicê* in July (chs. 39, 49, 56). Such a time of departure enables ships to take advantage of the generally northern wind in the summer in the Red Sea, and to use the south-west monsoon in the Gulf of Aden and the Arabian Sea in August and September when it is usually not so boisterous as it is in its earliest phase, March to June. As the *Periplus* says (ch. 39), the direct voyage can be risky, due to the strength of the monsoon. It could also be prudent to time departure from *Kanê* or Cape Guardafui so that the ship did not arrive in Indian waters until September for, as Pliny subsequently related (*NH 6. 24. 83*), the west coast of India and Sri Lanka had particularly stormy seas during the hundred days following midsummer, so much so that Sri Lankans avoided sailing in this period, i.e. mid-June to mid-September. In the early part of the twentieth century, it was reckoned that sailing off the west coast was practicable from the end of October on the Malabar coast, end of September off Bombay, and the end of August further north (Deloche, 1994: 212–14). Ships arriving from Arabia and Africa earlier in the summer months would face the hazards of a lee shore in strong winds: by September/October (depending on the precise destination) this danger was over, and the north-east monsoon, a foul, offshore wind on the west coast, did not begin until late November.

Those ships bound for the north-west of India and for the River Indus, the *Periplus* (ch. 57) tells us, 'hold out to the contrary for three days'—which probably means that for three days (say, 200 nautical miles) they took a south-east course across the direction of the monsoon wind to make ground to windward and get well clear of the island of Socotra and of Arabia. They then would have run on a north-east heading with the south-west monsoon across the Arabian Sea until they made a landfall in north-west India (*Periplus*, ch. 57). Ships bound for *Limyrikê* (the southern parts of India, well south of Bombay along the Travancore coast) on the other hand, turned 'the bows of the ship against the wind' (Huntingford, 1980: 53) or 'with the wind on the quarter' (Casson, 1989: 87) which must mean that these ships steered an easterly course, or even east-south-east, with the wind on their starboard quarter rather than astern, thus allowing for leeway (drift downwind) which would otherwise have taken them too far to the north.

The *Periplus* does not give the length of these open sea voyages but Pliny (*NH 6. 26*) says that, when sailing with the south-west wind, from *Ocelis* (Cella) it takes forty days to reach *Muziris* (Cranganore on the Malabar coast). This indicates an average overall speed of *c*.2 knots which seems relatively slow in a fair wind, but is probably due to the fact that they made ground to the south, away from Arabia, before turning north-east and running with the monsoon. Pliny also gives guidance about the timing of the return journey which is not mentioned in the *Periplus*—ships sail from India in December or early January: today this west coast has reasonable weather from December to March (Deloche, 1994: 212–14). Pliny says they do so with the south-east wind, however, the north-east monsoon is dominant in the Arabian Sea from the end of November to February: it would not be until they were closing the southern Arabian or north-east African coast in January or February that they would have a south-east wind, followed by a favourable southerly wind in the Red Sea. A return voyage to and from India could thus be undertaken from Egypt in less than a year, whereas that to east Africa took much longer (2.11.5.4.3).

### 6.3.3.1 NAVIGATIONAL TECHNIQUES

We can get some ideas of the navigational and pilotage techniques used on these voyages from a Sanskrit description of the duties of an Arabian Sea pilot, written in the first century AD (Tibbetts, 1971: 1; E. Taylor 1971: 85; Needham 1971: 555). Suparagā, the Indian pilot:

knows the course of the stars and can always orientate himself; he knows the value of the signs, both regular, accidental and abnormal, of good and bad weather; he distinguishes the regions of the ocean by the fish, the colour of the water, the nature of the bottom, the birds, the mountains and other indications.

Furthermore, Pliny (*NH 6. 24. 83*) noted that shore-sighting birds were used by Sri Lankan seamen to find the direction of land. Similar practices were described in the fifth century BC *Kevaddha Sutta* of Digha and the Hindu *Sutta Pitaka* (Hornell, 1946b: 143). Such non-instrumental methods were used worldwide into the medieval period, and indeed were used in Indian waters during the twentieth century (Arunachalam, 1987; 1996).

The *Periplus* contains useful pilotage information about several of the harbours mentioned. Thus the entries for *Barbariké* (in the Indus delta) state that it is near a small island up the middle channel of the seven channels in the delta of the River *Sinthos* (Indus). The approach to the Indus can be seen when still out of sight of land as a distinctively coloured outflow of water, and sea snakes can be seen (3.8.2.2.4) (*Periplus*, chs. 38, 39). Distances are given between ports: for example, from *Barbariké* to *Astakapra* (Hathab) opposite *Barugaza* (Broach) in the Gulf of Cambay (Fig. 6.1) is 3,000 stades i.e. *c*.300 nautical miles (*Periplus*, ch. 41). The actual distance is about 300 nautical miles to the entrance to the Gulf and 400 nautical miles to Broach. The overall length of the west coast of India (2,850 nautical miles) is said to be '40 days' sail' (Pliny *NH*, 6. 21) which makes a standard 'day's sail' of those times to be *c*.72 nautical miles.

The *Periplus* (ch. 40) warns seafarers on passage from the River Indus to the Gulf of Cambay to beware of the Gulf of *Eirinon* (Rann of Kutch—in those days it was a tidal bay, now it is a salt marsh) where the water is shoal and there are unpredictable tidal races and ships may readily be wrecked. The Gulf of *Baraké* (Gulf of Kutch—Casson, 1989: 196) is also hazardous. Deloche (1994: 56) notes that today this gulf is not usable by sailing vessels from May to September because of the south-west monsoon. Rao (1987: 252) has identified *Baraké* with a site now underwater off the Gujarat coast at Dwarka.

*Barugaza* (Broach in the Gulf of Cambay) is described in some detail (*Periplus*, chs. 41–6) suggesting this was the most significant port on the east coast of India at that time. *Barugaza* is said to be about 300 stades (30 nautical miles) up the River *Lamnaios* (Narbada) which flows into the eastern part of the bay (Gulf of Cambay—this is usable from September onwards—Deloche, 1994: 62). The *Periplus* states that the approach to *Barugaza*/Broach is difficult because of the narrowness of the bay and strong currents. The mouth of the River Narmada is difficult to find as the coast there is low-lying and there are shoals nearby. In addition, there is a great tidal range (difference in height between high and low water) at *Barugaza* with correspondingly strong tidal streams which can easily confuse the inexperienced mariner: ships can readily be

driven onto shoals and wrecked, and boats capsized. At the time of new moon (i.e. spring tides) these effects are particularly serious and a bore or *egre* can be heard and seen rushing in from seaward with the flood tide. For all these reasons the ruler of this region, *Arlake*, sends out pilots in their oared vessels *trappaga* and *kotymba*, to meet visiting ships in the bay. These pilots guide the ships into the river on the rising (flood) tide and moor them at *Barugaza* (where there is deeper water) at around the time of high water. When there is insufficient or unfavourable wind for this manœuvre, the pilot boats tow in the larger ships.

These ships would probably have berthed out of the main stream to minimize the effects of the tidal flows. The *Periplus* (ch. 46) advised that small vessels, which can enter during ebb (outflowing) tide and not have to wait for the deeper water associated with the flood tide, should be propped upright at their berths in the shallows so that they were not overwhelmed by the next flood tide as they could be if they were allowed to lie over on one side.

## 6.3.4 INDIAN LANDING PLACES

The *Periplus* (chs. 52, 53) mentions thirteen landing places, mostly of little commercial importance, along the coast (*c*.450 nautical miles) south of the Gulf of Cambay, including *Kalliena* (Kalyana) in what is now Bombay harbour. The most northerly ports in *Limuriké* (the southern part of the Malabar coast, i.e. the Travancore coast) are said to be *Naoura* (Cannonove) and *Tundis* (Tanor) in *Keprobotos* (Kerala). Further south is *Mouziris* (Cranganore on the River Periyar) which is also mentioned by Pliny (*NH* 6. 26) as the destination of ships from Egypt. *Nelkinda* (Kottayam on Lake Vembanad) is said to be an important town—up a river and *c*.120 stades (12 nautical miles) from the sea. Goods from this market town are carried by lighters down a shallow stream bordered by mudflats to ships waiting in the roadsteads at *Bakaré* (Vaikkarai) at the river mouth.

*Komar* is described in ch. 58 of the *Periplus* as a harbour with a fort and a renowned religious settlement: it is thought to be a site near Cape Comorin (Pliny's *Coliacum*, *NH* 6. 24. 86) the southernmost point of India (Casson, 1989: 224). This must have been a difficult cape to round but this is not mentioned in the

*Periplus*—perhaps suggesting that the author had no personal knowledge of the itinerary described beyond *Bakaré*.

In ch. 61 the island of *Palaisimoundou*, formerly *Taprobanê* (Sri Lanka) is mentioned, and in ch. 59 *Kolkhai* (Korkai on the River Tambraparni in Tinnevelly). *Kamara* (probably Puhar, now under sand), where there were Roman merchants (Casson, 1989: 25), *Poduké* (probably Arikamedu near Pondicherry) and *Sopatma* (near Madras); all these are on the Coromandel coast and are in ch. 60. *Masalia* (Masulipatnam) is mentioned in ch. 62, and in ch. 63, a port in the Ganges delta which has an annual flooding season like the Nile.

### 6.3.5 TYPES OF INDIAN RAFT AND BOAT

Local vessels, which are not named, from the Coromandel coast were in the coastal trade with *Limuriké* (Tranvancore coast). *Sangara* are also mentioned (ch. 60): Casson's (1989: 89) translation describes these as 'dug out canoes held together by a yoke', whereas Huntingford (1980: 54) gives 'vessels made of single logs bound together'. The Tamil word is *shangadam* which described a log raft: the Portuguese of the sixteenth century borrowed this term as *jangada* which they subsequently applied to the seagoing log rafts of Brazil (11.4.1). Huntingford's translation is preferred to Casson's here. The *sangara* may have a twentieth-century 'descendant' in the *sangadam*, a log raft of the Laccadive islands (Hornell, 1946a: 67).

The largest vessels working in these waters were *Kolandiophonta* which crossed over to *Khruse* (Burma and beyond) and the Ganges region. Christie (1957) has made the reasonable suggestion that this term is to be derived from the Chinese *kun lun po*, a term used in early Chinese writing for the ships of non-Chinese nations who traded in south-east Asia, and Manguin (1996) has recently argued for that interpretation. From this it follows that south-east Asian ships undertook the longer voyages in the Bay of Bengal, from the Indo-China region coastwise to southern India via the Ganges and possibly other major entrepôt.

*Masalia* (Masulipatnam between the Rivers Krishna and Godavari in Andrha Pradesh) is mentioned in ch. 62, but nothing is said here or in ch. 60 about sewnplank boats (*masula*) which are known to have been used extensively on this Coromandel coast from the

seventeenth century and probably much earlier (6.7.3). This may be another sign of the author's incomplete knowledge of the eastern coast of India.

The only other Indian vessels mentioned by name in the *Periplus* are the pilot-boats/tugs *trappaga* and *kotymba* used in the Gulf of Cambay (ch. 44). These are described as 'longships' which probably means they were oared (or possibly galleys, i.e. oars with auxiliary sails), and could be used on windless days. Hornell (1920) thought that the *kotymba* was probably like the modern *kotia* (6.7.4.3), but this seems unlikely as these are large, two-masted cargo ships similar in form to the Arab *baggala* and unsuitable as pilot-boats/tugs.

# 6.4

## Seafaring in the Bay of Bengal (First–Eighth Centuries AD)

(Figs. 6.12 and 8.1)

Pliny's remark (*NH* 6. 24. 82) that the distance from Ceylon to the River Ganges was equivalent to seven days' sail by 'our ships', shows that, by the first century AD, Roman ships sailed in the Bay of Bengal (Strabo: 15. 686). By *c.*166 AD they had sailed beyond Burma to Malaysia and possibly as far as Indo-China, but not necessarily in great numbers (Casson, 1988*b*).

When trade with the Mediterranean declined in the third century AD many towns in the western and north Deccan decayed but the lower Krishna valley remained prosperous—probably from new commercial ventures undertaken in south-east Asia (Ray, 1989: 46–7). By the fourth century AD the Pallavas of Tamil Nadu, south of the Deccan, were in ascendancy and one of the coins issued by them has a ship on the reverse (Ray, 1989: 46).

Evidence for early trade between India and southeast Asia is limited. Ray (1996) has suggested that cornelian, glass, and worked ivory may have been exported, and tin and aromatic wood imported. The earliest reference to the Andaman islands is by Ptolemy in the second century AD and the earliest human settlement is from around that era (Cooper, 1996). It is possible that the voyages on which Madagascar was colonized from south-east Asia in the mid-first millennium AD (8.2.2) involved a direct crossing of the Bay of Bengal at around the latitude of southern India and the Andaman/Nicobar islands (*c*.10°N). By the ninth century AD Arab seamen probably made this open sea crossing (3.8.1). In earlier times contacts between the east coast of India and south-east Asia were probably coastal voyages. Ray (1989; 1996) suggests that in the Mauryan period, when there is the first reference to south-east Asia in the second century AD *Arthaśāstra* of Kautilya, the route was probably from Orissa via Bengal to lower Burma. Certain materials noted in the *Periplus* as being embarked in Indian ports for the Mediterranean markets may well have originated further east: cinnamon and cassia may have originated in south-east Asia or southern China, and sandalwood may have come from eastern Indonesia (Casson, 1984: 237; Miller, 1969: 86–7).

Whether individual Indian ships went the whole way from eastern India to south-east Asia or the journey was undertaken by short-haul vessels with transshipments in certain harbours, is unclear. On the other hand, if the *kolandiophonta* of the *Periplus* was a large south-east Asian trading vessel (6.3.5), as seems likely, such voyages could have been undertaken by one such ship.

Evidence for trade around the northern coasts of the Bay of Bengal comes from finds of spherical red cornelian (a quartz) beads at sites such as Ban Don Ta Phet in west-central Thailand dated to about the first century BC. Bronze bowls, similar in form to those found at several contemporary sites in coastal Orissa and Bengal and in the Ganges valley have also been excavated from the Ban Don Ta Phet site (Ray, 1989: 50–1). Ray suggests that this evident trade is best explained by a coastal route via Orissa, Bengal, lower Burma, and then an overland route through the Three Pagodas Pass (south-east of Rangoon) into west-central Thailand. Similarities between artefacts excavated from Buni culture sites on the west coast of northern Java and from another site in western Bali dated to the first centuries BC/AD, and material recovered from graves at Adichanallur on the Tamil coast suggest that the Bay of Bengal coastal route may have extended along the western coast of Malaya to the Indonesian islands (Ray, 1989; 1990: 11–12).

In the early centuries AD the Indian sector of this coastal route was extended southwards from Orissa to the valleys of the Krishna and Godavari in Andhra Pradesh/Tamil Nadu. At the eastern end the route was extended around Malaya to the Mekong valley in Vietnam (Ray, 1989: 52–3). A fragmentary stone (*stuppa*) found in the state of Kedah, north-west Malaya has an inscription dated to *c.* AD 400 stating that it was set up by Buddhagupta, a *mahanavika* (master mariner) from *Raktamrttika*, which is thought to be Rajbadidanga on the River Bhagirathi a former arm of the Ganges (Ray, 1989: 53–4; 1990: 13). Excavations at Khuan Luk Pad in Krabi province, Thailand, have revealed evidence for trade to the west and to the east, and two coins from this region have a ship with two masts similar to those on Pallava coins found on the Coromandel coast.

The main evidence for overseas trade in Vietnam comes from the Oc-Eo site (Fig. 8.1) where second-to seventh-century Mediterranean intaglios and coins, cornelian seals with Brahmi inscriptions, and distinctive glass beads and statuary have been found. Indian influence may also be seen in the standardization of coinage in the Mekong region by *c.* AD 500, modelled, it has been suggested, on coins from south India (Ray, 1989: 52).

# 6.5

## Medieval European Contacts with India

The decline in Roman trade with India and beyond began in the third century AD, and from the fifth century onwards there is little information available in European sources concerning India. It seems likely that, from the beginning of Islamic expansion in the seventh century AD, east–west trade in the Indian Ocean was undertaken by Arabs. From the thirteenth and fourteenth centuries, however, we get glimpses of India from European travellers such as late thirteenth-century Marco Polo who also visited Sri Lanka and the Andaman and Nicobar islands, and the early fourteenth-century Franciscan friar, Odoric of Pordenone, who, in *c*.1320, sailed from the Persian Gulf to India and reported on the Malabar coast and Sri Lanka. Ibn Battutah, a Muslim cleric also of the mid-fourteenth century, travelled widely in northern and western India and visited the Andaman and the Laccadive islands.

In the mid-fifteenth century, the Portuguese sought a passage to India by circumnavigating Africa. Between 1432 and 1485 they gradually learned the best way of sailing into the southern Atlantic in order to make progress southwards along the western coast of Africa, and in 1488 Bartholemeu Dias rounded the southern point of Africa and sailed eastwards beyond Port Elizabeth. Nine years later Vasco da Gama rounded the Cape of Good Hope and sailed eastwards and then northwards into the Indian Ocean. After calling at Quelimane, Mozambique, and Mombasa, da Gama came to Malindi between Zanzibar and Lamu, in what is now Kenya. He sailed thence on 24 April 1498 with the Arab pilot Ibn Mājid of Gujarat (3.8.2), and, after a twenty-three day passage across the Arabian Sea, sighted the mountains of the Western Ghats in southern India. He anchored off Calicut (Kozhikode) on 21 May 1498, before the south-west monsoon had got into its stride. On his return voyage he left the Malabar coast at the end of August, had to tack against the monsoon and did not make the African coast until 3 January 1499, a voyage of four months. From this time onwards European knowledge of, and trade with, India grew, and with it came further knowledge of the boats and the seafaring practices of the subcontinent.

# 6.6
# Early Indian Water Transport

As in other parts of the world which the sixteenth-to nineteenth-centuries Europeans encountered, their reports on Indian boats and boatmanship are few in number, and incomplete and inexact. Furthermore, it seems likely that some of the later reports—from the seventeenth century and onwards—were made after Indian technology and seafaring had been influenced by European practices to a degree which it is difficult to determine. The descriptions of Indian rafts and boats that follow have been compiled from the representational and documentary evidence discussed earlier in this chapter, and from these post-medieval sources which range from travellers' tales on the one hand, to

technical reports prepared by competent observers working within their specialist field, on the other. An attempt has been made to discount any features which had probably been introduced from Europe, post-Vasco da Gama, seeking to deduce the state of the Indian nautical scene as it was before AD 1500.

## 6.6.1 BUNDLE RAFTS

The earliest evidence for bundle rafts is from the Harappan period site of Mohenjo-Daro in the Indus Valley, some 250 miles from the coast (Fig. 6.1). The depiction on a seal (Fig. 6.2) and on a baked clay or terracotta amulet (Fig. 6.3) have vertical lines across a well-curved hull, which, from Egyptian evidence (2.5.1, 2.6.3), almost certainly represent the bindings around the bundles of reeds or similar materials. There is no evidence for sail: these river craft were probably propelled by paddle or pole. Both representations have a steering oar on the quarter and some superstructure amidships. Neither find is well-dated, but they are ascribed generally to the Indus civilization of c.2500 to 1500 BC. One thousand and more years later, Herodotus (3. 98) tells us that such craft were used for river fishing in India.

Bowen (1956a: 280) and others consider a graffito on a Mohenja-Daro potsherd of c.2000 BC, also to represent a bundle vessel (Fig. 6.4), but its form is different from that usually given to bundle craft and there are no diagnostic 'binding' lines: this seems best interpreted as a representation of a planked boat with sail (6.7.1).

Pliny (NH 6. 24. 82), writing in the first century AD, but possibly here quoting Eratosthenes of the first century BC, describes how vessels made of reeds (papyraceis navibus), with rigging similar to that used by Nile boats, sailed between the River Ganges and Sri Lanka in twenty days. There is no known tradition of water-proofing reed bundles in India, and so it seems probable that these vessels were bundle rafts, which are indeed capable of sea voyages, as for example, off the coast of South America (11.4.2). Furthermore, Heyerdahl (1978: 28–34) has shown that, in certain circumstances, one-way trans-oceanic voyages can be made in this type of vessel. As these Indian bundle rafts took twenty days when Roman ships sailing continuously took only seven, we may conclude that these early Indian seamen remained in sight of land and went ashore

at intervals, possibly every night, to replenish and probably to allow their rafts to dry on the foreshore
between tides.

Reed-bundle rafts were still used earlier this century
by fishermen on the River Ganges and River Solani in
the north-east of India, and also on inland waters in the
south (Hornell, 1946a: 59–60). They may also have been
used on Lake Manchar in Sind, in the Indus valley.

Bundle rafts made of light poles were also used in
the Madras region where young cotton trees (*Bombax
malabaricum*) were used; and on the lower Ganges and
on the rivers of Bengal, Bihar, and Assam, where
bundles of plantain stems (*Kalār*) or sticks of *shola*
(*Aeschynomene aspera*) were used (Hornell, 1946a: 68).

## 6.6.2 FLOATS AND BUOYED RAFTS

The use of inflated skins as personal floats is depicted
on the first-century BC Stupa I at Sanchi (Mookerji,
1912: 32; Deloche, 1994: 133): such use—and that of
almost every other type of float—is known from
recent times (Hornell, 1946a: 22–5; plates II and III).

Rafts consisting of a light wooden platform given
extra buoyancy by inflated hide floats or by pots with
their mouths closed, have been noted in recent times
on inland waters in several parts of the subcontinent
(Hornell, 1946a: 22–5, 34–7; Greenhill, 1971: 140–2, 175–6;
Deloche, 1994: 132; McGrail, 1998: 189). Those with
floats are mainly from northern India—Kashmir, Punjab, the upper Indus, and the upper Ganges (Fig. 6.13).
The earliest documented reference to the use of float
rafts is in the *Memoirs* of Emperor Jahangir who
reigned from 1605 to 1627 (Hornell, 1946a: 24).

Rafts which gain their buoyancy from pots were
used in the lower reaches of rivers south of the Punjab
and the Himalayan foothills (Hornell, 1946a: 34–7;
Deloche, 1994: 32–3). These *gharnao* or *gharnai* ('chatty
rafts' in Anglo-Indian) had a light bamboo platform
under which were lashed several unglazed pots which
had had their mouths closed with a wad of *sal* leaves.
The earliest decription of their use also comes from the
seventeenth century, in *Storia do Mojor* by the Venetian,
Niccolao Manucci (Hornell, 1946a: 35).

## 6.6.3 LOG RAFTS

The earliest reference to log rafts in India is in the first-
century AD *Periplus of the Erythraean Sea* (ch. 60): the

Fig. 6.13. A twentieth-century
hide float raft on the River
Swat, northern Pakistan
(photo: Basil Greenhill).

Fig. 6.14. A seventeenth-century catamaran drawn by Thomas Bowrey (after Temple, 1905: plate 8).

*sangara* was a large raft of the Coromandel coast, made of logs bound together.

Gasparo Balbi and Fryer mentioned the log rafts of southern India in the sixteenth century (Hill, 1958: 210) but a more detailed account was given by Thomas Bowrey (*c*.1650–1713), a pepper merchant, who described several Indian vessels in his *Account* written in *c*.1690 (Temple, 1905). Amongst these was the *catamaran* (Fig. 6.14) which consisted of four, five, or six shaped logs seized or bound together with lashings. The centrally placed log(s) being longer than the others gave the raft the distinctive shape known in many parts of the world. Bowrey says that the smaller ones were used for fishing, whilst the larger ones could carry 3 or 5 tons of cargo. They were propelled by paddles and would, 'boldy adventure out of sight of the shore, but indeed they swimme as naturally as spanyall dogs' (Temple, 1905: 43).

Edye (1834), who was chief shipwright in the naval dockyard at Trincomalee in Sri Lanka, described similar *catamarans* from Madras and other parts of peninsular India. These were made of three logs so sized and positioned that they formed a hollowed shape with a rising bow. The logs were connected by three spreaders lashed to the logs through small holes. Overall, they measured 20–5 × 2.5–3.5 ft. (6–7.5 × 0.75–1 m). They were usually propelled by paddle but in monsoon times they were fitted with an outrigger and a sail.

In recent times similar rafts are used for fishing along the east coast of India from Orissa southwards to Cape Comorin and the southern part of Travancore, and around the northern coast of Sri Lanka (Deloche, 1994: fig. 37). On this Tamil coast (Hill, 1958: 210) they are known as *kattu maram* (logs bound-together). Some are simple log rafts but others, such as the seven-log *kola maram*, are shaped into the form of a boat and have an upturning 'bow' of short logs added (Fig. 6.15). *Kola marams* are log rafts used when taking flying fish. They are generally paddled but can be rigged with 'triangular lateen' sails on two masts stepped in the outer log on the lee side. In this role two large *guares* (8.3.1, 10.2.5, 11.4.1.2) are fitted between the logs to reduce leeway, and help with sailing balance, but evidently not to steer which is done with a large oar. The logs in this twentieth-century raft are bound together, as are the majority of the Indian ones, but some log rafts to the north of

Fig. 6.15. A twentieth-century catamaran (after Hornell, 1946*a*: plate IIA).

Fig. 6.16. A hide boat under construction near the River Bhavani in southern India (photo: Cambridge University Press).

the Coromandel coast are pegged together (Hornell, 1946a: 67).

In the Laccadive islands, on the southern island of Kavaratti, log rafts known as *tarappam* or *sangadam* were used in the early part of the twentieth century (Hornell, 1946a: 67–8).

## 6.6.4 HIDE BOATS

There appears to be no tradition or folklore memory of hide boats being used at sea in Indian waters; but they have been used on rivers and lakes. Hide boats are first mentioned in the late fourteenth century when they were used to ferry troops across the River Krishna in what is now Andhra Pradesh (Deloche, 1994: 138–9). In the same region, in the mid-seventeenth century, Tavernier saw large boats of oxhide on a basketry framework being used to ferry goods and people across rivers near Secunderabad (Hornell, 1946a: 95–6, 105). These craft were circular in plan with diameters of 10–20 ft (3–6 m), and were propelled by men with paddles, stationed on each quarter. Such boats were also used for river fishing

There are numerous accounts of similar hide boat usage from the eighteenth century through to the twentieth, mostly in the enormous catchment areas of the Rivers Krishna and Kaveri (Deloche, 1994: 137–40, figs. 1 and 24). By and large, this distribution is within the present-day states of Andhra Pradesh, Karnataka, and Tamil Nadu.

These boats were bowl or saucer-shaped (Fig. 6.16), and varied in size from one-man fishing boats, 1.5 to 1.8 m in diameter and 0.40 m deep, to boats of 4.2 m with a depth of 1 m which could carry 30 to 50 men or 4 tonnes of rice. The 'skin' of such boats was made of several oxen or buffalo hides stitched together and fastened to an open basketry framework of split bamboo by lashings just below the framework rim which had been reinforced by a stout bundle of bamboos forming, in effect, a gunwale. The primary framework of the larger of these boats was reinforced by secondary and, in some cases, tertiary framing (Palmer *et al.*, forthcoming).

In the late 1980s/early 1990s hides began to be replaced by a 'skin' made of two layers of plastic bags sewn together. At about the same time, the framework of at least some of these boats (notably the *parical* of

Hogenakal on the headwaters of the River Kaveri in Tamil Nadu) may have been simplified by omitting the teritary framing and reducing the number of bamboos in the secondary layer. This may have been due to a shift in the major role of these *parical* from carrying goods and animals to carrying tourists who are known to have significantly increased in numbers from around 1990 (Palmer, *et al.*, forthcoming).

The hide boat of southern Indian was evidently developed, from readily available bamboo, hide, and coir, to match its river environment and the several roles it was required to fill. The rounded shape means that it can be propelled and steered from any position, and has good manœuvrability. It thus is admirably suited for use on the fast-flowing, rock-strewn headwaters of the rivers of southern India, which, even in their lower reaches, can vary in course, depth, and flow during a single day. Furthermore, a circular form is also the simplest way of making a basket-type framework. A lightweight yet resilient structure facilitates the boat's use in shallow water and the carriage of relatively great loads, yet, when empty, it can be carried by one man.

### 6.6.5 POT BOATS

These are known in recent times, on the rivers of Bangladesh (Nishimura, 1936: 145, fig. 33); Hornell, 1946a: 98, fig. 9; Deloche, 1994: 140). This type of boat, known as a *tigari* or a *gamla*, is in reality a large earthenware basin, hemispherical in shape and 2½ ft (0.8 m) in diameter, with a reinforced rim. They are used by one person for crossing streams or flooded fields, and sometimes for tending fishing nets, and are propelled by paddle or by hand (Fig. 6.17). Strabo (17. 1. 4) noted the use of similar boats in the Nile delta where they were used as ferries.

Fig. 6.17. A Bengal *tigari*: a pot boat (after Hornell, 1946a: fig. 9).

### 6.6.6 LOGBOATS

A logboat found in the bed of the River Kelani near Colombo, Sri Lanka, in 1952 and now in the National Museum in Colombo has recently been dated by radiocarbon assay to 2300 ± 100 BP, that is, to the sixth to fourth centuries BC (Vitharana, 1992; Devendra, 1995). This boat has several paired holes near the top of the sides, *c.*1.10 m apart, which may be where a single outrigger was fitted.

The earliest documentary evidence for Indian logboats is found in Pliny (*NH* 6. 26. 105): pepper was brought in logboats from the district of Cottonara to the port of Pirakad on the Malabar coast. Similar boats, called *palegua* and *tomes* may be depicted in one of the drawings compiled by Linschoten in 1610 (Fig. 6.18). Apart from this, there appears to be no representational evidence for them, and no descriptions, until the early nineteenth century. Edye (1834) describes and illustrates five types of logboat from southern India: two logboats from the Malabar coast; two extended logboats, one from the Malabar coast and one from Point de Galle in Sri Lanka; and a group of paired logboats, *jangār*, also from Malabar.

The 'canoe' or logboat of the Malabar coast (Edye, 1834: 5–6) was made from a single log of *anjeli* (possibly *Artocarpus hirsuta*) or of *cherne-maram*, without embellishments, and measured 8–20 × 1.5–2.0 × 1.0–1.5 ft (2.5–2.6 × 0.45–0.6 × 0.3–0.45 m). These were used for fishing and cargo-carrying on rivers such as the Cochin, and were propelled by paddle. Such simple, yet useful, boats must have long been used in many parts of India, and Edye's boat may well be a linear 'descendant' of Pliny's 'pepper' logboat.

The *pambān manché* (Edye, 1834: 6–7, plate 4), also known as the 'snake boat' of Cochin (on the Malabar coast) was also made from a single log of *anjeli* wood. Edye's drawing, however, suggests that the high curving stern and possibly the drooping bow, must have been added to the parent log. It also seems likely that a capping or similar timber has been added to the top edge of the sides of this boat. These 'snake boats' measured 30–60 × *c.*3 ft (9–18 × 1 m) and were renowned for their speed: the largest ones, manned by about twenty paddlers (two at each station), are said to have reached speeds up to 11 knots. Twenty paddlers, double-banked, would leave space for passengers and goods—Edye's drawing shows a cabin towards the

Fig. 6.18. Boats off the Malabar coast (Linschoten, 1610: 108).

stern. Such speedy boats may have been used in former times by rulers, by their messengers and ambassadors, and perhaps by their fighting men. Special logs of above average size must have been chosen to give the length (necessary for speed) and breadth (necessary for double-banked paddlers); whilst the ordinary worka-day 'canoes' of the Malabar coast were made from logs of less-demanding specification.

The Cochin *bandar manché* (Edye, 1834: 7–8, plate 5) had one strake sewn onto each side and therefore was an extended logboat, although Edye does not mention this. These paddled boats measured 20–50 ft.(6–15 m.) in length and they could carry up to 18 tons of cargo. At Cochin they were used to supply visiting ships an-

chored in the roads. The 'ribs' that Edye says are spaced at *c.*5 ft (1.5 m) intervals appear to have been ridges, 6 × 2 in (150 × 50 mm) in section, worked from the solid log across the bottom of the boat. Similar ridges can be seen in the twentieth-century Malabar logboat (Hor-nell, 1946*a*: plate 26A). They were probably there as sta-tions for the paddlers, or to protect the cargo from bilge water or to divide the boat into functional spaces, rather than to give strength and support to the body of the boat as Edye suggested. Edye's drawings show a stern rudder fitted to this boat—most probably a sign of European influence.

The Point de Galle 'canoe' (Edye, 1834: 5, plate 2) is a double-ended logboat with sewn-on washstrakes and a single outrigger. The washstrakes give added free-board, the outrigger additional stability: thus these boats could be used at sea up to 25 nautical miles out from the coast of Sri Lanka to bring fresh fruit and veg-etables to passing ships. The basic logboat measures 18–30 × 1.5–2.5 × 2–3 ft (5.5–9.0 × 0.45–0.75 × 0.60–0.9 m) and is similar in form to the Malabar 'canoe'. The mast is fastened to the foremost of the two outrigger booms: no details of the sail are given by Edye, but, as the mast is significantly nearer the bow than the stern, this may have been a fore-and-aft sail. This sailing 'canoe' is steered by a paddle.

Hornell (1946a: 256) has described how simple log-boats, fitted with washstrakes and a single outrigger like the Point de Galle 'canoe', were used with a lugsail earlier this century in the strait between India and Sri Lanka. In such a boat the outrigger has to be kept to windward, otherwise the craft becomes unstable. These boats had an ingenious means of quickly mov-ing the outrigger across the boat so that it would be to windward after changing tack. There is no evidence that Edye's vessel had such a quick release outrigger, but if it did have this fitting, the mast, being attached to a boom, would have had to be refitted to the other boom when the outrigger system was changed to the other side.

The *jangār* (Fig. 6.19) was made from two ordinary Malabar logboats joined together side by side at a dis-tance of *c*.5 ft (1.5 m) centre to centre. Boards were placed across the midships areas of the two boats and kept in position by a bamboo structure which also kept the boats in a fixed relationship to one another and

acted as a barrier for live cargo. This is one of several methods known worldwide of pairing two boats so that greater stability and greater cargo space is obtained (McGrail, 1978: 44–51). The *jangār* was used to ferry cattle and bulky articles across rivers, and also military bullocks, horses, baggage, and carts. In the twentieth century, elsewhere in India and Ceylon, paired logboats were known as *jangada*, *jangadam* or even *sangadam* (Hornell, 1920: 187; 1946a: 81).

In early nineteenth-century southern India, from the Malabar coast to the Gulf of Mannar, a number of logboat types were used, including simple logboats and paired logboats on rivers carrying passengers, goods and animals, and a specialized form of logboat when speed was required. Close inshore, in anchorages off river mouths, paddled logboats extended with wash-strakes to give extra freeboard were used to service ships. At sea, in coastal water, extended logboats fitted with single outriggers for extra stability, were pro-pelled by sail and steered by paddle.

In Bangladesh today there are several examples of logboats extended by two or three strakes (Greenhill, 1971: 110–14). Others, for example, the *balam*, have so many strakes sewn on to a logboat base that, in effect, they become a sewn-plank boat. Paired logboats are also known in other parts of the Indian subcontinent, for example, the *donga*, used on the Rivers Krishna and Godavari in the Deccan, and in the Ganges drainage region: these are made of two trunks of the coconut or Palmyra palm (*Borassus flabellifornis*) linked by two transverse light timbers lashed to the upper surface of each hull (Hornell, 1946a: 190, fig. 28).

Logboat stability can be increased not only by pair-ing and by the addition of stabilizers and outriggers, but also by expanding the basic logboat so that its beam measurement at the waterline becomes greater than the diameter of the parent log (McGrail, 1978: 38–41). Logboats were expanded in India in recent times, for example, at Tinnevelly in Tamil Nadu where the sides of a hollowed log were made malleable by filling it with water heated by hot stones or by the sun (Hornell, 1946a: 192). After the sides have been forced apart, ribs were fastened inside the logboat to retain the new shape, and washstrakes added to regain height of sides. Only certain species of timber can be so treated with-out the boat splitting, and specialist supervision is required. There is no reason to think that both timber and expertise were not available in early India but

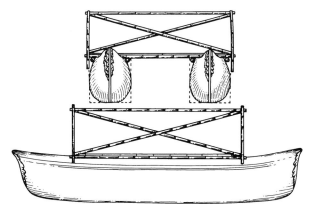

Fig. 6.19. Early nineteenth-century Malabar paired logboats: *jangar* (after Edye, 1834: plate 3).

whether this procedure was indeed used can only be demonstrated by some (as yet undiscovered) early documentary reference to the technique, or by some future excavation of an expanded logboat.

# 6.7
## Planked Boats and Ships up to the Twentieth Century

### 6.7.1 IN HARRAPAN TIMES

It is not possible to derive any structural information from the five pottery boat models excavated from the Indus civilization site on Lothal (6.1), but it seems likely that they represent planked vessels. Something may, however, be said about their shape. The only complete model ( Johnstone, 1980: 173, fig. 13.4) has a fine bow and a blunt stern. Rao (1965: 35–6) believes this model and a second one represent sailing vessels, but this is doubtful. The other three models appear to be flat-bottomed vessels with fine bows.

The graffito on an Indus potsherd from Mohenjo-Daro (Fig. 6.4) may also represent a plank boat with a mast near amidships, and a steering-oar on one quarter. This 'outline sketch' of a boat of *c.*2000 BC may be compared with the twentieth-century Indus 'punt', more correctly, the *quantel battella* (Greenhill, 1971: 34, 179–82; 1963) although these are propelled by sweeps rather than by sail. It may also be compared with some of the round-hulled boats of the Ganges delta which *are* sailed (Greenhill, 1963: 275).

### 6.7.2 THE LATE FIRST MILLENNIUM BC / EARLY FIRST MILLENNIUM AD

From the late first millennium BC/early first millennium AD there are depictions of what are probably planked vessels: some are large open boats (6.2.4); others are sailing ships. The depictions on coins, seals, and monumental stones give little information about hull structure and only slightly more about hull shape: they generally have a rising sheerline at the bow and some-

times at the stern. There are only two depictions giving information about plank fastenings—the second-century BC Bharhut medallion (Fig. 6.5) and the first-century BC Sanchi stupa (Fig. 6.6). Both show double-dovetail flat wooden clamps across the seams: the planking appears to fit together with joggles and projections, as seen in much earlier times on the Cheops ship (2.7.1), and also today in the *téna* whaling boats of Lamalera, Indonesia (Barnes, 1985: fig. 21.3).

These early depictions generally have steering-oars over each quarter, and they are propelled in the early days (first century BC) by a sail on a single mast, but subsequently they have two, and in some cases three, masts. These masts are supported by stays fore and aft, but shrouds are not depicted—this omission may be deliberate as shrouds tend to complicate illustrations and detract from other features. More can be learned from two depictions in the Ajanta caves. A vessel from cave 1 (Fig. 6.10) has hulc-like planking for which there are recent parallels from Bangladesh (Greenhill, 1971: 92) and from Orissa and Bengal (McGrail, Blue, and Kentley, 1999). This sailing ship also has *oculi* depicted at both ends. In cave 2 at Ajanta, a ship of *c.* AD 600 appears to have lugsails on three masts and an artemon-style sail over the bow (Fig. 6.11): this is probably a depiction of a south-east Asian ship, possibly the *kolandiophonta* (6.3.5) of the *Periplus of the Erythraean Sea* (ch. 60) which may well be *kun lun po*, the Chinese word for non-Chinese vessels (Manguin, 1996). With this exception, all the representations of early sailing ships in India appear to be of indigenous vessels.

### 6.7.3 SEWN-PLANK BOATS

Although the author of the *Periplus* mentions the sewn boats of Arabia and east Africa, he does not mention them in his chapters on India. Later Indian Ocean travellers, notably Marco Polo of the thirteenth century, Ibn Battutah, and Friar Odoric of the fourteenth century, and Vasco da Gama of the late fifteenth century, also mention only Arabian sewn vessels. The earliest traceable reference to Indian sewn boats appears to be from the early sixteenth century when Duarte Barbosa, a Portuguese who worked on the Malabar coast from 1500 to 1515, noted that sewn boats annually voyaged from Calicut on the Malabar coast to the Red Sea, some for Aden and some for Jeddah (the port for

Fig. 6.20. Early nineteenth-century sewn-plank boats off the Coromandel coast (Paris, 1843: plate 28).

Mecca), whence the goods were moved to Cairo and Alexandria. They sailed westwards in February, and eastwards between August and October in sewn-plank ships of 200 tonnes 'which have keels like the Portuguese' (Lane-Fox, 1875: 412–13).

Barbosa also recorded that sewn-plank boats were built from palm-tree timber in the Maldive islands (Hill, 1958: 203). These Maldive sewn boats also had keels and were of some size ('great burden') and there is an implication in Barbosa's account that they were sailed. At about the same time, an Italian, Gasparo Balbi, described 'certain boats (of the Coromandel coast) which are sown with fine cords' (Hill, 1958: 208). These oared vessels were used to take passengers and merchandise from ships through the heavy surf and land them on the beach (Fig. 6.20).

The earliest reference to the name *masula* (a term often used by Europeans to describe the sewn boats of India's east coast) appears to be by a Dutchman, Peter Floris, who worked in Masulipatnam (now Machilipatnam; the *Masalia* of the *Periplus*, ch. 62) on the Coromandel coast in AD 1611. He noted *masull* both at sea and in the harbour of St Thomas's Mount near Madras (Hill, 1958: 206). A more detailed description of the *massoola* was given by Thomas Bowrey (Temple, 1905: 42–4), a pepper trader in the late seventeenth century. These flat-bottomed boats (Fig. 6.21) had broad, thin planking sewn with *cayre* (coir); they had crossbeams

used as thwarts, but no other framing timbers. This brings to mind Strabo's remark (15. 1. 15) quoting Onesicritus, one of Alexander's commanders, that the boats of southern India and Sri Lanka were without floor timbers (*metrai*) and had poor sails. Bowrey noted how *masulas* were used through the surf carrying bales of calico or silk, and he remarked that their flexible structure was 'most proper for this coast'. Dr Fryer, a near contemporary of Bowrey, recorded that the *masula's* planking was fastened with rope yarn of the *cocoe* and that they were caulked with *dammar*—a tree gum or resin (Hill, 1958: 207–8).

Edye (1834) described and published drawings of five types of early nineteenth-century sewn boats: two from the Coromandel coast, the Madras *masula manché* and the Panyani *manché*; and three from the Malabar coast, the Mangalor and Calicut *manchés* and the smaller *patāmar*. The *masula* was double-ended and had a flat

Fig. 6.21. A seventeenth-century 'massoola' drawn by Thomas Bowrey (after Temple, 1905: plate 8).

bottom with some rocker and was generally similar in form to Bowrey's seventeenth-century boat (Fig. 6.21). These frameless *masulas* were sewn with coir yarn over coir wadding (a feature of twentieth-century *masulas*), and measured 30–5 × 10–11 × 7–8 ft (*c*.9–11 × 30 × 2 m). They were steered by two *tindals* (presumably with steering-oars over each quarter) and propelled by twelve men, two to each thwart, with bamboo oars. Rowing time was kept by a song, the rhythm of which was varied by the *tindal* to match the wave pattern in the surf. Edye emphasized (as also had Fryer) that these vessels were intentionally built with a pliable structure so that they would yield to the shock they received on taking the ground. It was necessary, however, to keep two men constantly bailing out water.

The four other types of sewn-plank boat had, by Edye's time, all been influenced to varying degrees by Arab techniques. The Mangalor *manché*, a river cargo boat propelled by pole, had retained the general shape of the *masula* but its stern post had been adapted to take a rudder. The Calicut *manché* was similar to that of Mangalor but had a raking Arab-style bow (see also F. Paris (1843: plate 10, figs. 7–10). It is unclear from Edye's descriptions whether these two boats were (unlike the *masula*) framed; but the Panyani *manché*, a coastal vessel, was indeed framed and also had a raked mast. The *patāmar* of the Malabar coast was generally nailed and bolted in the European fashion, but the smaller ones were sewn. Both sizes of *patāmar* were very similar in form to contemporary Arab sewn-plank *dows*.

Edye's *patāmar* of the Malabar coast (1834: plate X) was also very similar in form (with the long overhanging Arab bow) to the Malabar *patāmar* published by Admiral Paris (1843: plan 1C, figs. 1–6; Rieth, 1993: 42–3). Paris's detailed drawings show that the strake edges were interlocked in an N-shaped rabbet (an angular form of the more familiar rabbeted or half-lap joint) with a spike driven from inboard at an angle through the seam into the lower strake (Fig. 6.22); the strakes were also fastened by lashings, each one tightened by a wooden wedge. Stavorinus (1789), a Dutchman who visited the Gujarat coast (north of the Gulf of Cambay) in the eighteenth century noted that this technique was called *vadhera*. The rabbet was first lined with a cotton strip and resin, and the strakes lashed together at 5 ft (*c*.1.5 m) intervals in a diagonal manner through two holes in each strake: a thin wedge (Deloche, 1994: fig. 42G) was then driven into each lash-

Fig. 6.22. The *Vadhera* technique of plank fastening (after Deloche, 1994: fig. 42E).

ing (probably inboard). The strakes were then further fastened together by spikes at 200 mm intervals (Deloche, 1994: 192–3). Since the lashings are the first fastenings, this *patāmar* could be thought of as a sewn boat; the spikes are much closer spaced, but by themselves could not prevent the seams from opening.

Wilson (Deloche, 1994: 193), at the beginning of the twentieth century, found similar strake fastenings on Gujarat boats and also noted that the frames were fastened to the planking by large iron nails which were clenched by turning their points along the inner face of the frames. When Hornell (1930) examined Gujarat boats in the 1920s, he noted no lashings, but reported that after the strake seams had been spiked, the 'planks were spiked down to the frames' which had been 'first set up in the ordinary manner'. By that date, then, these Gujarat boats were built frame-first, although the planking was still edge-fastened by nails *vadhera* fashion, but no longer sewn or lashed.

Sewn-plank boats were in use in India into the twentieth century (Hornell, 1946a: 236): they are still in use today. There are large sewn-plank fishing boats on the Malabar coast, and large seagoing cargo boats known as *balam* in the lower Ganges and the Bay of Bengal (Greenhill, 1971: 105, 114–17). The *madel paruwa*, a sewn-plank boat with chine strakes, is used for beach seine-net fishing in Sri Lanka (Kentley and Gunaratne, 1987). The *masula* or *chelingue* of the Coromandel coast (Fig. 6.23) survives in form and in structure very similar to those described by Bowrey, Edye, and by Admiral Paris (1843: 36–7, plate 27, figs. 1–4) (Hornell, 1946a: 236; Deloche, 1994: 180–3; Kentley, 1985; 1996). In 1979 there were around 4,700 frameless sewn-plank boats in use on the east coast of India (Kentley, 1985: 303) between Cape Cormorin and Paradeep in Orissa. Bowrey's

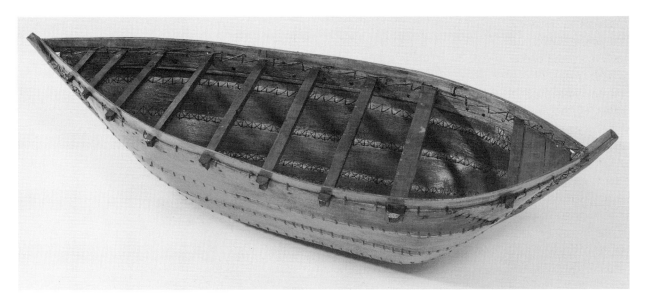

Fig. 6.23. A model of a *masula* sewn-plank boat (National Maritime Museum, Greenwich).

observation that *masulas* were 'most proper' for disembarking through surf onto a beach was echoed by the Royal Navy during the 1905 Somali campaign: *masulas* manned by Tamil crews proved 'eminently suitable for the work. They stood the knocking about better than the man-of-war boats . . . (which) required constant repair' (Brassey, 1905: 60–1). (See also Fig. 6.20.)

Another sewn-plank vessel recorded by Admiral Paris (1843: 29–31, plate 21) was the Sri Lanka *yāthrā-dhoni* or *yātrā-oruva* (Hornell, 1946a: fig. 60). In the early twentieth century, this double-ended, two-masted boat had a single outrigger to port, and a fixed stern rudder. This combination meant that if the outrigger was always to be to windward, as is normal, these vessels were limited to the west coast of Sri Lanka where they could always have the outrigger on the port side by using the alternating land and sea breezes (Hornell, 1946a: 258). R. Bowen (1953: 81–117, 185–211) suggested that the two-masted vessel on second-century AD coins from India's east coast (Fig. 6.7) may have been similar to the *yātrā-oruva*. But this is merely a superficial outline resemblance and could be said about many other vessels. To show any relationships over time, similarities in structural features would have to be demonstrated, and such details do not appear on these coins—not even the run of the planking.

Without head sails and with a steering-oar rather than a fixed stern rudder (both traits were probably brought to India by Arab or by European ships) it might have been possible to 'shunt' the early *yātrā-oruva*, as was done in the recent past in some of the single outrigger Micronesian boats when changing tack (9.3.6.3). Pliny (*NH* 6. 24. 82) appears to refer to such a manœuvre when he states that vessels that voyaged between India and Sri Lanka 'have bows at each end so as to avoid the necessity of coming about . . .'. An illustration (Fig. 6.18) published in the early seventeenth century by Linschoten (1610: 108) includes two double-ended sewn-plank boats (*almadias*) off Goa. The one with a single outrigger has no mast and is steered by a steering-oar; the other has a mast and sail near amidships, but no outrigger and is steered by a stern rudder. A conflation of these two boats—if it existed—could have been a forerunner of the nineteenth-century *yātrā-oruva*, and possibly a link with the boats Pliny described.

The Indian sewn-plank boat can be traced back only to the early sixteenth century. Since sewn boats were used in east Africa, Arabia, and south-east Asia in the late first millennium BC / early first millennium AD, it is reasonable to suggest that there may have been similar early use in India: the evidence, however, is lacking.

### 6.7.4 OTHER PLANKED VESSELS

The other Indian planked boats and ships described by Edye (1834), the large *patāmar*, the Arab *dow*, the *baggala* or *budgerow*, the *doni*, and the *boatila manché,* were all built in the European or late-Arab manner. There are, however, some earlier descriptions, brought together by Hill (1958), of Indian boats which were possibly entirely indigenous. These include: the double-ended *chaturi* of the Bay of Bengal, said to be swift under sail or oar—reported by Ludovico di Varthema in *c.*1507; and the *cature*, a small oared boat like a *bargatim* or cutter, noted by Duarte Barbosa in the period 1500–15 and by Tome Pires at about the same time. Tome Pires also noted *pagueres* which he described as ancient cargo vessels of southern India; these *pagueres* or *pagell* were also noted by Peter Floris in *c.*1611 in the harbour of Masulipatnam. Bowrey, in the late seventeenth century, recorded an *olocko*, an oared boat used as a ferry and to transport goods down the Ganges to ships in the Hugli. In Bowrey's drawing (Hill, 1958: fig. 3) this boat is steered by a side rudder and the oars have heart-shaped blades. Grant, writing in the mid-nineteenth century, states that the planks were laid edge-to-edge and fastened with iron staples or clamps. An evidently similar Bengal boat (but with sail) also had flush-laid planking fastened by iron staples (F. Paris, 1843: plate 32, figs. 6 and 7) both inboard and outboard. Greenhill (1971: 75–6) states that in the mid-twentieth century, these staples were known as *patam loha* and they were driven into shallow slots cut across the plank seams at intervals of *c.*2 in (50 mm): the seams were N-shaped rabbeted (Greenhill, 1957: fig. 8), similar to those in the *vedhera* technique of Gujarat (6.7.3).

Bowrey also described the Ganges *patella* (Temple, 1905: 225, plate 15). These were flat-bottomed, barge-like, clinker-built boats with protruding crossbeams, used to transport saltpetre downstream. They had a single mast and were steered by a large median rudder. Similar vessels were described and drawn by F. Paris (1843: 43, plan 35).

In more recent times, Greenhill (1971: 107–9) was told about the *patalia* cargo vessels of the upper Ganges which were flat-bottomed with the side planking overlapping in 'European-style' clinker fastened by iron spikes. In essential features this twentieth-century vessel seems to have been similar to Bowrey's *patella* of 300 years earlier. The distrib-ution of boats with conventional clinker planking is now limited to the upper Ganges, a coastal region of Bangladesh north of Chittagong, and Lake Chilka in Orissa (Deloche, 1994: fig.

35). The fastenings of, at least some of these boats are hooked nails.

Other boats mentioned by Bowrey include the *budgaroo* which is probably the *budgerow* of Edye; the *bagala* or *baghla* also mentioned by Edye; the *purgoo*; and the *boora*, evidently similar to the *bhar* of Hornell (1929: 193–4).

### 6.7.4.1 PLANK FASTENINGS

Plank fastenings already mentioned include: dovetail-shaped wooden clamps (Figs. 6.5, 6.6); sewing (Figs. 6.20, 6.21, 6.23); the *vedhera* technique using wedged lashings and iron spikes (Fig. 6.22); iron staples across N-rabbeted seams (Deloche, 1994: fig. 33é); 'European-style' clinker planking fastened by hooked nails or iron spikes. Other fastenings of recent times remain to be described: the sole use of iron spikes with planking laid edge-to-edge; treenails used similarly; and reverse-clinker planking.

#### 6.7.4.1.1 *Spikes with edge-to-edge planking*

Admiral Paris (1843: 18, plate 10, fig. 4) noted that, in flush-laid boats of the Malabar coast, notches were cut near the lower edge of each strake and spikes were driven in obliquely across the seam into the lower plank. Boats built on the Gujarat coast between Bombay and Cambay on the eastern shores of the Gulf of Cambay and the large seagoing sampans of Chittagong in Bangladesh were similarly fastened in recent times, the strakes meeting either in a half-lap or edge-to-edge (Hornell, 1930; Greenhill, 1971: 118).

#### 6.7.4.1.2 *Treenail fastenings*

The Calcuttan *manchés* of the Malabar coast (not to be confused with the Calicut *manchés* which were sewn boats) were fastened by tenons or treenails obliquely driven through the edges of flush-laid planking: the ends of the treenails can be seen in the plank faces (F. Paris, 1843: 20). Similar fastenings are known in the *punt* and the *bohatja* of the Indus valley (Greenhill, 1963; 1971: 178–80).

#### 6.7.4.1.3 *Reverse-clinker planking*

Reverse-clinker planking (Fig. 6.24), in which each succeeding strake overlaps *in*board the upper edge of the strake below (rather than *out*board, as in the European clinker), is depicted on eleventh- to twelfth-century

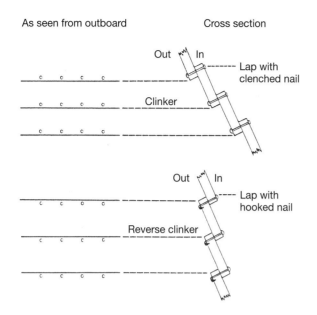

As seen from outboard          Cross section

Out          In

Lap with
clenched nail

Clinker

Out          In

Lap with
hooked nail

Reverse clinker

Fig. 6.24. Clinker and reverse-clinker planking (Institute of Archaeology, Oxford).

monumental carvings from Orissa (Blue *et al.*, 1997; McGrail, Blue, and Kentley, 1999). Two of these representations are now in museums—the Indian Museum, Calcutta (Fig. 6.25) and the Victoria & Albert Museum in London (Guy, 1995)—whilst the third remains in the black granite walls of the Jagamohana in the Jagannath temple, Puri (Mookerji, 1912: 36; Blue *et al.*, 1997: 195). The reverse-clinker planking is depicted in three dimension, although some of the other features are puzzling.

Two or three of the vessels depicted by Bowrey in the seventeenth century seem to have overlapping planking but this is probably European-style, rather than reverse-clinker. However, the *pettoo-a* 'from Balassora' depicted by Solvyns (1799) in the late eighteenth century undoubtedly had reverse-clinker planking (Fig. 6.26), and his *pataily* 'of Behar and Benares' also probably has. Some of the vessels from this east coast of India published by Admiral Paris in the early nineteenth century (1843) may also have been reverse-clinker.

Fig. 6.25. An eleventh/ twelfth-century monumental carving depicting reverse-clinker planking (Indian Museum, Calcutta).

Fig. 6.26.  A late eighteenth-century drawing of a *pettoua* by F. B. Solvyns (National Maritime Museum, Greenwich).

Fig. 6.27.  A reverse-clinker *nauka* under repair at Bolla Ghat, Sylhet District, Bangladesh in 1997 (photo: Society for South Asian Studies).

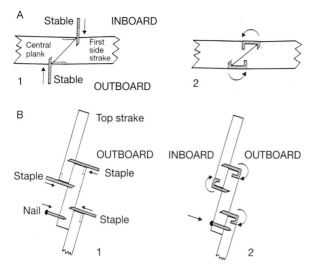

Fig. 6.28. Plank fastenings of the Sylheti *nauka* (Institute of Archaeology, Oxford).

Reverse-clinker boats were first identified in Sylhet, Bangladesh (Fig. 6.1) by Greenhill (1957, 1961, 1966, 1971, 1995a: 38–46, 254–5). During recent fieldwork in the subcontinent, some of these boats (Fig. 6.27) were further documented (McGrail, Blue, and Kentley, 1999). Furthermore, a *patia* group of reverse-clinker boats, in northern Orissa and southern West Bengal, has been recorded (Blue *et al.*, 1997; Kentley, McGrail, and Blue, 1999). The strakes of the *patia* are fastened together by nails which are driven through the overlap and clenched by hooking the emergent point back into the

planking (Fig. 6.24). The Bangladesh reverse-clinker strakes, on the other hand, are fastened by staples outboard alongside the upper edge of the lower plank, and also by staples inboard alongside the lower edge of the upper plank (Fig. 6.28).

The distribution of reverse-clinker vessels is from the Rivers Boro Bulong and Subarnarekha in northern Orissa north-eastwards to the great river system of the Ganges/Padma, the Brahmaput/Jumuna, and the Meghna in Bengal and Bangladesh. Although this technique can only be traced back for 200 years or so, it is possible that it may have its origins in much earlier times: for example, one of the vessels depicted in the Ajanta caves (Fig. 6.10) *may* have been built in reverse-clinker.

### 6.7.4.2 HULC PLANKING PATTERNS

A characteristic of the reverse-clinker boats of India and Bangladesh is that the lower planking does not end at posts but curves upwards to end on a near-horizontal line (Fig. 6.26). Such a planking pattern is similar to that of the medieval north-west European hulc (5.8.3) (McGrail, Blue, and Kentley, 1999; Greenhill, 2000).

Hulc planking in south Asia is not confined to reverse-clinker boats: in Orissa, Bengal, and Bangladesh there are edge-fastened, smooth-skinned boats (Fig. 6.29) (such as the *chhoat*, *salti*, *pallar*, and *pattam*) which have this planking pattern (Mohapatra, 1983;

Fig. 6.29. A Bangladesh *pallar* under repair in the 1950s. The lower hull has hulc planking that is capped by horizontal strakes in the upper hull (photo: Basil Greenhill).

Fig. 6.30. A Tuticorin *thoni* cargo ship, under all plain sail, leaving Columbo for Tamil Nadu in 1994 (photo: Captain A. W. Kinghorn).

Greenhill, 1971). Thus, without other evidence, depictions of hulc-planking patterns as in one of the Ajanta depictions (Fig. 6.10) cannot be interpreted as reverse-clinker planking. This historical-ethnographic research in India also has implications for historical-archaeological research in Atlantic Europe (5.8.3.3).

### 6.7.4.3 FRAME-FIRST VESSELS

All the boats discussed above were built plank-first which seems to have been the earliest building sequence used in all regions of the world. From the evidence presently available, the earliest use of the alternative sequence, frame-first, can be dated to the early centuries AD in north-west Europe (5.6.1). Subsequently this technique, in a somewhat different form, is found in the Mediterranean (4.15) and, by the fourteenth century, on the European Atlantic seaboard (4.16, 5.9). Frame-first may also have been used in south-east Asia and China from the fourteenth century (8.3.7.3, 10.5.1.4). Nowadays there is increasing use of frame-first building in India, but this seems to be a recent introduction, along with European designs, mechanization, and materials other than wood. In Tamil Nadu, however, there is a group of frame-first boats and ships which are designed by methods which were probably derived from those used by the Portuguese in the sixteenth century (4.16, 5.9.4): these are the merchant ships *thoni* (Fig. 6.30) of Tuticorin and *kotia* of Cuddalore, the fishing boats *vattai* of Palk Bay

and *vallam* from further south, and the *vattal* dumb lighter of Cuddalore (Blue, Kentley, and McGrail, 1998; Kentley *et al.*, forthcoming). Portuguese shipbuilders used a special wooden tablet inscribed with a geometrically spaced series of lines (Fig. 4.46) to derive the shape of the main frames from that of a master frame. Tamil builders use a simplified system (Fig. 6.31) based on a memorized formula, which is more suitable for their less-complex hull forms. Apart from this, the two design systems have much in common. Both are based on parameters such as a basic length module, and the total narrowing and rising of the designed hull. In each case hull shape is obtained from a combination of 'equal' (identical to the master frame) and 'unequal' frames; passive (non-designed) frames are subsequently added in the ends of the vessel. Furthermore, in both Atlantic and Tamil designs systems, the foremost and the aftermost designed frames are given special names (McGrail, forthcoming *a* and *c*).

### 6.7.5 SAIL AND RUDDER IN THE INDIAN OCEAN

There is no excavated evidence for sail but there appears to be an early representation of a vessel under sail dated to *c*.2000 BC (Fig. 6.4). The general impression from the early iconographic evidence is that a mast stepped near amidships was the norm: this probably means, as in Egypt (2.4, 2.7.4), the Mediterranean

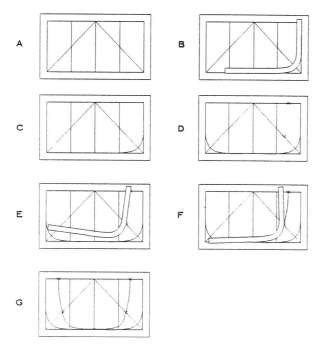

Fig. 6.31. Diagram illustrating the Tamil design sequence. A: preparation of the scrieve board; B, C, and D: drawing the shape of the master frame; E, F, and G: deriving the shape of another frame with its appropriate rising and narrowing (diagram: Society for South Asian Studies).

(4.7.2.1) and elsewhere, that the square sail was used. By the late first millennium BC–early first millennium AD (6.2.4, 6.7.2) there is clear representational evidence for sail: at first a single mast with a square sail, then two masts, and, by the fourth century AD, three masts. What type of sail the multi-masted ships had is not clear. Lugsails appear to be depicted on one Ajanta vessel (Fig. 6.11) but this is probably a ship from south-east Asia.

It has been claimed that the Arab lateen is *the* sail of the Indian Ocean, but this may not have been so until the twelfth–fifteenth centuries AD (3.6.5), although both types of lateen were known in the eastern Mediterranean from the Roman period (4.14.1). In Indian waters, the *patella* drawn by Bowrey (Temple, 1905: plate XV) in the mid-seventeenth century has a mast stepped well forward which may indicate a fore-and-aft sail, but this is by no means certain. In the early nineteenth century Admiral Paris (1843) recorded a wide range of sails and rigs on traditional vessels, including

sprits on small craft, square sails on river craft, and lugs and two types of lateen at sea.

A steering-oar, generally on both quarters, seems to have been the main, if not the only, means of steering seagoing vessels in pre-European times. Nowadays they are still frequently used on traditional craft: it is of some interest to note that, when only one steering-oar is fitted, it is generally to port.

# 6.8

# Medieval and Later Navigational Techniques

The pilotage and non-instrumental techniques used in Indian waters during the Graeco-Roman period (6.3.3.1) continued in use through medieval times and, by local fishermen, into the twentieth century (Deloche, 1994: 198–208). Navigational treatises by medieval Arab seamen and astronomers have survived from the times when instruments were beginning to be used (3.8.2), yet there is no known Indian equivalent; it is therefore not possible to say how much Indian seamen contributed to the development of instrumental techniques. From accounts compiled in recent years, however, it is clear that Indian quantitative methods of navigation were very similar to those used by Arabs (3.8.2): for example, both used the *zam* unit of distance measurement and the *isbâ* unit of angular measure (Arunachalam, 1987; 1996). Aleem (1980: 586) considers that the *zam* was an Indian unit adopted by Arabs.

Sailing manuals used by Gujarat seamen have survived from the mid-seventeenth century (Arunachalam, 1987; Varadarajan, 1979; Deloche, 1994: 205–8). These documents include summaries of astronomical observations, sketches of coastal profiles showing features in the vicinity of selected landing places and diagrammatic charts with routes and other features marked on them (Deloche, 1994: fig. 44a). It is clear that, by this time, Indian seamen were familiar with contemporary methods of navigation elsewhere.

# 7

# GREATER AUSTRALIA

New Guinea, Australia, Tasmania, and the western parts of Melanesia, as far as the Solomon islands, were first settled by people who came from south-east Asia and south-east China over 40,000 years ago (White and O'Connell, 1982). The islands of Japan may have been first settled at about the same time (10.10.1).

South-east Asia began to appear much as it is today from *c*.5,000 years ago, when mean sea level had risen to within today's tidal range, and the rate of this post-glacial rise in sea level had significantly slackened. Before that time, when sea levels were lower, many of today's islands were part of continental land masses, either south-east Asia or Australia, whilst those that were then islands were much greater in area. From the biogeographic viewpoint, this region is divided into three areas which conveniently form a framework for the discussion of its prehistory.

## 7.1

## The Early Environment

### 7.1.1 SUNDALAND

In the west of the region (Fig. 7.1) there is a continental shelf with shallow seas within which now lie Malaya, Sumatra, Java, Borneo, and Palawan (the westernmost island of the Philippines). This 'Sundaland' extends from what is now mainland south-east Asia as far east as the 'Huxley' line (Bellwood, 1985: 7, fig. 1.3), which is generally similar to the earlier 'Wallace' line (Harris, 1994: fig. 1.3) except that the latter ran south of the Philippines. The Huxley line, a transitional zone rather than a barrier, runs from the Pacific westwards between Taiwan and the Philippines, then generally southward: across the Sulu Sea; between Borneo and Sulawesi; and between the islands of Bali and Lombok, and on into the Indian Ocean. There are distinctive differences between the native fauna on either side of this line. At the time of maximum glaciation, *c*.18,000 BP, when mean sea level was 100 to 150 m below today's level, the Sundaland region (to the west of the Huxley line) was virtually all dry land (Bellwood, 1985: 7–8).

### 7.1.2 SAHULLAND

'Sahulland' or 'Greater Australia' is the Australian equivalent of Sundaland. At times of lower sea levels, New Guinea, Australia, Tasmania, and many smaller islands formed one land mass extending as far west as the 'Weber line' (Fig. 7.1), which runs from the Indian Ocean east of Timor, and generally north-eastwards through the Banda Sea; then west of New Guinea and east of the Moluccas, and on into the Pacific. This line marks a 50 : 50 balance between Oriental and Australian fauna. Sahulland thus extended from the Tropics in New Guinea and northern Australia to temperate Tasmania in the south.

### 7.1.3 WALLACEA

'Wallacea' is the name given to the region between Sundaland and Sahulland; it includes the Philippine

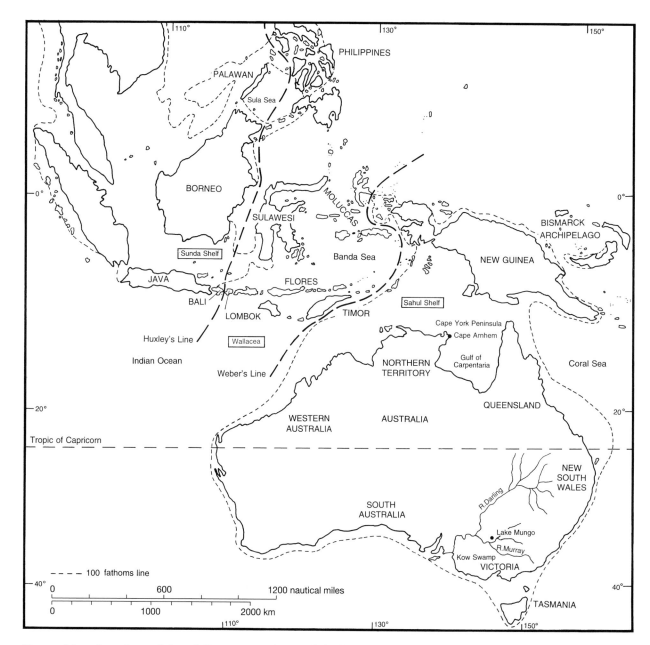

Fig. 7.1. Map of south-east Asia and Greater Australia: Sunda-land to the north-west; Sahul-land to the south-east; Wallacean archipelago between (Institute of Archaeology, Oxford).

islands (except Palawan), Sulawesi, the Moluccas, and the lesser Sunda islands from Lombok eastwards (Bellwood, 1985: 8). Geological and biogeographic evidence shows that, during the measurable past, this has been an archipelago of islands, even at the time of minimum sea level. Migrations through Wallacea, by flora and fauna (except those species that can fly or are air-dispersed) and by humans, must therefore have involved sea crossings.

## 7.2

# The Settlement of Greater Australia

Radiocarbon dates and other evidence show that parts of Sahulland were settled at remarkably early dates: sites on the northern coast of New Guinea from c.40,000 BP; New Ireland in the Bismarck archipelago from c.30,000 BP; and Buka island in the Solomons from c.28,000 BP. In northern Australia there are now dates in the range 30,000–40,000 BP, whilst in the temperate south there are coastal and riverine sites dated 35,000–40,000 BP (Bellwood, 1985: 99; Smith and Sharp, 1993). Dates of c.60,000 BP, and even 800,000 BP, have recently been suggested (Roberts, Jones, and Smith, 1994; Allen and Holdaway, 1995; Spooner, 1998; Morwood et al., 1998; Bednarik, 1998). These are based on thermo-luminescence and fission track methods of dating, but the accuracy of these innovative techniques is not yet proven, and dates derived from them are controversial. The generally accepted opinion is that the Wallacean archipelago was crossed and Greater Australia first settled some 50,000 years ago (Habgood, 1986; van Andel, 1989; Harris, 1994; R. Roberts et al., 1994; David et al., 1997).

The question whether there was just one founder population or numerous successive waves of migrants has long been discussed, and the matter is still in dispute. There seems to be general agreement, however, that these people came from Sundaland, having originated in Taiwan or the south-east coast of China (Bellwood, 1985: 99–100, 318).

Twenty-one years ago Birdsell (1977) identified two possible routes along chains of islands between the two continents: a northern route from Borneo to New Guinea via Sulawesi and the Moluccas; and a southern route from Java through Flores and Timor to northwest Australia (Fig. 7.2): these proposals have stood the test of time and are now generally agreed. Birdsell also estimated that, at the times of lowest sea level (c.53,000 and c.18,000 BP), the longest voyages would have been less than 60 nautical miles (100 km). At c.40,000 BP, although the sea level was higher, the channels between the Wallacean islands would have remained much the same in breadth, but at the beginning and end of these 'island-hopping' voyages there would have been longer passages through shallow seas over the shelves.

Van Andel (1989) has questioned whether New Guinea would necessarily have been part of Sahulland during the migration period and has estimated that, at a time when sea level was c.40 m. below that of today, the widest channel would have been 240 nautical miles (c.400 km) on the southern route, and 150 nautical miles c.250 km on the northern. Irwin (1992: 18–30) has also reinvestigated Birdsell's routes, this time at a sea

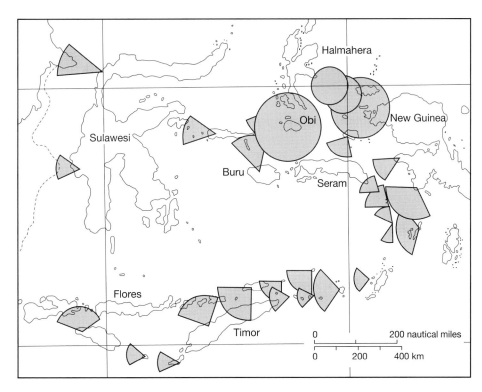

Fig. 7.2. Visibility sectors on routes across 'Wallacea' (after Irwin, 1992: fig. 8).

level of 50 m below today's, and he agrees that 60 nautical miles (100 km) would have been the maximum length of crossing via Borneo on the northern route. On crossings from New Guinea eastwards to the Solomon islands, however, he believes that there could have been passages up to 150 nautical miles (250 km); Harris (1994: 8), on the other hand, estimates the longest passage to have been only 100 nautical miles (c.180 km). Gosden (1993) considers that 50 nautical miles (90 km) would have been the maximum, although most passages would have been less than 6 nautical miles (10 km).

The mean of estimates for the northern route (other than those of van Andel) is c.72 nautical miles. Using paddles, average speeds of 1½ knots might be achieved; under oars, say three knots (4.4.5). Thus a paddled craft would take about two days for the maximum crossing; an oared craft, about one day. Using van Andel's estimate of 150 nautical miles, this crossing would have taken about four days under paddle, or two days under oars. These estimates of crossing times have both survival and navigational implications. Human survival would primarily depend on being able to carry sufficient fresh water. The structural survival of the vessel would depend on the materials used (7.3), and on the wind and sea state—the optimum choice of season would have been a period of calm, settled weather.

The navigational techniques needed on the first, exploratory voyages would have depended very much on whether land was, or was not, in sight during each passage. It is generally agreed (Irwin, 1992: 28–9) that these early migrations were purposeful and planned, rather than drift voyages or haphazardly selected routes across the open sea: before migrants left, they knew that there was land to be found.

Irwin (1992: 18–30) has shown that, on the northern route to New Guinea and as far east as New Ireland in the Solomons, a high point on an island to the east could always be seen from sea level before leaving each previous island (Fig. 7.2). Such 'intervisibility' is known as 'two-way', since throughout the passage, both home land and new land can be seen, and pilotage (i.e. visual) methods of navigation can be used in daylight hours. However, even the shortest of the crossings considered above includes night travel. On a clear tropical night it would probably have still been possible to maintain visual contact with land. Nevertheless, the possibility

that at some time during the night, or when there was poor visibility by day, contact could be lost, would probably have led these early voyagers to develop other means of maintaining a heading, such as relative to the wind, the swell, and even the stars (4.4.5).

On the southern route, on the other hand, there were certain channels where there was only 'one-way' intervisibility (Irwin, 1992: 18–30): that is, although new land could not be seen at sea level from the home land, it could be seen before voyagers had lost visual contact with their homeland. Methods that would-be migrants use to deduce that there is land over the horizon have been documented in Oceania (9.5.2—see also 4.4.4 and 4.4.6). Knowing the direction of new land by these indirect means, voyagers on the southern route across Wallacea could have used similar navigational methods to those used on the northern route, focusing first on the home land, and then on the new land.

The precise nature of this Pleistocene voyaging— the earliest sea crossings so far known, in any part of the world—depends upon the precise date of the migrations and upon factors such as mean sea level and heights of mountain peaks: such dates, levels, and heights are, at present, difficult to quantify with any precision. Moreover, whatever the date, past climates, winds and currents are, at best, known only in general terms.

Nevertheless, the primary evidence is clear: there were considerable channels to be crossed in the Wallacean archipelago, and humans evidently *did* cross them some 40,000 or more years ago. The overall distance from eastern Sundaland to western Sahulland is 600 nautical miles (c.1,000 km) which could be accomplished from island to island in less than a month: it is most unlikely that this happened. Islands visible from Sundaland, or of which there was early warning, would probably have been visited several times before they were settled. Similar exploratory voyages would have been undertaken in turn to other islands further east in the island chains—the whole crossing of Wallacea probably extending over many generations. There would have been no dramatic environmental changes to cope with: the coastal lands of north-western Greater Australia having a comparable range of marine resources to those of the Indonesian islands, with some continuity in marine and plant life, although some adaptation would have been needed in the south of Australia.

# 7.3
# Water transport

There is no direct evidence for the water transport used by the migrating voyagers when they crossed the Wallacean archipelago 50,000–40,000 years ago. There are no excavated remains of vessels in Wallacea or in Greater Australia (Sahulland) earlier than those of seventeenth-century European explorers. In Sundaland the earliest boats so far known are from the second century AD (8.3).

There are no Aboriginal oral histories ('dreamtime stories') which might throw light on the matter, as Oceanic sagas may be able to do for the very much later migrations from Melanesia to Polynesia (9.5). And there are no rock or bark paintings, or other representational evidence from the region which might be interpreted as early forms of water transport, except for some stone arrangements found near Cape Arnhem in the Northern Territory, which appear to be late representations of Indonesian boats (Mulvaney, 1975: plate 14). In late prehistoric times (that is before the eighteenth century AD) people from New Guinea and Sulawesi visited the Northern Territory and northern Queensland (Edwards, 1972: 10; Shutler and Shutler, 1975: 42–4; Bowdler, 1995). The metal axe and the extended logboat with double or single outrigger (Haddon and Hornell, 1937: ii. 179–93), and possibly the sail, appear to have been introduced at this time. This occasional contact with horticultural societies appears to have had limited effects in Australia: the new technology did not spread outside the north and north-eastern coastal strip, and it had little influence on cultural life—for example, the Australian Aboriginal never adopted formal agricultural techniques. Nevertheless, these possible external influences must be borne in mind when evaluating evidence from north and north-eastern Australia.

The best evidence so far available, for early water transport in this region, lies in descriptions compiled by Europeans of the vessels they saw being used in Australia at the time of 'first contact' in the seventeenth and eighteenth centuries. Tasmania is particularly important in this respect since it became isolated from the mainland by rising sea levels before 7000 BC—at about the time that New Guinea was separated from

Australia—and there was little, if any, subsequent cross-channel contact until the coming of Europeans. The Tasmanians' tool kit consisted of scrapers and simple percussion and bone tools and did not include the more advanced types found in mainland Australia. Notwithstanding the elementary nature of their tool kit, Tasmanians built and used log floats, log rafts, and seagoing bundle rafts. Tasmanians never had the new types of hafted tool which appeared on the mainland around 3000 BC; with this improved tool kit Australian Aboriginals were able to build technically advanced log rafts and bark boats.

## 7.3.1 LOG FLOATS

Single logs, on which the paddler sat, were used off the north-west coast of Australia to visit offshore islands, assisted by tidal flows and currents (Hornell, 1946: 72–3). Single driftwood logs were similarly used by Tasmanians to cross rivers (Birdsell, 1977: 135). Some of the logs used on the Australian north-west coast had a series of pegs driven into both sides around which were twined withies to form combined stabilizers and footrests at the waterline.

## 7.3.2 BUNDLE RAFTS

Tasmanians made bundle rafts from bark (a use not known elsewhere) and occasionally from reeds (Roth, 1899: 155; Hornell, 1946: 60; R. Jones, 1976: 239–60; 1977: 324–5; Birdsell, 1977: 135). The reed rafts were made of five bundles of what were probably bullrushes (*Typha* sp.). The bark rafts (Fig. 7.3) were made from 'stringy bark' (*Eucalyptus obliqua* or *regnans*), or from 'paper bark' of the tea tree shrub (*Melaleuca* sp.). The latter was preferred wherever it could be obtained, for rafts made of it not only resisted waterlogging longer, but were also lighter: a paper-bark raft weighed 350 lbs (160 kg) compared with the 500 lbs (230 kg) of a stringy-bark raft of similar size. This bark was not cut from the tree, rather loose pieces were picked up from the ground or pulled off the trunk; thus special debarking tools, as used when building bark boats in mainland Australia and in North America (11.4.4.3) were not required. Individual bundles of bark were bound into a cylindrical shape which tapered towards the ends, by a

Fig. 7.3. Early nineteenth-century Tasmanian bark bundle rafts. Lesueur and Petit's *Terre de Diemen*.

network of rope made from grass or inner bark. Three of these bundles were then lashed together, the two smaller bundles being positioned outboard and slightly above the larger, central bundle, to form a boat-shaped raft with upturned ends.

Most bark rafts seen in the early nineteenth century were up to 10 ft (*c*.3 m) long, 3–4 ft. (0.9–1.2 m) broad, with an inside depth of some 10 in (250 mm), and the larger ones carried three or four people. However, one large example measured 15 ft by 5 ft (4.5 by 1.5 m), and some of the coastal rafts were said to be 'the size of a whaleboat', able to carry seven or eight people and their dogs. Calculations by R. Jones (1976: 244–8) generally substantiate these early reports. In the shallows these rafts were propelled and steered by poles 8–16 ft (2.4–4.8 m) in length; poles were also used as double paddles in deeper water. At times, spears were used to pole or paddle rafts. Paddling was also done with the hands or using strips of bark; rafts were sometimes pulled or pushed by swimmers; and, whenever possible, use was made of favourable currents

and tidal streams. Progress against the wind was difficult.

Waterlogging was the principal limit on performance. Using laboratory data and experiments with full-size reconstructions, R. Jones (1976: 246–52; 1977: 324–5) has estimated that a paper-bark raft could be expected to retain sufficient buoyancy and manœuvrability for five to six hours, whereas for a stringy-bark raft this would have been less than an hour. Either raft could have been used to cross rivers and bays. Voyages to islands up to 5 nautical miles (8 km) offshore, which would have taken more than an hour, must have been undertaken in paper-bark rafts and with a fair wind and current, if Jones' deductions on waterlogging are correct.

### 7.3.3 LOG RAFTS

Roth (1899: 158) quotes, but questions the accuracy of, early nineteenth-century accounts of the occasional use of log rafts on large rivers and lakes, and on the coasts of Tasmania. These reports describe a raft of two logs (the simplest possible) with several transverse timbers lashed to them with bark strips. These rafts gained extra buoyancy and stowage space from wickerwork extensions—as used on the single-log floats of north-west Australia. There seems no good reason to reject these reports, *pace* Roth, especially since R. Jones (1976: 239–40) has noted an early account of the use of two-log rafts, lashed together with grass ropes, to cross Tasmanian rivers.

Both Roth and Jones point out that most Tasmanian tree species of today have a high specific density and thus would be unsuitable for rafts. Furthermore, they consider that the tools that the Aboriginals are thought to have had could not be used to fell trees or trim off branches. They therefore consider that log rafts would have been very rare in prehistoric times. However, the pines of Tasmania are of relatively low density; trees can be felled by controlled fire and by storms; and dried driftwood may also be used. There is every reason to believe that the prehistoric Tasmanians were able to build log rafts capable of being used in coastal waters.

On the Australian mainland, in the rivers of eastern Queensland, at isolated places on the north coast, and on the north-west coast and the rivers of the northern parts of western Australia, there is evidence for the recent use of three types of log raft (Hornell, 1946*a*: 71–2; Birdsell, 1977: 139–42).

### 7.3.3.1  RIVER RAFTS

On the rivers of eastern Queensland and along the north coast, simple, often temporary, rafts were made by using bark strips or grass cord, to lash together several mangrove saplings at their ends. By choosing different sizes of logs and placing them in specific relative positions, raft builders in the southern parts of the Gulf of Carpentaria made their rafts 'boat-shaped', with a narrower end (the bow) and a slightly hollowed form.

### 7.3.3.2  SINGLE RAFTS

On the north-west coast, 6–7 ft (1.8–2.1 m) rafts were made of mangrove logs pinned together by hardwood treenails, about 1 ft (0.30 m) in length. By placing the butt ends of all the logs at one end, these rafts were given a trapezoidal form in plan, with a narrow bow.

Near the stern, upright pegs formed a circular enclosure in which fish and fishing tackle were stowed—this is comparable with the tub of recent Taiwanese log rafts (10.2.5).

### 7.3.3.3  DOUBLE RAFTS

Offshore and in the estuaries of Australia's north-west coast, two of these single rafts were combined to form a *kalum* or double raft. A seven-log raft was positioned so that its narrow end partly overlapped the corresponding end of a nine-log raft. The two elements were not fastened together; they were kept in contact merely by the weight of the upper raft and the crew of one or two men. These composite rafts were used for fishing and turtle hunting in the rivers and bays, and for the exploration of islands up to 10 nautical miles (16 km) offshore. On such seagoing voyages, they were mainly propelled by tidal streams. A paddle, made from the lower stem of a mangrove with the fan-shaped root forming the blade, was used for steering and to move from and to shore, in and out of the tidal flow. A turtle spear was sometimes thrust down between the logs of the two units to secure the raft to bay or river bottom.

### 7.3.4  BARK BOATS

Bark boats were used on the rivers and coastal regions of Australia, in western Victoria, New South Wales, Queensland, and the Northern Territory (Lane-Fox, 1875: 420–1; Hornell, 1946: 182–6; R. Edwards, 1972: 7–9, 29–32; Birdsell, 1977: 136–9). Some were evidently made by cutting a complete cylinder of bark, thereby killing the tree, but many were probably made from half-cylinder strips, since today there are numerous 'canoe trees' surviving with an elongated barkless scar. Bark was usually taken from the stringy-bark tree (*Eucalyptus obliqua*) or the river red gum (*Eucalyptus camaldulensis*), during the rainy season in late spring/early summer when the sap was flowing. Special wedges and levers were needed to prise the bark from the bole and, for the larger strips, eight to ten men could be needed to lower the bark safely to the ground. Three general types of bark boat were built in continental Australia; all were propelled by paddles.

Fig. 7.4. Early nineteenth-century Australian lashed bark boats. Lesueur and Petit's Atlas to Peron's *Voyage of Discovery*.

### 7.3.4.1 SIMPLE BARK BOATS

In western Victoria, in the Murray/Darling basin, a thick section of bark in the form of an open-ended trough was fitted with a few transverse sticks to prevent the bark curling, and used as a boat in still waters, sometimes just for a single river crossing. If required for more demanding tasks, the ends were blocked with clay or mud. Such a boat could be built in less than half a day.

### 7.3.4.2 LASHED BARK BOATS

Of a higher technological standard were the lashed bark boats used in the rivers and creeks of coastal New South Wales and south-east Victoria (Fig.7.4). The outer surface of the bark was removed and the ends thinned, to produce a thin sheet which was then heat-

ed until it became pliable. The bark was then turned inside out and moulded in a hollow in the ground to a deeper shape wth upturned ends. These ends were then pleated and bunched, and tied with bark cord. Some of these boats are said to have had no framing, but this seems unlikely for anything but the simplest of shapes. Generally a few rod stretchers and some cord ties were fitted to maintain the shape and keep the sides a fixed distance apart. Superior models also had occasional flexible ribs, and a sapling or a cylindrical bundle of rushes along the top of each side to stiffen the rim. Such boats could carry two men, possibly more.

### 7.3.4.3 STITCHED BARK BOATS

The technologically most advanced bark boat was built up from several sections of bark sewn together—in this respect, and in its general structure, it is comparable with the bark boats of North and South America (11.4.4). Bark boats were built along the coasts of the Northern Territory and the tropical parts of Queensland. In fair weather they were used to visit offshore islands: for example, a documented 20 nautical mile (32 km) voyage in the Gulf of Carpentaria. A typical boat of this type was made from seven segments of eucalyptus bark: one long and wide sheet for one side of the boat; two wide pieces for the other side; and two pieces at each pointed end so that they could be made uprising. These were moulded to shape and then stitched together with bark strips or bast cord, and the seams caulked with gum. There was a supporting framework of stretchers, ties, and stick ribs. The largest boats noted measured 16–18 ft by *c*.2 ft (4.88–5.49 × 0.60 m), and could carry a crew of eight.

## 7.3.5 LOGBOATS

Outrigger craft—probably logboats with washstrakes—were seen off Cape York Peninsula by Captain James Cook on his first exploratory voyage in 1770 (Best, 1925: 201). Malay, possibly Bugis, seamen from New Guinea and Makassar in Sulawesi are believed to have been in contact with northern Australia during the fifteenth to seventeenth centuries AD, and to have introduced logboat building, and possibly the sail, to the Northern Territory (Lane-Fox, 1875: 402; Halls, 1961; R. Edwards, 1972: 10). This technique appears to have been confined to isolated places on the northern coast (Haddon and Hornell, 1937: ii. 179–93).

# 7.4
# Early Prehistoric Water Transport

If we set to one side logboats, which are thought to be late, the survey of water transport presented above probably gives as good a picture as is at present possible of early Australian nautical technology. In both Australia and Tasmania, the floats, rafts, and boats used during the period of early European contact were of a type and standard which matched the demands made

on them. In Tasmania, log floats, boat-shaped bundle rafts, and simple log rafts fastened by lashings were used for travel and exploration of lakes, rivers, and coastal islands up to 5 nautical miles (8 km) offshore. Lashed log rafts were also used in continental Australia, but there were also log rafts fastened together by treenails, and these were of greater size and are known to have made voyages to islands some 10 nautical miles (16 km) offshore. The bark boats of Australia—not found in Tasmania—ranged in complexity to match their roles: the most advanced technologically were used in the sea within the Gulf of Carpentaria, on voyages up to 20 nautical miles (32 km).

None of these rafts and boats appear to match the specification for the sort of seagoing craft needed to cross the Wallacean archipelago. It seems unlikely that any could have maintained their structural integrity and their buoyant nature long enough for them to be used on passages lasting at least twenty-four hours. Given that seagoing craft were needed by the first settlers of Greater Australia, and that eighteenth-century AD Australians no longer had them, it may be that, during the millennia after the migration across the Wallacean archipelago, there was some technological reversion (Bowdler, 1995). Without the stimulus of a requirement for sea voyages of more than a few miles, and in the possible absence of the optimum raw materials, the art of building substantial rafts was lost: craft of a lower level of technology were able to meet the Aboriginals' less ambitious aquatic requirements. Such a 'regression' is thought to have occurred during the last few centuries before European contact, the so-called 'Adaptive Phase', when the number and variety of stone tools evidently decreased in some parts of Australia (Shutler and Shutler, 1975: 37): there is another parallel in the way Tasmanians evidently stopped fishing in the pre-European phase. Possibly there was a comparable reduction in raft and boat-building techniques between 50,000–40,000 and, say, 3000 BC.

## 7.4.1 SEAFARING IN 40,000 BC

For long-range sea passages, bundle rafts have to be made of a reed species that do not readily become waterlogged—this characteristic may be enhanced by choosing a particular harvesting season (3.4.3). Furthermore, the reeds must be bound together in a way that ensures maximum compression and rigidity of each bundle (11.4.2). Seagoing qualities are improved if the bundles are bound together to form a boat-shaped raft. The logs chosen for seagoing lografts have to be relatively lightweight and resistant to waterlogging: in recent times, Taiwan log rafts were soaked in shark or tung oil to achieve this (McGrail, 1998: 49). As with bundle rafts, a boat shape is preferable. These log and bundle techniques are compatible with a Palaeolithic technology as in early Sundaland.

Bark boats, which the Tasmanians did not have, but the continental Australians did, are generally not used as seaboats. However, the technologically most advanced of North American bark boats were used for inter-island voyages of up to 50 nautical miles and, possibly over greater distances, from Newfoundland to Labrador (11.4.4.5). It seems unlikely, however, that such boats could be built using Palaeolithic techniques.

Bundle rafts have not been noted in any of the Sundaland countries, although the reeds of which they are generally made are readily available in many places. However, they are, and have been, used in Oceania (9.3.2). Log rafts have been, and are, widely used in south, south-east and eastern Asia, in Indonesia, and the Philippines, and extensively in Oceania (8.3.1, 9.3.4, 10.2.5). The rafts of the Indonesian islands, Sulu archipelago, New Guinea, the Bismarck archipelago, and the Solomons are made of bamboo or other lightweight timbers (Hornell, 1946: 70–5). The seagoing rafts of North Vietnam and Taiwan are made of a dozen or more large bamboos lashed together in a boat shape (Needham, 1971: 393; Doran, 1978; R. Bowen, 1956a: 288; Cairo, 1972; Aubaile-Sallenave, 1987). On balance then, whilst not eliminating the bundle raft, some form of log raft seems most likely to have carried the Palaeolithic migrants south-eastwards, across the Wallacean archipelago. Bamboo seems the most likely species to have been used: although not indigenous to Australia, it grows, and probably grew, in China, Vietnam, and Java, and generally along the proposed northern migration route. Bamboo has a strong but lightweight nodular structure, its silica-coated exterior delays waterlogging, and it can be lashed together.

After an appropriate form of water transport, the second principal requirement for the trans-Wallacean migration was the ability to hold a heading at night. The documented voyages of eighteenth- to twentieth-century Australians and Tasmanians all seem to have been within visual distance of land. Steering a course after dark by stars, wind, or swell may be another trait that has been lost due to non-use. However, Aboriginals undoubtedly have the ability to find their way about the desert interior of Australia, a technique which is similar in some respects to holding a course at sea (D. Lewis, 1994: 169). Thus there is no reason to think that the earliest Australians could not have successfully made their way across Wallacea, mostly by visual means, but holding a heading by other means when necessary.

# 8

# SOUTH-EAST ASIA

Maritime south-east Asia is taken here to include the Malay peninsula, the Gulf of Thailand, the deltas and lower reaches of the Chao Phraya, Mekong, and Red Rivers, and the myriad islands of the Indo-Malaysian archipelago, including the Philippines (Bellwood, 1985: 1–3). This region stretches from c.20°N (northern Vietnam, and Luzon in the Philippines) to c.12°S (Sumba and Timor in the Sunda islands); and from c.95°E (western Sumatra) to c.135°E (the Aru islands, south-west of New Guinea) (Fig. 8.1). It thus includes the 'Wallacea' and much of the 'Sundaland' of Chapter 7. A high proportion of this region is an archipelago, many of the islands being intervisible. In such a maritime zone, we would expect to find early evidence for sea voyaging. It also seems more likely, on theoretical grounds, that this region, rather than China to the north, would generate innovations both in boatbuilding techniques and in methods of propulsion and navigation, notwithstanding China's long coastline and three large river estuaries.

Away from the Equator, the region has a tropical climate, with clearly defined wet and dry seasons, and north-north-east monsoon winds during October–April, when it is relatively dry and cool; and south-south-west winds during the northern summer months of May–September, when it is hot and wet. Within 5° of the Equator there is an equatorial climate, with a number of prevailing winds: in the Celebes Sea, north-north-west in October–April, and south-south-east in May–September; and from the Java Seas to the Banda Seas, from the west in October–April, and from the east in May–September (Bellwood, 1985: 9–15). These seasonal winds, equatorial and tropical, have strongly influenced trading patterns throughout south-east Asia.

Hardwood timbers and bamboos suitable for rafts and boats are, and were, widely available throughout the region. Rattan palm and pandanus leaves were used to make mats, ropes, and baskets from early times, possibly as early as 8000 BC (Scarre, 1989: 90–1). In recent times, sails have been made from matting, rigging from rope, and some boats have been built using basketry techniques. Furthermore, the resins and dammar obtainable from tropical trees are invaluable in making vessels watertight. It is likely, therefore, that these techniques and raw materials were similarly used in earlier times.

## 8.1

## Early Population Movements

Between 18,000 BC, a time of minimum sea level, and 3000 BC, the rising sea level resulted in the ratio of coastline to land increasing by more than 3 : 1 (Glover, 1980: 152, 160). By that same date, the three major rivers of mainland south-east Asia had built up substantial deltas with seasonal flooding from the Himalayas, their margins were being settled (Higham, 1989: 1–3), and people had become increasingly dependent on resources from the maritime zone, both land and sea. Generally speaking, by c.3000 BC, with the sea level within the twentieth-century's tidal range, maritime south-east Asia appeared in physical terms much as it is today.

Using archaeological data and archaeo-linguistic

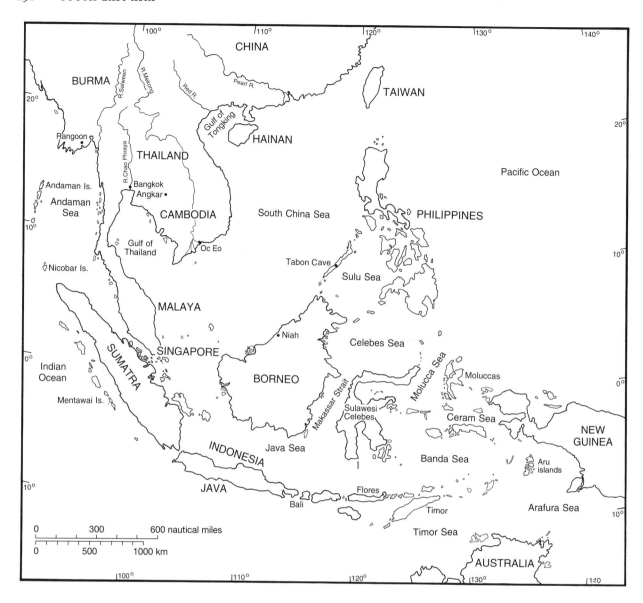

Fig. 8.1. Map of south-east Asia (Institute of Archaeology, Oxford).

techniques, Bellwood (1985: 223–33) has postulated the following sequence for the spread of peoples speaking early forms of the Austronesian group of languages—now spoken by the vast majority of the inhabitants of Indonesia, Malaysia, Philippines, Taiwan, parts of Vietnam, Oceania, and Madagascar (see also Rolett *et al.*, 2000):

4500–4000 BC   Austronesian settlement of Taiwan by Neolithic peoples from south China—Zhejiang or Fujian.

*c.*3000 BC   Expansion to Luzon, the northernmost island in the Philippines.

*c.*2500 BC   Further expansion through the Philippines, Borneo, Sulawesi, thence to the rest of Maritime south-east Asia.

There was then evidently a break in this expansion process, until the mid-second millennium BC, when the second great maritime migration from south-east Asia began: the Austronesian colonization of Oceania (9.1). A third overseas migration took place in the early centuries AD, this time westwards to Madagascar off the east coast of Africa (8.2.2).

The Neolithic colonization of maritime south-east Asia involved the use of rafts and/or boats, but there are no remains from this period to suggest what these might have been. If we may project backwards the evidence from later years, log rafts, and possibly bark boats and basket boats may have been used. The boat type which was to become, in European eyes, the characteristic of this region—the plank boat fitted with double outriggers—is another possibility: but this would seem to be less likely, if only because there is as yet no evidence anywhere in the world for plank boats before the Bronze Age, and no evidence for outriggers in south-east Asia until the late first millennium AD.

# 8.2

## Early Maritime Contacts

### 8.2.1 WESTWARDS WITH INDIA AND THE MEDITERRANEAN WORLD

The Graeco-Roman world imported a variety of raw materials and manufactured goods from south-east Asia (6.3). From the evidence now available, it is apparent that this trade was not direct but via Indian emporia, particularly those on India's west coast. The Mediterranean-based author of the first-century AD *Periplus of the Erythraean Sea* (6.3.1), one of the principal sources of evidence for this trade, seems to have had personal knowledge of the Malabar coast of south-west India, but his descriptions of India's east coast, the Bay of Bengal and beyond appear to be based on information he had gathered from Indian merchants and seafarers. Nevertheless, some Roman ships sailed the Bay of Bengal in the first century AD, and by the second century they had reached Malaya and possibly Indo-China (6.4). Locked mortise and tenon joints—a defining characteristic of the Mediterranean tradition of boat building (4.11.1)—were used to fasten the planking of the Chinese eleventh-century wreck from Wando (10.4.2.1) and the nineteenth- to twentieth-century wreck Johore Lama A (8.3.5.2.14), whilst the thirteenth-century Philippines wreck Butuan 2 has locked treenails (8.3.5.2.3). This evidence is inconclusive: it may be that this technique was indigenous to south-east and east Asia or it may be that it was transferred there during Roman times.

Chapter 56 of the *Periplus* tells us that the Malabar coast ports of south-west India held stocks of tortoise-shell which had been imported there from *Chryse*. From this and other passages it is clear that *Chryse*, a 'golden region', was a trading area, possibly an island, lying to the east of India, almost at the extremes of geographical knowledge (Casson, 1989: 235–6): it may have been in the Malay peninsula and/or Sumatra.

In chapter 60, we read that on the Coromandel coast of south-east India may be found, 'the very big *kolandiophonta* that sail across to Chryse and the Ganges region' (Casson, 1989: 89). Christie (1957: 347) has pointed out that this term is probably a version of the Chinese expression, *kun lun po*, meaning a 'large seagoing ship of south-east Asia'.

It is not clear from the *Periplus* whether such ships sailed direct between south-east Asia and India, or whether they sailed via the Ganges. It does seem likely, however, that these voyages were seagoing routes of one or, at the most, two legs, rather than a sequence of several short-haul coastal passages. This Bay of Bengal trade route is unlikely to have been the monopoly of south-east Asian seamen and merchants, indeed, by the fourth century AD, the sailing cargo ship was such an important feature of the economy of Tamil Nadu, on India's south-east coast, that its Pallavas rulers issued coins with ships on them (6.2.4). Moreover, an inscription dated to the same century on a stone at Kedah, north-west Malaya, refers to a master mariner with the Indian name, Buddhagupta, who may well have come from the River Ganges region (6.4). It is likely, therefore, that both Indian and south-east Asian ships undertook trading voyages in the Bay of Bengal.

There are references to south-east Asia in Indian literature possibly in the third century BC (Bellwood, 1985: 278), and certainly in the second century AD (Ray, 1989: 46–7). Evidence of trade, such as Indian cornelian beads and pottery, has been excavated from second century BC sites in south-east Asia (Ray, 1989: 52–3, 1990: 11–12; Ardika and Bellwood, 1991; Ardika *et al.*, 1997). Ray has suggested that there was a coastal route from India's east coast to Bengal and lower Burma, then overland from the Andaman Sea through the Three Pagodas Pass (south-east of Rangoon, north-west of Bangkok) into west-central Thailand, and onwards. By the early centuries AD there also appears to have been a coastal route along the west coast of Malaya to the Indonesian islands and to the Mekong valley in Cambodia and Vietnam (Ray, 1994: 157–8). At around this time, the direct route across the Bay of Bengal was probably taken (Ardika and Bellwood, 1991), as may be suggested in the *Periplus*. It is relevant to note here that an early tenth-century account by Abu Zaid states that it was ten days' sail from Sumatra to southern India (an average speed of *c.*4 knots) but twenty days in light winds (Hornell, 1941*a*: 250–1).

Despite the third-century AD, decline in demand from the Roman world, India's links with south-east Asia continued to develop (Ray, 1989: 46–7). In addition to cornelian beads and other semi-precious stones, Indian goods traded in the early centuries AD included glass, jewellery, coins, metalwork, and pottery. Flowing the other way were spices, perfumes, precious stones and pearls, silks and muslin, tortoiseshell, ivory and rhino horn, dyes and unguents, *ghi*, and *lac* (Glover, 1996).

These contacts with India led to the establishment of the first urban settlements in south-east Asia (Scarre, 1989: 258–9). *Oc Eo* (thought to be the *Funan* of Chinese literature) in the Mekong delta, Vietnam, is an example of one of these early trading towns (Presland, 1980: 274; Scarre, 1989: 258–9; Mukherjee, 1994). One of the maritime states which subsequently arose, known as *Sriwijaya,* probably based its power on its control of both sides of the Malacca strait between Malaya and Sumatra which it maintained from the seventh to the thirteenth centuries (Manguin, 1993*b*). Other trading places were established along the coasts of eastern Sumatra, northern Java, and the west coast of Malaya in response to the increasing India / Moluccas / China trade of the ninth to fourteenth centuries, which funnelled shipping towards the Malacca strait (Scarre, 1989: 258–9). Throughout subsequent changes in political power (even to today), this strait has retained its seafaring importance—for example, during the fifteenth to seventeenth centuries the Maritime Law Code of Malacca had widespread authority (Tibbetts, 1971: 62).

Indian ideas also had an impact on south-east Asia (Scarre, 1989; Bellwood, 1985: 137–43). There are traces of Buddhism from the fourth / fifth centuries AD, and by the eighth century it was well established in western south-east Asia (Ray, 1994: 154–61). Hinduism followed, slightly later (Bellwood, 1985: 137–43); whilst Islam was well established in northern Sumatra, for example, by the late thirteenth century (Bellwood, 1985: 143).

## 8.2.2 MADAGASCAR

An Austronesian language is spoken today in Madagascar but there is little direct evidence of how and when Austronesian speakers settled there (Bellwood, 1985: 103), presumably after an Indian Ocean voyage. The banana seems to have been brought from Indonesia to Madagascar before the tenth century AD, and south-east Asian artefacts of the ninth century AD have been excavated from east African coastal sites (Phillipson, 1980: 345). Other traits Madagascar has in common with south-east Asia include similar mythic themes, and the use of the blowpipe, the xylophone, and the extended logboat with double outriggers (Bellwood, 1985: 152; Ray, 1994: 120; Sherratt, 1980*a*: 345–6; Hornell, 1944*b*: 3–18; 1946*a*: 254–5).

Linguistic evidence suggests that Madagascar was settled from southern Borneo in the fifth or sixth century AD (Bellwood, 1985: 124; Ray, 1994: 120). south-east trade winds or the north-east monsoon, and the westerly set of the Equatorial Current would have facilitated a direct, near equatorial voyage across the Indian Ocean, possibly replenishing fresh water in the Maldive islands or the Chagos archipelago, to a landfall on the east coast of Africa; thence coastwise to Madagascar (12°–25°S, and some 200 nautical miles east of the mainland), which is thought to have been uninhabited at that time. However, such an ocean voyage presupposes that these migrants knew that there was land some 3,000 nautical miles to the west, that they had oceanic navigational abilities, and that their boat (or boats) could carry sufficient food and, especially, fresh water for a voyage which, at a speed made good of, say, 3.5 knots would have taken five or six weeks. Moreover, this boat, possibly an extended logboat with an outrigger on both sides (as on the eighth- / ninth-centuries reliefs in Borobudur, Java—Fig. 8.6) would not only have had to be able to sail with the wind on the beam, or even closer to the wind, but it would also have had to withstand the rigours of a lengthy oceanic voyage. A more likely alternative would have been to follow the west-bound trade route of the Indian and south-east Asian ships across the Bay of Bengal to Sri Lanka where they could learn of the recommended route to Arabia, and so south along the east coast of Africa until they encountered Madagascar.

In the late 1980s, a logboat-based boat, with the planks fastened by stitches and by treenails within the thickness of the planking, and with flexible ribs lashed to cleats, was built in the Sulu archipelago and sailed via Java to Madagascar (Manguin, 1985: 335). This attempt to 'reconstruct' the migratory voyages has yet to be published in detail, so its authenticity cannot be evaluated and its results cannot be assessed.

## 8.2.3 CONTACTS WITH CHINA

South-east Asia's links with India appear to have been mostly cultural and economic; links with China, on the other hand, seem to have been mainly political and military, at least until the late tenth century when the outward-looking Song Dynasty became economically powerful (Bellwood, 1985: 278–9). China became involved with northern Vietnam in the second century BC, enforcing tribute payments. In c.100 BC, China annexed this territory and it remained under Chinese rule until c. AD 900 (Scarre, 1989: 199).

There are Chinese texts surviving from the third and eighth centuries AD (10. 2. 11. 1) which describe those aspects of south-east Asian ships which were unusual to Chinese eyes; they also commented favourably on the maritime skills of south-east Asian seafarers. South-east Asian ships regularly visited ports in south China during this period mainly to embark Buddhist pilgrims for India via Sumatra (Bellwood, 1985: 279; Manguin, 1993a: 261). During the Song Dynasties (AD 960–1279) trade between the two regions increased, especially due to Chinese interest in the 'Spice Islands'—the Moluccas. The Mongol/Yuan dynasty of the fourteenth century sent several fleets as far as Java and Sumatra; and in the fifteenth century the Ming dynasty continued this involvement, culminating, between 1405 and 1433, in seven spectacular voyages under the command of the Grand Eunuch Zheng He (10. 10. 4).

# 8.3
# Water Transport

Until the 1980s, the only direct evidence for early water transport in south-east Asia came from two or three small boats excavated from ancient river beds (McGrail, 1981a: 61–4). There were also a number of representations of boats from various centuries: decorative stone carvings, rock paintings, and engravings on metal. Some of these were stylized and none could be interpreted in unambiguous detail. Unlike China and India, early south-east Asia had no tradition of literacy, so there were no indigenous descriptions of boats and maritime matters, but something could be learned from Chinese and, to a lesser degree, Indian sources. Much reliance had to be placed on sixteenth- and seventeenth-century accounts written by European seafarers and merchants, and on ethnographic accounts compiled in subsequent centuries: these also have interpretation problems.

In recent years, with the increasing capabilities of archaeologists working underwater, a number of wrecks from the fourteenth to the sixteenth centuries and later have been investigated. When the information from these sites is married to that from other sources, especially the documentary and ethnographic accounts, a more detailed picture of the later years of this south-east Asian boat and shipbuilding tradition emerges. However, these underwater sites, and others unknown to archaeologists, have often been looted by 'treasure hunters', which has meant that not only has information about cargo, trading patterns, and trade routes been lost, but it has also become much more difficult to interpret hull remains. None of these sites has yet been comprehensively recorded or published. Furthermore, the dates assigned to these wrecks are generally imprecise, often only within a range of two centuries and more. Nevertheless, the information from them has significantly added to our knowledge and has drawn attention to the importance of the south-east Asian tradition.

## 8.3.1 LOG RAFTS

No log rafts have been excavated, but bamboo log rafts are known to have been used for fishing in the harbours and rivers of the Philippines in the early nineteenth century (Paris, 1843: 112, plate 46). Admiral Paris also published paintings of small boats in Manila and in Java which had no less than nine bamboo stabilizers fastened to each side near the waterline (1843: 100, 180, plates 34, 97). These bamboo platforms were used for cargo and as poling walkways—for all practical purposes they were log rafts.

The *ghe be* is a bamboo log raft used in the present century for fishing on the rivers and the coasts of northern Vietnam (Bowen, 1956a: 288; Needham, 1971: 393; Aubaile-Sallenave, 1987: plates 20–3; Burningham, 1994: 229–32). Eight to ten bamboos were chosen and positioned alongside each other so that they gave the raft both transverse and longitudinal curvature—as in the Taiwan/Formosan log raft (10.2.5). The bamboos were bent under heat and held to shape by curved transverse bamboos lashed to them. The outermost bamboos were bigger than the others thereby giving the raft slightly raised 'sides' alternatively, two bamboos were fitted to each side. Three pole masts, each with a lugsail, were stepped in transverse timbers. There were also two or three wooden fins ( *guares*), which could be deployed downwards through the logs to combat leeway and assist steering (10.2.5, 11.4.1.2, 6.6.3, 5.8.2.2). These rafts were steered by a stern sweep which could also be used to propel the raft when not under sail. Small, five-bamboo, one-man rafts, propelled and steered by pole, were also used in rivers for cast-net fishing.

Hornell (1946a: 70) has noted that more workaday log rafts were recently used throughout island south-east Asia for lake and river transport. Haddon and Hornell (1938: iii. 15) have suggested that linguistic evidence points to early use of log rafts in Java and the Philippines, and in the light of these ethnographic accounts and the widespread availability of bamboo and other low-density-timbers, this seems likely. Polynesian use of seagoing log rafts (9.3.4) suggests that there may have been similar use in early south-east Asia.

## 8.3.2 BARK BOATS

Bark boats were recently used in Malaya, Borneo, and Java (Suder, 1930: plate 13; Doran, 1981: fig. 36). Nishimura (1931: 225) noted that Borneo Dyaks of the nineteenth century stitched together both ends of a bark cylinder and caulked them with clay to form a watertight bow and stern. Light timbers were then inserted tranversely to keep the sides a fixed distance apart. Earlier use of bark boats seems possible.

## 8.3.3 BASKET BOATS

Although boats of waterproofed basketry were used recently in east Java (Manguin, personal communication) their principal area of use is in Vietnam. Structurally these boats are equivalent to the hide boats of other regions. No example has been excavated, and there is no other documentation of them before early nineteenth-century reports. Nevertheless, the materials, tools, and techniques needed to build them are such that much earlier use is likely.

The two forms of simple basket boat (Fig.8.2)—round or elliptical in plan—are built in the same way (Hornell, 1946a: 109–11; Cairo, 1972; Aubaile-Sallenave,

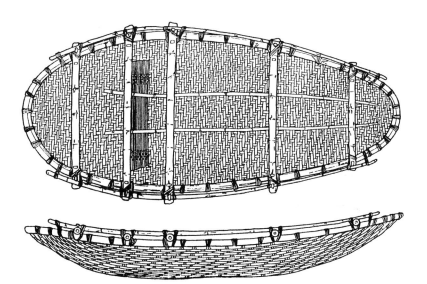

Fig. 8.2. A twentieth-century Vietnamese small basket boat (after Greenhill, 1976: fig. 45).

Fig. 8.3. An early nineteenth-century composite basket boat in Vietnamese waters (Paris, 1843: plate 45).

1987; Burningham, 1994). Strips of split bamboo, 1 in (25 mm) wide, are woven into a stiff matting of the required shape and size. The upper edge of this 'basket' is then reinforced by several split bamboos bound together with rattan strips. The hull is next made watertight by the application of paying/caulking, both inside and out. A number of different recipes are known, but the essential ingredient is resin which is mixed with one or more of the following materials: shredded bamboo, ground seashells, ground coconut husk, pulverized lime and water, buffalo dung, and *tram* bark (*Melalenca leucadendron*). The end product is a substance which can adapt to movement within the basket without cracking. The hull is subsequently coated with a vegetable oil. This supple, resilient, yet stress-resistant hull, is then further supported by bamboo framing timbers.

In the larger boats, a transverse plank is lashed to the bamboo 'rim', and a light pole fitted with a lugsail made from palm-leaf fibres is fitted through a hole in the plank and stepped in a timber on the bottom. When not under sail, the round boats are propelled by a paddle over the 'bow' or by a sculling oar over the 'stern'; the elliptical boats are often poled, but sometimes a sweep is used. Posts are lashed or pegged to the hulls of the larger sailing boats to support a deep rudder at the stern, and a rectractable wooden fin ( *guares*) at the bow, similar in shape to those used in log rafts (8.3.1). The *guares* is wedged in position within a verti-

cal groove: fully down when close hauled, part down on a reach, and up when running free.

The round boats can be up to 2 m in diameter; the others are generally in the range of 2 × 1 × 0.25 m to 4 × 1.25 × 0.65 m. They are used on the rivers of central and southern Vietnam and sometimes *c*.2 nautical miles out to sea, mainly for fishing. The small round ones are often used to tend rice crops and to harvest water vegetables. Two of the elliptically shaped boats are sometimes used as a pair, a wooden platform being fastened across the central parts of two boats which are about 1 m apart (Aubaile-Sallenave, 1987: plate 14). This stable pair can then ferry six or so horses, their riders and equipment across a river, propelled by a sweep on each quarter.

There is also a composite boat with basketry underwater parts and wooden topsides (Fig. 8.3). This is generally larger than any of the simple basket boats, has a more substantial framing and is used for a greater variety of tasks (Cairo, 1972). The upperworks (the wooden posts and strakes) are made separately from the basket bottom. The flush-laid strakes are fastened together by treenails within the thickness of the planking, and are fastened to the posts by treenails. These upperworks are then positioned over the basketry so that a strip of matting presses against the inboard faces of the strakes. Stringers are positioned inboard on this overlap, and the first strakes, the basketry, and the stringers are fastened together by treenails wedged outboard. Framing is then installed to support the basket.

### 8.3.4 LOGBOATS

There is one excavated and dated logboat from this region: that from Tanjong Rawa, Kuala Selinsing, Malaya, which has a calibrated radiocarbon date in the second or third century AD (*BM*-959). Fragments of three logboats, all used for burials, were found on this site, but only one could be excavated completely because of the degraded state of the timber and difficulties associated with the intertidal nature of the site (Sieveking, 1956: 203). No drawing of the boat has been published, merely a description. The excavated boat was 18 ft. 6 in. (5.6 m) in length, and broken off at both ends. Running up both sides were a series of integral,

pierced rectangular cleats, 6 in. (0.15 m) long, with a 2 ft (0.60 m) spacing between series. This is the earliest evidence for this feature which, in later years, seems to become a diagnostic characteristic of the south-east Asian tradition of plank boats. In recent plank boats, flexible ribs were lashed to such cleats, and the fact that the Selinsing logboat had cleats suggests that one or more strakes had been added to give her greater freeboard.

Sieveking (1956: 209) also noted two other logboats from Malaya, but these are undated. A 14 ft (4.3 m) boat from Batu Gajah had platform ends and four false ribs carved in the solid. The author suggests that this boat may have been expanded, but the false ribs make this unlikely. Another from the Tronoh Mines, Kamper, had a cargo of small tin ingots.

Excavations at the West Mouth site of the Niah caves in Sarawak in the late 1950s (Bellwood, 1985:

Fig. 8.4.  Coffin-logboats during excavations in the Niah caves, Sarawak, in the 1950s (Sarawak Museum).

254–8) revealed many graves dated from the mid-second millennium BC to the mid-first millennium BC with the bodies in log coffins with plank lids, or in coffins made of stitched bamboo strips. In a photograph of these excavations published by Johnstone (1988: 213, fig. 15.10), hollowed logs fashioned to recognizable log-boat shapes can be seen: these must be either logboats reused as coffins—as at Selinsing—or coffins made to resemble logboats (Fig. 8.4). In either case, these would have been important nautical finds if they had been fully recorded and dated. Similar burials are known in the Philippines (Manguin, personal communication); many others are known in Malaya and Vietnam, associated with bronze and iron artefacts (Manguin, 1993a: 255). Undated paintings on the walls of the Niah caves (Johnstone, 1988: 212, fig. 15.9) may depict logboats or possibly plank boats.

Higham (1989: 195) has noted 'opulent boat burials' excavated at Viet Khe and Chau Can, near the Red River in north Vietnam. His figure 4.5, however, shows that these were simple log coffins—as known in China (10.2.9)—with no attempt to represent nautical features.

In total, the evidence does not amount to much. Nevertheless, simple logboats, some with stabilizers, were found to be widely used on the rivers and sheltered waters of this region in the early nineteenth century (Dumont d'Urville, 1834, ii). Furthermore, expanded logboats have been used since at least the same date in the Mergui archipelago off the west coast of Malaya, on Malayan rivers, and in parts of Thailand (Sieveking, 1956: 210; Johnstone, 1988: 212). Elsewhere, such simple boats may well have gone unnoted by explorers and ethnographers. It seems likely that logboats, in all their variety, were widely used in early south-east Asia, alongside rafts, basket boats, and planked boats, each type built to carry out specific functions in a particular environment.

## 8.3.5 PLANKED VESSELS

### 8.3.5.1 BOATS WITH STITCHED PLANKS

#### 8.3.5.1.1 *Pontian and Khuan Lukpad*

In 1926, a boat in the bank of the river at Pontian, South Pahang, on the east coast of Malaya, was uncovered by a landslip (Gibson-Hill, 1952; Manguin, 1985: 333). The

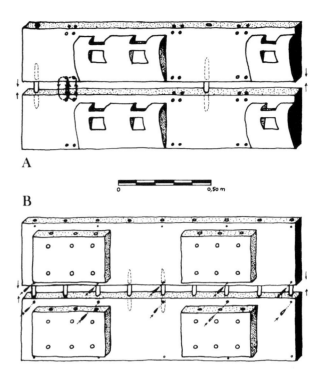

Fig. 8.5. Diagram showing: A: the Pontian boat plank fastenings; B: the Butuan fastenings. In both cases, the cleats are where frames were lashed to the planking (after Manguin, 1985: fig. 20.9).

fragmentary remains (some 12 m in length) consisted of part of a plank-keel and end post, two strakes from one side and one from the other, and seven slightly curved side timbers. The timber was *merawan* (*Ilopea* sp.), and the planking was 2 in (50 mm) thick. Holding the flush-laid planks together were treenails of *medang* and cord ties of *ijok* (*Arenga pinnata*)—both of which are common in the Malay peninsula and archipelago. No drawing of the remains has been published, but there are said to be two pairs of ties between each side timber, and Manguin (1985: 333) has noted that they pass through paired, L-shaped holes, 10 mm in diameter, within the thickness of the planking (Fig. 8.5A). A reconstruction drawing by Gibson-Hill (1952: 114) suggests that the ties are individual stitches rather than continuous sewing (Manguin, 1996: fig. 1). The treenails protruded from the edges of the planking, one between each side timber, which gives an average spacing of *c.*3 ft 2 in (*c.*1 m). Such a spacing suggests that the treenails were more for positioning the planking and resisting shearing forces than as the principal plank fastenings—in this respect they are similar to the early sewn-plank boats of the Mediterranean (4.9.4). The spacing of the pairs of ties is difficult to estimate, but it must average *c.*1 ft 7 in (0.5 m), which suggests that stitches rather than treenails were the important fastening.

At intervals of 3 ft 2 in (1 m) centre to centre, a series of cleats, each 1 ft 8 in (0.5 m) in length, had been left proud of the planking across its full width. 'Heavy' side timbers were lashed to the centre of these cleats, through paired holes (Gibson-Hill, 1952: 111).

Associated with the boat were pottery fragments from the Gulf of Siam region of the early centuries AD (Manguin, 1985: 333). The boat was subsequently dated by radiocarbon (*BM-958*) to AD 260–430 (calibrated) (Manguin, 1996). A fragment of a boat from Khuan Lukpad, Wat Khpong Thom museum, in south Thailand, may be fifth/sixth century AD, and has similar features to the Pontian find (Manguin, 1996).

### 8.3.5.1.2 *Kolam Pinisi*

Twenty-four planks recovered from a pond, Kolam Pinisi, near the River Musi, Palembang, southern Sumatra in 1990, also had stitched fastenings and cleats to which ribs had been lashed. This had been a 'large and sturdy' hull, and a radiocarbon assay (Gif-8483) gives a calibrated date of AD 434–631 (Manguin, 1993*b*: 27).

### 8.3.5.1.3 *Sambirejo*

In 1988, planks and a 5.94 m side rudder, from three or more boats, were recovered from Sambirejo near the River Musi downstream from Palembang, southern Sumatra (Manguin, 1989). Eight of the planks, average thickness 35 mm, length 14.50 m, from one vessel, dated by radiocarbon (Gif-7871) to AD 610–775 (calibrated) had been fastened edge-to-edge by treenails spaced at *c.*18 cm, and by individual lashings of *ijok* (the sugar palm—*Arenga pinnata*) through paired, L-shaped holes, at 0.76 m spacing. In this vessel, more reliance was evidently placed on the treenails as fastenings. Cleats, to which framing had formerly been fastened, were spaced at *c.*0.50 m.

In none of these boats were stitches the sole means of fastening the planking. In the Pontian boat of the third/fifth centuries, however, the treenails were clearly auxiliary and this boat can be considered to

be a 'sewn boat'. In the seventh-/eighth-centuries Sambirejo boat, on the other hand, the stitches supplement the unlocked treenails, ensuring that the planking is held fast in the plane of the hull, a plane in which unlocked treenails cannot, by themselves, effectively resist seam-opening stresses. The Sambirejo boat may be classified as a treenail-fastened boat. Both these boats had framing timbers lashed to cleats integral with the planking. The Pontian (and probably the Sambirejo) side framing was there to support the planking and to supplement the stitching by resisting the opening of seams.

### 8.3.5.2 VESSELS WITH TREENAILED PLANKING

In addition to the part-stitched boats discussed above, there are fourteen or so other wrecks from south-east Asian waters which have planking fastened by treenails within the thickness of the planking—these range in date from the fifth/seventh to the eighteenth/nineteenth centuries. Most of the descriptions published to date report incomplete projects, and much detail is missing. Moreover, wrecks found within south-east Asian waters were not necessarily built in that region and may have come from elsewhere, for example, from China. With the increasing trade links between south-east Asia and China in the twelfth to fifteenth centuries it is conceivable that features in one tradition were taken over by the other.

### 8.3.5.2.1 *Jenderam Hiler*

Fragmentary planking with treenail holes in the edges and cleats left proud of inboard faces have been recovered from a tin-mining site at Jenderam Hiler, south of Kuala Lumpur, Malaya, and dated (I-10757) to AD 465–655 (calibrated) (Manguin, 1996).

### 8.3.5.2.2 *Paya Pasir*

In 1989, timbers from a number of vessels were recovered from a flooded quarry site at Paya Pasir, Medan, northern Sumatra (Manguin, 1996). Chinese ceramics of the twelfth to fourteenth centuries were associated with these boats. The planking, up to 0.37 m breadth and 75 mm thick, had treenail holes, 18 mm in diameter, in both edges, and integral cleats with *ijok* lashing fibres in their holes. The end of one plank had a 'stepped' scarf. The floor and side timbers, up to 0.20 m across, had simple scarfs with a single treenail hole at their ends. This was not a flexible framing, but a reinforcing framing for a relatively large vessel, possibly up to 30 m in length (Manguin, 1996). It now seems likely that this site was once the harbour of the nearby settlement of Kota Cina of the twelfth to fourteenth centuries AD, and the wrecks may be from that period.

### 8.3.5.2.3 *Butuan*

In the late-1970s, during searches for Chinese porcelain (Scott, 1981: 1) or alluvial gold (Clark *et al.*, 1993: 143) near the River Masao, west of Butuan, Mindanao, Philippines, planking from at least two vessels was recovered. Subsequently, remains from seven other vessels were recovered. Of the nine, three (boats 1, 2, and 5) are now in the National Museum, Manila, and boats 2 and 5 have been dated by radiocarbon (Gak-7741–4) to the thirteenth/fourteenth centuries AD (Manguin, 1996: table 1). Interim reports have been published on boat 2 (Clark *et al.*, 1993) and on boats 1 and 5 (Green *et al.*, 1995). The principal features of these boats are:

1. The planking (which is thought to be *dongon* wood—*Heretiera litorales*) is edge-joined by 12–19 cm long treenails within the plank edges (Fig. 8.5B), *c.*13–20 m apart: selected treenails are locked by smaller treenails (dowels). (Manguin, 1996: fig. 3; Green *et al.*, 1995: fig. 14).

2. Cleat blocks, integral with the planking, are *c.*0.78 to 0.95 m apart. Each block has two or three pairs of holes through which the framing is lashed to the planking with palm-fibre rope (*Cabo negro*).

3. The plank-keel of Butuan 1 has groups of three 'cleats' disposed transversely: the central ones have no fastening holes. The plank-keel of boat 5 has one long 'cleat block' projection which runs from end to end.

These boats appear to have been relatively narrow and up to 15 m in length.

### 8.3.5.2.4 *Sha Tsui*

During the building of a reservoir between the Sai Kung peninsula and High Island, Hong Kong in 1974, the remains of a vessel were found near the village of Sha Tsui (Frost, Ho, and Ng, 1974). The site was reinvestigated in 1977 (Peacock, personal communication; Horridge, 1978: 52). The 3 in (76 mm) thick planks of this vessel were of *ch'iu-mu* (*Mallotus japonicus*), joined edge-to-edge by treenails of diameter 21.4–22.5 mm and lengths *c.*0.13 m. One end of these treenails was worked to a point whilst the other end was rounded. Some loose treenails were only 15–20 mm in diameter and more than 0.22 m in length. The planks within strakes were joined by stop-splayed scarfs on face, fastened together, with a 'yellowish putty' caulking, by nails or treenail. The plank seams were also covered by a putty caulking, over which a 3 in (76 mm) thick plank was fastened by square-shank iron spikes. Some of the planking also had integral cleats on the inboard face to which framing had been fastened (Peacock, personal communication). Associated finds included a wooden fragment possibly from a bulkhead, possibly part of a mast, and belaying pins or oar pivots.

A radiocarbon assay (HAR-867) gives a calibrated date of AD 1220–1430. Porcelain sherds of the fourteenth to sixteenth centuries were found with the planking. Using the plank scantlings, a local boat-builder estimated that the original vessel was probably 70–80 × 16 ft (*c.*21–24 × 5 m).

### 8.3.5.2.5 *Rang Kwien*

A wreck from Rang Kwien in the Gulf of Siam, possibly of the fourteenth/fifteenth centuries—has treenail-fastened planking (Manguin, 1983: 3; Green, 1994). No other details have been published.

### 8.3.5.2.6 *Pattaya*

A fourteenth-/fifteenth-century (Sua-2698) wreck at Pattaya off the east coast of the Gulf of Thailand, has been part-excavated after looting (Green and Harper, 1983; Green, Harper, and Intakosi, 1987; Green, 1994). This has features which are sometimes associated with Chinese shipping—multilayers of planking and bulkheads (10.5.1.2)—but the planking is edge-fastened by treenails, a feature which may well be characteristic of the south–east Asian tradition, in contrast to the Chinese use of iron nails.

Approximately 9 m of this round-hulled wreck were excavated, down to the keel which had a *c.*0.30 × 0.30 m cross-section, with bevels on the upper edges for the first strakes of the inner planking. There was a further timber on top of part of the keel, towards one end, which may have been a support for a keel-scarf. Eight strakes of inner planking, c.70 mm thick, survived each side, fastened to the keel and together by treenails, 20 mm in diameter at an interval of c.0.16 m. The scarfs in this primary planking were stop-splayed on face (Green and Harper, 1983: fig. 11b), and were all outboard of bulkheads. The second and third layers of planking, both 40 mm thick, were not edge-fastened, merely nailed by spikes to the inner planking, with a caulking of 'resin-lime' between them. Planks within these outer strakes were butted together.

The framing consisted of a series of bulkheads of beech (*Fagus* sp.) each with a floor timber or paired half-frames on the side nearer amidships. The bulkheads, at intervals, centre to centre, of 1.5–1.6 m, formed compartments 1.06–1.46 m. in length and were composed of several 70 mm thick planks, shaped to match the sides of the hull and fastened together by treenails, as in the primary hull planking to which they appeared to be nailed. Each bulkhead had a limberhole on either side of the keel. The frames were nailed to the hull planking and to their associated bulkhead. Two half-frames at one station were joined by a chock; floor timbers at the other stations were extended by side timbers to which they were scarfed.

On the assumed after side of one of the bulkheads was a mast-step timber straddling the keel. The two main holes in this step seem to be for timbers which would support the mast; the other notches may be for braces to the next bulkhead.

The fact that all scarfs recorded were outboard of bulkheads raises the question whether, despite the planking being edge-fastened, this vessel was built frame-first, i.e. were (some of) the bulkheads, floors, and half-frames fastened to the keel, and the inner planking then fashioned to match this shape, in lengths related to the bulkhead spacing? Similar questions are raised in connection with a fourteenth-century wreck from Chinese waters (10.5.1.4). Detailed examination of these remains is required before definitive answers can be given to such questions.

### 8.3.5.2.7 *Phu Quoc*

A wreck of about the same period and with similar features to the Pattaya ship has been part-excavated off Phu Quoc island in the Gulf of Thailand, Vietnam (Blake and Flecker, 1994). A c.25 m length of the keel survived, but no evidence for end posts. The keel had a rectangular cross section, 525 mm moulded by 300 mm sided, and had another 235 × 200 mm timber of indeterminate length fastened to its upper face by rectangular treenails.

The three layers of hull planking were of teak (*Tectona grandis*); the inner layer was 80/90 mm thick; the outer, 48 mm and 32 mm. Between each layer was up to 10 mm thickness of putty (*chu-nam*), there as much to prevent nail corrosion as to waterproof the planking. The inner planking was edge-fastened with treenails (c.150 mm in length and 25 mm diameter) of *sappan* (*Caesalpinea sappan*), spaced at c.180 mm. The plank scarfs that were recorded were not themselves fastened and were each at a bulkhead station. The excavators believe that this positioning 'may account for the irregular bulkhead spacing': this varied from c.1.06–1.46 m. An alternative explanation is that, as with the Pattaya find, planks ended at bulkhead stations because the vessel was built frame-first. The inner planking was fastened to each bulkhead by two iron spikes (15 mm square section, c.0.18 m long) and to the frames by a similar spike. The middle layer of planking, not being structural, was fastened to the inner planking, and the outer planking to the middle planking, by 90–110 mm spikes. The middle planking which was butted together, overlapped the seams in the inner planking.

Fifteen bulkheads were excavated, each extended to c.1.5 m above the keel. They were made of 110 mm thick horizontal planks of *padauk* (*Pterocarpus* sp.), edge-fastened with 25 mm treenails spaced at c.180 mm. Wedge-shaped timbers, 40 to 60 mm in section, and c.0.50 m in length, were driven through the planking from outboard and fastened (means unspecified) to the bulkhead within a rebate on the midships-facing face. These timbers ('bulkhead strengtheners') can only have been fitted after the bulkheads and before the middle layer of planking had been positioned. Bulkheads had limber holes either side of the keel and a central one at garboard level. A putty filler (*chu-nam*) was found between the bulkheads and hull planking—as the excavators observe, this was probably to delay the corrosion of nails, rather than to make the compartments watertight (G. Li, 1989).

Alongside each bulkhead, on the side away from

amidships, was a floor timber of 115–50 mm scantlings, with a layer of putty between bulkhead and frame. Near the ends of the keel, some 1.50 m beyond first and last bulkheads, more substantial floors of 230–40 mm scantlings were fitted.

Pottery and ingots of lead, tin, and copper were being carried in this vessel which the excavators consider was a cargo carrier up to 25 m in length. They also believe that this ship 'was probably built in Siam, with Chinese guidance or influence'. Origins of wrecks are difficult to establish generally, and in the light of present information it is especially difficult to differentiate between south-east Asian and Chinese vessels. As the Phy Quoc ship's inner planking was fastened together with treenails rather than iron nails, this wreck is taken to be a member of the south-east Asian tradition.

### 8.3.5.2.8 Bukit Jakas

A wreck on the margins of the Sungai Bintan estuary, at Bukit Jakas, Pulau Bintan, in the Riau archipelago off the north-eastern coast of Sumatra, was part excavated in 1981 (Manguin, 1982; 1983; 1993a). Of the lower hull 20 to 25 m survived, and this included a keel c.20 m in length, seven strakes of planking, mainly teak, framing elements and a mast step. The keel was 210 mm sided and 300 mm moulded, with a rabbet on the upper edges for the garboards. There were three layers of planking, the primary layer being c.0.10 m thick, and edge fastened by 20 mm diameter treenails, 0.20 m in length, spaced c.0.25 m apart. The two scarfs noted in the planking were both at bulkhead stations. The strakes were fastened to the frames by iron nails (spikes?) of 10 mm cross-section; it is not clear how the planking was fastened to the bulkheads.

The remains of seventeen bulkheads were found, at an average spacing of c.1.5 m. They were built of 0.10 m planks, edge joined by treenails, and had limber holes each side of the keel. The second plank of each bulkhead was set into a groove in the upper edge of the lowest one. Floor timbers alongside one or both sides of each bulkhead were fastened to the planking by square iron nails (Manguin, 1993a: 271); where there was only one, it seems to have been on the side nearer amidships. On the side away from amidships of one bulkhead towards an end, there were two mast-step timbers, similar to the step on the Pattaya wreck (8.3.5.2.6), with holes for two vertical mast partners and

notches for horizontal braces to the next bulkhead. Manguin (1989) considers that the original vessel was over 30 m in length. A radiocarbon assay (Gif-5774) gives a calibrated date of AD 1400–60.

### 8.3.5.2.9 Ko Si Chang 3

This wreck site, north-west of the island of Si Chang, in the Gulf of Thailand, north of Pattaya, was part-excavated in 1986 (Green, Harper, and Intakosi, 1987). The remains, which are dated by radiocarbon (Sua-2594) to the fifteenth/sixteenth centuries came from a trading vessel, more than 20 m in length. Elements investigated included: a keel; six strakes of inner planking, some outer planking and possible 'sheathing'; nine bulkheads and frames; and a mast-step timber.

The keel was 0.32 m sided and 0.24 m moulded, with a bevel for the garboards, and appeared to be in three sections. A reconstruction drawing (Green, Harper, and Intakosi, 1987: fig. 9) shows a hog or keelson timber on top of the keel. The keel is said to support several 'stanchions'.

The inner layer of planking was fastened edge-to-edge by 20 mm treenails, spaced 75–85 mm apart, and 'in most cases' scarfs were outboard of a bulkhead. Frames were on the side of the bulkheads nearer amidships, except in one case where seatings were needed for longitudinal timbers supporting the mast-step bulkhead. The reconstruction drawing appears to show the framing as two half-frames, meeting at the keelson, each with a limber hole. The compartments between bulkheads are c.1.20 m long; the bulkhead spacing, centre to centre, varies from 1.2–1.6 m. 'Bulkhead-locating pegs' were noted in the planking, at the 'fore' edge of two bulkheads: these may be what are called 'strengtheners' in reports on other wrecks.

### 8.3.5.2.10 Ko Kradat

Fragments of ship planking which had been fastened edge-to-edge by treenails, were excavated from a site off the island of Kradat off the north-eastern shores of the Gulf of Thailand (Green, Harper, and Prishan-chittara, 1981). Associated with the planking was 35 tonnes of granite ballast and pottery which is dated to the mid-to late sixteenth century.

### 8.3.5.2.11 *Ko Si Chang 1*

Only one layer of planking was excavated from this wreck, but caulking on the outer face of this inner planking showed that there had been at least one more layer (Green, 1983c; 1985; 1994; Green, Harper, and Intakosi, 1986). The 45 mm thick inner planking was fastened edge-to-edge by 10 mm treenails, spaced at c.0.19 m.

The bulkheads, at intervals of c.1 m, were made of 40 mm thick boards joined edge-to-edge by treenails spaced at c.0.60 m. Floor timbers, positioned next to bulkheads, had limber holes on either side of the keel, and were scarfed to side timbers on each side. Ceiling, planking, 25 mm thick, was attached to the hull planking between the floors.

A recent radiocarbon assay (Sua-2298) gives a sixteenth- to seventeenth-century date, and the excavator considers that this vessel may originally have been 20–25 m long.

### 8.3.5.2.12 *Ko Khram*

This wreck, from the Gulf of Thailand, south of Pattaya, had thirteen compartments and the planking was possibly fastened edge-to-edge by treenails. Radiocarbon gives a date in the sixteenth/seventeenth centuries (Green, 1987; 1994).

### 8.3.5.2.13 *Puerto Galera*

A looted wreck at Puerto Galera in northern Mindoro, Philippines, appears to have planking fastened edge-to-edge by treenails (Green, Harper, and Intakosi, 1987: 4; Clark *et al.*, 1989: 259). Guns from this site may be from the seventeenth/eighteenth centuries.

### 8.3.5.2.14 *Johore Lama*

In the sixteenth century, Johore Lama, on the River Johore near the southern point of the Malacca peninsula, was the fortified capital of Johore state, with a large harbour in the river mouth (Sieveking, 1954). In 1953, the remains of three boats were excavated from sites close to this river. The published report has no measured drawings and lacks structural details. One boat (C) was said to be a 'Malay boat', not much more than 30 years old. The second boat (B) from Sampan Tanjong had two layers of planking: the inner planking was fastened edge-to-edge by treenails, and the outer layer of machined planking was nailed to the inner by square iron nails. The excavator's identification of this as a nineteenth-century Chinese *twako* is doubtful as the latter had only a single layer of planking which was fastened together by angled spikes (Waters, 1947). On the evidence now available, boat B would seem to be a late but undated example of a boat with treenail fastenings, similar in some respects to the ships described above.

The third wreck (boat A), from Penkalan Raja, had part of a keel, a fragment of an end post and parts of two side strakes. One end of the 33 ft (10 m) keel had been cut short, the other end was mortised to the post. The planking was fastened edge to edge by 3–4 in (75/100 mm) treenails at 9–12 in (23–30 mm) spacing. At unspecified intervals there were 3 × 1¼ in (76 × 32 mm) tenons locked within mortises by one treenail per plank. The excavator considered that this boat might be a *perahu pukat* or sampan of the eighteenth/nineteenth centuries. A more cautious interpretation is that this was another undated example of the regional treenail-fastened tradition, this time with locked mortise and tenon auxiliary plank fastenings.

### 8.3.6 ICONOGRAPHIC EVIDENCE

There is some representational evidence to supplement that from excavation and early accounts: this is of limited use structurally, but can help with propulsion and steering. Reliefs in the eighth- to ninth-century Buddhist temple of Candi, Borobudur, Java depict two small boats and nine larger ones, five with outriggers and four without (Fig. 8.6). Those with outriggers have several masts with canted rectangular sails and two quarter rudders and may represent war vessels; the ones without outriggers have a single mast with a type of lugsail (Mookerji, 1912: 46, 48; Needham, 1971: 457–8, figs. 973–4; Manguin, 1980; Manguin, 1993a: 263; MacKnight, 1980: 123). Frescos in cave 2 at Ajanta in southern India (Fig. 6.11), dated to the early sixth century, include a vessel with several masts with high-aspect ratio lugsails, and two quarter rudders (6.2.4, 8.3.8). Opinions are divided on the origins of the vessel depicted—south-east Asian (most likely), Chinese, or even Indian (Manguin, 1980: 274; Ray, 1990: fig. 7; Horridge, 1978: 7).

Fig. 8.6. One of the vessels depicted on the eighth/ninth-century Buddhist temple at Borobudur, Java (photo: Sir David Attenborough).

The origin of the principal or 'foreign' vessel depicted in the twelfth century reliefs on the Bayon temple at Angkor Thom (8.3.8, 10.4.1) near the River Mekong in Cambodia (Needham, 1971: fig. 975) is also disputed (Manguin, 1983: 8–9; Gibson-Hill, 1952: 126–9).

Numerous large bronze drums have been excavated from early sites in south-east China and in south-east Asia, from north-east Thailand as far east as the Kei islands, including south-east Borneo, but not Sulawesi, the Moluccas, or Philippines (Bellwood, 1985: 272–80; Spennemann, 1985; Higham, 1989: 200). These were probably manufactured in northern Vietnam, during the Dong So'n cultural phase from c.500 BC to the first century BC, and their distribution gives some idea of the trading/exchange routes of that period or later. On some of these drums, stylized representations of fighting boats are engraved. These craft have rising ends and a quarter rudder or paddle (Fig. 8.7). Spennemann (1985) interprets them as logboats extended by stitched-on planks, whilst Horridge (1978) considers that some may represent bundle craft: such specific interpretations seem to outrun the evidence. Spennemann (1985) has also described a bronze boat model from Kampong Dobo in Flores. Again, this seems to represent a war boat, this time with a raised platform for marines and important people. The six pairs of men seated inside the hull appear to be paddlers. For stylistic reasons, Spennemann believes that this model has a date and origin similar to those of the Dong So'n drums.

Amongst other ship representations, Ray (1994) has noted two unprovenanced coins from Khuan Lukpad, Thailand, showing ships with two masts and quarter rudders (114, plate 12); and paintings of boats in lime-

Fig. 8.7. Boat engraved on a Dong So'n drum (British Museum).

stone caves near Phangna and Krabi, Thailand and on the island of Muna, south of Sulawesi (183–4). A fif-teenth-/sixteenth-century terracotta ship model from Wat Kaeng Paung, Thailand, now in the National Museum, Bangkok, has fore- and after- castles and transom bow and stern, but other aspects are unclear (Manguin, 1983: 10).

### 8.3.7 PLANKED VESSELS: STRUCTURE AND BUILDING SEQUENCE

The excavated evidence for plank boats and ships of south-east Asia, supplemented by documentary and representational evidence, can be presented in three chronological groups, each differentiated by structural characteristics. Although the resultant picture is one of increasing technological complexity, many of the earli-er features were never entirely superseded and were still used somewhere in this region during recent times. For example, in the nineteenth century, Wallace (1869: 321–2) noted that boats in the Kei islands (south of west New Guinea) had treenailed planking and flex-ible ribs fastened to cleats—by the twentieth century

the ribs had been replaced by rattan lashings (Aglion-by: 1991). In the late twentieth century, Barnes (1985) documented the *téna*, a whaling boat of Lambata (east of Flores and north of Timor) which was edge-fas-tened with treenails with frames lashed to cleats pro-truding from the planking (Fig. 8.8).

Although the three groups described below are given boundaries in the seventh and fourteenth cen-turies, some of the features thought to be characteris-tic of those times were first used in south-east Asia at an earlier date. For example: treenails were used as plank fastenings before the seventh century; and bulk-heads are documented before the fourteenth.

#### 8.3.7.1 UP TO THE SEVENTH CENTURY AD

From excavated evidence, the typical boat of this peri-od had planking fastened by individual lashings, with integral cleats (sometimes known as 'lugs') for lashed framing. A Chinese text of *c.* AD 300 on the flora of south-east Asia notes that the bark of the sugar palm (*Arenga pinnata*) was made into ropes which were used to bind boat's timbers (Manguin, 1993a: 261).

Although the second- to third-century AD logboat

Fig. 8.8. An early stage in building a Lambata *téna*. Cleat blanks have been left proud of the strakes (Robert Barnes).

the third-to fifth-century Pontian boat. The flush-laid planking of this boat is both lashed together and fastened with occasional treenails. The Pontian planking also had integral cleats to which framing timbers were fastened. The possibly fifth- to sixth-century Khuan Luk Pat boat and the fifth- to seventh-century planking from Kolam Pinisi had similar features. It thus seems likely that the earliest plank boats of south-east Asia—pre-third century AD—were stitched together and had framing lashed to integral cleats.

Sewn planking continued to be used into recent times. In Vietnam, Malaya, Borneo, Sarawak, Moluccas, and the Philippines, boats with the planking fastened by cords of bamboo fibres were recorded from the seventeenth to the twentieth century (Folkard, 1870: 261; Lane-Fox, 1875: 411–12; Manguin, 1985: 320–32). Nineteenth- and early twentieth-century Vietnamese boats are particularly well documented (Manguin, 1985): their planking was assembled with treenails across the seams and then fastened together with rattan stitches (Fig. 8.9).

That there were south-east Asian seagoing ships before the seventh century AD is clear from an account written by the Chinese monk, Wan Chen, in the third century AD. Wan Chen describes their sailing rig (10.2.11.1) but gives no details of the hull (Needham, 1971: 600–1).

## 8.3.7.2 SEVENTH TO FOURTEENTH CENTURIES AD AND BEYOND

The typical vessel of this period had treenail-fastened planking with integral cleat-blocks for lashed framing.

from Tanjog Rawa probably had added planking it is not known how that planking was fastened and the earliest fastenings that have been recorded are those on

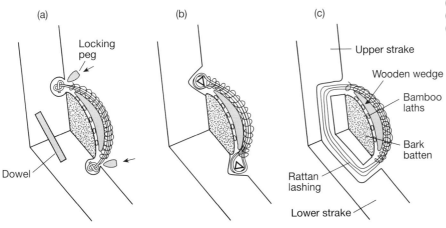

(a) 19th-century *ghe-nôc* of Huê.
(b) 20th-century *thuyên* of Cam-ranh.
(c) 20th-century *ghe-nôc* of Huê.

Fig. 8.9. Fastenings on Vietnamese sewn-plank boats (after Manguin, 1985: fig. 20.6).

The lashings were generally made of the bark of the sugar palm (*Arenga pinnata*)—known as *tali ijok* in the Malay and Indonesian languages and *cabo negro* in Filipino. Some craft had outriggers.

Although the seventh-/eighth-century vessel from Sambirejo had lashings between the planks, the primary fastenings were treenails within the thickness of the flush-laid planking. From this time onwards, treenail fastenings are features of every wreck so far excavated in south-east Asian waters. Treenail fastenings are also noted in descriptions of south-east Asian craft by Europeans: in 1544 by Antonio Galvao in the Moluccas (Horridge, 1978: 9); in 1582 by Nicolau Perreira SJ in Java (Manguin, 1980: 267–8); and in 1668 by Alcisco Alcina SJ in the Philippines (Horridge, 1982).

Alcina also described how these treenails were locked within the planking by smaller treenails of *ipil*. This locking technique has been found on the thirteenth-/fourteenth-century Butuan boats (Fig. 8.5B): it is known today in Madura and Bali (Horridge, 1982: 12); its apparent absence elsewhere, both today and more especially in antiquity, may be because few, if any investigators, have looked for it or an equivalent. In general terms, simple treenails within the thickness of the planking are unlikely to be relied upon, by themselves, as plank fastenings. To prevent the seams from opening either the treenails have to be modified or there have to be auxiliary plank fastenings. Tapered and/or oven-dried treenails may be driven into undersized holes in the plank edges and the next strake forced onto these treenails by some form of leverage (as is known today in south-east Asia) (Barnes, 1985). In this way there is controlled crushing of the wood fibres and an interference fit of treenails within holes. An alternative is to drive a small treenail through the ends of each fastening treenail, thus locking them in each plank and producing a positive fastening—as in Butuan boat 2. A third possibility is to use stitching (found in some of the early treenail-fastened south-east Asian boats) as auxiliary fastenings to prevent the seams opening. Another solution is to rely on the transverse framing to keep the planks in a fixed relationship with one another—flexible ribs, as found in some south-east Asian boats today (Horridge, 1978), are very effective in this respect (Fig. 8.10). Some of the excavated fourteenth-century and earlier south-east Asian boats may have had some of these features but, if they did, this was not noted by investigators.

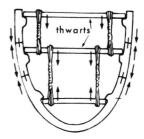

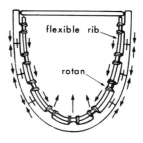

Fig. 8.10. Two south-east Asian methods of using framing to force planking together (after Horridge, 1982: fig. 2).

Horridge (1982: fig. 7) has described a simple method of forcing planks together before they are fastened, used today in the island of Bangka, which matches the seventeenth-century Philippines' techniques mentioned by Alcina. Horridge (1981: 78) and Barnes (1985: 355) have also published details of tools used in Indonesia to transfer the shape of the top edge of one plank to the bottom edge of another—such a simple device was probably used in much earlier times.

Framing lashed to planking cleat blocks, the other main feature of the earlier boats, also appears in seventh- to fourteenth-century wrecks: planking from Paya Pasir of the twelfth–fourteenth centuries; some, at least, of the thirteenth-/fifteenth-century boats from Butuan; and in thirteenth- to fifteenth-century planking from Sha Tsui. This technique was also probably referred to in the eighth century by Hui-Lin in his *I Chhieh Ching Yin I* (Needham, 1971: 459–60; Manguin, 1993a: 262). This Chinese monk said that, in the large seagoing ships of south-east Asia, ropes made from the bark of the coconut tree were used to 'bind the parts of the ship together'—it seems likely that this was a reference to frame lashings rather than to stitched planking (10.2.10.3). Framing lashed to cleats was clearly described by Gavao in 1544, and in 1668, Alcina mentioned that crossbeams/thwarts, as well as ribs, were lashed to cleats (Horridge, 1982).

The early twentieth-century *orembai* of the Moluccas was built with treenail fastenings and ribs lashed to cleats (Hornell, 1946a: 207–8), as were the boats of the Sea Dyaks of Borneo (Christie, 1957: 350) and the *prahu belang* of the Aru islands (Horridge, 1978: 24–30). *Prahus* are mentioned as one of several types of boat used for fishing and as ship's boats in Galvao's 1544 account cited by Horridge (1978: 10). This term is used by Europeans to describe any boat of south-east Asia and cannot now be linked with any specific tradition.

Outriggers are another feature of this period. They have not been excavated, but are first known from eighth-/ninth-century stone engravings at Borobudur, Java (Fig. 8.6); five of the boats depicted there have one, probably two, outriggers. The largest vessels known to have had double outriggers are Moluccan fighting craft known as *kora kora* (Hornell, 1946a: 259; Horridge, 1978, 1982). These vessels, which were notable for their stability and speed (8.3.8), were described and drawn by Europeans from the sixteenth century onwards (Haddon and Hornell, 1938: iii. 18). They were of galley proportions, double-ended with high extremities and a rockered keel. *Kora kora* were built with treenail plank fastenings and framing lashed to cleats. Crossbeams projected through both sides to form outrigger structures near the waterline and to them were fastened longitudinal timbers, the one furthest outboard being afloat. Rows of paddlers were stationed on these near-awash frameworks—up to 100 each side, it is said—and 100 marines manned the central raised platform inboard. In later, more peaceful, times, *kora kora* became 'royal barges', the fighting deck being replaced by a thatched cabin (Hornell, 1946: 259).

Double outriggers were widely encountered and reported by the sixteenth century and later Europeans (See Fig. 8.11), and they are in use today in south-east Asia and Madagascar (Hornell, 1944b; 1946a: 253–9). It seems likely that double outriggers were fitted to south-east Asian craft from before the eighth/ninth centuries through to the present day.

### 8.3.7.3 FROM THE FOURTEENTH CENTURY ONWARDS

The remaining finds in south-east Asian waters—some eight vessels from the fourteenth to the seventeenth centuries—were seagoing, keeled, round-hulled cargo ships 20 to 25 m in overall length. They all had treenail-fastened, flush-laid primary planking and, with one possible exception, there were one or two further layers. Furthermore, those finds with more than vestigial remains had bulkheads with associated framing to which the planking was nailed and, in two cases, (Phu Quoc and Ko Si Chang 3) also joined by 'bulkhead strengtheners' (10.5.1.2). In four finds, (Pattaya, Phu Quoc, Ko Si Chang 3, and Bukit Jakas) all or 'most' of the plank scarfs noted were outboard of bulkheads: this raises the strong possibility that these fourteenth- to sixteenth-century ships were built frame-first.

Keeled, round-hulled cargo vessels were also wrecked in Chinese waters during this period (10.4.2). The characteristics of vessels from both Chinese and south-east Asian waters, are not described in detail in the published reports at present available, but in general terms, and at that level of classification, the two groups seem to have several major characteristics in common. One distinction seems to be in the primary plank fastenings: treenails in south-east Asia; angled metal nails in Chinese waters. However, it should be noted that the fourteenth-century Chinese wreck Penglai 1 has treenails/dowels as well as spikes as plank fastenings (10.4.2.6.3). Other distinguishing features may be that Chinese vessels used a median rudder rather than the twin side rudders of south-east Asia; and the battened lugsail seems to be a Chinese characteristic, with the canted rectangular sail predominant in south-east Asia.

Of the other features—those that appear in both traditions: the earliest keel (rather than plank-keel) comes from thirteenth-century China (10.7.2)—but this is a relatively late date, and the apparent priority of 'invention' may be due to absence of evidence. Bulkheads are first known in China in the seventh–ninth centuries (10.7.2), but Hui-Lin of the eighth century, tells us that south-east Asian ships were 'divided fore and aft into three sections' which may be a reference to bulkheads. Furthermore, whilst the earliest wreck with multilayer planking is from thirteenth-century China, Hui-Lin states that the seagoing ships of south-east Asia were built 'by assembling (several) thicknesses of side-planks' (Needham, 1971: 459). Bulkhead 'strengthening' devices and the enigmatic feature of plank scarfs outboard of bulkhead, which may be a sign of frame-first building (8.3.7.3, 10.5.1.2, 10.5.1.4), both appear in Chinese wrecks at about the same time as they appear in south-east Asian waters. As with bulkheads, it is impossible to decide on present evidence precisely where the ideas for these features originated.

### 8.3.7.3.1 *The junco*

The seagoing, cargo-carrying ships discussed above may have been similar to ships known as *junco* (in Malay: *jong*) by Marco Polo and Odoric de Pordenone OFM, of the thirteenth and fourteenth centuries (Manguin, 1980: 266–7; 1993a: 266–7). In the sixteenth century, terms such as *junco, jonque*, and *junk* were widely used to describe the large ships encountered in south-east Asian waters. Duarte Barbosa, for example, mentioned that the Javanese *junco* had three or four layers of planking and rattan rope rigging (Hill, 1958: 203). Other sixteenth-century accounts describe large vessels ranging in size from 85–700 tons capacity, with two to four masts, up to four thicknesses of planking fastened with treenails and two quarter rudders. Among the sails used were lugsails, canted rectangular sails, and a square sail on a bowsprit. Such vessels were built in north Java and south Borneo close to the sources of teak (Manguin, 1980: 1993a).

### 8.3.7.3.2 *Small boats in this tradition*

Boats A and B excavated at Johore Lama, Malaya, were keel boats with treenail-fastened planking. Boat B had a second layer of planking nailed to the inner planking, similar in this respect to several of the ships described above. Boat A had only one layer of planking, and some of its fastenings were locked tenons in mortises: thus it was not precisely like the earlier boats discussed above.

No details have been published of these boats' framing but a small photograph appears to show that there were no cleats on boat B's planking and that she had several stout floors and a keelson (Sieveking, 1954: plate 4b). The primary plank fastenings suggest that both these boats were members of the regional, treenail-fastened tradition. Boat B could be a late example of a boat built during the period when ships were being built with bulkheads and frames, but, being a small craft, she had only framing. Without further details of boat A, it is not possible to suggest her status within this tradition.

## 8.3.8 PLANKED VESSELS: PROPULSION AND STEERING

Apart from the side rudder found at Sambirejo, south Sumatra, in association with sewn planking dated to the seventh/eighth centuries AD (8.3.5.1.3), and the few mast steps excavated in the fourteenth- to seventeenth-century wrecks, evidence for the propulsion methods and steering arrangements of early craft of south-east Asia comes entirely from documentary and iconographic sources. In the text, *Nan Chou I Wu Chih*, dated to the third century AD, Wan Chen, a Chinese Buddhist monk, described large seagoing south-east Asian ships, capable of carrying 600–700 people and possibly 260 tons of cargo (Needham, 1971: 600–1; Manguin, 1993a: 262). These vessels had sails woven from the leaves of the *lu-thou* tree, which were 'obliquely set on four masts', 'in a row from bow to stern'. These phrases seem to describe fore-and-aft sails set on four masts. It is thought that one of the ships depicted on sixth- to seventh-century frescos in cave 2 at Ajanta, India (Fig. 6.11), may represent a south-east Asian vessel, mainly because it has side rudders (Manguin, 1980). This vessel has high-aspect ratio sails, possibly lugsails, on three masts and a square sail on a bowsprit. In the eighth- to ninth-centuries galleries of a Buddhist temple at Borobudur, Java, two sizes of vessel are depicted: one of the larger ones (Fig. 8.6) which is fitted with outriggers, has canted rectangular sails on two bipod or tripod masts and a small square sail on a bowsprit. The other type of large vessel (Needham, 1971: fig. 974) is without outriggers and has a single mast with a sail of indeterminate form, but which Needham believes is a battened lugsail.

The principal ship represented on the twelfth-century reliefs at Angkor Thom, Cambodia (10.4.1) has features which make it difficult to decide whether it is 'Chinese' or 'south-east Asian'. For example, the sails appear to be battened lugsails, however, some see the rudder as a median one (Needham, 1970: fig. 975), whereas others see it as a single quarter rudder on the starboard side (Gibson-Hill, 1952: 126–9; Manguin, 1983: 9).

Some *kora kora* were propelled solely by paddle, whilst others were propelled by paddle and by sail which Galveo, in 1544, said were of sackcloth and matting (Horridge, 1978). Drawings of *kora kora* published by Horridge (1978: fig. 5) show bipod or possibly tripod

Fig. 8.11. A late sixteenth-century drawing of vessels in the Banda Sea: double outriggers in the foreground; the *jong* is to the right (de Bry, 1629: plate 28).

masts towards one end, and a drawing dated 1798 shows a canted rectangular sail with boom—see also de Bry (1601: plate xvi) and Paris (1843: plate 98). These features are also seen on the Borobudur vessels. The Javanese *junco* or, in Malay, *jong*, described by Perreira in 1582 had three masts with sails of woven rattan (Manguin, 1980: 267–8). The *jong* of the Banda Sea—illustrated by de Bry (Fig. 8.11)—had two canted rectangular sails as well as a square sail on a bowsprit. Another ship in this drawing clearly has a battened sail and so we may deduce that the *jong*'s sail was not battened. Similarly, in a drawing of Manila harbour (de Bry, 1619: plate xvi), the ship accompanying a *jong* has readily identifiable battened lugsails. Two *balotos* from the Philippines, illustrated by Alcina in 1668 (Horridge,

1982: fig. 3), one with and one without outrigger, appear to have canted rectangular sails.

This patchy evidence points to the conclusion that fore-and-aft sails of an unspecified form, set on two and more masts, were used by south-east Asian ships from the third century AD at the latest; this is earlier than these features are known on Chinese vessels (10.7.3). The canted rectangular sail was used on south-east Asian ships by the eighth / ninth centuries and continued in use in those waters until recent times, being 'matted' or of woven rattan from at least the sixteenth century (Manguin, 1980: 272); it does not appear to have been used in Chinese ships. The lugsail, specifically in its battened form, appears to have been mainly, if not exclusively, Chinese from the twelfth century (the carving on the Bayon at Angkor Thom, Cambodia—Needham, 1971: fig. 975); or earlier if the sixth-/seventh-century vessel represented in Ajanta cave 2 is thought to be Chinese. Battened lugsails appear on sixteenth-century and later European drawings of ships in south-east Asian waters, which have structural features which cannot easily be classified as Chinese, south-east Asian or otherwise. It is possible that the artists did not understand what they saw or misinterpreted what they were told. On the other hand, it may be that the battened lugsail had begun to be used on non-Chinese ships by this time, or earlier if the Angkor ship is taken to be from the south-east Asian tradition.

The median rudder was used in China from the first century AD (10.2.10.4) and was probably characteristic of Chinese seagoing vessels in later years. In Europe the quarter rudder preceded the median rudder and it may be that in China there was early use of quarter rudders, although, at present, there is only evidence there for steering sweeps (10.2.11.2). The median rudder does not seem to have been used in south-east Asian waters until the sixteenth century and later, when it is depicted on European drawings of at least one boat (by Alcina in the seventeenth century—see Horridge, 1982: fig. 3) and on illustrations of ships which may be Chinese or south-east Asian.

Some of the boats on the Dong So'n drums of the first century AD or earlier appear to have either paddles or quarter rudders (Fig. 8.7), and there is a side rudder from Sambirejo, south Sumatra (8.3.5.1.3) which is thought to be seventh/eighth century (Manguin, 1996: 185)—but the details of this have not yet been published. These apart, the earliest representations of quarter rudders are on the sixth- to seventh-century Ajanta ship (Fig. 6.11) and on the twelfth-century Angkor ship: in both cases there are problems in deciding whether other features of these representations are 'Chinese' or 'south-east Asian'. Europeans of the sixteenth and seventeenth century especially noted quarter rudders on the vessels of south-east Asia (Manguin, 1980: 270). Perreira in 1582 tells us that the Javanese *jong* had 'three rudders, one on each side and one in the middle': Manguin (1980: 270) believes that the latter was a steering sweep, however, a ship with both quarter and median rudders is depicted near Manila by de Bry (1602: plate xiii). In the seventeenth-century drawings published by Alcina (Horridge, 1982: fig. 3), one *balotos* has a quarter rudder, the other a median rudder. This evidence suggests that although paired quarter rudders may have been characteristic of south-east Asian craft in the sixteenth century, there may also have been (as with propulsion by sail), a degree of interchange of ideas about steering arrangements between south-east Asian and Chinese shipbuilders during this period, if not earlier.

Foil-shaped boards (*guares*) thrust down through the bottom of a vessel can also be used to steer by varying the number and position of foils and their immersed area. It has been suggested that some of the Dong So'n boats have such a device near the bow although Spennemann (1984) discounts this. *Guares* are used to oppose leeway as well as to steer, and today they are invariably found on sailing rather than paddled or oared craft. Furthermore, whilst they are known to have been used on boats, for example, Vietnamese basket boats (8.3.3)—they are much more frequently found on rafts (6.6.3, 8.3.1, 10.2.5, 11.4.1.2). It is thus unlikely that the paddled Dong So'n boats had them. On the other hand, on at least one of the eighth-/ninth-century depictions at Borobudur, one of the crew appears to be using *guares*, and as this vessel has a raft-like structure, this interpretation seems plausible.

# 9
# OCEANIA

Oceania is defined here as the islands of the southern Pacific Ocean and of the adjacent seas to the west; in cultural/linguistic terms these are the islands of Polynesia, Micronesia, and eastern Melanesia (Fig. 9.1). The Polynesian islands lie within a vast triangle with sides 3,500–4,000 nautical miles in length, and with apexes in New Zealand, Hawaii, and Easter island. The east Melanesian islands lie to the west of Polynesia and east-south-east of island south-east Asia; whilst Micronesia, with its nearly 3,000 islands, is to the north of Melanesia and east of the Philippines. These islands can be divided into two physical groups by reference to the 'Andesite Line' which runs northwards to the east of New Zealand and Tonga; generally north-westwards between Melanesia and Micronesia, passing to the north of Fiji, the Solomons, and the Bismarck archipelago; then northwards to the west of most of Micronesia (R. Green, 1991: fig. 1, 495; Irwin, 1992: fig. 1). West of this line the islands are remnants of the submerged margins of the continents of Asia and Australia (Sahulland). Islands to the east of this line, on the Pacific Plate, are of volcanic origin, and, in form, range from high islands still retaining their volcanic profile—examples are the Hawaiian, Society, Samoan, and Marquesas islands in Polynesia—to low-lying atolls with ring-shaped coral reefs enclosing a lagoon—examples are the North Cook and the Tuamotan islands of Polynesia, and many of the Micronesian islands (Bellwood, 1987: 10–14; Irwin, 1992: 4–5).

These Oceanic islands are mostly within the Tropics, the principal exceptions being Easter island and Rapa at $c.25°$ south, and New Zealand at 35–45° south. In terms of longitude, they extend from Micronesia at $c.140°$ east and eastern Melanesia at $c.160°$ east, across the International Date Line to Easter island at $c.110°$ west, only 2,000 nautical miles or so from the South American coast. With the exceptions of New Zealand in the south and the Hawaiian islands in the north, the Polynesian islands form an extension, as it were, of island south-east Asia, on a general alignment of east-south-east, with the great majority of them being in the southern hemisphere.

There is a tendency for islands to be smaller and more remote, and, apart from marine life, to have decreasing natural resources, the further they are east of the Solomons (Irwin, 1992: 18–23). These features may explain why people of the first maritime migration from south-east Asia (7. 2) in 40,000 BC or earlier, do not appear to have moved further east than the Solomons (Irwin, 1992: 18–21). It is also relevant that, between the easternmost Solomons and the Santa Cruz islands, there is a sea passage of $c.200$ nautical miles which includes a stretch where no land is in sight—a natural 'barrier' to expansion. There are similar or greater distances separating the Micronesian groups of islands from the Philippines to the west, and from western Melanesia to the south. A line drawn just to the east of the Philippines, north of New Guinea and the Bismarck archipelago, north and east of the Solomon islands, east of New Guinea and Australia, and west of New Zealand (R. Green, 1991: fig. 1) leaves 'Near Oceania' to the west and 'Remote Oceania' to the east (Fig. 9.2). Before Remote Oceania (that is, eastern Melanesia, Micronesia, and Polynesia) could be settled, it had to be appreciated that there were further islands beyond the horizon (9.5.2), and the technology of would-be migrants had to be such that boats could be built which were not only capable of longer voyages

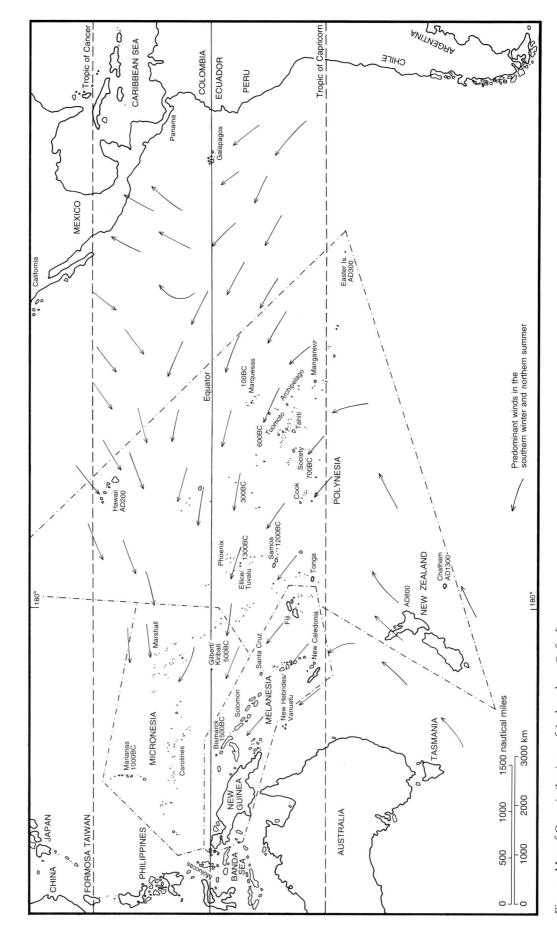

Fig. 9.1. Map of Oceania (Institute of Archaeology, Oxford).

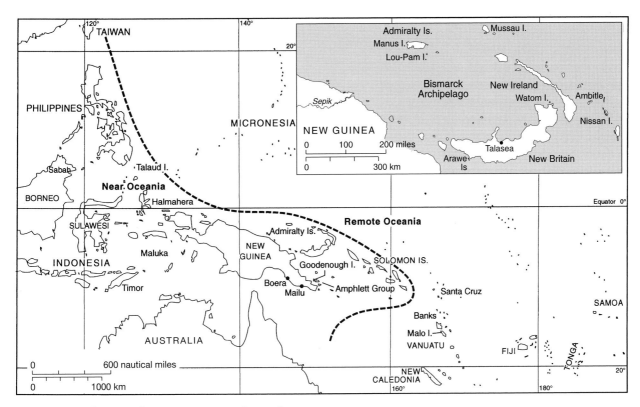

Fig. 9.2. Map of Near and Remote Oceania (after Ambrose, 1997).

than before, but also were able to carry plants and animals as well as people. Furthermore, an advanced form of navigation had to be perfected so that it could be relied upon when land was no longer in sight.

Although, from west to east, islands generally decrease in size and increase in remoteness, they mostly form clusters of islands grouped together in discrete archipelagos, with a high degree of intervisibility between islands within groups—either direct from island to island or from a boat between islands. To this extent, discovery and settlement problems were simplified: not only could several islands be reconnoitred on one exploratory voyage, but also these archipelagos formed a large target on which subsequent voyages of settlement could make a landfall; they could also act as a safety net for boats returning from further exploratory voyages as Polynesians ventured further into Remote Oceania. The major groups in Micronesia are the Marianas, Marshalls, Carolines, and Kiribati/Gilberts. In eastern Melanesia, there are the Santa Cruz, Vanuatu/New Hebrides, and Fijian groups. In western Polynesia, the Tongan, Samoan, and Tuvalu/Ellice groups; in central Polynesia, the Cooks, Society,

and Austral; and in eastern Polynesia, the Marquesas and Tuamotu groups (Fig. 9.1).

Apart from New Zealand, the Oceanic islands have a tropical climate—hot and fairly wet, with occasional hurricanes from the west in the southern summer, November to April. The predominant winds in the southern winter/northern summer are generally from the sector south-east to east-south-east over most of the region east of the Solomons, and east-south-east to east-north-east in Micronesia generally, with variables in the far west (Irwin, 1992: figs. 4, 42). In the southern summer, the north-east trades blow in Micronesian waters, whilst there are generally south-east to east winds in Polynesia (Irwin, 1992: figs. 33–4, 41). There are, however, seasonal and regional variations within this overall preponderance of easterly 'trade winds'. In the Bismarck–Solomon region there are monsoonal westerlies with a frequency of 50–70 per cent in the southern summer; around the tropic of Capricorn from New Caledonia to Easter island, there is a significant proportion (30–50 per cent) of winter days with westerlies; whilst nearer the Equator, as far east as central Polynesia, the chance of a westerlies is greater in summer (Irwin, 1992: figs. 35–6); further east in eastern Polynesia, outside the doldrums, westerlies blow occasionally (15–25 per cent) throughout the year.

In Polynesian waters there is a generally westwards flowing current of up to one knot in the southern winter, except in the far eastern region where it tends to set south-west. In the summer a weaker current flows towards the south-west. In Micronesian waters, an equatorial current sets easterly the year round, whilst away from the Equator the currents set westerly.

# 9.1

# The Oceanic Migration

By the second millennium BC, the migration south-eastwards of Austronesian speaking peoples, which had begun in Taiwan or the coast of south-east China some 2,000 years earlier, had reached as far east as the Solomon islands in western Melanesia (8.1). To the south and south-west, but unknown to them, was Australia, now separated from New Guinea by rising sea levels, which had been settled by Australoid peoples some 40,000 years earlier, as had New Guinea and most of the land to the west (7.2). To the north and east lay Remote Oceania: Micronesia to the north; eastern Melanesia and Polynesia to the east. All these islands appear to have been uninhabited before the mid-second millennium BC (Bellwood, 1987: 23–4; Irwin, 1992: 31–3).

The band of islands stretching in a generally east-south-east direction from mainland south-east Asia to the Solomon islands were in a relatively sheltered equatorial position between cyclonic areas, with predictable seasonal reversals of wind and current, forming a 'voyaging corridor' as Irwin (1992: 4–5, 24–5, figs. 6, 10, 11) has suggested. Furthermore, it was possible to voyage between most of these islands and remain in sight of land. With such advantages, this would have been an admirable 'nursery' in which to perfect seafaring and navigational skills and improve boat perfor-

mance. This vast archipelago was thus well placed to become a springboard for exploratory voyages to the north and to the east, with the island network from western Melanesia to the Solomons acting as a safety net on return.

Although some scholars, such as Heyerdahl (9.1.1), have argued that Oceania was populated from South America, there is convincing linguistic, biological, and archaeological evidence that it was from the west that the migrants came. Studies in physical anthropology show that Polynesians are mainly from southern Mongoloid stock with origins in south-east Asia, but there is also an Australoid element in their make-up, derived from the indigenous population of south-east Asia (Sunda) and north-east Sahulland (Bellwood, 1987: 23–6). Ethno-biological studies have shown that the Polynesian staples, taro, breadfruit, yams, and bananas were first domesticated in the south-east Asian region, as were Polynesian pigs, dogs, and fowl (D. Lewis, 1994: 7; Bellwood, 1987: 34). The sweet potato, which was found on first European contact to be an important element of diet in Hawaii, Easter island, and New Zealand, seems to have originated in the South American Andes (11.2). It is likely, however, that by the mid-first millennium AD, Polynesians were capable of sailing to South America from Easter island or possibly from the Marquesas: the sweet potato could have been brought back to Oceania at that time (Bellwood, 1987: 36). It may be relevant to note that, when in Valparaiso, Chile in 1831, Admiral Paris saw a small single-outrigger boat which he considered came from the Tuamotu archipelago (F. Paris, 1843: 198, plate 113).

Linguistic research has shown that the various Polynesian languages are similar to one another and related to the many Austronesian languages spoken in Indonesia, Micronesia, the Philippines, Madagascar, parts of Vietnam, and Malaya, and also marginally in New Guinea, the Bismarcks and Solomons where the main languages are of Australoid derivation, as are those of Australia (Bellwood, 1987: 27). This common language family reinforces the argument for the colonization of Oceania from the west.

A distinctive style of reddish earthenware pottery which, when decorated with pressed designs, can readily be distinguished from other ceramics, is now recognized as a prime characteristic of the Neolithic Lapita culture, which first becomes archaeologically visible in the Bismarck archipelago from the mid-second millennium BC (Bellwood, 1987: 47–52; Terrell and Welsch, 1997; Sand, 1997; Ambrose, 1997). Lapita pottery has also been excavated from many sites in eastern Melanesia and some in western Polynesia. Obsidian from the Talasea source in New Britain in the eastern Bismarcks, and from a source on Lou island in the Admiralty island region of the Bismarcks, has also been excavated from some Lapita sites further east (Bellwood, 1987: 51; Irwin, 1992: 29, 35). A pumice stone, with a large fragment of obsidian embedded in it, has been found amongst seaborne material which had drifted to Nadikdik atoll in the Marshall islands (Spennemann and Ambrose, 1997). Thus not all finds of obsidian far from their origin were transported by Man. Nevertheless, at least some of those finds testify to the seafaring mobility of these people. With some exceptions, radiocarbon dates for the earliest Lapita site on each island show an eastward trend: from c.1600 BC in the Bismarcks to c.1000 BC in Niuatoputapu, north of Tonga, in western Polynesia (Irwin, 1992: 39). East of the Solomons, Lapita sites appear to be the earliest signs of human occupation, thus, for this western region of the Pacific, Lapita pottery can be used as a marker for the movement eastwards of the earliest colonizers of Oceania.

The precise dating of the earliest settlements of Oceania outside the Lapita culture zone is still a matter of academic debate (Spriggs and Anderson, 1993; Kirch and Ellison, 1994). Nevertheless, from radiocarbon dates and other evidence summarized by Irwin (1992: 6–7, 80–2, 105–8, 124–32), the general pattern seems to have been:

*Polynesia*

- Between 1000 BC and 500 BC. From the Fiji/Tonga region to Samoa and the Cook islands.

- Between 500 BC and BC/AD. From the Cook region to the Society islands, the Tuamoto archipelago, and the Marquesas.

- Between BC/AD and AD 750. From the Cook/Society region or the Marquesas to Easter island; and from Tahiti and the Marquesas to Hawaii (Spriggs and Anderson, 1993; Cachola-Abad, 1993).

- By AD 1200. From the Cook/Society region to New Zealand (Anderson, 1991).

- By AD 1500. From New Zealand to Chatham island.

*Micronesia*

- Between 1000 BC and BC/AD. From the Philippines/East Indonesia region to the Marianas and the Carolines.

- Between BC/AD and AD 500. From the east Melanesia/west Polynesia region to East Micronesia.

## 9.1.1 MIGRATION STRATEGIES

The main thrust of the discovery and settlement voyages described above, to the islands of eastern Melanesia and Polynesia, is on a heading of approximately east-south-east which is within the sector (south-east to east) from which the predominant winds blow in that region. Voyages to Micronesia from the west are also into the predominant wind (east-south-east to north-east) in those waters; whilst voyages from the south are generally across the wind. Voyages from central Polynesia to Hawaii are across wind; whilst those to New Zealand are across and then into wind. There thus seems to be a preponderance of voyages which would have to be made into the predominant wind. To a landsman, this could well seem to be an impossible task: this sequence of voyages 'against the wind' defies Nature—hence the superficial attraction of Heyerdahl's theory which suggests that the colonizers of Oceania sailed *with* the wind, from east to west. However, three points can be made here: first, predominant winds do not blow continuously; second, at a certain level of technology and skill, boats can be sailed across and even make progress against the wind; and third, no seaman would sail with the wind on an exploratory voyage without being sure that he would have a fair wind to bring him back, either at a different time of year, or in an adjacent region. In AD 1492, Columbus used the easterly trade winds to cross the Atlantic confident that, further north, he would find westerlies for his return; Graeco-Roman seamen of the BC/AD period (and their Arab predecessors) used the westerlies to cross from Arabia to India, knowing that, later in the year, easterlies would bring them back (6.3). On the evidence of their achievements, the Polynesians and their predecessors must be considered self-confident, but not reckless, seamen, who would not unduly risk their lives.

This theory of the 'prudent Polynesian' has been

presented in some detail by Irwin (1990, 1992). He has formulated the proposition that, in the initial phase, Oceania was systematically explored in the direction which gave the best chance of survival, i.e. into the sector of the predominant wind but using non-predominant winds: should land not be sighted on an exploratory voyage, the predominant east-south-east wind could then be used for a relatively safe and speedy return home, probably with the wind on the quarter which usually results not only in maximum speed through the water but also in less violent boat motion than when the wind is dead astern. Irwin's proposition continues, that as experience was gained and sailing abilities improved, voyages were undertaken across wind to Micronesia and to Hawaii; and finally through regions of rotational wind systems associated with travelling depressions, out of the Tropics to New Zealand.

Irwin has investigated these hypotheses experimentally by using computer simulations of Oceanic voyages. 'Voyaging by computer' is a form of experimental archaeology in which thousands of voyages can be investigated, and reinvestigated using different parameters, rather than the handful of voyages that can be undertaken by actual boat reconstructions. Whether the results of such simulations are relevant to events in prehistoric Oceania depends on the appropriateness of the analytical techniques, on the authenticity of the data used, and on the validity of assumptions made about the ancient environment, the performance of the boats thought to have been used, and the navigational abilities of their crews (Coates et al., 1995).

Irwin's assumption that detailed meteorological and marine data collected during the recent past can be used to represent winds and currents in the later second millennium BC and the first millennium AD is not necessarily correct, but there is, as yet, no alternative (4.1). In such weather, Irwin's simulated boats leave the Solomons at the first signs of a fair wind and sail on predetermined headings within the sector from north through east to south-west. From east Melanesia similar voyages are subsequently made on headings within the sector from north-east through east to south—and so on across the Pacific. When the wind turns foul (i.e. returns to the predominant direction of east-south-east) the boats tack to the best of their ability aiming, at the least, to avoid being set westwards; they resume their easterly heading when the wind is again fair.

Two different strategies were programmed: (A) boats sailed until they sighted an island or exhausted their assumed supplies of fresh water; (B) they sailed until an island was sighted, or, after a set number of days, they turned for home with sufficient water for the return voyage. A general trend to emerge from these simulated exploratory voyages was that as they moved eastwards, strategy B (planned return) voyages became increasingly more successful at finding land than strategy A, due in part to sightings on return legs. As exploratory voyages moved further east where, in general, greater distances had to be covered, survival rates decreased; however, strategy B was invariably safer than A: in East Melanesia, 95–98 per cent compared with 70 per cent; in east Polynesia, 55–70 per cent compared with 25–45 per cent. The survival rates for strategy B were increased to 70–80 per cent when latitude sailing was allowed on the return leg, but whether early Polynesian seamen had this ability is debatable: the earliest known latitude sailing is in the tenth-century AD Indian Ocean where Arab seamen used a simple instrument known as a kamal to measure their latitude by the elevation of the Pole Star (3.8.2.2.3). Similarly, survival rates on voyages to the remote islands of Hawaii and Easter island were improved when it was assumed that explorers could return home via another island group which, in the prevailing conditions, was easier to reach than the home island, making the voyage into one with three legs—for this sort of voyaging, advanced geographical and navigational knowledge were required.

Some of the outcomes of these experiments challenged settlement theories based mainly on linguistic evidence, whilst others suggested that there could be gaps in the archaeological evidence. In general, however, the results of the thousands of voyages simulated supported the practicability of Irwin's hypotheses.

To understand how this Oceanic migration was undertaken, as well as to investigate the validity of some of Irwin's assumptions, it is necessary to examine the evidence not only for Polynesian navigational techniques, but also for the structure and performance of their vessels: the speeds they could achieve, their windward ability, and the crew and supplies they could carry are all important elements in such an enquiry.

## 9.2

# Evidence for Oceanic Water Transport

### 9.2.1 EXCAVATED EVIDENCE

Excavated nautical material is very rare in Oceania, there being only one group of finds of any importance. During excavations between 1973 and 1982 of water-logged deposits dated to the eighth/ninth centuries AD, at a coastal site near the town of Fare on Huahine, one of the leeward islands in the Society group, 100 nautical miles north-west of Tahiti, Dr Yoshihiko Sinoto of the B. P. Bishop Museum, Honolulu, uncovered wood-working tools, an unfinished steering paddle 3.6 m in length, a bailer, part of an outrigger boom, two log-boat fragments, pieces of sennit rope, and two adzed planks c.7 m in length (Sinoto, 1979, 1983, 1988; Bell-wood, 1987: 61–2). During subsequent excavations in 1980, a 12 m mast was uncovered. The two planks, of *Terminalia* sp., which were lifted for conservation in 1981, have an L-shaped cross section, lap joints at their ends, and holes for lashings through a face near one edge; they are thought to have been part of a paired (double hull) boat.

The only other known nautical artefacts excavated within Oceania are undated 'paddles and canoes' from Lake Horowhenua and Lake Mangakaware in New Zealand, a 0.76 m paddle from Ra'ivavae in the Austral islands (Bellwood, 1987: 90, 145), and a 'float from a small outrigger boat' from Monck's Cave, New Zealand (Haddon and Hornell, 1936: 199).

### 9.2.2 PETROGLYPHS

Many petroglyphs of nautical subjects exist in Oceania, but few have been published, and all are difficult to date. Three rock carvings on the island of Maui, in the Hawaiian group (D. Lewis, 1994: 65, 351, plate vi), depict the Tahitian 'half-claw' sail (Table 9.1, type 4) rather than the much more common Hawaiian 'claw' sail (Table 9.1, type 6): this suggests a voyage of a Tahitian boat to Hawaii at an unknown time in the past. A petroglyph in Kaingaroa shelter in central North Island, New Zealand, shows a boat with high ends, a project-ing forefoot and horizontal 'keel' and sheer lines (Scarre, 1989: 271): spiral decorations along the hull hide any other features. This depiction is thought to date to the period AD 1680–1780.

### 9.2.3 MUSEUM COLLECTIONS

In museums throughout the world there are innumerable models of Oceanic boats, many of unknown date and provenance, most of unknown scale and accuracy. There are also full-size boats, some made to order in recent times, but others are genuine work boats brought from Oceania by European navigators, some as early as the mid-eighteenth century. Hornell (1932, 1939) has described two boats from the latter group, and with Haddon in a monumental work on Oceanic craft (1936–8) he has published examples of nineteenth-century museum boats, as well as a wide range of twentieth-century boats still in use. Hornell (1932) believed that a small boat in the British Museum was the oldest complete Polynesian hull in existence; the oldest fragmentary hull being a logboat from South Island, now in the National Museum in Wellington, New Zealand. The British Museum boat (1771: 5–31.1) was obtained by Captain Wallace of HMS *Dolphin* from an atoll in the eastern Tuamotus in 1767. She measures 12 ft 9 in × 2 ft 3 in × 2 ft 1 in (3.90 × 0.69 × 0.63 m), and is a sewn-plank boat with a keel in three sections, and added ends carved from the solid. Her single outrigger has been lost. The other Oceanic boat was in the Cranmore Museum, Chislehurst, Kent when published by Hornell: its present whereabouts are unknown to the British Museum. This is a small, sewn-plank boat from Manihiki, Cook islands, measuring 5.64 × 0.36 × 0.354 m. It consists of four hollowed timbers which are butted and sewn together to form a log-boat base and to which a bow piece and washstrakes have been added. The boat also probably once had a single outrigger.

### 9.2.4 LINGUISTICS

Recent studies of the Austronesian group of languages, to which the Oceanic languages belong, have aimed at reconstructing the material culture vocabulary of proto-Austronesian (Bellwood, 1987: 27–30;

Lewis, 1994: 7). Amongst the words so reconstructed are those for 'sail', 'mast', 'outrigger', and 'outrigger boom'. Linguistic specialists claim that these words—and hence the artefacts they describe—are c.5,000 years old. It is doubtful whether accurate dating is possible by such methods; probably the most that can be said is that, at some early date—perhaps around 1500 BC when Austronesian people were probably established in the 'voyaging corridor' of island south-east Asia (9.1)—the ancestors of the Oceanic peoples had outrigger boats with mast and sail.

## 9.2.5 REPORTS BY EUROPEANS

European direct knowledge of the islands of Oceania began with Magellan and del Cano's circumnavigation voyage of 1520–2, during which they sailed through the northern Tuamotos (Disappointment island) and the northern Marianas (Ladrones). Other islands were 'discovered' by European navigators during the course of the next two centuries—for example, the Marquesas in 1595, New Zealand in 1642, and Easter island in 1722, and there are useful descriptions of the boats of the Marianas (Ladrones) observed by Pigafetta who sailed with Magellan in 1521, and by Dampier in 1686; of Marquesas boats by de Quiros in 1595; and of Tuamotu boats by Le Maire and Schoulten in 1616. The main thrust of European exploration came in the last forty years of the eighteenth century (Bellwood, 1987: 14–15): in this period, which was 'first contact' with Europeans for many islands, navigators such as Bougainville, La Perouse, de Surville, Cook, Wallis, and Bligh charted much of the Pacific and brought back accounts of traditional Polynesian societies and material culture. During the nineteenth century, life in most of the larger island groups was increasingly and irreversibly changed as European ideas, artefacts, technologies, and diseases were introduced by whalers, beachcombers, slavers, and missionaries.

Reports from the late eighteenth-century expeditions, by seamen who were familiar with boats and navigation, and by scientists who understood the importance of detailed recording, and illustrations by such artists as Sydney Parkinson, William Hodges, and James Webber who accompanied Cook, give as good an idea as it is now possible to have of the state of the boatbuilder's art and the seaman's craft in late prehistoric Oceania. The French hydrographer (and future Admiral), F.-E. Paris, who sailed with Captain J. S.-C. Dumont d'Urville onboard Astrolabe (1826–9) and with Captain C. Laplace in La Favorite (1829–32) and in L'Artemise (1837–40), published an incomparable collection of annotated illustrations of the water transport of Asia and the Americas, including many of Oceania (1843). Paris's recording was done at a time of increasing European cultural penetration of the south Pacific, nevertheless, comparison with Hodges' work in the late eighteenth century suggests that Oceanic boats had been only marginally affected by the early nineteenth.

There is a certain continuity between these eighteenth- and nineteenth-century reports on Oceanic boats and those by twentieth-century ethnographers such as Haddon and Hornell (1936–8). Although these later authors' reports are set within a context of emphasis on diffusion and on technological 'developments' over time, they do give detailed accounts and measured drawings of the boats then being used in Oceania, as well as summaries of earlier work by other researchers.

## 9.2.6 EXPERIMENTAL BOATS

Since 1935, a series of rafts and boats has been built with the aim of learning about aspects of Oceanic prehistory (Doran, 1981: 23–36; 63; Duncan, 1982). Such projects in experimental archaeology need to have clear aims and to use methods which are both logical and archaeologically / historically authentic, if the results in boat-building and in seafaring terms are to be relevant to maritime affairs in earlier times (Coates et al., 1995): such authenticity has seldom been demonstrable (McGrail, 1992b).

The double-hull / paired boat Hokule'a and the single outrigger boats Taratai 1 and 2 were built during 1975 to 1977 as 'replicas' of early Oceanic voyaging vessels. 'Hokule'a' is the Hawaiian name for Arcturus which is the zenith star for Hawaii, and the boat Hokule'a was built there by the Polynesian Voyaging Society (9.3.8). The aim of that society was to 'recreate' a twelfth-century AD east Polynesian voyaging boat (Finney et al., 1986; Finney, 1994: pp. xiii–xv) although there is, in fact, little evidence for such a vessel before the sixteenth century, apart from the eighth- ninth-century fragments from Huahine (9.2.1). Modern methods and materials were used to build a twin-hulled boat measuring 62 ft 4 in × 17 ft 6 in × 2 ft 6 in (draft) (19 × 5.33 × 0.76 m), based upon Tahitian/Tuamotan hull shapes as described in the eighteenth century, and on Hawaiian petroglyphs of 'crab-claw' sails (Doran, 1981; Stroup, 1985; Finney *et al.*, 1986). By their use of modern methods and materials, the Society implicitly decided not to investigate early boatbuilding methods and the structural aspects of performance. *Hokule'a* was steered by a central sweep and by quarter rudders. The two masts were stepped on the centreline of the 40 × 9 ft (12.19 × 2.74 m) platform which joined together the two hulls and which encompassed the living and working space for the twelve-man crew.

An unstated aim of the *Hokule'a* project must have been to learn something about the seafaring skills of earlier Oceanic communities. Learning to handle the gear and to operate the boat efficiently must have preceded the sailing trials; and learning to observe the night sky and comparable daytime phenomena must have preceded navigational trials.

The stated aims of the several voyages which were undertaken in *Hokule'a* were: (a) to establish the sailing ability of Oceanic double-hull boats; and (b) to investigate the feasibility of traditional navigation methods over long distances (Finney *et al.*, 1986). In so far as *Hokule'a* was representative of eighteenth-century Polynesian voyaging boats—and this seems difficult to establish—the first of these aims was evidently achieved in a variety of environmental conditions; her performance is discussed further below (9.3.8). The navigational aims of the project could, in general, have been achieved regardless of the vessel used—as David Lewis had demonstrated in the late 1960s (D. Lewis, 1970, 1994). However, navigational problems and solutions are, to a certain degree, influenced by the performance of the vessel—how close to the wind she can sail and so on. Furthermore, one of the greatest difficulties in experimental archaeology is to replicate the attitude of mind of early seamen and to replicate the natural interaction of man, boat, and environment. If these circumstances can be reproduced, the experimental results are much more likely to be relevant to earlier times (McGrail, 1975). To the extent that *Hokule'a* was an authentic reconstruction of an eighteenth-century vessel, the navigational trials were thus of more value to historical studies than if undertaken in a twentieth-century vessel.

The navigational results of these voyages are, in fact, only applicable to voyages undertaken *after* islands had been discovered (9.5.3). It would be much more difficult, if not impossible, to 're-enact' an exploratory voyage on which nothing was known (a) of what lay ahead, except the general direction of land possibly from the flight line of migrating birds (9.5.2); and (b) of the environmental conditions which would be experienced, except by weather forecasts based on recent experience and by extrapolation of the present night sky to foretell the future pattern of stars.

# 9.3
# Water Transport

From the range of evidence discussed above, descriptions of Oceanic floats, rafts, and boats can be compiled. Generally speaking, these descriptions apply to craft of the seventeenth century or later.

## 9.3.1 FLOATS

Broad flat planks hewn from hardwood *koa (Acaria heterophylla)* were used to ride the surf off Hawaii in the nineteenth century. These surf boards were also used off Easter island, as an aid to swimming, as were 'rush mats' (Hornell, 1946: 4).

## 9.3.2 BUNDLE RAFTS

Heyerdahl (1972: 20) has noted an Easter island tradition that bundle rafts were formerly used there, otherwise their only known use is in New Zealand and Fiji (Best, 1925: 140, fig. 100; Hornell, 1946a: 40, 78–9). Maoris paddled or poled temporary rafts across rivers. These were made from bound bundles of bulrushes (*raupo*; *Typha augustifolia*) or flax (*Phormium tenax*), and they ranged in size from one-man, sit-astride rafts to boat-shaped ones of five bundles. In Fiji, two great bundles of bamboos were lashed together, like the two hulls of a paired boat.

### 9.3.3 BUOYED RAFTS

In the Chatham Islands, south-east of New Zealand, in the late nineteenth century, boat-shaped wooden rafts (Fig. 9.3) were given extra buoyancy by packing dry fern stems and rolls of flax stalks against the bottom and sides (Hornell, 1946: 38–9). Larger sizes of raft also had inflated bladders of bull kelp (*rimu*) and with these they could be used for inter-island voyages of up to 12 nautical miles (Haddon and Hornell, 1936: 219, fig. 148). These seem to be the only example of buoyed rafts in Oceania.

### 9.3.4 LOG RAFTS

Early Europeans in Oceania noted log rafts in several places: in 1595, de Quiros (Mendana's pilot) saw them in the coastal waters of the Marquesas; Cook saw them in New Zealand in 1773; and Beachey saw seagoing ones off Mangareva in 1825 (Hornell, 1946a: 77–9; Best, 1925: 137). In addition to these sites, the twentieth-century distribution (Haddon and Hornell, 1938: 13–14; Hornell, 1946a: 71–9, plates 8b, 9; E. Doran, 1981: fig. 37) includes the Society islands, Tonga, Fiji, several islands in eastern Melanesia and occasionally in Micronesia.

These rafts were generally made from softwood logs, but in the western parts of the area, bamboo was used. They varied in shape and in structure with no obvious regional patterns: there may be functional or environmental reasons for these differences, but the available information is not sufficient for this to be decided. Some were given tapering ends using the natural taper of the logs and by positioning longer logs centrally—Fiji and Marquesas; others were rectangular—New Hebrides / Vanuatu. In some rafts the logs were lashed directly together—New Hebrides, New Ireland; others were lashed to transverse timbers—Mangareva; others again had their logs through-pinned or skewered by hardwood timbers—Marquesas.

Rafts seen by Paris (1843: pl. 114) in Santa Cruz were unusual in having an outrigger. In nineteenth-century New Zealand (Best, 1925: 136, fig. 97), rafts were made of two sets of two-tiered logs, each layer pinned together and the two layers lashed together, and connected by three transverse poles so that they were three to five feet (0.9–1.5 m) apart. The single crew manned the larger set, the smaller acting as a sort of outrigger float. These rafts were used for coastal fishing, and occasionally small domestic animals were carried.

All log rafts were paddled and, inshore, poled, but those of Mangareva, Tonga, and Yap also had sails; uniquely, some in the Society islands are said to have been towed by kites (E. Doran, 1981; Hornell, 1946a: 71–8). Steering was by pole, paddle, or steering-oar; wooden foils (*guares*) do not appear to have been used in Oceania for steering or for sail balance (9.3.7.3). The smaller rafts were used for fishing and as ferries on

Fig. 9.3. A boat-shaped buoyed raft from the Chatham Islands (Canterbury Museum, Christchurch, New Zealand).

Fig. 9.4. A sailing log raft from Mangareva, seen by Beechey in 1826 (National Maritime Museum, Greenwich).

rivers and in coastal waters. There were also seagoing rafts such as those of Mangareva in the Gambier islands seen by Beechey in 1826 (Fig. 9.4). These were sailing rafts 40–50 ft (12.19–15.24 m) long which carried twenty or so fighting men on voyages of over 25 nautical miles (Hornell, 1946a: 77). In Micronesia and Polynesia, especially Tonga, Samoa, Society, the Marquesas, and New Zealand, rafts were used to transport large blocks of stone and coral. Limestone discs, 1–12 ft (0.31–3.66 m) in diameter and used as currency on Yap were quarried some 350 nautical miles away in Babelthuap island, Palau, Micronesia: these could more readily have been moved on rafts than in a boat (Haddon and Hornell, 1938: 13-14).

## 9.3.5 LOGBOATS

Simple, unextended logboats are scarcely mentioned in 'first contact' and ethnographic accounts of Oceania; this may be because early observers were biased towards the more complex water transport. They are, however, known to have been used recently in New Zealand, Hawaii, and the Society islands. These were generally small boats with a crew of two to six men, used for fishing close inshore (Haddon and Hornell, 1936: 105). When this distribution is considered in conjunction with the fact that many Polynesian plank boats are logboat-based (9.3.6), it seems likely that logboats were once widely used in Oceania on those islands that had either suitable trees or driftwood logs. Best (1925: 5, 6, 22) stated that the simple logboats (*waka tiwa*) of New Zealand were much used in calm waters, 'in former times'. Hornell (1948: 47) has described logboat building in the Society Islands in some detail. The tree was felled and worked generally to a logboat shape, using stone tools and fire. After being soaked in fresh water for some days, the boat was given a final shaping, transverse timbers were inserted between the sides to prevent deformation, and the hull was smoothed with coral. The *tohuna* (master boatwright?) was in charge of all operations; he was the one who drew the outline of the intended boat upon the log in charcoal—to this extent he 'designed' the boat. In

Hawaii, the *kahuna* had a similar role; he also had a priestly function for, as occurred widely in Oceania, each stage of boatbuilding was begun and concluded by a ritual (Willis, 1922: 69).

### 9.3.6 PLANK BOATS

Europeans found three main types of planked boat in Oceania: the single boat; the boat with one outrigger; and the double-hulled or paired boat. These types were strikingly different from one another and within each type there were distinctive variants. However, these boats also had characteristics in common: for example, they were all built shell-first, the planks being sewn together and the framing lashed to the planking; the hulls were, in general terms, very similar in structure and in shape (the underwater lines of a Tongan *tomgiakia* and a Tahitian *pahi* recorded by James Cook were 'identical'—D. Lewis, 1994: 313); and the sails, although in detail different, were mainly variations on the triangular sail with its apex down (9.3.7.2).

The underwater parts of Oceanic boats were generally double-ended in shape, but above the waterline some were unequal-ended. Where large trees grew or became available as driftwood, the lowest element in a boat was a hollowed log (sometimes in two or more sections)—in other words, the hull was logboat-based. It is difficult to draw a line between a plank boat with a logboat base, and a logboat extended by the addition of several washstrakes. However, as in many, if not most Oceanic logboat-based hulls, the 'logboat' is in several sections, they are probably best thought of as plank boats with a logboat base. On islands not so well endowed with timber, boats had a conventional keel (again, sometimes in more than one piece) and were entirely planked. Where quality timber was especially in short supply, boats had many short and narrow planks: for example Easter island boats had planks which were only 2–3 ft (0.61–0.91 m) long and 4–5 in (0.10–0.13 m) wide.

Where a curved cross-section was required, planks were hollowed. Strakes were set edge-to-edge or with a protruding lap joint; planks within strakes were butted together. Strakes and scarfs were sewn, sometimes through holes in the planking, sometimes through projections from the planking, using, for example, three-ply sennit (coconut fibre) over a caulk-ing of green coconut husk mixed with sticky breadfruit gum which was held in place by a longitudinal lath or batten (Fig. 9.5). These fastenings had to be replaced after three months of seafaring or after two or three years if the boat was rarely used. Paris noted that the planking of Tuamotu boats in the early nineteenth century was held in position by wooden pegs before it was sewn (Haddon and Hornell, 1936: 83). This is similar to the methods used in Egypt (2.7.1, 2.8.3.2), in the Mediterranean (4.9.4), and in south-east Asia (8.3.5.1). It is not clear whether this technique was widely used in Oceania.

The framing timbers, which supported not only the planking but also the outrigger booms in those boats so fitted, and the transverse timbers which linked the two hulls in paired boats, were sometimes lashed to cleats proud of the planking and sometimes lashed direct to the planking. Where height at the ends was insufficient, bow and stern pieces hewn out of the solid were lashed in position (Best, 1925: 36–119, 217, 228; Haddon and Hornell, 1936–8; Greenhill, 1976: 27–8; P. Johnstone, 1988: 203–10; E. Doran, 1981: 61–2; D. Lewis, 1994: 53–9, 78–9).

The tools used for boatbuilding were essentially

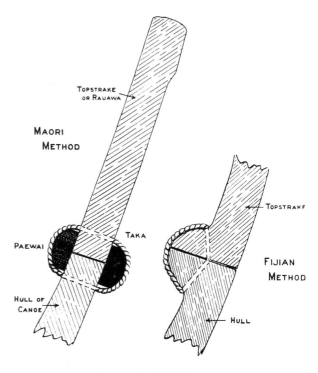

Fig. 9.5. Maori and Fiji methods of fastening a strake to a logboat hull (after Best, 1925: 84).

Fig. 9.6. Maori method of tightening sewn fastenings (after Best, 1925: 79).

Neolithic in character. Their precise nature and use varied regionally according to the raw mateials available; nevertheless, some general points can be made (Best, 1925: 50, 55, 79; Lewis, 1932: 146; Hornell, 1948: 46; Greenhill, 1976: 27–8; P. Johnstone, 1988: 206–9). Trees

were felled with stone axes and by controlled use of fire. In New Zealand, the Maori used ballista-powered or swing battering-ram devices to fell tough pines such as the *totara* and the *kauri*. Stone tools were mostly used, but axes, adzes, and blades were also made from the shells of sea snails and giant clams. Wallis has described how, in the Society Islands in 1767, one end of a log was heated until it began to crack; wedges were then used to split off planks (Haddon and Hornell, 1936: 105). Sharpened bones (sometimes human) set into a wooden handle were used as gouges and struck by a hard blackwood mallet to produce fastening holes. A special forked wooden lever (Fig. 9.6) was used to tighten stitches before they were wedged within these holes. Hulls were smoothed with the skin of a ray, and sometimes 'polished' with sandstone. Europeans frequently commented on the high standards of Oceanic boatbuilders and how effectively they used these 'primitive' tools. One major difference noted between these

Fig. 9.7. A twentieth-century reconstruction of a small Maori war boat (photo: *New Zealand Herald*, Auckland).

tools of stone, shell, and bone and European tools of iron, was that the Oceanic tools needed to be sharpened more frequently.

The Maori, who had the largest logs to contend with, had evolved ingenious methods of moving them safely from felling place to building site, using only rollers, skids, ropes, levers, wedges, handspikes, and parbuckles. The haulage ropes were five-stranded, made from the dried leaves of *ti torere* (*Cordyline banksii*) or *ti kauka* (*Cordyline australis*).

### 9.3.6.1 SINGLE-HULL BOATS

Europeans found single boats without outriggers in New Zealand, Tonga, Tuamotu, and the Austral and Society islands (Best, 1925: 5–6, 10, 23, 35, 190, 257–8; Hornell, 1946a: 209; Bellwood, 1987: fig. 12). These sewn-plank boats on a logboat base were of three different types, each with its own function. Simple small boats (*waka tete*) were used for coastal fishing in New Zealand. Much larger and more complex war boats were also used there; although not as stable as an equivalent paired/double-hull boat, they had reasonable stability because the large trees still available meant that a broad boat could be built. They are generally depicted propelled by paddles, but one seen on Cook's first voyage was under sail in a following wind (Rienits and Rienits, 1968: 43); and another depicted by Best (1925) was propelled by paddle and sail. These boats had a carved figure at the bow, and a prominent near-vertical stern (Fig. 9.7).

The third type of single-hull boat was not logboat-based but fully planked; it therefore could be built with the beam and hence stability appropriate to Ocean voyages. A late nineteenth century example of this type of 'voyaging canoe' has been published by Haddon and Hornell (1936: 76–8). These Tuamotuan boats (Fig. 9.8) (*c.*28 × 7 × 3.5 ft (8.53 × 2.13 × 1.07 m)) were propelled by sail on a mast stepped well forward, and steered by a steering oar over the stern.

### 9.3.6.2 DOUBLE-HULL/PAIRED BOATS

Paired boats were seen in many parts of Oceania by the first Europeans (Best, 1925): in eastern Melanesia—Santa Cruz (1595), New Caledonia (1773), and Fiji (1827); in the Carolines, Micronesia (1830); and in Polynesia—Tuamotu (1616), New Zealand (1642), Tonga (1643),

Tahiti (1769), Society (1770), Hawaii (1777), Cook (1777), Samoa, (1786), and Austral (1791). In certain places, there were great fleets of them, sometimes assembled as a display of power and prestige, at other times as a prelude to the invasion of another island. On Cook's first voyage, Banks saw 'some hundreds' near East Cape, New Zealand in 1769; at Tahiti in 1774, during Cook's second voyage, Forster counted 159 paired 'war canoes', 50–90 ft (15.2–27.4 m) long, with crews of 50–120 men, and also 70 smaller boats most of them also paired (Best, 1925: 23, 222–3; Haddon and Hornell, 1938: 43).

In these boats, two hulls were connected laterally some 2–8 ft (0.61–2.44 m) apart by transverse planks, beams or poles which were lashed to each hull. A platform was built on top of these and a matting shed was sometimes built there. Hatches in the platform gave

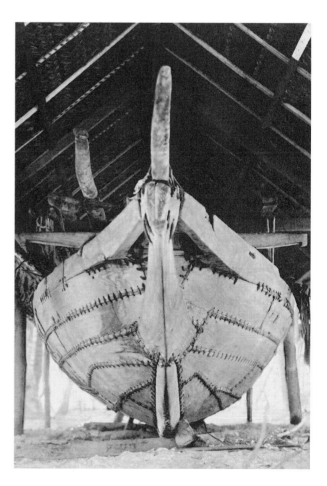

Fig. 9.8. A nineteenth-century Tuamotuan sewn-plank boat with a keel (Haddon and Hornell, 1936: 76–8).

Fig. 9.9. A double-hull boat seen off Tonga in 1616 (Haddon and Hornell, 1936: fig. 189).

access to the bilges for bailing. By this pairing of two hulls, each one of 2–3 ft (0.61–0.91 m) waterline beam, the boat's effective beam became 12 and more feet (3.66 m) (Haddon and Hornell, 1936: 19, 129). This not only increased stability, but also provided space for people and goods, and a wider base for rigging. Cook measured an average sort of boat which was 70 × 12 × 3.5 ft (21 × 3.7 × 1.1 m), whilst the average of measurements given by Admiral Paris is 14.5 × 2.01 × 0.98 m (Haddon and Hornell, 1936: 19). Such boats were generally permanent pairs, but temporary pairing of two similar single boats was known in the Society islands and in New Zealand (Haddon and Hornell, 1938: 41–2).

The earliest descriptions of paired boats come from the late sixteenth/early seventeenth centuries: an account of a Santa Cruz boat by Mendana in 1595; and a 1616 account by LeMaire and Schouten of a boat off Tonga (Johnstone, 1988: 204–5). A drawing from the latter expedition (Fig. 9.9) seems to show that the two hulls were similar in shape and size. This is confirmed by Tasman's drawing of another Tongan boat in 1643 (Haddon and Hornell, 1936: fig. 190; D. Lewis, 1994: plate V) and by Cook's 1777 measured drawing (D. Lewis, 1994: fig. 2; Haddon and Hornell, 1936: fig. 191).

Equal- or near-equal-hulled, paired boats were also seen in New Zealand in 1642 by Tasman (Haddon and Hornell, 1936: fig. 130); Hawaii in 1778–9 on Cook's third voyage (Haddon and Hornell, 1936: figs. 1 and 2); and in Tahiti on Cook's first (1769) and third voyages (Haddon and Hornell, 1936: 79, 131, fig. 87; Durrans, 1979: fig. 78).

Other paired boats had hulls of unequal length: differences of up to 20 per cent were noted in New Zealand and in Fiji and nearby islands (Best, 1925: 13, 203, 205, 241; Haddon and Hornell, 1938: 42). Banks, on Cook's first voyage, described the *pahee* of Raiatea in the Society Islands with one hull of 51 ft (15.55 m) and the other of 31 ft (9.45 m), a reduction of 35 per cent

(Greenhill, 1976: 27–8). The drawing by Parkinson of a similar boat also seen on the same voyage (Bellwood, 1987: fig. 13), shows the boat at an angle but the further hull does seem to be shorter. Paris's drawing of a Tongan paired boat with a midship mast shows hulls of significantly different sizes (F. Paris, 1843: plan 121; Rieth, 1993: 120–1, 162); and in the mid-nineteenth century, Thomas Williams drew a Fijian *ndrua* with unequal hulls (Durrans, 1979: fig. 80; D. Lewis, 1994: fig. 3).

Haddon and Hornell (1938: 41–2) identified two types of Oceanic paired boats from the data they collected:

A. With (near) equal length hulls and the mast stepped forward of amidships so that the boat had a definite bow and stern and therefore was tacked through the wind. These boats generally appear double-ended, but when precisely measured, as in Paris's measured drawing of an Hawaiian boat (Rieth, 1993: 166), they prove to be slightly fuller towards the stern.

B. Double-ended boats with hulls of unequal length, and the mast stepped amidships so that the boat can sail either way: such a vessel 'shunts' when changing tacks (9.3.6.3).

Of the boats described above, those from nineteenth- to twentieth-century Fiji are Haddon and Hornell type B. The boats from eighteenth-century Tahiti are type A with the mast set in the starboard hull; that from eighteenth-century Hawaii is type A with the mast in the port hull. The seventeenth-century New Zealand boat is type A but without a mast. Haddon and Hornell (1938: 41) state that type A boats were also used in Manihiki, Marquesas, Cook, and New Zealand. Tongan boats of the seventeenth/eighteenth centuries were type A, whilst some of those seen there by Cook in 1773–4 were type B (Haddon and Hornell, 1936: 265, 271–2). Paris evidently saw only type B.

Cook also saw both types in Samoa in 1768 (Haddon and Hornell, 1936: 241). Both also seem to have been in use in Tokelau, Ellice, and New Zealand (Haddon and Hornell, 1938: 41; Best, 1925). As by the nineteenth century, only type B boats were used in these islands, Haddon and Hornell (1938: 41–2) believe that type A was older and was replaced in certain islands from the late eighteenth century by type B which they think originated in Fiji.

On the evidence considered, it appears that the earliest known Oceanic paired boats had equal hulls with a single mast stepped forward, either on the starboard hull or, in Hawaii, between the hulls. This type of boat was seen in the mid-seventeenth century in New Zealand, but without a mast, and it was possibly seen in eastern Melanesia (Santa Cruz) in the late sixteenth century. It was certainly seen in seventeenth-/eighteenth-century Polynesia—in the west (Tonga), north (Hawaii), east (Tahiti), and south (New Zealand). Boats with *unequal* hulls and masts stepped amidships, or with two masts, were seen from the late eighteenth century onwards in the east Melanesia/west Polynesia region (Fiji, Tonga, Samoa), in central Polynesia (Society), and in south Polynesia (New Zealand).

### 9.3.6.3 BOATS WITH OUTRIGGERS

Boats with *two* outriggers have been used in western Melanesia and in Indonesia from at least the eighth century AD (8.3.7.2, 8.3.8). There are legends of their former use in New Zealand, and ambiguous reports suggesting that they have been used in the recent past in Oceania: Carolines and Palau in Micronesia; Samoa, Marquesas, Easter, and New Zealand in Polynesia (Best, 1925: 17, 201, 260). Haddon and Hornell (1936: 197–8; 1938: 15–16) considered this evidence and decided that early use was unlikely: moreover, double outriggers do not seem to have been used at any time in eastern Melanesia (Doran, 1981: fig. 42). Certainly it was the boat with the *single* outrigger that featured largely in early European reports from these regions.

In shape and in structure, the hulls of single outrigger boats are similar to those of paired boats (9.3.6.2). They are generally very narrow in relation to both length and depth—typical dimensions are: $c.11.5 \times 0.8 \times 1.10$ m. Such long, narrow and light boats (L/B = 14 : 1; L/D = 10.5 : 1) have high speed potential. In conventional boats, such an advantage is accompanied by limited transverse stability, but in the single outrigger boat adequate seagoing stability is achieved with only a slight increase in resistance to motion. The outrigger float, which may be a simple cylinder of wood or something of much more complex shape, is held out from the side of the boat at a distance equivalent to $c.1/3$ of the boat's length, by booms fastened to the hull's framing. These booms and their connectives are fashioned so that, under normal upright conditions, the float is close to the water where it acts to stabilize the boat transversely. Outrigger assemblages can vary in innumerable ways—they have been studied in some detail by Haddon and Hornell (1936–8).

Some Oceanic boats with single outriggers were double-ended, either end being usable as the bow. Others had a definite bow and stern and could be used only in one direction, with the outrigger usually to port. The dissimilar-ended boats invariably had their mast stepped towards the bow; double-ended boats had their mast either towards the bow or amidships, in all cases the aim being to achieve sail balance. The mast step position determined how the boat was handled when changing direction relative to the wind. A boat with the mast forward, was tacked: i.e. the bow was steered through the wind so that the wind now blew from the other side. The outrigger was first on the windward and then on the lee side of the boat. On the other hand, a boat with the mast amidships, was 'shunted': i.e. the bow became the stern by moving the rudder from end to end, and adjusting the mast and sail (still stepped amidships) to suit the new configuration. The new bow was then brought nearer the wind on the new tack. On old and new headings during such a shunting manoeuvre, the outrigger was always on the windward side of the boat. Paired boats with a mast amidships were also shunted (9.3.6.2).

With the outrigger to windward, the aim was to keep the float just skimming the water so that the turning moment due to its weight tended to oppose the heel due to the wind, and thus the boat was kept (near) upright. If this was insufficient, the righting moment could be increased by moving some of the crew (or cargo?) onto the outrigger booms or onto a platform on those booms. With the outrigger to leeward (as in the single outrigger boat with the mast forward), the aim was to keep the float just submerged so that its buoyancy acted to oppose the wind-induced heel.

Some boats with dissimilar ends had balance boards which jutted out from the boat on the side opposite the outrigger: when the float was to leeward, the boat could be brought nearer upright by stationing crew on this board. Greenhill (1971: 124, 157) has published a photograph of a Pakistan *ekdar hora* with an outrigger to leeward, counterbalanced by the crew on temporary balance boards, a condition in which she can be sailed closer to the wind than with the float to windward. The use of temporary balance boards or spars may have gone unrecorded in Oceania, but some of the

boats with masts amidships are known to have had a permanent board—a lee platform—fitted on the side opposite the outrigger. Haddon and Hornell (1936: 376) consider that this platform acted as 'a counterpoise to the outrigger frame'—which seems to imply that in no-wind conditions, such a boat would need a lee platform to stay upright. With the float to windward—as it generally is in these boats—this lee board could be used as a balance board only if 'fine tuning' were required to keep the float skimming, rather than in, the water.

Illustrations so far traced of Oceanic outrigger boats with their mast amidships show the outrigger to windward, with three exceptions. An early seventeenth-century drawing published by de Bry (1619: plate xv) of Dutch ships and local boats off the Marianas depicts several boats, under oars and under sail, with the outrigger to leeward—this may be an artist's mistake for, as Haddon and Hornell make clear (1938: 180), some artists of this period copied drawings they did not understand, whilst others worked up their illustrations at home. The second depiction is by Paris: the boat on the right of this illustration (Fig. 9.10), which has a list to starboard (outrigger side), clearly has its outrigger to leeward with the float submerged; three of the crew are on the lee platform which is to *windward*, presumably using their weight to correct the list. F. Paris (1843: 97–101) states that the boat had been taken aback and begun to capsize, and he has depicted her almost recovered from this incident and back on course. It thus seems that the crew of this vessel had, for some reason, chosen to sail with the outrigger to leeward, in a condition in which the weight of the outrigger has a destabilizing affect and the float has to be submerged to produce compensatory buoyancy. The third depiction of a leeward outrigger is on a small Tongan boat with her mast amidships drawn by Webber (Haddon and Hornell, 1936: 271, fig. 193).

The advantage of sailing in this state rather than 'shunting' to keep the outrigger to windward, which is inherently more stable, may be that it is possible to get closer to the wind (Greenhill, 1971: 124, 157); such tactics can, however, lead to being taken aback. Dampier stated that the boats he saw in Guam in 1686 had their outriggers to leeward, but this is usually interpreted as a mistake in his memory (Haddon and Hornell, 1936: 417; Shell, 1986). Nevertheless, it may be that some Micronesian single outrigger boats with mast amid-

Fig. 9.10. Single outrigger craft with balance boards in the Caroline Islands (Paris, 1843: plate 107).

ships were occasionally tacked, instead of the normal 'shunting', thus bringing the float to leeward on alternate legs. The advantages must have outweighed the obvious disadvantages of being less stable and with a potentially dangerous tendency to turn to leeward (Doran, 1981: 70, fig. 35).

The outrigger assemblage imposes asymmetric drag on the hull, more so when the float is immersed. To counteract this, a boat's quarter rudder was usually on the side opposite to the float. When such a boat was paddled—with or without sail—the effort was concentrated on that side. A more radical approach was taken in Micronesia (9.3.6.3.2) where certain boats had an asymmetric transverse section, being rounded on the outrigger side and near-vertical on the other (Goddard, 1985); such a section not only tends to compensate for the effects of the outrigger, but also reduces leeway.

### 9.3.6.3.1 Eastern Melanesia

Cook noted, on his first visit to Tanna in the New Hebrides in 1774, that all the boats had outriggers and some had sails (Haddon and Hornell, 1937: 14–15). A double-ended boat from Vanikoro, in the Santa Cruz islands, drawn by Admiral Paris (1843: plate 114; Rieth, 1993: 119, 160), is the earliest detailed evidence for an eastern Melanesian single outrigger boat. This vessel has a mast amidships, an outrigger to windward and a lee platform on the opposite side. An early twentieth-century boat from nearby also had these characteristics (Haddon and Hornell, 1937: 48, fig. 31). On the other hand, a modern boat from Fiji (Haddon and Hornell, 1936: 311, fig. 228), which was otherwise similar, had no lee platform. This latter type of boat was said by Haddon and Hornell (1936: 307) to be equal to the 'flying proa' of Micronesia (9.3.6.3.2) in excellence of design. Most of the other east Melanesian single outrigger boats illustrated or described by Haddon and Hornell (1936–7) have no mast.

From the very limited range of evidence available, it seems that the earliest known single outrigger boat in the Santa Cruz group was double-ended and had her mast amidships; she could thus be shunted. Her lee platform could have been used for fine adjustment of transverse trim—as one of the crew appears to be doing in Paris's illustration.

### 9.3.6.3.2 *Micronesia*

Single outrigger boats were seen in the Marianas in 1521 during Magellan's circumnavigation voyage (Fig. 9.11). These were double-ended with a steering paddle available at each end, and the mast was amidships. Magellan's chronicler Pigafetta, specifically noted that either end could be used as the bow. He also noted that they had an asymmetric cross-section and he commented favourably on their 'great swiftness'. The high speed of these Micronesian boats was invariably noted by subsequent Europeans and the boats came to be known as 'flying proas'. Similar boats were seen by Cavendish in 1588, Dampier in 1686, and Anson in 1742 (Haddon and Hornell, 1936: 413–17, fig. 300). By the early nineteenth

century, Carolines boats of this type had been fitted with a lee platform (Fig. 9.10) which nineteenth-century boats of the Marshalls also had (Haddon and Hornell, 1936: 362, 370, figs. 259; 266; D. Lewis, 1994: 60, fig. 4). These platforms were used to give a better lead to rigging, and, in Paris's drawing (Fig. 9.10), as a base for a small cabin for the crew or for the carriage of a small boat; a corresponding hut on the inboard end of the outrigger booms contained the boat's equipment. Paris also shows one of the five-man crew standing on the lee platform where his weight keeps the float on the opposite side just clear of the water.

This evidence suggests that, as in eastern Melanesia, the earliest outrigger boats known in Micronesia were sailed with their floats to windward. With an asymmetric transverse section and other fine points, this variant of the single outrigger design had a well-earned reputation for speed. By the early nineteenth century,

Fig. 9.11. A single outrigger-boat encountered by Magellan in the Marianas in 1521 (copyright, Bibliothèque nationale de France, 716 Fr. 24224. f. 20v).

lee platforms had been fitted to some Micronesian boats, which not only gave a better rigging lead and facilitated fine trimming of the height of the float above the sea, but also allowed the boat, like its unequal-ended cousin in Polynesia (9.3.6.3.3) to be tacked, with the lee platform used as a balance board when the float was to leeward. It is possible that this use of a more weatherly, if more risky tactic, began in the eighteenth century: with some boats tacking and some shunting.

### 9.3.6.3.3 Polynesia

During Mendana's visit to the Marquesas islands in 1595, de Quiros noted outrigger boats used in warfare and for fishing, the larger ones held thirty to forty paddlers. There is no mention of sail in this account, but Hodges drew a Marquesan boat with sail in 1774, during Cook's second voyage (Haddon and Hornell, 1936: 31, 35, fig. 21a). This boat had a definite bow, the outrigger is shown to port (i.e. into wind), and the mast was stepped forward of amidships. The outrigger structure appears to project also to leeward (starboard) where it could be used as a balance board.

De Quiros briefly mentioned boats seen in 1606 in the Tuamotu archipelago, but gave no details. Forster noted that boats seen there in 1772–5 were short, double-ended and built of planks on a keel; such a boat was brought by Captain Wallace in 1767 to the British Museum (9.2.3)—she probably once had an outrigger (Haddon and Hornell, 1936: 51, figs. 45–6).

The boat seen by Tasman in Tonga in 1643 (Haddon and Hornell, 1936: 261–2, fig. 187; Durrans, 1979: fig. 81) was double-ended but with the mast forward. The outrigger is depicted to windward (port). A platform with a hatchway, built on the inboard ends of the booms, projects out to starboard where it could be used to trim the boat. Cook, in 1773, confirmed much of this and added that hulls measured 20–30 ft × 20–22 in (6.1–9.1 × 0.51–0.56 m). In 1777, on Cook's third voyage, Weber drew a small outrigger boat with her sail partly furled (Haddon and Hornell, 1936: 271, fig. 193). This boat is double-ended with a canted mast amidships, but this time the outrigger is depicted to leeward (port). To windward there is a balance spar. Three crew are paddling, two to starboard, and two are seated on a platform on the outrigger booms. Paris's drawing and measured drawing of a Tongan boat (Rieth, 1993:

120–1, 161–2; Haddon and Hornell, 1936: 263, fig. 188) show that by the early nineteenth century, the mast was amidships. The platform, now with two hatches, still protrudes slightly from the non-outrigger side and could therefore have been used to trim the boat should she have been sailed with the outrigger to leeward.

Roggeveen noted a few 'poor and flimsy' boats when he visited Easter island in 1722. He did not mention outriggers, but subsequent Europeans, from 1770 onwards, described them (Haddon and Hornell, 1936: 96–9).

Wallis was the first to mention the single outrigger boats of Tahiti (Haddon and Hornell, 1936: 105). He gave no details except that the mast was 'in the middle'. As he was contrasting this mast with the two masts set up between the hulls of paired boats, it seems likely that the mast of outrigger boats was transversely in the middle of the hull, but (in the light of subsequent reports), longitudinally, forward of amidships. This Tahiti boat was first illustrated soon afterwards, during Bougainville's voyage (Haddon and Hornell, 1936: 115, fig. 77). In this drawing, the mast takes against the fore boom and is thus forward of amidships in this unequal-ended boat. On the starboard side, opposite the outrigger, which is shown to windward, there is an angled balance board. Bougainville clearly explains its twofold use: for shrouds, and to make the boat 'more stable by placing a man at the end of the plank'. Tobin, on Bligh's second voyage in 1792, drew a boat with similar features except that the balance board was abaft the fore boom, near the foot of the mast, and extended beyond the hull on both sides, a feature which Varela had already observed in 1772–6 (Haddon and Hornell, 1936: 114–15, 118–19, fig. 80). Ellis, who was a surgeon on Cook's third voyage (1776–80), stated that this board extended from the outrigger across the hull to project 5 or 6 feet (1.5 or 1.8 m) beyond the opposite side. In 1827, Paris made a measured drawing of a two-masted, unequal-ended boat with an outrigger to port (Haddon and Hornell, 1936: 117–19, figs. 78, 79; Rieth, 1993: 163). This boat had two balance boards, one forward of the mainmast, which was near amidships, and one abaft the foremast.

In 1777, Cook noted outrigger boats in Hawaii with a mast stepped upon the inboard part of the fore boom. Paris described similar boats in 1839 but by then they had been fitted with a European spritsail (Haddon and Hornell, 1936: 25; Rieth, 1993: 166, plan 127). Paris's drawing shows this near-double-ended boat with mast well forward and outrigger to port. These boats were tacked but there is no sign of a balance board to be used when the float was to leeward. The foreboom, however, projects to starboard and it may have been possible to use this.

An early nineteenth-century drawing by Turner (Haddon and Hornell, 1936: 228, fig. 156) shows a Samoan unequal-ended boat with a vertical mast amidships and the outrigger to windward (port); this would have been tacked. Outrigger boats were also noted by Cook in 1769 in New Zealand; where they were 'not common'. In Tubuai in the Australs, Cook, on his third voyage, noted that outrigger boats were not double-ended. In both cases, it seems that these boats did not have a mast (Haddon and Hornell, 1936: 151, 199).

On the assumption that the evidence for sailing outrigger boats reviewed above is representative of Polynesia over time and space, two groups can be identified:

(a) *Western*: In Tonga, from 1643 to 1777, boats were double-ended, the mast was forward, and the float was to port. Although the ends were similarly shaped, these boats had a definite bow as the mast was stepped towards one end. When on the starboard tack, it may have been possible to balance the boat from the windward side (starboard) of the platform which projected somewhat from the hull. Alternatively, temporary boards may have been used: see, for example, the small boat drawn by Webber (Haddon and Hornell, 1936: 271, fig. 193) with a balancing spar and other structure out to starboard. Early nineteenth-century double-ended Tongan boats with a canted mast amidships would have been shunted with the float always to windward. However, they could also have been tacked using the windward side of the platform (or temporary arrangements) to balance the boat when the outrigger was to leeward.

In Samoa, in the early nineteenth century, boats also had their mast amidships. These boats must have been tacked because they were not only unequal-ended, but also had masts which were stepped vertically. The balancing arrangements when the float was to leeward are not clear.

(b) *Central, eastern, and northern*: In Tahiti, from 1768 to 1827, boats were unequal-ended, their mast was forward, and the outrigger was always to port. They were

tacked, and when on a starboard tack, the fitted balance board was used to trim the vessel. By 1827, a two-masted rig had been evolved; apart from that, boats retained earlier characteristics.

Single outrigger boats were seen in the Marquesas in 1595, but details were not noted. In 1774, it was known that they were, like the Tahitian boats, unequal-ended, with the mast forward. When on the starboard tack, the vessel could be balanced from the projecting outrigger booms.

Outrigger boats were noted, but without details, in Hawaii in 1777. By 1839, a European spritsail had been adopted; however, the structural features were generally like those of contemporary Tahiti and Marquesas boats. The two ends of an Hawaiian boat were similar, but not precisely double-ended. Their mast was forward and they are known to have been tacked. When on the starboard tack it may have been possible to balance the boat from the fore boom which projected—otherwise there could have been temporary arrangements.

## 9.3.7 PROPULSION AND STEERING

In addition to the usual problems experienced when interpreting textual and iconographic evidence, there are special difficulties with the Oceanic material. European mariners naturally compared features on Pacific boats with those of their own ships (e.g. Dampier quoted by Haddon and Hornell, 1936: 415–16). As details of European fittings are sometimes not known and as it is almost always unclear whether the comparison is precise or merely general, it can be difficult to interpret such comparisons. Many of the illustrations are not measured drawings, and details which are necessary to an analysis of the rig are obscured. Furthermore, it is likely that details from several boats have sometimes been combined in one drawing, and the use of perspective may give a misleading impression of shapes, sizes, and relationships. At times, dubious features may be depicted, as in Hodges' painting of Matavai Bay, Tahiti (Rienits and Rienits, 1968: 99) during Cook's second voyage, where two boats have transom sterns: the question must then be asked whether this is a mistake and, if not, whether it is an indigenous Oceanic feature or a recent borrowing from European vessels.

## 9.3.7.1 BY PADDLE, POLE, AND SCULL

Paddling, with what to European eyes appeared to be large and unwieldy paddles, was encountered everywhere, mostly on its own but also in conjunction with sail. In the Marquesas, platforms for paddlers were sometimes fitted outboard of the hull. In shallow water, boats were punted (Haddon and Hornell, 1936: 7, fig. 2; 196, fig. 130; 1937: 10; D. Lewis, 1994: 55). European-style rowing was not known in Oceania, but there was a form of sculling (Haddon and Hornell, 1937: 8–10, fig. 4b). In eastern Melanesia, and perhaps elsewhere, Cook and others noted that 'sculls' (small oars) were thrust vertically into the water through holes in the platforms of paired boats, and through gaps between hull and outrigger; the blade of each oar was inclined and the loom pulled towards the oarsman to propel the vessel (Haddon and Hornell, 1936: 314, 318; 1937: 8–10). These paddles, poles and sculls were used on small boats, and on larger ones on short range voyages—longer voyages, whether by raft, or by paired or outrigger boats, were under sail.

## 9.3.7.2 PROPULSION BY SAIL

Sails were generally made of pandanus leaf or coconut palm-leaf matting. Individual cloths of this matting were sewn together, sometimes across (Haddon and Hornell, 1936: 261, 414) and sometimes along the length of the sail (F. Paris, 1843: 114–15; Rieth, 1993: 118, 118–19, 160). Sails were made fast to yards and booms, using paired cords rather than lacing, by ropes made from fibres of the plantain tree. There are also examples in the Marshalls of sails being fastened through holes bored through spars. The rigging was made of three or four strands of plantain rope bound together (Haddon and Hornell, 1936: 8–10, 122, 369).

Precisely how the mast was stepped at the time of first contact is difficult to say, but in early twentieth-century Fijian double-ended boats which shunt and therefore need the mast to be canted, alternately towards one end and then the other, the notched heel of the mast pivoted on a ridged chock which was itself lashed to the central outrigger boom or to a central crossbeam in a paired boat. The mast was sometimes supported some way above its heel by a shore which had a fork at its lower end so that it could also pivot about a beam or boom (Haddon and Hornell, 1936: 311–15). In other types of boat which were tacked rather than shunted, the mast remained generally vertical and there was a more substantial step. Most tacking boats had their mast step fastened to the forward outrigger or, in paired boats, to a forward crossbeam. In this latter case, the mast was sometimes in the port hull as in Hawaii, or starboard as in Tonga and Tahiti (Haddon and Hornell, 1936: figs. 1, 2, 87, 189, 191). These effective, yet simple, arrangements for the single mast may well be similar to those of much earlier times. In paired boats with two masts (9.3.7.2.2, 9.3.7.2.4) one could be port forward and the other starboard aft, or both could be between the hulls (Bellwood, 1987: fig. 13; Haddon Hornell, 1936: 105).

Masts were supported by shrouds, often in pairs and sometimes up to six or seven, and by stays, the base for the former being made as broad as possible using outriggers, lee platforms and balance boards, where fitted, and outrigged balance spars (Haddon and Hornell, 1936: 266–72, figs. 189, 190–3). Hodges, on Cook's second voyage, drew a Tahiti boat with a ladderlike fitting on the mast, also seen on a paired two-masted Tuamotu boat (Haddon and Hornell, 1936: figs. 58–9, 86): this was the equivalent of ratline-fitted shrouds on European ships.

The standing rigging was thus generally comparable with that of European rigs; the running rigging was, however, somewhat different. Generally speaking, there were no reef points or sheets, although Anson thought that 'running stays' were used as sheets to a boom—see also some of Paris's drawings and models (Haddon and Hornell, 1936: 13, 414; Rieth, 1993: 118–21). Anson also thought that sails could be reefed by rolling them around the boom (Haddon and Hornell, 1936: 415). The effective area of a triangular sail was varied by tricing up a spiller line, which ran from the boom, via the masthead or the yard, to the deck; this brought the boom and sail nearer the yard and mast (Haddon and Hornell, 1936: 266). Cook thought that, in Tongan boats that tacked, the sail might be shifted to leeward after unlacing the lower part of the sail from the yard (Haddon and Hornell, 1936: 269). In the earliest drawings of Oceanic vessels with yards, the yard rests in a crutch at the mast head (Fig. 9.9); later a halyard was introduced and it was then possible to hoist and to send down yard and furled sail (Rieth, 1993: 161, plan 118)—this may have been a European-inspired modification.

The first Europeans to see Oceanic sails described them by names familiar to them, for example, 'lateen'. Such sails were like lateens in having the yard at an angle to the deck, with the tack of the sail forward of the mast; in other respects they differed. Other types of sail seen in the Pacific were scarcely comparable with European sails but attempts were made to do so. In the recent past, scholars have tried to bring order and logic into the naming of Oceanic rigs—Haddon and Hornell (1938: 45–50), E. Doran (1981: 40) (Fig. 9.12), Horridge (1986) and D. Lewis (1994: 63). For one reason or another each scheme has proved unsatisfactory. Classification schemes are not an end in themselves, but a means of organizing data so that underlying patterns may

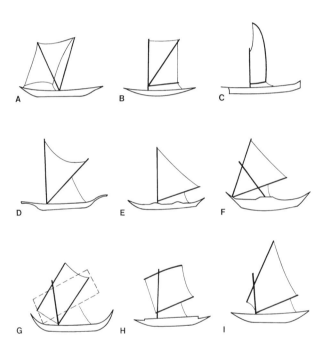

Fig. 9.12. Doran's classification scheme for Oceanic rigs (after Doran, 1981: fig. 21).

emerge. Classification also standardizes terminology and thus makes it easier for scholars to understand one another. Generally speaking, such schemes are temporary and they need to be reassessed when new data is obtained or new techniques become available (McGrail, 1995b).

It is necessary to simplify if every individual description or representation of an Oceanic rig is not to be regarded as a distinct type. Simplification involves identifying those variables which are considered (usu-

ally subjectively) to be important. In a new classification scheme (Table 9.1), mast, yard, and sail shape are identified as the important variables: the main types of Oceanic rig can be differentiated by reference to these three features. European sail names are not used; instead, each Oceanic rig is identified by the place and date of the earliest reliable European description and/or illustration. There is no implication of origins in this identification. Nor is there any implication of development of one rig from another; such speculations have bedevilled some of the earlier schemes. An analysis based on such data leads to the identification of six types of Oceanic rig.

### 9.3.7.2.1 *Type 1 rig: Marianas, 1521*

It is difficult to identify the rig on a vertical mast amidships depicted in Pigafetta's illustration (Fig. 9.11) of the double-ended outrigger boats he saw in the Ladrones/Marianas in 1521. However, Pigafetta emphasized in his text that either end was used as the bow and that there was a steering paddle available at both ends; he also described the boats' asymmetric transverse section. The sail was said to be a 'lateen' on an angled yard, 'in shape resembling a shoulder of mutton'. All these features appear subsequently in outrigger boats of this region, which were shunted rather than tacked. This strongly suggests that Magellan's boat had a Type 1 rig, despite the vertical mast depicted in the stylized illustration.

In 1686, at Guam in the Marianas, Dampier saw similar boats with a 'boomed lateen rig' and the heel of the yard held in a notch forward (Haddon and Hornell, 1936: 416; Johnstone, 1988: 203–4). This was also undoubtedly a Type 1 rig. Anson's 1742 measured drawing of a Marianas 'flying proa' (Haddon and Hornell, 1936: 414, fig. 300; Rieth, 1993: 157) shows an outrigger boat with a vertical mast with the yard suspended from the masthead at a point close to the yard's upper end. There were sockets at each end of the hull to take the heel of the yard, according to which end was the bow when the boat was shunted. Showing the mast vertical is probably a European convention; all indications are that the early 'flying proa' had a canted mast and was shunted (9.3.6.3.2).

Outrigger boats in the Carolines and Marshalls are known to have had similar rigs from the early nineteenth century onwards (Rieth, 1993: 116–18, 156; Haddon and Hornell, 1936: 362, 370, figs. 259, 266; D. Lewis, 1994: fig. 4). These had lee platforms from which the boat could be balanced; earlier 'flying proas' probably had temporary balance boards or spars.

Schouten described and drew a Type 1 rig forward on a paired boat seen off Tonga in 1616 (Fig. 9.9). The yard rested in a crutch at the masthead, about one-third along its length from its heel which was itself lashed to the fore part of one hull. This boat was probably tacked. The paired boats seen by Tasman off Tonga in 1643 had a Type 1 rig stepped forward between the hulls (Haddon and Hornell, 1936: fig. 190). The yard rested in a masthead crutch and its heel was held between the hulls by lines to each fore part. Paired boats noted by Cook and illustrated by Hodges in 1772–5, had similar rigs except that the mast was stepped in the starboard hull (Haddon and Hornell, 1936: 268–71, figs. 191–2;

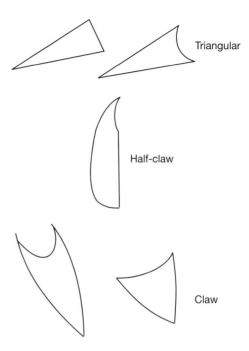

**Table 9.1** Six types of Oceanic rig

| Type and date* | Illustration | Variables | Alternative designations | | |
|---|---|---|---|---|---|
| | | | Doran (1981) | H & H (1938) | Lewis (1994) |
| 1. Marianas, 1521 | Fig. 9.11 | Canted mast + yard + triangular sail | Fig. 9.12, 'F' | Oceanic lateen | — |
| 2. Tonga, 1643 | H & H (1936), Fig. 187 | Vertical mast + yard + triangular sail | | | |
| 3. Tonga, 1777 | H & H (1936), Fig. 193 | Canted mast + yard + claw sail | — | As above | Reef Island claw |
| 4. Tahiti, 1768 | H & H (1936), Fig. 77 | Vertical mast; no yard; half-claw sail | Fig. 9.12, 'C' | Boom sprit | Tahiti half-claw |
| 5. New Zealand, 1769 | Rienits & Rienits, 1968: 43 | Vertical mast; no yard; triangular sail | Fig. 9.12, 'D' | Simple sprit | — |
| 6. Marquesas, 1774 | H & H (1936), Fig. 21A | Vertical mast; no yard; claw sail | ? | ? | ? |

*Earliest European description or illustration.

H & H = Haddon and Hornell.

*Notes:*
*Mast.* The spar which mainly transmits sailing forces to the hull. Where there is no yard, the mast additionally fulfils that function. Masts may be vertical or canted.
*Yard.* The spar to which the upper edge (head) or leading edge (luff) of a sail is laced. Some rigs have yards, some do not.
*Boom.* The spar to which the lower edge (foot) or trailing edge (leach) of a sail is laced. All known Oceanic sails have booms, some straight, some curved. With data at present available, this is a redundant variable and not used in the analysis.
*Sail shape.* Mainly from illustrations in Haddon and Hornell (1936–7) and Rieth (1993). Divided into 3 groups: triangular; half-claw; claw. See the diagrams, upper right.

D. Lewis, 1994: fig. 2). An additional detail is that the yard was kept within the masthead crutch by cleats on each side. By the time Paris visited Tonga in the early nineteenth century, the double-ended paired boats had the yard suspended on a halyard from a mast stepped amidships in the longer hull; the heel of the yard was fastened to the forepart of that same hull. These boats were probably shunted, the smaller hull acting in some sense as an outrigger (Rieth, 1993: 121, 162). Paris also noted outrigger boats with Type 1 rigs suspended from midship masts with the heel of the yard stepped in a hole forward (Rieth, 1993: 120–1, 161–2; Haddon and Hornell, 1936: 263, fig. 188). These were also shunted, balance could be achieved from the platform which projected to leeward.

Fijian early nineteenth-century double-ended paired boats and twentieth-century outrigger boats had similar rigs to those of early nineteenth-century Tonga (D. Lewis, 1994: fig. 3; Haddon and Hornell, 1936: 311, 315, figs. 228, 232).

### 9.3.7.2.2 *Type 2 rig: Tonga, 1643*

It is possible that the representations of all the boats in this class are conventionalized—as Anson's drawing (9.3.7.2.1) seems to have been—and show the mast vertical when in most modes of operation it would have been canted. Until that theory is proven, however, rigs of the following boats cannot be included in Type 1. The double-ended Tongan outrigger boat seen by Tasman in 1643 had a Type 2 rig stepped forward with the yard resting in a masthead crutch at about its mid point (Haddon and Hornell, 1936: 261, fig. 187). If the mast was permanently vertical, this boat was probably tacked. An early nineteenth-century double-ended paired boat of the Tuamotu archipelago, drawn and modelled by Paris (Haddon and Hornell, 1936: 81–2, figs. 58–9) had two masts each with a Type 2 rig with halyards, although Paris was informed that only one sail was ever used on whichever mast was appropriate for the tack. The heel of the forward yard fitted into a 'step' on the fore end of the smaller hull.

A late nineteenth-century double-ended paired boat of New Caledonia had a Type 2 rig stepped amidships (Haddon and Hornell, 1937: 9, fig. 4a). The yard on this vessel was suspended from the masthead on a halyard. It is not clear whether this boat would have been tacked or shunted.

### 9.3.7.2.3 *Type 3 rig: Tonga, 1777*

The boats seen by de Quiros, Mendana's pilot, off Santa Cruz in 1595, may have had Type 3 rigs (Johnstone, 1988: 204). The first definite sighting was in 1777 when Cook saw Type 3 rigs suspended from midships masts on Tongan double-ended outrigger and paired boats (Haddon and Hornell, 1936: 271, fig. 193). These boats were probably shunted. Single outrigger boats of Santa Cruz had similar rigs from the early-nineteenth century onwards (Rieth, 1993: 119, 160; Haddon and Hornell, 1937: 48, fig. 31). These boats had lee platforms; earlier outrigger boats probably used outrigged spars for balance.

Mangarevan (Gambier Islands) log rafts (Fig. 9.4) seen by Beechey in 1826 and by Dumont d'Urville in 1838 had a Type 3 rig. As these craft were clearly not double-ended, they must have been tacked or, more likely, the sail was only used in a fair wind.

### 9.3.7.2.4 *Type 4 rig: Tahiti, 1768*

Type 4 rigs stepped forward were seen on Society islands (mostly Tahitian) outrigger boats by Bougainville in 1768, by Cook on his second and third voyages and by Bligh in 1792 (Haddon and Hornell, 1936: 116–22, 130–1, figs. 77, 80, 81a, 86–7). Over time, the curvature of the head and the foot of the sail appears to have changed, but this may be due to the artists' differing appreciation of technical detail. As these boats had balance boards and were not double-ended, they would have been tacked. In 1768–71, Cook saw a Society islands paired boat rigged in this way on two masts, one amidships, one forward; they had two balance boards. Similar boats were known in recent times (Bellwood, 1987: 41, fig. 13; Lewis, 1994: fig. 1). Paris saw a two-masted Tahitian outrigger boat similarly rigged in 1827 (Haddon and Hornell, 1936: 116–17, figs. 78–9).

### 9.3.7.2.5 *Type 5 rig: New Zealand, 1769*

Single hull New Zealand boats, broad in the beam, were seen to have Type 5 rig stepped forward when Cook first visited there in 1769 (Rienits and Rienits, 1968: 43). Similarly rigged boats were also noted by D'Urville and by Paris in the early nineteenth century (Haddon and Hornell, 1936: 210–11, fig. 141; Rieth, 1993: 158, 160). In that same period, Samoan outrigger boats had this rig stepped amidships (Haddon and Hornell, 1936: 228, fig. 156). Type 5 rig generally appears to have been used in conjunction with paddling when there was a fair wind. These boats were not double-ended and, if required to sail to windward, would have been tacked.

### 9.3.7.2.6 *Type 6 rig: Marquesas, 1774*

Cook encountered this rig forward on Marquesan outrigger boats in 1774 (Haddon and Hornell, 1936: 35, fig. 21a). On his third voyage, he saw this rig, but with a more curved boom, on Hawaiian paired boats; similar boats were seen by Paris in 1839 (Haddon and Hornell, 1936: 6, 7, 13, 25, figs. 1, 2, 7; Rieth, 1993: 166). Both types were tacked; in outrigger boats the booms projected to starboard (on the opposite side to the float) and could have been used for balance.

### 9.3.7.3 STEERING

It is clear from observations and illustrations by Europeans that steering was often done by the paddlers when propelled solely by paddle, and by sail balance when under sail. When manœuvring or making large alterations of heading, and when in confined waters, freely held steering paddles were used, from the stern where practicable, otherwise from the platform. In the early sixteenth century, Pigafetta noted that steering paddles were like a baker's shovel, a 'staff with a board at the end'. His illustration of a Marianas outrigger boat (Fig. 9.11) shows such a paddle being used over the quarter, on the same side as the float (Johnstone, 1988: fig. 15.1; Haddon and Hornell, 1936: 413). Schouten's 1616 (Fig. 9.9) and Tasman's 1643 illustrations of Tongan paired boats show a large steering paddle being used from the platform on each quarter (Haddon and Hornell, 1936: 266–7, figs. 189, 190).

Illustrations by Tobin of small outrigger boats in late eighteenth-century Tahiti, and by Paris in early nineteenth-century Carolines, show paddles being used by a steersman sitting in the stern (Haddon and Hornell, 1936: 118; Rieth, 1993: 118). Large paddles used on the quarter by steersmen standing on the platforms of outrigger and paired boats, are shown in nineteenth-century drawings from the Marshalls, Tonga, and New Caledonia (Rieth, 1993: 120; Haddon and Hornell, 1936:

370; 1937: 9). Such paddles were 10 ft (3.05 m) long and, in boats that were shunted, were fastened by a long lanyard under the platform so that they could be floated from one end to the other on changing ends (Haddon and Hornell, 1936: 370).

Larger, nineteenth-century Carolines outrigger craft had what appears to be a side rudder on the quarter opposite the float (Rieth, 1993: 116–17, 118, 156). It is unclear how such rudders were pivoted, but they seem to have been usable either from inboard with a thwartships tiller, or by a helmsman sitting on the gunwale with one leg outboard. E. Doran's distribution map (1981: 85, fig. 48) shows no quarter rudders in use in Oceania outside the Carolines. It seems likely that they were unknown in prehistoric Oceania. A drawing of the 'reconstructed' paired boat *Hokule'a* (E. Doran, 1981: fig. 6) shows an oar or large paddle in two positions—over the stern and on the port quarter. These may be what Finney *et al.* (1986: 66, 81; Finney, 1994: 172–6) describe as a 'steering sweep' and 'quarter paddles'. D. Lewis (1994: 320) states that *Hokule'a*'s 'steering paddle' was used by increasing and decreasing its immersed area—in the manner of the *guares* or 'variable drop keels' used on Indian, Vietnamese, South Chinese, and South American log rafts (6.6.3, 8.3.1, 10.2.5, 11.4.1.2). It is not clear what evidence was used to justify their inclusion in the reconstruction.

### 9.3.8 THE PERFORMANCE OF OCEAN-GOING CRAFT

The great distances between island groups in the South Pacific, which the Polynesians undoubtedly sailed at an early date, testify to one aspect of the performance of both boats and crew. Factors that determine a vessel's range include how close to the wind she is sailed, speeds achievable on various headings relative to the wind, and the ability to sustain life at sea for a sufficient number of days without land-based replenishment. Other major factors which affect ability to undertake oceanic voyages include the navigational ability of the crew (9.5), the structural soundness of the boat in testing conditions, and her cargo capacity which would be of greater importance on colonization voyages than on voyages of exploration and discovery.

As there are only insignificant archaeological remains of vessels, evidence for performance comes only from the observations of European navigators such as Cook, and recent ethnographic accounts. The performance of reconstructions such as *Hokule'a*, a paired, two-masted boat with Type 4 rig, may be noted (Stroup, 1985; Finney *et al.*, 1986; D. Lewis, 1994: 319–20; Finney, 1994: 163–254). However, this and other Oceanic 'replicas' do not seem to have been designed, built, and tested in accordance with the generally agreed principles of experimental boat archaeology (Coates *et al.*, 1995). Although Finney *et al.* (1986) claim that the aims of the *Hokule'a* project included recreating a twelfth-century east Polynesian voyaging canoe and establishing its sailing ability, E. Doran (1981: 240) states that, '. . . modern materials were used in its construction, and Hawaiian topsides are superimposed on a Tahitian or Tuamotuan hull shape . . .'; whilst Duncan (1982) tells us that this vessel was 'performance accurate' and not 'technology accurate'. At best these Oceanic experiments may give a general impression of the seafaring abilities of Oceanic crews and their boats in *c*. AD 1800. The main usefulness of *Hokule'a*, however, seems to have been in the field of navigation (9.2.6, 9.5.3); such use can undoubtedly make a valuable contribution to knowledge of the past.

### 9.3.8.1 WINDWARD PERFORMANCE

There are no detailed early European accounts of Oceanic windward performance, but D. Lewis (1994: 71–5) believes that, in general, the Micronesian outrigger boat could probably point higher than the Polynesian paired boat. In practice, however, Lewis found that Oceanic craft were never sailed as close as possible to the wind, rather 'a good full and by': that is, with the sails invariably full, and not lifting or shaking. Sailing for long periods as close as possible to the wind ('close-hauled') is a product of twentieth-century racing. Sailing full and by imposes less stress on boat and crew; it was the usual state for voyaging boats and ships everywhere, in the eighteenth century and earlier. Lewis estimates that Oceanic boats in general were sailed 75°–80° (7 points) off the wind in this full and by condition. The 'replica' boat *Hokule'a* could be sailed 70° (including 10° leeway) off the true wind in calm to moderate open sea conditions; and 75° off (including 15° leeway) in rough seas (D. Lewis, 1994: 319; Finney, 1994: 38–9, fig. 5).

### 9.3.8.2 SPEED

Cook trailed a patent log from a Tongan paired boat (*tongiaki*) sailing on the wind and recorded a mean speed of 7 knots (D. Lewis, 1994: 70). Estimates given to Cook for the time taken in favourable conditions for certain ocean passages were equivalent to 130–50 nautical miles a day, whilst Cook estimated that a Tahitian *pahi* with paired hulls and two masts, which was much faster than his own ship, could sail more than 120 nautical miles a day. E. Doran (1981: 62) has summarized other early European comments on the speeds of Oceanic boats: Polynesian paired and outrigger boats were reasonably good, whilst the Fijian paired boats and the Micronesian outrigger boats were unusually fast. In favourable conditions, one Fijian boat made 12 knots and a Gilbertese 'flying proa' touched 17 knots, whilst a Carolines outrigger boat is said to have averaged 12.5 knots between Guam and Manila 1,200 nautical miles to the west (Hornell, 1936: 327, 350, 417). This latter figure appears to have been exceptional for a lengthy voyage, and D. Lewis's conclusion that Polynesian twin-hull and Micronesian outrigger boats of the eighteenth / nineteenth centuries could achieve 100–150 nautical miles a day in a fair wind (i.e. an average speed of 4 to 6 knots), seems to be a reasonable estimate (1994: 71). *Hokule'a* achieved 120–30 nautical miles a day (D. Lewis, 1994: 319): on an 118-day broken passage, she averaged over 100 nautical miles a day (Finney, 1994: 97). When sailing full and by, she averaged 4.5 knots in light winds, 6 knots in strong winds; off the wind, she could make 8 knots, and occasionally, 9 knots.

### 9.3.8.3 CAPACITY

On his second voyage to Tahiti, Cook saw paired boats, 50–90 ft long (15–27 m), each carrying 50–120 passengers; larger ones had a crew of 8–10, and 144 passengers (Haddon and Hornell, 1938: 43). Samwell, who sailed with Cook, considered that Tongan paired boats which could carry 80–100 people were capable of remaining at sea for a very long time. A Fijian paired boat of the late eighteenth century could carry a ton of copra (D. Lewis, 1994: 80). Marquesan outrigger boats carried 40–50 people on fishing and war expeditions, whilst a Micronesia outrigger boat from Faraulep in the Carolines, presumably on a conventional voyage, brought twenty-four men and women to Guam in the northern Marianas in 1721 (D. Lewis, 1944: 79).

This short review of load-carrying capacity suggests that both types of Oceanic boat (paired and outrigger) of the eighteenth and early nineteenth centuries were able to carry sufficient people and stores for a lengthy Oceanic reconnaissance voyage. However, outrigger boats of those times would not have been large enough for settlement voyages, when livestock, tools and other implements, and utensils, as well as a greater number of people would probably have to be carried. There is every reason to think that both outrigger and paired boats of the voyaging kind were structurally suitable for Oceanic voyages, and Micronesian and Polynesian crews of those times certainly had the seafaring skills to cope with adverse weather (Johnstone, 1988: 210).

### 9.3.8.4 VICTUALS

In recent times, Oceanic seamen carried a variety of long-life foods in sufficient quantity for lengthy voyages (Johnstone, 1988: 210; D. Lewis, 1994: 80–1). When operating from atoll regions such as Kiribati, pandanus fruit, cooked, dried to form a paste, and then wrapped in leaves, formed the staple diet and could last for up to two months. From volcanic islands such as the Carolines, pounded breadfruit or taro was allowed to ferment so that it remained unspoilt for a long time when stored in large leaf packages. Dried shellfish kept indefinitely. Water was carried in large bottle gourds with wooden stoppers, or in coconuts or lengths of bamboo. Drinking and eating coconuts were also carried. The water supply was topped up with rain water, and the standard diet was supplemented by fish caught at sea. Cook noted that Fijian paired boats had a fire hearth on their platforms laid on a bed of sand, stone, or clay: coconut husks were burnt (Haddon and Hornell, 1937: 8; D. Lewis, 1994: 57, 80). Fires can be seen on Schouten's 1616 drawing of a paired boat off Tonga (Fig. 9.9), and on Tasman's 1644 drawing of another Tongan boat (Haddon and Hornell, 1936: fig. 189, 190).

After a review of this and other evidence, and drawing on his personal experience, D. Lewis (1994: 81) concluded that 'there would be no real difficulty in adequately provisioning a large voyaging canoe for a month, and that this period could be extended, without undue hardship, for another fortnight.' Irwin (1992: 57) has suggested that, on such a voyage on an east-south-east heading 'against' the predominant wind, it would be safe to allow about a week of return for every two or three out. On the assumption that these early Polynesian boats could make a minimum of 100 nautical miles a day, this would give a safe radius of action of 1,500–2,000 nautical miles in two to three weeks out, and one week of return in the event that no land was found, leaving a fortnight on hard tack for contingencies.

# 9.4
# Early Ocean-Going Boats

Voyages east of the Bismarck archipelago are thought to have begun c.1500 BC (Spriggs and Anderson, 1993; Ambrose, 1997). In order to undertake these Oceanic voyages, these proto-Polynesians had to have ocean-going vessels of good capacity which could be sailed, at least, on a fine reach (say, 75° to 80° off the wind)—i.e. they could make good a track across the wind and thus not lose ground to leeward in the event of foul winds. They also needed to be able to navigate when out of sight of land. As voyages went further eastwards (and north and south), distances became greater, thus over a period of many centuries improved vessel performance was needed, especially in endurance.

Some scholars have suggested that search and settlement were undertaken on the same voyage; this implies that a founder population of would-be colonists with all necessary 'infrastructure' embarked on the first voyage into unknown waters. This would seem to aggravate an already difficult task, and, although incapable of proof, it seems more likely that the 'prudent Polynesian' would initially explore, and only when suitable land was found would a colonizing voyage be undertaken. Thus two types of craft would be required, the second more demanding in capacity and perhaps in sea-kindliness qualities. The archaeological evidence for the craft of the period 1500 BC to, perhaps, AD 1300, is negligible. There are only very minor remains of boats from this period (9.2.1), and the few known petroglyphs (9.2.2) are either undated or eighteenth century and later. Linguistic arguments suggest, at best, that at the beginning of Oceanic voyaging, the proto-Polynesians had outrigger boats with sail. We are thus left with evidence amassed by Europeans in the sixteenth–nineteenth centuries (principally late eighteenth/early nineteenth) in the form of descriptions, illustrations, and models. The Polynesians' ability to navigate without instruments is known to have decreased, certainly in extent and probably also in detail, as the requirement for long-range voyaging decreased. It seems likely that boatbuilding capabilities were similarly reduced in extent, perhaps limited to key centres, and boatbuilders generally may have been less ambitious. From this it follows that, in terms of technology and of ocean-going performance, the craft used during the most demanding period in Oceanic voyaging, say, 500 BC–AD 500, were at least equivalent to, and probably better than, those used in the heyday of European exploration, say, 1760–1840, before there was any significant transfer of European technology.

There were four types of ocean-going vessel in use in Oceania during the late eighteenth/early nineteenth centuries: the log raft; the single-hull plank boat; the single-hull plank boat with an outrigger; and the paired-hull plank boat.

The log raft seems unlikely to have been used on settlement voyages, but its potential for exploratory voyages should not be overlooked although its cross wind performance is questionable. The logboat-based single-hull boats generally in use were not ocean-going, but those used in New Zealand, where the large trees available meant that broad and hence stable boats could be built, were so used. However, as New Zealand was not settled until the final phase of Polynesian expansion, the use of this type of boat on the early voyages seems unlikely. Plank boats, not logboat-based but with a keel (Fig. 9.8), were used as 'voyaging canoes' in late nineteenth-century Tuamotu (9.3.6.1); although these boats appear to be out of the mainstream of Oceanic boatbuilding, there is no technological reason why one could not have been built in earlier times. On the other hand, there is a strong possibility of European influence by this date and, on balance, early use seems unlikely.

The choice thus seems to be limited to outrigger boats and paired boats, the most advanced of which were clearly capable of ocean voyages when Europeans encountered them. Doran (1981) has attempted to demonstrate, by an assessment of relative seaworthiness and study of the present distribution of boat and sail types, that paired boats preceded outrigger boats, but his arguments are not convincing and there does not seem to be any method of establishing a relative chronology. Both types may have been used for ocean voyages during the settlement of Oceania; however, for reasons of speed, manœuvrability and capacity, it may have been that outrigger boats were preferred for exploratory voyages, and paired boats for colonization. D. Lewis (1994: 54) has made the point that the preferred size of vessel was probably in the 50–75 ft (15–23 m) range for, as Cook's chief scientist, Joseph Banks, said, 'the middling sized ones' were least liable to accident in stormy weather.

From the evidence reviewed above, and in the light of evidence from the few early boats excavated in south-east Asia (8.3.5.1), it seems likely that early Oceanic voyaging boats had sewn planking on a logboat base, possibly with the planking initially aligned by treenails within the edges; the framing was probably lashed to cleats integral with the planking. By comparison with other parts of the world, it is possible that the earliest seagoing sailing rig in western Melanesia was a square sail on a midship mast. By 1500 BC, when the proto-Polynesians were ready to explore eastern Melanesia, it is possible that the rig consisted of a mast, yard, and boom with a triangular sail, apex down. On the grounds of simplicity, this single mast may have been stepped forward and the vessel tacked; shunting with the mast near amidships may have come later, but still within the migration period. Steering was probably achieved by sail balance generally, otherwise by freely held paddle; leeway was minimized by immersed steering paddle.

Such a 'reconstruction' is hypothetical; more factually based hypotheses may emerge if and when substantial early remains are excavated.

# 9.5

# Navigation

Early Europeans in Oceania were astounded to find that widely separated groups of islands within an enormous ocean had been settled by people having only a Stone Age technology. When Europeans needed compass, chart, astronomical tables, and a range of other aids, how had these Polynesians and Micronesians navigated without instruments? After 200 years of research, it is now reasonably clear how this was done. In fact, Cook gave the essential elements of the answer to this puzzle in the late eighteenth century when he wrote:

In these Navigations the Sun is their guide by day and the Stars by night, when these are obscured they have recourse to the points from whence the Wind and waves of the Sea come upon the Vessel (Beaglehole, 1967: 164).

Cook's chief scientist, Joseph Banks, enlarged on the Polynesians' astronomical knowledge:

. . . of these [stars] they know a very large number by name, and the cleverest among them will tell in what part of the Heavens they are to be seen in any month when they are above the horizon. They know also the time of their annual appearance and disappearance to a nicety . . . The people excel much in predicting the weather (Hooker, 1896: 162).

A more detailed account was given by Andia y Varela who led a Spanish expedition to Tahiti in 1772–6 (Haddon and Hornell, 1936: 144–5; D. Lewis, 1994: 84). He noted that voyages of 200 nautical miles and more were undertaken by sailing masters known as *faatere*. These Oceanic navigators divided the horizon into sixteen 'points' based on an east/west line between sunrise and sunset. During the day, bearings were known relative to the sun, and also to the directions of the wind and the swell, both of which were checked early on in the voyage, before losing sight of land. Pennants of feathers and bark were used to gauge the wind direction which they knew varied more than that of the swell. At night they steered by the stars, which they clearly distinguished from the planets. They knew which stars rose and set on the bearings of all the islands around; and they used these stars—each of which was given the name of its associated island—to navigate with 'as much precision as the most expert navigator of civilised nations could achieve'. In addition, they could forecast the next day's weather with some accuracy.

That Oceanic navigational knowledge was not limited to the local area is clear from Cook's conversation with Tupaia, a dispossessed chief and navigator-priest from Raiatea in the Society islands (Haddon and Hornell, 1936: 104; D. Lewis, 1994: 8–9). Tupaia gave Cook sailing directions for nearly all the Austral, Cook, and Tuamotus islands and others as far away as Rotuma and Fiji. This list included islands in most of the major groups, except Hawaii and New Zealand, in an area which extended for c.2,600 nautical miles east to west, and c.1,000 nautical miles north to south. Included were many islands not at that time known to Europeans, but which were eventually encountered. A chart based on Tupaia's knowledge, which Cook subsequently drew (Fernandez-Armesto, 1991: 171; Finney, 1994: fig. 3) shows seventy-four islands arranged in concentric circles according to their bearing and sailing time (not distance) from Tahiti.

Unknown to Cook and his contemporaries, the non-instrumental methods described above were generally similar to the ones that had been used millennia earlier by mariners in the Indian Ocean, Mediterranean, and eastern Atlantic (3.8.2, 4.14.2, 5.7.3). The principles of this 'environmental' navigation were evidently the same throughout the world; their application varied due mainly to differences in latitude and in weather patterns. As voyaging in the south Pacific was mostly within twenty degrees of the Equator, Oceanic navigators had the advantage that the night sky apparently rotated much less obliquely than in, for example, northern Europe; thus stars appeared to rise and set much closer to the vertical and could therefore be used longer as directional aids. There were comparable advantages when using the sun by day.

Europe was mainly settled over land and—apart from the Viking voyages of the early medieval period (5.7.3)—exploratory and colonization voyages in European waters were relatively short. The Micronesian and Polynesian settlements, on the other hand, were entirely by sea, many voyages being over great distances. Before the age of instrumental navigation, the only voyages comparable with those of the Polynesians are the trading voyages of the early centuries AD (and probably earlier) in the western Indian Ocean (6.3).

### 9.5.1  DRIFT VOYAGES?

It is sometimes suggested that the exploration and colonization of the South Pacific could be accounted for by drift voyages—either accidental or deliberate: both Greenland and North America were first encountered by Viking seamen who had been blown westwards in a storm far beyond their intended destination. Computer simulations by Levison, Ward, and Webb (1973), using Pacific wind and current data, have shown, however, that the major crossings—from western Melanesia to Fiji; and from eastern Polynesia to Hawaii, Easter island, and New Zealand—could not have been undertaken by drifting: there must have been deliberate voyaging. These simulations also showed that drift voyages from west to east Polynesia, and from west Polynesia to the Marquesas region were possible, but with a very low probability (D. Lewis, 1994: 16). The possibility remains that some islands may have been found on accidental drift voyages: as with the Vikings, Oceanic seamen so placed would need navigational skills to return home so that their discovery could be of use to a colonizing group, and there is no reason to think that they could not have done this. It seems probable, however, that most Oceanic exploration (and settlement) was undertaken deliberately; and on such voyages, navigational ability of a high order was required.

## 9.5.2  PRIOR KNOWLEDGE OF NEW LANDS

Irwin's hypothesis is that, for safety reasons, the South Pacific was progressively explored and settled by voyaging against the predominant wind—i.e. generally on a heading of east-south-east—so that, in the event that land was not found, a safe and speedy return could be made home. In fact, from the Solomon islands in western Melanesia, the great majority of eastern Melanesian and Polynesian island groups lie within the sector between east and south-east, the principal exceptions being Kiribati, Hawaii, and New Zealand (as well as the Micronesian islands). Exploratory voyages within that upwind sector would thus sooner or later discover new lands, as Irwin's simulations showed (1992: 133–73).

The proto-Polynesians of c.1500 BC were heirs of seafarers who had made their way eastwards through western Melanesia from island to island whilst, in the main, remaining in sight of land. In contrast, the nearest land to the east of San Cristobal, the easternmost island in the Solomons, was 200 nautical miles away (Fig. 9.1), and it was not possible to sail to within visible

range of that land (Santa Cruz) before losing sight of the Solomons (Irwin, 1992: 66–7). It may therefore be asked whether these proto-Polynesians (and their successors who had to make much longer voyages out of sight of land) could deduce by some means that there was land in the sector between east and south-east (i.e. upwind). If they had this ability, the area of ocean they had to search would have been considerably reduced.

D. Lewis (1994) has coined the phrase 'expanded target' to describe the combined effect of a number of environmental phenomena which 'signpost' the way to land over the horizon at a range greater than the normal sighting distance, even when that is increased by refraction (McGrail, 1998: 278; Haddon and Hornell, 1936: 145–6; D. Lewis, 1994: 25, 91, 152, 166, 195–261, 371). Atolls may be sighted at c.10 nautical miles in good conditions, whilst high islands can be sighted at greater ranges. Early warning of land at greater ranges than these visual distances can be given by:

- the flight line of groups of birds which feed at sea and nest ashore; terns and noddies out to 20 nautical miles, boobies out to 30 nautical miles;
- the predominant sea swell can be reflected and refracted by an island—the stick charts used by navigators in the Marshalls were aids to memorizing swell patterns around specific islands (D. Lewis, 1994: 239);
- in certain sun conditions lagoons on atolls appear as a reflected pale, shimmering column in the sky;
- certain types of cloud form over islands; other types break up;
- naturally occurring fires;
- changes in water colour can indicate a reef; for example, from deep blue to a light green over a reef in 20–30 fathoms;
- land breezes, the smell of land, and drifting fresh timber can all give early warning of islands.

Of these adventitious aids, only swell refraction, cloud formation and dispersal, and possibly lagoon reflection might be expected to extend the range (say, 25 nautical miles) within which birds would be the main indicator. None of these extensions would be sufficient for the presence of land to be recognized before losing sight of the homeland, on the long-range exploratory voyages the Polynesians are known to have made.

It is possible, however, that, as in the Irish discovery

of Iceland (5.7.3), migratory birds, year after year, out and back on the same route, may have indicated the direction of lands beyond the horizon to some of the would-be migrant Polynesians. For example, golden plover that breed in Alaska migrate in the autumn to south-east Polynesia via the Aleutians, Hawaii, Fanning, Christmas, and the Society islands (Hornell, 1946b: 144). Thus Tahiti and Raiatea islanders could well have deduced there was land to the north (i.e. the Hawaiian group). It should be noted that this argument can be used in reverse to suggest Hawaiian knowledge of the Society islands. A second example: the long-tailed cuckoo and the shearwater migrate from the New Zealand region to the Society islands: both outward and inward flights would tell Raiateans that there was land to the south-west (Hornell, 1946b: 144; Irwin, 1992: 107).

Archaeological and ethnographic studies tend to suggest that Hawaii and New Zealand were indeed settled from the Society islands. By following the flight line of migratory birds, searches for these island groups could have been restricted to a narrow sector, resulting in an increased chance of success. However, these voyages were late in the migration period and were generally orientated across the predominant wind: they therefore can throw little light on whether, in earlier times, explorers from east Melanesia and west Polynesia had similar indications of the direction in which islands over the horizon lay, and thus could narrow down their search area to a sector, say, 20° either side of the predominant wind.

### 9.5.3 NAVIGATIONAL TECHNIQUES

Traditional methods of navigation did not long survive the European arrival in Polynesia, but they did continue to be used into the twentieth century in Micronesia where they were taught in special schools (Haddon and Hornell, 1936: 145). Through the efforts of Dr David Lewis and others, from the 1960s onwards, these non-instrumental techniques were not only documented but also tested at sea (D. Lewis, 1994). Whilst this work has thrown considerable light on some of the navigational practices of the early Oceanic voyagers, it has not increased our knowledge of the special techniques needed on *exploratory* voyages when searching unknown seas for land beyond the horizon. On such

exploratory voyages, the navigator had to maintain a 'mental plot' of his position relative to home base; if land was found that also had to be 'plotted'; and when he successfully returned home and thereby completed the geographical closure, his first estimate of the outbound track could be amended. On subsequent voyages to this 'new found' land, both track and distance (however these were measured) would be known, and positions could be 'plotted' as deviations from this track and as a distance from the destination island—a different approach from that needed on the initial, exploratory voyage. Experimental voyages (9.2.6) can replicate the conditions of such repeat voyages, but not those of an exploratory voyage into the unknown, except to some degree when sailing close-hauled, when the wind's changing velocity determines the boat's course and the navigator has to keep a running plot of the consequent alterations in the boat's track—as the experimental navigators found, this required long hours of almost constant attention—see, for example, Finney *et al.* (1986: 66).

It is clear from the navigational experiments, that the process of navigating without instruments is greater than the sum of its parts; in fact it cannot in practice be compartmentalized into such aspects as 'direction' and 'speed', although for analytical and instructional purposes this may have to be done (D. Lewis, 1994: 48, 323; Finney *et al.*, 1986: 86). The position of the boat is deduced from nearly simultaneous observations of several phenomena, none of which need be measured precisely. It is pertinent to note, in this context, that two important works on the history of navigation (E. Taylor, 1971; Waters, 1978) include in their titles the phrases 'haven-finding art' and 'art of navigation' where 'art' implies personal skills. Non-instrumental navigation was an art *par excellence*: practitioners used past experience to analyse recent observations of the states of several independent variables—the relative position of heavenly bodies, the wind velocity and other aspects of weather, the swell direction, the movement of the boat through the water, the wake angle, and so on.

The summary exposition given below, of the non-instrumental techniques used in Oceania must necessarily deal with individual aspects separately; however, the holistic approach used in practice should be remembered. It is also important to note that, although the techniques described are consistent with

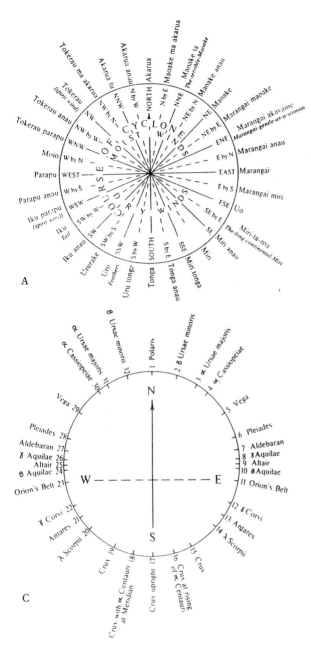

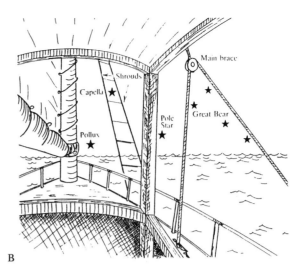

Fig. 9.13. Diagrams of directional aids to navigation. A: Cook Islands wind compass; B: steering by Polaris and Ursa Major; C: Carolinian star compass (after Lewis, 1994: figs. 19, 14, 16).

North Pole; likewise the Southern Cross for the Southern Pole.

### 9.5.3.1 TAKING DEPARTURE

Well before embarkation, the bearing of sunset or sunrise was checked against landmarks and the weather outlook ascertained. At embarkation, the velocity of the wind and the current were noted. Once clear of land, the direction of the wind and the swell, and the bearing of the sun or notable stars, were noted and any current set confirmed. With a fair wind, course was laid for the destination, allowing for estimated set and leeway; with a foul wind, the boat was sailed full and by, and estimates made of the deviation from the direct track. Before losing sight of land, the navigator 'took departure' by estimating his position relative to landmarks—this became the first datum on his 'mental chart'. Whenever possible this departure was timed so that landfall would be made in daylight. Sighting stones from which departure was taken are said to have been identified in Kiribati and Tonga (Haddon and Hornell, 1936: 25, 156; D. Lewis, 1994: 101, 119, 147–9, 363; McGrail, 1983b; 1998: 277–8).

### 9.5.3.2 DIRECTIONS

Directional systems may be based on the wind, the swell, the sun, and notable stars (Fig. 9.13), and Micro-

the methods noted in general terms by Cook and other Europeans in the late eighteenth century (9.5), they are not necessarily those of 2,000 or even 500 years earlier. Nevertheless, the fact that several of these techniques are known to have been used in other parts of the world at an early date (4.14.2, 5.7.3) tends to make early Oceanic use likely. A third caveat is that the methods described are mainly those of Micronesia, between the Equator and 20° north; whereas Polynesian voyages were generally between the Equator and 20° south, whence Polaris and the celestial North Pole cannot be seen. However, the circumpolar constellation Ursa Major can give an idea of the position of the celestial nesians are known to have used all of these. Each system can be used only for a limited period because of intrinsic qualities or because of worsening observational conditions. Selected rising and setting stars were used within $c.15°$ of the horizon, ten or so stars being so used in succession each night. A key star was the one known to rise or set over the destination. Circumpolar constellations were used to identify the celestial poles, the null points around which the night sky appears to revolve. In certain meteorological conditions, the swell came from an obvious direction and could be used as a datum for lengthy periods; at other times, complex swell patterns had to be analysed by 'feel' to identify the direction of the dominant swell. The wind changed in direction more frequently than the swell, and was best used in conjunction with other systems. The directions of sunrise and sunset changed slightly each day, but could be used as datums with a variable but known angular displacement ('amplitude') from east and west. In tropical latitudes, the sun was used for $c.$three hours around sunrise and sunset, and also at its zenith (i.e. noon).

A course which allowed for leeway and set was steered relative to whichever directional datum was dominant at a particular time. For example, by leaving the celestial pole on the port beam, or the predominant swell on the starboard beam, the wind on the starboard bow, the destination's horizon star fine on the bow, or the rising sun dead ahead. Courses were held by maintaining the mast or an element of rigging in line with the required datum (Fig. 9.13B), or by the feel of the wind.

Each of these systems can be generalized by noting, for example, the directions from which blow all winds that can be identified: the result is a wind 'rose' (Fig. 9.13A). A star 'compass' can similarly be generated (Fig. 9.13C). Because such natural phenomena are not spaced at regular intervals around the horizon, the winds, swells, and horizon stars seldom divide the horizon into equal sectors. The resulting roses, when turned into a diagram, are unfamiliar to European eyes, but in Oceania these roses or compasses are not instruments but concepts, and there is little problem in incorporating them into the indigenous navigational system. The directional system using the celestial pole is more familiar to twentieth-century Europeans. Once that fixed direction is recognized, the horizon can be divided into segments by successively halving the azimuth circle, resulting in eight, sixteen, or thirty-two equal sectors or 'points'.

As latitude is changed, the night sky also changes and familiar constellations drop below the horizon astern, and new ones appear ahead. The celestial North and South Poles remain on the same bearing, as does the east–west configuration of Orion's Belt; otherwise all star bearings change as ground is made to north or south (D. Lewis, 1994: 82–136, 157; Irwin, 1992: 44–8, 216–18; McGrail, 1983b, 1998: 280–1).

### 9.5.3.3 DISTANCE, SPEED, AND TIME

The estimation of distance made good in the direction of the target island is a complex process, involving, *inter alia*, the integration of time and speed. Although Lewis himself used the Dutchman's log to estimate speeds by counting seconds or chanting a standard phrase whilst passing a patch of foam, Micronesian navigators appeared to judge it by eye—probably by an integrated assessment of spray, turbulence, and wind pressure. Distance was understood as so many days' sail—an averaging out of several voyages on the same route. During each day, there were recognizable fixed points in time such as sunrise, noon, and sunset. The passage of time could be estimated from the sun's position between times; at night by the regularity of the sky's rotation from east to west at $15°$ an hour (D. Lewis, 1994: 159–62; McGrail, 1983b, 1998: 281–2).

### 9.5.3.4 KEEPING THE RECKONING

Micronesians kept their reckoning whilst on passage by a system known as *etak*. This may be thought of as a mental process by which information from many sources—wind, sea, sun, stars; estimates of time and speeds; and summations of leeway and drift—were integrated and then 'plotted' on a mental chart which gave the boat's position relative to a distant island (more or less on the beam) which apparently moved from one 'point' of the compass (rose) to another, on a reciprocal course to that of the boat which was considered to be stationary. As the voyage progressed, so different reference islands were used.

As new information became available to the navigator so the boat's position was updated. During twilight (a short period in the Tropics), most, if not all, sources of navigational information could be observed.

Towards the end of a day during which the sun, wind, and sea had been the principal aids, the night sky could also be used simultaneously; an integration of all this data produced a more reliable position. Leeway estimates were revised by looking at the wake angle—for the 'average' boat sailing full and by this was *c*.15°. Currents were usually taken to flow with the predominant wind, but could also be judged by the shape and size of waves, e.g. a short steep sea meant that the current was set against the swell.

From his experience, Lewis considers that a longer voyage does not mean greater inaccuracy. Errors due to unperceived environmental changes or to misestimates of direction or speeds do not necessarily accumulate in one direction; in fact, over a long journey, they seem to cancel out (D. Lewis, 1994: 173–91, 265; Irwin, 1992: 43–52, 218; McGrail, 1998: 282).

### 9.5.3.5 STAR ALTITUDES AND LATITUDE SAILING

It has sometimes been suggested that Micronesians used a form of latitude sailing, i.e. sailing to the 'latitude' of a target island and upwind of it; then maintaining that 'latitude' and sailing downwind to landfall. By 'latitude' is meant either: (a) that position where the altitude of the Northern Pole is the same as at the target island, or (b) that position where a known star directly overhead of a boat was also the zenith star for the target island. The altitude of the Pole may be measured in hand spans (Finney, 1994: figs. 15 and 16), each of which at arms' length subtends *c*.15° at the eye—this may be compared with the use of a *kamal* by medieval Arab seafarers (3.8.2.2.3). To determine when a particular star is directly over a boat it is necessary to sight up the mast when sailing on an east/west heading, or some such means. Accuracy down to a ½° (equivalent to a 30 nautical miles radius on the ocean) has been claimed, but has not yet been substantiated. In any case, there is little, if any, evidence that Micronesians did use latitude sailing (D. Lewis, 1994: 186, 277–89; Irwin, 1992: 50–3; McGrail, 1998: 279). On the other hand, it *is* conceivable that *approximate* polar altitudes and zenith stars were used, *along with other data*, in the *etak* evaluation process. It is doubtful, however, whether the ability to use latitude sailing can justifiably be included as a Polynesian navigational technique, as Irwin has done in his Strategy 4 (1992: 139).

### 9.5.3.6 LANDFALL

The phenomenon of the expanded target and the fact that islands in the South Pacific were often found to be in groups meant that 'dead on the nose' navigation was not essential to ensure a landfall. Land could be sighted anywhere forward of the beam, and if it proved to be the wrong island, course could be altered for other visible islands. To ensure that a boat was not downwind of its target at landfall, the courses steered towards the end of a voyage could be intentionally biased upwind and, if possible, up-current. Similarly, if there was any possibility of overrunning the target during the night, the boat would be hove-to until daylight (D. Lewis, 1994: 92–3, 201, 286; Irwin, 1992: 47).

### 9.5.4 NAVIGATION IN PREHISTORIC OCEANIA

The techniques outlined above provide a coherent system for navigating without instruments in tropical latitudes, as has been demonstrated in trials by Lewis and others. The apparent inaccuracies and approximations evident in individual aspects were offset by the *etak* method of evaluating all available data before reaching a conclusion, and by the cushioning effects of the extended range at which early warning could be obtained of target islands. Nevertheless, successful navigators had to have extraordinary capabilities, including the ability to memorize vast quantities of detailed information—possibly in verse form—and apply it in circumstances which never quite repeated themselves. They were truly master navigators.

As summarized above, the navigation system applies to Micronesia in, at best, the late eighteenth century AD. Whether it can be applied to the migration period is a moot point. Moreover, it is implicit in the system that the navigator knows where he is going, and is familiar, either personally or through handed-on experience, with the route, with lands invisible on passage, and with the general region of the target island. Although it is possible to see how aspects of this system could be used on an exploratory voyage into unknown seas, the detailed application is not yet clear.

# 10
# CHINA

## 10.1
## The Environmental Background

### 10.1.1 INNER AND OUTER CHINA
(Fig. 10.1)

China's topographical features had a strong influence on her communication links with the rest of the world. The core of the Chinese region—that of the historical Chinese empire until the end of the Ming dynasty in the mid-seventeenth century, is a relatively low-lying area extending *c*.1,000 miles from the coast between the Gulf of Chichli (Bo Hai) in the north, and the Gulf of Tonking in the south, with three great river systems, the Yellow River (Huang Ho) in the north, then the Yangtze (Chang Chiang = long river), and the smaller but important Pearl River (Bei Chiang) in the south. Surrounding this Inner China, and politically separate from it until the expansionist policies of the Qing or Manchu dynasty (1644–1912), is Outer China, a highland zone stretching in a semicircle from Manchuria in the north-east, through Gobi and Mongolia to the mountains and jungles of eastern Burma and northern Indo-China. The rivers and the coast of Inner China form a complex water transport network underpinning the economy, whereas in Outer China the rivers either flow out of China or, being headwaters, are usable only with difficulty.

The generally inhospitable Outer China, with its mountains, fierce deserts, and huge swamps, thus effectively cuts off Inner China, with its alluvial valleys and rolling hills, from contacts with the rest of the Asian continent, the only practicable way to the West

being the 'Silk Road', a hazardous and difficult caravan route which ran from the middle reaches of the Yellow River (Huang Ho) along the Gansu corridor and through the Jade Gates pass; then either north or south of the Tarim basin and westwards to southern and central Asia and thence to Europe. China's best outlets to the world have thus been by sea: across the Yellow Sea to Korea and Japan (Ma, 1991: 189); by the East China Sea to the Ryukyu islands and Taiwan; and by the South China Sea to maritime south-east Asia, thence to India and beyond.

Along the Chinese coast, in the summer months May to September, the prevailing wind is generally from the southern sector. Typhoons with storm-force winds occur during this period mainly in June to August (Ma, 1991: 188). In the winter months, October to March, there is a seasonal monsoon wind from a northerly direction in both the Yellow Sea and the South China Sea, whilst in the East China Sea the north-east trades prevail.

Two main sea currents affect the area: the Black Current, a warm current forming in the Malacca strait flows northward along the Chinese coast past the Ryukyu islands to the Korean strait where it becomes known as the Tsushima Current. From there it flows along the east coast of the Japanese archipelago to the Tsugaru strait between Honshu and Hokkaido and the Soya strait, north of Hokkaido. This current is generally visible as a black stream some 48 km (30 nautical miles) wide: it flows at *c*.1.5 knots. The cold current, Liman, forms in the Tartar strait between Sakhalin islands and the Russian mainland and flows southwards along the east coast of Korea to enter the East China Sea near the Jizhou peninsula.

The best time for a southerly voyage with a favour-

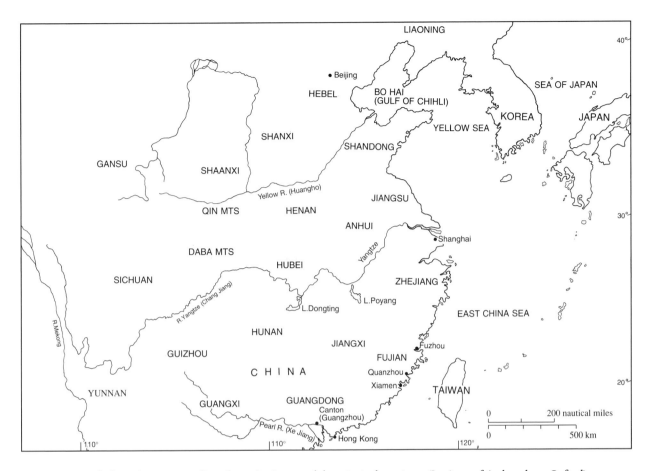

Fig. 10.1. Map of China showing coastline, the main rivers, and the principal provinces (Institute of Archaeology, Oxford).

able wind, albeit against the current, is thus during the period October to March, and it is noteworthy that the Chinese admiral Zheng He, on his series of early fifteenth-century voyages to south-east Asia, the Indian Ocean and beyond (10.10.4), invariably timed his departure from the northern ports so that he entered open water in January or February (Willetts, 1964: 27–30). Furthermore, Zheng He's return voyages from the south were timed so that he was in northern waters by July, thereby using southerly winds and the north-flowing current, but keeping ahead of the main season of typhoons.

## 10.1.2  NORTH AND SOUTH CHINA

As well as an Inner and Outer China, there is also a geographical division between North and South, the dividing line being north of the valley of the Yangtze as it crosses the East China Plain, and the Qin Ling and Daba mountain ranges to the west—a latitude of c.35°N. Although there is much more rain on average in the south than in the north, flooding and drought are more common in the north.

In the north the Yellow River (Huang Ho) flows in its upper reaches through the loess ('yellow earth'), a fine wind-blown soil which it deposits as silt in its lower reaches—this leads to frequently shifting channels and the general fluvial instability of the region. During the second millennium BC, the Yellow River entered the sea at the north end of Bo Hai (Gulf of Chihli). The principal mouth gradually moved southward so that, by the thirteenth/fourteenth centuries AD it entered the Yellow Sea south of the Shandong peninsula. Subsequently it has moved north and south in an irregular fashion (Blunden and Elvin, 1983: 16). On the other hand, this readily cultivated soil facilitated the earliest appearance of agriculture in the Chinese Neolithic

Age. The general instability of this loess region has meant, however, that although there was locally intensive use of water transport inland, extensive water communications were difficult.

Further south, the Yangtze and the Pearl Rivers are more stable. The Yangtze, in fact, discharges more water than the Yellow River but two great lakes in its middle reaches, Dongting and Poyang, act as reservoirs and thus even out the flow (Blunden and Elvin, 1983: 16). The Pearl River with its west, north, and east tributaries forms a very fertile delta region where it enters the South China Sea. Much of this southern region, from the Yangtze to the Pearl, is crossed by navigable rivers leading to the intensive and extensive use of water transport.

## 10.1.3 COASTAL WATERS AND THEIR INFLUENCE ON HULL SHAPE

The coastal waters of China may also be divided into northern and southern regions by physical features. In the Yellow Sea region, as far south as Hangzhou Bay at c.30°N, the coastal waters and river mouths are shallow, often with shifting sandbanks. South of Hangzhou Bay, on the other hand, in the East China Sea and the South China Sea regions, the rockbound coast has deeper waters with fjord-like harbour entrances and offshore islands (Donnelly, 1924: 8; Needham, 1971: 429; Liu and Li, 1991: 275). These very different waters appear to have led to the development of two different types of vessel.

In descriptions and illustrations from the early part of the twentieth century (Audemard, 1957–69; Greenhill, 1976: 103–5; 1995a: 83–4; Maitland, 1981: 54–9), we can see that Chinese ships, north and south, had several characteristics in common:

*Form*: All had fore-and-aft rocker, a transom stern and, generally, a smaller transom bow (above the waterline).

*Structure*: They were built in the frame-first sequence, but with the planking also fastened together (10.7.2). The sequence of building was: bottom planking (and keel); bulkheads; side planking.

*Propulsion*: They had multiple masts with battened lugsails and multiple sheets with which the crew could finely tune the sail shape. Leeboards were used, especially in the north.

*Steering*: They had a median (hoistable) rudder in a well.

The differences were partly structural but mainly in form. The northern ship had a keel-less, flat bottom with a sharp chine, bluff, stem-less bows, and a bluff, overhanging stern. The southern ship was generally bigger, with greater draft and more beam at the waterline. She had a keel (*lung ku* = dragon spine), a V-shaped lower hull with rounded bilges and a sharper entry, more rounded stern and, in general, her hull was more finely moulded and curvaceous than the northern ship (Greenhill 1976: 100–6; Donnelly, 1924: 8–10; Peng, 1988: 81; Zhou, 1983: 479–81; Liu and Li, 1991: 275). These differences in form and in structure, appear to have arisen because of the differences in coastal geography. Of the two types, the southern ship was the more suitable for overseas voyages, whereas the northern type was better for coastal and estuary work, and in particular, could take the ground well within tidal harbours.

The example of the southern ship most frequently quoted by twentieth-century Chinese authors is the *Fuchuan* ship from the Fujian Province. The *Guangdong* (Canton) ships from the Pearl River region were similar and this is the type best known to Europeans. Chinese authors (e.g. Zhou, 1983: 479) believe that they can trace this Fuchuan/Guangdong seagoing ship-type back to the Song dynasty (AD 960–1279).

It is also believed that the northern type can be traced back to the medieval *shachuan* ship (sand ship). Its origins are said to lie in the lower reaches of the Yangtze River in the T'ang dynasty (AD 618–909), or even in the period of the Warring States (481–221 BC) (Peng, 1988: 73; Zhou, 1983: 479–81). These authors give no references for their statements, but they appear to be using documentary and iconographic evidence. There are, however, documentary references from the Qing dynasty (1644–1912) to the use of a thousand and more *shachuan* to transport grain from the southern region (presumably down the Yangtze River) to Beijing via the coastal route and then a canal (Peng, 1988: 73). The fourteenth-century 'official inspecting boat' excavated in Liangshan, Shandong province in 1956 (10.4.2.8) is said to be of this type (Peng, 1988: 78). Zhou (1983: 480) also claims that *shachuan* were used in the tenth century AD for voyages to Java, and that early depictions of Chinese vessels in India and Indonesia also are of these 'sand ships'.

Whatever the origins of these two types of vessel, the northern *sachuan* and the southern *Fuchuan*, the differences between them, as they were perceived in the late nineteenth/early twentieth centuries, appear to be clear. The question now to be asked is whether a similar division can be seen in earlier times.

## 10.2
# Early Water Transport

### 10.2.1 SOURCES OF EVIDENCE

Professor Needham, polymath author of the major study of Chinese science and civilization (1971: 374–486; Ronan, 1986: 60–127) and Chinese authors such as Zhou (1983) argue that twentieth-century Chinese ships are the result of a monolinear development and that the distinctive features of recent Chinese ships can be traced back to early times.

When investigating an ancient culture like China which has been literate for millennia, there is a strong temptation for historians to build theories based entirely and almost uncritically on literary and representational evidence, forgetting that early accounts of seafaring are not precise descriptions such as appear in twentieth-century manuals of seamanship and navigation, and that early illustrations and models are not craftsmen's drawings or scale models from which a ship could be built. In his introductory paper to the Proceedings of the first international conference on sailing-ship history, held in Shanghai in December 1991, Yang Yu succinctly described this situation:

As the relics of ancient ships are scarce, the descriptions in old literature are usually ambiguous, sometimes even contradictory, so that to find out the realities of their existence is a troublesome affair. A lot of arguments arise from the differences of understanding. (Yang, 1991: 1).

The early Chinese annals, encyclopaedias, drawings, models, and other representational evidence were not produced with the aim of informing twentieth-century investigators: on the contrary, one of their main aims was to impress contemporary readers, listeners, and observers with the importance, the magnificence, and often the uniqueness of what they describe, so that exaggeration was permitted and uncertainties recorded as fact—this equally applies to medieval European history. To obtain a more authentic view of Chinese maritime history it is essential that these sources be assessed critically and be dated accurately so that a consistent and reliable framework is established. Furthermore, it is necessary to search out, record, and publish excavated examples of boats and ships and other maritime artefacts. Archaeology can frequently illuminate the historical record and reveal aspects of ancient times not otherwise documented. Without the control of excavated evidence, wrong conclusions can be drawn from limited historical information. Needham (1971: 392; Ronan, 1986: 67) believed that, ' . . . while it is not possible to say that dugout canoes (logboats) occur nowhere in the Chinese culture-area, they are in occurrence and distribution exceedingly sparse. Generally speaking, too, they seem to have disappeared during or before the Han' (i.e. second century AD or earlier). Recent archaeological research has revealed many early examples of logboats which suggests (*pace* Needham) that, as in many parts of the world, they were used widely in early China and continued in some places to be used into recent times (10.2.9). Archaeological evidence for other types of vessel and the use of naval architectural principles and scientific dating methods may similarly show that, for example, early Chinese ships were not as large as documentary and illustrative evidence has heretofore led some to believe, and that some of the Chinese nautical innovations are not dated as precisely as has been thought.

### 10.2.2 THE EARLIEST CRAFT

The main foci of Early Neolithic China were in the North-Central region, in the middle reaches of the Yellow River (Huang Ho) around the confluence where that river was joined by the Wei River and Fen River; and in the Ch'ing lien kang region of the Lower Yangtze (Glover, 1980: 156). In c.1850 BC the earliest Chinese Bronze Age civilization, known as the Shang, emerged out of that Neolithic culture (Bayard, 1980), in what is now western Henan province, on high ground clear of the Huang Ho's flood plain. This was a riverine-based civilization with a need for water transport.

In the late Shang (or Yin) period from *c.*1400 BC the characteristic Chinese ideographic script evolved, examples of which have been found engraved on bone (the so-called 'oracle' bones) and tortoiseshell, and sometimes on bronzes and on pottery (Bayard, 1980). Amongst these ideograms was the earliest form of the word *chou* (*zhou*) = 'boat' (Fig. 10.2) (Needham, 1971: 439; Ronan, 1986: 102; Liu, 1991: 321). Whether this demonstrates that boats of those times were rectangu-

Fig. 10.2. The earliest Chinese ideogram for *chou*: boat (after Ronan, 1986: 102).

lar in shape as Needham believed or whether this ideograph was merely an arbitrary scribal convention, is difficult to say. It is also difficult to decide whether this symbol represents a planked boat or some other form of water transport such as a log raft or possibly a logboat. There is a similar difficulty in the interpretation of the 'canoe-shaped' pottery vessels excavated from Neolithic sites of *c.*4000 to 5000 BC on the east Liaoning peninsula on the shores of the Yellow Sea (Xu, 1986: 1–2; Peng, 1988: 15–16) and the Lower Yangtze (Liu, 1991: 324–5): if they are models of boats, what type of boat do they represent?

Paddles have also been excavated from Neolithic sites (Liu, 1991: 324; Peng, 1988: 14–15). These may have been used for boat propulsion: on the other hand, they may have been used in the bakery, dairy, brewery, or field (McGrail, 1998: 206).

On theoretical grounds almost all types of water transport (float, raft, or boat) ever devised by Man were technologically feasible by Neolithic times (Table 1.2). The direct archaeological evidence for Chinese rafts and non-plank boats is very sparse, being limited to logboats—in this it is very similar to Europe. However, in the recent past the following have been used in Greater China (Peng, 1988: 12–27; Needham, 1971; Ronan, 1986):

- bundle rafts, and bark boats in north-east China (Manchuria);

- buoyed rafts and hide boats in the upper reaches of the Yellow River;
- hide boats in the upper Yellow, Yangtze, Yalung, Mekong, Heilong Rivers, and in Korea;
- log rafts in Taiwan and Fujian province, and also on the major rivers for downstream transport of logs;
- logboats on the Riyueton River in Taiwan; on the Heilong River (Amur) in north-east China (Manchuria); the middle and upper reaches of the Yellow River and on Lake Bosten in Xinjiang province; and on the rivers of Yunnan, Guizhou, Guangxi, and Guangdong provinces in southern China.

With the exception of the fishing log rafts of the coasts of Fujian province (Peng, 1988: 20), all these simple rafts and boats are, or were, used in Outer China: Manchuria in the north-east; Gansu and Qinghai in the north-west; Tibet in the west; Yunnan to Guandong in the south; and in Taiwan to the south-east. However, the fact that these craft are not used today in Inner China does not necessarily mean that they were not used there in earlier times, and although there is direct evidence for the earlier use only of logboats, there is other evidence to suggest that the distribution of rafts, and those boats that are neither logboats or plank boats, may have formerly been wider than it is today.

## 10.2.3 BUNDLE RAFTS

Nowadays bundle rafts are limited to north-east China where they have an unusual form with reed bundles fastened at right angles to one another to make an open framework pattern (Peng, 1988: 21) rather than all bundles being parallel as in other parts of the world (McGrail, 1998: 163–72). Needham (1971: 390, 396) states that reed-bundle rafts (*phu fa*) are 'not unknown' in China, but does not discuss them further. The only, very minor, evidence for their use in antiquity is an engraving on a possible third-century BC bronze bell (Nishimura, 1925: 114–15, fig. 33).

## 10.2.4 BUOYED RAFTS

Rafts buoyed by hide floats (*mu ying*) were used by a Han dynasty (206 BC–AD 220) army to cross the Yellow River, and similar use is described in an eleventh-centu-

ry text and illustrated in Ming (AD 1379–1644) encyclopaedias (Needham, 1971: 387). A similar raft, but
buoyed by pots, is illustrated in another Ming text
(Nishimura, 1936). The buoyed raft is now restricted to
the upper reaches of the Yellow River in Gansu
province—see de Courcy-Ireland (1991) for a recent
account. Worcester (1966: 122) noted that, after this
voyage downstream, the framework of buoyed rafts
was sold and the floats returned to their region of origin—as also known in Mesopotamia (3.4.5).

## 10.2.5  LOG RAFTS

Confucius, who lived c.551–479 BC in the Chou dynasty,
is said to have used a sailing raft (Needham, 1971: 396),
but the earliest known literary reference to log or bamboo rafts is from c.472 BC (Needham, 1971: 390). The sailing log raft known today in Taiwan and on the Fujian
coast opposite (Peng, 1988: 20), may not be indigenous,
as it was used by Taiwan aborigines in the twelfth and
thirteenth centuries BC (Needham, 1971: 393), some 500
years before the Chinese began to settle Taiwan. A similar raft used today in northern Indo-China (8.3.1) has
two or three masts and three or more *guares* (6.6.3, 8.3.1,
9.3.4) or movable leeboards, whereas the smaller Taiwan or Formosan sailing raft has only two *guares* and
but one mast, on which is hoisted a single balanced lugsail with battens (Fig. 10.3). This raft is made of a dozen
or so large bamboos lashed together and to curved
thwartship bamboos so that the bottom is curved both
transversely and longitudinally. Two steering-oars are
used over the stern and the *guares* are used to assist
steering and to reduce leeway when close-hauled.

Doran (1978) has documented something of the Taiwan raft's performance. On short, exploratory voyages, he found that they were sea-kindly, unsinkable,
and capable of being righted if capsized. Doran estimated that sailing with the wind they could achieve c.3
knots and they made best progress to windward when
c.6 points (67½°) off the wind.

## 10.2.6  BARK BOATS

Bark boats have only been noted on the Amur River in
China's Manchurian province of Heilongjiang. The
only other sign of the use of bark boats in this region is

Fig. 10.3. A model of the Taiwanese sailing log raft (National Maritime Museum, Greenwich).

some very minor evidence from Japan (Nishimura,
1931: 203–7).

## 10.2.7  HIDE BOATS

Hide boats are used today in the headwaters of the
Yangzte, Yellow, Yalung (Brahmaputra), and Heilong
(Amur) Rivers, and in Korea. These are mostly circular
in form (although rectangular ones are known in
Tibet—Hornell, 1946a: 99–100), and small in size.
There are several references in Chinese literature to
them from the fourth century AD onwards and Needham (1971: 386) has identified depictions on the walls of
a cave at Chhien-fo-tung as round hide boats of the Sui
dynasty (c.AD 581–618). A dictionary of the Ming dynasty (seventeenth century AD or earlier) defines *pi
chhuan* as a hide over a framework of bamboo or wood
(Nishimura, 1931: 180) and boats of this type seem to
have been used by the invading Mongols of the thirteenth century AD (Needham, 1971: 386).

## 10.2.8 BASKET BOATS

These boats are made from closely woven basketwork split bamboo which is caulked with a waterproof mixture of dung and coconut oil. Although unknown in China, they have been used extensively in Indo-China both inland and at sea (8.3.3).

## 10.2.9 LOGBOATS

Contrary to Needham's assertion (1971: 392), logboats have been used widely in twentieth-century China, although mostly in Outer China. They are known in Manchuria in the north-east, Xinjiang, Gansu, and Qinghai in the north-west and Yunnan in the south-west, in the remote parts of Guizhou, Guangxi, and Guangdong in the south and south-east, and in the island of Taiwan (Peng, 1988: 24–77).

Records of thirty-five excavated logboats have been traced, all from the eastern and southern coastal provinces: twenty-one from Jiangsu; five from Zhejiang; one from Fujian; seven from Guangdong; and one from Guangxi (Lin, 1991: 324–6; Peng, 1988: 25–7). This distribution is probably due to recent developments in the lower reaches of rivers rather than a reflection of the true picture. Only two of these are dated by radiocarbon assay, the others for which dates are given appear to be dated by association or by stratigraphy. Two fragments of logboats from Zhejiang are from the Neolithic at c.4250 BC; the twenty-one boats from Jiangsu and three from Zhejiang are

from the Late-Chou or Warring States period (c.722–221 BC). One boat from Guangdong is from the Qin dynasty (c.221–206 BC); one from Fujian and one from Guangxi are from the Western Han dynasty (260 BC–AD 10); six from Guangdong are from the Eastern Han (AD 10–220); and one from Zhejiang is from the Tang dynasty (AD 618–909).

The timber species is given only in two cases: a boat from Fujian province (c.7.1 × 1.6 × 0.83 m) and a boat from Guangdong province (c.10.7 × 1.3 × 0.8 m) are of camphor wood. The longest boat for which measurements are given is from Jiangsu province, c.11 × 0.90 × 0.42 m; the shortest is from Guangxi, c.4.7 × 0.5 × 0.3 m. From photographs published by Peng (1988) and from some measured drawings published by Dai (1985) these Chinese logboats seem to have features in common with European logboats (5.3.1): rounded and rectangular transverse sections; rounded and angular ends; beam ties across the ends; enigmatic holes through the sides; ridges across the bottom; washstrakes and stabilizers fastened on by treenails; and some may be paired and some extended in length.

More than twenty log coffins (chuanguan), similar in shape to logboats but with a partly hollowed half-log for a lid, have been found in Sichuan and Fujian provinces (Fig. 10.4). They are dated to the Warring States period, i.e. before c.221 BC (Peng, 1988: 27; Needham, 1971: 388–9; Johnstone, 1988: 187, fig. 14.2). One of these, now in the Fujian Museum, Fuzhou, was recovered from a cave in a cliff high above a river in the Wuyi Mountains of the Fujian province. The lower part of this log coffin measured c.4.5 m overall and resembled

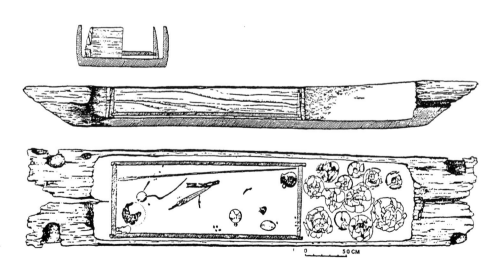

Fig. 10.4. A coffin-logboat from Pao-lun-yuan, Sichuan (after Needham, 1970: fig. 30).

a logboat with bulkheads and upturned ends. A male skeleton with grave goods was lying between the two bulkheads (*Fujianwenbo* 2 (1980)).

As in China, the use of logboats in Japan and Korea is more widespread than previously thought. Earlier authors (e.g. Suder, 1930: 11) assumed that they were only used by the Ainu peoples of Hokkaido: in fact they are now known to have been used in Honshu, Kyushu, and Korea, and also in the Ryuku islands between Japan and Taiwan (Deguchi, 1991: 197; Nishimura, 1931: 204; Worcester, 1956b). Simple logboats are still used for fishing in the north of Japan at Akita and in the south in Kagoshima Wan (Deguchi, 1991: 199). The Ainu logboats had one or two washstrakes sewn on to the sides in overlapping fashion (Deguchi, 1991: 201).

More than 200 logboats have been excavated in recent times from Japanese sites which include Osaka, Chiba, and Tokyo, the oldest known being a simple logboat of *sugi* wood from Torihama, Fukui, which is dated to the Upper Joman period of the Neolithic at *c.*3500 BC (Deguchi, 1991: 198, 203).

## 10.2.10 PLANK BOATS

### 10.2.10.1 PICTOGRAMS

Pictorial characters from the Shang dynasty (late second millennium BC) engraved on bone and on tortoiseshell (Fig. 10.2) represent the oldest known Chinese word for boat (*chou*). This element is also contained in contemporary pictograms for 'ship' (*chhuan*), 'transport' (*pan*), 'caulk (or to sew) a seam' (*chen*), and for 'propel by oar' (Peng, 1988: 31). There is also a related pictogram (*fan*) which has been interpreted as 'sail' (10.2.11, Fig. 10.8). Needham (1971: 439–40) and others believe that the *chou* pictogram may be derived from the shape and structure of the type of boat used in those days, i.e. a rectangular boat, built of planks and with bulkheads: in other words, the 'traditional' Chinese junk or sampan. An alternative hypothesis is that this symbol represents a log raft, which is likely to have preceded the planked boat as the main form of river transport. The interpretation of such symbols is fraught with difficulties (10.2.2).

### 10.2.10.2 COMPLEX LOGBOATS

Dai (1984; 1985) has described a wide range of complex logboats in China, in use in the recent past and today,

and Deguchi (1991) has described a comparable range in Japan and Korea. These are logboats extended vertically in height of sides by the addition of washstrakes, and in length by the addition of separate bow and stern portions. Other logboats have been extended in breadth by the insertion of bottom planking between logboat sides. There are also many examples of increasing the effective beam (and hence improving stability) by pairing two logboats, although there are no examples of the use of stabilizers or outriggers, or of increasing the beam measurement by expansion after heat treatment as can be found elsewhere in the world (5.3.1.6). This array of evidence leads both Dai and Deguchi to question the theory that the Chinese plank boat was developed from the raft (Needham, 1971), and to suggest that it was based on the complex logboat. Although this is plausible, there is little early archaeological evidence to support either theory, as is also the case in other regions of the world. Dai (1985) gives only one unambiguous excavated example of a complex logboat, one with holes near the top edges of both sides; this is undated, but other logboats he describes are dated by radiocarbon to the period *c.*1620 BC–*c.* AD 205. Deguchi (1991) describes two logboats with holes near their top edges, from Tomakomai, Hokkaido, Japan, dated *c.* AD 1400. Such holes need not be fastening points for washstrakes, as both authors believe, but may be where two logboats were paired or where temporary fittings were needed to hold the sides of the boat together during construction.

Deguchi also describes three other boats which had been broadened by inserting a bottom plank between the two sides of a logboat: a medieval find from Hachiro Lagoon, Japan, in which the planking was fastened by iron clamps and sealed by lacquer; a seventh–ninth-century AD boat from Anapchi Pond, Kyongju, South Korea, with nail and wooden fastenings (10.2.10.3); and a Han period (*c.*200 BC–*c.* AD 200) boat from near the Yangtze at Wujinxian, Jiangsu, China, where the planking was fastened by treenails. Peng (1988: 32) illustrates a similarly broadened boat excavated from Yanghe, Chuansha Co., Shanghai, but with a hollowed log which projected below the boat keel-fashion between the logboat sides, rather than a simple bottom plank. This boat also had holes along the sides near the top edge and an extended bow scarfed to the main hull. A similar logboat from Wujin Co., Jiangsu, is dated to the Han period. Deguchi mentions two logboats, possibly medieval, from Osaka, Japan, and from Shandong, China, which also had added bow and stern. These finds undoubtedly throw light on the range of wood-working and boatbuilding techniques used in medieval and earlier east Asia, but they cannot in themselves be direct evidence for the evolution of the plank boat, rather they suggest one possible line of development and this theory can only be taken further if and when excavation provides evidence for hybrid logboat/plank boats of an appropriately early date.

### 10.2.10.3 SEWN-PLANK BOATS

In Egypt, Britain, Denmark, and south-east Asia, the oldest known plank boats have their planking sewn or lashed together (2.7.1, 5.4, 8.3.7.1). There are other exca-vated sewn-plank boats from the Mediterranean, dated sixth/seventh century BC (4.9.4), and they are also known to have been used in east Africa and Arabia in the first century AD (2.11.5.3, 3.6). Sewn-plank boats were encountered by sixteenth- to seventeenth-cen-tury European explorers in Siberia, the South Pacific, India, south-west Chile, southern California, and the West Indies (9.4, 6.7.3, 11.4.7). Wherever they are found they seem to be amongst the earliest, if not *the* earliest, form of plank boat known. This may also have been the case in China; however, there appears to be mini-mal early documentary reference or representational evidence for them. This lack of evidence may be due to the fact that, by the time that technical descriptions and drawings of boats and ships began to be made (possibly in the Han dynasty(?)—*c.*200 BC–AD 200), sewn-plank boats were only used in the margins of China, having been mostly replaced by wooden and metal-fastened plank boats. In recent times sewn-plank boats have indeed been used in such peripheral places: by the Ainu in Japan; in Thailand, Vietnam and Burma, Taiwan/Formosa, Baoqing in Hunan Province (where there is a sailing boat known as *maobanchuan*); and Hainan island in Guangdong province (Lane-Fox, 1875: 408–12; Nishimura, 1920: 19; Manguin, 1985: 327; Peng, 1988: 31).

In a short article in the *China Daily* (8th Sept. 1982), Dai Kaiyuan described sewn-plank, oared fishing boats (*c.*10 × 2 × 1 m) he had found in use off Hainan island (see also Dai, 1983). Their planks were fastened togeth-er with coconut-fibre ropes or threads over a bamboo lath, and cogon grass was used to caulk the seams (Fig.

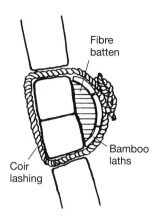

Fig. 10.5. Sewn-plank fastenings of a Hainan island boat (after Manguin, 1985: fig. 20.6).

10.5). In the same article, Dai quoted an early reference to sewn-plank boats: a text on plant life in south China published in *c.* AD 304 (*Nan Fang Raomur Huang*) states that foreigners used *gomuti* palm to fasten their ships. Needham (1971: 459) has also noted that Hui-Lin, an eighth-century AD Chinese monk, described in his *I Chhieh Ching Yin I*, how *Ku-Lun* people (from south-east Asia) used coconut-tree bark to fasten together parts of their ships; a similar statement was made by Ling Piao Lu I in the late ninth century AD (8.3.7.2).

During the Tang Dynasty (AD 618–909), Arab and Persian traders came to southern China in their sewn-plank ships (3.8.1). And by the twelfth/thirteenth cen-turies AD, during the Southern Song dynasty (AD 1127–1290), Zhou Qufei wrote in his *Linwaidaida* that large, seagoing sailing ships were being built of sewn planking in Guangdong province. Both Needham (1971: 459) and Dai (*China Daily*, 8 Sept. 1982) believe that traditional Chinese shipbuilders, at least as far back as the eighth century AD, used iron nail plank fas-tenings with a caulking of tung oil and lime. From the discussion above it would seem that sewn-plank fasten-ings were known in what is now southern China (pos-sibly culturally south-east Asia at that time) from at least the fourth century AD, and were used there from the twelfth century AD. Whether, in prehistoric times, sewn fastenings were used in other parts of China can only be investigated through excavation, or by meticu-lous investigation of the early logboats with holes through their sides (10.2.9).

An unusual plank boat, of the seventh to ninth cen-turies AD, excavated in 1975 from the Anapchi Pond in Kyongju, Southern Korea, is known from brief notes by Deguchi (1991: 202) and by Kim (1989: 7). This is said to be a *shilla* (a Korean dynasty) boat, *c.*5.9 m in length and made of a central bottom plank with upturned ends and two half-log, bilge strakes of 'L' cross-section (Fig. 10.6). The central bottom plank has cleats projecting upwards and through holes in them are transverse timbers—evidently generally similar in this respect to the Ferriby Bronze Age sewn-plank boats of the Humber region (5.4.2). There are lines across the seams on Kim's drawing but these are not described in his text:

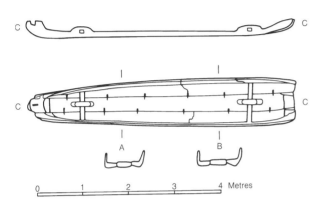

Fig. 10.6. Plans of a seventh/ninth-century AD plank boat from Anapchi Pond, Kyongju, Korea (after Kim, 1989: fig. 3).

by analogy with the Ferriby boats, they have been taken by some scholars to represent sewing. However, Deguchi's description (1991: 202) makes clear that these planks are fastened by metal nails, although the precise method is not given. On photographs in W. Lee (1990: 20) and in a companion volume in the Korean language on the Anapchi excavations (p. 77), no sewn fastenings are visible on the upper or underneath surfaces.

## 10.2.10.4 EARLY PLANK BOATS AND MODELS

The earliest direct evidence for plank boats comes from the Han dynasty (second century BC–early third century AD) remains of three boats excavated from Yanghe, Chuansha Co., Shanghai, from Wujin Co., Jiangsu, and from Guangzhou (Peng, 1988: 32). From the published photograph the Guangzhou find appears to be a three-plank boat with rising ends. The other two finds are also three-plank boats but of unusual construction: the central longitudinal member is effectively a thick plank-keel with a hollowed upper surface, with a horizontal scarf towards one end; the side

planks, also slightly hollowed, fit into rabbets along the top edges of the plank-keel—the fastening method is not shown—and horizontal holes at regular intervals near their top edges may be where crossbeams or benches were formerly fitted. These side planks are said to be 'nailed together'. The three vessels appear to be examples of river boats propelled by paddle.

The only other artefactual evidence for early boats comes from tomb models. The earliest of these models appear to be dated to the fourth to first centuries BC; they had steering oars rather than rudders, but Needham gives no further details (Ronan, 1986: 228).

A fragmented wooden tomb model from Changsha of the first century BC, now in the National Historical Museum in Beijing, has a flat bottom and overhanging punt-shaped ends (Peng, 1988: 35; Ronan, 1986: 105, fig. 196). This is an oared river boat, the oars being used through ports in the sides, with a steering oar worked in a notch at the stern. There is no indication of how the planking was fastened and no bulkheads or other framing are apparent.

Several pottery models excavated in the 1950s from first-century AD tombs in the vicinity of Guangzhou have the same general shape as the Changsha model (Ronan, 1986: 105–6, 228–9, figs. 197, 234, 235, 241; Peng, 1988: 36). Most evidence comes from one particular model made of grey clay and now in Guangzhou Museum (Fig. 10.7). This boat has two hatchways covered by awnings and giving entrance to the hold, and a cabin aft. Details of the structure cannot be deduced, but there appears to be no framing. This model probably represents a river cargo boat propelled by oars worked against tholes at deck level, and by poles used from the walkways which run along each side. There is no direct evidence for a mast but if, as Needham believes (Ronan, 1986: 166, 229), there was one, it was almost certainly a towing mast.

This boat was steered by an axial rudder slung under the overhanging stern. The trapezium-shaped, balanced rudder appears to be the earliest evidence for the use of a rudder on the centreline. There is an anchor suspended from a bollard in the bows—it appears to represent an anchor stone with wooden flukes attached.

An earthenware model boat from a tomb of *c.* AD 260 in Fanglu, Jintan Co., Jiangsu and now in the Changzhou Museum is of the same general shape but has no fittings other than a seat near one end and an

Fig. 10.7. Pottery boat model of the first century AD: the bow is to the left (Guangzhou Museum).

awning (Peng, 1988: 32). The model is not unlike the twentieth century *wupenchuan*, 'Black awning' boats used in many parts of China to carry cargo and passengers along and across rivers and canals. This small punt-shaped boat is nowadays propelled by one man sitting in the stern where he works a paddle with his hands over one side, and an oar with his feet over the other.

## 10.2.11 EARLY EVIDENCE FOR PROPULSION, STEERING, AND ANCHORING

### 10.2.11.1 PROPULSION

Seven wooden paddles have been excavated associated with a logboat from a fifth-millennium BC site at Lo Jin Corner Hermuda and Tong Xiang (Lin, 1991: 324, fig. 1). One of these has geometric patterns engraved at the junction of handle and blade.

One of the first-century AD pottery boat models from Guangzhou (Fig. 10.7) has walkways along each side which would have been used by men walking aft from forward, pushing on poles ('quanting') to propel the vessel in shallow waters. Use of poles is seen on rock carvings in a Eastern Han dynasty tomb (AD 25–221) at Xiaotangshan (Peng, 1988: 35).

Sixteen model oars were found in the first-century BC model boat from Changsha (10.2.10.4). They were pivoted through oarports in the top strake but whether the oarsmen were seated or standing, and whether they pulled or pushed their oars is not clear: today in Chinese rivers and harbours, oarsmen frequently stand and push (Wang, 1989: 52; Zhou, 1983: 490).

It has been claimed that this model also shows the use of a *yuloh* (sculling oar over the stern) but the model oar, pivoted in a central notch at the stern (Needham, 1971: fig. 961) is twice the length of the propulsion oars and seems more likely to be a steering-oar or sweep, than a yuloh. Needham (1971: 623) also considers that the yuloh was used in the Han dynasty (206 BC–AD 220), but the evidence he quotes is very meagre. However, a relief on a Han brick, noted by Peng (1988: 34) may depict a yuloh in use. A brief account by Lecomte, at the end of the seventeenth century, appears to be the earliest unambiguous reference to the yuloh system, although Needham (1971: 624) claims that there is a fourteenth-century painting by Yen Hui 'which clearly depicts the yuloh and its rope': Needham does not reproduce this painting.

There is no early direct evidence for sail, but ideograms on oracle bones and tortoiseshell of the Shang dynasty (Fig. 10.8) appear to suggest that sail was used before 1200 BC (Needham, 1971: 601; Sun, 1986). This argument turns on the interpretation of these pictorial characters, and Lin (1991: 321–2) has advanced alternative explanations for them. Other scholars have argued from early documents (Lin, 1991: 322–4; Wang, 1989: 52) that sails were first used during the Han dynasties (206 BC–AD 220). It is clear from the *Shih Ming* dictionary

Fig. 10.8. An early Chinese ideogram for *fan*: sail (after Ronan, 1986: 192).

compiled in *c.* AD 100 by Liu Hsi that sails of matting and cloth were in use by that time (Needham, 1971: 600). Lin (1991: 327, fig. 5) has published an engraving on an artefact excavated in Hunan and dated to the Warring States period (480–221 BC), which may depict a sail on a mast stepped amidships on a simple vessel. From this evidence he concludes that sail began to be used in China between 770 and 260 BC. The earliest certain period for the Chinese use of sails appears to be the Han dynasty: use in earlier periods is a matter of dispute.

Although the battened lugsail is nowadays closely associated with the Chinese maritime culture, it does not follow that this was the earliest form of Chinese sail. Indeed, by analogy with Europe and elsewhere it would be more likely that the earliest sail was a simple square sail. Such a sail may be described in the *Shih Ming* dictionary and depicted on the Hunan artefact—both from Han times. Square sails are almost certainly depicted on seagoing ships (10.4.1) on the fifth- or sixth-centuries AD Buddhist stone stele sculpture in a temple at Chengdu, Sichuan Province, and on the seventh-century frescos in the cave temples at Dunhuang in Gansu province (Needham, 1971: 455, 457, figs. 968, 970).

Needham (1971: 600–1; Ronan, 1986: 193–4) believes that a third-century AD text *Nan Zhou Yi Wu Zhi* by Wan Chen indicates that southern Chinese ships had matting fore-and-aft sails. However, this text is ambiguous and it could equally well be referring to south-east Asian ships with canted rectangular sails (8.3.8) rather than Chinese ships with lugsails (Xin and Yuan, 1991: 66–7). One of the sixth-/seventh-centuries AD ships on the Ajanta frescos, India (Fig. 6.11) has high-aspect ratio (possibly lug) sails on three masts slightly radiating like a fan, a feature traditionally associated with Chinese shipping (Needham, 1971: 454–5, fig. 967) but other aspects of this ship appear to be from the south-east Asian tradition. Dr Needham has claimed that one of the ships in the series depicted on the late eighth-century temple reliefs at Borobodur, Java (Needham, 1971: 457–8, fig. 974) is the 'oldest representation of a Chinese seagoing ship'. This ship is certainly different from the others at Borobodur (Fig. 8.6) in having no outrigger and only one mast (and that a pole mast). However, the sail on this vessel is scarcely visible: it may be 'a rigid Chinese lugsail with the matting texture clearly indicated' as Needham claims, but this is by no means certain.

The earliest depiction of a battened lugsail on a vessel with Chinese characteristics appears to be that carved in stone on the Bayon at Angkor Thom in Cambodia (8.3.6, 8.3.8, 10.4.1) and dated to *c.* AD 1185 (Needham, 1971: 460–1, fig. 975). This vessel is different from the others on the monument which are mainly paddled boats. This planked ship appears to have a keel with an angled stempost, an overhanging stern-gallery, two masts with battened sails of high-aspect ratio and multiple sheets, and a median rudder forward of the stern and protruding well below the hull: the flags at bow and stern are typically Chinese. These hull characteristics can be found either in the Quanzhou ships of the late thirteenth century (10.4.2) or in Chinese illustrations from later centuries and thus it seems likely that this sculpture was intended to be that of a Chinese ship: possibly here is the 'oldest representation of a Chinese seagoing ship with lugsails' which, from sometime in the medieval period, appear to have generally superceded the square sail.

Leeboards, lowered over the leeward side of a vessel so that they protrude below the level of the keel, can significantly improve windward performance. Writing in *c.* AD 759, Li Quan in his *Tai Bei Yin Ching* described a 'seahawk' warship which had to port and starboard 'floating boards shaped like the wings of a bird which help the ship so that even when wind and waves arise in fury they are neither driven sideways nor overturned' (Xin and Yuan, 1991: 72). Leeboards do not float: as translated, this eighth-century text seems to refer to stabilizing timbers, which float at the waterline and thus increase transverse stability rather than reduce leeway. However, stabilizers do not improve a boat's resistance to sideways motion which *is* the function of a leeboard, and a leeboard with a cross-section like a bird's wing (i.e. an aerofoil) would be a most effective one. All in all, this text is enigmatic: if it were to be translated again by someone aware of the nautical implications, perhaps the true nature of these floating boards would emerge. Meanwhile it seems premature to quote this as the earliest Chinese use of leeboards and the earliest clear reference must then be from the seventeenth century (Xin and Yuan, 1991: 72).

With a deep rudder, leeboards, and fore-and-aft sails, Chinese vessels could be expected to have a reasonable windward performance. Xin and Yuan (1991: 73) quote an early twelfth-century AD text, *Ping Zhou Ko Tan* by Zhu Yu to support their contention that Chinese vessels of that era could not sail closer than with the wind on the beam (i.e. 8 points off the wind) which is reasonable. Another text of *c.* AD 1562 suggests to Xin and Yuan that tacking closer to the wind may have been possible in Chinese vessels from the end of the Yuan dynasty, i.e. late fourteenth century AD. Zhou (1983: 490), however, quotes a Song dynasty writer of the thirteenth century for the observation that Chinese ships could sail much closer to the wind than other ships. These opinions, based as they are on questionable translation of texts written by authors of doubtful nautical knowledge, must remain speculative: more soundly based opinions may emerge should it ever prove possible to build and sail an authentic full-scale reconstruction model of a medieval Chinese ship, based on excavated evidence.

Marco Polo describes the towing of river craft in late thirteenth-century China, and it seems very likely that this form of propulsion was used from early times. Paintings by Zhang Zeduan of *c.* AD 1125 show large river boats being towed from a towing mast approximately one-third the overall length, from the bows, by men on the riverbank (Needham, 1971: fig. 976; Peng, 1988: 60–1). Needham (1971: 448) believes that one of the Guangzhou pottery model boats of the first century AD (10.2.10.4) formerly had a mast towards the bow: if it did, this could have been for towing rather than sailing.

River warships, propelled by treadmill paddle wheels, are said to have been invented by Li Gao during the Tang dynasty (AD 618–909) (Zhou, 1986: 492). Fleets of these man-powered paddle-wheel vessels are said to have been built in the Southern Song dynasty (1127–1290) (Zhou, 1986: 492). Illustrations survive from this period showing vessels with from two to twenty-two wheels on each side (Peng, 1988: 56–7), some are depicted used in conjunction with oars and/or sails. Vessels with a treadmill paddle wheel fitted at the stern under the helmsmen's deck were in use in south China in the early twentieth century (Peng, 1988: 58).

### 10.2.11.2 STEERING

The first-century BC tomb model boat from Changsha (10.2.10.4) has a steering sweep pivoted in a notch at the stern (Needham, 1971: fig. 961). A bas-relief of the Han dynasty (206 BC–AD 220) also depicts the use of a steer-ing sweep (Peng, 1988: 36) and they continued in use on certain river craft up to the present century.

One of the first-century AD pottery tomb models from Guangzhou has a median rudder slung under the overhanging stern, which could be raised and lowered within a well (Fig. 10.7). It may reasonably be assumed that they continued to be used on appropriate vessels, from this time onwards. The balanced median rudder is first seen on paintings by Zhang Zeduan dated *c.* AD 1125 (Xin and Yuan, 1991: 71; Xi, 1985: 44). That part of a balanced rudder which is forward of the pivot protrudes into the water flow when the rudder is turned and thus reduces the steering force required.

### 10.2.11.3 ANCHORS

The first-century AD tomb model from Guangzhou (Fig. 10.7) has an anchor with a stone stock and two wooden flukes suspended from a bollard (possibly a capstan) in the bows (Peng, 1988: 36). Three stone stocks from similar anchors found near Quanzhou have been dated to the twelfth and thirteenth centuries AD (Kapitän, 1990; 1991: 245). A twelfth-century report describes such an anchor suspended from a windlass in the bows by a rattan rope (Kapitän, 1991: 246). As in other parts of the world, it seems likely that simple anchor stones not only preceded the use of stone-stocked anchors but also continued in use until today.

# 10.3
# Early Inland Waterways

China has no natural land routes between the populous and frequently politically dominant north and the fertile south (10.1.2). The natural link between the south-east and the west is the Yangtze (Fig. 10.1), but the upstream journey could only be undertaken regularly and economically on those stretches where boats could be towed from the river banks. In the deeply-cut gorges of this swiftly flowing river, such towing was impossible until towing paths or haulways were cut into the cliffs during the Tang dynasty (AD 616–909) (Blunden and Elvin, 1983: 19–20, 104).

Canals were cut from at least the fifth century BC (Loewe, 1980: 248). Many of these were local ones in the south, but attempts were also made around this time to link the south with the north (Blunden and Elvin, 1983: 104–5). In this early work lie the origins of the Grand Canal (*Da Yunhe*) which began to take more obvious shape in the Sui dynasty *c*. AD 607–610: the Shanyang canal was cut to connect the Yangtze to the

Huai River; and the Tongji canal cut to connect the Huai to the Huang Ho/Yellow River near Luoyang, one of the two capital cities (Fig. 10.9).

Another canal (Yongji) linked the Huang Ho with Beijing whilst the Jiangnan canal extended south from the Yangtze to the Fuchun River at Yuhang/Hangzhou (Blunden and Elvin, 1983: 105), with a further stretch from west of the Sanmen gorges of the Huang Ho to

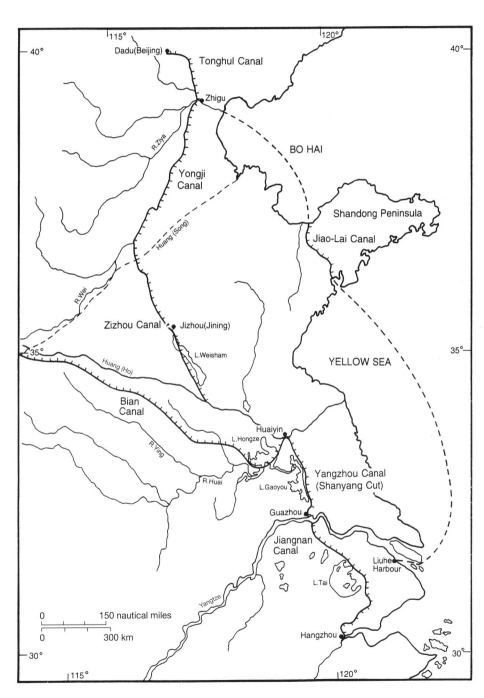

Fig. 10.9. Canals in northern China (Institute of Archaeology, Oxford).

the other capital at Daxingcheng (Xian). This canal system, over 1,000 km in length, became the main north–south route for the state transport of grain, and also a commercial artery linking the north with the south. It is thought that, generally speaking, flash locks, and inclined planes with winches were used on these early canals but by the eleventh century, pound locks with double gates had been introduced (Blunden and Elvin: 1983, 104).

The Mongols of the Yüan dynasty (1290–1379) revitalized the canal system, particularly the Grand Canal. When they moved the capital to Dadu (Beijing), a new canal was cut to the east of the Shandong hills from the Huang Ho (then flowing generally eastwards from the Sanmen gorges rather than north-east as in earlier times) northwards to the capital (Blunden and Elvin, 1983: 16, 105). Another canal, Jiao-Lai, was cut across the base of the Shandong peninsula. Ships bringing grain northwards from the Yangtze estuary could then either sail around Shandong in fair weather or discharge their cargo into barges at the south end of the Jiao-Lai canal: other ships moved the grain from the north end of the canal across Bo Hai towards Beijing. It seems likely that a vessel similar to the *shachuan* (10.1.3) would have been used on these coastal voyages.

After the Mongols had been ousted in 1368, the Ming dynasty recovery programme included further canal building. The problem of keeping the higher parts of the Grand Canal (maximum height above the mean level of the Yangtze, 138 ft. (42 m) supplied with water was solved during this period by the engineer, Sung Li (Blunden and Elvin, 1983: 19; Needham, 1971: 526).

# 10.4

# Seagoing Vessels

The evidence so far considered, both archaeological and ethnographic, is mainly of inland water transport. The recent and present-day use of bundle rafts, buoyed rafts, log rafts, bark boats, hide boats, basket boats, and sewn-plank boats (also used in coastal waters), mainly in Outer China, suggests that these craft may also have been used in former times, possibly with a wider distri-

bution than today, wherever they were environmentally suitable. There is some literary evidence for the Chou and Han periods to support this hypothesis; but so far no firm excavated evidence to give substance to it.

There is evidence for the early use of logboats from Neolithic times right up to the twentieth century. Although there is some evidence for complex logboats, this is from a late period, and the early logboats so far known would not have been seagoing craft.

Plank boats fastened by iron nails are known from the Han period (10.2.10.4) but these, and the tomb models which are interpreted as representing plank boats, are all river craft. In sum, then, there is no direct evidence for early seagoing craft. Nevertheless overseas voyages did take place within this region, as we know from other evidence that many islands in the China Seas were inhabited from Neolithic times onwards (Glover, 1980: 161). Some of the impetus for these colonizing voyages came from south-east Asia, northwards through the Philippines, Formosa, Ryuku islands, Japanese islands, and so on. However, there is also evidence that the early Chinese undertook coastal voyages: see, for example, Needham's summary of the literary evidence from *c*.500 BC onwards (Ronan, 1986: 102–4). In this respect the Chinese situation is very similar to that in north-west Europe: overseas voyages were undoubtedly undertaken from Neolithic times onwards yet there is no unchallengeable direct evidence for indigenous seagoing vessels until much later.

The Chinese evidence for seagoing vessels may be considered under three headings: iconographic, excavated, and documentary, none earlier than the fifth century AD.

## 10.4.1 ICONOGRAPHIC EVIDENCE

A carving of a ship on a Buddhist stone stele of the fifth or sixth century AD in the Wan Fu Si temple at Chengdu (Ronan, 1986: fig. 232) may be the earliest known representation of a Chinese seagoing ship. This vessel has a built-up superstructure and a single square sail. The ships depicted on seventh-century Buddhist frescos in the cave-temples at Dunhuang may also be seagoing. They have blunt ends above the waterline, are propelled by a single square sail set on a pole mast stepped well forward of amidships (restricting sailing to a following wind), as well as by oars, and they appear to be steered by two steering-oars pivoted on the quarters (Ronan, 1986: 225, fig. 231; Needham, 1971: fig. 968).

River ferries depicted on a painting by Zhang Ze-Duan (Ronan, 1986: fig. 200) dated *c.* AD 1125 are probably not seagoing but they show structural characteristics which may be common to all vessels of that period. There is a bipod towing mast forward of amidships supported by many stays, both forward and aft, a relatively large, balanced, median rudder, and a transom stern surmounted by a stern gallery.

One of several vessels depicted in stone on the late twelfth-century Bayon temple at Angkor Thom (8.3.8, 10.2.11.1) in Cambodia (Ronan, 1986: fig. 199) is obviously different from the others which are generally of the enlarged logboat style associated with south-east Asia (8.3.6). This is a planked ship with a keel and a stem (or possibly a small transom above the waterline) and an overhanging stern, two matted sails with battens and multiple sheets, a slung rudder extending below the level of the keel, and an anchor suspended from a windlass in the bows. This could be indigenous or it might be a visiting ship from south China since Needham believes that the flags at bow and stern have typical Chinese designs (Ronan, 1986: 112).

Small drawings of Chinese ships on the Catalan World Map of *c.*1375 and that of Fra Mauro Camaldolese of *c.*1459 (Needham, 1971: 471–3) seem to show that seagoing *jonqs* of those times were bluff or transom—ended above the waterline—as in the wreck Quanzhou 1 (10.4.2.2); that they had up to five masts with high-aspect ratio sails (lugsails?) probably made of matting; and that they had a median rudder within a well in the after hull.

## 10.4.2 EXCAVATED MEDIEVAL VESSELS

Liu and Li (1991: 280) have published a brief note on two T'ang period (seventh- to ninth-century AD) vessels: one from Yangzhouo, Jiangsu excavated before 1974; and one from Rugao, Nanjing excavated before 1961. G.-Q. Li (1989: 282) and J. Green (1986*a*) have described aspects of the latter vessel: she was flat-bottomed, with eight bulkheads nailed to the planking (or vice versa?), and the gaps were sealed with lime and tung oil. Another brief report (Xi and Xin, 1991: 233)

mentions an early wreck from Xingan which evidently had overlapping planking.

### 10.4.2.1 THE WANDO ISLAND SHIP

More is known about a small vessel of the eleventh century, excavated in 1984 at Wando island on the southwestern coast of Korea. Kim (1991: 56–8) and Green and Kim (1989: 39–41) consider that this ship has 'features associated with traditional ship constructional methods of "Old Korean Ship"' and that these features are 'quite different from the Chinese ship-construction method'. As this Wando ship is the earliest ship to be excavated in the China Sea region, and as there is no other vessel with which it may be compared for another 200 years, these statements seem premature. It is possible, in the light of present knowledge, that the Wando ship's technological features may be representative of eleventh-century seagoing ships in that region. Furthermore, the Anapchi Pond boat (10.2.10.3) may have been an earlier member of this tradition. Chinese ships of the thirteenth century, as known at present, are generally similar to the Wando ship but different in detail; Chinese ships of the tenth century, if they were to be found, would probably also be generally similar to the Wando island ship, but different in detail. If tenth-or thirteenth-century Chinese ships built for service in different waters or for a different function were to be found in future, then again, we should expect them to be somewhat different.

The Wando island ship was carrying a cargo of over 30,000 caledons which have been identified as coming from a kiln in Hainan province, and are dated to the period AD 1050–1100. Much of the bottom (*c.*6.5 m) and side planking (*c.*7.4 m) of this vessel were recovered after the exacavation, but not the ends; nor is there any mention in the excavation report of any framing timbers. The timber species are said to be Korean but no details are given. The overall dimensions of the original vessel have been estimated as 9 or 10 × 3.5 × 1.7 m. This is a flat-bottomed vessel with flared sides (Fig. 10.10). The central part of the bottom consists of five strakes *c.*0.18–0.20 m thick. Each strake consists of two or three planks: the three planks in the central strake are joined in a 'protruding-tongue scarf' with no obvious fastenings; the other scarfs in the bottom planking are pierced by horizontal plank fastenings.

The three central strakes of the bottom planking are

Fig. 10.10. Measured drawing of the eleventh-century AD vessel from Wando Island, Korea (after Green and Kim, 1989: fig. 14).

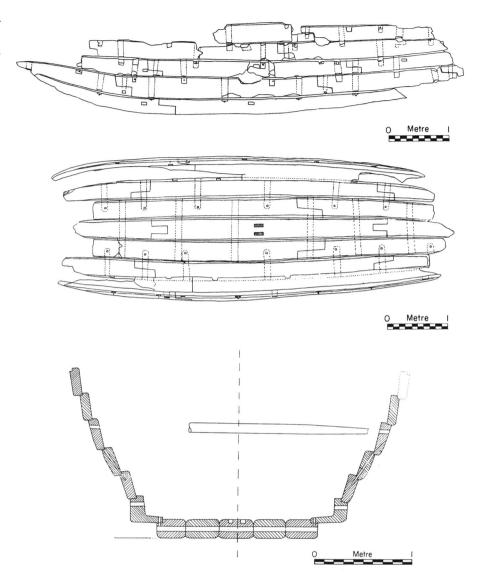

fastened together edge-to-edge almost in raft fashion, by six transverse timbers ('tenons') which go through the thickness of each strake—any locking method is not described. The two outer bottom strakes are fastened to the inner bottom planking by six or seven similar transverse timbers which pass right through the outer strakes but only a short distance into the inner strakes where they are locked within their mortises by a vertical treenail.

The outer bottom strakes have a square rabbet cut along their outer edge into which an L-shaped transition or chine timber fits: this is fastened there by vertical tenons (treenails?). The single scarf shown in these chine timbers is not locked. There are remains of four more side strakes each side, of thickness *c*.0.10 m and

breadth 0.28–0.33 m. The scarfs in these side strakes are pierced by vertical tenons (treenails?). In the upper edge of the chine strake and in the other five side strakes are rabbets, into which the next side strake is fastened by tenons which pass right through the breadth of the upper strake but only a short distance into the lower strake where they are locked within their mortises by horizontal treenails. The rabbeted-lap planking makes the sides 'apparently clinker'.

The uppermost surviving side strake has a rabbet along its top edge and thus this ship must have had at least six side strakes (including the chine strake). The chine (first side strake) and the fourth side strakes have rectangular horizontal holes through them, in one case at an interval of *c*.1.75 m to which framing (possibly

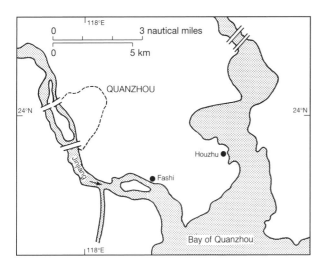

Fig. 10.11. Map of the Quanzhou region (Institute of Archaeology, Oxford).

floors, bulkheads, side timbers, crossbeams) could have been fastened in position. The central bottom plank has two vertical holes worked into it near the centre of the surviving length: this is possibly where a mast step was fastened.

## 10.4.2.2 QUANZHOU SHIP I

In 1974, the remains of a ship were excavated from Houhzou harbour in Quanzhou, Fujian (*Quanzhou Ship Report*, 1987 (in Chinese); G.-Q. Li, 1986, 1989; Green, 1983a; Green and Burningham, 1998). Although not the first seagoing wreck to be excavated in China, it was the first to be widely published and the first to throw direct light on Chinese medieval shipbuilding. Coins in the wreck date it to *c.* AD 1277.

The port of Quanzhou was probably medieval *Zaytun* (10.6.1, 10.6.2), noted by several European travellers

for its harbour and its shipping and international trade (Fig. 10.11). The impressive remains of this ship (Fig. 10.12)—almost the full length of the hull, up to and beyond the turn of the bilge at about the loaded waterline, and much of the internal structure (Fig. 10.13)—are now reassembled and displayed in a building east of the Kai Yuan Temple in Quanzhou, as an outstation of the Museum of Overseas Communications History which moved into new buildings by the eastern lake in 1990. As the excavated remains have been reassembled it is not now possible to examine the hull fastenings and the internal structure. Description and deduction must therefore rely heavily on such information as has been published in the English language and on questions asked through interpreters.

Green and Burningham (1998) have recently reported on examinations of the remains undertaken between 1983 and 1994. The only substantial addition to the information already published by Green (1983a), G.-Q. Li (1986, 1989), and in Chinese sources is that all plank scarfs identified in the remains of Quanzhou 1 are at bulkhead stations (Green and Burningham 1998: 287, figs. 11, 15). Green and Burningham's plans of the remains (1998: fig. 5) differ from those in earlier Chinese publications: for example, the forward extension of the keel rises at 20° to the horizontal (formerly 25°), and the after extension rises at 15° (formerly 10°). Green and Burningham's text (1998: 282), however, gives these angles as 35° (forward) and 27° (aft). In view of these anomalies, Chinese sources published in 1987 are used here for Fig. 10.14, rather than those of Green and Burningham.

When found, the vessel measured 24.02 × 9.15 m and the highest surviving planking was *c.*2 m above the bottom, measured vertically. The remains consisted of: a main keel with an extension at both ends, the forward extension is probably part of the lower stem; part of

Fig. 10.12. Quanzhou 1 during excavation in 1974 (Museum of Overseas Communication History, Quanzhou).

Fig. 10.13. Internal view of Quanzhou 1 showing mast step timber, bulkheads and floors (photo: Jeremy Green).

Fig. 10.14 (*below*). Plan and longitudinal section of Quanzhou 1 (after *Quanzhou Ship Report* (in Chinese), 1987: 17).

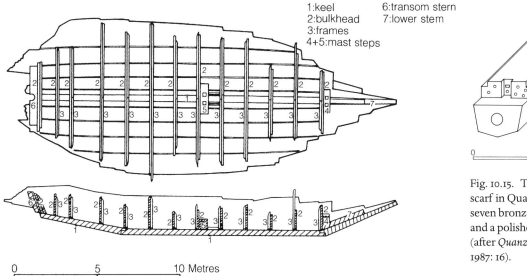

1:keel          6:transom stern
2:bulkhead   7:lower stem
3:frames
4+5:mast steps

0                    5                    10 Metres

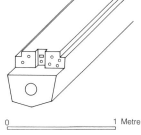

Fig. 10.15. The forward keel scarf in Quanzhou 1 with seven bronze coins (above and a polished disc (below). (after *Quanzhou Ship Report*, 1987: 16).

0                                    1 Metre

the stern transom; twelve bulkheads with adjacent frames; sixteen strakes of planking to starboard and fourteen to port; and two mast steps.

### 10.4.2.2.1 *The keel and stempost*

The main section of the camphor-wood keel is *c*.12.5 m long and is joined to an after-section of pine, some 5 m in length and rising at *c*.10°, in a horizontal, half-lap scarf (with a gradient of about 1 in 1) reinforced by a

dovetail joint in the upper half. The keel is similarly scarfed at its forward end to the lower part of the pine stem, in length *c*.5 m (and rising at an angle of *c*.25°). Both scarfs are reinforced by knees. Within the forward scarf (Fig. 10.15), on a vertical face, are set seven bronze coins thought to represent Ursa Major, and a polished bronze disc probably representing the moon (Green, 1983*a*: 254). In the after scarf there are thirteen coins and a disc. The keel near the midship station is *c*.0.35 m moulded and *c*.0.30 m sided. Rabbets have been worked along its upper edges to receive the garboard strakes. The three exposed faces of the keel are protected by a light sheathing (G.-Q. Li, 1989: fig. 3).

### 10.4.2.2.2 *The planking*

The hull has double planking up to, and including, the eleventh strake and then triple planking up to the top of the surviving remains (Fig. 10.16). The inner planking

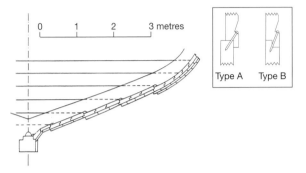

Fig. 10.16. Quanzhou 1: transverse section, with two types of plank fastening.

(80 mm thick) is primary and is edge-joined and fastened; the other layers (50 mm thick) are secondary: they are not edge-joined or fastened, but are placed edge-to-edge (subsequently caulked) and nailed to the primary planking and to the half frames (G.-Q. Li, personal communication) and bulkheads.

The lower edge of the first or garboard strakes of the primary planking is fashioned to fit into the rabbet cut along the keel and fastened there by obliquely driven nails used as spikes, spaced at *c*.0.15 to 0.20 m. A rabbet has been fashioned along the upper edge of the garboard into which fits a rabbet along the lower edge of the second strake, forming, in effect, a half-lap joint (type B in Fig. 10.16) which is fastened by angled spikes spaced at *c*.0.2 m and driven from above. The upper edge of the second strake is left square and a rabbet is cut in the lower edge of the third strake, thereby forming a rabbeted lap joint (type A in Fig. 10.16). The next two strakes are laid in half-lap joints; then a rabbeted lap seam followed by two half-lap seams; another rabbeted lap seam followed by two half-lap seams; finally, a fourth rabbeted lap seam and five half-lap seams to the edge of the surviving remains (upper edge of the sixteenth strake).

The effect of this sequence of joints (Fig. 10.16) is to form an *apparently* clinker-laid hull with overlaps at every rabbeted lap seam along which reinforcing battens are nailed inboard. In this primary 'clinker' hull the *apparent* first strake is two actual strakes broad; the second, third, and fourth are each of three actual strakes; and the fifth is of at least six actual strakes.

The first strake of the second layer of planking has a bevelled lower edge to take against the side of the keel. The remaining strakes, edge-to-edge, but in an angled seam, are positioned so that in general they overlap the seams of the primary planking. This second layer is fastened to the framing through the primary planking, and the apparent clinker nature of that planking is reflected in this second layer. The third layer of planking begins at the level of the twelfth primary strake, and is positioned and fastened in a similar manner.

The primary planking is of Chinese fir, pine, and camphor, or possibly cedar (Green and Burningham, 1998: 284). Drawings published by G.-Q. Li (1989: fig. 4) show that planks were fashioned from half logs and were orientated in the ship so that alternate strakes had the pith of the log inboard and then outboard. The average breadth of planking is 0.28 m, and the largest plank is 13.5 m in length. Planks are joined together within each strake by diagonal, hooked scarfs (stop-splayed on edge) of variable length, or by butted joints (G.-Q. Li, 1989: 277, fig. 4). All scarfs so far noted are at bulkhead stations. G.-Q. Li (1989), but Green and Burningham (1998) do not make clear whether the primary planking had both types of scarf or only diagonal ones, with butted scarfs in the second and third layers. The planking iron nails were of varied cross-section, and measured between 120 and 200 mm in length. Their heads were driven below the plank outer face by a nail set (a nail punch 0.16 m long was found inside the hull) and the resulting depression outboard of them filled with *chu-nam*, a putty made of jute fibre (*Corchorus capsularis*), shredded bamboo, lime, and oil from the tung tree (*Aleurites fordii*). By sealing the nails in this way, corrosion due to salt water was minimized (G.-Q. Li, 1989). This *chu-nam* was also used to caulk the plank seams (ibid)—presumably this was a true caulking in the second and third layers; if it was used in the primary planking it may only have been as a sealant. A putty of lime and tung oil, without the fibre, was used to 'fill irregularities and gaps in the surfaces of the hull planks'. It was also applied to the planking faces between the three layers. This putty or luting was applied with a wooden spatula (one was found inside the ship measuring 0.40 m in length) and the surface was cleaned and smoothed as the putty set (G.-Q. Li, 1989: 278–9, fig. 5).

The second and third layers of planking were subsidiary planking, adding to hull strength and making the total thickness c.0.180 m. It may be that this thickness was only maintained over the loaded waterline region of the hull by restricting the third layer to strakes 12–16: this would have increased both longitudinal strength and transverse stability. If, as seems likely, caulking was forced into the butted seams of this flush-laid subsidiary planking, then it would have become, in effect, a second load-bearing 'shell', adding to the strength of the primary planking shell.

### 10.4.2.2.3 *The transom, framing, and bulkheads*

This vessel had a transom stern, angled aft slightly and probably surmounted by a stern gallery as the side planking extends beyond the transom (Green, 1983a: 256). The transom has an inner layer of horizontally laid planking and an outer layer of much thicker horizontally laid camphor wood planks into which a vertical groove has been cut for the rudder stock (Green, 1983a: fig. 10). It is unclear how this planking is joined and fastened.

Twelve frames, joggled to fit the 'apparent clinker' primary planking, are fitted to the hull at intervals ranging from c.1.30–1.90 m. These are half frames which meet on the centre line where there is a limber hole. They extend up to (in one case, beyond) the upper edge of the surviving planking (Fig. 10.14). They are substantial, being sided c.0.15 m and moulded c.20 m. Higher framing elements do not appear to have survived. The second and third layers of planking are fastened to the half frames by iron nails used as spikes: it is not clear how the frames and primary planking are fastened together, or whether the frames are fastened to the keel.

On the after side of the six after frames and on the forward side of the six forward frames, bulkheads are positioned (Fig. 10.14). They survive, in some cases, up to the height of the surviving sides and are made of several horizontal cedar planks c.80 mm thick with half-lap joints fastened by diagonally driven iron nails: the seams are sealed with the *chu-nam* putty. The bulkhead planking is further reinforced by near-vertical

battens fastened to it by iron nails (G.-Q. Li, personal communication). A limber hole is cut in each lowest plank of these bulkheads, except for the foremost and aftermost, in line with the frame limber holes. The edges of the bulkheads are joggled to take against the 'apparent-clinker' primary planking, and nails fasten the second and third layers of hull planking to these edges. It is not clear whether the bulkheads were fastened to the keel, but they were fastened to the primary planking (or vice versa) by L-shaped metal brackets ('stiffeners' or *gua-ju* nails) which were 0.30–0.60 m in length and c.80 mm broad (Fig. 10.17). A hole was worked through the primary planking near the bulkhead position at (almost) every strake and a corre-

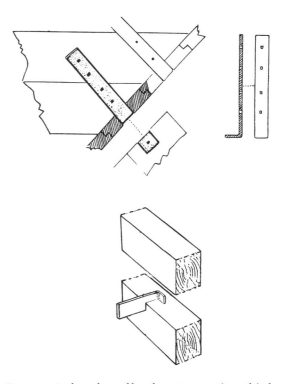

Fig. 10.17. L-shaped metal brackets (*gua-ju* or '*ju* nails') that fastened the primary planking to the bulkheads in Quanzhou 1 (upper), and in the Penglai wreck (lower) (after *Quanzhou Ship Report*, 1987: 20; and Xi and Xin, 1991: fig. 5).

sponding 10 mm deep groove worked across the bulkhead planking runs at right angles to the hull. The angled iron fitting was then passed through the primary planking, where its shorter arm was fastened outboard by an iron nail, and its longer arm fastened to the bulkhead planking by four or five nails. These metal fittings were then treated with the lime and tung oil mixture. Each bulkhead was thus sandwiched between a pair of half-frames on one face (the one nearer amidships) and, on the other face, by iron brackets connecting it to the *primary* planking.

Contrary to 'received wisdom' (e.g. Needham, 1971), bilge water *was* able to flow almost the full length of the vessel through limber holes cut in the half-frames and bulkheads above the keel, as was common in contemporary European building. This would make it simpler to pump out excess water in the bilges. It seems likely that, apart from any role they may have had in design, the primary role of the bulkheads was to increase the transverse and the longitudinal strength of the hull. The fact that they were also *moderately* watertight (up to the loaded waterline) would mean that, if the hull planking in one compartment were to leak, the incoming seawater would flow only slowly into adjacent compartments via the small limber holes and the unavoidable spaces left between framework and hull planking; without bulkheads, such leakage would have spread quickly to all compartments, once the water had reached the upper surface of the frames near the centreline (unless any ceiling planking was watertight).

Such an arrangement of bulkheads would (as is traditionally claimed) provide convenient stowage modules for the goods of several merchants travelling in the same ship; on the other hand, except in the smaller ships, if these bulkheads were to be built up much above the loaded waterline they would impede the movement of people along the length of the ship, below the upper deck.

### 10.4.2.2.4 Mast steps

There were two mast step timbers, joggled to match the inner profile of the planking, each of them with two vertical, rectangular-section holes disposed athwartships. The main mast step timber, with holes sided c.0.20 m and 0.40 m apart, was fastened to the keel c.1 m forward of amidships, forward of, and supported by, the sixth bulkhead. It was braced to the fifth frame by longitudinal timbers each side of the keel. The foremast timber, with holes c.0.15 m sided, was forward of the first bulkhead, on top of an inner stem which was itself above the keel scarf between stem and keel. A square hole cut out of the uppermost plank in bulkhead no.5 has been interpreted as a notch to allow

the mainmast to be lowered forward to an angle of c.25° to the horizontal.

### 10.4.2.2.5 Sequence of building

There is an apparent paradox in the published data on this ship: the primary planking is edge-fastened, yet the plank scarfs within strakes are invariably at bulkhead stations. Edge-fastened planking usually, but not always (see, for example, Greenhill (1976: 65) and Coates (1985)) implies a plank-first sequence of building; whereas having plank scarfs at bulkhead stations suggests that the bulkheads were in position before planking began, that is, a frame-first design and building sequence. Given certain assumptions it would be possible to outline building sequences, which would be either plank-first or frame-first. However, there are too many uncertainties: it is not known whether half-frames and bulkheads are fastened to the keel; nor how the half-frames and the bulkheads (apart from *ju* nails) were fastened to the primary planking. It may be, in fact, that the primary planking was fastened to half-frames and bulkheads, but this could only be determined by recording whether any strake fastenings or scarf fastenings were immediately outboard of half-frames or bulkheads.

### 10.4.2.2.6 Equipment and cargo

No other elements of the ship were recovered, but fragments of ropes made of bamboo, rattan, flax, and palm were found, and some evidence that there had been a windlass. Among finds from within the hull were a metal chisel, a wooden spatula for use with *chunam*, a nail punch, and a wooden measuring stick calibrated in units approximating to one inch, i.e. one thumb breadth (display in Quanzhou ship museum).

The cargo of this ship included pepper, cinnabar, and other spices and medicines from south-east Asia, special timbers such as sandalwood and *Lignum dalbergiae, aquilariae,* and *santali*, tortoiseshell, olibanum (?), ambergris (possibly from east Africa), and cowrie shell currency from the South China Sea region. There were also many cargo tallies and the remains of sacking. Food remains included: coconut, olives, peaches, plums and lychee, birds, fish, dog, goat, pig, and cow. Rat bones were also found. Pottery, a stoneware wine jar, a hat, and Chinese chessmen may have belonged to the crew.

### 10.4.2.2.7 *Reconstruction*

A hypothetical reconstruction of Quanzhou I gives her overall dimensions as 34.5 × 9.9 × 3.27 m, with a displacement of 374.4 tonnes (Zhou, 1983: 482): whether this is loaded or lightship displacement is not stated. G.-Q. Li (1989: 277) gives her 'estimated load capacity' as 'over 200 tonnes' whilst Yang and Chen (1990: 85) estimate 250 tonnes.

### 10.4.2.3 QUANZHOU 2 (FASHI)

In 1976, the remains of a wreck were encountered at Fashi off the northern bank of the River Jinjiang, 5 km south-east of Quanzhou. Part of this *wreck*, *c*.7.5 × 4 m in area, was excavated during 1982, recorded and then back-filled. The stern was located, with evidence for a transom, but neither transom nor rudder were found. There was only one layer of planking, some 95 mm thick, probably edge-fastened in a similar manner to the planking of Quanzhou wreck No. 1.

Three bulkheads (and frames?) were excavated, with spacings of 2.06 and 1.90 m. For the first time in Chinese waters, fragments of sail were recovered, a mat sail stiffened by bamboo: the remains are now on display in the ship museum at Quanzhou (see also 4.14.1). The wreck is dated by pottery to the Southern Song period, twelfth–thirteenth centuries AD. It is estimated that her original full length would have been *c*.23 m and that she could have carried *c*.120 tonnes of cargo (Yang and Chen, 1990: 83–6, figs. 1 and 2).

### 10.4.2.4 NINGBO

A small ship of the Song dynasty (tenth–thirteenth centuries AD) was found at Ningbo, Zhejiang in 1979. The superstructure and the ends were missing, as is frequently the case, but about half of the bottom in length and in height was recorded. It proved impossible to lift and conserve the entire remains so a few planks were recovered and the rest left *in situ* (He, 1991: 237–8; Peng, 1988: 101; Xi and Xin, 1991; Lin, Du, and Green, 1991). This was a round-hulled vessel with a relatively sharp bow. Mast steps for the foremast and mainmast were found, and it is presumed that there

was a third mast in the missing stern. The keel was a substantial timber, 0.26 m sided and 0.18 m moulded, which protruded below the bottom planking. The stem post was fastened by 'mortise and tenon' and by iron nails to the keel. The framing appears to have consisted of bulkheads built on top of floors—seven of these combinations survived. Bulkhead 5, immediately aft of the main mast step, was reinforced by a timber projecting upwards from the keel against its after face. The single layer of planking was nailed to the frames. Planks within strakes were joined in oblique scarfs up to 1.55 m in length; the strakes seem to have been joined together by 'mortise joints' fastened with oblique iron nails (Lin, Du, and Green, 1991: 306)—possibly these were half-lap joints as in Quanzhou I. Xi and Xin (1991: 233) state that there was 'tongue and groove joining of adjacent shell planks'—see 10.4.2.2.5. The seams were caulked with a *chu-nam* mixture. A wale, of half-log cross-section, was nailed outboard along the seam between the seventh and eighth strakes: this may have been below, rather than at, the waterline.

### 10.4.2.5 SHINAN

A wreck, found off the south west-coast of Korea in the Shinan district, was excavated between 1976 and 1982, and the hull was recorded and lifted in sections during 1983–4 (Green, 1983*b*; Green and Kim, 1989; Hoffman, Choi, and Kim, 1991; C.-E. Lee, 1991). A wooden tally on a cargo crate gives the probable date of her sinking as AD 1323 (Green and Kim, 1989: 34).

There are differences between the measurements given on the plan and sections, without scales, published by C.-E. Lee (1991) and those derived from the scale drawings of Hoffman, Choi, and Kim (1991). Furthermore the drawing of keel and stem published by Green and Kim (1989: fig. 8) shows the overall length as 24.6 m whereas Hoffman's drawing gives *c*.14 m. For these reasons, Hoffman's plan and sections (similar in detail to C.-E. Lee, 1991: fig. 2) are reproduced here but without his scale (Fig. 10.18).

The timber species used in this vessel are said by Hoffman, Choi, and Kim (1991: 59) to be Chinese red pine (*Pinus massoniana*) and Chinese fir (*Cunninghamia lanceolata*). The pines in particular were large trees, 60–100 years old. The keel, planking and other external timbers were covered by 15–20 mm thick 'protective boards' of cedar (C.-E. Lee, 1991: 161)—probably

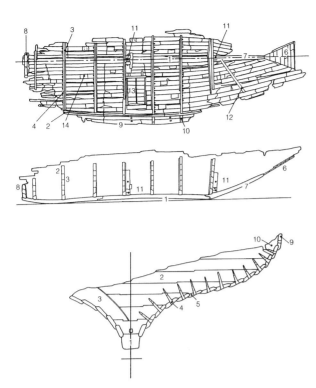

Fig. 10.18. Plan and sections of the Shinan wreck. 1: keel; 2: bulkhead; 3 and 12: frames; 4:*ju* nail; 5 and 9: planking; 6 and 8: transoms; 7: stem; 10: sidetimber; 11: mast step; 13: liquid tank; 14: butt strap (after Hoffman, Choi, and Kim, 1991: fig. 1).

the equivalent of a second layer of planking in other vessels.

### 10.4.2.5.1 *Keel*

The main keel measured *c*.11.8 × 0.71 (sided) × 0.5 m (moulded) and was found on excavation to be hogged by 0.54 m (C.-E. Lee, 1991) or by 0.22 m. (Green and Kim, 1989: 36, fig. 8). The after section was *c*.8.2 m in length and curved upwards over its aftermost third. Rabbets were worked along the upper outer edges of this keel to take the garboard. The two parts of the keel were fastened together in a number of ways: first, by a horizontal hooked scarf with a gradient of *c*.73 per cent, and by a vertically worked dovetail. A wooden wedge was then driven transversely through the hook of the hooked scarf, and two iron staples were driven into each side of the keel across this scarf (Green and Kim, 1989: fig. 9). It is also likely that nails were driven through the upper surface of the keel fastening the upper and lower parts of the hooked scarf together.

Coins and a polished disc similar to those in Quanzhou 1 wreck (10.4.2.2.1) had been inserted between the near-horizontal surfaces of this scarf (Green and Kim, 1989: 36).

### 10.4.2.5.2 *Stern and bow*

The lower part of the transom which consisted of horizontal planks (sloping aft at *c*.10°) was found set into a transverse groove near the end of the keel (Hoffman, Choi, and Kim, 1991: fig. 1). There were some nail holes in the after end of the keel which C.-E. Lee (1991) states were for rudder fittings.

A stem, some 6 m in length, was joined to the main keel at an angle of *c*.20°, by a scarf similar to the after one, but without the dovetail. A triangular-shaped transom was fastened in an unspecified way to the foremost end of the stem, inclined at an angle of *c*.33°. This transom was made of two layers of horizontal planks—butted inboard, half-lapped outboard. A rabbet was cut along stem and transom edges to receive the planking.

### 10.4.2.5.3 *Planking*

Red pine and black pine strakes were excavated, twelve to starboard, plus two 'bulwark strakes', and six to port. This planking was, in general, some 0.12 m thick and 0.40–0.60 m broad. Planks within strakes were mostly scarfed together in half-laps, but there were also some 'tongued and grooved' scarfs (Green and Kim, 1989: fig. 3). Wooden butt straps, 1.06 by 0.40 × 0.8 m, were fastened (means unknown) over these plank scarfs, inboard. These scarfs were generally staggered throughout the hull (Fig. 10.18): Green and Kim (1989: 35) state that some were outboard of framing timbers. Strakes were fastened together in a rabbeted-lap joint (giving a 'clinker' effect), the rabbet being cut out of the lower inner edge of the upper plank (Fig. 10.18). Towards the bow this rabbeted-lap gradually changed to a half-lap so that the bow planking appears to be flush-laid, both inboard and outboard (C.-E. Lee, 1991: fig. 27). These lap joints were fastened by square-section nails driven from outboard diagonally through the lap (Green, 1983*b*: fig. 4).

Two planks and a fragment from the starboard side of the wreck have been identified as 'bulwark' planking and a fragment of decking or a coaming (Green and

Kim, 1989: 38–9, fig. 13). This 'bulwark' strake appears to be fastened by pairs of diagonal nails through its lap joints. These strakes have both square and round holes cut through them: the round holes, being 0.15 m in diameter, have been tentatively interpreted as either for scuppers or for oars.

C.-E. Lee (1991) has noted that there was 'caulking' of 'oakum and calcium putty' which requires further analysis. The precise use of this putty is unclear, but it seems more likely to be a sealant or used as a stopping rather than a true caulking.

### 10.4.2.5.4 *Bulkheads and frames*

Bulkheads were set into grooves cut into the keel and planking (Green and Kim, 1989: 35, figs. 8 and 9; C.-E. Lee, 1991: fig. 6) alongside frames no. 1 (aft) to no. 7. Bulkheads no. 1–no. 4 are aft of their associated frame; nos. 5–7 forward. The bulkheads are made up of six or seven horizontal planks; the lowest plank at 0.24 m is thicker than the others and has a 30 mm limber hole above the keel, probably in line with a similar gap between the two adjacent half-frames. Figure 4 in Green and Kim (1989: 34) illustrates a half frame (mistakenly captioned as a butt plate) which is also figured by C.-E. Lee (1991: fig. 22): this timber has two lines of horizontal holes in its vertical faces which were probably where a bulkhead was nailed to it (or vice versa).

Planks in the bulkheads were joined to the one below in a broad dovetail (C.-E. Lee, 1991: fig. 12) and by paired angled nails driven from opposite sides (Green, 1983b: fig. 5): there may also be tenons or treenails across some seams (C.-E. Lee, 1991: figs. 26 and 29). The bulkheads were fastened to the planking (or vice versa) by long wooden treenails or pegs (Hoffman *et al.*, 1991: fig. 1; C.-E. Lee, 1991: fig. 29) which were driven through circular holes in the centre of the planking (Green, 1983b: fig. 4) at every strake. These 'stiffeners', some 0.80 m in length, were fastened by four nails (Green and Kim, 1989: fig. 2) to the face of the bulkhead away from its associated frame. Bulkheads were thus sandwiched between a frame and a line of 'stiffeners'. The stiffeners do not seem to be wedged, but have an enlarged head outboard so that they make an interference fit within the planking.

Eight frames were fitted inside the planking, fashioned to match the clinker-effect contours of the hull. Where necessary, bevels were worked along their edges to match the longitudinal curve of the sides; the foremost frame (no. 8), which was found detached, appears to have been canted (i.e. at right angles to the rising stem and bow planking). These frames were spaced at an average of *c.*3 m apart and they extend up to the twelfth strake (C.-E. Lee, 1991: fig. 16; Hoffman, Choi, and Kim 1991: fig. 1). Lee shows them as one-piece frames, but this hardly seems likely considering the curves involved, and fig. 22 in C.-E. Lee (1991) appears to show a half-frame (published upside down?) which seems more likely. It is not clear whether these frames were fastened to keel and planking, and if so, how. From figs. 2 and 4 in Green and Kim (1989) it seems that the frame's cross-section was *c.*0.15 m sided × 0.40 m moulded.

In the fourth hold between bulkheads 4 and 5, on either side of the mainmast step timber, are structures which C.-E. Lee (1991: 162, fig. 31) has called watertight 'liquid tanks'. Drawings showing more details are required so that the function of these structures may be investigated.

### 10.4.2.5.5 *Mast steps*

This ship had two transverse mast-step timbers, each with two vertical holes (Green and Kim, 1989: fig. 10; Hoffman, Choi, and Kim, 1991: fig. 1). The mainmast step timber, 1.85 × 0.55 × 0.60 m stands on the keel forward of frame 4, with a limber hole 0.15 × 0.15 m, and was checked to fit against the first, second, and third (port) strakes. The foremast step timber, of smaller dimensions, is similarly fitted forward of bulkhead 7. It is not clear how these timbers were fastened to keel, planking, and framing. Fragments of the masts survived, sufficient to show that they were composite masts with four spars bound together: two of these projected downwards into the holes in the mast step timber. The four elements of the mast were then held in position by an angled, tapering pin, some 0.15 m in diameter, which was locked by a key through a hole near its lower end.

### 10.4.2.5.6 *Building sequence*

Green and Kim (1989, 35: fig. 3) state that some of the plank scarfs with butt plates on their inner face are outboard of a frame, which suggests that these particular frames had been fitted after the planking had been fastened together. However, Hoffman's plan (1991: fig. 1) and Lee's plans (1991: 2 and 16) show several plank scarfs not at frame or bulkhead stations, and none are evident at such stations. A detailed examination of the hull is required so that the likely building sequence can be determined.

### 10.4.2.5.7 Function

The ship had been carrying metal and stone objects, pottery, sandalwood and twenty-eight tonnes of coins (Hoffman, Choi, and Kim, 1991: 59). The keel appears to have become hogged during service, which is a common problem in wooden seagoing ships. The fact that her timbers were infested with the marine borers *teredo* and *limnoria*, despite her sheathing of cedar wood, also argues for her having been seagoing, as does her transverse sections with a protruding keel and her sharply set lower strakes. The species of timber used to build her are natives of west and south China (C.-E. Lee, 1991: 156). This all suggests that this cargo vessel, having been built in southern China, undertook many trading voyages in the East China Sea before being wrecked off the Korean coast.

### 10.4.2.5.8 Reconstruction

A 1 : 5 model has been built to investigate how this ship was built, her shape, and her size (Green and Kim, 1989: fig. 7)—this research is still underway. C.-E. Lee (1991: 162) however has estimated that the ship was originally *c.*32 m overall length with a maximum breadth of 10.3–10.9 m. At a draft of *c.*2.95 m she would have had a displacement of *c.*187 tonnes, with a dead-weight tonnage of *c.*150 tonnes. Hoffman, Choi, and Kim (1991: 59) estimate her to have had a cargo capacity of 200 tonnes.

### 10.4.2.6 PENGLAI I

In 1984 a wreck was found during dredging in the mouth of the River Huahe off Dengzhou Port, near Penglai, Shandong. Timber species suggest that this ship was built in southern China and Xi and Xin (1991: 230–1) believe that she was sunk before AD 1376. The remains measured *c.*28.6 × 5.6 m (Fig. 10.19) and consisted of keel, stem, planking, framing, mast steps, rudder seating, anchors, some rigging, and the 'window of a deck house' (Yuan and Wu, 1991: 170).

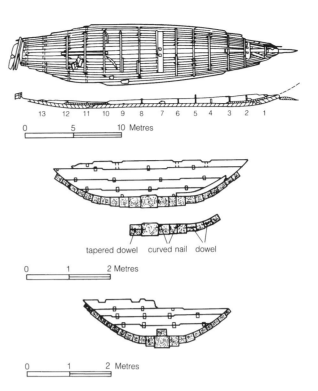

Fig. 10.19. Plan and sections of the Penglai wreck (after Xi and Xin, 1991: figs. 1–3).

### 10.4.2.6.1 Keel, stem, and stern

The main keel of pine (*Pinus masoniana lanib*) was 17.06 m in length, 0.40 sided and 0.30 moulded, and was joined to a 5.58 m 'stern keel' of camphor wood (*Cinnmomum camphora*) by a 'tongue and groove joint with iron bands and spade nails' (Yuan and Wu, 1991: 170). Xi and Xin (1991: 226) call this joint a 0.72 m 'oblique scarf'. As they also say this scarf was similar to that on Quanzhou 1, it probably was a half-lap scarf, as evidently shown on fig. 1 in Xi and Xin (1991: 235). A dovetail-shaped tenon was driven transversely through the scarf (Yuan and Wu, 1991: 171). This scarf had a gradient of *c.*2 : 1, half the gradient of the Quanzhou keel scarfs. The after keel had a cross-section of 0.40 × 0.30 m tapering to 0.20 × 0.28 m and at its upper end was *c.*0.60 m higher than the main keel. The camphorwood stem, 3.96 m in length, was similarly scarfed to the keel and rose to a height of *c.*2 m above the keel. Strengthening timbers, measuring *c.*2 × 0.26 × 0.16 m were fastened over these two keel scarfs.

It is not clear whether a transom stern was found on

excavation, but the published drawings show a group of transverse timbers close to the after end of the surviving planking. These timbers may be the three described as 'rudder seats' by Xi and Xin (1991: 228). These rudder seating timbers were positioned on top of each other, the lowest being 0.26 m thick and the other two, 0.10 m. The hole for the rudder stock (vertically through these timbers?) was 0.30 m in diameter.

### 10.4.2.6.2 *Bulkheads and frames*

There were thirteen bulkheads installed in this ship at an average spacing of *c*.2 m. These were made of 0.16 m thick planks of *Castanopsis*: those with the most remains had four such planks and were up to 1 m in height. These planks had joggled edges and were fastened to each other by four or five flat tenons driven oversize into mortises 80 mm long, 30 mm wide, and 60 mm deep within the thickness of each plank. A limber hole 80 × 60 mm was cut into the lowest plank in each bulkhead, above the keel. Notches were cut into the upper edge of the top plank in bulkheads no. 3 and no. 5—possibly for longitudinal beams (carling) to support decking. Neither descriptions nor drawings indicate whether or not the bulkheads were fastened to the keel.

Curved framing timbers (*c*.0.25 m moulded and 0.15 m. sided), some 1.30 m in length, were positioned to port and starboard against the planking at the turn of the bilge, from about the third to the ninth strake, alongside the bulkheads. It is unclear how they were fastened. They were positioned aft of the forward bulkheads and forward of the after bulkheads. On the published drawings, framing timbers are not shown in association with bulkheads 1, 2, 3, 6 and 7, but it seems likely that originally they were.

### 10.4.2.6.3 *Planking*

The strakes were of Chinese fir (*Cunninghamia lanceolata*) and the remains of ten survived to port and eleven to starboard. They ranged in length 3.7–18.5 m, breadths 0.20–0.44 m and thickness 0.12–0.28 m (probably thick enough to hold caulking). The garboard strakes were thickest, being almost rectangular in cross-section. From the transverse sections published by Yuan and Wu (1991: figs. 2 and 3) and by Xi and Xin (1991: figs. 2, 3 and 4) many of the planks seem to have been fashioned from a whole log with the pith near their centre.

Planks within strakes were scarfed together by 0.56 m 'inverse hooked scarfs' (Xi and Xin, 1991: 227) or by 'agnail tongue and groove joints' (Yuan and Wu, 1991: 170). The published drawings seem to show that these were horizontal hooked scarfs.

On the published drawings, there are no scarfs other than at bulkhead stations. It may be that strakes met edge to edge in a half-lap. They were fastened by dowels/treenails at 0.60 m spacing, and by 'staples' (Xi and Xin, 1991: 227), or by slant-inserted iron spade nails (Yuan and Wu, 1991: 170) every 0.15–0.20 m. Figure 4 in Xi and Xin (1991) appears to show that these dowels were driven right through the breadth of a strake and partly into the strake below (similar in this respect to the eleventh century Wando ship—10.4.2.1). The metal nails were driven at an angle into the inboard face of a strake and on into the upper edge of the strake below. The seams were caulked with *chu-nam* (Yuan and Wu, 1991: 172).

The strakes were also fastened to the bulkheads: spikes were driven through plank scarfs into the edges of bulkheads nos. 4, 5, 6, 8, 10, 11, and 12. It is not clear whether all planking was fastened to all bulkheads, but this seems likely. Indeed, Xi and Xin (1991: 235, fig. 2) show fastenings between the second strakes each side and the lowest plank of no. 3 bulkhead.

The bulkheads and planking were further held relative to one another by L-shaped metal brackets similar to those in Quanzhou 1 but used in a different way. The shorter leg of these *ju* nails was inserted to half its breadth into L-shaped holes in the inboard face and upper edge of each strake adjacent to bulkheads, before the next strake (with matching L-shaped holes) was positioned. The longer leg thus protruded inboard from the seam, its broader surface taking against one face of the bulkhead (Fig. 10.17B). Forward bulkheads (nos. 1–8) had *ju* nails against their after faces whilst the after bulkheads (nos. 9–13) had them against their forward faces. It is not clear how these *ju* nails were fastened to the bulkheads; their outer end, embedded within the thickness of the planking, was hardly likely to pull through. This arrangement means that the bulkheads were almost certainly in position *before* the planking.

### 10.4.2.6.4 *Mast steps*

Mast steps of *nanmu* wood (*Phoebe zhennan*), similar to those in Quanzhou 1 (10.4.2.2.4), were fastened by iron spikes to the bottom planking either side of the keel and to the forward faces of no. 2 and no. 7 bulkheads. The mainmast step measured 3.88 × 0.54 × 0.26 m and had two square holes of side 0.26 m; the foremast step was 1.6 × 0.46 × 0.20 m and had 0.20 m holes. The published plan shows two longitudinal timbers in the second hold which may have been used to brace the forward mast step against no. 1 bulkhead.

### 10.4.2.6.5 *Building sequence*

This ship—on the evidence available in the English language—may have been built frame-first in the skeleton sequence, i.e. the shape of the lower hull, at least, was determined by the bulkheads, in addition to the keel, stem, and transoms. The main features supporting this hypothesis are: the plank scarfs are all at bulkhead stations; the position of the *ju* nails fastening planking to bulkheads; and the planking being significantly thicker than the primary planking of comparable ships (120–280 mm compared with 80–120 mm) thus being able to hold inserted caulking.

### 10.4.2.6.6 *Function*

Military equipment such as iron swords, stone shot, fire bottles filled with powder, and a copper blunderbuss of 0.102 m calibre were excavated, leading to the hypothesis that this ship had been an 'anchovy' ship, an offshore patrol warship known from medieval documents (Xi and Xin, 1991).

### 10.4.2.6.7 *Reconstruction*

Reconstruction drawings have been published by Xi and Xin (1991: 236, figs. 6, 7 and 8) in the spirit of 'throwing stones to bring back jade'. These show a three-masted vessel with battened lugsails, of slender lines and a L/B ratio of *c.*6 thus suggesting a design for speed, which would have been appropriate to a warship. The overall length is estimated to be between 32 and 38 m with a maximum breadth of *c.*6 m. At a draft of 1.8 m she would have had a loaded displacement of 173.5 tonnes.

### 10.4.2.7 PENGLAI 2

Xi and Xin (1991: 229) note that there was another, longer, wreck not far from Penglai 1: this wreck has not yet been investigated. Xi and Xin suggest that the two wrecks may have been intentionally sunk in the late-fourteenth century as part of harbour works.

### 10.4.2.8 LIANGSHAN

This wreck was excavated from a former bed of the River Songjin at Liangshan Hsien, Shandong, in 1956. Much of the vessel survived, including fragments of the hatch covers, but no superstructure; all hull timbers are southern pine. She is now on display in Shandong Museum at Jinan (Needham, 1971: 479, fig. 979; He, 1991: 237–44). Although she was probably a vessel for inland waters, aspects of her structure are of wider interest. She is dated to the late fourteenth century from inscriptions on a gun and on an anchor.

### 10.4.2.8.1 *Planking*

This vessel has a flat bottom of nine strakes laid edge-to-edge. There is no keel, but the central three bottom strakes, of total breadth 0.675 m, are thicker (0.165 m) than the others (0.08 m) and constitute a plank-keel. The hooked scarfs in these three keel strakes are staggered, being under no. 5, no. 9 and no. 11 holds (He, 1991: fig. 3): the scarfs have a gradient of *c.*35 per cent—no fastenings are shown on the diagram. There are four bilge strakes and eight strakes in the slightly flared sides. The strakes are flush-laid, butt-jointed, and are fastened by nails (presumably driven in diagonally). The top strake is much more substantial than the others, being 170 mm sided and 138 mm moulded. An extra thickness of planking (a wale of two timbers) is nailed to the sides just above the loaded waterline. At the lightship waterline (lower down the sides) floating 'girdles' or stabilizers were fastened—additionally, these would have protected the planking when using canals.

### 10.4.2.8.2 *Bulkheads and frames*

Twelve bulkheads were fitted to this vessel at an average spacing of *c.*1.7 m. The vertical gaps between the thicker keel strakes and the remaining bottom strakes acted as limber holes under these bulkheads. The bulkheads were each built of four or five 65 mm-thick planks, joined by (angled?) nails; upper planks in two bulkheads had been repaired. There is an opening, 1.3 × 0.96 m, through the tenth bulkhead from the bow, thereby making no. 9 and no. 10 holds virtually one compartment 3 m in length. Bunk boards were found in the forward part of this compartment which was just forward of the helmsman's station (He, 1991: 243).

Frames were fitted adjacent to the bulkheads, probably on the sides nearest the midships station. How they were fastened is not recorded.

### 10.4.2.8.3 *Hatchways and decking*

Substantial timbers were used to form hatches over each hold, extending over approximately 40–50 per cent of the breadth of the vessel. The upper surfaces of these structures were notched to receive hatch covers.

Longitudinal planks, of 60 mm thickness, and laid from bulkhead to bulkhead, formed a decking around the hatches. Outboard of the hatches were walkways which could also have been used as poling galleries.

### 10.4.2.8.4 *Propulsion and steering*

The foremast was stepped on the bottom of the vessel forward of no. 3 bulkhead, and the mainmast forward of no. 7 (near amidships). The mainmast step is 1.87 × 0.29 × 0.10 m; the foremast step, 1.38 × 0.30 × 0.85 m. The lower portions of these masts were recovered: the foremast has a section 0.30 × 0.09 m; the mainmast, 0.28 × 0.195 m. A notch had been cut in the top of no. 2 bulkhead so that the foremast could be lowered into it. It is probable that the mainmast was held in position by a transverse near-horizontal timber (64 × 40 mm)—similar to that in the Sinan wreck (10.4.2.5.5).

Two vertical wooden pillars, 75 mm in diameter, protrude from the after face of the transom forming a channel, c.0.20 m wide, for the rudder stock. It seems that an unbalanced rudder was used (He, 1991: 243).

### 10.4.2.8.5 *Function*

In addition to the gun, swords, arrows, and armour were found with this wreck, suggesting that this vessel had a military use. He (1991) considers that the holds in this vessel were too small for this to be a troop transport, rather an army supply boat, able to defend herself.

### 10.4.2.8.6 *Reconstruction*

This boat measures 21.9 × 3.49 × 1.24 m with an L/B ratio of over 6 and an L/D of c.18. She was thus suitable for use on canals and rivers propelled by sails or, by poles, and possibly by oars. At a draft of 0.75 m, He (1991: 239, 241) estimates that she had a displacement of 33.1 tonnes, including 13 tonnes of equipment, stores, etc.

# 10.5
# Characteristics of the Excavated Ships

The total evidence is not large: only six medieval wrecks, and none of them comprehensively published in the English language. Of the six, only three, Quanzhou 1, Shinan, and Penglai 1 have been documented in any detail, and some of these reports, when translated, are ambiguous. Nevertheless, it is possible to see certain features present in these wrecks which can form the basis for a preliminary definition of a Chinese medieval shipbuilding tradition.

## 10.5.1 SEAGOING SHIPS OF THE THIRTEENTH/FOURTEENTH CENTURIES

### 10.5.1.1 FORM

These ships were not double-ended, having a relatively sharp bow underwater and a transom-shaped stern. Above the waterline there was more symmetry apparent, with a transom-shaped bow above the fore-stem. In longitudinal section there was an angular, rather than smooth, transition between fore-stem and keel, as well as between keel and transom stern. There was a transverse structure high in the stern, projecting aft of the after transom. In transverse section these vessels had a generally rounded bottom with flaring sides.

## 10.5.1.2 STRUCTURE

These vessels were not open boats but ships with decks, with all that implies for structural strength. Two-part keels were joined together, and to the lower stem, by complex horizontal scarfs, either half-laps or hooked. The after-keel was inclined upwards at $c.10°$ to the main keel, the lower stem at $c.20°$. Planks within strakes were joined in horizontal scarfs, half-laps or hooked. Strakes were generally edge-joined together in half-laps or rabbeted laps fastened by angled nails; the Penglai ship had long dowels/treenails as well as angled nails. None of these strake fastenings were 'positive' fastenings comparable with the locked mortise and tenon of the Mediterranean (Fig. 4.23) and the clenched nails of north-west Europe (Fig. 5.50). On the other hand, the *ju* nails between primary planking and bulkheads could be considered 'positive' as they were (probably) fastened by spikes at both ends (Fig. 10.17).

The framework consisted principally of half-frames and associated bulkheads (each with limber holes). These frames were spaced more or less evenly, throughout the length, at intervals which varied from $c.1.5$ to 3.0 m. Planking and framework were generally fastened together by nails driven from outboard. In addition, frames and bulkheads were nailed together, and bulkheads and planking were linked by *ju* nails or a wooden equivalent hooked to the outer face, or jammed within the thickness, of the planking. The second and third layers of planking in the Quanzhou 1 wreck were not primary structure, although they strengthened the hull and enhanced its integrity. It is unclear whether the third layer of planking was 'designed' into the vessel or whether it was added as a reinforcement during the ship's working life, as Marco Polo had suggested was done in his day (10.6.1).

## 10.5.1.3 PROPULSION AND STEERING

These vessels had two composite masts stepped in a timber positioned across the keel and lower planking, at stations 17–22 per cent of the overall length of the ship from the bow for the foremast: and 52–7 per cent for the mainmast. These mast steps had two vertical holes disposed athwart ships as the characteristic housings for each mast.

It seems likely that steering and sailing balance would require a third mast further aft (a mizzen)—this smaller mast need not have been stepped on the keel. A median rudder was hung near the stern positioned so that its stock could rotate within a groove in the stern transom.

## 10.5.1.4 BUILDING SEQUENCE

With the information at present available it is not possible to work out the sequence in which these medieval Chinese ships were built with any certainty: arguments can be advanced that they were built bulkhead-first and also that they were built plank-first. There is a similar dilemma with four fourteenth–sixteenth-centuries wrecks from south-east Asian waters which appear to have had a very similar hull structure (8.3.7.3).

The strakes of the Quanzhou 1 and Penglai 1 ships described above were edge-fastened, yet their plank scarfs were generally at bulkhead stations. Furthermore, they had *ju* nails or similar fastenings between planking and bulkheads: these were so positioned that, in Penglai 1, the bulkheads were almost certainly in place before the planking was fashioned, fitted, and fastened. If this hypothesis proves to be true on further examination of the remains, the lower hull of Penglai 1 was built in the frame-first (actually, bulkhead-first) sequence: her hull shape was determined by the framework of bulkheads and not by her planking. It is possible that Quanzhou 1 was similar.

For Penglai bulkheads to be used in this 'active' way they would probably (though not certainly) have had to be fastened to the keel, but this information is not in the published report. This is but one of several structural features of all these ships (Chinese and south-east Asian) that need to be clarified. Others are: whether plank scarfs were fastened together or merely fastened to the bulkheads; the precise spacing of the bulkheads, centre to centre; whether there are any strake fastenings immediately outboard of bulkheads; whether all strakes were fastened to all bulkheads; and whether caulking was inserted before or after the planking was fastened.

It has been suggested that medieval Chinese ships could not have been built bulkhead-first because their planking was edge-fastened. Generally speaking, edge-fastened planking does indicate that a hull was built plank-first—for exceptions see 10.4.2.2.5. However, it is entirely practicable to fasten planking together with angled nails or treenails after the strakes have been individually fastened to a bulkhead framework: indeed, twentieth-century Chinese junks were built in this manner (10.1.3); and boats in Gujarat, western India, in the early twentieth century, were built frame-first yet had edge-fastened planking (6.7.3).

A provisional sequence of building the lower hull of Penglai 1 may be outlined on the assumption that her bulkheads were fastened to her keel.

- Main keel timber scarfed to the after keel and to the lower stem post. Strengthening timbers fastened to this 'backbone', immediately above the two scarfs.
- All (or some) bulkheads built up to the designed shapes and fastened to the keel. The transom stern similarly built up and fastened in position. After this framework had been faired, it was supported by temporary longitudinal and transverse battens, and by shores and props.
- Holes for dowel fastenings bored into the sides of the keel and the stem at *c*.0.60 m intervals. Planks forming the garboard strakes prepared so that scarfs would lie outboard of a bulkhead, and holes bored in their lower edges to match those on the keel. Garboards fitted to the keel and fastened by dowels, then by angled nails at 0.15 to 0.20 m intervals. Garboards also fastened by nails to the bulkheads. L-shaped holes cut in the inner/upper edge of garboards, adjacent to bulkheads, and *ju* nails part-set into them.
- Planks in the second strakes prepared in a similar manner, and L-shaped holes were cut in their inner/lower edge to match those on the garboard. Planking was then positioned on the protruding *ju* nails and fastened to garboard by angled spikes and treenail/dowels, and to bulkheads by spikes. Strake fashioning, fitting, and fastening continued in this manner, plank scarfs being staggered so that those in adjoining strakes were not fastened to the same or a nearby bulkhead.

## 10.5.2  OTHER MEDIEVAL WRECKS

The Wando cargo ship of the eleventh century (10.4.2.1) does not conform to the specification of the thirteenth- and fourteenth-century ships but it does have some of the diagnostic features: rabbeted-lap side planking; the use of angularly driven fastenings through the lapped planking; and possibly bulkheads. Some scholars consider that this ship is from a tradition other than that of the thirteenth- and fourteenth-century ships because the rabbeted lap joints are formed in a different way (rabbet worked in the outer, upper edge of the lower strake (Wando) rather than in the inner lower edge of the upper strake). In view of the limited evidence available to date, and the sparse record of the Wando wreck, this proposed division is premature: it seems more appropriate to consider the Wando ship to have been a forerunner of the thirteenth- and fourteenth-century ships, with some early features, and possibly with some regional and functional differences.

The military supply vessel from Liangshan (10.4.2.8) similarly does not have some of the characteristic features of the east Asian tradition but she does have regularly spaced frames and bulkheads, horizontal hooked 'keel' scarfs, two typical mast steps at the 17 per cent and 55 per cent stations, and the use of angled nails to fasten the side planking. Deviations from the 'norm' (e.g. the 3-element plank-keel) may be explained by her specialist use on canals.

## 10.5.3  CHANGES OVER TIME

### 10.5.3.1  KEEL SCARFS

Scarf gradients become less steep, from 100 per cent down to *c*.35 per cent: with more wood in contact at the scarf, there was a potentially stronger joint. Scarfs were made more complex and thus less liable to work in a seaway: from simple half-lap joints to hooked scarfs, sometimes wedged and stapled, and with an additional dovetail element. Scarfs were further strengthened by fastening a reinforcing timber across their upper surface.

### 10.5.3.2  ANTI-LEEWAY PROPERTIES

There is a significant technological change in the 'design' of the keel and lower planking between the Quanzhou wreck 1 of the late thirteenth century and the Shinan wreck of the early fourteenth century. The Shinan keel is more leeway-resistant as its d/b ratio is 0.8 compared with 0.6 (McGrail, 1998: table 8.1). The more-steeply inclined lower strakes on the Shinan hull add to this leeway resistance.

## 10.5.3.3 BUILDING SEQUENCE

The published evidence from which the building sequence might be deduced, is equivocal: the planking is edge-fastened, yet there are signs of a bulkhead-first approach. The strongest case for this bulkhead-first sequence can be made for the late fourteenth-century Penglai ship (10.5.1.4); see also several contemporary ships of south-east Asia (8.3.7.3). A comparable change from plank-first to frame-first seems to have occurred at about the same time in the Mediterranean (4.16) and in Atlantic Europe (5.9.4), although framing-first methods had been used by Celtic shipbuilders during Roman times (5.6.3), and also in the Mediterranean from c. seventh century AD (4.15). In China, as in Atlantic Europe, this medieval shift may have been due to several factors: worsening supplies of timber; skilled labour at a premium; recently acquired ability to develop the shape of a hull from a single template, and to repeat 'designs'. In Atlantic Europe, this led to the building of ocean-going vessels capable of encircling the globe. Similar changes in east Asia may have led to the early fifteenth-century ocean-going ships of Admiral Zheng He (10.10.4).

# 10.6

# Documentary Evidence

Until the mid-1970s, accounts by late thirteenth to fourteenth-century European visitors to China, such as Marco Polo and Ibn Battutah, were virtually the only evidence available about medieval Chinese ships. These accounts may now be more readily interpreted in the light of the excavated evidence discussed above.

## 10.6.1 MARCO POLO

Marco Polo is thought to have lived in China during AD 1275–1292 (around the time that Quanzhou 1 was wrecked), and his observations on Chinese life were set down in c.1295, after his return to Italy. It is not clear how technically minded Polo was, nor is it known how well he was acquainted with European shipbuilding and seafaring before he left Italy for China. It must also be borne in mind that Needham (1971: 466–75; Ronan, 1986: 115–18) whose commentary on the maritime aspects of Polo's narrative is often quoted by others, tended to accept Polo's remarks at face value, and almost invariably claimed that features of Chinese ships noted by Polo were unknown in European waters until centuries later. Nevertheless, Polo's descriptions, and those of the Arab traveller and geographer, Ibn Battutah, do provide technological details which can be compared with the evidence from excavated vessels of about the same date.

Polo tells us that, in the lower reaches of the River Yangtze, there were many ships and countless lografts. These river ships were decked, had one mast with a single sail, and carried 4,000–12,000 quintals which Needham (1971: 466) equates with 200–600 tonnes weight of cargo. When these ships could not be sailed, they were towed (by boats or men?) upstream using ropes of split bamboo.

Seagoing ships are mentioned several times in Polo's account, the most detailed descriptions being in his section on the port of *Zaytun* (Quanzhou in Fujian Province). These were large ships generally with four masts, each with a single sail, but with two extra masts which could be stepped and rigged in fair weather. Sweeps, each manned by four seamen, could also be used to propel these ships, presumably in conditions of no wind, or when manœuvring in a confined space, or off a lee shore. This use of sweeps necessarily limits the ship's freeboard, i.e. the height of the sides above the waterline. Polo noted that some of these seagoing ships had a draught of c.4 paces (which Needham (1971: 467) translates as c.20 ft or 6 m) and that their crew varied in size from 'fewer than 150' to 'more than 300' seamen; both of which suggests sizeable ships. These ships are said to have had only one deck on which were up to sixty cabins for merchants: such 'cabins' were probably enclosed bunks as found in the twentieth-century Antung trader (Waters, 1938: 55–6).

Polo noted that these ships could carry up to 6,000 'baskets of pepper': the European equivalent is not known but if we presume that each basket could be carried by one man, the cargo of the largest of these ships would have been c.300 tonnes, which is of the same order as estimates (200–50 tonnes) made for the cargo capacity of Quanzhou ship 1. However, a crew of

150 seems to be far too many for such a vessel (perhaps some were marines) and a draught of *c.*10 ft (*c.*3 m) would seem more appropriate than the 20 ft quoted.

The largest of these seagoing ships had two or three large boats and up to ten smaller boats as tenders. The large boats seem to have been about one-quarter the size of their parent ship and were used, under oar or sail, to tow her. On passage these large boats were themselves towed by the ship. The smaller boats were carried on board the ship, lashed outboard, and were used for fishing and like tasks, and during anchoring. These seagoing ships had iron fastened, double-thickness pine or fir planking, caulked (and possibly also payed) with *chu-nam.* The ship's hold was divided into up to thirteen watertight compartments by (up to twelve) bulkheads made with 'strong planks fitted together' (Needham, 1971: 467).

The fact that the four medieval Chinese wrecks from Quanzhou, Penglai, Shinan, and Liangshan (10.4.2) had bulkheads at an average spacing of 1.50–3 m suggests that the seagoing ships noted by Marco Polo probably had a similar spacing. Thus Polo's largest ships with thirteen compartments were, at most, *c.*40 m in length. Indeed, as Quanzhou 1 also has thirteen compartments and is thought originally to have measured *c.*35 × 10 × 3.5 m (10.4.2.2), Polo's largest ships would seem to have been of this size.

Using excavated evidence again, it seems probable that in the lower holds of Polo's ships where cargo was stowed (probably on a 'deck' of ceiling planking), there would have been waterways for the free passage of bilge water through limber holes in bulkheads and floor timbers. In this sense, such compartments would not be completely watertight, as Needham (1971) and many subsequent authors thought. Nevertheless, such a system of bulkheads would reduce the flow of sea water from one damaged or leaking compartment to others, in addition to their primary role of strengthening the ship.

When ships had been at sea for a year or more, or needed to be repaired for some other reason, Polo tells us that a third layer of planking was fastened on top of the original double-thickness planking. This method of repair seems entirely plausible, especially in the light of the evidence from Quanzhou 1. However, Polo goes on to state that an extra layer of planking was similarly fastened to the hull annually until there were six layers: at this stage, the ship was relegated to estuary and coastal voyages in fair weather only (Needham, 1971: 468). This procedure would limit seagoing ships to five years or so useful life: furthermore, such a thickness of planking throughout the hull would significantly reduce the ship's freeboard and/or payload. Perhaps it is more reasonable to conclude that such layers of planking were added to the original double-thickness hull only when and where necessary. The Quanzhou 1 ship appears to have had just one extra layer of planking added to the double-planked hull, possibly only over the region of the loaded waterline.

### 10.6.2 IBN BATTUTAH

Ibn Battutah visited China in *c.* AD 1347 and noted three sizes of seagoing vessel: *jonq,* the largest with twelve sails; *zaw,* medium-sized; and *kakam,* the smallest with three sails. The largest vessels were built only in Zayton (Quanzhou) and Sin-Kilan/Sin al Sin (Guangzhou/Canton): Battutah considered Zayton to be the largest port known to him, with 100 large *jonq* and innumerable smaller vessels. These large *jonq* had four decks, each one with merchant's cabins and were said to be manned by 600 seamen and 400 marines. Each *jonq* had three tenders of varying sizes. As well as sails, which were made from split-bamboo matting, sweeps could also be used: each sweep—there were about twenty—was manned by about thirty men, standing in two rows either side of the sweep. The looms of these sweeps were too thick to be grasped (said to be 'as big as masts'—Needham, 1971: 469) and rope lanyards were fitted along both sides of the sweep for the men to pull. Needham (1971: 470) claimed that these 'huge oars' were 'yulohs' (10.2.11.1) but *yulohs,* as known today, can only be used effectively over the stern of a vessel and it would be impossible to fit in twenty there. These 'huge oars' were undoubtedly sweeps used in the conventional manner, widely spaced along the length of the ship, ten to a side, on the deck nearest the waterline.

From Battutah's account (Needham, 1971: 469) the sequence of building these seagoing vessels of the mid-fourteenth century seems to have been plank-first, at least in the lower hull. After this had been built of thick planking (possibly double-thickness?), very thick planks were fastened across the ship (as bulkheads?) by large nails, said to be three ells in length. The lowest deck was then fastened in position and the ship was fitted out for service after being launched. It is possible that this is a description of the frame-first sequence of building being used for the upper hull, but the interpretation is by no means clear.

It seems, then, that if allowance is made for the ambiguities in Polo's and Battutah's accounts, and if their exaggerations are disregarded, there is a general concordance between these late thirteenth- and mid-fourteenth-century descriptions, and the recently excavated Chinese seagoing ships of approximately the same date.

# 10.7
# The Chinese Shipbuilding Tradition

The earliest Chinese nautical evidence is of boats from inland waters, but by the fifth or sixth century AD representational evidence appears for seagoing sailing ships. A number of well-documented seagoing wrecks are dated to the thirteenth and fourteenth centuries and there are descriptions of Chinese ships by Europeans and by Chinese authors from the thirteenth to the sixteenth centuries. The iconographic evidence is mainly for hull shape above the waterline, propulsion, and steering; the excavated ships tell us more about the structure and shape, especially below the waterline; whilst the documentary evidence throws light on several aspects. The context of this evidence suggests that it is mainly concerned with the ship capable of *overseas* voyages, that is, in twentieth-century Chinese terminology, we are dealing with the southern ship, the *Fuchuan* or *Guangzhou* ship and not the northern variant, the *shachuan* or sand ship which was more suitable for coastal and estuary work (10.1.3). Although there are some structural differences between these two types as seen in recent centuries (for example, the northern ship is keel-less), the main difference seems to be in shape and size. The Lianshan wreck is thought by Chinese scholars to be a *shachuan* or northern type of vessel, but many of her structural characteristics are similar to those of the other thirteenth- to fourteenth-

century wrecks which appear to be of the southern or overseas type.

## 10.7.1 SHAPE

The characteristic silhouette of the above-water hull of this Chinese seagoing shipbuilding tradition may be seen in ships depicted in the seventh-century Buddhist frescos at Dunhuang: built-up bow and stern, with a projection astern (10.4.1). This projection may be a stern gallery which later became a common feature, and which is first seen clearly on a painting of river craft dated *c.* AD 1125. Square ends in plan, again above the waterline, are also seen on one of the Dunhuang frescos. The earliest representations of square ends are on the first-century AD pottery models of river craft from Guangzhou (Fig. 10.7): one of these models also has a transom stern. The European travellers' accounts of the thirteenth and fourteenth centuries do not mention shape, but from wrecks of this time, we see that the underwater hull had a relatively sharp bow and a squared-off stern. There was an angular junction between keel and stern and between keel and forestem, and the transverse section was generally rounded with flaring sides, but with a relatively sharp lowest section.

There seems to be continuity in the characteristic *above*-water shape of seagoing ships, from the fifth to seventh centuries AD through to the depiction of fourteenth- and fifteenth-century Chinese ships on European maps (10.4.1). The shape of the *under*water hull from the thirteenth century at least is, as one should expect, more conventional and generally similar to contemporary hulls elsewhere.

## 10.7.2 STRUCTURE AND BUILDING SEQUENCE

Lu Xun, a shipwright of the Jin dynasty (AD 265–420) is said to have built a warship with eight watertight compartments (Zhou, 1983: 483, 489). However, the earliest clear evidence for hull structure comes from a briefly reported seventh- to ninth-century *wreck* from Ju-Kao, Jiangsu (10.4.2) which has bulkheads and iron-fastened planking, caulked with *chu-nam*. Keel and stem are seen on the late twelfth-century ship carved on the

Bayon Temple, Angkor Thom, Cambodia (10.4.1), and two-part keels and lower stems are found in the several excavated wrecks of the thirteenth and fourteenth centuries. Planking, edge-joined in half-laps or rabbeted laps, fastened by angled nails, and caulked with *chunam*, is also found on these wrecks. Marco Polo noted that the planking of seagoing ships was usually doubled and sometimes there were even more layers: this is confirmed by evidence from the wreck Quanzhou 1. The thirteenth- to fourteenth-century wrecks had bulkheads (which Polo and others noted), but also half-frames.

The sequence of building these ships is not yet entirely clear, but, at the least, there are signs that Chinese shipwrights were moving towards a bulkhead-first approach, and it may be that Penglai 1 of the late fourteenth century was indeed designed and built in this manner (10.5.1.4). As Chinese ships were also built bulkhead-first with edge-fastened planking in the late nineteenth/early twentieth century (Audemard, 1957–69: ii; Greenhill, 1976: 103–5; 1995a: 83–4; Maitland, 1981: 54–9), it seems that this probable fourteenth-century innovation persisted into the present day.

## 10.7.3 PROPULSION AND STEERING

The single square sail was used on seagoing ships from at least the fifth/sixth century AD and it is not until the late twelfth-century carving at Angkor Thom (10.4.1) that there is evidence for Chinese lugsail-shaped sails, probably made of matting and with battens and distinctive multiple sheets. It is possible that such a sail is depicted on the seventh-century Ajanta frescos (Fig. 6.11) and in the eighth-century Borobodur temples (Fig. 8.6), but the ships with these sails may well have been of the south-east Asian tradition rather than Chinese. All forms of evidence suggest that, from the twelfth century onwards, the lugsail was the predominant Chinese sail. The Angkor Thom ship has two masts, whilst Marco Polo, a century later, describes Chinese ships with four permanent and two temporary masts, and in the mid-fourteenth century, Ibn Battutah claimed to have seen ships with twelve sails (10.6). The thirteenth- to fourteenth-century Chinese wrecks generally appear to have had two, probably three, permanent masts.

The seagoing ship depicted in the seventh-century Dunhuang temples (10.4.1) is propelled by oars or sweeps as well as by sail, and this practice is referred to by both Marco Polo and Ibn Battutah. This means that these medieval seagoing ships had at least one weather deck (possibly a gallery deck) from which it was possible to row, with several standing oarsmen manning each sweep, when it was impracticable to rely solely on sails: in a calm, against headwinds, or when manœuvring near land.

The Dunhuang ship is steered by two steering oars or sweeps, pivoted on each quarter. A median rudder is fitted to one of the first-century AD Guangzhou pottery models of a riverboat (Fig. 10.7), and balanced median rudders are depicted on the early twelfth-century paintings of river ferries by Zhang Ze-Duan (10.4.1). However, the earliest evidence for median rudders at sea appears to be on the late twelfth-century Angkor Thom carvings (10.4.1). The thirteenth- to fourteenth-century wrecks show evidence for a median rudder near the stern: these rudders do not appear to be inset within a well under the overhanging stern as is known to have been used in later times; nor do they appear to have been balanced.

## 10.7.4 SIZE

Marco Polo emphasized the great size of the Chinese seagoing ships he saw, but he stated that they had only one deck. Moreover, the figures for cargo that he gives suggest that these ships had a cargo capacity of *c*.300 tonnes and that they cannot have been longer overall than 40 m (10.6.1). Ibn Battutah claimed that Chinese vessels had four decks, but it seems likely that some of these were in the superstructure. Three wrecks of the thirteenth/fourteenth centuries, Quanzhou 1, Shinan, and Penglai, are all thought to have been less than 35 m in overall length, and to have had cargo capacities within the range 100–250 tonnes (10.5.1). It is possible that these ships originally had three or more 'decks': a decking of ceiling planking in the bottom of the hold; a full length deck on top of the bulkheads; with further decks within the superstructure aft.

The great size of some of Zheng He's Indian Ocean ships of the early fifteenth century has also been stressed by certain authors (10.10.4), however, a more rational, but speculative, assessment suggests overall lengths not greater than *c.*70 m and cargo capacities of *c.*2,000 tonnes for the few, relatively large, ships in these Chinese fleets.

## 10.7.5 SHIP DESIGN

Needham (1971: 413) has noted that traditional Chinese boatbuilding was 'by eye'. This is commonly and widely said about plank-first traditions, but there are indications in Europe that, although plank-first builders often have in their mind's eye an ideal boat shape which they attempt to translate into three-dimensional reality, they also supplement their visual acuity by rule-of-thumb and by building aids (4.15.3, 5.9.4). There is a suggestion of such a possibility in Needham's remark (1971: 409) that in *c.* AD 1158, Zhang Zhongyan, made a small 'demonstration model' before building a ship; his contemporary, Zhang Hsueh, is said to have built a similar model which appears to have been at 1 : 10 scale. These models may have been used as building aids to get the required shape for the ships.

Ibn Battutah's description of how Quanzhou (*Zaytun*) ships were built in *c.* AD 1347, appears to be that of a plank-first sequence, at least for the lower hull, and aspects of plank-first techniques are evident in Chinese (and south-east Asian) wrecks of around that time. The Penglai wreck, a military ship dated to the mid-fourteenth century (probably a decade or so after Ibn Battutah's visit to China), on the other hand may well have been built in the bulkhead-first sequence (10.5.1.4, 10.5.3.3). In early twentieth-century China, bulkheads were installed and fastened to the bottom planking before the side planking was added (10.7.2): this was the frame-first sequence with the bulkheads determining the form of the hull, nevertheless the flush laid planks were edge-fastened by angled nails and then by clamps across the seams (Audemard, 1957: ii; Greenhill, 1976: 104).

Some idea of the rules that may have been used in earlier times to determine the *overall* shape and size of Chinese ships may be gained from the 'traditional' rules-of-thumb used to build Guandong wooden junks in recent centuries (Liu and Li, 1991). The basic unit was the breadth of the vessel to be built. If this waterline midships breadth is B, the overall length L, and the depth of hold amidships D, then:

- L = K × B (where K = 3.5 to 4 for coastal, and 5.5 to 6 for deep sea vessels)
- D = 0.5 B
- cargo capacity = LBD × $K_2$ ($K_2$ = 0.35 coastal; and 0.30 deep sea)
- stem height = B; stern height = 1.5 B
- transom breadth = 1.1 B
- bottom breadth = 0.6 B
- height of mainmast = 3 B to 3.3 B.
- height of foremast = 2.4 to 2.6 B.
- the size and shapes of the sails and their yards were also related to B, through the height of their masts (Liu and Li, 1991: figs. 5 and 6)
- leeboard length = B; leeboard breadth = L/20
- length of rudder post = B; Rudder area = $(B/2)_2$
- nail length = 2 × plank thickness
- nail spacing = nail length.

It is not difficult to visualize simple versions of such rules being used in earlier times in China. Furthermore, comparable rules were a feature of the system used to design fifteenth-century ships in the Mediterranean and on the Atlantic coast of Europe (4.16, 5.9.4) and subsequently in India (6.7.4.3).

In the official archives of Wenzhou prefecture is a document dated to the Song dynasty (i.e. before *c.* AD 1290) which refers to 'two volumes of drawings of ships'. However, Zhou (1983: 484) has explained that these were probably sketches and specifications rather than scale drawings. Scale drawings for at least parts of the design seem to have been used in Manchu times: in early Qing documents (seventeenth/eighteenth century AD) concerning the Fujian 'arrow pursuit ship' (*ganzen chuan*), the length of the keel is said to be related in an unspecified manner to the length of the ship, and instructions are given how to draw the keel's longitudinal profile: for every *zhang* (3.33 m) of keel, the fore keel (lower stem) rises 5 to 5.2 *cun* (16–17 cm) whilst the middle keel (main keel) rises at 2.6 *cun* (8 cm); the after keel appears to lie in the same plane as the main keel (Zhou, 1983: 484–5). Instructions were also given for drawing the transverse sections of this vessel at four bulkhead stations: in the bow, by the mainmast, by the 'official stateroom', and at the stern (Zhou, 1983: 485–6).

## 10.8

# Other Plank-Boat Traditions

### 10.8.1 DRAGON BOATS

Racing in long and relatively narrow-planked boats called *lung chuan* (dragon boats) is undertaken widely today in the Chinese cultural region, especially at the May festivals. These *lung chuan* are not to be confused with the cruising boats which actually have a dragon figurehead in the bows and are sometimes also known as 'dragon boats'. *Lung chuan* have this name because they are said to have a dragon's shape (Fig. 10.20). Their great length and overhanging ends are given extra support by a bamboo-rope cable which runs, low down, from end to end and acts as a hogging hawser (Needham, 1971: 436–7; Worcester, 1956b). These boats have a central longitudinal strength member, which either projects below the planking as a keel or is internal, acting as a keelson. Into this keel or keelson, simple bulkheads are slotted to form the framework of the boat: in these aspects they have similarities with the mainstream shipbuilding tradition (10.7.2). *Lung chuan* are double-banked, propelled by 18–36 paddlers each side. They have a maximum beam of *c.*4 ft (*c.*1.2 m) and have lengths of over 100 ft (*c.*30 m): an L/B of *c.*25 : 1. There

is representational evidence stretching back for over 2,000 years of a form of boat which may be an early type of dragon boat, i.e. a planked boat of high L/B ratio, capable of high speed when propelled by many paddlers. Such a boat probably had war uses and despatch boat duties before being used for competitive races.

The earliest representation of what may be a dragon boat is a painting on silk excavated from a Chu tomb dated to the period 475–221 BC (Peng, 1988: 48). The first reference to racing boats also comes from the state of Chu—a legend describing dragon boat races commemorating a poet's death during the Warring States period (480–221 BC). During the Han period (third–first century BC) lively scenes of boats—thought to be dragon boats—were engraved on bronze drums which are now found widely distributed from Indo-China in the south to Guangxi and Sichuan provinces in north China (Fig. 8.7) (Rawson, 1980: 171–2). These representations are stylized and some aspects are difficult to interpret, but their common features appear to be: a long boat with rising ends, propelled by several paddlers, steered by a steering oar, and sometimes with an anchor hanging over the bows (Peng, 1988: 36, 39, 45, 47, 48). It is not apparent from these engravings whether the boats represented were logboats or plank boats.

In a now-lost book *Fu-Nan Chuan* of the third cen-

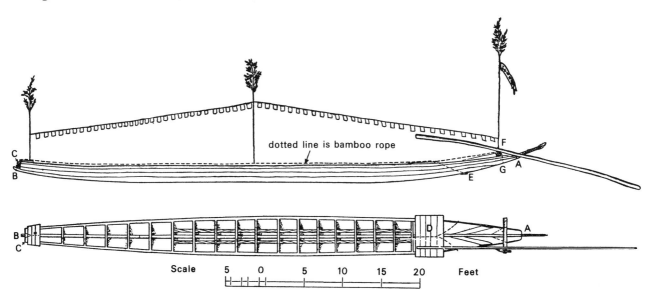

Fig. 10.20. Measured drawing of a Yangtze Dragon Boat. The hogging truss of bamboo rope passes from the bow (B) over chock (C) to the platform (D) where it divides: one portion is made fast to chock (E) and the other continues over the transom (F) to the counter at (G) (after Worcester, 1956c).

tury AD there is a description of boat building in Cambodia and Cochin-China (Needham, 1971: 450). The dimensions given, *c.*70 × 6 ft (*c.*21 × 1.8 m), suggest that these may have been plank boats rather than logboats, although trees of such a size are not beyond the bounds of credibility. The crew of up to 100 men appear to have been double-banked (i.e. two men side by side) and each are said to have had an oar, a paddle, and a pole: although paddling, and perhaps poling, seem just practicable by fifty men each side within a length of 70 ft, rowing would appear not to be so.

Li and Lin (1985: 18–24) consider that a logboat with rising ends excavated at Ningbo, Zhejiang, was a dragon boat of the T'ang period (AD 618–909), whilst Deguchi (1991: 199) believes this boat was used ceremonially in the Iris Festival. A scale drawing shows this boat to have been *c.*11.5 × 0.95 × 0.35 m, a suitable size for a relatively speedy craft with thirty-six or so double-banked paddlers.

The earliest depiction of long boats used for competitive racing appears to be by a Song-dynasty (tenth–thirteenth centuries AD) painter Zhang Zeduan which is entitled 'Striving for the Championship in the Jimming Dragon Boat Racing Pool'.

This multifaceted evidence shows that there has been a history of long boats propelled by many paddlers in China since the late first millennium BC. It seems likely that at first these were logboats and that they were used in war. By the early second millennium AD, at the latest, warcraft were of a different form and these paddled long boats (by now known as dragon boats) were relegated to ceremonial and competitive occasions (as happens worldwide). When the change from logboat to plank boat occurred is not clear: it may have been relatively late. The use of planks would mean that much longer, and therefore potentially faster, dragon boats could be built. Their very length meant that the keel/keelson structure with a hogging hawser had to be used.

## 10.8.2 VESSELS WITHOUT BULKHEADS

Needham (1971: 437) has drawn attention to twentieth-century boats from the Chinese cultural region which do not have bulkheads. Boats from Lake Erh Hai in south-west Yunnan have frames instead of bulkheads;

whilst the 'snake-boats' (*shê chhuan*) of the River Kungthan also have no bulkheads.

## 10.8.3 UNUSUAL PLANK-FASTENINGS

Deguchi (1991: 204–5) has recorded an edge-fastened boatbuilding tradition in nineteenth-/twentieth-century Honshu, Japan. The planking of these boats was fastened edge-to-edge by wooden tenons within mortises in the thickness of the plank (later replaced by iron nails) and by double dovetail wooden clamps across the seams (Fig. 10.21). These clamps and tenons were not locked in position but were fashioned slightly oversize to make an interference fit. The planking was further fastened and the seams made watertight by an adhesive, made from lacquer (*urushi*) and powdered saw-

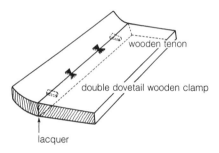

Fig. 10.21. Plank fastenings in a recent boat from Honshu, Japan (after Deguchi, 1991: fig. 16).

dust or flour, which was spread along the plank edges before fastening. This mixture was also used to waterproof knots.

The wooden tenons within mortises may have similarities with the plank fastenings of the eleventh-century Wando ship (10.4.2.1). Otherwise, there is, as yet, no evidence for early use of these techniques elsewhere in the Chinese cultural region, but varnish trees (e.g. *Rhus succedanea* and *Rhus verniciflora*) grow in a forest zone which extends from Japan to South Korea, south and south-west China and into Vietnam and it may be that their usefulness to boatbuilders had formerly been widely appreciated. Lin (1991: 326) has quoted from a legend concerning King Zao of the Zhoa dynasty (900–400 BC) who was given a 'glued boat' by the people of the River Han region; whilst Deguchi (1991: 205) claims that there is evidence for the use of lacquer to pay the underwater planking of Chinese vessels in the T'ang dynasty (AD 618–909).

Another type of edge-fastened boat has been noted by Lin (1991: 326). Three plank-built 'royal barges', each measuring c.13.1 × 2.3 × 0.76 m, were excavated in 1978 from the tomb of King Zhongshan in Pingshan, Hebei, and are dated to c.310 BC. The planks, which were said to be 0.40–0.60 m broad and 0.10–0.15 m thick, were fastened together by iron 'hoops' (possibly staples) and the seams were filled with a mixture of wooden chips and molten lead. Secondary structure was said to be fastened to the hull with 'bone nails'. The thickness of the planking and the use of lead suggests that these boats may have been specially built for the funeral ceremonies, rather than have been working boats, nevertheless, the fastening techniques may have been used in contemporary vessels.

### 10.8.4 TUB BOATS

Plank-built small boats in the shape of a tub or basin, without bulkheads or any other mainstream characteristic, are used today on the Yangtze at Wuhu, fifty miles upstream from Nanjing and by inshore fishermen in Japan where they are known as tarai-buné (Hornell, 1946a: 108–9). These boats are elliptical in plan and measure 6 to 8 ft in length, c.4½ ft in breadth and are about 2 ft in height of sides (c.1.8–2.4 × 1.4 × 0.6 m). They are built of short staves like a barrel, but bound together with bamboo or rattan ropes rather than iron hoops. The Chinese boats are paddled, whilst Japanese fishermen use a single scull over the stern where there is a grooved cleat and grommet.

# 10.9

# Boat and Shipbuilding Sites

As in most regions of the world, informal building sites, which leave little or no archaeologically detectable remains, were used in China from earliest times and continue to be used in the less-advanced regions today—The 'shipbuilding factory' established by Fuchai in the Spring and Autumn period (770–476 BC) at Fuzhou, in the estuary of the River Ming, was probably of this type (Chen and Chen, 1991: 298). However, excavations in Guangzhou in 1974 (Zhou, 1983: 488) revealed the remains of a third-century BC/third-century AD shipbuilding site with three timber structures of blocks up to 1 m in height, upon which ships up to 8.4 m in breadth could be built; vessels were subsequently launched via a slipway into the sea. Shipbuilding tools, such as plumbs and squares, chisels, axes, and caulking irons, were also excavated, and nearby was a timber yard with an 'ox' used to bend timbers heated by fire.

From the early centuries AD, therefore, some of the references to 'dockyards' may well be concerned with formal rather than informal building sites. For example, there are references from the Three Kingdoms era (AD 220–80) to a shipbuilding area at Zhixiang, east of the Kaiyuan temple in Fuzhou. By the Song dynasty (AD 960–1290), the state shipyard at Fuzhou seems to have been moved to Hekou beside the Maitreya Temple (Chen and Chen, 1991: 298–9). Other shipyards, both state and private, were at Mingzhou, Quanzhou, Kwangzhou, and in Chejiang province (C.-Q. Li, 1989: 282–3). Lin (1991) has described wharfs and a 'shipyard' dated to the Song dynasty (tenth–thirteenth century AD) which were excavated at Ningbo in 1978/9.

In the Ming period (fifteenth century) the most important state shipbuilding yards seem to have been near the capital Nanjing between the Hanzhong and Yijiang city gates (Zhou, 1983: 486; Peng, 1988: 73; Needham, 1971: 483, fig. 981). A sixteenth-century account, Long Jiang Chuan Chang Zhi, of the shipbuilding yards on the Dragon River near Nanjing, includes plans of the yards where the ships of Zheng He's fleets were built and fitted out during the period 1401–3 (10.10.4). In the mid-twentieth century this site consisted of large rectangular ponds c.1 m deep, the largest being 240 × 35 m in area; presumably these were the silted-up remains of docks. Excavations were undertaken there in 1953 and 1965 (Zhou, 1983: 486–7): the report does not mention whether any structures were found, only the remnants of a windlass, a large rudder stock (10.10.4) and 'other component parts of the vessel'.

## 10.10

# China and the World Overseas

### 10.10.1 CHINA AND JAPAN

Japan was settled *c*.50,000–60,000 years ago (Scarre, 1989: 69) at a time of lower sea levels. This must have involved a sea voyage which may have been either across the Korean strait, which was much narrower than it is today, or along the island chain which extended from the Philippines (then part of continental south-east Asia), and northwards along the Ryukyu islands to Kyushu (Fig. 10.22). These voyages may well have been undertaken on log rafts, as seems to have been the case in the first colonization of Australia (7.2) at about the same time. The hunter-gatherer economy then established in Japan began to be replaced by millet and rice agriculture, and by bronze and then iron technology from the mid-first millennium BC, by which time there was a much higher sea level (Scarre, 1989: 196). The initial impetus for this cultural change appears to have come from east China and Korea, at a time when the coastlines, currents, and winds were similar to those obtaining today. These later incomers would have been capable of building any of the basic types of water transport: which vessels were used for sea passages must await some future excavation, but, in those times, planked vessels are a possibility.

Ma (1991: 189), quoting work by Kinomiya, gives three routes which were used in the Sui and Tang dynasties (AD 581–909) to cross from the Chinese mainland to Japan:

- coastal: from Dengzhou on the Shandong peninsula northwards to the Liaodong peninsula, then coastwise to south-west Korea and across the strait to Kyushu;
- intermediate: from the Yangtze estuary, northwards to the Shandong peninsula, then across the Yellow Sea to south-west Korea, thence to Kyushu;
- open sea: from Ningbo, south of the Yangtze estuary, across the East China Sea to Kyushu.

It seems likely that a similar range of routes would have been open to earlier seamen as far back as, say,

1500 BC: the choice of route and time of year would depend not only on winds and currents but also on the type of vessels used and on the navigational skills of the crew. Hsu Fu, a legendary figure of the Qin dynasty (*c*.220 BC), is said to have been sent eastwards by the first emperor of the Qin with a group of young people, including artisans, and with a supply of grain seed, to search for medicinal herbs (Ma, 1991; Severin, 1994: 45–7). The numbers of people sent and their equipment suggest that this was more a migration than a herb-hunting sortie. In later times, Hsu Fu was honoured in Japan as the god of farming, medicine, and sericulture. It therefore seems likely that the Hsu Fu legends incorporate folk memories of a migration, for which there is archaeological evidence, from north China and Korea to Japan in the late first millennium BC which introduced crop cultivation, metal working, silkworm farming, and probably Chinese writing characters to Japan.

### 10.10.2 CHINA AND THE AMERICAS?

Needham (1971: 540–53), Lin (1991: 321), Severin (1994) and others have argued that there were Chinese contacts with the Americas between the seventh century BC and the sixteenth century AD. Needham focused his attention on the Qin period (third century BC), and specifically on Hsu Fu's legendary voyage. Whether Chinese seamen of this period crossed the Pacific is very uncertain. Nevertheless the possibility of an isolated, probably accidental, crossing cannot be ruled out.

In 1993, Tim Severin (1994), known for his Brendan, Sindbad, and Jason voyages, had a sailing raft built in Hong Kong and sailed via Taiwan, the east coast of Japan and eastwards across the Pacific in latitudes 40°–36°N. This raft was based on the Formosan (Taiwanese) raft shape known in the early twentieth century (10.2.5), but had three layers of rattan-lashed bamboos rather than one. It measured *c*.60 × 15 ft (*c*.18 × 4.5 m), had three masts, each rigged with a battened lugsail, and a crew of five or six. Severin's plans for this trans-Pacific voyage were based on Needham's interpretation of the Chinese literary evidence for trans-Pacific voyages. The raft averaged only 35–40 nautical miles each day and encountered such severe weather that, more than three months after leaving Japan, the

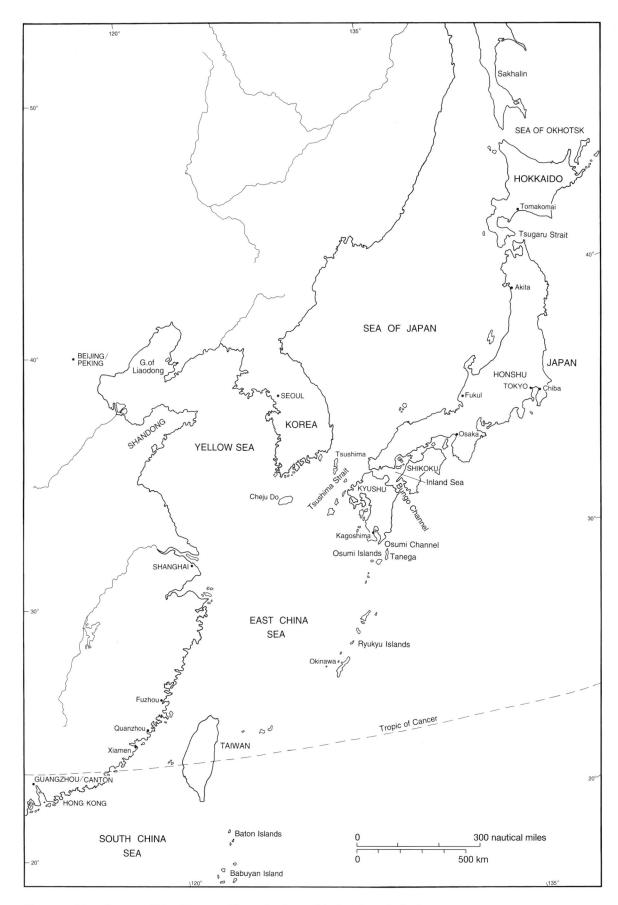

Fig. 10.22. Map of eastern China, Korea, and Japan (Institute of Archaeology, Oxford).

raft had to be abandoned when more than 1,000 nautical miles west of the Americas, when it began to break up. As with some of Heyerdahl's oceanic voyages, Severin's voyage tells us little about early maritime history, but does tell us something about the seagoing capabilities of log rafts and the skills of twentieth-century human beings.

## 10.10.3 CHINA AND THE INDIAN OCEAN

Towards the end of the *Periplus of the Erythraean Sea*, a merchant's guide to maritime trade in the Red Sea and the Indian Ocean (2.11.5, 6.3.1), the unknown first-century AD author mentions the River Ganges, *Chrysê* (probably Burma and the Malay peninsula), and then, 'a very great inland city called *Thina*' from which silk was sent to India. The *Periplus* (ch. 64) continues: 'It is not easy to get to this *Thina*, for rarely do people come from it, and only a few'. The place name *Thina*, known to Ptolemy (7. 3. 6) as *Sinai* or *Thinai*, is thought to be derived, through Sanskrit, from *Ch'in* (Ts'in or Qin) the name of the dynasty which, in the period 221–206 BC, began the unification of the Chinese people (Needham, 1954: 168–9).

The final sentence in this *Periplus* (ch. 66) reads, 'What lies beyond this area, because of extremes of storm, bitter cold and difficult terrain and also because of some divine power of the gods, has not been explored' (Casson, 1989: 93). These quotations encapsulate European knowledge of China at the beginning of the first millennium AD. Little was known other than its general location to the east and north of *Chrysê*, and that it was the source of such highly desirable goods as silk, fur, and *malabathran*, the leaves of the cinnamon tree used in Mediterranean medicines and in cooking (*Periplus*, chs. 39, 65).

### 10.10.3.1 THE SILK ROAD

Although at this time, and later in the first millennium AD, traded goods may have been carried from east Asia to Europe by several relays of ships on short-haul routes (6.4, 3.8.1), the main route for trade between China and the Mediterranean appears to have been overland via the so-called 'Silk Road', a group of caravan routes from China westwards to *Bactria* (Afghanistan), thence either westwards to the Mediterranean

via Mesopotamia and Syria to Antioch, or through Palmyra to the Lebanon; or southwards from *Bactria* to the River Indus or to *Barygaza* in the Gulf of Cambay in western India; or down the River Ganges to its delta. The final leg of this last route was presumably by sea, southwards along the east coast of India, around Cape Comorin and up the west coast to *Limyrikê* (the Malabar coast). At the western termini of these routes (Antioch, the Levant ports, *Barbarika* in the Indus estuary, *Barygaza*, and *Limyrikê*), Chinese goods could be bought by traders and shipped to the Mediterranean markets (Casson, 1989: 26; Newby, 1982: 34–5). Sections of this Silk Road had been opened up as early as the fifth century BC and it was to remain a major link between eastern and western Asia, until the Sung dynasty (AD 960–1279) when, because of severe disruptions in central Asia, the maritime route proved to be both safer and cheaper (Scarre, 1989: 191; Twitchett, 1980: 271).

### 10.10.3.2 THE MARITIME SILK ROUTE
(Fig. 10.23)

It is often difficult to determine from archaeological, and indeed early documentary, evidence the nationality of the ships undertaking overseas trade: voyages between two countries may be made by the ships of one or other country, or of both, or indeed, of a third country. However, Chinese texts of the second century BC do seem to describe overseas trading voyages by Chinese ships to the eastern islands of south-east Asia (Scarre, 1989: 198–9). From there the goods were taken to India by Indonesian and then by Indian vessels. By the mid-fourth century AD, there were direct maritime links with Malaya and by the end of that century with Sri Lanka (Fernandez-Armesto, 1991: 22). These voyages were probably undertaken by Chinese ships, but it is clear from the travelling Bhuddist monk Fa Xian's account of his journey home to China from Sri Lanka via Java, that there were also non-Chinese vessels on this route (Snow, 1992: 58).

Chinese merchants are also said to have visited Batanea on the Euphrates in the mid-fourth century (Fernandez-Armesto, 1991: 22; Guy, 1992: 71), but these voyages may have been in Persian or Arab ships. Hornell (1946: 231), quoting the tenth-century Arabs, Hamza of Ispahan and Al Ma'sudi, claimed that, in the early fifth century, Chinese ships (along with Indian

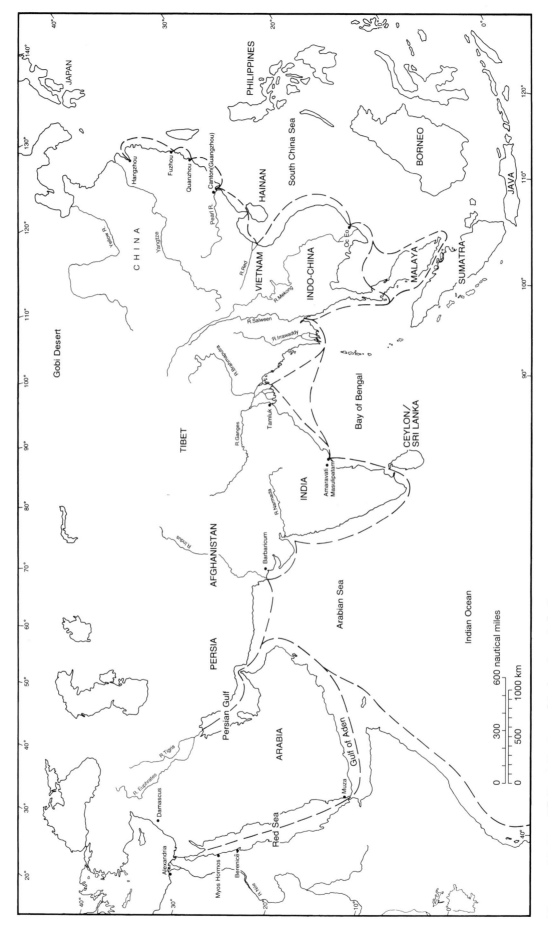

Fig. 10.23. Maritime Silk Route (Institute of Archaeology, Oxford).

ships) could be seen on the River Euphrates at Hira near Kufa, some 45 miles south-west of Babylon—this interpretation is by no means certain.

By the seventh century, Persian and Arab traders were established in several ports in south-east China (Hornell, 1941a: 254; 1946a: 231; Blunden and Elvin, 1983: 189; Scarre, 1989: 190–1). It seems likely that they came in their own ships for I. Ching noted that in AD 671, he left Guangzhou (Canton) in a *possu* or Persian ship (Fernandez-Armesto, 1991: 20). Chinese accounts from the seventh to the ninth centuries, on the other hand, describe the sea route between Guangzhou and Arabia and possibly as far as the African east coast (Hornell, 1946a: 231; Snow, 1992: 57), and the ninth-century Arab merchant Suleiman refers to Chinese ships at Quilon in south-west India and at Siraf and Oman in the Persian Gulf (Snow, 1992: 58). Furthermore, artefacts from China, dated to the ninth century and later, have been excavated from Gulf ports such as Obola (*Apologus*), Basra, Siraf, Kish, and Hormuz (Hornell, 1946a: 231; Fernandez-Armesto, 1991: 22). These facts suggest that some Chinese, as well as Persian and Arab, ships voyaged to and from Arabia in those centuries.

The communities of foreign traders in China (Muslims, Persians, Zoroastrians, Christians, and Jews) continued to prosper into the Sung dynasty and beyond, apart from a temporary check in Guangzhou during the ninth century (Hornell, 1946a: 232). This probably means that there was considerable use of Arab shipping—a view supported to some degree by the Sindbad story and other Arab tales which originated at about this time (3.8.1). Moreover, the ninth-century scholar, Li Chao, claimed that, 'the ships that sail the southern seas are foreign ships' (Snow, 1992: 58): this was probably an exaggerated view but it seems likely that the majority of the ships on this maritime silk route were non-Chinese.

There is a comparable difficulty in deciding whether Chinese ships visited Africa during this period. Chinese annals of the mid-ninth century describe the south coast of the Gulf of Aden and the Somali coast and there is significant archaeological evidence for the import of Chinese products to the African east coast: coins dated from the seventh century onwards with a peak in the Song dynasty (AD 960–1279); and porcelain from the tenth to the fourteenth centuries (Needham, 1971: 494–8; Newby, 1982: 58). Whether this demonstrates direct contact with these regions by Chinese

seamen and traders on board Chinese ships is difficult to say.

During his early tenth-century voyages in the Indian Ocean, Al Mas'udi learned that Arab shipping from Oman and Siraf met ships from the China Seas at Kalah Bar in the Malayan peninsula (Fernandez-Armesto, 1991: 32). In the twelfth century Al Edrisi recorded that such meetings were at *Debal* in Sind probably near Karachi (Hornell, 1946a: 232). This may reflect the general situation in earlier times: most Chinese vessels undertook only the eastern stages of the maritime silk route as far as Malaya or India where goods were transshipped to Persian and Arab (and possibly Indian) ships; however, some Persian and Arab ships must have undertaken the complete voyage, Persian Gulf to China and return.

This two-way, and probably two-part, maritime silk route became very prominent later in the Song, Yuan, and early Ming dynasties (twelfth–early fifteenth centuries) (B. Li, 1991: 330; Snow, 1992: 58). During this time there was further extensive and intensive Muslim settlement in the coastal lands of south-east China, in the Fujian province in particular, suggesting a preponderance of Arab shipping at that time. That India was also involved in this Chinese trade is demonstrated by finds of porcelain in such places as Kayal in the Gulf of Mannar, Quilon in South Travancore, and Calicut and the Bay of Mount Deli on the Malabar Coast (Hornell, 1941a: 255).

Chinese ships and seamen were also undoubtedly involved—see, for example, the thirteenth-century wreck Quanzhou 1 with her cargo from south-east Asia and possibly east Africa (10.4.2.2.6). Increasingly detailed Chinese reports on foreign countries were compiled, indicating greater familiarity with overseas lands from Indo-China to India and possibly as far as Malindi and Madagascar (Needham, 1971: 499; Newby, 1982: 58; Snow, 1992: 59). In the fourteenth century, Chinese seamen gave precise names to the seas they sailed, rather than the earlier general term 'southern seas': from China southwards to Borneo was 'the Greater Eastern Ocean'; then 'the Lesser Eastern Ocean' to Malacca; 'the Lesser Western Ocean' was probably what we now call the Bay of Bengal, and 'the Greater', the Arabian Sea.

Early fourteenth-century maps compiled by Zhu Siben and a map published in Korea in 1402 show Africa ending in a point more or less to the east of Sumatra

(Snow, 1992: 59–60). Needham (1971: 499–503) believes that this demonstrates that Chinese seamen must have rounded the southern tip of Africa by that time, but other scholars do not rule out the possibility that these maps were based on the reports of others (Fernandez-Armesto, 1991: 23).

Taken as a whole, this evidence from the second century BC to the fourteenth century AD suggests an increasing Chinese awareness of the values of overseas trade: first with south-east Asia; then, by the fourth century AD, with the countries of the Bay of Bengal; and, from the seventh century AD, with the maritime silk route with its western terminals in the eastern Mediterranean and on the east coast of Africa. The knowledge of foreign lands displayed by Chinese geographers and travellers in their texts and on their maps suggests that, by the thirteenth century at the latest, some Chinese merchants and seamen had travelled in Chinese ships along all these routes. Nevertheless, on balance, Chinese ships never seem to have dominated the silk route, except possibly in the earlier centuries and then only on the South China Sea section: Persian, Indian, and, increasingly, Arab ships and seamen were probably used in the greatest numbers.

## 10.10.4 OVERSEAS VOYAGES IN THE FIFTEENTH CENTURY

In 1368, the Mongols were driven from China and the Yüan dynasty was replaced by the Ming. The new emperor, T'aitsu, sent diplomatic missions to India in the following two years, and the third emperor, Yong'le, did the same in 1402 and 1403. These overseas expeditions were a prelude to a series of seven spectacular voyages throughout the Indian Ocean region which Chinese fleets undertook between 1405 and 1433 under the command of the Grand Eunuch of the Three Jewels, Zheng He (Willetts, 1964; Needham, 1971; Snow, 1992). This period of evident Chinese maritime dominance, almost a 'thalassocracy' from Timor in the east to Aden and east Africa in the west, has been regarded as a high point in Chinese affairs by twentieth-century scholars: B. Li (1991) recently calculated that, since 1904, over 900 theses and academic papers on Zheng He and his times have been published in China, and 863 others translated into Chinese.

In 1405, Emperor Yong'le ordered Zheng He to lead a fleet to the 'Western Ocean' ostensibly to search for his nephew whom Yong'le had deposed in 1402, but this could scarcely be the main reason for assembling a fleet of 62 ships and 240 auxiliary vessels, with a total complement said to be over 30,000.

Zheng He's accounts of his voyages, which he deposited in the state archives, were probably destroyed by anti-maritime zealots in 1477 (Ronan, 1986: 146), but aspects of these voyages are described on memorial stones erected in south-east China and at Devundara in Sri Lanka, in accounts written by participants, and in reports written by official historians. From these it is clear that the principal reason for these seven voyages was to impress the rulers of the known world with the power and wealth of the recently established Ming dynasty. A secondary reason was to learn more about Indian Ocean countries and the routes to them, and to explore the possibilities of trade. Gold, silver, and silk were taken as presents from the emperor to foreign rulers but the emperor also allowed some private trading in such things as porcelain, lacquerware, musk, and camphor. The Chinese sought to bring back spices and oils and even elephant tusks and rhinoceros horns which they used in medicines. Although there were fighting men on board these ships, who on occasions boarded pirate ships and fought on shore, neither colonization nor domination appear to have been amongst the emperor's aims.

Most of the routes taken, and places visited, by these seven fleets were in waters which had been known, to a greater or lesser extent, to the Chinese for centuries. It was only in the far west of the Indian Ocean, in Arabia and on the African east coast, that Zheng He's fleets could be said to be truly exploring. The first three voyages (1405–7; 1408–9; 1409–11) were to maritime south-east Asia, Sri Lanka, and south India as far north as Calicut and Quilan. On the fourth voyage (1413–15) the fleet split into two: one squadron visited the East Indies; the other went westwards across the Bay of Bengal to Sri Lanka, Maldives, south-west India, and across the Arabian Sea to the Persian Gulf at Ormuz. Ships of the fifth voyage (1417–19) again formed into several squadrons: some went to the Ryukyu islands, Borneo, and Java; whilst others headed west for Ormuz and Aden, then to the east coast of Africa, to Mogadishu, Brawa, and Malindi—a coastal trading route used by Greeks and Arabs since at least the first century AD (2.11.5.4). One of the principal aims of the sixth voyage (1421–2) was to return a number of 'ambassadors' to their own countries, and ships visited now-familiar ports from Borneo to Mogadishu and Brawa.

In 1426, Emperor Yong'lo was succeeded by his grandson, Xuan Zong, who authorized Zheng He's seventh and final voyage (1431–3). This again took the fleet as far west as Ormuz: on parts of this voyage they averaged nearly 100 nautical miles a day (Willetts, 1964: 30).

It has been suggested that ships of Zheng He's fleets may have reached Australia (Ronan, 1986: 152–3), but the evidence is very slight. More substantial, although indirect, evidence points towards the possibility that these Chinese ships may have approached or even rounded the tip of southern Africa and entered the South Atlantic (Ronan, 1986: 132–8; Snow, 1992: 69). In 1628, Mao Yuanyi published a copy of an earlier chart based on the results of Zheng He's voyages, which showed ports on the African eastcoast well to the south of Malindi—Mombasa, and possibly Mafia island, south of Dar es Salaam, and Quitangouha island, off Mozambique. Furthermore, an atlas, compiled by the Venetian cartographer, Fra Mauro Camaldolese in 1459, shows a Chinese-type vessel off the southern tip of Africa with an accompanying note referring to a 'junk of the Indies' which, in 1420, sailed for forty days (c.2,000 miles) 'more or less SW and W' of Cape Sofala near Beira in Mozambique, and Diab in Madagascar without sighting land: if true, this could have brought the junk to the South Atlantic.

Attempts have recently been made in China to compile reconstruction drawings and to make models of the ships in Zheng He's fleets (for example, Chen, Yang, and Chen (1986), Huang (1991) and B. Li (1991)) but it is very doubtful whether there is, at present, sufficient information to do so. Needham (1971: 480–2) gives the sizes of the largest of the ships in Zheng He's first fleet as 440 ft (137 m) in length and 186 ft (56 m) in breadth and quotes their cargo capacity variously as 2,540 tonnes or 510 tonnes. Barker (1989) and Sleeswyk (1996) have pointed out the inconsistencies in these and other estimates which suggest that either the dimensions are exaggerated or that they have been converted incorrectly from Chinese *zhang* units into metres. As the dimensions quoted by Needham are from the official history of the Ming dynasty, *Ming Shih*, published

in 1767, and not fifteenth-century estimates, their value is indeed questionable.

In two recent papers, Yang (1986, 1991: 2) has suggested that the Ming dynasty annals' accounts of the size of Zheng He's ships are to be treated cautiously. He has pointed out that a fragment of a memorial stone in the Jing Hai temple at Nanjing, which may be fifteenth century, states that Zheng He's seagoing ships had eight oars and a cargo capacity of 2,000 *liao*— where one *liao* is equivalent to c.60 kg rice: this indicates a capacity of c.120 tonnes. Yang considers that Zheng He's ships were probably similar to the Kiangsu traders and the Fujian junks known from recent centuries, and not more than 30 m in length overall. In the early twentieth century, Fujian traders were c.25 m in length overall and had a capacity of c.150 tonnes (Donnelly, 1924: 103–4, 111–12).

Needham (1971: 481) notes other estimates of the size of Zheng He's ships based on a large rudder stock (now in the National Museum, Beijing) discovered in 1962 near Nanjing on the site of a Ming shipyard: these calculations suggest an overall ship length between 538 ft (164 m) and 600 ft (183 m). It should be noted in this context that Ronan's (1986) shorter version of Needham's work overlooks the fact that Needham used Ming units (1.02 ft) and Huai units (1.12 ft) rather than imperial feet units. It is undoubtedly true that this rudder stock must have come from a large ship, but overall lengths of this magnitude are scarcely credible.

Needham (1971: 481, fig. 980) does not explain the details of the calculations used to get ship length from the rudder stock parameters, but he does give the stock's dimensions (in Huai feet units) and it is possible to apply to this data the rules of thumb used to build Guangdong junks in recent centuries (10.7.5) and investigate the possible dimensions of the rudder stock's parent ship. Using these rules, the minimum overall dimensions of the ship become 67.38 × 12.25 × 6.12 m; and the maximum, 80.88 × 13.48 × 6.74 m Using an extension of these rules (Liu and Li, 1991: 276), it may be estimated that the cargo capacity of the parent ship lay between 1,515 and 2,204 tonnes. Sleeswyk (1996), using naval architectural concepts, has recently argued that the largest of He's ships was c.62 m in length and c.11.2 m breadth, with a displacement tonnage of c.1,100 tonnes.

These dimensions and tonnage, although large, are nevertheless credible and bear comparison, for example, with estimates made for Henry V's warship, *Grace Dieu*, built between AD 1418 and 1420, which is thought to have been *c*.40 × 15 × 6.5 m overall and to have had a cargo capacity of *c*.1,400 tonnes (McGrail, 1993*c*: table 1).

The late sources quoted by Needham (1971: 480) say that the largest of Zheng He's ships had three decks above the main deck in the raised superstructure at the stern, and several decks below the main deck: they were also said to have had nine masts. Marco Polo of the late thirteenth century describes Chinese ships with four permanent and two temporary masts whilst the ships seen by Ibn Battutah of the mid-fourteenth century had twelve sails and four decks. Nine masts, permanent and temporary, and four or five decks do not therefore seem unreasonable for the largest ships of the early fifteenth century. Nevertheless, in Zheng He's fleet there were probably few of these nine-masted, multiple-decked ships, measuring 60–70 m overall length, with a cargo capacity of up to 1,000 tonnes: the majority of the ships would have been significantly smaller with, perhaps, four to six masts and a cargo capacity of, say, 150–500 tonnes.

# 10.11

# Pilotage and Navigation

As in other parts of the world (4.4.6, 5.2, 5.4.9, 6.8), early navigation in Chinese waters was essentially environmental or non-instrumental (Needham, 1971; Yan, 1983): use of the sounding lead and steering by Polaris and other heavenly bodies are mentioned in the early centuries AD: doubtless they were in use much earlier.

In European waters the change from non-instrumental navigation to quantitative or geometric methods began not later than the twelfth century with the use of the mariner's compass at sea. By the mid-thirteenth century Mediterranean seamen had sand-glasses for time measurement, charts marked with a network of magnetic bearings (rhumb lines) and distances, dividers and a straight-edge (ruler), written sailing directions including tide tables, and traverse tables

for calculating courses and distances made good when sailing in various winds; furthermore, Arabic numerals began to be used instead of Roman, which made calculations easier (Waters, 1988: 1989).

Comparable changes occurred in Chinese waters at a somewhat earlier date. The properties of the magnetized needle appear to have been known in China from Han times (206 BC–AD 200): the mariner's compass, a 'south pointing' magnetized iron sheet in the form of a fish, floating on water, was first used at sea sometime between AD 1099 and 1102 (Yan, 1983: 498) (see also 3.8.2.2.1). The azimuth plane of this compass was divided into twenty-four equal sectors: these sectors or 'points' were then divided into 'intermediate-points', each equal to $7\frac{1}{2}°$, in twentieth century terminology. This reflects the Han dynasty pre-compass method of dividing the horizon, and may be compared with the European points system in which each point is the equivalent of $11\frac{1}{4}°$, which by the eighteenth century was divided into $\frac{1}{4}$-points ($c.2\frac{3}{4}°$). The European thirty-two points division was obtained by dividing the horizon, again and again, five times into equal halves. Chinese 'points', on the other hand, cannot be obtained by such regular division, but require thirds of a right angle ($30°$) to be estimated after the initial two divisions into equal halves.

By the late thirteenth century, compass headings for various destinations were being recorded in China, and by the late fourteenth century, compilations of these compass headings were published. Charts with these compass courses noted on them are thought to have been used in the thirteenth century, but the earliest surviving chart is from the early Ming, say, fifteenth century (Yan, 1983: 502). A schematic diagram of the Indian Ocean with what appears to be the track of Zheng He's seventh voyage in 1430 marked on it, and with compass bearings noted, was published in a seventeenth-century treatise by Mao Yuan; it is not clear whether this is an exact transcription of fifteenth-century material or whether there are later intrusions.

A book of sailing directions has survived from the fifteenth century. In this *rutter* or 'pilot's handbook', compass bearings are given for destinations in the South and West Oceans and distances are given in *keng* ('watches' of 2.4 hours each, i.e. one-tenth of a day). *Keng* are mentioned from the twelfth century onwards and they were possibly measured by the burning of calibrated incense sticks. This *Shung Feng Xiang Song* was written by an anonymous mariner in c.1430: it also gives soundings in fathoms, tables of monthly and seasonal winds, tide tables (an earlier example is known from the eleventh century), meteorological information, and tables giving the azimuth rising and setting bearings of four constellations.

The Chinese measurement of distance in keng (watches) may be compared with the European use of a 'day's sail', the distance generally sailed in twenty-four hours; or with the later use of leagues—the distance a ship could sail in one hour. Use of a 'Dutchman's log' was first recorded in the third century AD (Yan, 1983: 499) when timing the thrown-overboard log was done by 'running quickly to the stern': this may be compared with the European practice of timing by chanting a standard refrain (McGrail, 1983b: 318). These early measurements, both European and Chinese, would not have resulted in an estimate in units of speed (e.g. knots or miles per hour) but would have been in terms of being 'more than' or 'less than' or 'equal to' a standard speed, which, if regularly achieved, would get them to their destination in the standard time. Sand clocks may have been used at sea in Chinese ships from the fourteenth century: the speed of a ship could then be estimated more accurately.

Estimates of latitudinal position on land by measuring sun-shadow lengths are known to have been used by AD 724 when the Chinese astronomer-royal was sent to Hanoi by the Emperor. In Egypt, this method was used in the second millennium BC. A means of estimating latitude at sea by measuring the altitude (vertical angle) of the Pole Star does not appear, either in the Mediterranean or in China, until medieval times, although rough estimates do seem to have been made using the mast as a datum in Roman times (McGrail, 1983b: 308, 318). Hands held at arm's length could also have been used to measure the Polaris altitude in hand spans or palms. An instrument, which subsequently came to be known as the kamāl (3.8.2.2) was used by Arab seamen to measure this altitude at sea in c. AD 850–900 (Fatimi, 1996).

Chinese seamen were certainly able to estimate latitude with some accuracy by the sixteenth century. In the treatise Xi-Yang Chao Gong Dian Lu, written in 1520 and based on fifteenth-century accounts of Zheng He's expeditions, Polaris altitudes are given for each stage of the voyage (Ronan, 1986: 170). These altitudes were measured in chih (a finger breath) and chio (¼ or ⅛ of

chih) and may be compared with the Arabic isbâ (finger breath or inch = 1°36′) and zam (⅛ isbâ) (3.8.2.2.5). It seems likely that the Chinese learned of the Arab kamal sometime after the ninth century, and used it at sea to estimate Polaris altitudes. That they used the kamal from the sixteenth century is clear from Li Xu's Jie Am Lao Ren Man Bi, published in 1606. Each one of a set of twelve ebony tablets, when held at arm's length, subtended at the eye the angle between star and horizon from 1°36′ to 18°56′: they were thus suitable for measuring Polaris altitudes anywhere between Hainan and the Malacca strait, or off the Coromandel and Malabar coasts of southern India. The European equivalent of the kamāl was the cross-staff which was first mentioned in 1321; it may well have been developed from the Arab instrument.

From this survey of the evidence (variable both in quality and in quantity, and also in dating accuracy) for Chinese, Arab, and European means of navigation when out of sight of land, it seems reasonably certain that the earliest step towards the use of quantitative methods was made by the Arabs with the invention of the kamāl in the late-ninth century. This instrument was possibly based on ideas and practices used by Greek scientists and seamen of the later Roman Empire (3.8.2.2). The use of the mariner's compass almost certainly spread from the Chinese to the Arab and Mediterranean worlds, sometime in the twelfth century. The measurement of distance/speed was improved by the introduction of the sand-glass which happened in the Mediterranean in the eleventh or twelfth century (Waters, 1978: 308). The sea chart, on which information from compass, kamāl or equivalent, and sand-glass could be plotted, first appeared in the Mediterranean in 1311 or possibly 1270 (Ronan, 1986: 161): something similar may have been used in the Chinese and Arab world at about the same time.

It thus seems that no one region can be credited with being leader in the art of navigation as Needham (1971) appears to believe. Chinese, Arabs, and Europeans each introduced and developed aspects of the subject. Arab knowledge was based on that of Persia which in turn probably drew much from Greek sources; and doubtless contributions were made by south-east Asian and Indian mariners. The state of navigation in the fifteenth century thus owed something to all these regions and their interaction by sea with one another.

# 11

# THE AMERICAS

It is generally agreed that America was populated across what is now the Bering Strait (Fig. 11.1) from the Chukot/Koryak/Kamchatka region in the north-eastern part of Siberia to Alaska (Guilaine, 1991: 107–14). On present evidence human beings appear to have moved into Siberia from the south in *c*.33,000 BC, or possibly as early as 40,000 BP (Klein, 1980: 94).

The earliest evidence of Man in the north-west region of the American continent is thought to come from the Old Crow Flats site in north-west Yukon where bones said to be associated with stone artefacts have been dated to *c*.29,000 BC (Klein, 1980: 95): this claim has frequently been challenged, as has the date of another early site in North America, the Meadow-croft Rock shelter (Adovasio, Donahue, and Stukenrath, 1990). The traditional view is that it was not until the Canadian ice sheets began to melt, some time after 18,000 BP (a time of lowest sea levels) that Man could spread from this north-western region eastwards and southwards (Fig. 11.2). Dates from excavations in other parts of the Americas appear to support this late date: mid-tenth millennium BC for Chile; the southern tip of South America in the mid-ninth millennium BC; the Arctic regions from *c*.9000 BC (G. Clark, 1977: 353; Street, 1980: 56); and Greenland from *c*.2000 BC (McGhee, 1993).

However, evidence for settlements in Brazil possibly as early as 30,000 BC (Bray, 1986; Guidon and Delibrias, 1986; Guilaine, 1991) have caused a reassessment of this late chronology, and recently published dates from the Monte Verde (Adovasio and Pedler, 1997) site in southern Chile in the range 12,500–13,000 BP seem to imply that the first human settlement in Alaska was well before that date, the leading point in an advance northwards and eastwards which had begun in the centre of the Eurasian land mass (Bednarik, 1989; Meltzer, Adovasio, and Dillehay, 1994; Adovasio and Pedler, 1997).

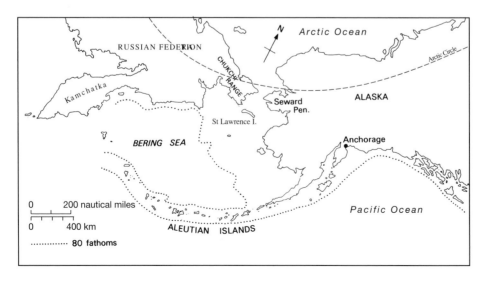

Fig. 11.1. Map of the Bering Strait region (Institute of Archaeology, Oxford).

Fig. 11.2. Map of the Americas (Institute of Archaeology, Oxford).

## II.I

# The Earliest Settlement

The question of precisely when the first humans travelled from Siberia to Alaska is important to maritime studies because sea levels changed significantly during this period. Before *c*.45,000 BP, a land 'corridor', some 500 miles (1,000 km) wide, connected the two continents. As ice sheets melted, sea levels rose worldwide, tending to flood such regions of relatively low land. This was not a steady continuous rise, rather there were significant fluctuations in relative sea levels regionally as land, now without the weight of ice, tended to rise. Due to these effects, the Siberian/ Alaska tundra-covered 'corridor', 'Beringia', is thought to have re-emerged between 25,000 and 14,000 BP (Klein, 1980: 87; Guilaine, 1991: 109–12). A subsequent further rise in sea level meant that, by *c*.10,000 BP, the Bering Strait was more or less as it is today (Street, 1980: 56).

This environmental evidence, which cannot yet be considered definitive, suggests that the transit from Siberia to Alaska could have been undertaken over land before 45,000 BP, or between 25,000 and 14,000 BC; or across water between 45,000 and 25,000 BP, and after 14,000/10,000 BP.

A technological assessment of the sort of water transport that might have been used during the period 45,000–25,000 BP suggests that, in this upper Palaeolithic period, the range of water transport is likely to have included only floats, simple log rafts, and simple, frameless, hide boats (Table 1.2). The use of floats (log, bundle, or hide), when the man is necessarily part-immersed in the water, would be impracticable in these cold northern latitudes (*c*.65°N) even on rivers and lakes. Log rafts may have been usable for short periods on inland waters but not at sea, even in summer. Only boats can give the necessary protection and prevent extreme wetness and coldness leading to hyperthermia. However, the protection afforded by the simple hide boat it was then technologically possible to build would probably have been inadequate and, in any case, it is doubtful if such a boat would have been sufficiently substantial for an open sea voyage.

By Mesolithic times, from *c*.9000 BP, when the Bering Strait had been formed, more substantial boats could have been built (Table 1.2). If trees of sufficient size had grown, simple log boats could have been built, but, like the log and bundle rafts, these would not have been seagoing even in the somewhat milder climate then prevailing. On the other hand, framed hide boats built from several skins would have been sufficiently seaworthy and afforded sufficient protection to be used to cross the Bering Strait, or possibly used on a route further south along the line of the Aleutian islands, from Kamchatka to the Alaska peninsula (Fig. 11.1).

A synthesis of this, admittedly tentative environmental and nautical technology data, suggests a range of possibilities:

- before 45,000 BP—overland travel;
- 45,000–25,000 BP—travel generally impossible unless suitable boats could have been built;
- 25,000–14,000 BP—overland travel;
- 14,000–10,000 BP—overland or by hide boat intermittently;
- after 10,000 BP — by hide boat.

'Overland travel' does not mean that a land 'corridor' could have been used 'dryshod': on the contrary, the River Yukon would have meandered across Beringia, and generally this would have been difficult, probably impassable, terrain without water transport (Engelbrecht and Seyfert, 1994: 223).

That contact could be established, whatever the date, and maintained between Asia and America in these northern latitudes is clearly demonstrated by the generally homogenous nature of the circumpolar cultures which became established from North Cape in Norway eastwards across Eurasia to the Chukchi Sea in north-east Siberia, to Alaska, and across northern Canada to Greenland (Bandi, 1969). Aspects of this similarity can be seen today when the Siberian hide boats *baidara* and *baidarka* are compared with the Inuit/Eskimo *umiak* and kayak; and the bark boats of the River Kutenai region of British Columbia (Coulton, 1977) are compared with those of the River Amur region of south-east Siberia (Brindley, 1919: 101–4).

Movement overland south and east from Alaska, appears to have been blocked by the vast ice sheets of the Cordillera, Laurentian, and Greenland glaciers until *c*.18,000 BP (Guilaine, 1991: 112). However, the Mesolithic hide boat, and possibly the Palaeolithic simple hide boat, could have been used on a coastal route in summer, close inshore in the shelter of islands wherever possible and with some boat portages across headlands. As Engelbrecht and Seyfert (1994) have pointed out, on such coastal routes there would be more and varied food resources and a more equable climate, and driftwood would be available on the foreshore. In this way Man could have gradually spread southwards to warmer latitudes. Although much of the remainder of the Americas could then, in theory, have been explored and settled by overland travel, it is clear that this movement would have been greatly facilitated by the use of floats, rafts, and boats: indeed, the settlement of islands, both in lakes and offshore, and known from early dates (Engelbrecht and Seyfert, 1994: 224) could not have been undertaken without water transport.

# II.2

# Later Settlements

The main thrust of archaeological opinion is that the aboriginal population of the Americas remained generally free from external influences until the late fifteenth century AD, apart from two-way traffic across the Bering Strait between Alaska and Siberia. From *c*.3000 BC, and probably much earlier, there was regular contact between Asians and Americans across this strait. The 50 nautical mile channel, with St Lawrence island and the Diomedes islands conveniently located (Fig. 11.1), was a link and not a barrier to communication—and continues to be so. Giddings (1967, 46) noted, for example, that in AD 1711 native Americans sailed *umiaks* to Siberia in one day. Thus was cultural interchange maintained within the circumpolar zone from Greenland to east Siberia: the transfer of technology into and out of this zone seems to have been negligible.

In the medieval period, from *c*. AD 900–1400, Scandinavians settled on the south and west coast of Greenland (11.4.5.2.1). Around AD 1000, they briefly settled in Newfoundland and they made occasional voyages to the Labrador coast until the mid-fourteenth century (Clausen, 1993; Graham-Campbell, 1994: 174–9). The impact on native culture in general and specifically on technology, seems to have been minimal.

It has also been suggested that there were pre-Columbian contacts across the Atlantic by Greek,

Phoenician/Carthaginian, Roman, Irish, British, and Portuguese ships. Morison (1971, 3–31) sums up the minimal evidence for these hypothetical voyages and demonstrates their improbability. A case for contacts across the Atlantic from the prehistoric Mediterranean has also been argued by Heyerdahl (1978) based in part on Elliot Smith's (1915–16) diffusionist ideas concerning the influence of Egypt on South American civilization, and on his own remarkable transatlantic voyages in bundle rafts RA 1 and 2 (Heyerdahl, 1972). Heyerdahl has certainly demonstrated that, in certain conditions, twentieth-century man can make one-way voyages from north-west Africa to the Caribbean in bundle rafts propelled by sail and helped by the west-south-west current. But this is very far from proving that this was actually done in pre-Columbian times (or indeed later). The general similarities between certain features of South American cultures and those of Ancient Egypt, which Heyerdahl and others (for example, see Johnstone, 1988, 229) use to support this theory, are not sufficiently specific to make pre-Columbian contact likely.

Kehoe (1971) has pointed out that there are certain similarities between the tools used by peoples of the Laurentian Archaic culture of north-east America and by Scandinavians in the third millennium BC and suggested this might be explained by unintentional drift voyages by fishermen across the North Atlantic. But, again, there are only general similarities, nothing incompatible with independent invention.

It is possible that Oceanic people made contact with the west coast of South America, but this was probably in medieval or later times (9.1). Botanical arguments have sometimes been advanced as indirect evidence for contacts between Africa and the east coast of South America. Bottle gourds (*Lagenaria siceraria*) are found in early levels on some South American sites (Bray, 1980: 372) used as dishes, net floats, or rattles. This plant has no known American ancestor and all the wild species known are native to Africa: it is suggested that it may have been brought across the Atlantic in pre-Columbian times. However, experiments have demonstrated that the plant will remain viable after floating for a long time in salt water (Bray, 1980: 372) and thus it seems more likely that bottle gourds have appeared in South America by natural means.

The sweet potato (*Ipomoea batatas*) is generally considered to be a native plant of America yet was widely found in the islands of Oceania during the period of earliest European contact (9.1). Hornell (1945; 1946c) and others have argued that this widespread distribution may indicate pre-Columbian voyages, intentional or accidental, between, say, Chile/Peru and Polynesia. Heyerdahl and Skjölsvold (1956) have argued that there must have been early voyages from the west coast of South America to the Galapagos islands some 600 miles away, as they excavated pre-Columbian mainland pottery there. Furthermore, Heyerdahl's (1963) Konti-ki voyage has demonstrated that, in certain circumstances, a log raft, assisted by westerly surface currents, may be sailed 4,000 miles from Peru to Raroia in the Tuamotu group of Polynesia.

On the other hand, the dates of the early reports of sweet potatoes in Oceania are late enough for the first plants to have been taken there by westward sailing Spanish ships—and this seems the most likely explanation in the light of present evidence.

A stronger case for pre-Columbian contacts across the Pacific is based on intriguing stylistic similarities between pottery from Valdivia in Ecuador, and other sites in coastal Peru, dated as early as 3000 BC (G. Clark, 1977: 443; Johnstone, 1988: 223) and Jomon pottery of an even earlier date found in shell-midden sites on the Japanese island of Kyushu. These middens also contained fish remains which show that Jomon fishermen ventured to distant sea-fishing grounds at certain seasons. Some supporting evidence comes from the fact that the wooden foil known as a *guares* is used to steer and give sailing balance to seagoing log rafts in Peru, India, Indo-China, and south-east China (11.4.1.2, 6.6.3, 8.3.1, 10.2.5), suggesting this trait may have been dispersed to America across the Pacific (Johnstone, 1988: 228–9). However, the dates when such usage was first noted are such that this dispersal could be associated with the sixteenth-century European circumnavigation voyages.

As G. Clark (1977, 443), Johnstone (1988, 223) and others have pointed out the general trend of surface currents from Japan is towards the north-west coast of America; thence in a clockwise direction southwards to Mexico; and then generally back eastwards to Micronesia and the Philippines. However, the northwest monsoon wind might theoretically take a vessel from Mexico, south-eastwards to Ecuador, thence to Peru (G. Clark, 1977: 443). There are examples of recent unplanned drift voyages by Japanese junks which became stranded in American waters between the Aleutians and northern Mexico, but none is known to date to have reached South America (Heizer, 1938: 214; Johnstone, 1988: 223–4). Such a voyage of not less than 8,000 nautical miles, at, say, 2 knots (which would be good for a drift voyage), would take about six months: a more likely estimate is that it would take at least a year. Johnstone (1988: 223) quotes such a drift voyage across the Pacific in 1815 from Japan to California which took seventeen months, and three of the crew were found to be still alive. Severin's (1994) planned voyage by sailing raft took him from Japan towards the Californian coast (10.10.2). Drift voyages to the north-west coast of America in pre-Columbian times cannot be ruled out entirely, but the likelihood of this happening, and the vessel being carried onwards to Ecuador seems very low indeed.

Whatever the practicability and likelihood of Japanese cultural influences and technology being brought to America by such a method, evidence from recent excavations now seems to suggest that pottery was, in fact, a local development in South America, as simpler ceramics have been found in levels underlying Valdivia-style pottery (Morris, 1980: 395).

## II.3

# European Settlements in the Fifteenth–Eighteenth Centuries

During the long period of isolation, from first settlement to the late fifteenth century AD, indigenous Americans developed many forms of water transport. In general this development was along the same lines as in Eurasia, but there are notable differences of emphasis, mainly due to the differences in the relative abundance of certain raw materials, and there are some variant forms which appear to be unknown elsewhere.

Only in recent years has there been any excavated evidence for the water transport of the Americas, some of which throws light on the period before the time of first contact with Europeans. More information comes from European accounts written in the late-fifteenth century and later. The societies these Europeans encountered were at different stages of development, ranging from Stone Age to what may be called medieval technologies. All these societies were theoretically capable of building the complete array of water transport from log floats to plank boats and, with the exception of bundle boats and basket boats which have a very restricted distribution in the world, there is evidence for the use of all these types of craft somewhere in the Americas.

The European observers did not necessarily understand all that they saw—some had no knowledge of boatbuilding themselves and were evidently technologically illiterate. Some could readily appreciate the virtues of the craft they encountered; others dismissed them as 'primitive'. Thus there are difficulties in interpreting some of these 'first contact' accounts of the building and use of indigenous American rafts and boats.

## II.3.1 SAIL: INDIGENOUS OR INTRODUCED?

An especially difficult question to answer is whether or not sails were used before the coming of Europeans. Sails on indigenous craft were not reported until 1526 (C. Edwards, 1965: 66–9): these were triangular sails. Square sails were noted on South American log rafts in 1571 and on Arctic *umiaks* in 1576–8 (Leshikar, 1988: 14). Both triangular (lateen) and square sails were used in the European explorers' vessels. Furthermore, even as late as 1605 it was possible for a shipwrecked Franciscan friar to save his life by showing the Carib inhabitants of the island of Dominica how to use sails (McKusick, 1960). However, the precise method of setting triangular sails, and their rigging, makes it unlikely that they were copied from European rigs. Although Vasco de Balboa's band were the first Europeans to see the Pacific Ocean in 1513 from Darien (in what is now Panama), and the first European ships to enter the Pacific Ocean from the east were in Magellan's expedition of 1520, Pizarro and Almagro became the first Europeans to sail along the west coast of America. In 1524, in ships built on the west coast of the isthmus, they made the first of three voyages to Peru from Panama. From the second of these voyages, in 1526, we have a description of large seagoing log rafts with a cotton sail and hemp-

like rigging (C. Edwards, 1965: 67, 70, 105, 113; Currie, 1995). These cotton sails were said to be of the same shape as those on Spanish small ships which Edwards (1965: 67) has demonstrated would have been lateen (i.e. triangular) sails on ships of this size, and not the square sails which Prescott (1847: 244), the historian of the Spanish conquest of Peru, and many subsequent authors, assumed.

Subsequently other sailing log rafts were seen off Ecuador and Peru and noted by Oviedo and by de Santa Clara (C. Edwards, 1965: 68), and illustrations were published by Madox in 1582 and van Spilbergen in 1619 (Fig. 11.3). The illustrations show that, although these were indeed triangular sails (and thus similar to a lateen), they were not rigged as lateens but in a way unknown in European waters: the sail was bent to a spar which acted as both mast and yard.

Also seen in Spilbergen's drawing (Fig. 11.3) is the use of *guares*, long, foil-shaped timbers, aids to steering, which are inserted between the logs of a raft at positions and to depths which can both be varied. Wooden objects excavated from pre-Columbian graves in Peru (Fig. 11.7) are most likely *guares* (Heyerdahl, 1978: 204–8; C. Edwards, 1965: 110–14), and as such devices are only needed on sailing vessels the case for indigenous sail in the Americas seems to be proved beyond reasonable doubt. The distinctive rig and distinctive method of steering can also be seen today on *jangada* rafts off the Brazil coast (Fig. 11.4).

Sails were also seen in use on a logboat from Ecua-

Fig. 11.3. A seventeenth-century sailing log raft off the west coast of South America. Detail from Spilbergen's drawing of Paita harbour (de Bry, 1619: plate 12).

Fig. 11.4. A twentieth-century sailing log raft (*jangada*) off the coast of Bazil (photo: Paul Johnstone).

dor in 1531 during Pizarro's second voyage, and on *umiaks* in the Arctic by Frobisher in 1577 (C. Edwards, 1965: 35; Leshikar, 1988: 14). Furthermore, Heyerdahl (1978: 199) has noted that a model log raft from a twelfth-century AD grave near Arica, Chile, has a square sail of reed matting. Such widespread use of different types of sail on different craft in different regions, and used very competently, makes it most unlikely that sail was not known in pre-Columbian America.

# 11.4

# Water Transport

Almost all the types of craft in American waters, inland and coastal, which so impressed Europeans, were in use somewhere in the Europe that these fifteenth- to seventeenth-centuries explorers had left: hide boats in Ireland and Britain; logboats in many places; log rafts on the Rhine and other continental rivers; bundle rafts off Corfu and Sardinia; sewn-plank boats in Finland.

The exceptions were bark boats and buoyed rafts, although the latter had been used in much earlier times in the Mediterranean. Columbus and his successors were evidently unfamiliar with most of these European craft. Planked boats and ships dominated their lives: hide boats, logboats, log and bundle rafts, and sewn-plank boats had, well before the fifteenth century, been marginalized and used only in economically disadvantaged regions where the technological impact of the plank boat and ship was still to be felt. European explorers and settlers, therefore, could not evaluate the American rafts and boats in relation to their own experience.

## 11.4.1 LOG RAFTS

Great seagoing rafts were seen off the coast of northern Peru during Pizarro's second voyage in 1525 (Nelson, 1961: 163-6; C. Edwards, 1965: 67, 70; Currie, 1995: 511–3). They consisted of several *balsa* logs, the longest one in the centre, lashed together by rope of *henequen*, probably sisal, with one or two triangular cotton sails. Goods and equipment which had to be kept dry were carried inside a wooden structure on top of the basic raft. Miguel de Estete, of Pizarro's second voyage, tells us that the logs were of balsa which is 'as soft and light on the water as a cork' (C. Edwards, 1965: 70). Balsa (*Ochroma* spp.) is indeed lightweight, its specific density being 0.04–0.32 compared with oak's 0.70–0.80. In 1680, William Dampier and his surgeon, Lionel Wafer, gave more details of the structure of these Peruvian, Ecuadorian, and Panamanian rafts which seem most unlikely to have been influenced by European technology, even at that late date. Twenty or thirty great logs up to 40 ft (12 m) long were used for the lowest layer, bound together with ropes. A second layer was spaced out across these logs and fastened to them by hardwood pins. Above this, a series of vertical posts supported one or two more 'decks' of logs so that the raft had about 10 ft (3 m) of superstructure above the waterline (Nelson, 1961: 163-6; C. Edwards, 1965: 95). At the lowest level robust cargo was carried; at the middle level was a 'room' for the crew and their possessions; whilst cargo which could be damaged by sea water was carried on the 'deck' above them. Dampier estimated that these rafts carried 60–70 tons of cargo on 1,500 mile voyages between Lima and Panama (C. Edwards, 1965: 72, 105). Earlier Spanish reports estimated that these west coast sailing rafts could carry thirty large casks (*toneles*) of cargo, or fifty men and three horses.

Similar seagoing rafts were seen on the east coast in Brazilian waters (C. Edwards, 1965: 97; Johnstone, 1988: 227) where they came to be known as *jangada* (Lane-Poole, 1940). This is a Tamil word derived from Sanskrit (6.6.6) and this fact led Doran (1971: 133) to believe that this sailing raft was introduced to the east coast of South America by the Portuguese. However, the similarity between these rafts and those on the west coast (a triangular sail on a yard/mast; the use of *guares*) suggests that those Brazilian rafts were pre-Columbian in origin. The term *jangada* was probably applied to them by Portuguese seamen who had served time in Indian waters.

In 1540, de Ulloa saw seagoing log rafts in Mexican waters off lower California (Best, 1925: 142). Thus this seagoing tradition lay between the latitudes of 30°N and 20°S, mainly on the west coast between Mexico and Peru.

In inshore and inland waters simple forms of log raft were also used for fishing and for passengers and cargo. They were propelled by paddle and pole and sometimes by sail, and used extensively on the rivers of Chile, Peru, Ecuador, Colombia, Panama, and Mexico.

Fig. 11.5. Sixteenth-century log rafts off Puerto Viejo, Ecuador (after Benzoni, 1857).

Benzoni documented some of these inshore rafts in 1572 in Ecuadorean waters (Fig. 11.5). He noted that they were shaped at the ends by using an odd number of logs (3–11) with the longest in the middle (Benzoni, 1857; C. Edwards, 1965: 62, 64, 71). Such a shape has hydrodynamic advantages and is found in many parts of the world (McGrail, 1998: 45–6); it is often combined with a taper towards the bow end, which is achieved by using the natural taper of the logs so that the raft is broader aft than forward. Other observers reported that rafts on inland waters had raised platforms amidships for goods or important passengers, and occasionally they carried straw huts as shelters.

### 11.4.1.1 SAILS

Van Spilbergen's log raft (Fig. 11.2) of 1619 had two triangular sails, whilst Benzoni's raft (Fig. 11.5) had a square sail on masts which appear to be sheers (pivoted spars), a feature noted also by Hall and by Smyth in the early nineteenth century (Hall, 1824). Since these South American sails were not set on a conventional European pole mast it is unlikely that they had been copied from European prototypes.

### 11.4.1.2 *GUARES*: IMMERSED STEERING FOILS

The early seventeenth century drawing by George van Spilbergen (Fig. 11.2) of a sailing raft in Paita harbour,

Peru, shows three of the crew adjusting *guares*. How these steering aids were used in South America was first noted in the 1730s by the Spanish navigator, Juan (C. Edwards, 1965: 73–4). An Ecuadorean raft off Guayaquil was seen to have six *guares* which were variable in position and in depth of immersion: thus course could be altered, and sailing balance attained, as well as leeway reduced. For example, if a *guares* near the bow was immersed more deeply or it was moved even closer to the bow the raft would turn towards the wind; raising or removing one nearer the stern would have a similar effect (Heyerdahl, 1978: fig. 16). The ability of these rafts to make progress across the wind was favourably commented on by early Europeans (C. Edwards, 1965: 73–7). *Guares* projecting to varied depths may be seen on the drawing of a sailing raft from Guayaquil which Admiral Paris published in 1843 (Fig. 11.6).

Boards some 2 m in length, which are most probably *guares* (Fig. 11.7), have been excavated from coastal grave sites at Ica in Peru (C. Edwards, 1965: 110–12; Heyerdahl, 1978: 102, 204–13). They have an aerofoil cross-section, and a decorated handle at one end, and the

Fig. 11.7. *Guares*: variable leeboards of *c*.300 BC from graves at Ica, Peru (Museum für Völkerkunde, Berlin).

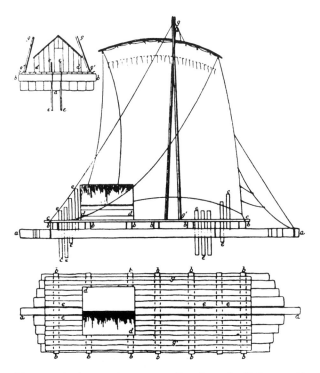

Fig. 11.6. A nineteenth-century sailing log raft off Guayaquil, Ecuador (after Paris, 1843).

earliest have been dated to *c*.300 BC: this steering technique is thus pre-Columbian.

### 11.4.1.3 EARLIEST LOG RAFTS

It is clear from the foregoing discussion that a range of log rafts was in use in American waters in pre-Columbian times: from simple rafts on the upper reaches of rivers to complex seagoing 'freighter' rafts with a distinctive sailing rig and a distinctive method of steering. Johnstone (1988: 232–3, figs. 2.2, 16.14) has drawn attention to the wooden models of rafts from the Arica graves of *c*. AD 1200 in North Chile, and to the pre-Columbian ornate golden models of rafts from Lake Guatavita, Columbia. There is also a golden disc from the Cenote of Chichen Itza, Yucatan, on which may be a representation of a log raft (but see 11.4.3). Pottery models of Moche- and Gallinazo-ware suggest the use of log rafts in the period AD 200–700, whilst *guares* from Peruvian graves (Fig. 11.7) take the use of seagoing, sailing log rafts back to at least 300 BC.

## 11.4.2 BUNDLE RAFTS

Rafts made of reed bundles were also sighted during Pizarro's 1531 voyage, fishing in coastal waters from Ecuador southwards along the coast of Peru (C. Edwards, 1965: 1). Subsequently early European explorers noted them off the coast of northern Chile and they were encountered in subsequent centuries off the coast of California as far north as San Francisco (Leshikar, 1988: 19; Brindley, 1931: 11, 16–17). They were also seen on rivers and lakes in the earliest European times: at Otavalo in Ecuador; Junin in Peru; Lake Titi-caca on the Peru/Bolivia border; Lake Poopo in Bolivia; and at Huarpe in west-central Argentina (C. Edwards, 1965: 107, map 1); and subsequently north-west of San Francisco on Lake Pyramid, Nevada (Brindley, 1931: 15); Lake Klamath, Oregon (Hornell, 1946a: 45); north-west of Vancouver on the River Thompson, British Columbia (Hornell, 1946a: 45); Lake Tulare, California, north of Los Angeles; Lake Clear, north of San Francisco (Hornell; 1946a: 45); and on the River San Francisco in eastern Brazil (C. Edwards, 1965: 13). Like the log rafts this distribution is west coast except for Brazil, and their use at sea lies between c.40°N and c.35°S.

These craft ranged in complexity: at one end of the range there was the one-man *caballito* c.6 ft (1.8 m) in length which were used as tenders to ships anchored in open roadsteads, off the southern Peru coast, and those of the nineteenth-century Lima coast where rafts weighed only a few pounds, 'so that on one mule

Fig. 11.8. A twentieth-century bundle raft from Lake Titicaca, Peru (photo: S. McGrail).

the fisherman can carry his boat, his net, and even sufficient materials to build his hut' (C. Edwards, 1965: 3). At the upper end of the range are the 15–20 ft (4.5–6 m) bundle rafts of Lake Titicaca which have a sail (Fig. 11.8) and can carry up to twelve passengers and their baggage. Occasionally two of these Lake Titicaca craft were paired for greater stability by lashing one alongside another with leather thongs (Brindley, 1931: 8); in the mid-seventeenth century Peruvian coastal paired rafts were capable of carrying horses and cattle. Mitman, in his *Catalogue of the Watercraft Collection* in the US National Museum, recorded that an outrigger was sometimes used in recent times (Brindley, 1931: 8): this is the only known use of outriggers in the Americas. At sea, bundle rafts seem to have been propelled mainly if not entirely by paddles made from split canes; whereas in inland waters, poles and sail were also used.

### 11.4.2.1 RAW MATERIALS

Bundle rafts were made of reeds (*Phragmites communis* and *Scirpus riparius*), rushes (*Typha augustifolia*), and palm (*Maurita vinifera*) (C. Edwards, 1965: 13–14). Leshikar (1988) states that the bulrush (*tule*) was used in California, whilst Brindley (1931: 7) says rush (*totura*) was used in the Lake Titicaca region and *tule* grass in Nevada (Brindley, 1931: 15). In the early eighteenth century, du Pratz noted rafts on the lower Mississipi made of bundles of canes, in two layers (Roberts and Shackleton, 1983: 5). A type of cane known as *carrizo* was both buoyant and water-resistant (Roberts and Shackleton, 1983: 7).

### 11.4.2.2 STRUCTURE

At their simplest these rafts consisted of two bundles lashed together side by side, so narrow that the paddler could sit astride. The more complex ones were 'boat-shaped' either tapered at both ends or with a pointed bow and transom stern, and the ends were turned up. Some 'freeboard' was achieved in these 'boat-shaped' rafts by lashing smaller bundles on the upper outer sides of two bottom bundles (Fig. 11.9). In general the seagoing rafts were of the smaller size, whilst the full range of sizes was found on inland waters.

There were several methods of building these craft, but the basic features they all had in common were:

- The reeds or similar raw materials were gathered at a certain time and place, sometimes from cultivated stands (C. Edwards, 1965: 14–16).
- The tools required were a sharpened mussel shell to cut the reed, a pounder to separate cord fibre from the stalks, and a wooden stick to turn the butt ends of the reed back into the bundle.
- Individual bundles were bound tightly to compress them so that the craft becomes more rigid and the bundles less liable to waterlogging (Fig. 11.10).
- These bundles were then joined together by lashings using coiled basketry techniques (McGrail, 1998: 167–8). The lashings were made of cotton, grass, rush, yucca fibre, vines, animal hair, and even hide (C. Edwards, 1965: 9–12; Roberts and Shackleton, 1983: 10).
- The Chumash Indians of the California coast, where there was only low-quality reed, coated their bundles with a boiled mixture of bitumen and pine pitch, dusted with fine clay (Roberts and Shackleton, 1983: 10).

### 11.4.2.3 EARLIEST BUNDLE RAFTS

Pre-Columbian, and indeed, pre-Inca, use of bundle rafts is evidenced by pottery models from Peru (Leshikar, 1988: 28–9, fig. 29; C. Edwards, 1965: 1; Johnstone, 1988:14); and is possibly encapsulated in the legends of the Muisca Indians of Lake Guatavita region, Colombia (Leshikar, 1988: 24, 28). A model (Fig. 11.11) excavated by Professor J. C. Spahni from an Atacama culture burial site near the mouth of the River Loa in northern Chile, and dated to the beginning of the Christian era (BC / AD), is evidence for earlier use of bundle rafts.

C. Edwards (1965: 1) and Johnstone (1988: 13–14) believe that there is evidence for even earlier use off the west coast of South America at early coastal sites such as Huaca Prieta, Peru (of *c.*2000 BC) where nets weight-

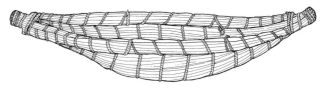

Fig. 11.9. A simple 4-bundle reed raft (Institute of Archaeology, Oxford).

Fig. 11.10. Compressing a reed bundle so that it can be bound tightly (photo: Clinton Edwards).

ed by stone sinkers and supported by gourd floats have been found (G. Clark, 1977: 432). However, this is more likely to be evidence for river fishing, and the midden contents of seaurchin and shellfish suggests that other seafood was gathered from the foreshore. The cold waters of the Humboldt Current, which flows northwards along the west coast from northern Chile to the Equatorial zone, support an immense quantity of fishes as well as sea mammals, water birds, and shellfish. On the other hand, the deep-sea fish bones in Ecuadorean middens do suggest the use of water transport on open seas as G. Clark (1977: 444) has argued, but this evidence is of much later date, although still pre-Columbian, of c. AD 200–700; moreover, this deep-sea fishing need not have been undertaken from bundle rafts as log rafts were also widely used on this west coast (11.4.1).

### II.4.3 BUOYED RAFTS

Two types of buoyed raft were indigenous to the Americas, both of them in Central and Southern America (C. Edwards, 1965: 17–18, 59–60, 89–90, 92–3; Hornell, 1946a: 32–3, 38–9). The less distinctive of the two types is the one consisting of gourds (often called 'calabash' from *calabaza* = dried fruit) netted or lashed together with a decking of light timbers on top—similar use of gourds is known from Egypt and central and eastern Africa (McGrail, 1998: 188). The other type is a member of the worldwide family of rafts buoyed by hide floats but it is distinctive and probably unique in having only two large multi-hide floats.

### II.4.3.1 HIDE FLOAT RAFTS

The hide float rafts were in use at first European contact in the rivers and along the coast of southern Peru and northern Chile, south of the coast where the log raft was used (11.4.1). This use extended from the River Ica at 15°S to Talcahuano at 37°S, some 250 miles south of Valparaiso (C. Edwards, 1965: 107). They were first noted in 1553 by Cieza da Léon but were not described in detail until Thomas Cavendish's voyage of 1587.

Fig. 11.11. A model of a bundle raft, some 2000 years old, excavated in northern Chile (photo: Paul Johnstone).

Cavendish tells us that the coastal fishermen of southern Peru lashed together two inflated multi-hide bladders to form a seagoing raft (Hornell, 1946a: 32). Father Acosta in 1590 described how such rafts were also used on rivers such as the Ica. In 1653 Father Bernarbé Cobo noted that paddles were the sole means of propulsion. Frezier, in the early eighteenth century, recorded that these paddles were double ones and that small cotton sails were occasionally used. He also gave the first detailed description of how hides were joined together to make large floats, using fishbone awls, wooden or bone toggles, and lashings of seals' intestines (McGrail, 1998: 187–91). Frezier also noted that the decking on top of the two floats was made of light timbers covered by a skin. Admiral Paris (1843) published a drawing of a sealskin float raft he had seen in Valparaiso, Chile, in 1834 (Fig. 11.12). From this one can see how the two floats were tied tightly together at the bow but somewhat apart at the stern, thus giving the structure something of a boat shape in plan. The average size of these rafts seems to have been *c.*2–3 m in length and *c.*1.25 m across the stern.

Captain George Shelvocke noted that buoyed rafts were used as tenders of visiting sailing ships in 1720, and Amat y Junient in the 1770s (Edwards, 1965: 18) recorded their use as ferries across the river estuaries of central Chile. The latter also noted that, with a double paddle, such a raft 'required little energy to send it skimming through the water'. Captain Basil Hall found that they were used in 1821 to take goods from ships through the surf in conditions in which a European boat would be swamped (C. Edwards, 1965: 19). It was not until the early twentieth century that anyone recorded how the hide seams were first sealed with grease and then each was payed with two or three coats of an impermeable mixture of red clay, grease, and oil (Hornell, 1946a: 33). These float rafts continued in use into the mid-twentieth century, the last recorded use being in 1944 (C. Edwards, 1965: 17).

### 11.4.3.2 NETTED GOURDS

Float rafts of netted gourds were used as ferries on the rivers of northern Peru and of Mexico (C. Edwards, 1965: 59, 92). In 1531, members of Francisco Pizarro's expedition crossed the River Saña, Peru in them; and in 1579, Francisco de Aguero reported them in use on the River Armeria near Zapotitlán in Jalisco, Mexico.

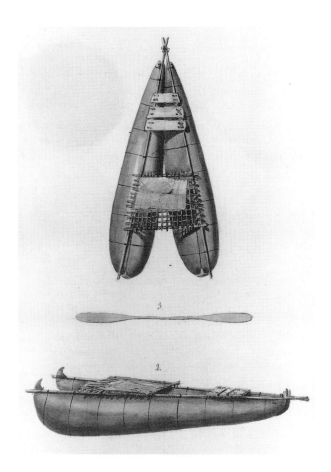

Fig. 11.12. A float raft seen in Valparaiso, Chile in 1834 (Paris, 1843: plate 112).

These rafts measured *c.*1.25 × 1.50 m and were propelled by swimmers, the one in front pulling by means of a sling around his shoulders, the one astern pushing. The net was made from plant fibre cord and the species of gourd used was probably *Lagenaria vulgaris* which has a tough durable shell (C. Edwards, 1965: 60, 93). Sometimes a platform of light sticks was fastened to the upper side of the net. Such rafts were still in use in Mexico on the River Balsas in the 1940s when Pedro Hendrichs noted that a raft with a platform measuring *c.*1 × 1 m needed eight large gourds in its net. Thompson (1949: 73) has argued that the representations of rafts with hemispherical attachments underneath on a gold disc from the early site of Chichen Itza, were in fact buoyed by gourds: this would take their use back to 1,000 years or so before European first contact. If this interpretation is correct, such float rafts would have been used in western Mexico or elsewhere as there are no rivers or lakes in Yucatan (C. Edwards, 1965: 92).

## II.4.4  BARK BOATS

Early European explorers encountered bark boats in three distinct areas of the Americas: in a region across North America, south of the hide boat zone; on the rivers of Guiana and Brazil, especially the Amazon; and on the west coast of southern Chile, south of the plank boat region.

The French explorer, Jacques Cartier, saw bark boats on the St Lawrence River on his first voyage to the New World in 1534, and they were noted again in 1603 by Samuel de Champlain, on the St Lawrence near Quebec, and by Captain George Weymouth off the coast of Maine (Adney and Chapelle, 1964: 7).

These Europeans were most impressed by the speed of the paddle-propelled bark boats—Weymouth, for example, noting that a bark boat with a crew of three or four could overtake his ship's boats with four oarsmen. Other explorers commented favourably on the bark boat's usefulness on shallow rivers, especially in the vicinity of rapids, as well as in deep rivers and at sea. They were impressed by its lightweight construction which meant that not only could it be readily carried overland around difficult stretches of river (as Champlain noted in 1603) but also that it was very buoyant which in turn led to good speed potential and cargo capacity. In 1603, Captain M. Pring noted that a 17 × 4 ft (5.2 × 1.2 m) boat on the River Piscataqua in New England weighed only 60 lbs (25 kg) yet it carried nine men standing upright (Roberts and Shackleton, 1983: 170). Bark boats were found to be especially useful in 'wilderness travel' as they could be repaired by materials ready to hand; indeed, new boats could be built using the resources of the land immediately adjacent to the rivers.

So impressed were Europeans by the bark boats of North America that they themselves used them as the most suitable boat to explore the vast areas of inland waters. By the middle of the eighteenth century the French were building bark boats in a factory near Montreal, so economically dependent had they become on them (Adney and Chapelle, 1964: 8–13).

### II.4.4.1  DISTRIBUTION AND RAW MATERIALS

Bark boats were found to be used by indigenous Americans in a vast area extending almost across the continent from Newfoundland and New England in the east to Alaska and British Columbia in the west. This region from c.60°N–45°N in the west and to c.35°N in the east (Fig. 11.13), almost coincides with the range of the paper birch tree (*Betula papyrifera*), the bark of which had been found to be the most suitable for boats (Waugh, 1919: 23). The bark of buttonwood (*Platanus occidentales*), red elm (*Ulmus* sp.), cottonwood (*Populus* sp.), basswood (*Tilia americana*), hickory (*Carya* sp.), chestnut (*Castenea dentata*), and yellow cedar (*Thuja excelsa*) was used to the south-east of the paper birch region; and pine (*Pinus* sp.) and spruce (*Picea* sp.) bark were used in southern British Columbia (Waugh, 1919: 23–4; Adney and Chapelle, 1964: 14–15). But these species were clearly seen as second-rate to the paper birch bark, and boats built of them were said to be 'heavy and loggy, inconvenient for portage and generally short-lived' (Waugh, 1919: 24). The paper birch, on the other hand, had a resinous bark which was flexible when green or damp but which did not shrink or stretch unduly. This bark also had a horizontal grain which was compatible with sewing together several bark sheets, and it did not have a rough surface which in many other species had to be scraped away to make the bark flexible (Adney and Chapelle, 1964: 14–15, 24).

Materials used to fasten bark sheets together included roots split into four strands, of spruce, cedar, larch, and pine (McGrail, 1998: 90, table 7.3; Roberts and Shackleton, 1983: 167). The framing, which was forced into and supported the shell of bark, was made from cedar, spruce, maple, larch, ash, and willow trees (McGrail, 1998: 90, table 7.4). Framing of white cedar (*Thuja occidentalis*) and fastenings of black spruce (*Picea mariana*) roots were preferred.

### II.4.4.2  STRUCTURE

The earliest explorers described more about the performance of the North American bark boat than about its construction, and it was not until 1684 that the earliest surviving account was written of how these boats were built (Adney and Chapelle, 1964: 8–10): Baron de la Hurtan described the method then in use in what is now eastern Canada. By this date there had been more than a century of French influence in that area and it is difficult to assess what effect this had on indigenous boatbuilding methods. In the late nineteenth century and early twentieth century, E. T. Adney made a detailed record of the methods then in use throughout

Fig. 11.13. Twentieth-century distribution of hide boats and bark boats (Institute of Archaeology, Oxford).

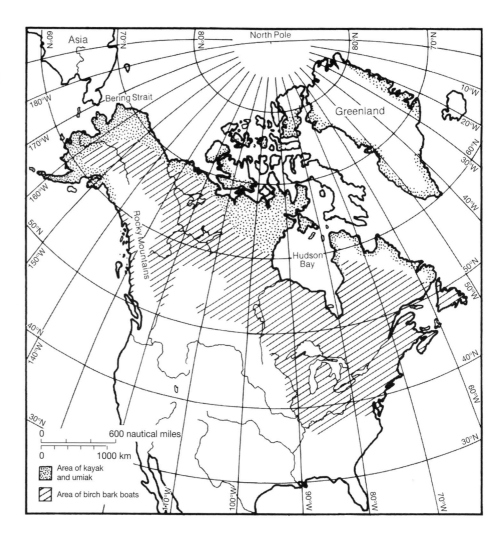

North America and his notes and drawings were subsequently published by H. Chapelle (Adney and Chapelle, 1964): this volume forms a firm basis for discussion.

Materials used by different tribes varied, and shapes and sizes differed but, with the possible exception of those bark boats of the Kutenai (on the north-west coast) which have a protruding forefoot, the building methods that have been documented in the past 100 years or so followed a standard pattern (Adney and Chapelle, 1964; Hansen and Madsen, 1981; Hornell, 1946a: 186; Waugh, 1919). A bark sheet, extended in length and breadth by sewing additional pieces of bark where necessary, had appropriate gores cut which were then sewn to obtain the required shape of hull and sheerline; the framework of stringers, thwarts, and ribs was then inserted into the bark shell and lashed into position. The seams were then payed with resin or gum. Thus in general terms this was a shell sequence (McGrail, 1998: fig. 7.4). However, the shape of the bark shell was obtained from part of the framework: two stringers and several transverse members (thwarts) were assembled to the shape required for either the sheerline plan or the bottom plan of the boat, and used as a temporary (sometimes permanent) mould or former, around which the bark shell was shaped: this is a feature of the skeleton sequence of building. In the early twentieth century, sticks ('memory sticks'—Roberts and Shackleton, 1983: 157) marked with the principal dimensions were used to achieve the required shape of framework, and to check the final form of the boat. There was also sometimes a shaped building-bed to give the required hog or sag to the bottom of the boat (Adney and Chapelle, 1964: 36–57). These features are in the skeleton, rather than the shell, tradition.

Whether these aspects of skeleton building were

introduced under European influence or were part of the pre-Columbian repertoire of techniques, is difficult to say. It seems likely—using parallel evidence from the less-developed forms of bark boat built in 'first contact' South America and Australia—that the North American bark boat was, in earlier times, built in the shell sequence, the shape of the hull being determined by the bark sheet. This almost certainly must have been the case with the prototype bark boat, the simple boat made from a single sheet of bark. The question remains: when the complex bark boat of more than one sheet was evolved, was a form of skeleton building evolved at the same time or did the hull shape continue to be obtained by eye and simple rule-of-thumb? The problems of building by eye (i.e. in the shell sequence) increase markedly with the size and complexity of the vessel, but the North American bark boat probably never reached the critical size.

### 11.4.4.3 TOOLS

The tools required to build a complex bark boat include those necessary for stripping the bark from the tree (knives, wedges, scrapers, and wooden rollers); binding and sewing the bark shell (knives, awls); and making, assembling, and fastening in the framework (axes, knives, mallets). Stone axes, knives, wedges, and scrapers; wooden rollers and mallets; and awls of bone or stone were all used in other trades in pre-Columbian North America and so would have been available for bark-boat building. Ritzenthaler (1950) has drawn attention to a distinctive curved knife used by twentieth-century bark-boat builders to shape the ribs. If such a knife is truly diagnostic of bark-boat building this may assist interpretation of the archaeological

record. Gidmark (1988: 13) noted that curved knives had been excavated from sites in the River Ottawa: these were made of slate on the Alumette islands, and of beaver's incisor teeth on Morrison island.

### 11.4.4.4 SIZE AND SHAPE

An Algonkin bark boat measured by S. de Champlain near Quebec in 1603 was about 20 ft (6 m) in length and 3 ft (0.9 m) in maximum breadth, whilst one noted by J. Guy in 1612 measured 20 ft × 4 ft 6 in (6 × 1.4 m). The seagoing boats of the Beothuk were 20 ft (6 m) or less in length (Ritzenthaler, 1950: 60); and Gidmark (1988) states that Algonkin boats were rarely longer than 6 m (20 ft), and he gives the greatest known as 7.54 m (25 ft). On the other hand, the largest boats de le Hontan noted were 33 × 5 × 2 ft (10 × 1.5 × 0.61 m), whilst Dunphy (1979: 80) states that the trading bark boats of colonial times could be up to 36 ft (10.97 m) in length, and Ritzenthaler (1950: 62) states that these 'freighter canoes' were 40 ft. (12.2 m) in length. Thus the evidence seems to support Adney and Chapelle's belief that the longest bark boats encountered by Europeans in the early years were only about 30 ft (9 m) in length (1964: 8–10), and the production of the larger 'war canoes' and 'freighters' of the later period was stimulated by the French.

Although the bark boats of each tribe or tribal grouping could be recognized primarily by *detailed* differences in shape, the great majority seem to have conformed to a general shape which may be seen in the lines of a mid-eighteenth-century boat from New England which was brought to Chatham, England, and recorded there in 1749 (Fig. 11.14). This boat is generally double-ended, i.e. symmetrical about the midships ver-

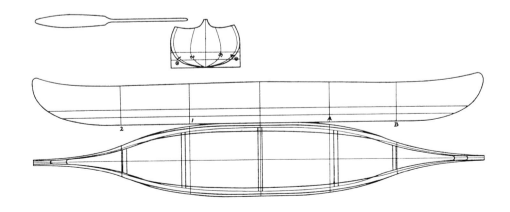

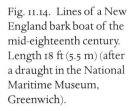

Fig. 11.14. Lines of a New England bark boat of the mid-eighteenth century. Length 18 ft (5.5 m) (after a draught in the National Maritime Museum, Greenwich).

Fig. 11.15. A bark boat
of the River Kutenai,
British Columbia (after
Coulton,1977: fig. 1D).

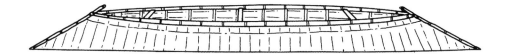

tical axis; in plan, the breadth is maintained over the working area of the boat with a marked decrease in breadth towards the ends, resulting in 'hollow' lines at bow and stern; in long section, the sheer remains parallel to the bottom over the working area with a slight rise to the rounded bow and stern; in section, the boat is generally rounded throughout; she has the following overall shape ratios— L/B = 6.4, L/D = 11.8, B/D = 1.8; this is a design for speedy passages in relatively calm waters. The exceptions to this general shape are three types of seagoing bark boats, and the river boats of the River Kutenai and River Columbia region of the northwest Pacific coast.

### 11.4.4.5 SEAGOING BARK BOATS

The Beothuk people of Newfoundland built a 20 ft (6 m) seagoing boat which was broader than average (i.e. c.4 ft (1.22 m) rather than 3 ft (3.3 m) and which had a sharp V-shaped lower cross-section with a longitudinal timber which has been described as a 'keelson' (Roberts and Shackleton, 1983: 168). These were used for inter-island voyages in the Gulf of St Lawrence, and on coastal voyages of up to 50 nautical miles in the Newfoundland/Labrador region (Adney and Chapelle, 1964: 94, 96, 98; Ritzenthaler, 1950: 61). Stones were loaded as ballast on these passages (Engelbrecht and Seyfert, 1994: 227–8).

From the New Brunswick coast, the Micmac Indians hunted whale and seals in large bark boats 18–24 ft (5.5–7.3 m) long, with sides which were, like the Beothuk boats, 'up-curved and turned in towards the centre to exclude heavy seas' (Waugh, 1919: 28). An early nineteenth-century picture (published by Roberts and Shackleton, 1983: 169) shows that the paddlers plied their blades away from this midships part where the tumblehome would have made paddling difficult. The tumblehome cross-section made it easier to lift seals into the boat. Early French explorers noted sail on some of these Micmac boats, but did not give details.

The bark boats of the Yahgan and Alacaluf of the Chilean archipelago were also seagoing (11.4.4.7).

### 11.4.4.6 RIVER KUTENAI BOATS

The bark boats of the region around the River Kutenai in southern British Columbia and the River Columbia in Washington, Montana, and Idaho states are unusual in shape in that they have a protruding forefoot (Fig. 11.15) sometimes described as, 'sturgeon nosed' or 'monitor-shaped' (Waugh, 1919: 24; Brindley, 1919: 106; Ritzenthaler, 1950: 61; Adney and Chapelle, 1964: 168–73; Gidmark, 1988: 14).

This shape is also seen in the bark boats of Goldi, Ottascha, Tungar, and Yakut peoples of the River Amur which, over much of its length, forms the present-day boundary between Russia (Chita-Amur) and China (Mongolia and Manchuria), but in its lower reaches turns northwards at Khabarovsk to enter the Sea of Okhotsk in the Bay of Sakhalin to the west of the Kamchatka peninsula. Waugh (1919: 24) believed that the protruding forefoot shape enabled these bark boats to be used in fast-flowing rivers.

Amongst the several reasons why protruding forefoots are incorporated into a boat design (McGrail, 1990b: 43) are: to increase speed potential; to improve directional stability; to keep up the boat's head in a short, steep sea. Any one, and indeed all, of these effects would be useful to a boat in a fast flowing river, especially in the lower reaches. Whether this is a case of independent invention in the British Columbia and in the River Amur regions, or whether the protruding forefoot design was part of the cultural property brought to the Americas from Siberia, is impossible to say on present evidence.

### 11.4.4.7 SOUTH AMERICAN BOATS

In South America complex bark boats were found to be used in the south-west, on the coast of southern Chile and around the islands, from the Taitao peninsula at c.46°S, southwards to Cape Horn (56°S) south of Tierra del Fuego, and to Elizabeth island in the east (C. Edwards, 1965: 21–5, 107–8). Simple bark boats were found in the north-east on the many rivers of Brazil (M. Brindley, 1924; Hornell, 1946a: 183–6).

The first Spaniards to visit southern Chile noted the bark boats of the Alacalufs and the Yahgansu, which had a sheerline curved 'Like the moon of four days', i.e. they had rising ends. The segments of bark 'as thick as a finger' were caulked with straw or reed at the seams, and sewn together with strips of baleen (whalebone) over thin wooden battens—quoted by C. Edwards (1965: 21) from the account of Miguel de Goiçueta who accompanied Francisco de Ulloa on his voyage in 1553. Subsequent explorers such as Wallace in 1767 and Antonio de Córdoba in 1785/6 added further details of the construction methods. Three segments of bark less than one inch in thickness were used, one for the bottom and one for each side; the tools were of stone or bone. The three pieces were worked to the required shape and sewn together with hide thongs—possibly of sealskin (M. Brindley, 1924)—or dry reeds or baleen. The caulking in the seams was a mixture of straw and mud; at a later date, M. Brindley (1924: 131), states that moss was used. A framework was subsequently sewn or lashed into the bark shell, consisting of fifteen or more slender branches curved to the transverse shape of the hull and extending from sheer to sheer, with poles along each side as sheerline stringers fastened together at bow and stern, and a few transverse timbers which were used as thwarts by the paddlers. The shell of bark was then lined with strips of bark running transversely around the boat from sheer stringer to sheer stringer. A framework of tranverse and longitudinal sticks formed a deck about 6 in (150 mm) above the bottom, with a space amidships from which water could be bailed.

These mid-eighteenth-century bark boats were 15–25 × 3–4 × 2–3 ft (4.6–7.6 × 0.9–1.2 × 0.61–0.9 m), and could carry up to nine or ten men (Fig. 11.16). When used in coastal waters, stones were loaded as ballast (Engelbrecht and Seyfert, 1994: 227–8). Although these descriptions were written more than 250 years after first European contact, C. Edwards (1965: 22–5) believes that, apart from the sealskin sail mentioned by de Córdoba, the methods of construction were most probably those of pre-Columbian times. The continuity of design and building techniques which this belief implies receives support from a description of an Alacaluf bark boat built in 1903 and exhibited in the Salesian Museum in Punta Arenas (C.

Edwards, 1965: 24–5). This 12 × 2 ft (3.7 × 0.6 m) boat had been built in the same general way as those described by de Córdoba with the minor difference that pithy vines were used to caulk the seams.

From his examination of this 'Salesian' boat, C. Edwards (1965: 25) was able to fill in some of the details of construction of this general type of craft. The three bark sheets were from the southern beech (*Nothofagus* sp.) and the bottom length had been tapered at the ends to give pointed bow and stern to the boat. The side bark sheets were turned inboard over the sheer stringers and fastened to them by spiral stitching. Edwards notes that the last bark boat known to be in use in this part of the world was sighted in 1917 just north of the western end of the Strait of Magellan.

In the early twentieth century simple bark boats were still in use by Arawaks in British Guiana in the upper creeks of the River Mazzaruni and River Pomeron and on the headwaters of the many rivers that rise on the Brazilian plateau of Matto Grosso (M. Brindley, 1924; Worcester, 1956a).

These boats were similar in size to those of southern Chile, for example, one measured by M. Brindley (1924: 126) was 15 ft 6 in × 4 ft 3 in (4.7 × 1.3 m), but they were made from a single sheet of bark. The tree from which this bark was taken was *Mora* or 'purple heart'

Fig. 11.16. Bark boats from Tierra del Fuego (Paul Johnstone, 1988: fig. 3.3).

(Worcester, 1956a) which grows up to 200 ft (61 m) and has a diameter near the ground of 7–9 ft (2.13–2.74 m): this suggests that the Alacalufs and Yahgans of southern Chile probably used bark from these trees because only relatively small trees were available to them. Being of only one sheet, the Arawak bark boats were shaped firstly by varying the extent to which the upper edges of the curved bark sheet were spread by inserted slender wooden poles—broader amidships, less at the ends; and secondly by cutting gores (V-shaped sections) out of the upper edge of the sheet near the ends and sewing the sides of these cuts together. By these spreading and folding operations the open ends of the boat were forced to rise so that they would be clear of the water. Split cane was used to sew up these gores and to lash in the light framework of transverse poles and cane rod sheer stringers. Transverse cords from sheer to sheer were also sometimes used to prevent the ends spreading (M. Brindley, 1924). Such boats were light enough to be carried around rapids, nevertheless, Brindley noted that they were often used with only 3 in (76 mm) of freeboard amidships, in which condition they could hold three people and two or three hunting dogs.

## 11.4.5 HIDE BOATS

Two main types of hide boat were encountered by early Europeans: simple hide boats used on some of the rivers of both North and South America; and complex boats used at sea, and in the rivers of the Arctic and sub-Arctic.

### 11.4.5.1 SIMPLE BOATS

The *pelota* is a simple boat made from a single hide, sometimes without a framework, used on the rivers of Colombia, Venezuela, Brazil, Bolivia, Paraguay, Uruguay, and Argentina (Hornell, 1941c; 1946a: 150–4). The first account of them appears to be as late as 1782, well after the time that cattle and horses had been introduced by Europeans. The explorer, Antonio Viedma, saw one made from hides and sticks to cross the River Chico in Patagonia (Hornell, 1941c: 27). In 1822, Father Martin Dobrizhoffer, SJ, gave a more detailed description of the frameless boats built by the Adipones of the Gran Chaco in Patagonia. A hairy, raw

bull's hide was shaped into a square by cutting off the feet and the neck; the four sides were then bent to stand upright and each corner tied with a thong so that the boat retained its squareness of form. A thong was then passed through a hole in one of the sides, and the boat, loaded with a passenger sitting on top of his luggage, was then towed across the river by a swimmer. This frameless boat evidently retained its form except when many days of continuous rain made it soft—in which event boughs of trees were placed under the four sides and across the bottom to form a simple framework (Hornell, 1941c: 27–8; 1946a: 150).

These simple boats have been used in the twentieth century (Hornell, 1941c; Moura, 1988: 496–9) in South America, and accounts of these confirm the early reports and add some details. The hide was shaped with the hairy side outwards as it was easier to bend that way. When of square or rectangular form there was generally no framework; when of rounded form the upper edge of the hide was supported by curved sticks to which the hide was laced by thongs, and the bottom reinforced by further sticks. In other instances, sub-rectangular shaped boats were made by lacing a rawhide thong through holes around the edges of the hide: pulling the two ends of the thong drew the sides upwards (Hornell, 1941c: 28).

There were no horses or cattle in pre-Columbian South America from which hide boats could have been made and Hornell has suggested that, if this was a pre-Columbian form of water transport as seems likely, hides from the *guanaco* were used instead. The Amerinds are known to have hunted the *guanaco* and to have used the hides for cloaks (Hornell, 1941c: 29). The *guanaco* is a llama-like camelid, 7–8 ft (2.1–2.4 m) in length but only some 4 ft (1.2 m) at the shoulder—it would therefore probably have been necessary to sew two *guanaco* hides together to make the minimum size of *pelota*. An alternative hypothesis is that sea mammal hides were used after being treated in some way to make them sufficiently stiff.

A similar form of boat, again sometimes frameless, was used by the Plains Indians of North America and became known to Europeans as the 'bull boat' (Hornell, 1946a: 148–50; Adney and Chapelle, 1964: 220). Early travellers and settlers on the central plains noted them but recorded few details (Hornell, 1946a: 149). In the early nineteenth century, they were seen in use as ferries on the Missouri (Catlin, 1841): they were des-

Fig. 11.17. An early nine-teenth-century hide boat (bull boat) of the Plains Indians (Department of the Library, American Natural History Museum).

cribed as being made 'in the form of a large tub of a buffalo skin stretched on a frame of willow boughs' and were towed by a swimmer. Subsequent study of some of the boats that survive from this era shows that the framework consisted of widely spaced withies bound together where they crossed and turned upwards along their length with their ends joined by a circle of withies to form the 'rim' of the boat. A further circle of withies was added to form the bottom of the sides. This open lattice was then covered by one or two buffalo hides turned in over the 'rim', and lashed in position (Fig. 11.17) to form a bowl shape some 4–5 ft (1.2–1.5 m) in diameter, with flattened bottom and vertical sides. Such boats could be built in a few hours with material ready to hand, providing hides were available. Subsequently they were regularly smoked and oiled to preserve the hide. When not towed by a swimmer they were propelled by a kneeling paddler. They were readily portable.

A type of hide boat was sometimes built by Malecite, Algonkin, and other Indians of the north-east maritime provinces, who usually built bark boats. When boats were needed in early spring, before suitable bark could be obtained (early summer being the best time), simple boat-shaped frameworks were built and covered with hides. Adney and Chapelle (1964: 193, 219–20) call these 'emergency' hide boats, and describe how they were built in the bark-boat sequence, that is,

using the top stringers as a mould, the hide shell was shaped first and then the light framework inserted.

### 11.4.5.2 COMPLEX BOATS

Complex hide boats, perhaps the apogee of hide boat development, were used in the Arctic and sub-Arctic of North America, not only on rivers but also at sea. The *umiak* was a double-ended, open boat, flat-bottomed and deep sided (Fig. 11.18). The kayak was also double-ended but of an elongated lanceolate shape with very little freeboard and was almost unique amongst small boats in having a complete deck with an opening for its typically one-man crew (Fig. 11.19). *Umiak* and kayak have their counterparts in the *baidar* and *baidarka* of Siberia, with which Alaska and the Aleutian islands have had cultural continuity since prehistoric times (Dumond, 1980).

#### 11.4.5.2.1 *European encounters*

Hide boats of these two types are also used today in Greenland (Petersen, 1986). From the *Graenlandinga* and *Eirik* sagas, first written down in Iceland in the late-twelfth and mid-thirteenth centuries (see Clausen, 1993), we learn that Greenland was first sighted by Europeans in the late tenth century from the Norwegian ship of Gunnbjorn Ulfson blown off course to the westwards when bound for Iceland. After exploratory

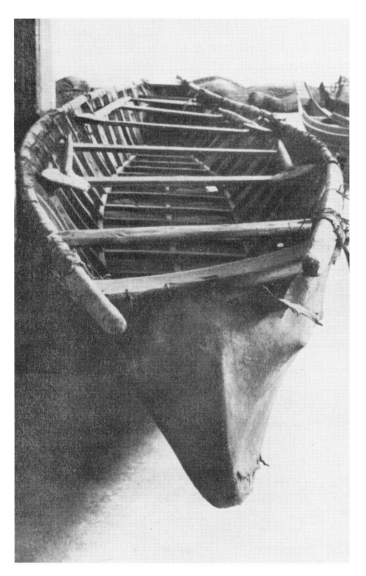

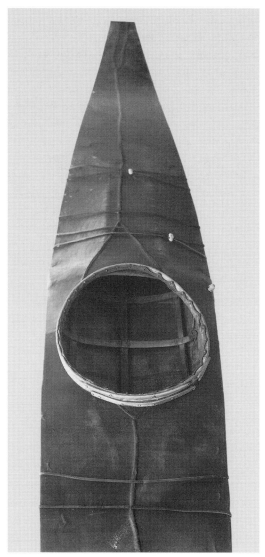

Fig. 11.18. A *umiak* from Greenland (National Museum of Ethnography, Stockholm).

Fig. 11.19. Cockpit of a Greenland kayak (The Smithsonian Institution).

voyages during AD 982–5, Eric the Red led an expedition from Iceland in 986 and established settlements on the west coast of Greenland—settlements which continued until the fifteenth century when, after deteriorating weather and loss of contact with Iceland and Norway, they were overwhelmed by indigenous Inuit. These settlers were in contact with the Inuit from their earliest days and must inevitably have encountered their boats, but no record of them has survived.

In the year AD 986, Biarni Heriulfson, en route from Iceland to Greenland and unsure of his longitude, sighted land well to the west of Greenland; this was probably Labrador or Baffin island. Leif Ericsson,

second son of Eric the Red, sailed from Greenland in AD 1001 to retrace Biarni's voyage and visited 'Helluland', 'Markland' and 'Vinland' which are generally thought to be Baffin island, Labrador, and Newfoundland.

Subsequently a settlement was established by Thorfinn Karlsefni, probably near the northern tip of Newfoundland (Clausen, 1993). The sagas tell us that in a bay in Vinland, Thorfinn Karlsefni saw *hud-keipr*—literally 'hide-tholes' but taken to mean 'hide boats'—approaching him in great numbers so that the estuary seemed to be covered with bits of charcoal (Magnussen and Palsson, 1965: 29–41, 60, 99, 100). In other sections of the *Graenlandinga* saga, we learn that three beached boats of these *skraeling* (weathered, darkly-tanned skin) people, had three men under each of them. Arima (1975: 95) has suggested that these descriptions best fit the hide boats of the Algonkin Indians rather than the typically one man kayak or the large capacity *umiak* of the Eskimos. However, if *keipr* (thole or rowlock) is taken at face value, the description seems more readily to apply to *umiaks*.

In the fourteenth and fifteenth centuries, kayaks and possibly *umiaks* appeared in Norway. Olaus Magnus recorded in 1505 that he had seen two hide boats which King Haakon VI (1355–1380) was said to have captured: probably these were kayaks. In 1430, Claudius Clavus noted that there was a kayak in the cathedral at Nidaros (Trondheim), and a further remark seems to refer to a *umiak*. Such boats can only have come from eastern Siberia or North America, and the probability is that they were from Greenland where there were Norwegian settlements.

Martin Frobisher made two exploratory voyages to North America in 1576 and 1578, searching for the elusive North-West Passage to India. He 'rediscovered' Greenland, crossed Baffin Bay and landed on Baffin island and on the Labrador coast, where he encountered both *umiaks* and kayaks. The *umiaks* were open boats and had sails of animal skins. Frobisher captured one of the one-man kayaks (Whittaker, 1977: 43) and the expedition's artist, John White, painted a picture in 1577 of an encounter between a European oared-boat, kayaks, and Inuit armed with bows and arrows (Leshikar, 1988: fig. 7; Bray, 1989: 77). From this painting we can see most of the characteristic features of the *kayak* that have persisted until this century: a double-ended, relatively long boat of low freeboard and with a maximum breadth not much greater than that of the human body; the ends are pointed and rise out of the water; the boat is decked with hide of a piece with the hides forming the hull; and the sole crew is sealed at waist level into his cockpit, becoming as one with the boat and propelling her with a double-bladed paddle (Fig. 11.20).

The earliest modern account of North American hide boats is that by Hans Egede (1745) based on his stay in Greenland in *c*.1729. He noted that *umiaks* had sails of seals' intestines, and claimed that the largest boats were almost 60 ft (18.3 m) in length (Adney and Chapelle, 1964: 190). The kayaks were about three fathoms (5.5 m) in length and at most ¾ yard (0.69 m) broad. The framework of this double-ended, one-man boat was made of thin laths of wood fastened together with sinews, and was covered with dressed, hairless sealskins. Egede emphasized that the paddler was fastened into his cockpit so that no water could penetrate. He also noted that kayaks were used in stormy seas and when they were upset the man was often able to right the boat again using his paddle—possibly the earliest reference to the 'kayak roll' (Hornell, 1946a: 163).

A number of kayaks are now held in European museums, some of them having been brought from North America in recent times—for example, the one in Lincoln Museum (Vernon, 1984). A few, however, are from the seventeenth century, at a time when Europeans were increasingly fishing and whaling in the seas around Greenland and the Davis Strait. The earliest one is probably the one in Trinity House, Hull, which seems to have been acquired about 1613: the framework is thought to be of bone rather than wood (Souter,

Fig. 11.20. A sixteenth-century kayak (after Leshikar, 1988: fig. 7).

1934). The one in the Royal College of Surgeons in Edinburgh was acquired before 1696 (Souter, 1934: 12). Others are to be found in Netherlands' museums (Nooter, 1971)—Netherlands' ships were whaling in Arctic waters from the early seventeenth century—and Nooter (1971: 5) has noted that a Greenlander gave a kayak demonstration in an ornamental lake in The Hague in 1625.

It used to be thought that those kayaks said to have been captured in the North Sea region with their crew on board, had been forced there from Greenland or indeed Labrador by contrary winds and seas—see, for example, Whittaker (1954). However, Whittaker (1977) has recently suggested that it is more probable that they were captured in Arctic waters by European whalers and fishing boats and subsequently escaped when in European waters; or they were released when in sight of Orkney, Britain, or continental Europe by a friendly crew.

From a study of some of the reports of early European explorers and settlers, of actual kayaks and *umiaks* acquired during the post-medieval period, and from recent ethnographic records of the building of recent hide boats in Arctic and sub-Arctic America, for example, by Arima (1975) and by Zimmerley (1980), a picture can be built up, incomplete in parts, of the *umiaks* and kayaks of the early European settlement phase, how they were built and something about how they were used.

### 11.4.5.3  THE *UMIAK/BAIDARA*

There were differences in detail over time and space, but the essential core of features was found in all *umiaks* and indeed, in the *baidara* of Siberia (Sauer, 1802). The Arctic and sub-Arctic peoples relied on driftwood for their timber, fir (*Abies* sp.) and spruce (*Picea* sp.) being the principal species (Adney and Chapelle, 1964: 185). Currents take trees from the rivers of the Pacific coast of Asia to the Arctic, and other currents bring trees from northern Russian and Siberian rivers into the Arctic Sea and then westward with the ice to the east coast of Greenland, then southwards and then north-westwards along the west coast of Greenland and then to the north-east coast of America (Souter, 1934: 9).

The framework of the *umiak* was made of three central longitudinal members, the 'keelson' and the stem and stern posts, to which were fastened, by sinew or hide thong lashings widely spaced flat floor timbers and a chine stringer on each side, thus forming the bottom. One or two light stringers were similarly fastened to side timbers which had themselves been fastened to the chine stringers. The topmost stringer, the 'gunwale', was formed of poles which in some designs protruded beyond the ends to form handles. Crossbeams, five or six of which acted as thwarts, were lashed to stringers each side and completed the framework. This open framework was thus lighter than the more closely arranged, and even interwoven, framework of the Irish currach (5.3.3).

The framework was then covered with a multi-hide assembly of two to five seal or walrus skins (Souter, 1934: 10), the upper edge of which was turned inboard over the top stringers and lashed as a unit to a pair of stringers. Many people, mostly women, were involved in preparing and fastening several hides together to form the boat's 'skin'. Green, untreated hides were taken and, depending on their thickness, were split to give the required weight of hide (Adney and Chapelle, 1964: 188). These hides were then shaped and sewn together using caribou sinews or hide thongs or sometimes fish gut (Arima, 1975: 104; Roberts and Shackleton, 1983: 135), a hidden stitch (Johnstone, 1988: fig. 9.23) being used which did not penetrate either hide in the seams. This unit of several skins was then stretched to the shape of the framework and lashed in position, covering the entire frame including the keelson, except for handles protruding at each end. The hides were then dressed with seal oil and caribou fat (Adney and Chapelle, 1964: 182, 188), and the seams were payed with blubber or other animal fats. Such a treatment delays degradation of the hide and ensures watertightness of the unit but it does not cause a permanent change of the hide structure as does tanning. The *umiak* hide in the North Atlantic and Pacific thus can remain watertight for no longer than four to seven days (Adney and Chapelle, 1964: 188) as the prolonged soaking leaches out the preservatives.

The fact that the hide 'cover' is fastened to the framework only along its top edge means that when disturbed by, say, meeting ice, the whole 'skin' moves relative to the framework. Thus the 'skin' absorbs shock by distortion. The lashed joints also give the framework a certain resilience. The combination of light, resilient framework with a semi-independent rel-

Fig. 11.21. Drawing of an early nineteenth-century *umiak* (Paris, 1843: plate 132).

atively lightweight hide cover is a significant feature of this design.

Available timber lengths determine the precise length of individual *umiaks* but Hornell (1946a: 155–9) considered that the average in the nineteenth and early twentieth centuries was about 30 × 5–6 ft (9.1 × 1.5–1.8 m), and Adney and Chapelle (1964: 183) give 36–40 ft (11–12 m) as an average length. Hans Egede claimed to have noted a Greenland *umiak* in 1729 that was close on 60 ft (18.2 m) in length, whilst David Crantz in the mid-eighteenth century stated that they were generally 36 ft, 48 ft and even 54 ft (11, 14.6, 16.5 m) (Adney and Chapelle, 1964: 176, 190). The largest of the *umiaks* described by Adney and Chapelle (1964: 181–90) and Hornell (1946a: 155–163) measured 10.67 × 1.37 × 0.61 m, the smallest was 6.30 × 1.45 × 0.46 m; the mean of their L/B ratios was 5.7 whilst that of their L/D ratios was 12.1 (McGrail, 1998: table 10.1).

*Umiaks* were steered by a steering-oar over the stern. They were paddled or rowed by oars pivoted against bone tholes or in thong loops (Adney and Chapelle, 1964: 186–7): this was difficult in strong winds; *umiaks* being lightweight and having deep sides, had much windage. They were also sailed—Martin Frobisher

noted this in 1576. The mast was stepped in a block on the keelson; there was no mast thwart but the mast was steadied with stays and shrouds of hide (Adney and Chapelle, 1964: 175). The square sail, without braces but with sheets, seems to have been set on a mast stepped well forward (Fig.11.21)—in this case its use was probably restricted to a near-following wind as an aid to rowing. In later times, and probably under European influence, the mast was moved further aft and a sprit sail was set—this may have allowed the boat to be sailed across the wind.

In recent times, *umiaks* have been used exclusively for the movement of cargo and passengers, as needed for example, on a migration, permanent or seasonal. In former times, however, smaller, handier versions were also used for whaling: in this role inflated floats were fastened to the top stringer to prevent capsizing (Hornell, 1946a: 156; Adney and Chapelle, 1964: 183). Stefansson (1942), writing about the late nineteenth century, states that Yankee whalermen working in north-west Alaskan waters preferred these whaling *umiaks* to their own planked whaleboats. He also noted that a 35–45 ft (10.7–13.7 m) *umiak* could carry 2 tons yet could itself be carried by two men. When not in use, *umiaks* were

Fig. 11.22. One-man and two-man *baidarka* of the Aleutian Islands (National Maritime Museum, Greenwich).

stored bottom up in a sheltered place, often on a pile of stones to prevent them from being damaged by dogs and other animals.

### 11.4.5.4 THE KAYAK/*BAIDARKA*

The kayak also combines strength with lightness. Its elongated lanceolate form and compact size give it the potential speed required in its specialized hunting role. However, the resulting narrow beam and low free-board reduce its natural transverse stability to the very minimum: this disadvantage is offset to a degree, and seaworthiness maintained, by having a watertight deck and by the Inuit wearing a watertight coat fastened to the cockpit coaming. The *baidarka* of Siberia is generally similar to the kayak (Fig. 11.22).

As with the *umiak*, there were differences in detail, but there is a core of attributes that defines these boats as kayak/*baidarka*. Hornell (1946a: 166–75) considers that there were seven regional types including the Koryak and Chukchi types of eastern Siberia. One very obvious difference was that, although most kayaks had only one cockpit, some of the Alaskan boats had two or even three, thereby exhibiting spatial continuity with some of the east Siberian boats (Fig. 11.22).

The kayak was built in the skeleton sequence (as the *umiak*): a framework was built and then covered entirely by a 'skin' of hides which was only pierced by a tailor-made cockpit for the crew. A French captain who met kayaks in the Davis strait in the late seventeenth century recorded that the coaming around the cockpit was made of whalebone.

Fig. 11.23. Measured drawing of an eighteenth-century kayak from north-eastern Canada. Length 21 ft 6 in (6.6 m) (after an original drawing in the National Maritime Museum, Greenwich).

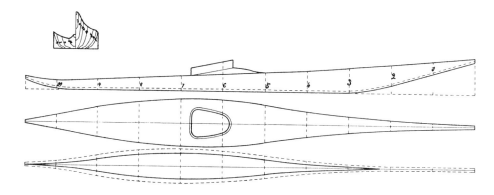

In transverse section, the kayak hull was rounded or rather multi-chine, as the hide 'cover', enveloping the stringers closely, took up this form (Fig. 11.23). In longitudinal section the boat was very low overall, with a slightly rising stern and a more pronounced rise at the bow. The dimensions of the cockpit were related to the individual man who was to use the boat—Zimmerley (1979: p. xxi) states that the diameter of the cockpit in the Hooper Bay kayak equalled the distance from the armpit to the first finger joint (c.2 ft (0.61 m)). Other dimensions of the boat were similarly anthropometric: the length of boat forward of the cockpit was approximately one fathom plus one cubit/ell (c.7 ft 6 in (2.28 m)); that aft of the cockpit was one fathom plus a palm (c.6 ft 4 in (1.92 m)). Other examples are that the central deck beams were spaced at one cubit/ell (1 ft 6 in (0.46 m)); the depth or moulded dimension of the lower stern piece was a span from thumb to middle finger (c.7 in (0.18 m)) and its breadth or sided dimension was three fingers (c.2 in (51 mm)). Petersen (1982: 8) states that Greenland kayaks today have an overall length equal to three times the height of the paddler, which would be c.15 ft 6 in (4.72 m). It seems highly likely that similar rules were used in the days before European influence to produce a boat that fitted the individual as closely as possible—recent kayak users have emphasized how they have most confidence when man and boat feel and act as one.

The raw materials needed for a kayak were similar to those for a *umiak* with the addition that willow or similar timber was required for the bent frames. Two to five hides were joined together to form the all-enveloping 'skin' of the kayak over a framework which had been lashed together and of which the top stringer or gunwale was the primary strength member.

The smallest kayak noted by Adney and Chapelle (1964: 181–90) and Hornell (1946a: 155–63) measured 4 × 0.50 × 0.24 m; the largest, 10 × 0.80 × 0.50 m. The thirty-three kayaks in British museums have lengths and breadths within these ranges; their heights vary from 1 ft 1 in to 6 in (0.32–0.15 m) (Souter, 1934: 11). Others measured in Alaska and the Bering Strait region in the late nineteenth century had similar measurements. Some of the bigger ones may not be hunting kayaks but ones specially built for travelling, as described by Arima (1975). Not only do these latter have greater overall dimensions so that they can carry stores and even passengers inside the hull but also the cockpit is enlarged to take two people back to back; in quiet waters other passengers may travel spreadeagled on top of the kayak.

The L/B ratio for the group of North American kayaks described by Adney and Chapelle (1964) and Hornell (1946a) ranges from 15 to 9.5 and the L/D, from 40 to 10: these figures highlight the fact that kayaks are long, narrow, and low boats. Hornell (1946a: 167–72) estimated that kayaks weigh only 15–20 kg which ties in with Souter's statement that the thirty-three kayaks in British museums weighed between 25 and 50 lbs (c.11–23 kg). This may be compared with a typical small plank boat built in the Viking tradition which weighed 110–134 kg and could carry three men (McGrail and McKee, 1974). The planked boat carried c.1.5 times its own weight, whereas the one-man kayak carried c.3.5 times.

Kayaks were and are propelled and steered by a double-bladed paddle (Fig. 11.20). In earlier times it was sometimes reported that kayaks were sailed. However, this seems to have been the misidentification of a white screen rigged to hide the paddler's silhouette as he approached his prey. On rare occasions, most often in rivers, two or even three kayaks, lashed together side by side to give extra transverse stability, were rigged with a makeshift sail (Zimmerley, 1980: 694; Hornell, 1946a: 66).

A single kayak underway is maintained in a stable state by small adjustments of the paddler's body and paddle. It is more difficult to maintain stability when the kayak is at rest on the water: the usual way is to place one blade of the paddle on the water surface. A special routine has to be used to man a kayak because of this great 'tenderness' in transverse stability. Another special routine has been evolved to recover from the not infrequent capsize, the 'kayak roll': the paddler stays with his boat and uses his paddle to roll her upright again (Adney and Chapelle, 1964: 223–9).

Early Europeans remarked on the speeds that one-man, hunting kayaks could achieve; they could, for example, keep up with European ships which would have been doing about four knots. Arima (1975: 138–9) and Zimmerley (1980) agree that the kayak's maximum speed in fair weather conditions was 4–6 knots. Speed was necessary to travel the long distances between base and hunting grounds with minimum effort, but the low profile and the good manœuvrability characteristics of the kayak were invaluable when actually hunting—stealth rather than speed was needed when stalking seals, walruses, or whales at sea, or waiting at river crossing points for migrating herds of caribou.

## II.4.5.5 ARCHAEOLOGICAL EVIDENCE

The archaeological evidence for the use of hide boats in North America is mostly indirect until *c.* AD 500 (Arima, 1975) when more substantial evidence becomes available. This indirect evidence generally takes the form of whaling and sea mammal hunting equipment which it is deduced must have been used in hide boats owing to the shortage of timber in the Arctic and sub-Arctic. Further support for such arguments comes from the fact that, in historic times, hide boats have been the only form of water transport used by the indigenous peoples of the Arctic and sub-Arctic from eastern Siberia to Greenland. Hide boats are in concord with their environment in this circumpolar zone where there are few, if any, trees, yet a good supply of hides from land or sea mammals, and where life can be sustained by sea fishing and hunting.

Although it is possible that the earliest Americans crossed the Bering Strait from Siberia to Alaska as early as 12,000 BC or even 40,000 BC (II.1), the earliest evidence of Man in the Arctic comes from sites in western Alaska ascribed to the Denbigh culture of 3000–2000 BC, where thin worked points similar to the end blades of recent toggling harpoons have been excavated (Giddings, 1964: 240; 1967: 274). A site at Onion Portage on the River Kobuk is near a natural crossing point for caribou, which leads to the suggestion that hunting kayaks may have been used here in the third millennium BC, as they have been in recent times (G. Clark, 1977: 413).

By 2000 BC, the Inuit were well established in Alaska, and by 1000 BC had moved eastwards as far as Greenland (Bray, Swanson, and Farrington 1989: 75). From a site at Cape Krusenstern in western Alaska dated to the period 1800–1500 BC came a large whaling harpoon, lance blades, and toggle harpoon heads of whalebone (Giddings, 1967: 226–43; Arima, 1975). An engraving on an ivory bodkin (Johnstone, 1988: fig. 16.2)) from House 7 at Cape Krusenstern depicts a hunting scene and what is probably a *umiak*, although Arima (1975) has suggested it may be a kayak or even a bark boat (G. Clark, 1977: 423).

Artefacts similar to those recently used by Inuit hunters, including an inflation mouthpiece for a harpoon float, have also been excavated from Chaluka on Umnak Island in the Aleutians dated to *c.*1700 BC. Similar artefacts came from culturally equivalent sites further east (Bandi, 1969: 138–9, 157–62).

From several sites of the Dorset culture in the east and the contemporary Choris and Norton culture in the west, hunting weapons, ivory crutches (possibly to hold spears on board a kayak) and the remains of seal, walrus, and caribou suggest the continuation of hunting by hide boat down to the beginning of the Christian era. Giddings (1967: 126, 199) has suggested that whaling probably began *c.*100 BC.

Sites on St Lawrence island in the Bering Strait, of the Obvik culture (*c.*300 BC–*c.* AD 600) taken together with evidence from sites of the contemporary Old Bering Sea culture on the Chukchi peninsula of eastern Siberia, reveal a society highly specialized in sea mammal hunting (Arima, 1975: 230–4). Harpoon supports, bird darts, and plugs for harpoon floats suggest the use of kayak-type boats; whilst whaling harpoons suggest *umiaks* or similar craft (Bandi, 1969: 69–70).

From St Lawrence island also comes an ivory model of a kayak with moderate sheer and a rockered bottom, and a face engraved in the cockpit. Apart from the face, this model is similar to the model kayaks found on an Old Bering Strait site near Uelen on the Asian side of the Bering Strait. Model *umiaks* and full size paddles and fragments of boat framework were also found at the Ekven site near Uelen (Arima, 1975: 234). The excavator of the Asian material, Arutyunov, dated the graves from which these artefacts came to the third–fifth centuries AD, whereas Arima (1975: 234) believes they may be as early as the first century BC / AD. At another Old Bering Sea site on St Lawrence island, bark models of kayaks and fragmentary *umiaks* have been found (Collins, 1937); and large harpoons, probably whaling size, came from a site dated *c.*AD 500 near Deering in the Seward peninsula of Alaska (Bandi, 1969: 102).

Bark models of kayaks and *umiaks* dated to AD 500–900 have been excavated from Point Barrow in northern Alaska. The kayaks have rounded bottoms and flared sides, whilst the *umiaks* have flat bottoms. Bird darts and seal darts and a short waterproof hooded jacket of gutskin, which could have been used to seal a man into a kayak cockpit, were also found. From the early Punuk phase of *c.* AD 600–900 come two ivory

Fig. 11.24. The fourteenth/
fifteenth-century framework
of a Greenland *umiak* found
in 1949 (Danish National
Museum).

models of a hooded man in a kayak with paired seal-skin floats, excavated from a mound near Gamball on St Lawrence island (Arima, 1975: 238–9).

The Thule culture, which began in *c.* AD 900 in Alaska during the late Punuk phase of the Bering Strait region, had spread eastwards to east Greenland before AD 1100. This is the culture that the sixteenth-century Europeans encountered in the Arctic and it was the precursor of the late nineteenth/early twentieth-century culture which has been documented ethnographically (Arima, 1975; Zimmerley, 1980). From the early phase of Thule there is further archaeological evidence for both kayaks and *umiaks* (Arima, 1975: 240–2). From north-west Hudson Bay, Southampton island, north Baffin island and north-west Greenland have come engravings on artefacts, wooden models, and fragments of boats such as a harpoon rest, a top stringer, and a cockpit coaming fragment of baleen. An engraving on a bow-drill handle from the Pond Inlet site shows a *umiak* and a kayak approaching two whales. On the other side of the handle a caribou in the water faces three kayaks, whilst there are five tents in the background, undoubtedly the depiction of a summer hunting camp at a caribou crossing.

In 1949 Egil Knuth found the greater part of a *umiak* framework on the beach at Herlufsholm in northern Greenland (Fig. 11.24). The framework which was *c.*11 m in length had many of the characteristics of the nineteenth-/twentieth-centuries *umiak*, but it has been dated by radiocarbon to (K-352) the fourteenth/fifteenth century AD (Johnstone, 1988: 221; Knuth, 1980: 18; Bandi, 1964: 168).

Arima (1975: 242–4) considers that this archaeological evidence from 2000 BC onwards, shows that, throughout Arctic and sub-Arctic Canada, the kayak and the *umiak* had very similar characteristics with some local differentiation in detail. There was also a continuity in time, as well as space, with some features of both kayaks and *umiaks* continuing in use for several centuries, possibly for 1,000 years or more. It would thus seem that the kayak and the *umiak* attained their optimum design during the early first millennium AD, or possibly earlier. They retained these characteristics into recent times, with some minor changes, because they near-perfectly matched both the environment in which they were used and the function which they were required to fulfil.

## 11.4.6 LOGBOATS

On his first voyage to the Caribbean in 1492, Columbus found that logboats of great size were widely used (Ife, 1990). Some were as long as a 'galley of 15 benches', i.e. *c*.50 ft (15 m). None had sails, but were propelled by paddles. Their breadth was not as great as that of a European planked galley of comparable length as they were limited by the diameter of the parent log, sizeable though these cedars were (Thompson, 1951: 70–1). Nevertheless, if there was room to accommodate two paddlers abreast they would have had a minimum beam of *c*.4 ft (1.22 m), and a maximum at the stern, if one allows for the natural taper of the log, of *c*.6 ft (1.8 m). On his second voyage, Columbus recorded an even larger logboat, some 96 ft (29 m) long and 8 ft (2.5 m) in breadth (McKusick, 1960: 7). If true, such a boat would have been over twice the size in length and breadth of the Hasholme boat, one of the largest of the British prehistoric logboats (5.3.1.5). With such beam measurements these large Caribbean logboats, unlike those in Europe, would have had adequate stability for use on inter-island voyages, as indeed they were used. A pamphlet published soon after Columbus' second voyage (Roberts and Shackleton, 1983: 16–18) states that the larger logboats had a washstrake fastened on each side. These would have given the boats the extra freeboard they needed for seagoing.

Logboats were also seen during the early sixteenth century in the coastal waters and rivers of most of the countries bordering the Caribbean Sea and the Gulf of Mexico: Florida, Mexico, Honduras, Panama, and Columbia (C. Edwards, 1965: 35–7); Thompson, 1951: 69–72; Durham, 1955: 34; Quinn and Quinn, 1973: 6; Johnstone, 1988: 234–5). Several of these boats were under sail, but the details of their rig and their abilities relative to the wind were not documented.

On his fourth voyage in 1502, Columbus encountered a large cargo-carrying logboat off Honduras, which was some 8 ft (2.44 m) in beam and propelled by twenty-four paddlers. She had a palm-leaf awning amidships and carried cargo and passengers (Leshikar, 1988: 16–18). Thompson (1951; 1964) has suggested, from the cargo she was carrying, that her route was probably from the Aztec entrepôt at Xicalango in the Bay of Campech, Mexico, around the Yucatan peninsula to the River Ulua in Honduras. This route was probably one section of a much longer coastal route along the eastern coast of Central America, from north of Mexico City to the Panama/Colombia border (Hammond, 1981); there may well have been another branch through the Antilles, from Cuba to Trinidad. Leshikar (1988: 22) has suggested that Mayan shrines and watch towers along the Yucatan coast were where beacons were lighted to guide this coastal trade at night and in conditions of poor visibility.

Excavations during the 1970s at Moho Cay and Wild Cane Cay, islands off the Belize coast, and the island of Cozumel off the east coast of Yucatan, revealed a trade in such goods as obsidian, metalwork, and pottery during the period *c*. AD 400–900, the Classic and Late-Classic Mayan phases, thus confirming the existence of at least part of this coastal trade route in pre-Columbian times. Engravings on bones from Guatemala and models from Belize dated to *c*. AD 700 tend to suggest that this earlier trade was also undertaken in logboats (Hammond, 1981). The excavation of traded goods from inland sites in this densely forested part of central America suggests that this was a combined riverine and coastal route.

Further north, in Mexico, a boat model carved from jade from Vera Cruz (Leshikar, 1988: fig. 19) suggests that the Olmecs of the Gulf coast had logboats. Written sources (e.g. the Codex Mendoza) show that the Aztecs also used boats, especially in and around their city of *Tenochtitlan* (now Mexico City) which was built on several islands and from which they controlled the Valley of Mexico. Some of these boats may have been logboats since two stone carvings on a temple in *Tenochtitlan* appear to depict punt-shaped logboats as well as representations of a fish spear and a paddle. A similarly shaped logboat measuring 5.31 × 0.61 × 0.36 m was excavated from a site in Mexico City in 1959: this is not yet dated, but there is a strong possibility that it is of pre-Columbian date (Leshikar, 1988: 25–6). Such sizes of logboat would have been useful for transporting men and materials needed to build the many Aztec dykes, dams, bridges, causeways, canals, and floating gardens. They could also have been used for riverine trade as described in the Codex Mendoza, for fishing and as ferries, and possibly for war as shown on an illustration of 1521 depicting Aztecs, in what may be logboats, fighting the invading Spaniards (Leshikar, 1988: 25–6).

Logboats were also encountered on inland waters in the sixteenth century outside this Central American region in Ecuador, on the River Mississippi, in North

Carolina and Virginia (Leshikar, 1988: 17); on the north and east coast of South America, and on the great rivers Orinoco, Amazon, and de la Plata. In recent years, logboats have been excavated (most of them in a non-archaeological way) from sites in Ontario, Quebec, Wisconsin, Michigan, Lake Eerie, New Brunswick, Vermont, Ohio, Kentucky, North and South Carolina, Georgia, Alabama, Mississippi, Louisiana, Florida, and possibly Texas (Plane, 1991; Leshikar, 1988: 17; Waugh, 1919, 30). They have usually been of cypress (*Cupressus* spp.) or pine (*Pinus* sp.)—but one from Lake Eerie of *c.*1600 BC and one from Lake Savannah, Ohio of *c.*1500 BC, are of white oak (*Quercus alba*). The oldest boat, from De Leon Spring, Florida, is dated *c.*5120 BC (Engelbrecht and Seyfert, 1994: 222); the most recent a pine (*Pinus strobus*) logboat from the Tyendinaga Indian Reserve, Ontario, *c.* AD.1500 (S-1724). Taken with the evidence from Central and South America, this distribution shows that logboats were used within a large zone on the eastern side of North America: from the Great Lakes to the Mississippi and Florida; within the Gulf of Mexico and the Caribbean Sea; and in northern and eastern South America. The logboats of Peru and Chile on the west coast seem not to be indigenous but to have been introduced there by the Spaniards (C. Edwards, 1965: 108).

Although many of the accounts of early European encounters with indigenous logboats give no details, two or three provide valuable information about how these boats were built and used. For example, Thomas Harriot (1590) described Virginian logboat building in 1548. The chosen tree was felled by burning through the bole just above the roots (wet moss was probably used to prevent the fire spreading). The crown of the tree was then burnt off and the log laid on simple stocks where the bark was removed and the log hollowed by alternately burning and scraping with shells sharpened on a sandstone (Fig. 11.25). In Virginia and in North Carolina these boats were used mainly for fishing in shallow waters. They were propelled by paddles, sometimes with the paddlers standing to their task (Fig. 11.26) (Quinn, 1973: 6; Waugh, 1919: 32; C. Edwards, 1965: 3, 7, 104).

T. de la Vega described how logboats were used on the River Mississippi in the sixteenth century. The smaller ones (*c.*10 m in length) had twenty-eight paddlers who were stationed two abreast, so they must have been at least 1.00 m broad. The larger ones appear to have been used for warring raids: they held fifty paddlers and twenty-five to thirty warriors and so must have been of the order of 25 m. in length. De la Vega recorded that the paddlers kept time by chanting, and that they could propel their boats as fast as a horse at full speed, say, 8–12 miles an hour.

Fig. 11.25. A late sixteenth-century drawing of logboat building in Virginia (de Bry, 1619: plate 21).

Fig. 11.26. A Virginian logboat under paddles (de Bry, 1619: plate 22).

## 11.4.6.1 SEAGOING LOGBOATS

In addition to the Caribbean logboats seen by Columbus (11.4.6), logboats were also used at sea in the British Columbia/Washington state region. This region included the River Columbia in Washington state, the River Fraser in British Columbia, and the archipelago of islands in the Strait of Georgia and Puget Sound. Logboats were first noted by Cook, and were drawn by Weber in 1778 (Rienits and Rienits, 1968: 140). These boats belonged to the Haida Indians of Queen Charlotte island, off British Columbia, and Prince of Wales island, off southen Alaska, the Nootka Indians of Vancouver island, and the Wishram, Kwakiutls, and Tlingit Indians of the region between. These people lived on an abundance of marine resources including whales, seals, sea lions, sea otters, seabirds and fish, especially the river salmon, but also sea fish such as halibut and cod (G. Clark, 1977: 385; Madsen, 1985; Waugh, 1919; Durham, 1955). Excavations at the Five Miles Rapids site, near the confluences of the River Deschutes and River John Day with the River Columbia, show that it had been an important salmon-catching station as early as the eighth millennium BC (G. Clark, 1977: 385). Similar sites have been identified in the lower reaches of the River Fraser.

The logboats used for this fishing and hunting in historic times were made from the red cedar (*Cedrela odorata*), and they varied in size from small ones suitable for one man, to large seagoing ones up to 18 m (60 ft) in length. The most seaworthy were 9–11 m (30–5 ft) in length, and were used by the Nootka as whale-hunting boats (Fig. 11.27). European seamen such as Captain Cook were impressed by the seaworthiness of such boats and the seamanship of their crew (Roberts and Shackleton, 1983: 97–118).

The cedar logs (sometimes half-logs) were hollowed using stone tools and fire, and given a flattish bottom with flared sides. End pieces were lashed or fastened by mortises to seagoing boats giving them a distinctive rising sheerline at bow and stern (Fig. 11.27). In recent times, when logs of the minimum diameter (*c*.2 m) to ensure adequate transverse stability at sea were no longer available, the hollowed log was expanded to give a greater beam at the waterline. The hollow was first filled with water which was then heated by hot stones; when the timber had become sufficiently malleable, the sides were gently forced apart and framing timbers were inserted to ensure the boat retained this expanded shape when it cooled. This technique has been used in many parts of the world (5.3.1.6.1, 6.6.6, 8.3.4): Finland, Estonia, India, Burma, Siam (McGrail,

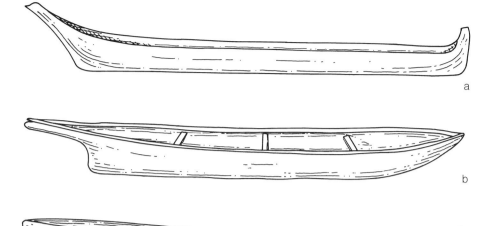

Fig. 11.27. Logboats of north-western America.
(a): offshore Nootka boat;
(b): offshore Salish boat;
(c): riverine Salish boat.
Not to the same scale
(after Waugh, 1919).

1998: 66–70); it was also used in recent times in Guyana, Brazil, Tierra del Fuego, and Alaska in the Americas (McGrail, 1978: i.38–9). The procedures used vary in detail but in all of them the stage of forcing out the sides the final few degrees is the most critical: Hurault (1970: 65) has noted that one in every four or five logboats built by twentieth-century Guyanans burst during expansion and became unusable.

Expansion is well worth the effort since a much beamier boat is obtained: Bidault (1945: 175) quoted an expansion from 0.9 to 1.5 m beam (67 per cent increase); whilst Hurault (1970: figs. 24–40) recorded a change in beam measurement from 0.31 m to 0.67 m (116 per cent increase) Such increases in waterline beam give the boat sufficient stability to be used at sea (McGrail, 1978: ii, fig. 187). The process of expansion also causes the ends of the boat to rise, thus giving it a rising sheerline; the height of sides over the midships region is also invariably reduced—for example, in the case of the Guyana logboat recorded by Hurault this change was from 0.48 m to 0.24 m (50 per cent). If the new height of side results in insufficient freeboard, washstrakes may be added. Roberts and Shackleton (1983: 103) have noted that the Nootka avoid having to add washstrakes by shaping the hollowed log before expansion with a hogged 'keel line' and sheerline. After expansion, the bottom and the sides of the boat became nearly horizontal.

The last recorded whale hunt in Nootka logboats was in 1908 (Madsen, 1985). In those days, two or three boats were used, each one having a steersman and six paddlers, with a harpooner in the bow. The traditional harpoon had a 5 m yew shaft with a head consisting of a point made from a large seashell, and barbs from moose antlers which were stuck to the shaft with resin and bound with whale sinew. The line consisted of 1,000 m or so of rope made from the *bast* (inner bark) of the thuja, and spaced out on it were floats of inflated seal skins which slowed down the harpooned whale and also enabled the whalers to trace the whale's progress through the water.

The transverse stability of logboats built from logs of small diameter, can be increased (hence their potential for seagoing improved) without recourse to expansion. Hornell (1928) recorded in the early years of this century a class of logboat in Charca, Colombia, and off the nearby island of Gorgona, which had a balsa log lashed to each side at the waterline. Similar boats had been drawn by Admiral Paris in Valparaiso, Chile (Fig. 11.28). These stabilizers effectively increase the logboat's beam, hence stability.

## 11.4.7 SEWN-PLANK BOATS

### 11.4.7.1 THE CHILEAN DALCA

Sewn-plank boats were first encountered in South America during de Ulloa's 1553 expedition along the coast and among the islands north of the bark-boat region: that is, from *c*.47°S near the Gulf of Penas, northwards through the Chonos archipelago to *c.*42° 30′S in the Gulf of Coranados, north of the island of Chiloé (C. Edwards, 1965: 25-30, 103, 124; Heizer, 1938; 1966; Lothrop, 1932). In 1558, fifty of these *dalca* were commandeered by a Spanish expedition and used to cross the Chacao channel to invade the island of Chiloé (C. Edwards, 1965: 25). From these early accounts we learn that these boats were built from three planks: a long thick central bottom plank which gave rising ends to this double-ended boat; and two side planks which converged towards the ends, giving a shape which was similar to that of the bark boats further south but somewhat broader at the ends. Whether these early boats had stem or stern posts is not mentioned in these early accounts, but later boats appear not to have had them, instead the bottom plank continued up to, and sometimes beyond the sheerline, and the ends of the side planks were fastened to it. The *dalcas* described by Alonso de Góngara Marmolejo in 1560 were 30–40 ft (9–12 m) in length and about 3 ft (0.9 m) broad amidships.

The plank seams were coated with a caulking of the inner bark of the *maqui* tree (*Aristolelia maqui*), or of leaves of the *tiaca* (*Caldeluvia paniculata*), or of grass rolls, or sometimes of a herb and clay mixture, and the planks were then sewn together over a longitudinal split-cane batten. The sewing material was not noted at that time, but later *dalcas* are said to have been sewn with bamboo (*Chusquea coley*). The timber used for the earliest known *dalca* is also unknown but Lothrop (1932) has shown that it was probably larch (*Fitzroya patagonica*), cypress (*Libocedrus tetragona*), or beech (*Nothofagus betuloides*). The tools used were of stone or shell, and wooden wedges were used to split the planking from the log (Lothrop, 1932: 244–5).

The only framework in these boats appears to have been transverse roundwood timbers used as thwarts. *Dalcas* were propelled by single-bladed paddles, and Lothrop (1932: 245) has estimated that they could carry nine to eleven men.

In 1675/6, Antonio de Vea requisitioned nine *dalcas* from the island of Chiloé and modified them for use under oars by strengthening the top edge of the sides and adding wide thwarts. Antonio de Vea also dismantled several *dalcas* and carried them in pieces across the isthmus of Ofqui so that he could use them further south. C. Edwards (1965: 26) thinks that this may reflect contemporary Indian practice. Portages using bottom runners (Heizer, 1966: 24) may also have been undertaken. The stitching in the *dalca* is above any part that might touch the ground: boats could thus readily be dragged over portage tracks or up beaches without damage to the plank fastenings.

By the time of Antonio de Córdoba's voyage in

Fig. 11.28. An early nineteenth-century extended logboat with stabilizers (Paris, 1843: plate 130).

1788–9, to survey the Strait of Magellan, many European features had been incorporated into the *dalca*, including floor timbers (C. Edwards, 1965: 26–7), and five-plank and then seven-plank *dalcas* were built.

However, the features which did not change were the use of sewn fastenings and the materials used for caulking. The last *dalca* (with many European innovations) in use in the Chiloé region was recorded in *c*.1900. Under European influence the use of the *dalca* had spread southwards along the coast of Chile, and Mrs Brassey (1878: 133), cruising in *Sunbeam*, saw one in English Reach in the Magellan Strait in the mid-1870s. The very last *dalca* of South America was seen in the Magellan Strait in 1915 (C. Edwards, 1965: 30).

## 11.4.7.2 THE CHUMASH *TOMOL*

In the waters of the Santa Barbara channel, north of Los Angeles, from Point Conception in the north (34°50′N) to Point Mugu to the south-east (34°N), the Chumash Indians used a sewn-plank boat known as the *tomol* or *tomolo* (Heizer, 1938; 1966; Kroeber, 1925: 812; Hudson, Timbrook, and Rempe, 1978). The narrow strip of coastal land settled by the Chumash had a mountainous hinterland, but its inshore waters were protected by a string of islands to the south and west, including Santa Barbara, Santa Rosa, and San Miguel. The *tomol* was used for fishing in these waters and also in the open sea (Davenport, Johnson, and Timbrook 1993).

This type of boat was first encountered by Juan Cabrillo in 1542 near Santa Catalina island and was described by Sebastian Vizcaino in 1602 as being made of cedar and pine and having a crew of fourteen or fifteen, including eight paddlers (Heizer, 1938: 194). Other sewn boats encountered on this voyage were described as being paddled 'so swiftly that they seemed to fly'. A further sewn boat was said to be 'so well constructed and built that since Noah's Ark a finer and lighter vessel with timbers better made has not been seen'. Other features singled out for mentioning were that the paddles had a blade at each end; and that the boats were higher at the ends than amidships. *Tomol* used for fishing usually had two paddlers, stationed near each end so that they could paddle on both sides alternately, and a boy was stationed amidships to bail out the boat.

It is not until the late eighteenth century that more details of construction were noted, and by this time the Chumash Indians had been subjected to European influence for over 200 years; they were rapidly Hispanicized soon after the Christian missions appeared (Heizer, 1966). One of the most detailed accounts was written by Father Pedro Font in 1776 and this, and other accounts, seem to show that, notwithstanding their Hispanicization, they had adopted few, if any, European techniques in boatbuilding—for example, they were using 'no other tools than their shells and flints' (Heizer, 1938: 198). The *tomol* in the late eighteenth century was built of twenty or more long and narrow planks joined at the seams by deer-sinew lashings which were then waterproofed with pitch. These boats had no ribs and only one transverse timber which was near amidships where it preserved the shape of the boat and acted as a thwart. The ends were pointed and higher than amidships. All the boats were painted red with haematite, and some of them were decorated with shells.

One *tomol* measured by Father Font, 'was 36 palms long and somewhat more than three palms high': Heizer (1938: 198) translates this as 24–6 ft by 2–3 ft which must be based on a 'handspan' of eight inches rather than a palm of the usual four inches. These late eighteenth-century *tomolos* were propelled in the manner first noted in the sixteenth century, by one man near each end of the boat with a double-bladed paddle. They were used for fishing and could be taken, 'through rough seas with much boldness', and they were so light that ten or twelve men could carry a boat loaded with fish on their shoulders (Heizer, 1938: 212).

*Tomol* boats measured during Gaspar de Portola's overland expedition in 1769–70 were seven to eight *vara* (5.2–6.7 m) in length and one to one and a-half *vara* in breadth (0.91–1.20 m). It was noted that the sewing was payed with bitumen which was readily available from nearby surface springs (Heizer, 1938: 195). Father Juan Crespi, who was on this expedition, recorded that these boats were so light that two men could launch boats of 20–24 ft (6–7 m) in length.

In 1793, A. Menzies, the naturalist on Captain Vancouver's voyage to the west coast, recorded that *tomol* of the Santa Barbara channel measured about 12–18 ft in length by 4 ft wide amidships (3.7–5.5 × 1.2 m), and that the double-bladed paddles were about half the length of the boat. In addition to confirming many of the features mentioned by Father Font, Menzies stated that the planking was sewn with 'thongs and sinews

Fig. 11.29. *Helek*: a reconstruction sewn plank *tomol*, built in 1976 (Museum of Natural History, Santa Barbara).

and glewed so close as to be quite watertight and preserve its shape as well as if it had been made of one piece', and he noted that these boats could carry a crew of up to six (Heizer, 1938: 200).

The little archaeological evidence there is for the *tomol* was reviewed by Heizer (1938: 203–5), but this evidence cannot bear the weight of the conclusions Heizer drew from it as the excavations were poorly documented and there was no precise dating.

The *tomol* appears to have continued in use in this region of the Santa Barbara channel until the 1860s, possibly by then influenced by European techniques. Even at this late date it was not fully documented. However, in the early twentieth century, J. P. Harrington interviewed elderly Chumash Indians and compiled a mass of notes on the *tomol*. These notes were recently edited and published by the Santa Barbara Museum of Natural History (Hudson, Timbrook, and Rempe, 1978) in a book which includes a further review of the archaeological evidence. The editors undertook an extremely difficult task as Harrington's notes were disorganized, repetitive, contradictory, and incomplete. Nevertheless, they seem to have produced a reasonably accurate account of the late nineteenth-century *tomol* which, in general, reinforces the picture of the 'first contact' *tomol* compiled from European accounts.

Two recently built *tomolo* are described in this Santa Barbara publication: one which Harrington had built in *c*.1914 known as the '*Highland* replica'; and one called *Helek* built in 1976 (Fig. 11.29). This account casts doubt on the archaeological evidence as some of the fragments previously thought to be from ancient *tomol* now seem to have been taken from the *Highland* replica (Hudson, Timbrook, and Rempe, 1978: 26, 56, 101–2).

In the early twentieth century tools used to build *tomolos* included: clam-shell adze and chisels; a sharpened bone or flint as an auger; a shell scraper and dried sharkskin to smooth the planking. The planking was first 'glued' together with *yop*, a hot mixture of bitumen (*wogo*) and pine pitch; then it was sewn together with *tok*, a string of red milkweed fibre. The seams were then caulked with *yop*.

The knowledge of early *tomol* gained from the accounts of sixteenth- to eighteenth-centuries explorers, although incomplete, does present a picture of a seagoing plank boat which matched a particular function—fishing and communications with offshore islands—in a particular operational environment of inshore waters protected by a chain of islands. They were built from readily obtainable timber, possibly some of it driftwood, and the local supply of natural bitumen on which the water-tightness of the boat was dependent. This was a boat in tune with its environment, natural and technological. The local topography, the local source of bitumen, and a supply of driftwood may not only have stimulated the original formulation of the idea of a sewn-plank boat, but may also have ensured that the idea did not subsequently spread outside this c.100 miles coastal zone: the coastal waters north and south of the Santa Barbara channel were not protected by offshore islands, and the people living there did not have such ready access to the indispensable bitumen.

# II.5
# America's Earliest Water Transport

The general picture that emerges from the evidence considered in this chapter is that, at the time of European 'first contact' with the Americas in the late fifteenth century AD, a wide range of water transport was used on rivers, lakes, and coastal waters. Owing to the enormous range of latitude encompassed by the Americas, from c.85°N to c.55°S, there is a wide range of raw materials and of operating environments, thus similar types of water transport had been developed at widely separated locations. For example, hide boats were used not only in the Arctic regions and adjacent waters (Fig. 11.13) but also on the inland waters of the Great Plains of North America around 30°–40°N, and in much of South America between 10°N and 35°S. Bark boats were in use throughout a vast area of North America, extending almost across the continent from c.60°–45°N in the west and to c.35°N in the east (Fig. 11.13); but also in Guyana on the north-east coast of South America, on the River Amazon in Brazil, and in southern Chile as far south as Tierra del Fuego.

Given that the Americas were peopled from northwest towards the east and south over a period of millennia, and that outside influences of any significance seem to be most unlikely before the late fifteenth century, the discontinuity in these distributions suggests that, as Man progressed southwards, types of water transport were conceived to match the available raw materials and the differing aquatic environments. For example, simple hide boats, which may well have been used in the earliest movements southwards from Alaska (11.1), probably left a relict population in the Great Plains of North America and in the Amazon basin of South America. When the time came to explore and exploit the Arctic rivers and seas, say, in the third millennium BC, the complex hide boat was brought to perfection.

As far as can be deduced from inadequate 'first contact' reports, the bark boats of southern Chile, although generally similar in structure to those of the North American Indians, were not comparable in performance with the more specialized of the northern types. The bark boats of the north-east of South America were of a very simple kind and were used only on inland waters. The hide boats of the Plains Indians and of the inland South American Indians although, again, recognizably of the same general type, were much less developed structurally and scarcely comparable in performance with those of the northern and Arctic regions. When compared with hide boats and bark boats around the world, the boats of North America are amongst the very best, being seagoing and having high performance within their individual functional, operational, and environmental boundaries. Perhaps the only boats of comparable excellence have been the hide boats of north-west Europe (5.3.3), and the recent hide boats (and possibly the bark boats) of Arctic Siberia which are, in fact, part of the same circumpolar culture as Arctic North America. The other American hide and bark boats, used only on inland water, were much simpler in structure and were restricted in their achievements. Nevertheless, they have analogs in some parts of the world: for example, Mongolian hide boats and Australian bark boats.

The logboat distribution is less clear than that of hide and bark boats as it is not certain that all of the first sighting reports—some of them as late as the mid-nineteenth century—can be taken to reflect the pre-Columbian distribution: it is especially important to be aware of this as some scholars (for example, C. Edwards, 1965: 110) consider that the Spaniards introduced logboats into Peru and Chile. Nevertheless there appear to be two distinct groups: those of the west coast of North America, from southern Alaska to northern California, the biggest and best of which were seagoing; and those of the east and south, from the region of the eastern Great Lakes south to Florida and Louisiana, and the coastlands and islands of the Gulf of Mexico and the Caribbean Sea, the north-east coast of South America from Guatemala to Guyana, in the two great east coast rivers, Amazon and del Plata, and in Colombia and northern Ecuador on the west coast. Where very large trees were available (to give breadth of boat, hence inherent stability), and where other environmental conditions were right, this form of water transport was also taken to the limits of excellence in the seagoing logboats of the Nootka and Haida Indians of the British Columbia / California region, and those of the Caribbean.

The distribution of rafts is generally limited to the western coast in a zone between 40°N and 40°S, although some were also used on rivers inland from this coastal region. Bundle rafts, mainly of reeds or rushes, but some of palm leaves, were used on the west coast and on inland waters from California to northern Chile. Buoyed rafts, with hide floats at sea and gourds inland, were used in the southern parts of this region but not north of Mexico. Log rafts, on the other hand, were not only used on the west coast at sea, and on the greater rivers between British Columbia and northern Chile, but also in Brazilian waters and possibly in the Caribbean.

Whenever and howsoever Man first entered the Americas (11.1), there would have been no discontinuity, no significant change in the general environment and in the raw materials available between eastern Siberia and western Alaska. Whether this initial colonization was over a land 'corridor' or across a strait, some form of water transport would have been needed: simple hide boats and lografts would probably have sufficed, if overland; complex hide boats would have been needed for a sea crossing.

From that time onwards as the climatic conditions ameliorated and as different environments were encountered in the migrations south and east from Alaska, a range of rafts and boats was developed which paralleled achievements elsewhere in the world. There is a possibility that ideas for different types of water transport could have spread from Asia to America via 'Beringia' or across the Bering Strait, but apart from improvements and embellishments to the hide boats of the Arctic and sub-Arctic (possibly a two-way flow of ideas), this seems unlikely. The probability is that the rafts and boats of the Americas were developed independently, sometimes more than once, as the need arose, as the environment permitted, as raw materials facilitated, and as and when human ingenuity and technological competence determined.

## 11.5.1  NAUTICAL ACHIEVEMENTS

In certain regions of the Americas where raw materials of extraordinary quality were available, types of raft and boat which harmonized well with their operating environment, and the function required of them, were developed to rival any produced elsewhere in the world. Thus we see the seagoing logboats of the northwest, and of the Caribbean; the bark boats of North America; the Arctic hide boats; the seagoing log rafts with their *guares*; and the bundle rafts of the Pacific coast. A distinctive craft which in some ways is unique, is the float raft from Peru and Chile. Another probably unique feature is the early use of double-bladed paddles on the kayak, the *tomol* sewn-plank boat, and on buoyed rafts (11.4.3.1., 11.4.5.4, 11.4.7.2). Although some scholars have had doubts, the sail was almost certainly used in American waters in pre-Columbian times.

The major surprising feature of the early American scene is the relatively insignificant position of the plank boat: two small groups of sewn-plank boat, the *dalca* and the *tomol*, in widely separated places on the western seaboard off southern Chile and off southern California. In general it appears that economic and social requirements throughout pre-Columbian America could be satisfied by rafts and non-plank boats and it was only in very restricted zones where there were special circumstances that plank boats (small ones) were built.

If Europeans had not arrived in the fifteenth century and if American economic, political, and social life had developed, as in other parts of the world, to the point where large seagoing vessels were required, in the search for new sources of raw materials and for long-range trade other than could be undertaken in their coastal log rafts and logboats (11.4.1, 11.4.6), it is of some interest to speculate how indigenous American boat-builders would have responded to the challenge to build *ships*, which as far as is known can only be built from wooden planks (at least until the advent of the metal ship). Would the coastlands of southern Chile and parts of southern California have become centres of innovation? Or were these two regions so marginalized, self-sufficient and in such a stable symbiotic relationship with the environment that the stimulus for bigger and more seaworthy *dalca* and / or *tomol* (leading to ships) would never have arisen there?

# 12

# EARLY WATER TRANSPORT

## 12.1

## The State of Research

### 12.1.1 THE EXCAVATED EVIDENCE

The direct evidence for early water transport is both sparse and late in date: worldwide, there are only a few hundred logboats and, perhaps, a hundred well-documented plank boat and ship remains from before AD 1500. The earliest logboat is dated to the eighth millennium BC; the earliest plank boat to the third millennium. There are no excavated examples of the other five basic types of boat (hide, bark, bundle, basket, and pottery); no bundle or buoyed rafts; and only five documented log rafts—the earliest from Roman times. Clearly there is much missing, especially from the earlier periods, since there is indirect evidence for the use of water transport at sea from at least 40,000 BC, and it is likely to have been used on inland waters from much earlier times.

The virtual absence from the archaeological record of rafts and of non-plank boats, other than those made from logs, is especially to be regretted since these are likely to have been the craft used in earliest times about which we know least. This absence is not merely due to non-recognition of vestigial remains of such water transport (although that must have played its part): rafts and the simpler forms of boat may never enter the archaeological record in identifiable form. In recent times—and probably for centuries past—buoyed rafts built in the Arabian and Chinese uplands were taken apart after a single voyage downstream and the timber sold (3.4.5, 10.2.4). Hide boats were similarly disman-

tled in fifth-century BC Mesopotamia (Herodotus, 1. 194) and in early twentieth-century Tamil Nadu (Deloche, 1994: 139). When twentieth-century Arabian bundle rafts became irreversibly waterlogged they were used as building material or for fuel.

Plank boats are also dismantled and reused. When medieval European boats and ships were no longer usable afloat, their planking and their framing timbers were used to embank rivers or to build waterfront structures: log rafts and simple forms of plank boat were, no doubt, similarly reused in prehistoric times. Sometimes medieval remains of reused boat timbers have been recognized, recorded, and published (Milne and Hobley, 1981; A. E. Christensen, 1985; Herteig, 1985; McGrail, 1993b; Marsden, 1994, 1996), but undoubtedly much has been lost. Flat-bottomed boats, poorly represented in excavation reports, are especially likely to be reused as they are built mainly of straight planking. Since such planks have few distinctive features, their nautical origins can easily be lost for ever (Greenhill, 1995a: 188–9).

Our knowledge of early water transport is thus very incomplete, with only four or five examples worldwide of groups of vessels ('traditions') that we can claim to be able to understand and can describe in any detail. Our knowledge is also very much biased towards planked boats and ships. It is also biased towards Europe.

At the present time, the overwhelming majority of documented boat and ship remains are from only three regions: Egypt, the central and eastern Mediterranean, and the north-western waters of Atlantic Europe. Some early boats have been excavated in the south-east Asian region, and there are a dozen or so medieval ships from south east Asian and Chinese waters. In the

Americas, pre-European logboats are known, and there is fragmentary evidence for hide boats in the Arctic north. Both south Asia and Oceania have only one find of any consequence. Arabia and Australia appear to have none. Overall, the evidence is thus overwhelmingly from Europe.

This very obvious bias is reflected in the relative lengths of the regional chapters in this study. Different resources and different research standards compound this bias, as does differential survival; with the result that it is not yet possible to compile a balanced, comprehensive, worldwide view of the subject. It is also questionable whether, even within relatively well-endowed Europe, the small group of boats that are well documented fully represents the ancient range of types, sizes and functions (Crumlin- Pedersen, 1983*b*: 6; 1997*b*: 185).

Outside Europe, low rates of discovery and excavation of ancient water transport are probably at least partly due to non-recognition of the importance of boat and ship remains. Moreover, the resources that nations allocate to research and training in the excavation, conservation, display, and publication of ancient boats and ships vary greatly from region to region: the worldwide sum is clearly inadequate. Furthermore, the full potential of many of the wrecks that have been uncovered, worldwide, has not been realized; this is mainly due to inadequate resources and know-how: examples of such projects can be found in several chapters of this study. Steffy (1995*a*: 423) recently noted that, of twenty-seven Mediterranean wrecks he investigated in a desk-based study, '. . . few had been recorded well enough to permit a complete analysis of the hull structure'. This is a clear illustration of the generally low standards of research on underwater wreck sites that obtained until recent times.

## 12.1.2 TARGETED RESEARCH

Only a few research units are capable of pursuing ancient boat investigations consistently and rigorously through all the stages of a research programme from pre-excavation research to publication, and on further to reassessment, as shown in Figures 1.2 and 1.3.

The research centres at Roskilde, Denmark, and Bodrum, Turkey, have led the way in selecting specific sites for research, so that answers may be sought to questions about selected types of vessel, and about certain periods of time. Further excavations are now needed to determine the full range of variability within the apparent near-uniformity of both the Nordic tradition during the Viking age, and the Mediterranean 'mortise and tenon' tradition during the Classical period. Other excavations in Europe should be aimed at clarifying understanding of: sewn-plank boats; the Romano-Celtic tradition; the pre-Classical phase in the Mediterranean; and the change from plank-first to frame-first in both Atlantic Europe and in the Mediterranean. Comparable programmes of research need to be undertaken outside Europe wherever resources and expertise are available.

## 12.1.3 ETHNOGRAPHIC RESEARCH

There are other regions of the world, however, where it is not yet possible to pursue such a systematic programme of archaeological research. Indeed, in many places, resources are such that chance finds of water transport cannot be dealt with adequately, either in the physical care of remains, or in their scholarly publication. The best course in these circumstances is probably to undertake research which does not involve excavation. Traditional rafts and boats, propelled by muscle power or sail, are still widely used in those regions, but are being rapidly replaced by plastic craft with engines. These traditional craft should be documented in an ethnographic manner as an element of life in the early twenty-first century. Such documentation can then become the basis for research backward in time into the history of water transport in each region, using documentary and iconographic sources. The results of these investigations, together with environmental research into past climates, sea levels, river courses and coastlines, may then lead to surveys of estuary regions and former river beds. In this way, the experience and the infrastructure needed to tackle an ancient boat project may be accumulated, perhaps leading, in the fullness of time, to a research excavation of early water transport.

Archaeologists and others who undertake the documentation of traditional boats and their uses, as suggested above, should gain from such work an understanding of nautical and seafaring matters, boat-building techniques, and the general lifestyle of small-scale, essentially non-industrial maritime communities which will stand them in good stead when the time comes for archaeological research.

## 12.1.4 INTERNATIONAL CO-OPERATION

This study has shown that there are several issues that need to be tackled internationally. Even within one language different terms are used for what are evidently the same, or very similar, artefacts: for example, in English, *treenail*, *peg*, and *dowel*. Furthermore, a single term may have several meanings: to a Scandinavian a 'clenched nail' is one that has had its tip deformed over a rove, as in the Nordic clinker tradition (Fig. 5.50); whereas to someone working on Mediterranean material that term means a nail that has had its tip turned through 180° ('hooked') (Fig. 5.27). An illustrated technical glossary, with agreed terms in several languages, would dispel misunderstanding and increase effectiveness of research.

Standardized terminology is also needed in the naming of wreck sites. Generally, in northern Europe wrecks at the same location are given suffixes '1' to 'n' in the order of their discovery. There are different practices in the Mediterranean and elsewhere, some using alphabetical suffixes rather than numbers, others numbering wrecks in order of their presumed building date rather than in discovery sequence. Furthermore, boat-grave sites with the same place-name identification as nearby wrecks, as at Hedeby near Schleswig (5.8.1), are omitted from the numbering sequence. At Utrecht the earliest boat find has been similarly omitted (5.8.3.2), whilst at Sutton Hoo in East Anglia (5.7.1.3) two buried vessels seem to have been numbered in order of assumed importance (by mound size) rather than discovery.

There are a number of instances in this study where it seems clear that the recording of a find *in situ*, and again during post-excavation research, was not undertaken to internationally acceptable standards. This criticism applies to excavated depictions of water transport as well as to excavated boats and ships. The nearest archaeologist is not necessarily the best person to undertake the excavation, research, and publication

of an important find. Those charged with heritage responsibilities should strive to ensure that the best possible hands and brains work on such sites.

The international forum known as ISBSA (International Symposia on Boat and Ship Archaeology) has, during its twenty-five years of existence, concerned itself mainly with the organization of triennial conferences and the publication of the subsequent proceedings (McGrail, forthcoming b). Perhaps it is now time for ISBSA to become active in the field of international standards and co-operation? By its very nature, maritime archaeology has to be international in its outlook. Topics that need to be tackled on a worldwide basis include:

- increased environmental research, especially into former sea levels, coastlines and weather patterns.
- a scientific dating programme, especially of vessels now in museums.
- the application of rigorous standards to experimental ship and boat projects (Coates *et al.*, 1995).
- the re-examination, by an international team, of representations of boats for which competing interpretations have been proposed: an example is the Thera fresco (4.7.2.2).
- the re-recording, by an international team, of certain boat and ship remains which are not yet fully understood. Examples are: vessels thought to be Romano-Celtic (5.6); vessels said to be cogs (5.8.2); and the medieval ships from south-east Asian and Chinese waters (8.3.5.2; 10.4.2);
- the encouragement of boat and ship archaeological research in countries such as India, once the necessary infrastructure is in place.

## 12.2

# Inter-Regional Comparisons

Notwithstanding that there is bias within the data presented in this study, that some well-documented boats may not be fully representative of their time, and that not all boat finds have been recorded to the highest standards, it can be useful to search the evidence, as it stands now, for similarities and distinctive differences.

## 12.2.1 INVENTION, DIFFUSION, AND EVOLUTION

Similarities may arise by chance, by convergence due to innate human characteristics worldwide, or by the transfer of technology from one culture to another. In this study, several examples have been given of the transfer of technology by raft, boat, and ship: the settlement of new lands such as Greater Australia and Japan before 40,000 BC (7.2; 10.10.1) and that of Oceania from the second millennium BC (9.1); and intrusions into territories already populated, such as Bronze Age voyages between Egypt and *Punt* (2.7.7.1, 2.9.1), those by Phoenicians and Greeks in the Iron Age Mediterranean (4.9), and by the medieval Chinese and Arabs in the Indian Ocean (3.8.1, 10.10.3). As a result of such voyages maritime technological innovations were probably dispersed.

It might be thought that, in the remote past, the idea of building specific types of water transport (log rafts, bundle rafts, or buoyed rafts; boats of logs, planks, bark, hide, pottery, bundle, or basketry) may have originated in a specific place and, from there, spread outwards by virtue of the mobility conferred. This seems unlikely in view of the American experience: the development of a wide range of raft and boat types (11.5) within the Americas over millennia seems clearly to be the result of independent invention. A similar sequence of inventions probably occurred in other regions of the world, reflecting Man's innate ingenuity: as different environments were encountered, as different raw materials became available, and as different functions were required of water transport, so new types of raft and boat were visualized and built whenever the prevailing technology allowed. And these types proved to be remarkably similar throughout the world.

Nevertheless, there was probably a degree of diffusion around centres of innovation. Like the wagon and other forms of land transport, rafts, boats, and ships are their own advertisement: ideas may be transferred from place to place not only by passengers and crew, but also by the vessels themselves: boat-building and boat-handling techniques are there for all to see and to copy.

## 12.2.2 UNIVERSAL SIMILARITIES

### 12.2.2.1 BASIC TYPES OF WATER TRANSPORT

The three basic types of raft and the seven basic types of boat appear almost everywhere in the world. Indeed, two raft types (log and bundle) and four boat types (log, bark, hide, and plank) were probably built and used at an early date in every region of the world, apart from Australia, and even there *some* of these basic types were used. Such a wide distribution is probably due to common solutions to common problems rather than to technological transfer. There is no reason to think, however, that the same development path was taken everywhere. For example, in contradistinction to the rest of the world, the plank boat was used in the Americas on a very limited scale (11.4.7), and coastal trade was undertaken by sailing log rafts or sailing logboats. Furthermore, trees were of such great dimensions that seagoing logboats could be constructed there without recourse to stability-enhancing techniques (11.4.6); the double-bladed paddle seems to have been used there before any other region; and a unique variant of the buoyed raft originated there (11.4.3.1).

It is sometimes suggested that the plank boat may have been developed from another, simpler, form of water transport. There is little evidence for or against this hypothesis. Nevertheless, if such development did take place, there is no reason to suppose that the same process took place in all regions. The idea of building a plank boat could have been based, for example, on the bark boat in the Americas, the bundle raft in Egypt, the log raft in China, the hide boat in Atlantic Europe, and perhaps the logboat in the Baltic.

### 12.2.2.2 NAVIGATIONAL TECHNIQUES

The methods used to navigate when out of sight of land ('non-instrumental' or 'environmental') are also remarkably similar throughout the world. The differences in detail and emphasis between the techniques documented for Oceania (9.5), the China Sea (10.11), the Indian Ocean (3.8.2, 6.3.3.1, 6.4, 6.8), the Mediterranean (4.4.6, 4.9.3.2.1, 4.14.2), and Atlantic Europe (5.2, 5.4.9, 5.6.6, 5.7.3) are mainly due to differences in latitude, and to other aspects of the maritime environment.

### 12.2.2.3 SYMBOLIC USES OF WATER TRANSPORT

Another widespread feature is the symbolic use of water transport. In early Egypt, boats and ships were entombed in pyramids and other burial sites, as were boat models in later times (2.6.1, 2.7.1, 2.8.3, 2.8.4). Boats, and indeed ships, have been widely used as coffins: in south-east Asia, from northern Vietnam to Sarawak and the Philippines (8.3.4); in China (10.2.9); and in Atlantic Europe (5.4.8, 5.7.1.3, 5.7.1.4.1). In medieval Europe, and indeed later, models of boats were frequently hung as offerings in churches and shrines.

### 12.2.3 SPECIFIC SIMILARITIES

#### 12.2.3.1 SIMILARITIES OF FORM

It has sometimes been claimed that certain boats, widely separated in time and space, are 'alike': for example, early twentieth-century Portuguese boats are said to resemble those of ancient Mesopotamia (Filgueiras, 1977) with the implication that this demonstrates early overseas contacts between the two places. Such similarities are almost invariably in terms of shape, especially of the main hull, and this apparent affinity may be explained without having to postulate some prehistoric diffusion of ideas.

Evidence from around the world, some of it presented in this study, suggests that, where there are similar operating environments and similar functional requirements, similar hull shapes are used. Other things being equal, a boat with a rectangular transverse section carries a greater payload than one with a rounded section, but has more resistance to motion; a relatively broad boat has more inherent stability than one that is narrow; overhanging bows are useful for a river ferry, but can be impractical in a sea boat; a flat-bottomed boat can readily take the ground on a foreshore, but a rounded hull with a projecting keel is preferable in a vessel that has to be worked to windward. Thus boatbuilders and boat users in different cultures, seeking efficiency in their boats by modification and experiment, may independently converge towards the use of similar hull shapes. Rather than being due to a specific transfer of technology, most similarities of hull form are probably due to structural, hydrostatic, and hydrodynamic requirements, and our common human ingenuity.

#### 12.2.3.2 PROPULSION BY SAIL

Sails have only rarely been excavated (10.4.2.3), and rigging is only slightly more evident archaeologically. Thus we are almost entirely dependent on iconographic evidence (McGrail, 1996d: 84–9). The earliest representation of a sail, anywhere in the world, is on an Egyptian pot of c.3100 BC (Fig. 2.5). Other representations give a date of c.2000 BC for earliest sail use in the eastern Mediterranean (Fig. 4.16), the late first millennium BC for north-west Europe (Fig. 5.12), and the seventh century AD for the Baltic (5.6.6, 5.7.1.3.1). The corresponding dates east of Egypt are: Arabia, the late third millennium BC (Figs. 3.8, 3.9); India, c.2000 BC (Fig. 6.4); and China, possibly c.1200 BC (Fig. 10.8; 10.2.11.1). Superficially, these dates suggest that the idea of using a sail originated in Egypt, and was subsequently disseminated to the west and to the east. However, Egypt was certainly not the only origin for the use of sail, since early European explorers of the Americas found a range of sail types and rigs in use on rafts and boats on both east and west coasts, from the Arctic to Brazil and Peru (11.3.1). Correspondingly, there may have been several regional origins for the use of sail in the Old World, in addition to Egypt, with some diffusion around each centre of innovation.

#### 12.2.3.3 STEERING BY *GUARES*

Steering and achieving sail balance using *guares* (adjustable, foil-shaped lee-boards) is known widely in the Tropics of south Asia, south-east Asia, China, and the Americas (6.6.3, 8.3.1, 10.2.5, 11.4.1.2). It has been suggested that this trait may have been transferred from region to region by sixteenth- and seventeenth-century Europeans. This seems unlikely, however, since the usage is unknown in Oceania (9.3.4) through which these European explorers sailed on voyages connecting the Atlantic, Pacific, and Indian Oceans. There may have been some, now unknown, diffusion of this practice, but the possibility of independent invention must also be considered.

## 12.2.3.4 FASTENINGS

### 12.2.3.4.1 *Lashed and sewn planking*

Lashed or sewn-plank fastenings are, or have been, used almost worldwide: only Australia is without examples, but boats of sewn bark were used (7.3.4). Plank boats fastened together by individual lashings are known in Atlantic Europe (5.4.5), south-east Asia (8.3.5.1.1), and the Americas (11.4.7), and seem to have been earlier than boats with running sewing. One characteristic common to all types of lashed and sewn fastenings is that, in one way or another, the stitches/lashings in the lower hull are protected so that they are not damaged when the boat takes the ground. Another widespread feature is the association of both techniques with lashed framing. This is not now a universal association, but may once have been.

In Egypt (2.7.1, 2.8.3.2), the Mediterranean (4.9.4), the Arabian Sea (3.6), and south-east Asia (8.3.5.1) planks that are to be sewn together are first aligned by treenails within the plank thickness across the seam. Examples of this technique are also known in Oceania (9.3.6) but it is not clear how widespread this technique was in that region. In Atlantic Europe, Sri Lanka, and the Indian Bay of Bengal coast, on the other hand, this use of treenails is unknown. In Atlantic Europe, planks could be aligned before being lashed or sewn together by means of transverse timbers through cleats proud of each plank's inboard face (5.4.5). The Indian and Sri Lankan sewn-plank boats are frameless (6.7.3).

All boats with lashed or running sewn fastenings have a general, but not necessarily a specific, affinity with one another (McGrail, 1996c: 225–7). Kentley (1996) has published pioneering studies of sewn-plank boats on India's east coast, and identified two distinct sewing patterns. Prins (1986) has looked for regularities and patterns over a broader field. However, sewn-plank boats have been used for at least 5,000 years, and from almost every river and coast in the non-American, non-Australian world (McGrail, 1996c: Fig. 2), and much more research is required if they are to be compared and contrasted effectively, patterns recognized, and perhaps distinctive traditions identified.

### 12.2.3.4.2 *Mortise and tenon plank fastenings*

Flat, wooden, loose tenons within mortised holes in the plank thickness were used, in conjunction with other types of fastening, to fasten planking together in third-millennium BC Egypt (2.7.1, 2.8.3). Similar fastenings, but with the tenons locked in position by trans-piercing pegs, were used in the Mediterranean from c.1500 BC for over 2,000 years (4.8.3, 4.13.3). This type of locked fastening has also been found in vessels wrecked or abandoned in the Thames and Rhine regions in the early centuries AD (5.5). The simplest explanation of this distribution in time and space is that this plank fastening originated in Egypt, spread into the eastern Mediterranean, possibly via the Canaanites/Phoenicians (4.9.3.2.3), thence to the Graeco-Roman world. The Romans probably took the idea to the north-western parts of their Empire and, even beyond, to Ireland (5.5.3).

Comparable plank fastenings are found outside the Roman Empire in south-east Asia, Korea, and Japan. Reports on these vessels are not unambiguous, and drawings or photographs of the fastenings are not always available, so precisely how similar these fastenings are to those of the Mediterranean is not clear. A nineteenth-/twentieth-century Honshu tradition in Japan (10.8.3) appears to have used unlocked mortise and tenon joints as auxiliary fastenings; whilst a boat of the eighteenth/twentieth centuries excavated from Johore Lama, Malaya (8.3.5.2.14) used locked fastenings similarly. On the other hand, the plank fastenings used in the eleventh-century wreck from Wando island, Korea (10.4.2.1) were clearly only distantly related to the Mediterranean mortise and tenon: the tenons passed right through one strake and a short distance into the adjacent strake where they were locked by a peg. The thirteenth-century Butuan boats from the Philippines (8.3.5.2.3) had treenails as auxiliary fastenings within the plank thickness, and some of these were locked by a trans-piercing peg—a similar concept to the Mediterranean locked mortise and tenon joint but not necessarily derived from it. The case for the transmission by Roman ships of the mortise and tenon locked joint to the Indian Ocean and beyond is not proven. The medieval and later fastenings found there may be derived from an indigenous prototype.

### 12.2.3.4.3 *Hooked nail fastenings*

Nails that are clench-fastened by turning the point back through 180° ('hooked') are found in wrecks of the Mediterranean mortise and tenon tradition from the fifth/fourth century BC onwards: copper nails fastened frames to planking (4.9.4.6). Iron nails were similarly used from the first to the fourth century AD in Romano-Celtic vessels, where they fastened planking to frames (5.6.4). This may be a case of technological transfer via Roman shipping from the Mediterranean to Atlantic Europe. On the other hand, as Arnold (5.6.4) has pointed out, hooked and turned iron nails were used before 500 BC in the manufacture of cartwheels in Halstatt, central Europe. Any technological transfer from central Europe to the Mediterranean could have been via the River Po and the River Rhône. Whether there was technological transfer, and if so, in which direction, cannot be decided on the evidence available.

Hooked iron nails appeared again in north-west Europe, about 1,000 years later, as fastenings of the cog's clinker-laid side planking (5.8.2.6). This usage appears to be similar to that in the Romano-Celtic Zwammerdam 2 boat of the second/third centuries AD, which, unusually, has overlapping side strakes (5.6.2.1.3). Evidence for use within that thousand-year period is needed, before we can begin to consider any idea of transmission.

### 12.2.3.5 CLINKER AND REVERSE-CLINKER PLANKING

Hooked iron nails were used to fasten together 'conventional' clinker planking in the River Ganges region of India in the early years of the twentieth century (Hornell, 1946a: 249–50: Greenhill, 1971: 107–9). This south Asian practice can be traced back to the early nineteenth century and possibly to the eighteenth or seventeenth century (McGrail, Blue, and Kentley, 1999: 124–5). The European form of this 'conventional' clinker fastening seems to have its origins in the western Baltic in the early centuries AD (5.7.1.1). It is impossible, therefore, to decide, on this evidence alone, whether the south Asian clinker plank fastening method was indigenous or was brought there by post-medieval Europeans.

Boats built in reverse-clinker planking—that is, with the upper plank inboard (rather than outboard) of the lower—are known in the Bay of Bengal region today (6.7.4.1.3): in northern Orissa, southern West Bengal and in Bangladesh (Blue et al., 1997; Kentley, McGrail, and Blue, 1999; McGrail, Blue, and Kentley, 1999). The Orissan and West Bengal boats are fastened by hooked nails, those of Bangladesh by boatbuilders' staples. Although boats with reverse-clinker planking have

been built in the United States, Sweden, and Britain, this has been only during the last fifty years or so, and they were very few in number. It does seem, therefore, that the reverse-clinker technique may have had a unique origin in the deltas and estuaries to the north and north-west of the Bay of Bengal.

Why one form of overlap should be used rather than the other is not immediately obvious. Many builders of reverse-clinker boats in India and Bangladesh are not aware that the other form of clinker exists: there is probably a comparable situation in Atlantic Europe. Theoretically, it would seem that the 'conventional' form of overlap could emerge when adding planking to a keel with a good moulded dimension (i.e. 'plank on edge'), whereas when starting with a plank-keel ('plank on face') or a keel-less flat bottom, the natural way to make an overlap would be in reverse-clinker fashion. In practice, there seems to be no structural or operational advantage of one type over the other. The choice between the 'conventional' form of overlap and the reverse-clinker form may never have arisen in Europe or in India or, if ever the two methods were both visualized, the choice may have been a purely cultural one.

# 12.3

# Boat and Ship Archaeology

The study of water transport is one element, probably the core element, of maritime archaeology. In its turn, maritime archaeology is a specialization within the discipline of archaeology which may itself be defined as, 'the study, through material remains, of the nature and the past behaviour of Man in his environmental setting'. (McGrail, 1989a). The archaeologist's intentions, when studying a boat find, must be the same as when addressing any other excavated artefact or structure: to learn as much as possible about the whole range of human experience, from the boat itself, from its associated finds and immediate context, and from its wider environment. 'Human experience' is a variable combination of elements which integrate and interact, and is therefore difficult to define. For the purposes of analysis, however, it may be divided into five aspects: technological, environmental, economic, socio-political, and the sphere of thoughts and aspirations (Hawkes, 1954). Since archaeology deals directly with material remains of the past, excavation can usually throw more light on those aspects of life that are dependent on material things, and less on those aspects that are mainly in the realm of ideas. In other words, from the average investigation we learn most about technology and least about cognitive matters, although every attempt should be made to redress that balance.

The evidence described in this study confirms that general rule: boat and ship excavations answer more questions about technology (and answer them more readily and confidently) than about any other sphere of life. With varying degrees of confidence, depending on the methods used, we can establish the date of the boat, the circumstances of her deposition, the range of raw materials used, the tools and techniques used to convert these materials into a boat and, in fortunate cases, the methods of propulsion and steering. In certain projects, the full original form of the boat can be deduced, and her performance estimated in different conditions at sea, due regard being taken of the source of the data used, the appropriateness of the chosen methods, and the rigour of the arguments advanced (Coates *et al.*, 1995). The reconstruction of excavated remains is not an exact science, if only because of the nature of the source material; reconstruction drawings and models can never be other than hypothetical, and doubt must remain about certain aspects of every reconstruction even after the most rigorous research.

Answers to some technological questions can be enhanced by reference to comparative evidence from other boat finds, from documentary sources and iconographic interpretations, and from ethnographic studies. In the longer term, new research projects may have to be initiated to search for answers to questions that arise during the course of post-excavation research (Fig. 1.2).

After technology, most information recovered from a boat excavation is about the environmental and economic aspects of former times. Problems concerned with the maritime environment are increasingly being tackled during excavations; however, answers to questions are often given only within broad limits of time and space, rather than in the detail needed if we are to understand the elements that ancient mariners had to

face at a given time and place: the mean sea level coastline, the tidal regime, river channels and gradients, and the likelihood of winds from different sectors. In the sphere of economics, the sources of raw materials used to build a boat, and of goods carried on board, can be identified with increasing confidence, leading to speculation about a wrecked vessel's origins and her final voyage, and about trade routes in general. However, as with environmental matters, a much broader database than a single boat find is needed to answer the many questions that can be posed about economic life.

Finds associated with excavated boats have been used to investigate socio-political matters, such as social differences within the crew, and the nature of trade—was it controlled by the state or by individual merchants? Answers based solely on boat finds are seldom convincing but the evidence may be used to supplement other documentation.

Finally, boat excavations can throw light on human thoughts and aspirations. There are three main areas:

*First*: As the structure of an excavated boat is investigated, the results of decisions made by the ancient boatbuilder are revealed. The sequence in which a boat was built is important technologically and diagnostically, but it also reflects the builder's mindset: it may prove possible, for example, to deduce how the builder visualized the shape of the boat he intended to build, either in terms of the planking or the framing (1.4.1.1). Furthermore, if it proves possible to reconstruct the boat and assess its performance, we may glimpse something of the builder's aspirations for his boat.

*Second*: informed speculation about how an excavated boat had been used can lead to consideration of the problem of how early navigators kept their reckoning when out of sight of land (12.2.2.2). The essence of that research is to determine how the navigator, with only environmental clues to guide him, visualized his position as his boat progressed across the trackless sea: how might he have constructed a 'mental chart'? Since, by definition, there are no navigational instruments to be excavated which might point towards an answer to that question, research has to move far from the material world of the excavated boat, into the sphere of human cognition.

*Third*: symbolic features have been found on some excavated boats—for example, the anthropomorphic appearance of the stern of the Iron Age logboat from Hasholme (5.3.1.5) and the *oculus* on her bow (Fig. 5.8).

Boats have also been used as coffins or in entombment ceremonies (12.2.2.3). Such features and actions further illuminate the non-material world of former times.

## 12.3.1 MARITIME ARCHAEOLOGY WITHIN THE ARCHAEOLOGICAL DISCIPLINE

Maritime archaeology, the study of Man's early encounter with the rivers and seas of the world, has only become established as a suitable subject for academic study in the last twenty-five years, almost a century after its parent discipline, archaeology, achieved that status. The study of Man as primarily a landsman is thus light years ahead of the study of Man the seafarer, in terms of numbers, resources, and academic prestige (but perhaps not in public interest). Yet there were seamen before there were farmers, navigators before potters, and boatbuilders before wainwrights. Furthermore, until the advent of the railways and motorized road transport (and, latterly, the aeroplane) water transport (riverine as well as seagoing) was the principal means of communications and trade for the greater part of the habitable world.

Rafts and boats have been of immense importance to the social and economic lives of countless communities in every region, from equatorial lands to the Arctic. Seagoing vessels have been of similar importance, but on a broader canvas and have thus had correspond-

ingly more influence on world affairs, not least in the earliest settlements of Greater Australia, Japan, Oceania, and possibly the Americas. Millennia later, an explosive outburst of European activity in the late fifteenth/early sixteenth centuries AD resulted in the transfer of aspects of European culture (material and metaphysical) to a large part of the world, with results that deeply influence our lives today. This most significant event was achieved by sea in ships that were, as water transport always had been, the most complex artefacts of their time and at the leading edge of contemporary technology.

Boats and ships also facilitated the spread of Christianity from the first century AD, and of Islam from the eighth. It is not inconceivable, therefore, that there were comparable voyages in prehistoric times by which there was wide transmission of ideas which are now only archaeologically visible as 'monuments', as 'rituals', and as technological innovations.

Of the unique importance of water transport to mankind there can thus be no doubt. But this importance is not reflected in the knowledge we have today of early maritime matters. As this study shows, much has been achieved, but the potential for learning more about the maritime past is immense. The archaeological discipline worldwide now needs to seek ways of correcting the imbalance between its investigations into terrestrial and maritime aspects of the past.

# Bibliography

ADAM, P. (1977). 'Attempted reconstruction of the Marsala Punic ship', *MM* 63: 35–7.

ADAMS, J. (1990). 'Oskarshamm cog: Part II', *IJNA* 19: 207–19.

ADNEY, E. T. and CHAPELLE, H. I. (1964). *Bark Canoes and Skin Boats of North America*. Washington: Smithsonian Museum.

ADOVASIO, J. M. and PEDLER, D. R. (1997). 'Monte Verde and the antiquity of humankind in the Americas'. *Antiquity*, 71: 573–80.

—— DONAHUE, J., and STUCKENRATH, R. (1990). 'Meadowcraft Rock Shelter radiocarbon chronology'. *American Antiquity*, 55: 318–54.

AGLIONBY, J. (ed.) (1991). *Oxford University expedition to Kei Kecil, Maluku Tenggara, Indonesia, 1990*. Oxford: Aglionby.

ÅKERLUND, H. (1963). *Nydamskeppen*. Göteborg: Elanders Boktrycheri Aktiebolag.

ALEEM, A. A. (1967). 'Concepts of currents, tides and winds among medieval Arab geographers in the Indian Ocean'. *Deep Sea Research*, 14: 459–63.

—— (1968a). 'Concepts of marine biology among Arab writers in the Middle Ages' *Bulletin of Institute of Oceanography Monaco*, 2: 359–67.

—— (1968b). 'Ahmad Ibn Magid: Arab navigator of the 15th century and his contribution to marine sciences' *Bulletin of Institute of Oceanography Monaco*, 2: 565–80.

—— (1980). 'On the history of Arab navigation', in M. Sears and D. Merriman (eds.) *Oceanography: The past*. Proceedings of the 3rd International Congress on the History of Oceanography. New York: Springer-Verlag, 582–95.

—— (1989). 'Wonders of the Sea of India: An Arabian book of sea tales from the 10th century and the St Brendan Legend', in J. de Courcy Ireland and D. C. Sheehy (eds.) *Atlantic Visions*. Dun Laoghaire: Boole Press, 61–6.

ALLCHIN, B. and ALLCHIN, R. (1997). *Origins of a Civilisation*. New Delhi: Penguin Books.

ALLEN, J. and HOLDAWAY, S. (1995). 'Contamination of Pleistocene radiocarbon determinations in Australia'. *Antiquity*, 69: 101–12.

ALONSO, F. (1994). 'Prehistoric boats in the rock paintings of Cadiz and in the rock carvings of north-west Spain', in Westerdahl (ed.): 11–19.

AMBROSE, W. R. (1997). 'Contradictions in Lapita pottery, a composite clone'. *Antiquity*, 71: 525–38.

ANDERSEN, E., CRUMLIN-PEDERSEN, O., VADSTRUP, S., and VINNER, M. (1997). *Roar Ege*. Roskilde: Viking Ship Museum.

ANDERSEN, S. H. (1987). 'Mesolithic dugouts and paddles from Tybrind Vig, Denmark'. *Acta Archaeologica*, 57: 87–106.

—— (1994). 'New finds of Mesolithic logboats in Denmark', in Westerdahl (ed.): 1–10.

ANDERSON, A. (1991). 'Chronology of colonization in New Zealand'. *Antiquity*, 65: 767–95.

ANDERSON, A. O. and ANDERSON, M. O. (eds.) (1961). *Adamnan's Life of St Columba*. London.

ANDERSON, B. W. (1978). *Living World of the Old Testament*, 3rd ed. London: Longman.

ANDERSON, R. C. (1925). 'Italian naval architecture in *c*.1445'. *MM* 11: 135–63.

—— (1928). 'English galleys in 1295', *MM* 14: 220–41.

—— (1934). 'Bursledon ship', *MM* 24: 112–13.

—— (1945). '"Jal's Memoire No 5" and the manuscript "Fabbricca di Galere"', *MM* 31: 160–7.

ANON (1946). *Western Arabia and the Red Sea*. BR 527. Geographical Handbook Series. London: Naval Intelligence Division.

ARDIKA, I. W. and BELLWOOD, P. (1991). 'Indian contact with Bali'. *Antiquity*, 65: 221–32.

—— —— SUTABA, M. I., and YULIATI, K. C. (1997). 'Sembiran and the first Indian contacts with Bali: An update'. *Antiquity*, 71: 193–5.

ARIMA, E. Y. (1975). 'Contextual study of the Caribou Eskimo kayak'. *Canadian Ethnology Service Paper*, No. 25. Ottawa.

ARKELL, A. J. (1959). 'Early shipping in Egypt'. *Antiquity*, 33: 52–3.

ARNOLD, B. (1977). 'Some remarks on caulking in Celtic boat construction and its evolution in areas lying NW of the Alpine arc'. *IJNA* 6: 293–7.

—— (1978). 'Les barques celtiques d'Abbeville, Bevaix et Yverdun'. *Archeologia*, 118: 52–60.

—— (1985). 'Sewn boats in Switzerland: A clue', in McGrail and Kentley (eds.): 163–4.

—— (1990). 'Some objections to the link between Roman boats and the Roman foot (*pes monetalis*)'. *IJNA* 19: 273–7.

—— (1991). 'Gallo-Roman boat of Bevaix and the bottom-based construction', in Reinders and Paul (eds.): 19–23.

ARNOLD, B. (1992). 'Batellerie gallo-romaine sur le lac de Neuchâtel'. *Archéologie Neuchâteloise*, 2 vols. 12/13.

—— (1995–6). 'Pirogues monoxyles d'Europe centrale', *Archéologie Neuchâteloise*, 2 vols. 20/21.

—— (1998). 'Embarkations romano-celtiques et construction sur sole', in E. Rieth (ed.). *Concevoir et construire les navires*. Paris: Eres.T.I.P., 75–90.

—— (1999a). 'Some remarks on Romano-Celtic boat construction and Bronze Age wood technology'. *IJNA* 28: 34–44.

—— (1999b). 'Altripa: Archéologie expérimentale et architecture navale gallo-romaine'. *Archéologie Neuchâteloise*, 25.

—— (1996c). 'Les pirogues néolithiques de Paris-Bercy', in Pomey and Rieth (eds.): 73–8

—— (2000). 'Carpenters, logboats and Bronze Age villages on Lake Neuchâtel' in Litwin (2000): 201–6.

ARUNACHALAM, B. (1987). 'Haven-finding art in the Indian navigational traditions and cartography', in S. Chandra (ed.). *Indian Ocean*. Delhi: Sage, 191–221.

—— (1996). 'Traditional sea and sky wisdom of Indian seamen and their practical applications', in Ray and Salles (eds.): 261–82.

ASHE, G. (1962). *Land to the West*. London: Collins.

ATKINSON, R. J. C. (1960). *Stonehenge*. Harmondsworth: Penguin.

AUBAILE-SALLENAVE, F. (1987). *Bois et bateaux du Viêtnam*. Ethnosciences, 3. Paris: SELAF.

AUBET, M. E. (1993). *Phoenicians and the West*. Cambridge: Cambridge University Press.

AUDEMARD, L. (1957–1969). *Les jonques chinoises*. Rotterdam: Maritiem Museum.

AVIENUS, R. F. (1977). *Ora Maritima*, ed., J. P. Murphy. Chicago: Ares.

AYERS, J. (1978). 'Discovery of a Yuan ship at Sinan, SW Korea'. *Oriental Art*, 24: 79–85.

BALLARD, G. A. (1920a). 'Sculptures of Deir-el-Bahari'. *MM* 6: 149–55, 162–74, 212–17.

—— (1920b). 'Transporting of the obelisks at Karnak'. *MM* 6: 264–73, 307–14.

BANDI, H. G. (1964). *Eskimo Prehistory*. Anchorage: University of Alaska.

—— (1969). *Eskimo Prehistory*. London: Methuen.

BARKER, R. (1989). 'Size of the "Treasure Ships" and other Chinese vessels'. *MM* 75: 273–5.

—— (1991). 'Design in the Dockyard c.1600', in R. Reinders and K. Paul (eds.), *Carvel Construction Techniques*, Monograph 12. Oxford: Oxbow, 61–9.

—— (1993). 'J. P. Sarsfield's *Santa Clara*: An addendum'. *IJNA* 22: 161–5.

BARNES, R. H. (1985). 'Whaling vessels of Indonesia', in McGrail and Kentley (eds.): 345–66.

BARNETT, R. D. (1958). 'Early shipping in the Near East'. *Antiquity*, 32: 220–30.

BASCH, L. (1969). 'Phoenician oared ships'. *MM* 55: 139–62, 227–45.

—— (1972). 'Ancient wrecks and the archaeology of ships'. *IJNA* 1: 1–58.

—— (1973). 'Golo wreck and sidelights on other ancient ships culled from Admiral Paris's *Souvenirs de marine conserves*'. *IJNA* 2: 329–44.

—— (1976a). 'Pirogues du Proche-Orient'. *Sefunim*, 5: 10–14.

—— (1976b). 'Le navire cousu de Bon-Porté'. *Cahiers d'archéologie subaquatique*. 5: 37–42.

—— (1981). 'Carthage and Rome: Tenons and mortices'. *MM* 67: 245–50.

—— (1983a). 'When is a ram not a ram?' *MM* 69: 129–42.

—— (1983b). 'Bow and stern appendages in the ancient Mediterranean'. *MM* 69: 395–412.

—— (1985). 'Appendix A: Response to Gillmer'. *MM* 71: 413–15.

—— (1986). 'Aegina pirate ships of *c*. BC 1700'. *MM* 72:415–37.

—— (1987a). *Le musée imaginaire de la marine antique*. Athens: Institute Hellénique pour la Préservation de la tradition nautique.

—— (1987b). 'Review article: A review of Coates and McGrail (eds.) 1984, and Morrison and Coates 1986'. *MM* 73: 93–105.

BASS, G. F. (1967). 'Cape Gelidonya: A Bronze Age shipwreck'. *Trans. American Philosophical Society*, 57/8.

—— (ed.) (1972). *History of Seafaring*. London: Thames & Hudson.

—— (1980). 'Marine archaeology: A misunderstood science'. *Ocean*, 2: 137–52.

—— (1987). 'Oldest known shipwreck reveals splendours of the Bronze Age'. *National Geographic*, 172: 692–733.

—— (ed.) (1988). *Ships and Shipwrecks of the Americas*. London: Thames & Hudson.

—— (1991). 'Evidence of trade from Bronze Age shipwrecks', in Gale (ed.): 69–82.

—— (1997). 'Mediterranean Sea', in Delgado (ed.): 268–74.

—— PULAK, C., COLLON, D., and WEINSTEIN, J. (1989). 'The Bronze Age shipwreck at Ulu Burun'. *American Journal of Archaeology*, 93: 1–29.

BAYARD, D. (1980). 'East Asia in the Bronze Age', in Sherratt (ed.) (1980a): 168–73.

BAYKOWSKI, U. (1994). 'Kieler Hanse-Cog: A replica of the Bremen Cog', in Westerdahl (ed.): 261–4.

BEAGLEHOLE, J. C. (1967). *Journals of Captain Cook on his Voyages of Discovery*, ii. Cambridge: Cambridge University Press.

BEAUDOUIN, F. (1970). *Les bateaux de l'Adour*. Bayonne: Museée Basque.

BEDNARIK, R. G. (1989). 'On the Pleistocene settlement of South America'. *Antiquity*, 63: 101–11.

—— (1998). 'Experiment in Pleistocene seafaring'. *IJNA* 27: 139–49.

BEGLEY, V. (1996). *Ancient Port of Arikamedu*. Memoirs

Archaeology, 22. Pondicherry: École Français Extrème Orient.

BEHERA, K. S. (1994). 'Maritime contacts of Orissa: Literary and archaeological evidence'. *Utkal Historical Research Journal*, 5: 55–70.

BELL, M., CASELDINE, A., and NEUMANN, H. (2000). *Prehistoric Intertidal Archaeology in the Welsh Severn Estuary,* CBA Research Report 120.

BELLABARBA, S. (1988). 'Square-rigged ship of the *Fabbrica di Galere* manuscript'. *MM* 74: 113–30, 225–39.

—— (1993). 'Ancient methods of designing hulls'. *MM* 79: 274–92.

—— (1996). 'Origins of the ancient methods of designing hulls: A hypothesis'. *MM* 82: 259–68.

BELLWOOD, P. (1985). *Prehistory of the Indo-Malaysian Archipelago*. Australia: Academic Press.

—— (1987). *Polynesians*. London: Thames & Hudson.

BELTRAME, C. (2000). '*Sutiles naves* of Roman age', in Litwin (2000): 91–6.

BENZONI, G. (1857). *History of the New World.* trans. Rear Admiral W. H. Smyth. London: Hakluyt Society.

BEST, E. (1925). *Maori canoe*. Bulletin 7. Wellington: Dominion Museum.

BIAGI, P., TORKE, W., TOSI, M., and UERPANN, H-P. (1984). 'Qurum: A case study of coastal archaeology in northern Oman'. *World Archaeology*, 16: 43–61.

BIDAULT, J. (1945). *Pirogues et pagaies*. Paris.

BILL, J. (1994). 'Iron nails in Iron Age and medieval shipbuilding', in Westerdahl (ed.): 55–63.

—— (1995). 'Gedesby ship under sail'. *Newsletter from Roskilde*, 5: 3–8.

—— (1997a). 'Ships and seamanship', in P. Sawyer (ed.) (1997). *Oxford Illustrated History of the Vikings*. Oxford: Oxford University Press, 182–201.

—— (1997b). 'Gedesby ship', in Delgado (ed.): 166.

—— (1998). 'Seafaring farmers in the Middle Ages'. *Newsletter from Roskilde*, 11: 4–10.

—— and VINNER, M. (1995). 'Gedesby ship under sail'. *Newsletter from Roskilde*, 5: 3–8.

BIRDSELL, J. H. (1977). 'Recalibration of a paradigm for the first peopling of Greater Australia', in J. Allen, J. Golson, and R. Jones (eds.). *Sunda and Sahul*. Canberra: Australian National University Press. 113–68.

BISHOP, M. C. and DORE, J. N. (1988). 'Corbridge: Excavations of the Roman fort and town, 1947–1980'. English Heritage Archaeological Reports, 8. London: English Heritage.

BISWAS, S. S. (1981). *Terracotta Art of Bengal*. New Delhi.

BLACK, E. (1996). 'Where have all the sails gone?'. *Tropis*, 4: 103–12.

—— and SAMUEL, D. (1991). 'What were sails made of?'. *MM* 77: 217–26.

BLAKE, W. and FLECKER, M. (1994). 'Preliminary survey of a South East Asian wreck, Phu Quoc island, Vietnam'.

*IJNA* 23: 73–91.

BLUE, L. (1995). 'A topographical analysis of the location of harbours and anchorages of the eastern Mediterranean in the Middle and Late Bronze Age'. Oxford D. Phil. thesis.

—— KENTLEY, E., and McGRAIL, S. (1998). '*Vattai* fishing boat and related frame-first vessels of Tamil Nadu'. *South Asian Studies*, 14: 41–74.

—— —— —— and MISHRA, U. (1997). '*Patia* fishing boat of Orissa: A case study in ethnoarchaeology'. *South Asian Studies*, 13: 189–207.

BLUNDEN, C. and ELVIN, M. (1983). *Cultural Atlas of China*. Oxford: Phaidon.

BOETTO, G. (2000). 'New technological and historical observations on the Fiumicino 1 wreck from Portus Claudius (Fiumicino, Rome)', in Litwin (2000): 99–102.

BONDE, N. (1994). 'De norske vikingeskibsgraves alder'. *Nationalmuseets Arbejdsmark*, 128–48.

—— and JENSEN, J. S. (1995). 'Dating of a Hanseatic cog- find in Denmark', in Olsen, Madsen, and Rieck (eds.).: 103–22.

—— BARTHOLIN, T., CHRISTENSEN, K., and ERIKSEN, O. H. (1993). 'Dendrokronologiske daterings'. *Arkaeologiske Udgravninger i Danmark*, 294–310.

BONINO, M. (1985). 'Sewn boats in Italy', in McGrail and Kentley (eds.): 87–104.

—— (1989). 'Notes on the architecture of some Roman ships: Nemi and Fiumicino'. *Tropis*, 1: 37–53.

—— (1990). 'Neolithic boat in the Adriatic', *MM* 76: 113–15.

—— (1995). 'Sardinian, Villanovan and Etruscan craft between 10th and 7th centuries BC from bronze and clay models'. *Tropis*, 3: 83–98.

BOON, G. C. (1977). 'Greco-Roman anchor stock from North Wales'. *Antiquaries Journal*, 57: 9–30.

BOOTH, B. (1984). 'Handlist of maritime radiocarbon dates': *IJNA* 13: 189–204.

BOUND, M. (1985). 'Early observations on the construction of the pre-Classical wreck at Campese Bay, island of Giglio', in McGrail and Kentley (eds.): 49–66.

BOURRIAU, J. and OATES, J. (1997). 'Spinning or sailing?: The boat models from Eridu'. *Antiquity*, 71: 719–21.

BOWDLER, S. (1995). 'Offshore islands and maritime exploration in Australian prehistory'. *Antiquity*, 69: 945–58.

BOWEN, E. G. (1972). *Britain and the Western Seaways*. London: Thames & Hudson.

BOWEN, R. LE BARON (1952). 'Primitive watercraft of Arabia'. *American Neptune*, 12: 186–221.

—— (1953). 'Eastern sail affinities'. *American Neptune*, 13: 81–117, 185–211.

—— (1956a). 'Boats of the Indus civilisation'. *MM* 42: 279–90.

—— (1956b). 'European sewn boats'. *MM* 42: 256–8.

—— (1956c). 'Earliest lateen sail'. *MM* 42: 239–42.

—— (1960). 'Egypt's earliest sailing ships'. *Antiquity*, 34: 117–30.

BRANDT, H. and HOCHKIRCH, K. (1995). 'Saiing properties of

the Hansa cog in comparison with other cargo sail ships'. *Technology Research Schiffstechnik*, 42/1: 1–20.

BRASSEY, Mrs (1878). *Voyage in the 'Sunbeam'*. London: Longman Green.

BRASSEY, T. A. (ed.) (1905). *Naval Annual*. London: Brassey.

BRAY, W., (1980). 'Early agriculturalists in the Americas', in Sherratt (ed.) (1980*a*): 365–74.

—— (1986). 'Finding the earliest Americans'. *Nature*, 321: 726.

BRAY, W. M., SWANSON, E. H., and FARRINGTON, I. S. (1989). *Ancient Americas*. Oxford: Phaidon.

BRIGHT, L. S. (1979). 'Recovery and preservation of a freshwater canoe'. *IJNA* 8: 261–3.

BRINDLEY, H. H. (1919–20). 'Notes on the boats of Siberia'. *MM* 5: 66–72, 101–17, 130–42, 184–7; 6: 15–18, 187.

—— (1931). 'Sailing balsa of Lake Titicaca and other reed bundle craft'. *MM* 17: 7–19.

BRINDLEY, M. D. (1924). 'Canoes of British Guiana'. *MM* 10: 124–32, 307–8.

BRØGGER, A. W. and SHETELIG, H. (1971). *Viking Ships*. Oslo: Dreyers Forlag.

BRONSON, B. (1980). 'SE Asia: Civilisations of the tropical forests', in Sherratt (ed.) (1980*a*): 262–6.

BROODBANK, C. (1989). 'Longboat and society in the Cyclades in the Keros-Syros Culture'. *American Journal of Archaeology*, 93: 319–37.

—— and STRASSER, T. F. (1991). 'Migrant farmers and the Neolithic colonisation of Crete'. *Antiquity*, 65: 233–45.

BROOKS, F. W. (1929). 'King's ships and galleys mainly under John and Henry III'. *MM* 15: 15–48.

—— (1933). *English Naval Forces 1199–1272*. London: Brown and Son.

BRUCE-MITFORD, R. (1974). 'Snape boat', in R. Bruce-Mitford (ed.). *Aspects of Anglo-Saxon Archaeology*. London.

—— (1975). *Sutton-Hoo ship burial*, i. London: British Museum.

BRUSIĆ, Z. (1968). 'Istrazivanje anticke luke kad Nina'. *Diadora* 4: 203–9.

—— and DOMJAN, M. (1985). 'Liburnian boats: Their form and construction', in McGrail and Kentley (eds.): 67–87.

BUCHOLZ, H-G. (1988). 'Archäologische Holzfunde aus Tamassos, Zypern'. *Acta Praehistorica et Archaeologica*, 20: 75–157.

BUDGE, E. A. W. (1907). *The Nile: Notes for Travellers in Egypt*. London: Thomas Cook.

BURL, A. (1998). *Great Stone Circles*. New Haven: Yale University Press.

BURNINGHAM, N. (1994). 'Notes on the watercraft of Thanh Hoa province, northern Vietnam'. *IJNA* 23: 229–38.

BUTLER, J. (1963). 'Bronze Age connections across the North Sea'. *Palaeohistoria*, 9: 166.

CACHOLA-ABAD, C. K. (1993), 'Evaluating the orthodox dual settlement model for the Hawaiian islands', in M. W. Graves and R. C. Green (eds.) (1993). *Evolution and Organi-*

*sation of Prehistoric Society in Polynesia* Monograph 19. Auckland: New Zealand Archaeological Association, 13–32.

CAIRO, R. F. (1972). 'Note on S. Vietnamese basket boats'. *MM* 58: 135–53.

CALCAGNO, C. (1997). 'Aspects of seafaring and trade in the Central Mediterranean region *c*. BC 1200–800'. D. Phil. thesis, University of Oxford.

CAMPS, G. and D'ANNA, A. (1980). 'Recherches sur les navigation prehistoriques en Méditerranée Occidentale', *Navigation et gens de mer en Méditerranée*. Aix-en-Provence: Maison de la Méditerranée, 1–16.

CARR LAUGHTON, L. G. (1923). 'Bayonne ship'. *MM* 9: 83–7.

CARRAZÉ, F. (1977). 'Mediterranean hulls compared: 3. Jeanne-Garde B'. *IJNA* 6: 299–303.

CARRELL, T. L. and KEITH, D. H. (1992). 'Replicating a ship of discovery', *IJNA* 21: 281–94.

CARTER, J., KENCHINGTON, T., and WALKER, D. (1982). 'A dugout log canoe in Uniacke Lake, Nova Scotia'. *IJNA* 11: 245–9.

CARVER, M. O. H. (ed.) (forthcoming). *Sutton Hoo Cemetery and its Context*.

CASSON, L. (1956). 'Fore-and-aft sails in the ancient world'. *MM* 42: 3–5.

—— (1964). 'Odysseus' boat'. *American Journal of Philology*, 85: 61–4.

—— (1971). *Ships and Seamanship in the Ancient World*. Repr. with corrections 1996. Princeton: Princeton University Press.

—— (1975). 'Bronze Age ships: The evidence of the Thera wall paintings'. *IJNA* 4: 3–10.

—— (1978). 'Thera ships'. *IJNA* 7: 232–3.

—— (1980). 'Two-masted ships'. *IJNA* 9: 68–9.

—— (1984). *Ancient Trade and Society*. Detroit: Wayne State University Press.

—— (1988*a*). 'Rome's trade with the eastern coast of India'. *Cahiers d'histoire*, 33: 303–8.

—— (1988*b*). 'Rome's maritime trade with the Far East'. *American Neptune*, 48: 149–53.

—— (1989). *Periplus Maris Erythraei*. Princeton: Princeton University Press.

—— (1991). 'Ram and naval tactics', in Casson and Steffy (eds.): 76–82.

—— (1992). 'Odysseus' boat. (Homer, *Od.* 5. 244–53)'. *IJNA* 21: 73–4.

—— (1996). 'New evidence for Greek merchantmen'. *IJNA* 25: 262–4.

—— and LINDER, E. (1991). 'Evolution and shape of the ancient ram', in Casson and Steffy (eds.): 67–71.

—— and STEFFY, J. R. (eds.) (1991). *Athlit Ram*. College Station: Texas A & M University Press.

CASTIGLIONE, C. O. (1967). 'Le piroghe preistoriche italiane'. *Natura*, 58: 5–48.

CATLIN, G. (1841). *Manners, Customs and Conditions of the*

*N.' American Indians*. 2 vols. London.

CEDERLUND, C.-O. (1985). '*Lodja* and other vessels', in McGrail and Kentley (eds.): 233–52.

—— (1995). 'Ledung ships, cogs and other medieval types in northern Europe', in C. O. Cederlund (ed.). *Medieval Ship Archaeology*. Stockholm: University of Stockholm, 11–17.

CHAKRABARTI, D. (1980). 'Early agriculture and the development of towns in India', in Sherratt (ed.) (1980a): 162–7.

CHEN, Q. and CHEN, Y. (1991). Chinese Fu-chuan , in Zhang (ed.): 298–308.

CHEN, Y., YANG, Q., and CHEN, X. (1986). 'Study for the replica of Zheng He's Treasure Ship'. *Marine History Research*, 2: 47–58.

CHERRY, J. F. (1990). 'First colonization of the Mediterranean islands: A review of recent research'. *Journal of Mediterranean Archaeology*, 3/2: 145–221.

CHESNEY, F. R. (1850). *Expedition for the Survey of the Rivers Euphrates and Tigris in 1835–37*. London.

—— (1868). *Narrative of the Euphrates Expedition*. London.

CHEVILLOT, C. and COFFYN, A. (1991). *L'âge du bronze atlantique: Ses facies, de l'Ecosse à l'Andalousie et leurs relations avec le bronze continental et la Méditerranée*. Paris.

CHITTICK, N. (1979). 'Early ports in the Horn of Africa'. *IJNA* 8: 273–7.

—— (1980a). 'Stone anchor-shanks in the western Indian Ocean'. *IJNA* 9: 73–6.

—— (1980b). 'Sewn boats in the western Indian Ocean and a survival in Somalia'. *IJNA* 9: 297–309.

CHRISTENSEN, A.-E. (1968a). *Boats of the North*. Oslo: Norske Samlaget.

—— (1968b). 'Sjovollen ship'. *Viking*, 32: 131–53.

—— (1972). 'Boat-building tools and the process of learning', in Hasslöf, Henningsen, and Christensen (eds.) (1972b): 235–59.

—— (1974). 'Klåstadskipet'. *Tjolling Bygdebok*, 1: 542–6.

—— (1985). 'Boat finds from Bryggen'. *Bryggen Papers*, 1: 47–280. Oslo University Press.

—— (1986). 'Tools used for boatbuilding in ancient and more modern times', in Crumlin-Pedersen and Vinner (eds.): 150–9.

—— (1987). 'Medieval ship model'. *IJNA* 16: 69–70.

—— (1989). 'Hanseatic and Nordic ships in medieval trade', in Villain-Gandossi, Busutil, and Adam (eds.): 17–23.

—— (1996). 'Proto-Viking, Viking, and Norse craft', in A. E. Christensen (ed.), *History of the ship: Earliest Ships*. London: Conway Maritime Press, 72–88.

—— (1997). 'Gokstad ship'; 'Oseberg ship'; 'Tune ship', in Delgado (ed.): 172–4, 302–3, 428–9.

—— and LEIRO, G. (1976). *Klåstadskipet*. Saertrykk av Vestfoldminne.

CHRISTENSEN, C. (1990). 'Stone Age dugout boats in Denmark', in D. E. Robinson (ed.), *Experimentation and Reconstruction in Environmental Archaeology*. Oxford: Oxbow,

119–42.

CHRISTIE, A. (1957). 'An obscure passage from the Periplus'. *Bulletin of the London School of African Studies*, 19: 345–53.

CICILIOT, F. (1998). 'Genoese *cocha*', in Pomey and Rieth (eds.): 191–4.

CLARK, G. (1977). *World Prehistory*, 3rd edn. Cambridge University Press.

—— and PIGGOTT, S. (1976). *Prehistoric Societies*. Harmondsworth: Penguin.

CLARK, J. G. D. (1953). 'Archaeological theories and interpretation: Old World', in A. L. Kroeber (ed.), *Anthropology Today*. Chicago: Chicago University Press, 343–60.

CLARK, P., CONESE, E., NICOLAS, N., and GREEN, J. (1989). 'Philippines archaeological site survey, February 1988'. *IJNA* 18: 255–72.

—— GREEN, J., VOSMER, T., and SANTIAGO, R. (1993). 'Butuan 2 boat known as *balangay*, in the National Museum, Manila, Philippines', *IJNA* 22: 143–59.

CLARKE, R., DEAN, M., HUTCHINSON, G., McGRAIL, S., and SQUIRRELL, J. (1993). 'Recent work on the River Hamble wreck near Bursledon, Hampshire'. *IJNA* 22: 21–44.

CLAUSEN, B. L. (ed.) (1993). *Viking voyages to North America*. Roskilde: Viking Ship Museum.

COATES, J. (1984). 'Naval architecture of the trireme', in Coates and McGrail (eds.): 51–74.

—— (1985). 'Some structural models for sewn boats', in McGrail and Kentley (eds.): 9–18.

—— (1989a). 'Triereis: Its design and construction'. *Tropis*, 1: 83–90.

—— (1989b). 'The reconstruction', in Morrison and Coates (eds.): 16–25.

—— (1990a). 'Pentekontors and Triereis compared'. *Tropis*, 2: 111–16.

—— (1990b). 'The ship', in Coates, Platis, and Shaw (eds.): 3–9.

—— (1993). 'Design of an experimental trireme', in Shaw (ed.) (1993a): 21–8.

—— (1995a). 'Tilley's and Morrison's triremes:Evidence and practicality'. *Antiquity*, 69: 159–62.

—— (1995b). 'Trieres reconstruction, *Olympias*: Some unresolved questions'. *Tropis*, 3: 135–46.

—— (1996). 'Appendix F', in Morrison and Coates (eds.): 347–8.

—— (1997). 'Experimental archaeology', in Delgado (ed.): 146–8.

—— (forthcoming). 'Planking tenons in ancient Mediterranean ships built shell-first'. *Tropis*, 6.

—— and McGRAIL, S. (eds.) (1984). *Greek Trireme of the 5th century BC*. Greenwich: National Maritime Museum.

—— and MORRISON, J. (1987). 'Authenticity in the replica Athenian trireme', *Antiquity*, 61: 87–90.

—— and MORRISON, J. (1993). 'Summary of lessons learned', in Shaw (ed.) (1993a): 108–9.

—— PLATIS, S. K., and SHAW, J. T. (eds.) (1990). *Trireme Trials*

1988. Oxford: Oxbow Books.

COATES, J., McGRAIL, S., BROWN, D., GIFFORD, E., GRAINGE, G., GREENHILL, B., MARSDEN, P., RANKOV, B., TIPPING, C., and WRIGHT, E. (1995). 'Experimental boat and ship archaeology: Principles and methods', *IJNA* 24: 293–301.

COGHILL, N. (ed.) (1951). *Canterbury Tales*. Harmondsworth: Penguin.

COLEMAN, J. E. (1985). '"Frying Pans" of the Early Bronze Age Aegean'. *American Journal of Archaeology*, 89: 191–204.

COLES, B. (1990). 'Anthropomorphic wooden figures from Britain and Ireland'. *PPS* 56: 315–33.

COLES, J. (1993). 'Boats on the rocks', in J. Coles, V. Fenwick, and G. Hutchinson (eds.) *Spirit of Enquiry*. Exeter: University of Exeter Press, 23–38.

COLLINS, H. B. (1937). *Archaeology of St. Lawrence Island*. Smithsonian collection, vol. 96.1.

COOPER, Z. (1996). 'Archaeological evidence of maritime contacts: Andaman Is', in Ray and Salles (eds.): 239–46.

COULTON, R. L. (1977). 'Preserved aboriginal canoes in western Canada'. *MM* 63: 249–52.

CRAWFORD, H. (1997). 'The site of Saar: Dilmun reconsidered'. *Antiquity*, 71: 701–08.

CRUMLIN-PEDERSEN, O. (1965). 'Cog-kogge-kaag'. *Handels-og Søfartsmuseet på Kronborg Årbog*, 81–144.

—— (1969). *Das Haithabuschiff*, BAH 3.

—— (1977). 'Some principles for the recording and presentation of ancient boat structures', in McGrail (ed.), *Sources and Techniques in Boat Archaeology*. Oxford: BAR. S.29, 163–78.

—— (1978). 'Ships of the Vikings'. in T. Andersson and K. I. Sandred (eds.) (1978). *The Vikings*. Acta Universitatis Uppsaliensis, 8. Uppsala: 33–41.

—— (1979). 'Danish cog finds', in McGrail (ed.) (1979): 17–34.

—— (1981). 'Skibe på havbünden'. *Handels-og Søfartsmuseets Årbog*: 28–65.

—— (1983a). 'Schiffe und Seehandelsrouten im Ostseeraum 1050–1350'. *Lübecker Schriften zur Archäologie und Kulturgeschichte*, 7: 229–37.

—— (1983b). 'From Viking ships to Hanseatic cogs'. Third Paul Johnstone Lecture. Greenwich: National Maritime Museum.

—— (1985). 'Cargo ships of northern Europe, AD 800–1300', in A. E. Herteig (ed.). *Conference on Waterfront Archaeology*. Bergen: Historisk Museum, 83–93.

—— (1986a). 'The "Roar" project', in Crumlin-Pedersen and Vinner (eds.): 94–103.

—— (1986b). 'Aspects of Viking-age shipbuilding'. *Journal of Danish Archaeology*, 5: 209–28.

—— (1986c). 'Aspects of wood technology in medieval shipbuilding', in Crumlin-Pedersen and Vinner (eds.): 138–49.

—— (1986d). 'Discussion', in Crumlin-Pedersen and Vinner (eds.): 157–8.

—— (1988). 'Schiffe und Schiffahrtswege im Ostseeraum während des 9–12 Jahrhunderts'. in M. Müller-Wille (ed.). *Bericht der Römisch-Germanischen Kommission, 69*. Mainz am Rhein: P. von Zabern; 530–63.

—— (1989). 'Wood technology and forest resources in the light of medieval shipfinds', in Villain-Gandossi, Busutil, and Adam (eds.): 25–42.

—— (1990). 'Boats and ships of the Angles and Jutes', in McGrail (ed.) 1990a: 98–116.

—— (1991a). 'Badgrave og gravbade pa Slusegard'. *Slusegarde-Gravpladsen*. Jysk Arkaeologisk Selskabs Skrifter, 14.3, 3: 93–263.

—— (1991b). 'Ship types and sizes AD 800–1400', in O. Crumlin-Pedersen (ed.). *Aspects of Maritime Scandinavia*. Roskilde: Viking Ship Museum, 69–82.

—— (1994). 'Medieval ships in Danish waters', in Westerdahl (ed.): 65–72.

—— (1997a). *Viking Age Ships and Shipbuilding in Hedeby/Haithabu and Schleswig*. Roskilde: Viking Ship Museum.

—— (1997b). 'Large and small warships of the North', in A. N. Jørgensen, and B. L. Clausen (eds.). *Military Aspects of Scandinavian Society*. Copenhagen: National Museum, 184–94.

—— (2000). 'To be or not to be a cog: The Bremen cog in perspective' *IJNA* 29: 230–46.

—— and THYE, B. M. (eds.) (1995). *Ship as a Symbol*. Copenhagen: National Museum.

—— and VINNER, M. (eds.) (1986). *Sailing into the Past*. Roskilde: Viking Ship Museum.

—— —— (1993). 'Roar og Helge af Roskilde'. *Nationalmuseets Arbejdsmark*. 11–29.

—— NYMARK, L., and CHRISTIANSEN, C. (1980). 'Kyholm 78', *IJNA* 9: 193–216.

CULVER, H. B. (1929). 'A contemporary 15th century ship model'. *MM* 15: 213–21.

CUMMINS, W. A. (1979). 'Neolithic stone axes', in T. H. Clough and W. A. Cummins (eds.). *Stone Axe Studies*, CBA Research Report 23. 5–12.

—— (1980). 'Stone axes as a guide to Neolithic communications in England and Wales'. *PPS* 46: 45–60.

CUNLIFFE, B. (1982). 'Britain, the Veneti and beyond'. *OJA* 1: 39–68.

—— (1984). 'Relations between Britain and Gaul in the first century BC and the early first century AD', in S. MacReady and F. Thompson (eds.). *Cross-Channel Trade between Gaul and Britain in the Pre-Roman Iron Age*. Occ. Papers, 4. London: Society of Antiquaries, 3–23.

—— (1988). *Greeks, Romans, and Barbarians*. London: Batsford.

—— (ed.) (1994). *Prehistory of Europe*. Oxford: Oxford University Press.

—— (2001). *Facing the Ocean*. Oxford: Oxford University Press.

CUNNINGHAM, A. (1879). *Stupa of Bharhut*. London.

CURRIE, E. J. (1995). 'Archaeology, ethnohistory and exchange along the coast of Ecuador'. *Antiquity*, 69: 511–26.

DAI, K. (1983). 'Guangdong fenghe muchuan' (Preliminary study of sewn-plank boats from Guangdong). *Haijiaoshi Yanjiu*, 5: 86–9.

—— (1984). 'Dug-out and the origin of junk in ancient China'. *ICHCS* 3. Beijing.

—— (1985). 'Notes on the origination of ancient Chinese junks based upon study of unearthed dug-out canoes'. *Maritime History Research*, 1: 4–17.

DAKORONIA, F. (1990), 'Warships on sherds of LH3C kraters from Kynos'. *Tropis*, 2: 117–22.

DAVENPORT, D., JOHNSON, J. R., and TIMBROOK, J. (1993). 'Chumash and the swordfish'. *Antiquity*, 67: 257–72.

DAVID, B., ROBERTS, R., TUNIZ, C., JONES, R., and HEAD, J. (1997). 'New optical and radiocarbon dates from Ngarrabullgan Cave, a Pleistocene archaeological site in Australia'. *Antiquity*, 71: 183–8.

DEACON, M. (1968). 'Bosporus undercurrent'. *MM* 76: 207–10.

DE BOE, G. and HUBERT, F. (1977). 'Une installation portuaire d' époque romaine à Pommeroeul'. *Archaeologia Belgica*, 192: 5–57.

DE BRY, T. (1601–1629). 1601, Petits Voyages, pt. 5; 1602, Grands Voyages, pt. 9; 1619, Grands Voyages, pt. 11; 1629, *Petits Voyages*, pt. 3.

DE COURCY-IRELAND, J. E. (1991). 'Skinboats'. *MM* 77: 182–3.

DE GRAEVE, M. C. (1981). *Ships of the Ancient Near East*. Orientalia Lovaniensia Analecta, 7. Leuven: Katholieke Universiteit Leuven.

DEGUCHI, A. (1991). 'Dugouts of Japan: Hull structure, construction and propulsion', in Zhang (ed.) (1991): 197–214.

DELANEY, J. (1976). 'Fieldwork in south Roscommon', in C. O'Danochair (ed.). *Folk and Farm*: Dublin. 15–29.

DELGADO, J. P. (ed.) (1997). *Encyclopaedia of Underwater and Maritime Archaeology*. London: British Museum Press.

DELOCHE, J. (1994). *Transport and Communications in India*, ii. *Water Transport*. New Delhi: Oxford University Press.

—— (1996). 'Iconographic evidence on the development of boat and ship structures in India: A new approach', in Ray and Salles (eds.): 199–224.

DELPINO, F. (1991). 'Siderurgia e protostoria italiana'. *Studi Etruschi*, 56: 3–9.

DE MORGAN, J. (1894–1903). *Fouilles à Dahchour*, 2 vols. Vienna: Adolphe Holzhausen.

DENFORD, G. T. and FARRELL, A. W. (1980). 'Caergwrle bowl'. *IJNA* 9: 183–92.

DENNELL, R. (1983). *European Economic Prehistory: A New Approach*. London: Academic Press.

DE SÉLINCOURT, A. (ed.) (1954). *Herodotus: The Histories*. rev. J. Marincola, 1972. Harmondsworth: Penguin.

DEVOY, R. J. (1982). 'Analysis of the geological evidence for Holocene sea-level movements in SE England', *Proceedings of the Geologists' Association*, 93: 65–90.

DEVENDRA, S. (1995). *Pre-modern Sri Lankan Watercraft: The Twin-hulled Longboats*. Sesquicentennial Commemorative Volume of Royal Asiatic Society of Sri Lanka. Colombo: 211–38.

DE WEERD, M. (1987). 'Velsen: The medieval logboat', in R. W. Brandt, W. Groenman-van Wateringe, and S. van der Loeuw (eds.) (1987), *Assendelver Polder Pap*, 1: 265–83.

—— (1988). *Schepen voor Zwammerdam*. Amsterdam: de Weerd.

—— (1990). 'Barges of the Zwammerdam type and their building procedures', in McGrail (ed.) (1999a): 75–6.

—— (1994). 'Rib insertion in phases', in Westerdahl (ed.): 43–4.

—— and Haalëbos J. K. (1973). 'Schepen voor het opscheppen'. *Spiegel Historiael*, 8: 386–97.

DICK-READ, R. (1964). *Sanamn*. London.

DILKE, O. A. W. (1985). *Greek and Roman Maps*. London: Thames & Hudson.

DILLEHAY, T. D. (1989). *Monte Verde: A Late Pleistocene Settlement in Chile*, i. Washington: Smithsonian Institution Press.

—— (1997). *Monte Verde: A Late Pleistocene Settlement in Chile*, ii. Washington: Smithsonian Institution Press.

DIMMOCK, H. L. F. (1944). 'Points of the compass: Arabian style'. *MM* 30: 154–61.

DOE, B. (1980). 'Emergence of Arabia', in Sherratt (ed.) (1980a): 212–15.

DONNELLY, I. A. (1924). *Chinese Junks and Other Native Craft*. repr. 1988. Singapore: G. Brash.

DORAN, E. (1971). 'Sailing raft as a great tradition', in C. L. Riley J. C. Kelley, C. W. Pennington, and R. I. Rauds (eds.) (1971). *Man Across the Sea*. Austin: University of Texas Press, 115–38.

—— (1973). *Nao, Junk and Vaka: Boats and Culture History*. Texas: Texas A & M University.

—— (1978). 'Seaworthiness of sailing rafts'. *Anthropological Journal of Canada*, 16: 17–22.

—— (1981). *Wangka: Austronesian Canoe Origins*. Texas: Texas A & M University Press.

DORAN, J. E. and HODSON, F. R. (1975). *Mathematics and Computers in Archaeology*. Edinburgh: Edinburgh University Press.

DOUMAS, C. (ed.) (1978). *Thera and the Aegean World*, i. London.

DRACK, W. (1989). 'Das rad in der Eisenzeit'. *Katalog zur Sonderausstellung des Schwiezerischen Landesmuseums*: 31–42.

DUBOIS, C. (1976). 'Remarques sur les quilles des navires romains'. *Revue archéologique de Narbonnaise*, 9: 155–75.

DUFF, A. J. (1998). 'Reality of long-distance rowing'. Paper presented to the Trireme Conference at Oxford, Aug. 1998.

DUMOND, D. E. (1980). 'Colonisation in the Arctic', in Sherratt (ed.) (1980a): 361–4.

DUMONT D'URVILLE, J. S. C. (1834–5). *Voyage pittoresque auteur du monde*. 2 vols. Paris: Tastu.

DUNCAN, L. (1982). 'Experimental voyaging in the Pacific'.

*Journal of the Polynesian Society*, 91: 455–65.

DUNPHY, W. P. (1979). 'Bark canoes of N. America'. *MM* 65: 77–82.

DURHAM, G. (1955). 'Canoes from cedar logs'. *Pacific Northwest Quarterly*, 46: 33–9.

DURRANS, B. (1979), 'Ancient Pacific voyaging: Cook's views and the development of interpretation'. *Captain Cook and the South Pacific*, British Museum Yearbook, 3. London: British Museum, 137–66.

EDWARDS, C. R. (1965). 'Aboriginal watercraft on the Pacific coast of S. America'. *Ibero-Americáná*, 47. Berkeley and Los Angeles: University of California Press.

EDWARDS, R. (1972). *Aboriginal Bark Canoes of the Murray Valley*. Adelaide: South Australia Museum.

EDYE, J. W. (1834), 'Native vessels of India and Ceylon'. *Journal of the Royal Asiatic Society*, 1: 4–14.

EGEDE, H. (1745). *A Description of Greenland*. Copenhagen.

ELGEE, H. W., and ELGEE, F. (1949), 'An EBA burial in a boat-shaped coffin from NE Yorkshire'. *PPS* 15: 87–106.

ELLMERS, D. (1972). *Frühmittelalterliche Handelsschiffahrt in Mittel und Nordeuropa*. Neumünster: Karl Wachholtz Verlag.

—— (1979). *Cog of Bremen and Related Boats*, in McGrail (ed.): 1–15.

—— (1984). 'Earliest evidence for skin boats in Palaeolithic Europe', in McGrail (ed.) (1984a): 41–85.

—— (1990) 'Frisian monopoly of coastal transport in the 6th–8th centuries AD', in McGrail (ed.) (1990a): 91–2.

—— (1994). 'Cog as a cargo carrier', in Unger (ed.): 29–46.

—— (1996). 'Celtic plank boats and ships, 500 BC–AD 1000', in A.-E. Christensen (ed.): 52–71.

EMANUELE, P. D. (1977). 'Ancient square rigging, with and without lifts'. *IJNA* 6: 181–5.

EMERY, W. B. (1963). *Archaic Egypt*. Edinburgh.

ENGELBRECHT, W. E. and Seyfert, C. K. (1994). 'Palaeo-Indian watercraft: Evidence and implications'. *North American Archaeologist*, 15: 221–34.

ENGELHARDT, C. (1865). *Nydam Mosefund*. Copenhagen.

ENGLERT, A., INDRUSZEWSKI, G., JENSEN, H., GIÜLLAND, T., and GREGORY, D., (1998). 'Sailing in Slavonic waters'. *Maritime Archaeology Newsletter*, 11: 14–27.

ERNSTON, J. (1985). 'Ship procession fresco: The pilots'. *IJNA* 14: 315–20.

EVANS, A. (1935). *Palace of Minos at Knossos*. London.

EVANS, A. C. (1994). *Sutton Hoo Ship Burial*. London: British Museum.

EWE, H. (1972). *Schiffe auf Siegeln*. Rostock.

FACEY, W. and MARTIN, E. B. (1979). *Oman: A Seafaring Nation*. Muscat: Ministry of Information and Culture, Oman.

FAGAN, B. M. (1996). *Oxford Companion to Archaeology*. New York: Oxford University Press.

FARRAR, A. (1987). 'Spray deflectors'. *MM* 73: 271–2.

—— (1988). 'Spray deflectors: A sequel'. *MM* 74: 160–2.

—— (1989). 'Marsala Punic ship: The shape to be re-lofted'.

*MM* 75: 368–70.

—— (1990). 'Ancient Mediterranean boatbuilding'. *Ship and Boat International*, Mar.: 15–18; May: 27–30.

FARRELL, A. W. and PENNEY, S. (1975). 'Broighter boat: A reassessment'. *Irish Archaeological Research Forum*, 2,2: 15–26.

FATIMI, S. Q. (1996). 'History of the development of the *kamal*', in Ray and Salles (ed.): 283–92.

FENWICK, V. (ed.) (1978). *Graveney Boat*. Oxford: BAR 53.

—— (1983). 'New Anglo-Saxon ship'. *IJNA* 12: 174–5.

—— (1997). 'Graveney boat', in Delgado (ed.): 175–6.

FERNANDEZ-ARMESTO, F. (1991). *Atlas of World Exploration*. London: The Times.

FILGUEIRAS, O. L. (1977). 'Xavega boat', in McGrail (ed.): 77–111.

—— (ed.) (1988). *Local Boats*. Oxford: BAR. S. 438, 2 vols.

—— (1990). 'Barco do Mar and the Thera boats breed'. *Tropis*, 2: 143–73.

FINNEY, B. R. (1982). 'Early sea-craft, transoceanic voyagers and Stone Age navigators'. *Archaeoastronomy*, 5: 30–6.

—— (1994). *Voyage of Rediscovery*. Berkeley: University of California Press.

—— KILONSKY, B. J., SOMSEN, S., and STROUP, E. D. (1986). 'Relearning a vanishing art'. *Journal of the Polynesian Society*, 95: 41–89.

FITZGERALD, M. A. (1994). 'The ship', in J. P. Oleson (ed.) (1994). *Harbours of Caesarea Maritima*, Oxford: BAR. S. 594.

FITZPATRICK, A. P., ELLIS, C, and ALLEN, M. J. (1996). 'Bronze Age "jetties" or causeways at Testwood Lakes, Hampshire'. *Newswarp*, 20: 19–22.

FLEMMING, N. C. (1996). 'Sea level, neo-techtonics and changes in coastal settlement', in E. E. Rice (ed.), *Sea and History*. Stroud: Sutton Publishing, 23–52.

FLETCHER, J. (1984). 'Date of the Graveney boat'. *IJNA* 13: 151.

FLIEDNER, S. (1964). *Die Bremer Kogge*. Bremen: Focke Museum.

—— and POHL-WEBER, R. (1972). *Cog of Bremen*. Bremerhaven: Deutsches Schiffahrtsmuseum.

FOLKARD, H. C. (1870). *Sailing Boat*. 4th edn. Repr. 1973. Wakefield.

FORBES, R. J. (1964). *Bitumen and Petroleum in Antiquity*. i. 2nd. edn. Leiden: E. J. Brill.

FORSELL, H. (1983). *Fynd av Sydda Båtar i Finland*. Båtar 1. Helsingfors: Skärgårdmuseet.

FORSELL, H. (1985). 'Sewn boats in Finland', in McGrail and Kentley (eds.): 195–210.

FRAKE, C. O. (1994). 'Dials: A study in the physical representation of cognitive systems', in C. Renfrew, and E. B. W. Zubrow (eds.), *Ancient Minds: Elements of Cognitive Archaeology*. Cambridge: Cambridge University Press, 119–32.

FRESCHI, A. (1991). 'Note tecniche sul relitto greco arcaico di Gela'. *Atti*, 4: 201–10.

FRIEL, I. (1993). 'Henry V's *Grace Dieu* and the wreck in the River Hamble near Bursledon, Hampshire'. *IJNA* 22: 3–19.

—— (1995). *Good Ship*. London: British Museum Press.

FROST, R. J., HO, C. H., and NG, B. (1974). 'Sha Tsui, High Island'. *Journal of the Hong Kong Archaeological Society*, 5: 23–33.

FROST, H. (1975a). 'Another Punic wreck in Sicily'. *IJNA* 4: 209–28.

—— (1975b). 'Discovery of a Punic ram'. *MM* 61: 23–5.

—— (1975c). 'Pharos site, Alexandria, Egypt'. *IJNA* 4: 126–30.

—— (1976). *Punic Ship: Final Excavation Report*. Supplement to *Natizie degli Scavi di Autichita*, 30.

—— (1977). 'Progressing towards the reconstruction of the Punic ship'. *MM* 63: 33–4.

—— (1981). 'Punic ship museum, Marsala'. *MM* 67: 65–75.

—— (1990). 'Where did they build ancient warships?'. *Tropis*, 2: 181–6.

—— (1996). 'Old saws'. *Tropis*, 4: 189–97.

—— (1997). 'Marsala Punic warship', in Delgado (ed.): 260–2.

—— (1999). 'Simulated Clinkers in the Third Century BC Mediterranean', in Pomey and Rieth (eds.): 161–3.

FRY, M. F. (2000). *Coiti*. Northern Ireland Archaeological Monograph, 6. Belfast: DOE.

GAIRDNER, J. (1889). *Sailing Directions for the Circumnavigation of England and for a Voyage to the Strait of Gibraltar*. 1st ser., vol. 79. London: Hakluyt Society. repr. New York (n.d.).

GALANG, R. E. (1941). 'Types of watercraft in the Philippines'. *Philippines Journal of Science*, 75, 3: 291–306.

GALE, N. H. (ed.) (1991). *Bronze Age Trade in the Mediterranean*. Studies in Mediterranean Archaeology, 90. Jonsered: Paul Åströms Förlag.

GARMONSWAY, G. N. (ed.) (1967). *Anglo-Saxon Chronicle*. London: Dent.

GASPAR, A. T. and VALLEJO, E. A. (1992). 'Lessons from the Canaries'. *Antiquity*, 66: 120–9.

GASSEND, J.-M. (1989). 'La Construction navale antique de type alterne'. *Tropis*, 1: 115–27.

GEORGIOU, H. S. (1996). 'Rigging of Bronze Age ships'. *Tropis*, 4: 213–27.

GIBSON-HILL, C. A. (1952). 'Further notes on the old boat found at Pontian in S. Pahang'. *Journal of Malayan Branch of Royal Asiatic Society*, 25: 111–33.

—— (1954). 'Malayan fishing boats'. *Journal of Malayan Branch of Royal Asiatic Society*, 27: 149–50.

GIDDINGS, J. L. (1964). *Archaeology of Cape Denbigh*. Providence, RI: Brown University.

—— (1967). *Ancient Men of the Arctic*. London.

GIDMARK, D. (1988). *Algonquin Birchbark Canoe*. Princes Risborough: Shire Ethnography.

GIESECKE, H.-E. (1983). 'Akrotiri ship fresco'. *IJNA* 12: 123–43.

GIFFORD, E. (1993). 'Expanding oak logboats: Is it possible?', in Coles, Fenwick, and Hutchinson (eds.): 52–3.

—— and GIFFORD, J. (1995). 'Sailing characteristics of Saxon ships as derived from half-scale working models with special reference to the Sutton Hoo ship'. *IJNA* 24: 121–31.

—— —— (1996). 'Sailing performance of Anglo-Saxon ships as derived from the building and trials of half-scale models of the Sutton Hoo and Graveney ship finds'. *MM* 82: 131–53.

—— —— (1997). 'Probable sailing capabilities of Middle Minoan Aegean ships'. *MM* 83: 199–206.

GILBERT, E. (1998). 'Mtepe: A regional trade in the late survival of sewn ships in E. African waters'. *IJNA* 27: 43–50.

GILLMER, T. C. (1975). 'Thera ship'. *MM* 61: 321–9.

—— (1978). 'Thera ships: A reanalysis'. *MM* 64: 125–133.

—— (1985a). 'Thera ships as sailing vessels'. *MM* 71: 401–13.

—— (1985b). 'Appendix B: Reply to Basch 1985'. *MM* 71: 415–16.

—— (1989). 'Theories on ship configuration in the Bronze Age Aegean'. *Tropis*, 1: 129–38.

—— (1995). 'Further identification of functional parts of Thera fresco's ships'. *Tropis*, 3: 177–92.

GLOVER, I. C. (1980). 'Agricultural origins in E. Asia', in Sherratt (ed.) (1980a): 152–61.

—— (1996). 'Recent archaeological evidence for early maritime contacts between India and SE Asia', in Ray and Salles (eds.): 129–58.

GODDARD, D. (1985). 'Proas of Kiribati', in McGrail and Kentley (eds.): 367–86.

GOOD, G. L., JONES, R. H., and PONSFORD, M. W. (eds.) (1991). *Waterfront Archaeology*. CBA Research Report 74. London: CBA.

GOODBURN, D. M. (1986). 'Do we have evidence of a continuing Saxon boatbuilding tradition?' *IJNA* 15: 39–47.

—— (1987). 'Medmerry: A reassessment of a migration period site on the south coast of England'. *IJNA* 16: 213–24.

—— (1994). 'Anglo-Saxon boat finds from London: Are they English?', in Westerdahl (ed.): 97–104.

—— (2000). 'New light on the construction of early medieval "Frisian" seagoing vessels', in Litwin (2000): 219–24.

GORDON, R. K. (1949). *Anglo-Saxon Poetry*. London: Dent.

GOSDEN, C. (1993). 'Understanding the settlement of Pacific islands in the Pleistocene', in M. A. Smith, M. Spriggs, and B. Faukhauser (eds.) (1993). *Sahull in Review*. Australian National University, Dept. of Prehistory Occasional Paper 24. Canberra: Australian National University Press, 131–6.

GOWLETT, J. (1984). *Ascent to Civilisation*. London: Collins.

GRAHAM-CAMPBELL, J. (ed.) (1994). *Cultural Atlas of the Viking World*. Oxford: Andromeda.

GREEN, J. (1983a). 'Song dynasty shipwreck at Quanzhou, Fujian Province, People's Republic of China'. *IJNA* 12: 253–61.

—— (1983b). 'Shinan excavation, Korea: An interim report on the hull structure'. *IJNA* 12: 293–301.

—— (1983c). 'Ko Si Chang Excavation Report'. *Bulletin of the Australian Institute for Maritime Archaeology*, 72: 9–37.

GREEN, J. (1984). 'Maritime archaeology of shipwrecks of the Indian Ocean: 50 years on'. Paper presented to the 2nd International Conference of Indian Ocean Studies, Perth.

—— (1985). 'Ko Si Chang 1 shipwreck excavation 1983–5'. *Report on SPAFA Technical Workshop on Ceramics*. Bangkok: 311–35.

—— (1986a). 'Eastern shipbuilding traditions: A review of the evidence'. *Bulletin of the Australian Institute for Maritime Archaeology*, 122: 1–6.

—— (1986b). 'Chinese shipbuilding traditions, new evidence from maritime archaeological sites'. Paper presented to the 4th International Conference on the History of Chinese Science, Sydney.

—— (1994). 'Maritime archaeology and maritime ethnography of the Indian Ocean, SE and E. Asia'. Paper presented to the International Seminar on Techno-Archaeological Perspectives of Seafaring in the Indian Ocean, New Delhi.

—— and BURNINGHAM, N. (1998). 'Ship from Quanzhou, Fujian Province, People's Republic of China'. *IJNA* 27: 277–301.

—— and HARPER, R. (1983). *Excavation of the Pattaya Wreck Site and Survey of Three Other Sites*, Thailand 1982. Australian Institute for Maritime Archaeology, Special Publication 1. Albert Park, Victoria.

—— —— (1987). *Maritime Archaeology of Shipwrecks and Ceramics in SE Asia*. Australian Institute for Maritime Archaeology, Special Publication 4. Albert Park, Victoria: 1–37.

—— and KIM, Z. G. (1989). 'Shinan and Wando sites: Further information'. *IJNA* 18: 33–41.

—— HARPER, R., and INTAKOSI, V. (1986). 'Ko Si Chang 1 shipwreck excavation 1983–5: A progress report'. *IJNA* 15: 105–22.

—— —— —— (1987). 'Ko Si Chang 3 shipwreck excavation'. Australian Institute for Maritime Archaeology. Special Publication 4. Albert Park, Victoria: 39–79.

—— —— and PRISHANCHITTARA, S. (1981). *Excavation of the Ko Kradat Wreck Site, Thailand, 1979–1980*. Special Publication, Dept. of Maritime Archaeology. Perth: Western Australian Museum.

—— CLARK, D., SANTIAGO, R. and ALVARES, M. (1995). 'Interim report on the joint Australian–Philippines Butuan boat project'. *IJNA* 24: 177–88.

GREEN, R. C. (1991). 'Near and Remote Oceania', in A. Pawley (ed.) (1991). *Man and a Half*, Polynesian Society Memoir, No. 48. Auckland: 491–502.

GREENHILL, B. (1957). 'Boats of East Pakistan', *MM* 43: 106–34; 203–15.

—— (1961). 'More evidence for the separate evolution of the clinker-built boat in Asia'. *MM* 47: 296–7.

—— (1963). 'A boat of the Indus'. *MM* 49: 273–5.

—— (1966). *Boats of East Pakistan*. London: Society for Nautical Research.

—— (1971). *Boats and Boatmen of Pakistan*. Newton Abbot: David and Charles.

—— (ed.) (1976). *Archaeology of the Boat*. London: A. & C. Black.

—— (1988). *Evolution of the Wooden Ship*. London: Batsford.

—— (1995a). *Archaeology of Boats and Ships*. London: Conway Maritime Press.

—— (ed.) (1995b). *Evolution of the Sailing Ship*. London: Conway, Maritime Press.

—— (2000). 'The mysterious Hulc'. *MM*. 86: 3–18.

GRENIER, R. (1988). 'Basque whalers in the New World', in Bass (ed.): 69–84.

—— LOEWEN, B., and PROULX, J.-P. (1994). 'Basque shipbuilding technology c.1560–1580', in Westerdahl (ed.): 137–42.

GROSSMAN, E. (1994). 'Sounding leads from Apollonia, Israel'. *IJNA* 23: 247–53.

GUÉROUT, M., RIETH., E., and GASSEND, J. M. (1989). 'Le navire Génois de Villefranche: Un naufrage de 1516?'. *Archaeonautica* 9.

GUIDON, N. and DELIBRIAS, G. (1986). 'Carbon-14 dates point to man in the Americas 32,000 years ago'. *Nature*, 321: 769–71.

GUILAINE, J. (ed.) (1991). *Prehistory*. Oxford: Facts on File.

GUY, J. (1992). 'China and the Maritime Silk Route conference'. *IJNA* 21: 70–3.

—— (1995). 'Sculptural boat model from eastern India', *South Asian Archaeology*, 769–78.

HABGOOD, P. J. (1986). 'Aboriginal migrations: They came to a land down-under'. Paper read at the World Archaeological Congress, Southampton.

HADDON, A. C. and HORNELL, J. (1936–8). *Canoes of Oceania*, 3 vols. Special Publications. Honolulu: B. P. Bishop Museum, 27–9. repub. as one vol. Honolulu, 1975.

HAGUE, D. B. (1973). 'Lighthouses', in D. J. Blackburn (ed.). *Marine Archaeology*. London: Butterworth, 293–314.

HAGY, J. W. (1986). '800 years of Etruscan ships'. *IJNA* 15: 221–50.

HALDANE, C. W. (1988). 'Boat timbers from El-Lisht'. *MM* 74: 141–52.

—— (1993). 'Ancient Egyptian hull construction'. Doctoral diss. Texas A & M University.

HALDANE, C. W. (1996). 'Ancient Egyptian hull construction'. *Tropis*, 4: 235–44.

—— (1997a). 'Dahshur boats', in Delgado (ed.): 122–3.

—— (1997b). 'Khufu Ships', in Delgado (ed.): 222–3.

—— and SHELMERDINE, C. W. (1990). 'Herodotus, 2. 96. 1–2 again'. *Classical Quarterly*, 40, 2: 535–9.

HALE, J. R. (1980). 'Plank-built in the Bronze Age'. *Antiquity*, 54: 118–27.

HALL, B. (1824). *Extracts from a Journal Written on the Coasts of Chili, Peru, and Mexico*. 2nd edn. Edinburgh.

HALLS, C. (1961). 'Origin and distribution of the dug-out canoe in Australia'. *MM* 47: 208–9.

HALLSTRÖM, G. (1960). *Monumental Art of Northern Sweden*

*from the Stone Age*. Stockholm.

HAMILTON, A. (1727). *A New Account of the East Indies*. 2 vols. London.

HAMMOND, N. (1981). 'Classic Maya canoes'. *IJNA* 10: 173–85.

—— (1989). 'Introduction', in W. M. Bray, E. H. Swanson, and I. S. Farrington (1989). *Ancient Americas*. Oxford: Phaidon, 1–8.

HANSEN, K. and MADSEN, J. S. (1981). *Barkbåde*. Roskilde: Viking Ship Museum.

HARRIOT, T. (1590). *Briefe and True Report of the New Found Land of Virginia*. repub. 1972. New York:

HARRIS, D. R. (1994). 'Pathways to world prehistory'. *Proceedings of the Prehistoric Society*, 60: 1–13.

HARRIS, J. W. K. (1980). 'Early man', in Sherratt (ed.) (1980a): 62–70.

HASSLÔF, O. (1963). 'Wrecks, archives and living tradition'. *MM* 49: 162–77.

—— (1972a). 'Main principles in the technology of shipbuilding', in Hasslôf, Henningsen, and Christensen (eds.) (1972b): 27–72.

—— HENNINGSEN, H., and CHRISTENSEN, A.-E. (eds.) (1972b). *Ships and Shipyards, Sailors and Fishermen*. Copenhagen: Copenhagen University Press.

HAWKES, C. F. C. (1954). 'Archaeological theory and method: Some suggestions from the Old World'. *American Anthropologist*, 56: 155–68

—— (1977). *Pytheas*. 8th J. N. L. Myres Memorial Lecture. Oxford: Blackwell.

—— (1984). 'Ictis disentangled and the British tin trade'. *Oxford Journal of Archaeology*, 3: 211–33.

HE, G. (1991). 'Measurement and research of the ancient Ming dynasty ship unearthed in Liangshan', in Zhang (ed.): 237–44.

HEINSIUS, P. (1956). *Das Schiff der Hansischen Frühzeit*. Hanseatic Historical Society, NS 12. Weimar: Herman Bolan.

HEIZER, R. F. (1938). 'Plank canoe of the Santa Barbara region California'. *Ethnological Studies*, 7: 193–227.

—— (1966). 'Plank canoes of S. and N. America'. *Kroeber Anthropological Society Papers*, 35: 22–39.

HENKEL, X. (1901). 'Die sichtbarkeit im Mittelmeergerbiet'. *Petermann's Geographische Mittelungen*.

HERRMANN, G. (1980). 'Parthion and Sasanian Iran', in Sherratt (ed.) (1980a): 278–83.

HERODOTUS. *The Histories*, trans. A. de Sélincourt (1954). rev. J. Marincola, 1972. Harmondsworth: Penguin.

HERTEIG, A. E. (ed.) (1985). *Conference on Waterfront Archaeology in North European Towns*. Bergen: Historisk Museum.

HEYERDAHL, T. (1963). *Kon-Tiki Expedition*. London: Penguin Books.

—— (1972). *Ra Expeditions*. London: Penguin Books.

—— (1978). *Early Man and the Ocean*. London: Allen & Unwin.

—— and SKJÖLSVOLD, A. (1956). 'Archaeological evidence for pre-Spanish visits to the Galapagos Islands'. *Memoir of the Society of American Archaeologists*, No. 12.

HIGHAM, C. (1989). *Archaeology of Mainland SE Asia*. Cambridge World Archaeology. Cambridge: Cambridge University Press.

HILL, A. H. (1958). 'Some early accounts of the Oriental boat'. *MM* 44: 201–17.

HIRTE, C. (1987). 'Zur Archäologie monoxyler Wasserfahrzeuge im nördlichen Mitteleuropa'. unpub. thesis, University of Kiel.

HOCKER, F. (1991). 'Cogge en Coggeschip: Late trends in cog development', in R. Reinders (ed.) (1991). *Bouwtraditie en Scheepstype*. Groningen: 25–32.

—— (1995). 'Lead hull sheathing in Antiquity'. *Tropis*, 3: 197–206.

HOCKMANN, O. (1982). 'Spatromische schiffsfunde in Mainz'. *Archeol. Korrespond*, 12: 231–50.

—— (1989). 'Römische schiffsfunde westlich des Kastells Oberstimm'. *Sonderdruck qus Bericht der Römasch–Germanischen Kommission*, 70: 322–50.

—— (1997). 'Roman river patrols and military logistics on the Rhine and the Danube', in A. N. Jorgensen and B. L. Clausen (eds.). *Military Aspects of Scandinavian Society*: Studies, 2. Copenhagen: National Museum, 239–47.

HODGE, A. T. (1983). 'Massalia, meteorology, and navigation'. *Ancient World*, 7: 67–88.

HODGES, H. (1964). *Artefacts*. London: J. Baker.

HOEKSTRA, R. E. (2000). 'Cog of Kampen: Rebuilding of the wreck OZ36', in Litwin (2000): 117–20.

HOEKSTRA, T. J. (1975). 'Utrecht'. *IJNA* 4: 390–2.

HOFFMANN, P., CHOI, K.-N, and KIM, Y.-H. (1991). '14th century Shinan ship: Progress in conservation'. *IJNA* 20: 59–64.

HOHEISEL, W. D. (1994). 'Full-scale replica of the Hanse Cog of 1380', in Westerdahl (ed.): 257–60.

HOOKER, J. D. (ed.) (1896). *Journal of Sir Joseph Banks During Captain Cook's First Voyage in HMS* Endeavour *(1768–71)*. London.

HÖRBERG, P. U. (1995). 'Nuts, bricks and pewter', in Olsen, Madsen, and Rieck (eds.): 123–6.

HORNELL, J. (1910). 'Report on the feasibility of operating deep-sea fishing boats on the coasts of the Madras presidency'. *Madras Fishery Bulletin*, 4: 33–70.

—— (1920). 'Origins and ethnological significance of Indian boat design'. *Memoirs of the Asiatic Society of Bengal*, 7: 139–256.

—— (1928). 'South American balanced canoes'. *Man*, 28: 129–33.

—— (1929). 'Boats of the Ganges'. *Memoirs of the Asiatic Society of Bengal*, 8: 185–94.

—— (1930). 'Tongue and groove seam of the Gujarati boatbuilders'. *MM* 16: 310–12.

—— (1932). 'Oldest complete Polynesian canoe hull in existence'. *Man* 32: 266–96.

—— (1936). 'British coracles'. *MM* 22: 5–41, 261–304.

HORNELL, J. (1937–8). 'Curraghs of Ireland'. *MM* 23: 78–83; 24: 5–39, 148–75.

—— (1938a). 'Coracles of the Tigris and Euphrates'. *MM* 24: 153–9.

—— (1938b). 'Boat occuli survivals: Additional records'. *Journal of the Royal Anthropological Institute*, 68: 339–48.

—— (1939). 'Canoe hull from Manihiki'. *Ethnologia Cranmorensis*, 4: 6–12.

—— (1939–40). 'Frameless boats of the Middle Nile'. *MM* 25: 417–32; 26: 125–44.

—— (1941a). 'Sea trade in early times'. *Antiquity*, 15: 234–56.

—— (1941b). 'Seagoing *mtepe* and *dau* of the Lamu archipelago'. *MM* 27: 54–68.

—— (1941c). 'Pelota or hide-balsa of S. America'. *Man*, 41: 27–30.

—— (1942a). 'Tentative classification of Arab sea-craft'. *MM* 28: 11–40.

—— (1942b). 'Floats: A study in primitive water transport'. *Journal Royal Anthropological Institute*, 72: 33–44.

—— (1943a). 'Outrigger devices: Distribution and origin'. *Journal of the Polynesian Society*, 52: 91–100.

—— (1943b). 'Fishing and Coastal Craft of Ceylon'. *MM* 29: 40–53.

—— (1943c). 'Sailing ships in Ancient Egypt'. *Antiquity*, 17: 27–41.

—— (1944a). 'Constructional parallels in Scandinavia and Oceanic boat construction'. *Journal of the Polynesian Society*, 53: 43–58.

—— (1944b). 'Outrigger canoes of Madagascar, E. Africa and the Comoro Islands'. *MM* 30, 3–18, 170–85.

—— (1945). 'Was there pre-Columbian contact between the peoples of Oceania and S. America?' *Journal of the Polynesian Society*, 54, 4: 167–91.

—— (1946a). *Water Transport*. Cambridge: Cambridge University Press. repr. 1970, Newton Abbot: David and Charles.

—— (1946b). 'Role of birds in early navigation'. *Antiquity*, 20: 142–9.

—— (1946c). 'How did the sweet potato reach Oceania?' *Journal Linn. Society Botany*, 53: 41–62.

—— (1948). 'Making and spreading of dugout canoes'. *MM* 36: 46–52.

HORRIDGE, G. A. (1978). *Design of Planked Boats of the Moluccas*. National Maritime Museum Monographs, 38. Greenwich.

—— (1979). *Konjo Boatbuilders and the Bugis prahus of S. Sulawesi*. National Maritime Museum Monographs, 40. Greenwich.

—— (1981). 'Ancient plank boats of the islands east of Asia', in D. Howse (ed.) (1981). *Five Hundred Years of Nautical Science, 1400 to 1900*. Greenwich: National Maritime Museum, 241–58.

—— (1982). *Lashed-lug Boats of the Eastern Archipelagos*. National Maritime Museum Monograph, 54. Greenwich.

—— (1986). 'Evolution of Pacific canoe rigs'. *Journal of Pacific History*, 21/2: 83–99.

HORTON, M. (1997). 'Mare Nostrum: A new archaeology in the Indian Ocean'. *Antiquity*, 71: 747–9.

HOURANI, G. F. (1963). 'Arab seafaring in the Indian Ocean'in Ancient and Early Medieval Times'. Beirut: Khayats. (repr. from Princeton Oriental Studies, No. 13: 1951). repr. with notes, 1995. Princeton: Princeton University Press.

HUANG, B. (1991). 'Overall design of the official ship in the style of the ancients: "Zheng He"', in Zhang (ed.) (1991): 286–97.

HUDSON, T., TIMBROOK, J., and REMPE, M. (eds.) (1978). *Tomol: Chumash watercraft as described in the ethnographic'notes of John P. Harrington*. Anthropological Papers, No. 9. Santa Barbara Museum: Ballena Press.

HUMBLA, P. (1934). 'Båtfyndet vid Äskekärr'. *Göteborgs och Bohusläns fornminnes förenings tidskrift*. Göteborg: 1–21.

HUNTINGFORD, G. W. B. (1980). *Periplus of the Erythraean Sea*. London: Hakluyt Society.

HURAULT, J. (1970). *Africains de Guyane*. The Hague.

HUTCHINSON, G. (1991). 'Early 16th century wreck at Studland Bay, Dorset', in Reinders and Paul (eds.): 171–5.

—— (1994). *Medieval Ships and Shipping*. Leicester: Leicester University Press.

—— (1995). 'Two English side-rudders', in Olsen, Madsen and Rieck (eds.): 97–102.

IFE, B. W. (ed.) (1990). *Christopher Columbus' Journal of the First Voyage*. Warminster: Aris and Phillips.

INSKEEP, R. (1980). 'Final stages of hunting and gathering in Africa', in Sherratt (ed.) (1980a): 174–8.

IRWIN G. (1992). *Prehistoric Exploration and Colonisation of the Pacific*. Cambridge: Cambridge University Press.

—— BICKLER, S., and QUIRKE, P. (1990). 'Voyaging by canoe and computer: Experiments in the settlement of the Pacific Ocean'. *Antiquity*, 64: 34–50.

JAMES, T. G. H. (1983). *Introduction to Ancient Egypt*. London: British Museum.

JANSSON, S. (1994). 'Hjortspring boat from northern Sweden?' *Maritime Archaeology Newsletter from Roskilde*, 2: 16–17.

JELLEMA, D. (1955). 'Frisian trade in the Dark Ages'. *Speculum*, 30: 15–36.

JENKINS, N. (1980). *Boat Beneath the Pyramid*. London: Thames & Hudson.

JENSEN, J. (1989). 'Hjortspring boat reconstructed'. *Antiquity*, 63: 531–5.

JESTIN, O. and CARRAZÉ, F. (1980). 'Mediterranean hull types compared: An unusual type of construction: The hull of wreck I at BonPorté'. *IJNA* 9: 70–2.

JEZEGOU, M. P. (1985). 'L'épave 2 de l'anse St. Gervais à Fos-sur-mer'. *Tropis*, I: 139–46.

JOFFREY, R. (1978). 'Note sur deux ferrets Mérovingiens de collection du Musée des Antiquités Nationales', in M. Fleury and P. Périn (eds.) (1978) *Problèmes de chronologie rel-*

*ative et absolue concernant les cimetières mérovingiens d'entre Loire et Rhine*. Paris.

JOHNSON, C. (1927). 'London shipbuilding, AD 1295'. *Antiquity*, 7: 424–37.

JOHNSTON, P. F. (1997). 'Thera', in Delgado (ed.): 419–20.

JOHNSTON, S. (1994). 'Making mathematical practice'. Ph.D. diss. University of Cambridge.

JOHNSTONE, P. (1972). 'Bronze Age sea trial'. *Antiquity*, 46: 269–74.

—— (1973). 'Stern first in the Stone Age?'. *IJNA* 2: 3–11.

—— (1988). *Sea-craft of Prehistory London*. 2nd edn. London: Routledge.

JOHNSTONE, T. M. and MUIR, J. (1962). 'Portuguese influences on shipbuilding in the Persian Gulf'. *MM* 48: 58–63.

JONES, D. (1990). *Model Boats from the Tomb of Tut'ankhamun*. Oxford: Griffith Institute.

—— (1995). *Boats*. London: British Museum Press.

JONES, R. (1976). 'Tasmania: Aquatic machines and offshore islands', in G. Sieveking, I. H. Longworth, and K. E. Wilson (eds.) (1976). *Problems in Economic and Social Archaeology*. London: Duckworth, 235–63.

—— (1977). 'Sundering of the Bassian bridge', in Allen, Golson, and Jones (eds.). *Sunda and Sahul*.

JØRGENSEN, A. N. and CLAUSEN, B. L. (eds.) (1997). *Military Aspects of Scandinavian Society*. Studies in Archaeology and History, 2. Copenhagen: National Museum.

KAHANOV, Y. (1994). 'Sheathing and caulking of ancient ships in the Mediterranean from the 6th century BC to the 5th century AD'. *CMS Newsletter*, 21: 12–13.

—— (1996). 'Conflicting evidence for defining the origin of the Ma'agan-Michael shipwreck'. *Tropis*, 4: 245–8.

—— (1999). 'Ma'agan-Michael ship (Israel)', in Pomey and Rieth (eds.): 155–60.

—— (forthcoming). 'Ma'agan-Michael ship'. *Proceedings of the 8th ISBSA Conference at Gdansk, 1997*.

—— DOHERTY, C., and SHALEV, S. (1999). 'Metal nails from the Ma'agan-Michael ship'. *IJNA* 28: 277–88.

—— (2000). 'Herodotus 4.42: The sun direction'. *MM 86*: 66–72.

KAPITÄN, G. (1969–71). 'Ancient anchors and lead plummets'. *Sefunim*, 3: 55–61.

—— (1990). 'Ancient two-armed stone-stocked wooden anchors: Chinese and Greek'. *IJNA* 19: 243–5.

—— (1991). 'Ancient two-armed stone-stocked wooden anchors: Chinese and Greek', in Zhang (ed.): 245–8.

KATZEV, M. L. (1989a). 'Kyrenia 2: Building a replica of an ancient Greek merchantman'. *Tropis*, 1: 163–75.

—— (1989b). 'Voyage of Kyrenia 2'. *INA Newsletter*, 161: 4–10.

—— (1990). 'Analysis of the experimental voyages of Kyrenia 2'. *Tropis*, 2: 245–55.

—— and KATZEV, S. W. (1986). 'Kyrenia 2'. *INA Newsletter*, 133: 2–11.

—— —— (1987). *Kyrenia 2: An Ancient Ship Sails Again*.

Piraeus: Hellenic Institute for the Preservation of Nautical Tradition.

KAUL, F. (1998). *Ships on Bronzes*, 2 vols. Copenhagen: The National Museum.

KAY, H. E. (1971). *Science of Yachts, Wind and Water*. Henley-on-Thames: Foulis.

KEHOE, A. B. (1971). 'Small boats upon the N. Atlantic', in Riley, Pennington, and Rands (eds.): 275–92.

KEITH, D.H. (1988) 'Shipwrecks of the explorers', in Bass (ed.): 45–68.

—— and BUYS, C. J. (1981). 'New light on medieval Chinese seagoing ship construction'. *IJNA* 10: 119–32.

KENNEDY, D. H. (1978). 'Further note on the Thera ships'. *MM* 64: 135–7.

KENTLEY, E. (1985). 'Some aspects of the *masula* surf boat', in McGrail and Kentley (eds.).: 303–18.

—— (1993). 'Sewn boats of the Indian Ocean: A common tradition?', in Coles, Fenwick, and Hutchinson (eds.): 68–71.

—— (1996). 'The sewn boats of India's east coast', in Ray and Salles (eds.) (1996): 247–260.

—— and GUNARATNE, R. (1987). '*Madel Paruwa*: A sewn boat with chine strakes'. *IJNA* 16: 35–48.

—— McGRAIL, S., and BLUE, L. (1999). 'Further notes on *patia* fishing boats in the Bay of Bengal'. *South Asian Studies*, 15: 151–8.

—— —— PALMER, C., and BLUE, L. (2000). 'Further notes on the frame-first vessels of Tamil Nadu'. *South Asian Studies*, 16: 143–8.

KIM, Z.-G. (1989). 'Outline of Korean shipbuilding history'. *Korean Journal*: 4–17.

—— (1991). 'Wreck excavated from Wando island', in Zhang (ed.) (1991): 56–8.

KIRCH, P. V. and ELLISON, J. (1994). 'Human colonisation of remote Oceanic islands'. *Antiquity*, 68: 310–21.

KLEIN, R. (1980). 'Later Pleistocene hunters', in Sherratt (ed.) (1980a): 87–95.

KNAPP, A. B. (1993). 'Thalassocracies in Bronze Age eastern Mediterranean trade'. *World Archaeology*, 24: 332–47.

KNAPP, F. V. (1924). 'Canoe-building tools of the Tasman Bay Maoris'. *Journal of the Polynesian Society*, 33: 103–13.

KNUTH, E. (1952). 'Outline of the archaeology of Peary Land'. *Arctic*, 51: 17–23.

—— (1980). 'Umiaq'en fra Peary Land'. Roskilde: Viking Ship Museum.

KRAMER, S. N. (1963). 'Dilmun: Quest for Paradise'. *Antiquity*, 37: 111–15.

KROEBER, A. L. (1925). *Handbook of the Indians of California*. Washington: Smithsonian Museum.

KUNIHOLM, P. I. (1990). 'Overview and assessment of the evidence for the date of the eruption of Thera'. *Thera III*, 3, 3: 13–18.

—— and STRIKER, C. L. (1987). 'Dendrochronological investigations in the Aegean and the neighbouring regions'.

*Journal of Field Archaeology*, 144: 385–98.

LABAREE, B. W. (1957). 'How the Greeks sailed into the Black Sea'. *American Journal of Archaeology*, 61: 29–33.

LAHN, W. (1992). *Die Kogge von Bremen*, i. Hamburg: Kabel.

LAMB, H. H. (1977). *Climate*, ii. London: Methuen.

LAMBROU-PHILLIPSON, C. (1995). 'Smiths on board Late Bronze Age ships'. *Tropis*, 3: 243–8.

—— (1996). 'Reliability of ships' iconography: The Theran miniature marine fresco as an example. *Tropis*, 4: 351–65.

LANDSTRÖM, B. (1961). *The Ship*. London: Allen & Unwin.

—— (1970). *Ships of the Pharaohs*. London: Allen & Unwin.

LANE, F. C. (1934). *Venetian Ships and Shipbuilders of the Renaissance*. Baltimore.

LANE-FOX, A. (1875). 'On early modes of navigation'. *Journal of the Royal Anthropological Institute*, 4: 399–437.

LANE-POOLE, R. H. (1940). 'Primitive craft and medieval rigs in S. America'. *MM* 26: 333–8.

LANTING, J. and BRINDLEY, A. (1996). 'Irish logboats and their European context'. *Journal of Irish Archaeology*, 7: 85–95.

LAYARD, A. H. (1849). *Nineveh and its Remains*. 3rd edn. 2 vols.

—— (1853) *Discoveries in the Ruins of Nineveh and Babylon*. London: John Murray.

LEBECQ, S. (1990). 'On the use of the word "Frisian" in the 6th–10th centuries written sources', in McGrail (ed.) (1990a): 85–90.

LEE, C.-E. (1991). 'Study on the structural and fluid characteristics of a rabbeted clinker-type ship', in Zhang (ed.): 154–68.

LEE, W. (1990). *Boats of Korea*. Daewonsa, Korea.

LEHMANN, L. T. (1978). 'A flat-bottomed Roman boat from Druten, Netherlands'. *IJNA* 7: 259–68.

LESHIKAR, M. E. (1988). 'Earliest watercraft: From rafts to Viking ships', in Bass (ed.) (1988): 13–32.

LEVISON, M., WARD, R. G., and WEBB, J. W. (1973). *Settlement of Polynesia: A Computer Simulation*. Minneapolis: University of Minnesota Press.

LEWIS, A. (1973). 'Maritime skills in the Indian Ocean 1368–1500'. *J. Economic and Social History of the Orient*, 162–3: 238–64.

LEWIS, A. B. (1932). *Melanesians*. Chicago: Natural History Museum.

LEWIS, D. (1970). 'Polynesian and Micronesian navigation techniques'. *J. Institute of Navigation*, 23: 432–47.

—— (1994). *We the Navigators*, 2nd edn. Honolulu: University of Hawaii Press.

L'HOUR, M. and VEYRAT, E. (1994). 'French medieval wreck from Aber Wrac'h', in Westerdahl (ed.): 165–80.

LI, B. (1991). 'Notes on the design of replica models of Zheng He's Treasure Ship fleet', in Zhang (ed.): 330–40.

LI, G.-Q. (1986). 'Investigation on the application of watertight seam-sealing putty on the Song vessel excavated at Quanzhou Bay'. *Marine History Research*, 2: 32–8.

—— (1989). 'Archaeological evidence for the use of "chunam" on the 13th century Quanzhou ship, Fujian Province, China'. *IJNA* 18: 277–83.

LI, S. and LIN, S. (1985). 'Textual study on the Dragon Boat unearthed in Ningbo, Zhejiang'. *Marine History Research*, 1: 18–24.

LIN, H. (1991). 'On the origin of sails in China', in Zhang (ed.): 320–9.

LIN, S., DU, G., and GREEN, J. (1991). 'Waterfront excavations at Dongmenkou, Ningbo, Zhe Jiang Province, PRC'. *IJNA* 20: 299–311.

LINDER, E. (1972). 'Seafaring merchant-smith from Ugarit and the C. Gelidonya wreck'. *IJNA* 1: 163–4.

LINSCHOTEN, J. H. van (1610). *Histoire de la navigation*. Amsterdam.

LIPKE, P. (1984). *Royal Ship of Cheops*. Oxford: BAR.S. 225.

LITWIN, J. (1985). 'Sewn craft of the 19th century in the European part of Russia', in McGrail and Kentley (eds.): 253–68.

—— (1995). 'Boats, cogs, hulcs and other medieval ship types in the south of the Baltic', in C. O. Cederlund (ed.) (1995) *Medieval Ship Archaeology*. Stockholm: University of Stockholm Press, 19–25.

—— (1997). 'Medieval Baltic ships', in P. Beck (ed.), (1997). *L'innovation technique au Moyen Age*. Paris: Editions Errance, 88–97.

—— (ed.) (2000). *Down the River to the Sea*. Gdańsk: Centralne Muzeum Morskie.

LIU, L. and LI, C. (1991). 'Characteristics of Guangdong wooden junks', in Zhang (ed.): 275–85.

LIU, P. (1991). 'Viewing Chinese ancient navigation and shipbuilding through Zheng He's ocean expeditions', in Zhang (ed.) 176–80.

LOEWE, M. (1980). 'Growth of a Chinese empire', in Sherratt (ed.) (1980a): 246–51.

LOEWEN, B. (1997). 'Bayonne, 1419: Lapstrake and moulded frames in the same hull?'. *MM* 83: 328–31.

—— (1999). 'Morticed frames of 16th century Atlantic ships and the "Madeiras da Conta" of Renaissance texts'. *Archaeonautica*, 14: 213–22.

LOSEBY, S. T. (1992). 'Marseille: A late antique success story'. *Journal of Roman Studies*, 82: 165–85.

LOTHROP, S. K. (1932). 'Aboriginal navigation off the west coast of S. America'. *Journal Royal Anthropological Institute*, 62: 229–56.

LOVEGROVE, H. (1964). 'Remains of two old vessels found at Rye, Sussex'. *MM* 50: 115–22.

LUND, N. (ed.) (1984). *Two Voyagers at the Court of King Alfred*. York: Sessions.

MA, X. (1991). 'Xu Fu, one of the navigation forerunners in the world', in Zhang (ed.): 181–90.

MAARLEVELD, T. J. (1992). *Archaeology and Early Modern Merchant ships*. Rotterdam Papers, 7. Rotterdam: ROB/AAO.

—— (1994). 'Double Dutch solutions in flush-planked shipbuilding', in Westerdahl (ed.): 153–64.

McCaughan, M. (1988). 'Ethnology and Irish boatbuilding traditions', in O. L. Filgueiras (ed.) (1988). *Local Boats*. Oxford: BAR.S. 438(i), 101–17.

—— (1991). 'Enigma of Carvel building traditions in Ireland', in Reinders and Paul (eds.): 133–6.

McCusker, J. J. (1966). 'Wine prise and medieval mercantile shipping'. *Speculum*, 41: 279–96.

McGhee, R. (1993). 'Skraellings of Vinland', in Clausen (ed.): 43–53.

McGowan, A. (1981). *Tiller and Whipstaff*. London: HMSO.

McGrail, S. (1975). 'Models, replicas and experiments in nautical archaeology'. *MM* 61: 3–8.

—— (ed.) (1977). *Sources and Techniques in Boat Archaeology*. Oxford: BAR.S 29.

—— (1978). *Logboats of England and Wales*'. Oxford: BAR. 51, 2 vols.

—— (ed.) (1979). *Archaeology of Medieval Ships and Harbours in Northern Europe*. Oxford: BAR.S 66.

—— (1981a). *Rafts, Boats and Ships*. London: HMSO.

—— (1981b). *Brigg 'Raft' and Her Prehistoric Environment*. Oxford: BAR. 89.

—— (1981c). 'A medieval logboat from the River Calder at Stanley Ferry, Wakefield, Yorkshire'. *Med. Arch.* 25: 160–4.

—— (1983a). 'The interpretation of archaeological evidence for maritime structures', in P. Annis (ed.) (1983). *Sea Studies*. Greenwich: National Maritime Museum, 33–46.

—— (1983b). 'Cross-Channel seamanship and navigation in the late-1st millennium BC'. *Oxford Journal of Archaeology*, 2: 299–337.

—— (ed.) (1984a). *Aspects of Maritime Archaeology and Ethnography*. Greenwich: National Maritime Museum.

—— (1985a). 'Brigg "raft": Reconstruction problems', in McGrail and Kentley (eds.): 165–94.

—— (1985b). 'Towards a classification of water transport'. *World Archaeology*, 163: 289–303.

—— (1988a). 'Assessing the performance of an ancient boat: The Hasholme logboat'. *Oxford Journal of Archaeology*. 7: 35–46.

—— (1988b). 'Foreword', 2nd edn. of Johnstone, 1988: pp. xiii–xviii.

—— (1989a). 'Maritime archaeology in Britain'. *Antiq. Journal*, 691: 10–22.

—— (1989b). 'Shipment of traded goods and of ballast in Antiquity'. *Oxford Journal of Archaeology*, 8: 353–8.

—— (1989c). 'Boatbuilding characteristics', in P. Marsden (ed.). 'Late-Saxon logboat from Clapton'. *IJNA* 18: 89–111.

—— (1989d). 'Pilotage and navigation in the times of St. Brendan', in J. de Courcy-Ireland and D. C. Sheehy (eds.). *Atlantic Vision*. Dun Laoghaire: Boole Press, 25–35.

—— (ed.) (1990a). *Maritime Celts, Frisians and Saxons*. CBA Research Report, 71. York: CBA.

—— (1990b). 'Boats and boatmanship in the late-prehistoric southern North Sea and Channel region', in McGrail (1990a): 32–48.

—— (1991a). 'Early sea voyages'. *IJNA* 20: 85–93.

—— (1991b). 'Bronze Age seafaring in the Mediterranean', in N. H. Gale (ed.) (1991). *Bronze Age Trade in the Mediterranean*: Studies in Mediterranean Archaeology, 90. Jonsered: Paul Åströms Förlag. 83–91.

—— (1992a). 'Columbus' trans-Atlantic voyages in 1492–3'. *Medieval History*, 23: 76–91.

—— (1992b). 'Replicas, reconstructions and floating hypotheses'. *IJNA* 21: 353–5.

—— (1993a). 'Prehistoric seafaring in the Channel', in C. Scarre and F. Healy (eds.). *Trade and Exchange in Prehistoric Europe*. Oxford: Oxbow, 199–210.

—— (1993b). *Medieval Boat and Ship Timbers from Dublin*. Dublin: Royal Irish Academy.

—— (1993c). 'Future of the designated wreck site in the River Hamble'. *IJNA* 22: 45–51.

—— (1995a). 'Celtic seafaring and transport', in M. J. Green (ed.). *Celtic World*: London: Routledge, 254–84.

—— (1995b). 'Romano-Celtic boats and ships: characteristic features'. *IJNA* 24: 139–45.

—— (1995c). 'Training maritime archaeologists', in O. Olsen, J. S. Madsen and F. Rieck (eds.) (1995), *Shipshape*. Roskilde: Viking Ship Museum, 329–34.

—— (1996a). 'Navigational techniques in Homer's Odyssey'. *Tropis*, 4: 311–20.

—— (1996b). 'Bronze Age in N. W. Europe', in A.-E. Christensen (ed.): 24–38.

—— (1996c). 'The study of boats with stitched planking', in Ray and Salles (eds.): 225–38.

—— (1996d). 'Ship: Carrier of goods, people and ideas', in E. E. Rice (ed.) (1996). *Sea and History*, Stroud: Sutton, 67–96.

—— (1997a). 'Early frame-first methods of building wooden boats and ships'. *MM* 83: 76–80.

—— (1997b). 'Boat fragments', in N. Nayling (ed.) (1997). *Excavations at Caldicot, Gwent*. CBA Research Report 108. 210–17.

—— (1997c). *Studies in Maritime Archaeology*. Oxford: BAR. 256.

—— (1998). *Ancient Boats in NW Europe*. 2nd edn. London: Longman.

—— (2000). 'ISBSA: Past, present and future'. in Litwin (2000): 269–72.

—— (forthcoming a). 'Portuguese-derived ship design methods in India?' *Proceedings of the Conference on the Iberian/Atlantic Shipbuilding Tradition in Lisbon, 1998*.

—— (forthcoming b) (ed.) *The Boats of South Asia*. London: Society for South Asian Studies.

—— and Farrell, A. (1979). 'Rowing: Aspects of the ethnographic and iconographic evidence'. *IJNA* 8: 155–66.

—— and Kentley, E. (eds.) (1985). *Sewn-Plank Boats*. Oxford: BAR.S. 276.

McGrail, S. and McKee, E. (1974). *Building and Trials of the Replica of an Ancient Boat*. Pts 1 and 2. Monographs and Reports 11. Greenwich: National Maritime Museum.

—— and Roberts, O. (1999). 'Romano-British boat from the shores of the Severn Estuary'. *MM* 85: 133–46.

—— and Switsur, R. (1979). 'Medieval logboats of the River Mersey', in S. McGrail (ed.) (1979). *Medieval Ships and Harbours in Northern Europe*. Oxford: BAR.S. 66.

—— Blue, L., and Kentley, E. (1999). 'Reverse-clinker boats of Bangladesh and their planking pattern'. *South Asian Studies*, 15: 119–49.

McKee, E. (1976). 'Identification of timbers from old ships of north-western European origins'. *IJNA* 5: 3–12.

—— (1978). 'Recording details of the hull; Draughtsman's notes; Reconstructing the hull; Model planks; Drawing the replica; Tentative sequence for building the replica', in Fenwick (ed.): 35–46, 49–104, 265–302, 307–10.

—— (1983). *Working Boats of Britain*. London: Conway Maritime Press.

McKusick, M. B. (1960). *Aboriginal Canoes in the West Indies*. Publications in Anthropology, 63. New Haven: Yale University Press.

MacKnight, C. C. (1980). 'Study of praus in the Indonesian archipelago'. *Great Circle*, 22: 117–28.

MacLaurin, E. C. B. (1978). 'Phoenician ship from Tyre described in Ezekiel 27'. *IJNA* 7: 80–3.

McPherson, N. (1877/8). 'Notes on antiquities from the Isle of Eigg'. *Proceedings of Society of Antiquaries of Scotland*, 12: 594–6.

Madsen, J. S. (1985). *Stammebåde*. Roskilde: Viking Ship Museum.

—— (1991). 'Fribrødre: A shipyard site from the late-11th century', in Crumlin-Pedersen (ed.). *Aspects of Maritime Scandinavia*. Roskilde: Viking Ship Museum, 183–206.

Magnusson, M. and Palsson, H. (eds.) (1965). *Vinland sagas: The Norse discovery of America*. Harmondsworth: Penguin.

Maitland, D. (1981). *Setting Sails*. Hong Kong: South China Morning Post.

Malmer, M. P. (1981). *Choronological Study of North European Rock Art*. Kungl. Vitterhets Hist. och Antikvitets Akad. Antikvar, 32. Stockholm.

Mandal, S. and Cooney, G. (1996). 'Irish stone axe project'. *Journal of Irish Archaeology*, 7: 41–64.

Manguin, P.-Y. (1980). 'South East Asian ship: An historical approach'. *Journal of South East Asian Studies*, 112: 266–76.

—— (1982). *Buket Jakas wreck Site: Provisional Report*. Jakarta: École Française d'Extrême-Orient.

—— (1983). 'Relationship and cross influences between SE Asian and Chinese shipbuilding traditions'. Paper read at International Association of Historians of Asia, 9th Conference, Manila, 1983.

—— (1985). 'Sewn-plank craft of SE Asia', in McGrail and Kentley (eds.): 319–44.

—— (1989). 'Trading ships of insular SE Asia'. *Proc. Perte-muan Ilmiah Arkeologi V*. i. Jakarta: Ikatan Ahli Arkeologi Indonesia, 200–18.

—— (1993a). 'Trading ships of the S. China Sea'. *Journal Economic and Social History of the Orient*, 36: 253–80.

—— (1993b). 'Palembang and Sriwijaya: An early Malay harbour-city rediscovered'. *Journal Malaysian Branch of the Royal Asiatic Society*, 661: 23–46.

—— (1996). 'SE Asian shipping in the Indian Ocean during the 1st millennium AD', in Ray and Salles (eds.): 181–98.

Mantzourani, E. K. and Theodorou, A. J. (1991). 'An attempt to delineate the sea-routes between Crete and Cyprus during the Bronze Age', in V. Karageorghis (ed.) (1991). *Civilizations of the Aegean and Their Diffusion in Cyprus and the Eastern Mediterranean, 2000–600 BC*. Larnaca: Piendes Foundation, 39–56.

Mao, Y. (ed.) (1983). *Ancient China's Technology and Science*. Beijing: Foreign Languages Press.

Marangou, C. (1990). 'Rowers paddling sailing ships in the Bronze Age Aegean'. *Tropis*, 2: 259–71.

Marchaj, C. A. (1964). *Sailing Theory and Practice*. London: Adlard Coles.

Marcus, G. J. (1953–4). 'Factors in early Celtic navigation'. *Études Celtiques*, 6: 312–27.

Marinatos, N. (1984). *Art and Religion in Thera*. Athens.

Marinatos, S. (1974). *Excavations at Thera VI (1972 season)*. Athens.

Marincola, J. (ed.) (1996). *Herodotus: The Histories*. Harmondsworth: Penguin.

Mark, S. E. (1991). 'Odyssey (5. 234–53) and Homeric ship construction'. *American Journal of Archaeology*, 95: 441–5.

—— (1996). 'Odyssey (5. 234–53) and Homeric ship construction: A clarification'. *IJNA* 25: 46–8.

—— (1997). *From Egypt to Mesopotamia*. College Station: Texas A & M University Press.

Marsden, P. (1976). 'Boat of the Roman period found at Bruges, Belgium in 1899, and related types'. *IJNA* 5: 23–56.

—— (1994). *Ships of the Port of London*, i. London: English Heritage.

—— (1996). *Ships of the Port of London*, ii. London: English Heritage.

Marstrander, S. (1963). *Ostfolds Jordbruksristninger Skebjerg*. Oslo: Institute for Sammenliguende Kulturforskning.

Martinez, P. V. C., Surinach, S. G., Marcen, P. G., Lull, V., Perez, R. M., and Herrada, C. R. (1997). 'Radiocarbondating and the prehistory of the Balearic Islands'. *PPS* 63: 55–86.

Martinez-Hidalgo, J. M. (1966). *Columbus' Ships*. Massachusetts: Barre.

Mathews, J. (1984). 'Tax law of Palmyra'. *Journal of Roman Studies*, 74: 157–80.

Mazzarino, S. (1987). 'Sul nome del vento *hipalus* ("ippalo"), in Plinio', *Helikon*, 22–7: pp.vii–xiv.

Medas, S. (1993). 'Imbarcazioni e navigazione preistorica nel Mediterraneo', *Bollettino di archeologia subacquea*, 1:

103–47.

MEIGGS, R. (1982). *Trees and Timber in the Ancient Mediterranean World*. 2nd edn., 1998. Oxford: Clarendon Press.

MEIJER, F. (1986). *History of Seafaring in the Classical World*. London: Croom Helm.

MELTZER, D. J., ADOVASIO, J. M., and DILLEHAY, T. D. (1994). 'On a Pleistocene human occupation at Pedra Furady, Brazil'. *Antiquity*, 68: 695–714.

MERCER, P. (1986). 'Neolithic in Cornwall'. *Cornish Archaeology*, 25: 35–80.

MILLER, J. (1969). *Spice Trade of the Roman Empire*. Oxford: Oxford University Press.

MILLETT, M., and MCGRAIL, S. (1987). 'Archaeology of the Hasholme logboat'. *Archaeological Journal*, 144: 69–155.

MILNE, G. (1996). 'Blackfriars ship 1: Romano-Celtic, Gallo-Roman or *Classis Britannicae*?'. *IJNA* 25: 234–8.

—— and GOODBURN, D. (1990). 'Early medieval port of London AD 700–1200'. *Antiquity*, 64: 629–36.

—— and HOBLEY, B. (eds.) (1981). *Waterfront Archaeology in Britain and Northern Europe*. CBA Research Report 41. London: CBA.

MOHAPATRA, P. (1983). *Traditional Marine Fishing Craft and Gear of Orissa*. Madras: Bay of Bengal Programme.

MOOKERJI, R. (1912). *Indian Shipping*. Bombay: Longman, Green. repr. 1999. New Delhi: Munshiram Manoharlal.

MOORE, A. (1970). *Last Days of Mast and Sail*. Newton Abbot: David and Charles.

MOOREY, P. R. S. (1980). 'Mesopotamia and Iran in the Bronze Age', in Sherratt (ed.) (1980a): 120–7.

MOORTEL, A. VAN DE (1991). 'Construction of a cog-like vessel in the Late Middle Ages', in Reinders and Paul (eds.). 42–6.

MORELAND, W. H. (1939). 'Ships of the Arabian Sea about AD 1500'. *Journal of the Royal Asiatic Society*, 63–74, 173–92.

MORGAN, L. (1988). *Miniature Wall Paintings of Thera: Study in Aegean Culture and Iconography*. Cambridge: Cambridge University Press.

MORGAN, R. A. (1990). 'Reconstructing a neolithic mortuary chamber from the fens of Eastern England through tree-ring study', in D. E. Robinson (ed.) 101–17.

MORISON, S. E. (1971). *The European Discovery of America: The Northern Voyages*. New York: Oxford University Press.

MORRIS, C. (1980). 'Andean S. America: From village to empire', in Sherratt (ed.) (1980a): 391–7.

MORRISON, J. S. (1976). 'The Classical tradition', in Greenhill (ed.): 155–73.

—— (ed.) (1995a). *Conway's History of the Ship. ii. Age of the Galley*. London: Conway Maritime Press.

—— (1995b). 'Ships and boats of the Mediterranean from 3000 to 500 BC', in Greenhill (ed.) (1995a): 131–50.

—— (1995c). 'Warships of the Mediterranean 500–31 BC', in Greenhill (ed.) (1995a): 151–72.

—— (1995d). 'The trireme', in Morrison (ed.) (1995a): 49–65.

—— and COATES, J. F. (1986). *Athenian Trireme*. Cambridge: Cambridge University Press.

—— —— (1989). *Athenian Trireme Reconstructed*. Oxford: BAR.S. 486.

—— —— (1996). *Greek and Roman Oared Warships*. Oxford: Oxbow.

—— —— and RANKOV, N. B. *Athenian Trireme*. 2nd edn. Cambridge: Cambridge University Press.

MORWOOD, M. J., O'SULLIVAN, P. B., AZIZ, F., and RAZA, A. (1998). 'Fission-track ages of stone tools and fossils on the east Indonesian island of Flores'. *Nature*, 392: 173–9.

MOTT, L. V. (1994). 'A three-masted ship depiction from 1409'. *IJNA* 23: 39–40.

MOURA, C. F. (1988). 'Boats used by the settlers of Mato Grosso in the 18th and 19th centuries', in Filgueiras (ed.): 473–505.

MOWAT, R. J. C. (1996). *Logboats of Scotland*. Monograph 68 Oxford: Oxbow.

MUCKELROY, K. (1981). 'Middle Bronze Age trade between Britain and Europe'. *PPS* 47: 275–97.

—— HASELGROVE, C., and NASH, D. (1978). 'Pre-Roman coin from Canterbury and the ship represented on it'. *PPS* 44: 439–44.

MUIR, J. (1965). 'Early Arab seafaring and rudders'. *MM* 51: 357–9.

MUKHERJEE, B. N. (1994). 'Maritime contacts of ancient Bengal with SE Asia: New epigraphic data'. Paper presented to the International Seminar on Techno-archaeological Perspectives of Seafaring in the Indian Ocean, New Delhi.

MÜLLNER, A. (1892). 'Ein schiff im Laibacher Moore'. *Argo*, 1: 1–7.

MULVANEY, J. (1975). *Prehistory of Australia*. London: Penguin.

MURPHY, J. P. (ed.) (1977). *Rufus Festus Avienus: Ora Maritima*. Chicago: Ares.

MURRAY, O. (1993). *Early Greece*. Fontana.

MURRAY, W. M. (1987). 'Do modern winds equal ancient winds?' *Mediterranean Historical Review*, 22: 139–67.

MYHRE, B. (1980). 'Ny datering av våre eldste båtar'. *Arkeo*, Bergen: 27–30.

NAYLING, N. and CASELDINE, A. (1997). *Excavations at Caldicot, Gwent*. CBA Research Report, 108. York.

—— and MCGRAIL, S. (forthcoming). *The Barland's Farm Boat*. CBA Research Report.

—— MAYNARD, D., and MCGRAIL, S. (1994). 'Barland's Farm, Magor, Gwent: A Romano-Celtic boat', *Antiquity*, 68: 596–603.

NEEDHAM, J. (1954). *Science and Civilisation in China*, i. Cambridge: Cambridge University Press.

—— (1970). *Clerks and Craftsmen in China and the West*. Cambridge: Cambridge University Press.

—— (1971). *Science and Civilisation in China*, iv, pt. 3. Cambridge: Cambridge University Press.

NEGUERUELA, I., PINEDO, M., GÓMEZ, M., MIÑANO, A., ARELLANO, I., and BARBA, J. S. (1995). 'Seventh-century BC Phoenician vessel discovered at Playa de la Isla, Mazarron,

Spain'. *IJNA* 24: 189–97.

NELSON, J. G. (1961). 'Geography of the balsa'. *American Neptune*, 21: 157–95.

NEUMANN, J. (1988). 'References to the technique of tacking by sailing ships in Classical literature'. *MM* 74: 417.

—— (1991). 'Number of days that Black Sea-bound sailing ships were delayed by winds at the entrance to the Dardanelles near Troy's site'. *Studia Troica*, 1: 93–100.

NEWBY, E. (1982). *World Atlas of Exploration*. London: Artists House.

NICOLAYSEN, N. (1882). 'Viking ship discovered at Gokstad in Norway'. Oslo: Forlag af alb Cammermeyer.

NIGAM, R. (1988). 'Was the large rectangular structure at Lothal a "dockyard" or an "irrigation tank"?' in S. R. Rao (ed.) (1988). *Marine Archaeology of the Indian Ocean Countries*. Goa: National Institute of Oceanography, 20–1.

NISHIMURA, S. (1920). *Kumano-no-morota-bune or the Many-Paddled Ship of Kumano*. Tokyo: Society of Naval Architects.

—— (1925). *Ancient Rafts of Japan*. Tokyo: Society of Naval Architects.

—— (1931). *Skinboats*. Ancient Ships of Japan, vols. 5, 6, 7, 8. Tokyo: Society of Naval Architects.

—— (1936). *Hani-bune or Clay Boat: Kako-no-Kawa or Deerskin*. Ancient Ships of Japan, vol. 9. Tokyo: Society of Naval Architects.

NOOTER, G. (1971). *Old Kayaks in the Netherlands*. Medelingen 17. Leiden: Rijksmuseum voor Volkenkunde.

OATES, J. (1980). 'Emergence of cities in the Near East', in Sherratt (ed.) (1980a): 112–19.

—— DAVIDSON, T. E., KAMILLI, D., and McKERRELL, A. (1977). 'Seafaring merchants of Ur?'. *Antiquity*, 51: 221–34.

OATLEY, K. (1974). 'Mental maps in navigation'. *New Scientist* (19 Dec.): 863–6.

O'CONNOR, B. (1980). 'Cross-Channel relations in the Later Bronze Age'. Oxford: BAR.S. 91.

O'CONNOR, D. (1980a). 'Egypt and the Levant in the Bronze Age', in Sherratt (ed.) (1980a): 128–35.

—— (1980b). 'Late period Egypt and Nubia', in Sherratt (ed.) (1980a): 193–5.

OERTLING, T. J. (1989). 'Molasses Reef wreck hull analysis: Final report'. *IJNA* 18: 229–43.

O hEAILIDHE, P. (1992). 'The "Monk's Boat": A Roman period relic from Lough Lene, Co. Westmeath'. *IJNA* 21: 185–190.

OIKONOMIDES, A. N. and MILLER, M. C. J. (eds.) (1995). *Hanno the Carthaginian Periplus*. Chicago: Ares.

OLESON, J. P. (1988). 'Ancient lead circles and sounding leads from Israel coastal waters'. *Sefunim*, 7: 30–40.

—— (1994). 'Ancient lead sounding weight in the National Maritime Museum'. *Sefunim*, 8: 29–34.

OLSEN, O. and CRUMLIN-PEDERSEN, O. (1967). 'Skuldelev ships II'. *Acta Archaeologica*, 38: 73–174.

—— MADSEN, J. S, and RIECK, F. (eds.) (1995), *Shipshape*.

Roskilde: Viking Ship Museum.

OPPENHEIM, A. L. (1954). 'Seafaring merchants of Ur'. *Journal of American Oriental Society*, 74: 6–17.

OSBORNE, R. (1996). *Greece in the Making*. London: Routledge.

OSSOWSKI, W. (1999). *Studia nad Lodziami Jednopiennymi z obszaru Polski*. Proc. Polish Maritime Museum, 11. Gdansk: Marpress.

PALAIOLOGOU, H. (1989). 'Aegean ships from the 2nd MBC'. *Tropis*, 1: 217–28.

PALMER, C., BLUE, L., and McGRAIL, S. (forthcoming). 'Hide boats at Hogenakal on the River Kaveri, Tamil Nadu'. *South Asian Studies*, 17.

PALOU, H., RIETH, E., IZAGUIRRE, M., JOVER, A., NIETO, X., PUJOL, M., RAURICH, X., and APESTEGUI, C. (1998). *Excavacions arqueològiques subaquàtiques a Cala Culip 2: Culip 6*. Girona: Museu d'Arqueologia de Catalunya.

PAPALAS, A. J. (1997). 'Development of the trireme'. *MM* 83: 259–71.

—— (1999). 'Polycrates of Samos and the first Greek trireme fleet'. *MM* 85: 3–19.

PARIS, F. E. (1843). *Essai sur la construction navale des peuples extra-européens*. Paris: Bertrand.

PARIS, P. (1955). *Esquisse d'une ethnographie navale des peuples annamites*. Rotterdam.

PARKER, A. J. (1991). 'Review of McGrail (ed.), 1990'. *IJNA* 20: 363.

—— (1992). *Ancient Shipwrecks of the Mediterranean and the Roman Provinces*. Oxford: BAR.S. 580.

—— (1999). 'Review of Morrison and Coates, 1996'. *Antiquity*, 73: 477–8.

PEACOCK, D. P. S. (1969). 'Neolithic pottery production in Cornwall'. *Antiquity*, 43: 145–9.

—— (1990). *Myos Hormos: Quseir al-Qadim*. Southampton: University of Southampton.

PENG, D. (ed.) (1988). *Ships of China*. Beijing: Chinese Institute of Navigation.

PERLÈS, C. (1979). 'Des navigateurs méditerranéens il y a 10,000 ans'. *La Recherche*, 10: 82–3.

PETERSEN, H. C. (n.d.—1982?). *Instruction in Kayak Building*. Roskilde: Viking Ship Museum.

—— (1986). *Skinboats of Greenland*. Ships and Boats of the North, vol. 1. Roskilde: Viking Ship Museum.

PHILLIPSON, D. W. (1980). 'Iron Age Africa and the expansion of the Bantu', in Sherratt (ed.) (1980a): 342–7.

PLANE, A. M. (1991). 'New England logboats'. *Bulletin of Massachusetts Archaeological Society*, 521: 8–17.

PLAYDON, G. W. (1967). 'Significance of Marshallese stick charts'. *Journal of the Institute of Navigation*, 20: 155–66.

PLINY. *Natural History*. trans. H. Rackham (1969). 10 vols. Cambridge, Mass.: Harvard University Press.

POMEY, P. (1981). 'L'épave de Bon Porté et les bateaux cousus de Méditerranée'. *MM* 67: 225–43.

—— (1982). 'Le navire romaine de la Madrague de Giens'.

*Comptes Rendus de l'Académie des Inscriptions et Belles-Lettres*: 133–54.

—— (1985). 'Mediterranean sewn boats in Antiquity', in McGrail and Kentley (eds.): 35–48.

—— (1988). 'Principes et methodes de construction en architecture navale antique'. *Cahiers d'histoire*, 33: 397–412.

—— (1994). 'Shell conception and skeleton process in ancient Mediterranean shipbuilding', in Westerdahl (ed.): 125–30.

—— (1995). 'Les Épaves Grecques et Romaines de la Place Jules-Verne à Marseille'. *Académie des inscriptions et belles-lettres*: 459–84.

—— (1996). 'Un exemple d'évolution des techniques de construction navale antique: de l'assemblage par ligatures à l'assemblage par tenons et mortaises', in D. Meeks and D. Garcia (eds.) (1996). *Techniques et économie antiques et médiévales*. Paris: Editions Errance. 195–203.

—— (1997a). 'Bon-Porté wreck', in Delgado (ed.): 69.

—— (1997b). 'Madrague de Giens wreck', in Delgado (ed.): 252–3.

—— (ed.) (1997c). *La Navigation dans l'Antiquité*. Aix-en-Provence: Édisud.

—— (1998). 'Conception et réalisation des navires dans l'Antiquité méditerranéenne'. *Revue d'anthropologie des connaissances*, 13: 49–72.

—— (1999). 'Les Épaves Grecques du 6e siècle av. J.-C. de la Place Jules-Verne à Marseilles, in Pomey and Rieth (eds.): 147–53.

—— and RIETH, E. (eds.) (1999). 'Construction navale maritime et fluviale'. *Archaeonautica*, 14.

—— and TCHERNIA, A. (1978). 'Le tonnage maximum des des navires de commerce Romains'. *Archaeonautica*, 2: 233–51.

POSTGATE, N. (1980). 'Assyrian Empire', in Sherratt (ed.), (1980a): 186–92.

POTTS, T. (1994). *Mesopotamia and the East*. Oxford: University Committee for Archaeology.

PRADOS, E. (1997). 'Indian Ocean littoral maritime evolution'. *MM* 83: 185–98.

PRESCOTT, W. H. (1847). *History of the Conquest of Peru*. London.

PRESLAND, G. (1980). 'Forest cultures of S. and SE Asia', in Sherratt (ed.) (1980a): 272–6.

PRINS, A. H. J. (1965). *Sailing from Lamu*. Assen: Van Gorcum.

—— (1970). 'Origins of leeboards'. *MM* 56: 349–53.

—— (1986). *Handbook of Sewn Boats*. Monograph, 59. Greenwich: National Maritime Museum.

PRYNNE, M. W. (1968). 'Henry V's *Grace Dieu*', *MM* 54: 115–28.

PRYOR, J. H. (1992). *Geography, Technology and War*. Cambridge: Cambridge University Press.

—— (1995). 'Geographical conditions of galley navigation in the Mediterranean', in Morrison (ed.) (1995a): 206–16.

PRYTULAK, M. G. (1982). 'Weapons on the Thera ships?'. *IJNA* 11: 3–6.

PULAK, C. (1998). 'Uluburun shipwreck: An overview'. *IJNA* 27: 188–224.

*Quanzhou Ship Report* (1987) (in Chinese).

QUINN, D. B., and QUINN, A. M. (eds.) (1973). *Virginian Voyages from Hakluyt*. London.

QUALLS, C. (1981). 'Boats of Mesopotamia before 2000 BC'. Doctoral diss., Columbia University.

RABAN, A. (1989). 'Medinet Habu ships: Another interpretation'. *IJNA* 18: 163–71.

—— (1995). 'Sea People and Thera ships'. *Tropis*, 3: 353–66.

RAMIN, J. (1976). *Periplus of Hanno*. Oxford: BAR.S. 3.

RANK, G. (1933). 'Zwei seltene bootfunde aus Estland'. *Sitzungsberichte der Gelehrten Estinschen Gesellschaft*: 304–15.

RAO, S. R. (1963). '"Persian Gulf" seal from Lothal'. *Antiquity*, 37: 96–9.

—— (1965). 'Shipping and maritime trade of the Indus people'. *Expedition* 7: 30–7.

—— (1970). *Shipping in Ancient India*. Vivekananda Commemoration Volume. Madras.

—— (1981). 'Docks and wharves', in A. Ghosh (ed.) (1981). *Encyclopedia of Indian Archaeology*. unpub. Indian Council of Historical Research Project.

—— (1987). 'Submerged city and shipwreck in Dwarka'. *IJNA* 16: 252–3.

RATNAGAR, S. (1981). *Encounters: Westerly Trade of the Harappa Civilization*. New Delhi: Oxford University Press.

RAWSON, J. (1980). *Ancient China*. London: British Museum.

RAY, H. P. (1985). 'Trade in the western Deccan under the Satavahanas'. *Studies in History* 1: 15–35.

—— (1986). *Monastery and Guild: Commerce Under the Satavahanas*. New Delhi: Oxford University Press.

—— (1987). 'Early historical urbanisation: The case of the western Deccan'. *World Archaeology*, 19: 94–104.

—— (1988). 'Early trade in the Bay of Bengal'. *Indian Historical Review*, 14: 79–89.

—— (1989). 'Early maritime contacts between S. and SE Asia'. *Journal of South-East Asian Studies*, 201: 42–54.

—— (1990). 'Seafaring in the Bay of Bengal in the early centuries AD'. *Studies in History*, 6: 1–14.

—— (1993). 'East coast trade in peninsular India c.200 BC to AD 400'. *South Asian Archaeology* 1991: 573–84.

—— (1994). *Winds of Change*. New Delhi: Oxford University' Press.

—— (1996). 'Early coastal trade in the Bay of Bengal', in Reade (ed.).

—— and SALLES, J.-F. (eds.) (1996). *Tradition and Archaeology: Early Maritime Contacts in the Indian Ocean*. New Delhi: Manohar.

READE, J. (ed.) (1996). *Indian Ocean in Antiquity*. London: the British Museum and Kegan Paul.

REDNAP, M. (1984). *Cattewater Wreck*. Oxford: BAR. 131.

—— (1997). *Magor Pill Boat*, in Delgado (ed.): 254.

—— (1998). 'Reconstructing the Magor Pill boat', in

N. Nayling (ed.). *Magor Pill Medieval Wreck*. CBA. 115. York.

REINDERS, R. (1979). 'Medieval ships: Recent finds in the Netherlands', in McGrail (ed.): 35–44.

—— (1983). 'Excavation and salvage of a sixteenth century "Beurtschip" '. *IJNA* 12: 336–8.

—— (1985). *Cog Finds from the Netherlands*. Lelystad: Flevobericht; 248.

—— and PAUL, K. (eds.) (1991). *Carvel Construction Techniques*. Monograph 12. Oxford: Oxbow.

REISNER, G. A. (1913). *Models of Ships and Boats*. Cairo: Institute Français d'Archéologie Orientale.

RENFREW, C. (1967). 'Cycladic metallurgy and the Aegean'Early Bronze Age'. *American Journal of Archaeology*, 71: 1–20.

—— (1998). 'Word of Minos'. *Cambridge Archaeological Journal*, 8: 239–64.

REYNOLDS, C. G. (1978). 'Thera ships'. *MM* 64: 124.

RIECK, F. (1994). 'Iron Age boats from Hjortspring and Nydam', in Westerdahl (ed.): 45–54.

—— (1995). 'Ships and boats in the bog finds of Scandinavia', in Crumlin-Pedersen and Thye (eds.): 125–9.

—— (2000). 'New parts for the Nydam ships', in Litwin (2000): 207–12.

—— and Jørgensen, E. (1997). 'Non-military equipment from Nydam', in Jørgensen and Clausen (eds.): 220–5.

RIENITS, R. and RIENITS, T. (1968). *Voyages of Captain Cook*. London: Hamlyn.

RIETH, E. (1989). 'Le Clos des galées de Rouen lieu de construction navale à clin et à carvel', in Villain-Gandossi, Busutil, and Adam (eds.): 71–7.

—— (1991). 'L'épave du début de 16 siècle de Villefranche-sur-mer', in Reinders and Paul (eds.): 47–55.

—— (1993). *Voiliers et pirogues du monde au début du 19ᵉ siècle*. Paris: du May.

—— (1994). 'Flat-bottomed medieval (11th century) boat from Orlac, Charente', in Westerdahl (ed.): 121–4.

—— (1996a). *Le Maitre-Gabarit, La Tablette et Le Trébuchet*. Paris: CTHS.

—— (1996b). 'Le calfatage des barges et des galées au Clos des Galées de Rouen'. *Navalia Archeologia e Storin*. Savona: International Propeller Club, 55–67.

—— (1999). 'L'épave du caboteur de Culip 6', in Pomey and Reith (eds.): 205–12.

—— (2000). 'Medieval wreck from Port Berteau 2', in Litwin (2000): 225–8.

—— CARRIERRE-DESBOIS, C., and SERNA, V. (1996). 'L'épave du haut Moyen Age de Port-Berteau 2'. *Revue de la Saintonge et de l'Aunis*, 22: 13–47.

RIEU, E. V. (ed.) (1946). *Homer: The Odyssey*. Harmondsworth: Penguin.

—— (ed.) (1950). *Homer: The Iliad*. Harmondsworth: Penguin.

RILEY, C. L., KELLEY, J. C., PENNINGTON, C. W., and RANDS, R. I. (eds.) (1971). *Man across the Sea*. Austin: University of Texas.

RILEY, W. E. and GOMME, L. (1912). *Ship of the Roman Period Discovered on the New County Hall Site*. 2nd edn. London: London County Council.

RITZENTHALER, R. E. (1950). 'Building of a Chippewa Indian birch-bark canoe'. *Bulletin Public Museum of Milwaukee*, 192: 53–99.

RIVAL, M. (1991). *La Charpenerie navale romaine*. Paris: CNRS.

ROAF, M. and GALBRAITH, J. (1994). 'Pottery and p-values: "Seafaring merchants of Ur?" re-examined'. *Antiquity*, 68: 770–83.

ROBERTS, K. G. and SHACKLETON, P. (1983). *The Canoe*. Toronto: Macmillan.

ROBERTS, O. T. P. (1984). 'Viking sailing performance', in McGrail (ed.): 123–49.

—— (1987). 'Wind-power and the boats from the Cyclades'. *IJNA* 16: 309–11.

—— (1990). 'Rigging the Athenian trireme'. *Tropis*, 2: 287–300.

—— (1992). 'Brigg "raft" reassessed as a round bilge Bronze Age boat'. *IJNA* 21: 245–58.

—— (1993). 'Sailing rig of *Olympias*', in J. T. Shaw (ed.) (1993a): 29–38.

—— (1994). 'Descendants of Viking boats', in Unger (ed.): 11–28.

—— (1995). 'An explanation of ancient windward sailing: Some other considerations'. *IJNA* 24: 307–15.

ROBERTS, R. G., JONES, R., and SMITH, M. A. (1994). 'Beyond the radiocarbon barrier in Australian prehistory: A critique of Allen's commentary'. *Antiquity*, 68: 611–16.

ROBERTSON, J. (1925). *Laws of Kings of England from Edmund to Henry I*. Cambridge.

ROBINSON, D. E. (ed.) (1990). *Experimentation and Reconstruction in Environmental Archaeology*. Oxford: Oxbow.

ROBINSON, M. E., SHIMWELL, D. W., and CRIBBIN, G. (1999). 'Reassessing the logboat from Lurgan townland, Co. Galway. *Antiquity*, 73: 903–8.

RODWELL, K. (1993). 'The Cemetery', in M. J. Darling (ed.) (1993). *Caistor-on-Sea Excavations by Charles Green*. East Anglian Archaeology Report, No. 60. Norwich: Norfolk Museums Service, 252–5.

ROE, D. (1980). 'Handaxe makers', in Sherratt (ed.) (1980a): 71–8.

—— (1995). 'Orce basin and the Initial Palaeolithic of Europe'. *Oxford Journal of Archaeology*, 14: 1–12.

ROLETT, B. V., CHEN, W.-C., and SINTON, J. M. (2000). 'Taiwan, Neolithic seafaring and Austronesian origins'. *Antiquity*, 74: 54–61.

RONAN, C. A. (1986). *Shorter Science and Civilisation in China*, iii. Cambridge: Cambridge University Press.

ROSE, S. (ed.) (1982). *Navy of the Lancastrian Kings*. Navy Records Society. London: Allen & Unwin.

ROSEMAN, C. H. (ed.) (1994). *Pytheas of Massalia: On the Ocean*. Chicago: Ares.

ROSENBERG, G. (1937). *Hjortspringfundet Nord. Oldtidsminder* 3.1. Copenhagen: Kommission hos gyldendalske boghandel Nordisk Forlag.

ROSLOFF, J. P. (1991). 'One-armed anchor of *c*.400 BC from the Ma'agan Michael vessel, Israel'. *IJNA* 20: 223–6.

ROTH, H. L. (1899). *Aborigines of Tasmania*. 2nd edn., Halifax: F. King.

RUBIN DE CERVIN, G. B. (1977). 'Thera ship: Other suggestions'. *MM* 63: 150–2.

RULE, M. (1982). *Mary Rose*. London: Conway Maritime Press.

—— and MONAGHAN, J. (1993). *Gallo-Roman Trading Vessel from Guernsey*. Guernsey Museum Monograph, 5. St. Peter Port: Guernsey Museum Services.

RUNYAN, T. J. (1991). 'Relationship of southern and northern seafaring traditions in late-Medieval Europe', in C. Villain-Gandossi, S. Busutil, and P. Adam (eds.) (1991). *Medieval Ships and the Birth of Technological Societies.* Malta: Foundation for International Studies, ii. 197–209.

—— (1994). 'Cog as a warship', in Unger (ed.): 47–58.

SALISBURY, W. (1961). 'Woolwich ship'. *MM* 47: 81–90.

SALOMEN, A. (1939). *Die Wasserfahr-zeuge in Babylonien.* Helsinki.

SAND, C. (1997). 'Chronology of Lapita-ware in New Caledonia'. *Antiquity*, 71: 539–47.

SANDAHL, B. (1951, 1958, 1982). *Middle English Sea Terms,* i–iii. Uppsala: English Institute, Uppsala University.

SARSFIELD, J. P. (1984). 'Mediterranean whole moulding'. *MM* 70: 86–8.

—— (1985). 'From the brink of extinction'. *Wooden Boat*, 66: 84–9.

—— (1988). 'Survival of pre-16th century Mediterranean lofting techniques in Bahia, Brazil', in Filgueras (ed.), 63–86.

SAUER, M. (1802). *Account of an Expedition to the Northern Parts of Russia by Commodore Joseph Billings.* London.

SCARRE, C. (ed.) (1989). *Past Worlds*. London: *The Times*.

SCOTT, W. H. (1981). *Boat-building and Seamanship in Classic Philippine Society*. Anthropological Papers, 9. Manila: National Museum.

—— (1982). 'Boat-building and seamanship in Classic Philippine society'. *Philippine Studies*, 30: 335–76.

SCULLARD, H. H. (1974) *Elephant in the Greek and Roman World*. New York: Cornell University Press.

SEVERIN, T. (1978). *Brendan Voyage*. London: Hutchinson.

—— (1982). *The Sindbad Voyage*. London: Hutchinson.

—— (1994). *China Voyage*. London: Little, Brown.

SEYMOUR, T. D. (1907). *Life in the Homeric Age*. New York: Macmillan.

SHAW, C. T. (1980). 'Agricultural origins in Africa', in Sherratt (ed.) (1980a): 179–84.

SHAW, J. T. (ed.) (1993a). *Trireme Project*. Monograph 31. Oxford: Oxbow.

—— (1993b). 'Summary of the "trireme controversy"', in J. T. Shaw (ed.) (1993a): 1–3.

SHAW, M. C. (1982). 'Ship cabins of the Bronze Age Aegean'. *IJNA* 11: 53–8.

—— (1990). 'Review of Morgan, 1988'. *American Journal of Archaeology*, 94: 347–8.

SHELL, R. (1986). 'Chamorro flying proa'. *MM* 72: 135–43.

—— (1987). 'Early accounts of the Chamorro flying proa'. *MM* 73: 33–48.

SHEPPARD, T. (1901). 'Notes on the ancient model of a boat and warrior crew found at Roos in Holderness'. *Trans. East Riding Antiq. Soc.*, 9: 62–74.

—— (1902). 'Additional notes on the Roos Carr images'. *Trans. East Riding Antiq. Soc.*, 10: 76–9.

—— (1926). 'Roman remains in north Lincolnshire'. *Trans. East Riding Antiq. Soc.*, 25: 170–4.

SHERRATT, A. (ed.) (1980a). *Cambridge Encyclopedia of Archaeology*. Cambridge: Cambridge University Press.

—— (1980b). 'Interpretation and synthesis', in Sherratt (ed.) (1980a): 404–14.

SHETELIG, H. (1917). *Osebergfundet*, 1. Oslo.

—— (1917). *Tuneskibet.* Oslo.

—— (1930). 'Das Nydamschiff '. *Acta Archaeologica*, 1: 1–30.

—— and JOHANNESSEN, F. (1929). *Kvalsund fundet*. Bergen: John Griegs Boktrykker.

SHUTLER, R. and SHUTLER, M. E. (1975). *Oceanic Prehistory.* Berkeley: University of California.

SIEVEKING, G. DE G. (1954). 'Recent archaeological discoveries in Malaya (1952–3)'. *Journal of the Malayan Branch of the Royal Asiatic Society*, 27, 1: 224–33.

—— (1956). 'Recent archaeological discoveries in Malaya (1955)'. *Journal of the Malayan Branch of the Royal Asiatic Society*, 29, 1: 200–11.

SIMONE, L. (1990). 'Recupero di imbarcazioni monossili'. *Notiziario.* Soprintendenza Archeologica della Lombardia, 56–7.

SINOTO, Y. H. (1979). 'Excavations on Huahine, French Polynesia'. *Pacific Studies*, 3, 1: 1–40.

—— (1983). 'Archaeological excavations of the Vaito'otia and Fa'ahia sites on Huahine Island, French Polynesia'. *National Geographic Society Research Reports*, 15: 583–99.

—— (1983). 'Huahine: Heritage of the great navigators'. *Museum*, 35: 70–3.

—— (1988). 'Waterlogged site on Huahine Island, French Polynesia', in B. A. Purdy (ed.) (1988). *Wet Site Archaeology.* Telford, Pa.: Telford Press, 113–30.

SLEESWYK, A. W. (1980). 'Phoenician joints, *coagmenta punicana*'. *IJNA* 9: 243–4.

—— (1981). 'Ship of Harold Godwinson'. *MM* 67: 87–91.

—— (1983). 'On the location of the land of Pwnt on two Renaissance maps'. *IJNA* 12: 279–91.

—— (1986). '*Ever* or *boene rinses* and the origin of the lugsail in N.W. Europe'. *MM* 72: 78–81.

—— (1990). 'Engraver Willem a Cruce and the development of the chain-wale'. *MM* 76: 345–61.

SLEESWYK, A. W. (1996a). 'Some remarks concerning the Punic ram'. *Tropis*, 4: 91–9.

—— (1996b). 'The *liao* and the displacement of ships in the Ming Navy'. *MM* 82: 3–13.

—— (1999). 'Oarage of Phoenician biremes'. *Tropis*, 5: 383–92.

—— (forthcoming). 'Beyond *Olympias*: An outsider's view'. in N. B. Rankov (ed.). *Trireme Olympias: The Final Report, Sea Trials 1992–4*.

SMITH, E. (1915–16). 'Ships as evidence of the migrations of early culture'. *Journal Manchester Egyptian and Oriental Society*.

SMITH, M. A., and SHARP, N. D. (1993). 'Pleistocene sites in Australia, New Guinea and island Melanesia', in M. A. Smith, M. Spriggs, and B. Frankhauser (eds.) (1993). *Sahul in Review*. Occasional Papers in Prehistory, 24. Canberra: Australian National University, 37–59.

SMOLAREK, P. (1994). 'Aspects of early boat-building in the southern Baltic region', in Westerdahl (ed.): 77–82.

SNOW, P. (1992). 'Chinese Columbus: Zheng He and his predecessors'. *Medieval History*, 2, 3: 56–75.

SØLVER, C. V. (1936). 'Egyptian shipping c.1500 BC'. *MM* 22: 430–69.

SOLVYNS, F. B. (1799). *Les Hindoos*. Calcutta.

SØRENSEN, A. C. (1999). 'Ship-grave from Ladby'. *Newsletter from Roskilde*, 12: 9–13.

SOUTER, W. C. (1934). *Story of Our Kayak and Some Others*. Presidential address to the Aberdeen Medico-Chirological Society. Aberdeen: Aberdeen University Press.

SPENNEMANN, D. R. (1984). 'Some critical remarks on the boats depicted on the SE Asian kettledrums: An assessment of the daggerboard'. *IJNA* 13: 137–43.

—— (1985). 'On the Bronze Age ship model from Flore, Indonesia'. *IJNA* 14: 237–41.

—— and AMBROSE, W. R. (1997). 'Floating obsidian and its implications for the interpretation of Pacific prehistory'. *Antiquity*, 71: 188–93.

SPOONER, N. (1998). 'Human occupation at Jinmium, northern Australia'. *Antiquity*, 72: 173–8.

SPRIGGS, M., and ANDERSON, A. (1993). 'Late colonisation of East Polynesia'. *Antiquity*, 67: 200–17.

STAVORINUS, J. S. (1789). *Voyages to the East Indies*. London, ii. 28–30.

STEFANSSON, V. (1942). *Ultima Thule*. London.

STEFFY, J. R. (1982). 'In retrospect and an analysis of the hull', in G. F. Bass, and F. H. van Doorninck (eds.) (1982). *Yassi Ada* 1. College Station: Texas A & M University Press, i. 82–6.

—— (1983). 'Athlit ram'. *MM* 69: 229–47.

—— (1985a). 'Kyrenia ship: An interim report on its hull construction'. *American Journal of Archaeology*, 89: 71–101.

—— (1985b). 'Herculaneum boat: Preliminary notes on hull details'. *AJA* 89, 3: 519–21.

—— (1987). 'Kinneret Boat Project II'. *IJNA* 16: 325–9.

—— (1989). 'Role of three-dimensional research in the Kyrenia ship reconstruction'. *Tropis*, 1: 249–62.

—— (1991). 'Ram and bow timbers: A structural interpretation', in Casson and Steffy (eds.): 6–39.

—— (1994). *Wooden Shipbuilding and the Interpretation of Shipwrecks*. College Station: Texas A & M University Press.

—— (1995a). 'Ancient scantlings: The projection and control of Mediterranean hull shapes'. *Tropis*, 3: 417–28.

—— (1995b). 'Shipwreck archaeology: An essential medium for interpreting ancient ship construction', in V. Karageorghis and D. Michaelides (eds.) (1995). *Cyprus and the Sea*. Nicosia: University of Cyprus, 23–31.

STENTON, F. M. (1967). *Anglo-Saxon England*, 2nd edn. Oxford: Oxford University Press.

STEVENSON, W. H. (ed.) (1959). *Asser's Life of King Alfred*. Oxford: Oxford University Press.

STIEGLITZ, R. R. (1999). 'Phoenician ship equipment and fittings'. *Tropis*, 5: 409–19.

STRABO. *The Geography*. trans. H. L. Jones (1967). 8 vols. Cambridge, Mass.: Harvard University Press.

STRASSER, T. F. (1996). 'The boat models from Eridu: Sailing or spinning during the Ubaid period?' *Antiquity*, 70: 920–5.

STREET, F. A. (1980). 'Ice Age environments', in Sherratt (ed.) (1980a): 52–6.

STROUP, E. D. (1985). 'Navigating without instruments: Voyages of Hokule'a'. *Oceanus*, 28: 69–75.

SUDER, H. (1930). *Vom einbaum und floss zum Schiff*. Berlin.

SUN, G. (1986). 'On the possibility of the existence of Chinese sail in the pre-Christian era, and the earliest possible time-limit of their emergence'. *Marine History Research*, 2: 11–19.

SWITSUR, R. (1989). 'Early English boats'. *Radiocarbon*, 31: 1010–18.

—— and WRIGHT, E. V. (1989). 'Radiocarbon ages and calibrated dates for the boats from North Ferriby, Humberside: A reappraisal'. *Archaeological Journal*, 146: 58–67.

TAYLOR, D. A. (1988). 'Contemporary use of whole-moulding in the vicinity of Trinity Bay, Newfoundland', in Filgueras (ed.): 87–100.

TAYLOR, E. G. R. (1971). *The Haven-Finding Art*. London: Hollis and Carter.

TCHERNIA, A. (1995). 'Moussons et monnaies'. *Annales*, 505: 991–1010.

—— POMEY, P., and HESNARD, A. (1978). L'épave romain de la Madrague de Giens'. *Gallia*, 34th Supplement.

TEMPLE, R. C. (ed.) (1905). *Geographical Account of Countries Round the Bay of Bengal 1669–1679 by Thomas Bowrey*. London: Hakluyt Society.

TERRELL, J. E. and WELSCH, R. L. (1997). 'Lapita and the temporal geography of prehistory'. *Antiquity*, 71: 548–72.

THAPAR, R. (1980). 'India before and after the Mauryan empire', in Sherratt (ed.) (1980a): 257–61.

—— (1990). *History of India*. London: Penguin.

THESIGER, W. (1978). *Marsh Arabs*. Harmondsworth: Penguin.

THIRSLUND, S. (1987). 'Sailing directions of the North Atlantic Viking Age'. *Journal of Navigation*, 50: 55–63.

—— (1995). *Viking Navigation*. Copenhagen: Thirslund.

THOMAS, S. D. (1985). 'Navigating without instruments in Oceania'. *Oceanus*, 28, 1: 52–8.

THOMPSON, J. E. S. (1949). 'Canoes and navigation of the Maya and their neighbours'. *Journal Royal Anthropological Institute*, 79: 69–78.

—— (1964). 'Trade relations between the Maya highlands and lowlands'. *Estudios de Cultura Maya*, 4: 13–49.

THOMSEN, M. H. (2000). 'Studland Bay wreck, Dorset, UK: Hull analysis'. *IJNA* 29: 69–85.

THORNE, A. (1980). 'Arrival of Man in Australia', in Sherratt (ed.) (1980a): 96–100.

THORPE, R. S., WILLIAMS-THORPE, O., JENKINS, D. G., and WATSON, J. S. (1991). 'Geological source and transport of the bluestones of Stonehenge, Wiltshire'. *PPS* 57: 103–57.

THORVILDSEN, K. (1957). *Ladby-Skibet*. Copenhagen: National Museum.

THRANE, H. (1995). 'Penultima Thule', in J. Waddell and E. S. Twohig (eds.) (1995). *Ireland in the Bronze Age*. Dublin: Stationery Office, 149–57.

THROCKMORTON, P. J. (1973). 'The Roman wreck at Pantano Longarini'. *IJNA* 2: 243–66.

TIBBETTS, G. R. (1971). *Arab Navigation in the Indian Ocean Before the Coming of the Portuguese*. Oriental Translation Fund NS 42. repr. 1981. London: Royal Asiatic Society.

TILLEY, A. F. (1976). 'Rowing the trireme'. *MM* 62: 357–9.

—— (1992). 'Three men to a room: A completely different trireme'. *Antiquity*, 66: 599–610.

—— (1995). 'Warships of the ancient Mediterranean'. *Tropis*, 3: 429–40.

—— and JOHNSTONE, P. (1976). 'A Minoan naval triumph?' *IJNA* 5: 285–92.

TINNISWOOD, J. T. (1949). 'English galleys 1272–1377'. *MM* 35: 276–315.

TIPPING, C. (1994). 'Cargo handling and the medieval cog'. *MM* 80: 3–15.

TOBY, A. S. (1986). World's first warships: Tubs or ocean greyhounds? *IJNA* 15: 339–46.

TOOLEY, M. J. (1990). 'Sea-level and coastline changes during the last 5,000 years', in McGrail (ed.) (1990a): 1–16.

TROELS-SMITH, J. (1946). 'Stammebaade fra Aamosen'. *Fra Nationalmuseets Arbejdsmark*: 15–23.

TWITCHETT, D. (1980). 'Imperial China and its neighbours', in Sherratt (ed.) (1980a): 267–71.

TYERS, I. (1994). 'Appendix 6, Dendrochronology', in Marsden (1994): 201–9.

TZALAS, H. (1995a). 'Editor's note'. *Tropis*, 3: 187.

—— (1995b). 'On the obsidian trail: With a papyrus craft in the Cyclades'. *Tropis*, 3: 441–69.

TZAMTZIS, A. I. (1989). '"Ikria" on Minoan seals'. *Tropis*, 1:

275–84.

UNGER, R. W. (ed.) (1994). *Cogs, Caravels and Galleons*. London: Conway Maritime Press.

VALBJØRN, K. V., RASMUSSEN, H. P., and JORGENSEN, J. A. (2000). 'Reconstruction of the Hjørtspring boat', in Litwin (2000): 103–10.

VAN ANDEL, T. H. (1989). 'Late Quaternary sea-level changes and archaeology'. *Antiquity*, 63: 733–45.

—— (1990). 'Addendum to van Andel 1989'. *Antiquity*, 64: 151–2.

VAN DE MOORTEL, A. (1991a). Construction of a cog-like vessel in the late-Middle Ages', in Reinders and Paul (eds.): 42–6.

—— (1991b). *Cog-like vessel from the Netherlands*. Flevobericht, 331. Lelystad: Rijksdienst voor de IJsselmeer polders.

VAN DE NOORT, R., MIDDLETON, R., FOXON, A., and BAYLISS, A. (1999). '"Kilnsea boat" and some implications for the discovery of England's oldest plank boat remains'. *Antiquity*, 73: 131–5.

VAN DER MERWE, P. (1983). 'Towards a three-masted ship', in *Proceedings of the* 4th International Congress of Maritime Museums, 1981. Paris: Musée de la Marine, 121–9.

VAN DOORNINCK, F. H. (1976). 'The 4th century wreck at Yassi Ada'. *IJNA* 5: 115–31.

VAN NOUHAYS, J. W. (1931). 'Model of a Spanish caravel of the beginning of the 15th century'. *MM* 17: 327–46.

VARADARAJAN, L. (1979). 'Traditions of indigenous navigation in Gujarat'. Paper read at the International Conference on Indian Ocean Studies, Perth, Australia, 1979.

—— (1990). 'Maritime encounter of East and West: Indian shipbuilding techniques'. Paper read at the Conference on Silk Roads, Goa, 1990.

VEBAEK, C. L. and THIRSLUND, S. (1992). *Viking compass*. Copenhagen.

VERNON, J. (1984). 'The Lincoln kayak'. *MM* 70: 415–26.

VICHOS, Y. and PAPATHANASSOPOULOS, G. (1996). 'Excavation of an Early Bronze Age cargo at Dokos'. *Tropis*, 4: 519–38.

VIGIE, B. (1980). 'Les representations de bateaux dans le bassin Mediterraneen aux temps protohistoriques'. *Navigation et Gens de Mer en Méditeranée*. Aix-en-Provence: Maison de la Méditeranée, 17–32.

VILLAIN-GANDOSSI, C., BUSUTIL, S., and ADAM, P. (eds.) (1989). *Medieval Ships and the Birth of Technological Societies*. i. *Northern Europe*. Malta: Foundation for International Studies.

VINSON, S. (1994). *Egyptian Boats and Ships*. Princes Risborough: Shire Egyptology.

VITHARANA, V. (1992). *Oru and Yatra*. Colombo: Sri Lankan National Library Service Board.

VLEK, R. (1987). *Medieval Utrecht Boat*. Oxford: BAR.S. 382.

VOSMER, T. (1997). 'Indigenous fishing craft of Oman'. *IJNA* 26: 217–35.

WACHSMANN, S. (1980). 'Thera waterborne procession reconsidered'. *IJNA* 9: 287–95.

WACHSMANN, S. (1981). 'Ships of the Sea Peoples'. *IJNA* 10: 187–220.

—— (1990). 'Excavation of an ancient boat in the Sea of Galilee'. *Atiqot*, 19. Jerusalem: Israel Antiquities Authority.

—— (1994). 'INA/CMS joint expedition to Tantura Lagoon'. *Institute of Nautical Archaeology Quarterly*, 22, 2: 3–8.

—— (1995). 'Paddled and oared ships before the Iron Age'. in Morrison (ed.) (1995a): ii. 10–35.

—— (1998). *Seagoing Ships and Seamanship in the Bronze Age Levant*. College Station: Texas A & M University Press.

WAKEMAN, W. E. (1872–3). 'Curach'. *Journal Royal Society Antiquities of Ireland*. 4th ser., 2: 74–6.

WALKER, C. B. F. (1990). *Cuneiform*. London: British Museum Publications.

WALLACE, A. R. (1869). *Malay Archipelago*. London.

WALLINGA, H. T. (1993). *Ships and Sea Power before the Great Persian War*. Leiden: E. J. Brill.

—— (1995). 'Ancestry of the trireme', 1200–525 BC, in Morrison (ed.) (1995a): ii. 36–48.

WANG, Y. (1989). 'Investigation of Chinese ancient shipbuilding from archaeological discoveries'. *Marine History Research*, 4–5: 42–52.

WARD, R. (1995). 'Surviving charter-party of 1323'. *MM* 81: 387–401.

WARNER, R. (1954). *Thucydides: The Peloponnesian War*. Harmondsworth: Penguin.

—— (1996). 'Yes, the Romans did invade Ireland'. *British Archaeology*, 14: 6.

WARREN, P. (1984). 'Absolute dating of the Bronze Age eruption of Thera (Santorini)'. *Nature*, 308: 492–3.

WASKÖNIG, D. (1969). 'Billiche Darstellungen des Hulk im 15 und 16 Jahrhundert zur Typologie von Schiffen der Hansezeit'. *Jarbuch 1969*. Hamburg: Altonaer Museum: 139–66.

WATERS, D. W. (1938). 'Chinese junks: The Antung Trader'. *MM* 24: 49–67.

—— (1947). 'Chinese junks: The Twaqo'. *MM* 33: 155–67.

—— (1978). *The Art of Navigation in England in Elizabethan and Early Stuart Times*, 2nd edn. Greenwich: National Maritime Museum.

—— (1988). *Reflections on Some Navigational and Hydrographic Problems of the 15th Century Related to the Voyage of B. Dias 1487–8*. Monograph 201. Lisbon: Instituto de Investigacao Cientifica Tropical.

—— (1989). 'Intellectual challenge of oceanic navigation in the 15th century'. Congresso International Bartolomeu Dias e sua epoca, University of Porto. *Actas*, 2: 141–59.

WATKINS, T. (1980). 'Prehistoric coracle in Fife'. *IJNA* 9: 277–86.

WAUGH, F. W. (1919). 'Canadian aboriginal canoes'. *Canadian Field-Naturalist*, 33, 2: 23–33.

WEDDE, M. (1995). 'Bow and stern in Early Aegean Bronze Age ship imagery: A re-analysis'. *Tropis*, 3: 485–506.

WEHAUSEN, J. V., MANSOW, A., and XIMINES, M. C. (1988). 'Colossi of Memnon and Egyptian barges'. *IJNA* 17: 295–310.

WERNER, W. (1997). 'Largest ship trackway in ancient times'. *IJNA* 26: 98–117.

WESTERDAHL, C. (1982). 'Nytt om Åskekärrsskeppet'. *Meddelanden*, 1: 25–6.

—— (1985a). 'Sewn boats of the North'. *IJNA* 14: 33–62, 119–42.

—— (1985b). 'Sewn boats of Sweden', in McGrail and Kentley (eds.): 211–32.

—— (1992). 'Review'. *IJNA* 21: 84–5.

—— (ed.) (1994). *Crossroads in Ancient Shipbuilding*. Oxford: Oxbow. Monograph 40.

—— (1995). 'Society and sail', in Crumlin-Pedersen and Thye (eds.): 41–50.

WHEELER, R. M., GHOSH, A., and DEVA, K. (1946). 'Arikamedu: An Indo-Roman trading station on the east coast of India'. *Ancient India*, 2: 17–124.

WHITE, J. P. and O'CONNELL, J. (1982). *Prehistory of Australia, New Guinea and Sahul*. Sydney: Academic Press.

WHITEHOUSE, D. (1980). 'Expansion of the Arabs', in Sherratt (ed.) (1980a): 289–97.

—— (1983). 'Maritime trade in the Gulf: 11th and 12th centuries'. *World Archaeology*, 14: 328–34.

WHITTAKER, I. (1954). 'Scottish kayaks and the "Finn-men"'. *Antiquity*, 28: 99–104.

—— (1977). 'Scottish kayaks reconsidered'. *Antiquity*, 51: 41–5.

WHITWELL, R. J. and JOHNSON, C. (1926). 'Newcastle galley'. *Archaeologica Aeliana*, 4th ser., 2: 142–96.

WILKINSON, C. K. (1983). *Egyptian Wall Paintings*. New York: Metropolitan Museum of Art.

WILLETTS, W. (1964). 'Maritime adventures of Grand Eunuch Ho'. *Journal of SE Asian History*, 5: 25–42.

WILLIS, D. D. K. (1922). 'Development from log to clipper'. *MM* 8: 66–72, 133–40, 268–76.

WILSON, D. M. (1985). *Bayeux Tapestry*. London: Thames and Hudson.

WINKLER, H. A. (1939). *Rock Carvings of Southern Upper Egypt*. London.

WINLOCK, H. E. (1955). *Models of Daily Life in Ancient Egypt*. Cambridge, Mass.: Harvard University Press.

WOOLMER, D. (1957). 'Graffiti of ships at Tarxien, Malta'. *Antiquity*, 31: 60–7.

WORCESTER, G. R. G. (1956a). 'Notes on the canoes of British Guiana'. *MM* 42: 249–51.

—— (1956b). 'Four small craft of Taiwan'. *MM* 42: 302–12.

—— (1956c). 'Origin and observance of the Dragon Boat festival in China'. *MM* 42: 127–37.

—— (1966). *Sail and Sweep in China*. London: HMSO.

WORTHINGTON, E. B. (1933). 'Primitive craft of the central African lakes'. *MM* 19: 146–63.

WRIGHT, E. V. (1976). *North Ferriby Boats: A Guidebook*, Monograph 23. Greenwich: National Maritime Museum.

—— (1990). *Ferriby Boats*. London: Routledge.

—— (1994). 'North Ferriby boats: A final report', in Westerdahl (ed.): 29–34.

—— and Switsur, V. R. (1993). 'Ferriby 5 boat fragments'. *Archaeological Journal*, 150: 46–56.

—— Hutchinson, G. R., and Gregson, C. W. (1989). 'Fourth boat-find at North Ferriby, Humberside'. *Archaeological Journal*, 146: 44–57.

Xi, L. (1985). 'Comparison between Western and Chinese techniques in handling sails together with rudder'. *Marine History Research*, 1: 36–46.

—— and Xin, Y. (1991). 'Preliminary research on the historical period and restoration design of the ancient ship unearthed in Penglai', in Zhang (ed.): 225–36.

Xin, Y., and Yuan, S. (1991). 'Blue ribbon holder in the Medieval age: Chinese Junks', in Zhang (ed.): 65–75.

Xu, Y. (1986). 'On the emergence and operation of ancient canoes judging from the discovery of canoe-shaped earthwares along the coast of E. Liaoning peninsula'. *Marine History Research*, 2: 1–10.

Yan, D. (1983). 'Technique of maritime navigation', in Mao (ed.): 494–503.

Yang, Q., and Chen, D. (1990). 'Récentes découvertes à Quanzhou (Zaitun)'. *Archipel*, 39: 81–91.

Yang, Yu (1986). 'Further study of Zheng He's "Treasure Ships" for expedition to Western Ocean'. *Maritime History Research*, 2: 59–64.

—— (1991). 'On the study of ancient sailing ships', in Zhang (ed.): 1–4.

Yuan, X., and Wu, S. (1991). 'On the construction of the Penglai fighting sailship of Yuan dynasty', in Zhang (ed.): 169–75.

Zhang, S. (ed.) (1991). *Proceedings of the International Sailing Ships History Conference*. Shanghai: Society of Naval Architecture and Marine Engineering.

Zhou, S. (1983). 'Shipbuilding', in Mao (ed.): 479–93.

Zimmerley, D. W. (1979). *Hooper Bay Kayak Construction*. Canadian Ethnology Service Papers, 53. Ottawa: National Museums of Canada.

—— (1980). *Arctic Kayaks*. Canadian Studies Report 11C. Ottawa: National Museums of Canada.

# Glossary

**apron**: a centre-line timber reinforcing the joint between stem and keel.

**aspect ratio of a sail**: height²/area.

**batten**: (1) a light strip of wood fastened over a *seam*; similar to a *lath*; (2) a light flexible strip of wood used to lay out curved lines or establish hull contours.

**baulk**: a tree trunk which has been roughly squared.

**beam shelf**: a *stringer* which supports *crossbeams*.

**beam tie**: a transverse strengthening member at the ends of a logboat, may be in the form of a *crook*.

**beat**: to sail with the wind well forward of abeam.

**beitiass**: *tack*ing boom used in the Viking period to give a taut leading edge to a sail.

**bevel**: a surface which has been angled to make a fit with another.

**bilge**: region between the sides and the bottom of a boat.

**bireme**: an oared vessel with two levels of oarsmen.

**bitts**: vertical posts to which lines or cables can be belayed; similar to *kevel-heads*.

**blind fastening**: one in which the point of the nail does not protrude through the timber.

**bole**: main stem or trunk of a tree.

**bonnet**: auxiliary sail laced to the foot of a square sail to increase sail area and driving power in light airs.

**boom**: a spar to which the foot of a sail is bent.

**bottom boards**: lengths of timber fastened together and laid over the bottom of a boat as flooring.

**braces**: lines to trim *yard*. (Fig. G1)

**brail**: rope used to bundle a sail rapidly.

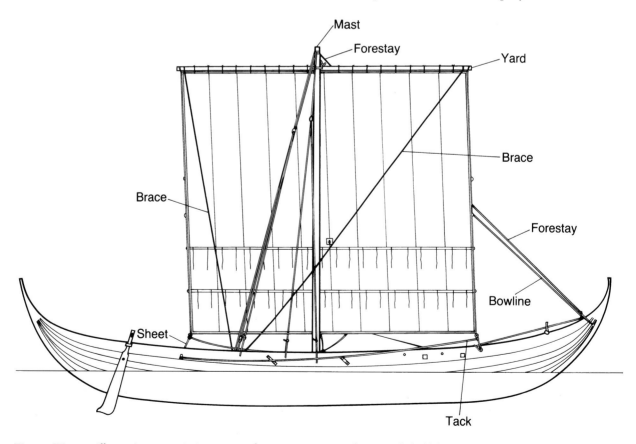

Fig. G1. Diagram illustrating some rigging terms (after a reconstruction drawing of Skuldelev 3 by Ole Crumlin-Pedersen; see also Fig. 5.48).

**breast hook**: a transverse timber across the centre line reinforcing the bow against spreading.

**bulkhead**: a transverse partition which divides the boat into compartments.

**carvel built**: there are several definitions in use; in particular, this term is sometimes taken to be synonymous with *frame-first* building with *flush-laid* strakes. The term is confusing and best avoided.

**cathead**: timber projecting outboard from the bow of a vessel, and from which an anchor can be hung.

**caulk**: to insert material between two members and thus make the junction watertight. Whether this is done before or after planking is fastened may be an important diagnostic trait.

**ceiling**: lining of planking over *floor* timbers and usually fastened to them.

**chock**: a straight-grained timber used to reinforce an angular joint between two timbers, or to fill a space at the apex of such a joint.

**clamp**: (1) a device for holding elements of a boat together (temporarily); (2) a *stringer* directly inboard of a *wale*, and fastened through the frames to it.

**cleat**: a projection to which other fittings may be fastened or a line made fast.

**cleat rail**: a longitudinal timber incorporating several cleats.

**clench, rivet**: to deform, hook or turn the end of a fastening so that it will not draw out—may be done over a *rove*.

**clew**: the lower after corner of a fore-and-aft sail, or the lower corners of a square sail.

**clinker built**: a form of boat-building in which the strakes are placed so that they partly overlap one another—usually upper strake outboard of lower strake, but occasionally the reverse arrangement is found.

**coak**: similar to *treenail*.

**construction plan**: a scale drawing of a boat with a longitudinal section, horizontal plan, and several transverse sections. The position and nature of the scarfs, and other important constructional details and scantlings, may also be given.

**couple**: pair of equal and parallel forces, acting in opposite directions, and tending to cause rotation.

**crook**: a curved piece of wood which has grown into a shape useful for boat-building.

**crossbeam**: a timber extending across the vessel.

**deadrise**: angle at which the bottom planking lies to the horizontal.

**dolly**: a metal billet held against the head of a boat nail whilst it is being clenched.

**double-ended**: a boat which is (nearly) symmetrical about the midship transverse plane.

**draft (draught)**: (1) the vertical distance between the water-

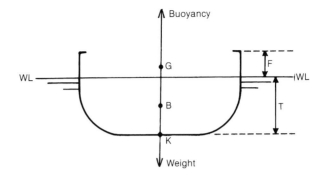

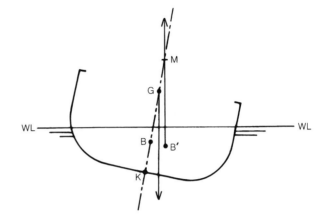

| B | centre of buoyancy | K | datum |
| B' | centre of buoyancy when heeled | M | metacentre |
| F | freeboard | T | draft |
| G | centre of mass | WL | waterline |

Fig. G2. Diagram illustrating transverse stability.

line and the lowest point of the hull (Fig. G2); (2) an alternative term for *lines*.

**draw-tongue joint**: a method of fastening flush-laid planking in which free tenons are fitted into mortises cut in the meeting edges of adjacent planks; after the planking is assembled the tenons may be pierced by two treenails, one through each plank. Sometimes known as *mortise and tenon*.

**fay**: to fit one timber carefully against another.

**feather edge**: tapering to nothing.

**fetch**: the distance of open water to windward of a stretch of coast.

**fibre saturation point**: a theoretical stage in wood–water relations when all the water (free water) has been removed from the cell cavities, but none from the cell walls. For most timbers this is at a *moisture content* of 25 per cent to 30 per cent.

**flare**: the transverse section of a boat increases in breadth towards the *sheer*.

**floor timber**: a transverse member, often a *crook*, extending from turn of *bilge* to turn of bilge, and set against the planking (see *frame*).

**flush-laid**: planking in which adjoining *strakes* are butted edge-to-edge and do not overlap.

**foundation plank**: the central bottom plank in a flat-bottomed boat.

**frame**: a transverse member made up of more than one piece of timber, usually *floor timbers* and pairs of *futtocks*, and set against the planking (see *rib* and *timber*).

**frame-first**: a vessel is said to be built frame-first when the hull shape is determined by the framing which is the prime element in design and strength.

**freeboard**: height of sides above the waterline (Fig. G2).

**futtocks**: pairs of timbers which, with a *floor timber*, constitute a *frame*; they support the side planking. See *side timber*.

**galley**: (1) a vessel capable of being propelled by oars and by sail; (2) a ship's kitchen.

**garboard**: the *strake* next to the keel.

**gripe**: (1) the tendency of a sailing vessel to come up into the wind; (2) the forefoot of a stem.

**grommet**: strand(s) of rope layed up in the form of a ring.

**guares**: a retractable wooden foil for combating leeway and for steering (a variable lee-board).

**halyard**: line to hoist and lower yard and sail.

**hog**: the bending or shearing of a hull in the vertical plane causing it to arch upwards in the middle and drop at the ends; opposite to sag.

**hogging hawser or stay**: tensioned rope or cable rigged on the centre-line high in the hull to prevent *hogging*.

**hooked nail**: a fastening nail that is *clenched* by turning the tip through 180° back into the timber.

**hold index**: ratio of length of hold to length of vessel; some measure of the importance given to cargo carrying.

**interference fit**: said of a *treenail* in a hole or a tenon in a mortise when the wood fibres interlock.

**joggle**: to cut out a notch in a piece of timber so that it will fit close against another member.

**keel**: the main longitudinal strength member, joined to the stems forward and aft.

**keelson**: centre-line timber on top of the floors adding to the longitudinal strength and stiffness. May have a *mast step* incorporated.

**kevel head**: the ends of a vessel's top timbers protruding above the *sheer line*, and to which lines may be made fast.

**knee**: a naturally grown *crook* used as a bracket between two members set at about right-angles to each other; hanging knee—vertically below; standing knee—vertically above; lodging knee—horizontally.

**land**: that part of a strake which is overlapped by the strake immediately above it in *clinker* building.

**lath**: a light longitudinal *batten* laid over caulking to protect it, and held in place by fastenings.

**layoff**: to draw out the lines of a boat full size.

**lee shore**: shore towards which the (predominant) wind blows.

**leech**: the after or lee edge of a fore-and-aft sail or the outer edges of a square sail.

**lift**: line running from *yardarm* to mast.

**limber hole**: notch cut in the underside of frames to allow free circulation of bilge water.

**lines**: the interrelation of sections in different planes which show the shape of a boat's hull. They usually consist of: (a) sheer plan with longitudinal section; (b) half-breadth plan with waterlines or horizontal sections; (c) body plan with transverse sections. Diagonal lines, longitudinal section lines on the half-breadth plan, and waterlines on the sheer plan, enable the three plans to be related to each other, and checked for fairness. Lines converted to numbers are known as a 'table of offsets'.

**loom**: that part of an oar inboard of the point of pivot. The section of an oar between the loom and the blade is called the shaft.

**luff**: the leading edge of a fore-and-aft sail.

**mast partner**: a structure, often a *crossbeam*, at deck level, locating and supporting a mast.

**mast step**: fitting used to locate the heel of a mast.

**mast step timber**: centre-line timber on top of the floors incorporating a *mast step*—not as long or as massive as a *keelson*.

**metacentre**: theoretical point (M) in the middle plane of a vessel through which the buoyancy force passes when the vessel in inclined at a small angle (Fig. G2).

**metacentric height**: distance from the metacentre (M) to the centre of mass (G) of a loaded boat (Fig. G2).

**moisture content**: the weight of water in a specimen of wood expressed as a percentage of the weight of oven-dry wood. Thus the figure can be greater than 100 per cent.

**mortise and tenon**: see *draw-tongue joint*.

**moulded**: dimension of a timber measured at right angles to the *sided* dimension.

**moulds**: transverse wooden patterns giving the internal shape of a vessel.

**painter**: light head-rope by which a boat is made fast; mooring rope.

**parrel**: a *crook* that holds a *yard* close to the mast, yet allows the yard to pivot and slide up and down.

**pay**: cover plank seams with a layer of hot pitch, or to coat a ship's bottom with tar or other waterproofing substance.

**peak**: the upper after corner of a four-sided fore-and- aft sail.

**pith**: the middle core of a *bole*.

**plank**: a component of a *strake* that is not all in one piece.

**plank-first**: a vessel is said to be built plank-first when the hull shape is determined by the planking.

**plank-keel**: a keel-like timber of which the ratio of its *moulded* dimension to its *sided* dimension is ≤ 0.70.

**rabbet, rabet, rebate**: a groove or channel worked in a member to accept another, without a lip being formed.

**radial plane**: a longitudinal section of a *bole* through the pith and at right angles to the growth rings.

**rays**: layers of parenchyma cells in horizontal strands running out from the centre of a tree towards the circumference.

**reach**: to sail with the wind from slightly forward of abeam to slightly aft.

**reef**: to shorten sail by tying up the lower portion using reef points.

**rib**: a simple form of frame. This term may be more appropriate than *frame* when applied to small open boats.

**ribband**: a flexible strip of wood, heavier than a *batten*, temporarily fastened to framing to assess fairness, and to establish the run of the planking.

**rocker**: fore-and-aft curvature of *keel* or bottom of vessel.

**rove, roove**: a washer-like piece of metal, which is forced over the point of a nail before it is *clenched*.

**rubbing strake**: an extra thick strake (*wale*); or a strake fastened outboard of an existing strake, near the top of a vessel's sides to protect the hull when alongside another vessel or a waterfront.

**run**: to sail with the wind from the stern sector.

**scarf, scarph, scarve**: a tapered or wedge-shaped joint between pieces of similar section at the join; hooked scarf: a scarf with a stepped *table*; keyed scarf: a scarf with a transverse key through a mortise across the *table*.

**seam**: juncture of two members required to be watertight.

**sheer, sheer line**: the curve of the upper edge of the hull.

**sheer strake**: the top *strake* of planking.

**sheet**: line used to trim the foot of a sail (Fig. G1).

**shelf (rising)**: a longitudinal timber or *stringer* fastened inside the planking and / or framing of a vessel to support the ends of *crossbeams*.

**shore**: stout timber used to support (part of) the hull of a vessel, internally or externally, when she takes the ground.

**shrouds**: ropes leading from the masthead to the sides of the boat to support the mast athwartships (Fig. 5.48).

**side timber**: a framing timber supporting the side planking at stations between the *floor timbers*; it may be adjacent to

a floor but is not fastened to it.

**sided**: dimension of a timber measured (near) parallel to the fore-and-aft plane of a vessel.

**spile**: to transfer a curved line on to a pattern which, when laid flat, will give the shape to cut a timber or a plank.

**stabilizers**: external longitudinal timbers fastened to a boat's sides at the loaded waterline to increase transverse stability.

**stays**: ropes leading from the masthead forward and aft to support the mast (Fig. G1).

**stealer**: a method of planking the ends of a boat so that a *strake* is gained or lost thus avoiding over-wide or narrow plank ends.

**stocks, set-up**: the temporary wooden support on which a boat is built.

**strake**: a single *plank* or combination of planks which stretches from one end of a boat to the other.

**stretcher, foot timber**: an athwartships length of timber against which a rower braces his feet.

**stringer**: a longitudinal strength member along the inside of the planking.

**table**: the meeting surface of the two main elements of a *scarf*.

**tack**: (1) the lower forward corner of a fore-and-aft sail (Fig. G1); (2) to alter course so that the bow of a sailing vessel passes through the wind.

**tangential plane**: a longitudinal section of a *bole* at right angles to the radial plane and tangential to the growth rings.

**thole**: a wooden pin projecting upwards at sheer level to provide a pivot for an oar.

**throat**: the upper forward corner of a four-sided fore-and-aft sail.

**thwart**: a transverse member (*crossbeam*) used as a seat.

**timber**: used generally referring to any piece of wood used in boat-building. One piece *ribs* or *frames*, especially those steamed or bent into place, are frequently called timbers.

**transition strake**: the strake at the transition between bottom and sides of a boat, especially when there is a marked change in the boat's transverse section (ile; chine girder).

**transom**: athwartship bulkhead. (In this text it is normally applied to a fitted bulkhead at the stern or the bow.)

**treenail, trunnel**: wooden peg or dowel used to join two members. It may be secured at each or either end by the insertion of a wedge.

**trireme**: an oared vessel with three levels of oarsmen.

**tumblehome**: the opposite of *flare*, the topsides narrow as they rise.

**turned nail**: a fastening nail that is *clenched* by turning the tip through 90° to lie along the face of the timber.

**volumetric coefficient**: ratio of displacement to the cube of waterline length; a measure of a vessel's potential speed.

**wale**: a *strake* thicker than the rest.

**washstrake**: an additional *strake* normally fitted to increase freeboard and to keep out spray and water.

**wear**: to alter course so that the stern of a sailing vessel passes through the wind.


**yard**: a spar suspended from a MAST, and to which the head of a square sail is bent (Fig. G1).

**yardarm**: the ends of a *yard*, and to which *braces* are made fast.

*Note*: Many of these definitions are taken from the glossary in my *Ancient Boats in N. W. Europe* (1998). Others are based on preliminary definitions in a glossary for medieval ships, under preparation at the Centre for Maritime Archaeology, Roskilde: I am very grateful to that institution.

# Index

Notes: numbers in italics denote illustrations (only where there is no corresponding text on the same page). References to common structural components, e.g. nails, cleats, are indexed only where a particular structural or developmental feature is involved.